Official Reference

to Visual Basic for

Applications Keywords in

Microsoft Excel 5 and

Microsoft Excel for

Windows® 95

Microsoft®
Excel/Visual Basic®
Reference Second Edition

Microsoft Press

PUBLISHED BY
Microsoft Press
A Division of Microsoft Corporation
One Microsoft Way
Redmond, Washington 98052-6399

Library of Congress Cataloging-in-Publication Data
Microsoft Excel / Visual Basic reference. -- 2nd ed.
         p.   cm.
      Includes index.
      ISBN 1-55615-920-X
      1. Microsoft Visual BASIC.   2. Microsoft Excel (Computer file)
      I. Microsoft Corporation.
      QA76.73.B3M544   1995
      005.369--dc20   95-34317
                                                               CIP

Printed and bound in the United States of America.

1 2 3 4 5 6 7 8 9   QMQM   0 9 8 7 6 5

Distributed to the book trade in Canada by Macmillan of Canada, a division of Canada Publishing Corporation.

A CIP catalogue record for this book is available from the British Library.

Microsoft Press books are available through booksellers and distributors worldwide. For further information about international editions, contact your local Microsoft Corporation office. Or contact Microsoft Press International directly at fax (206) 936-7329.

Acquisitions Editor: Casey D. Doyle
Project Editor: Brenda L. Matteson

Introduction

This manual is an alphabetic reference for Visual Basic for Microsoft Excel. The reference contains topics for all functions, methods, objects, properties, and statements in the language, and is essentially identical to the information contained in Microsoft Excel Visual Basic Help.

Unless otherwise noted, each topic in this manual is applicable to both Microsoft Excel 5 and Microsoft Excel for Windows 95. At the beginning of the reference, there is a section with lists of methods, objects, and properties that are new or changed in Microsoft Excel for Windows 95. References to other online and printed material refer to documentation for Microsoft Excel for Windows 95.

Where to Find Information About Visual Basic for Microsoft Excel

For general information about Microsoft Excel, see *Getting Results with Microsoft Excel for Windows 95* or *Getting Results with Microsoft Office for Windows 95*.

For in-depth information about using Visual Basic in Microsoft Excel, read the *Microsoft Excel/Visual Basic for Windows 95 Programmer's Guide*, available from Microsoft Press. If you're new to Visual Basic in Microsoft Excel, or if you prefer a task-oriented approach to learning, you might want to start by reading *Microsoft Excel Visual Basic Step by Step*, a self-paced tutorial also available from Microsoft Press. Another Microsoft Press book, *Developing Microsoft Excel Solutions*, contains expert development strategies, tips, tricks, and sample Microsoft Excel/Visual Basic macros and applications.

Note You can order the *Microsoft Excel/Visual Basic for Windows 95 Programmer's Guide*, *Microsoft Excel Visual Basic Step by Step*, and *Developing Microsoft Excel Solutions* directly from Microsoft Press. To place a credit card order, call 615-793-5090, or call 1-800-MS-PRESS toll-free. Please be sure to have your reference code FXL ready for faster order processing. CompuServe subscribers can also order through the Microsoft Press Electronic Book Store by typing **GO MSP**.

Tips on How to Learn Visual Basic

The following are suggestions for getting the most from the time you spend learning Visual Basic.

Learn Microsoft Excel first

The more you know about Microsoft Excel, the better prepared you'll be to venture into Visual Basic. Most macros perform a sequence of actions in Microsoft Excel, and most instructions in a macro are equivalent to commands or actions in Microsoft Excel. Consequently, working with Visual Basic is a little like working with Microsoft Excel without a user interface; instead of commands and dialog boxes, you use Visual Basic instructions. The statements and functions you use to write instructions are much easier to understand if you're familiar with the features they represent in Microsoft Excel.

Also, if you know Microsoft Excel well, you can better answer the question you're most likely to ask when writing a macro: "What's the best way to do this?" People have been known to write long macros for tasks that could have been handled by a single Microsoft Excel command.

Learn what you need, when you need it

Learn what you need for the task at hand. Visual Basic can seem overwhelming at first, particularly if you haven't had experience with a macro programming language. A great way to learn the language is to investigate how to implement a particular macro idea you have. As you gain experience writing different types of macros, you'll cover a lot of ground.

Use the macro recorder

The macro recorder can record the Visual Basic instruction for virtually every action you take in Microsoft Excel. You can use the macro recorder to see how actions in Microsoft Excel translate into Visual Basic instructions, and vice versa. Also, you'll find that recording part of a macro is often faster and easier than writing out the instructions.

Use Visual Basic Help

Help is a powerful tool for learning Visual Basic. In a Visual Basic module, you can type a Visual Basic keyword and—with the insertion point somewhere in the keyword—press F1 to immediately display Visual Basic Help for that keyword. The Visual Basic Help topic for most keywords includes an example you can copy and paste into your macro. For more information, see "Using Online Help" later in this introduction.

Code Samples

Your Microsoft Excel package includes code samples you can open and run. You can copy any part of the samples into your own applications, modifying them as necessary. These code samples are located in the Samples.xls workbook in the Examples folder in your Microsoft Excel folder.

Using Online Help

Microsoft Excel provides an extensive Help system for the Visual Basic language, the objects that Microsoft Excel supports, and the properties and methods of those objects.

If you clicked Typical when you installed Microsoft Excel, you'll need to run Setup again to install Help for Visual Basic for Microsoft Excel.

You can access Visual Basic Help in any of the following four ways:

- In a Visual Basic module, place the insertion point anywhere in an object, property, method, function, or other keyword, and then press F1 to get context-sensitive Help.

- On the Help menu, click Microsoft Excel Help Topics. You can then either click "Getting Started with Visual Basic" on the Contents tab, look up a specific topic or Visual Basic term on the Index tab, or perform a full-text search from the Find tab.

- On the Help menu, click Microsoft Excel Help Topics. You can then ask a question on the Answer Wizard tab and read the topics displayed in the Programming and Language Reference section of the dialog box.

- With a Visual Basic module active, click Object Browser on the View menu, and then click the Element Help button (appears as a question mark below the Objects/Modules box) for information about an object, method, property, or function.

Document Conventions

This book uses the typographic conventions shown in the following table. You might not recognize all the terms or Visual Basic keywords, but you'll learn more about them later.

Example of convention	Description
setup	Words or characters you're instructed to type appear in bold.
Sub, **If**, **ChDir**, **MsgBox**, **True**, **Add**, **Height**, **Application**, **Range**, **Row**	Words in bold with the initial letter capitalized indicate a language-specific term: a property, method, or object name; or another Visual Basic keyword.
propertyname	In syntax, italic type indicates placeholders for information you supply.
index	In syntax, bold italic type indicates placeholders for arguments when you can use either positional or named-argument syntax.
[*expressionlist*]	In syntax, items inside square brackets are optional.
{**While**|**Until**}	In syntax, braces and a vertical bar indicate a mandatory choice between two or more items.
ENTER	Small capital letters are used for the names of keys and key combinations, such as ENTER and CTRL+R.
CTRL+V	A plus sign (+) between key names indicates a combination of keys. For example, CTRL+V means to hold down the CTRL key while pressing the V key.
myVar	This font is used for example code.

Programming Style

This book uses the following programming style guidelines for code examples.

- The following font is used for code.

```
Sub HelloWorld
    Cells(1,1).Value = "Hello, world!"
End Sub
```

- An apostrophe (') introduces comments in code.

```
' This is a comment; these two lines
' are ignored when the program is running.
```

- Names of macros and user-defined functions appear with initial letters capitalized throughout this book. Note that macro and function names cannot include spaces, so if a name consists of more than one word, the other words in the name also have their initial letters capitalized.

```
' The AuditResult user-defined function is in the Finance module.
Function AuditResult(latestIncome, expenses, taxes, commissions)
```

Argument and variable names appear with initial letters lowercase (to distinguish them from macro, function, property, method, and object names).

- Keywords appear with initial letters capitalized, whereas built-in constants appear with an initial lowercase "xl" or "vb."

```
' Sub is a keyword.
Sub Title(titleText)
```

```
' xlManual is a built-in constant.
Application.Calculation = xlManual
```

- Control-flow blocks and statements in **Sub** and **Function** procedures are indented within the code that surrounds them.

```
Sub CheckRecordSound
    SoundRecordCapable = Application.CanRecordSounds
    If SoundRecordCapable Then
        Cells(1,1).SoundNote.Record
    End If
End Sub
```

- The line-continuation character—an underscore (_)—indicates that code continued from one line to the next is part of the same logical line. You can type these statements all on one line in the Visual Basic module. You can also divide lines of code and add the line-continuation character yourself.

```
ActiveSheet.Rectangles.Add _
    width:=200, _
    height:=200, _
    left:=50, _
    top:=50
```

Microsoft Product Support Services

Microsoft offers a variety of support options to help you get the most from your Microsoft product. For more information about Microsoft Product Support Services, see *Getting Results with Microsoft Excel for Windows 95* or *Getting Results with Microsoft Office for Windows 95*.

Outside the United States, contact Microsoft Product Support Services at the Microsoft subsidiary office that serves your area. Microsoft subsidiary offices and the countries they serve are listed in *Getting Results with Microsoft Excel for Windows 95* and *Getting Results with Microsoft Office for Windows 95*.

Changes to Visual Basic in Microsoft Excel for Windows 95

Existing properties and methods have been changed, and several new properties, methods, and objects have been added to Visual Basic in Microsoft Excel for Windows 95.

Changed Properties and Methods

The following properties and methods have been changed to support new Microsoft Excel features or to enhance existing features.

Topic	Description
GetOpenFileName Method	The new *multiSelect* argument allows you to select more than one filename in the Open dialog box.
HelpContextID Property	Added to the **ToolbarButton** object.
HelpFile Property	Added to the **ToolbarButton** object.
Names Method	Added to the **Worksheet** object to handle sheet-scoped names.
PasteSpecial Method	For the **Range** object, a new constant for the *paste* argument allows you to paste range content and formatting but not border formatting.
Protect Method	The new *userInterfaceOnly* argument allows you to specify protection from user changes while still allowing changes from Visual Basic code.
SaveAs Method	New arguments allow you to specify shared-mode access and how change conflicts are resolved.
StatusBar Property	Added to the **ToolbarButton** object.

AutoCorrect Support

The following new object, properties, methods have been added to support automatic corrections.

Topic	Description
AddReplacement Method	Adds a row to the array of AutoCorrect replacements returned by the **ReplacementList** property.
AutoCorrect Object	Contains AutoCorrect attributes (capitalization of names of days, correction of two initial capital letters, automatic correction list, and so on).
AutoCorrect Property	Returns an **AutoCorrect** object that represents the AutoCorrect attributes.

Topic	Description
CapitalizeNamesOfDays Property	**True** if the first letters of names (and abbreviations) of days are capitalized automatically.
DeleteReplacement Method	Deletes a row from the array of AutoCorrect replacements returned by the **ReplacementList** property.
ReplacementList Property	Returns or sets the entire array or one row of the array of AutoCorrect replacements.
ReplaceText Property	**True** if text from column one of the array of AutoCorrect replacements is automatically replaced with the text from column two.
TwoInitialCapitals Property	**True** if occurrences of two initial capital letters in a word are corrected automatically.

OLE Document Properties Support

The following new properties, methods, and objects have been added to support OLE document properties. Document properties allow Microsoft Excel to expose a standard set of built-in document properties and additional custom document properties added by the user.

Topic	Description
BuiltinDocumentProperties Property	Returns a **DocumentProperties** collection object that contains the built-in document properties for the object.
CustomDocumentProperties Property	Returns a **DocumentProperties** collection object that contains the custom document properties for the object.
DocumentProperties Object	Represents the collection of document properties (either built-in or custom).
DocumentProperty Object	Represents a single document property.
LinkedToContent Property	**True** if the value of a custom property is linked to the contents of the document it's contained in; **False** if the property is a static value.
LinkSource Property	Specifies the source of a custom document property that's linked to document contents.

AutoComplete Support

The following method and property have been added to support the AutoComplete feature.

Topic	Description
AutoComplete Method	Returns a completed string from the list, or returns an empty string if there was no completion or if more than one entry in the list matches.
EnableAutoComplete Property	**True** if the AutoComplete feature is enabled.

Protection Control

The following properties have been added to allow you to control the user's ability to change toolbars, filtered lists, PivotTables, and outlining.

Topic	Description
EnableAutoFilter Property	**True** if AutoFilter arrows are enabled when user-interface-only protection is turned on.
EnableOutlining Property	**True** if outlining symbols (show detail or hide detail) are enabled when user-interface-only protection is turned on.
EnablePivotTable Property	**True** if PivotTable controls and actions are enabled when user-interface-only protection is turned on
Protection Property	Controls what kinds of changes the user can make to a toolbar.

Appearance Control

The following properties and methods have been added to control the appearance of the mouse pointer, turn animated insertion and deletion on and off, create a password-entry edit box, and set the background graphic for a worksheet or chart.

Topic	Description
Cursor Property	Sets the appearance of the mouse pointer in Microsoft Excel.
EnableAnimations Property	**True** if animated insertion and deletion is enabled.
PasswordEdit Property	Causes an edit box to display its contents as a series of asterisks.
SetBackgroundPicture Method	Sets the background graphic for a worksheet or chart.

Miscellaneous

Topic	Description
AutoLoad Property	**True** if the OLE object is automatically loaded when the workbook that contains the object is opened.
CopyFromRecordset Method	Copies the contents of a DAO **Recordset** object into cells on a worksheet, beginning at the first cell of the specified range.
ListHeaderRows Property	Returns the number of header rows for the specified range.
MoveAfterReturnDirection Property	Controls the direction in which the active cell is moved after the user presses ENTER.
NetworkTemplatesPath Property	Returns the network path where templates are stored. If the network path doesn't exist, the property returns an empty string.
OnSave Property	Returns or sets the name of a Visual Basic procedure to run whenever the user invokes the Save or Save As command.
Post Method	Posts the specified workbook to a Microsoft Exchange public folder or a Lotus Notes database.
ProtectionMode Property	**True** if user-interface-only protection is turned on.
RangeSelection Property	Returns a **Range** object that represents the selected cells on the worksheet in the specified window even if a graphic object is active or selected on the worksheet.
RefersToRange Property	Returns the **Range** object referred to by a **Name** object.
TemplatesPath Property	Returns the local path where templates are stored.

& Operator

Description   Used to force string concatenation of two expressions.

Syntax   *result* = *expression1* **&** *expression2*

The **&** operator syntax has these parts:

Part	Description
result	Any numeric variable.
expression1	Any expression.
expression2	Any expression.

Remarks   Whenever an *expression* is not a string, it is converted to a **String** variant. The data type of *result* is **String** if both expressions are **String** expressions; otherwise, *result* is a **String** variant. If both expressions are **Null**, *result* is also **Null**. However, if only one *expression* is a **Null**, that expression is treated as a zero-length string when concatenated with the other expression. Any expression that is **Empty** is also treated as a zero-length string.

See Also   Operator Precedence.

Example   This example uses the **&** operator to force string concatenation.

```
MyStr = "Hello" & " World"          ' Returns "Hello World".
MyStr = "Check " & 123 & " Check"   ' Returns "Check 123 Check".
```

* Operator

Description   Used to multiply two numbers.

Syntax   *result* = *number1*∗*number2*

The ∗ operator syntax has these parts:

Part	Description
result	Any numeric variable.
number1	Any numeric expression.
number2	Any numeric expression.

Remarks The data type of *result* is usually the same as that of the most precise expression. The order of precision, from least to most precise, is **Integer**, **Long**, **Single**, **Double**, **Currency**. The following are exceptions to this order:

- When multiplication involves a **Single** and a **Long**, the data type of *result* is converted to a **Double**.
- When the data type of *result* is a **Long**, **Single**, or **Date** variant that overflows its legal range, *result* is converted to a **Variant** containing a **Double**.
- When the data type of *result* is an **Integer** variant that overflows its legal range, *result* is converted to a **Long** variant.

If one or both expressions are **Null** expressions, *result* is a **Null**. If an expression is **Empty**, it is treated as if it were 0.

See Also Operator Precedence.

Example This example uses the * operator to multiply two numbers.

```
MyValue = 2 * 2                  ' Returns 4.
MyValue = 459.35 * 334.90       ' Returns 153836.315.
```

+ Operator

Description Used to sum two numbers.

Syntax *result = expression1+expression2*

The **+** operator syntax has these parts:

Part	Description
result	Any numeric variable.
expression1	Any expression.
expression2	Any expression.

Remarks Although you can also use the **+** operator to concatenate two character strings, you should use the **&** operator for concatenation to eliminate ambiguity and provide self-documenting code.

When you use the + operator, you may not be able to determine whether addition or string concatenation will occur. If at least one expression is not a **Variant**, the following rules apply:

If	Then
Both expressions are numeric data types (**Boolean, Integer, Long, Single, Double, Date** or **Currency**)	Add.
Both expressions are **String**	Concatenate.
One expression is a numeric data type and the other is any **Variant** (except a **Null**)	Add.
One expression is a **String** and the other is any **Variant** (except a **Null**)	Concatenate.
One expression is an **Empty Variant**	Return the remaining expression unchanged as *result*.
One expression is a numeric data type and the other is a **String**	A `Type mismatch` error occurs.
Either expression is a **Null**	*result* is a **Null**.

If both expressions are **Variant** expressions, the underlying type of the expressions determines the behavior of the + operator in the following way:

If	Then
Both **Variant** expressions are numeric	Add.
Both **Variant** expressions are strings	Concatenate.
One **Variant** expression is numeric and the other is a string	Add.

For simple arithmetic addition involving only expressions of numeric data types, the data type of *result* is usually the same as that of the most precise expression. The order of precision, from least to most precise, is **Integer, Long, Single, Double,** and **Currency**. The following are exceptions to this order:

- When a **Single** and a **Long** are added together, the data type of *result* is converted to a **Double**.

- When the data type of *result* is a **Long, Single,** or **Date** variant that overflows its legal range, *result* is converted to a **Double** variant.

- When the data type of *result* is an **Integer** variant that overflows its legal range, *result* is converted to a **Long** variant.

- When a **Date** is added to any other data type, the data type of *result* is always a **Date**.

If one or both expressions are **Null** expressions, *result* is a **Null**. If both expressions are **Empty**, *result* is an **Integer**. However, if only one expression is **Empty**, the other expression is returned unchanged as *result*.

See Also

Operator Precedence.

Example

This example uses the **+** operator to sum numbers. The **+** operator can also be used to concatenate strings but to eliminate ambiguity, you should use the **&** operator instead.

```
MyNumber = 2 + 2                    ' Returns 4.
MyNumber = 4257.04 + 98112          ' Returns 102369.04.
Var1 = "34" : Var2 = 6              ' Initialize variables.
MyNumber = Var1 + Var2              ' Returns 40.
Var1 = "34" : Var2 = "6"            ' Initialize variables.
MyNumber = Var1 + Var2              ' Returns "346" (string concatenation).
```

- Operator

Description

Used to find the difference between two numbers or to indicate the negative value of a numeric expression.

Syntax 1

result = number1-number2

Syntax 2

-number

The **-** operator syntax has these parts:

Part	Description
result	Any numeric variable.
number	Any numeric expression.
number1	Any numeric expression.
number2	Any numeric expression.

Remarks

In Syntax 1, the **-** operator is the arithmetic subtraction operator used to find the difference between two numbers. In Syntax 2, the **-** operator is used as the unary negation operator to indicate the negative value of an expression.

The data type of *result* is usually the same as that of the most precise expression. The order of precision, from least to most precise, is **Integer**, **Long**, **Single**, **Double**, **Currency**. The following are exceptions to this order:

- When subtraction involves a **Single** and a **Long**, the data type of *result* is converted to a **Double**.
- When the data type of *result* is a **Long**, **Single**, or **Date** variant that overflows its legal range, *result* is converted to a **Variant** containing a **Double**.
- When the data type of *result* is an **Integer** variant that overflows its legal range, *result* is converted to a **Long** variant.
- When subtraction involves a **Date** and any other data type, the data type of *result* is a **Date**.
- When subtraction involves two **Date** expressions, the data type of *result* is **Double**.

If one or both expressions are **Null** expressions, *result* is a **Null**. If an expression is **Empty**, it is treated as if it were 0.

See Also   Operator Precedence.

Example   This example uses the - operator to calculate the difference between two numbers.

```
MyResult = 4 - 2              ' Returns 2.
MyResult = 459.35 - 334.90    ' Returns 124.45.
```

/ Operator

Description   Used to divide two numbers and return a floating-point result.

Syntax   *result = number1/number2*

The / operator syntax has these parts:

Part	Description
result	Any numeric variable.
number1	Any numeric expression.
number2	Any numeric expression.

Remarks

The data type of *result* is usually a **Double** or a **Double** variant. The following are exceptions to this rule:

- When both expressions are **Integer** or **Single** expressions, *result* is a **Single** unless it overflows its legal range; in which case, an error occurs.

- When both expressions are **Integer** or **Single** variants, *result* is a **Single** variant unless it overflows its legal range; in which case, *result* is a **Variant** containing a **Double**.

If one or both expressions are **Null** expressions, *result* is a **Null**. Any expression that is **Empty** is treated as 0.

See Also

Operator Precedence.

Example

This example uses the **/** operator to perform floating-point division.

```
MyValue = 10 / 4                    ' Returns 2.5.
MyValue = 10 / 3                    ' Returns 3.333333.
```

\ Operator

Description

Used to divide two numbers and return an integer result.

Syntax

result = *number1**number2*

The \ operator syntax has these parts:

Part	Description
result	Any numeric variable.
number1	Any numeric expression.
number2	Any numeric expression.

Remarks

Before division is performed, the numeric expressions are rounded to **Integer** or **Long** expressions.

Usually, the data type of *result* is an **Integer**, **Integer** variant, **Long**, or **Long** variant, regardless of whether or not *result* is a whole number. Any fractional portion is truncated. However, if any expression is a **Null**, *result* is also a **Null**. Any expression that is **Empty** is treated as 0.

See Also

Operator Precedence.

Example

This example uses the \ operator to perform integer division.

```
MyValue = 11 \ 4           ' Returns 2.
MyValue = 9 \ 3            ' Returns 3.
MyValue = 100 \ 3          ' Returns 33.
```

^ Operator

Description

Used to raise a number to the power of an exponent.

Syntax

result = *number^exponent*

The ^ operator syntax has these parts:

Part	Description
result	Any numeric variable.
number	Any numeric expression.
exponent	Any numeric expression.

Remarks

Number can be negative only if *exponent* is an integer value. When more than one exponentiation is performed in a single expression, the ^ operator is evaluated as it is encountered from left to right.

Usually, the data type of *result* is a **Double** or a **Variant** containing a **Double**. However, if either *number* or *exponent* is a **Null** expression, *result* is also a **Null**.

See Also

Operator Precedence.

Example

This example uses the ^ operator to raise a number to the power of an exponent.

```
MyValue = 2 ^ 2            ' Returns 4.
MyValue = 3 ^ 3 ^ 3        ' Returns 19683.
MyValue = (-5) ^ 3         ' Returns -125.
```

Abs Function

Description

Returns the absolute value of a number.

Syntax

Abs(*number*)

The *number* argument can be any valid numeric expression. If *number* contains no valid data, **Null** is returned; if it is an uninitialized variable, **Empty** is returned.

Remarks	The absolute value of a number is its unsigned magnitude. For example, ABS(-1) and ABS(1) both return 1.
See Also	**Sgn** Function.
Example	This example uses the **Abs** function to compute the absolute value of a number.

```
MyNumber = Abs(50.3)        ' Returns 50.3.
MyNumber = Abs(-50.3)       ' Returns 50.3.
```

Accelerator Property

Applies To	**Button** Object, **Buttons** Collection, **CheckBox** Object, **DrawingObjects** Collection, **GroupBox** Object, **GroupBoxes** Collection, **Label** Object, **Labels** Collection, **OptionButton** Object, **OptionButtons** Collection.
Description	Returns or sets the keyboard accelerator character for the control. Read-write.
Remarks	Each control has one accelerator character which the user can press in combination with the ALT key to activate a control while a dialog is running.
	The first text character of the control that matches the first accelerator text character will be underlined. The comparison for underlining is case-sensitive, but case is not considered when a key is pressed.
	On the Apple Macintosh, the accelerator character is only underlined when the **CommandUnderlines** property is **True**. If this property is **False**, the accelerator character is preserved, but it is not underlined.
	If the accelerator key doesn't match any text in the control, the accelerator is nonfunctional.
Example	This example sets the button text and accelerator key for button two on Dialog1.

```
With DialogSheets("Dialog1").Buttons(2)
   .Text = "Press Me"
   .Accelerator = "P"
End With
```

Activate Method

Applies To

Chart Object, **ChartObject** Object, **DialogSheet** Object, **MenuBar** Object, **Module** Object, **OLEObject** Object, **Pane** Object, **Range** Object, **Window** Object, **Workbook** Object, **Worksheet** Object.

Description

Activates the object, as shown in the following table.

Object	Description
Chart, **ChartObject**	Makes this chart the active chart.
DialogSheet, **Module**, **Worksheet**	Makes this sheet the active sheet. Equivalent to clicking the tab.
MenuBar	Activates the menu bar. There are certain restrictions on which menu bars you can activate at certain times. See the Remarks section for details.
OLEObject	Activates the object.
Pane	Activates the pane. If the pane is not in the active window, the window that the pane belongs to will also be activated. You cannot activate a frozen pane.
Range	Activates a single cell, which must be inside the current selection. To select a range of cells, use the **Select** method.
Window	Brings the window to the front of the z-order. This will not run any Auto_Activate or Auto_Deactivate macros that might be attached to the workbook (use the **RunAutoMacros** method to run those macros).
Workbook	Activates the first window associated with the workbook. This will not run any Auto_Activate or Auto_Deactivate macros that might be attached to the workbook (use the **RunAutoMacros** method to run those macros).

Syntax

object.**Activate**

object
    Required. The object to activate.

Remarks

When you activate a built-in menu bar, you can display only a menu bar appropriate for the object. For example, if you try to display a chart menu bar for a worksheet or macro sheet, this method returns an error and interrupts the current macro.

Activating a custom menu bar disables automatic menu bar switching when different types of documents are selected. For example, if a custom menu bar is displayed and you switch to a chart, the two chart menus are not displayed (they would be if you were using the built-in menu bars). Automatic menu bar switching is reenabled when a built-in menu bar is displayed.

See Also   **Select** Method.

Example   This example activates Sheet1 in the workbook BOOK1.XLS.

```
Workbooks("BOOK1.XLS").Worksheets("Sheet1").Activate
```

This example selects cells A1:C3 on Sheet1 and then makes cell B2 the active cell.

```
Worksheets("Sheet1").Activate
Range("A1:C3").Select
Range("B2").Activate
```

This example activates the workbook BOOK4.XLS. If BOOK4.XLS has multiple windows, the example activates the first window, BOOK4.XLS:1.

```
Workbooks("BOOK4.XLS").Activate
```

ActivateMicrosoftApp Method

Applies To   **Application** Object.

Description   Activates a Microsoft application. If the application is already running, this method activates the running application. If the application is not running, this method starts a new instance of the application.

Syntax   *object*.**ActivateMicrosoftApp**(*index*)

object
    Required. The **Application** object.

index
    Required. Specifies the Microsoft application to activate (one of **xlMicrosoftWord**, **xlMicrosoftPowerPoint**, **xlMicrosoftMail**, **xlMicrosoftAccess**, **xlMicrosoftFoxPro**, **xlMicrosoftProject**, or **xlMicrosoftSchedulePlus**).

Example   This example starts and activates Word.

```
Application.ActivateMicrosoftApp xlMicrosoftWord
```

ActivateNext Method

Applies To   **Window** Object.

Description   Activates the specified window and then sends it to the back of the window z-order.

Syntax   *object*.**ActivateNext**

object
    Required. The **Window** object.

See Also   **ActivatePrevious** Method, **Next** Property.

Example   This example sends the active window to the back of the z-order.

```
ActiveWindow.ActivateNext
```

ActivatePrevious Method

Applies To   **Window** Object.

Description   Activates the specified window and then activates the window at the back of the window z-order.

Syntax   *object*.**ActivatePrevious**

object
    Required. The **Window** object.

See Also   **ActivateNext** Method, **Previous** Property.

Example   This example activates the window at the back of the z-order.

```
ActiveWindow.ActivatePrevious
```

ActiveCell Property

Applies To   **Application** Object, **Window** Object.

Description   Accessor. Returns a **Range** object that represents the active cell in the active window (the window on top) or in the specified window. If the window is not displaying a worksheet, this property fails. Read-only.

Remarks   If you do not specify an object qualifier, this property returns the active cell in the active window.

Be careful to distinguish between the active cell and the selection. The active cell is a single cell inside the current selection. The selection may contain more than one cell, but only one is the active cell.

The following expressions all return the active cell, and are all equivalent.

```
ActiveCell
Application.ActiveCell
ActiveWindow.ActiveCell
Application.ActiveWindow.ActiveCell
```

Example   This example uses a message box to display the value in the active cell. Because the **ActiveCell** property will fail if the active sheet is not a worksheet, the example activates Sheet1 before using the **ActiveCell** property.

```
Worksheets("Sheet1").Activate
MsgBox ActiveCell.Value
```

This example changes font formatting for the active cell.

```
Worksheets("Sheet1").Activate
With ActiveCell.Font
    .Bold = True
    .Italic = True
End With
```

ActiveChart Property

Applies To   **Application** Object, **Window** Object, **Workbook** Object.

Description   Accessor. Returns a **Chart** object that represents the active chart (either an embedded chart or a chart sheet). An embedded chart is considered active when it is either selected or activated. When no chart is active, this property returns **Nothing**. Read-only.

Remarks   If you do not specify an object qualifier, this property returns the active chart in the active workbook.

Example   This example turns on the legend for the active chart.

```
ActiveChart.HasLegend = True
```

ActiveDialog Property

Applies To   **Application** Object.

Description   Accessor. Returns a **DialogSheet** object that represents the topmost running dialog sheet. If there is no running dialog sheet, this property returns **Nothing**. Note that the active dialog sheet is not necessarily the active sheet. Read-only.

Example   This example sets the height of the active dialog box.

```
ActiveDialog.DialogFrame.Height = 91
```

ActiveMenuBar Property

Applies To   **Application** Object.

Description   Accessor. Returns a **MenuBar** object that represents the active menu bar. Read-only.

Example   This example displays the name (**Caption** property) of the active menu bar.

```
MsgBox "The active menu bar is called " & ActiveMenuBar.Caption
```

ActivePane Property

Applies To   **Window** Object.

Description   Accessor. Returns a **Pane** object that represents the active pane in the window. Read-only.

Remarks   This property can be used only on worksheets and macro sheets.

      This property returns a **Pane** object. You must use the **Index** property to obtain the index of the active pane.

See Also   **ActiveWindow** Property.

Example
This example activates the next pane for the active window in BOOK1.XLS. You cannot activate the next pane if the panes are frozen. The example must be run from a workbook other than BOOK1.XLS. Before running the example, make sure that BOOK1.XLS has either two or four panes in the active worksheet.

```
Workbooks("BOOK1.XLS").Activate
If not ActiveWindow.FreezePanes Then
    With ActiveWindow
        i = .ActivePane.Index
        If i = .Panes.Count Then
            .Panes(1).Activate
        Else
            .Panes(i+1).Activate
        End If
    End With
End If
```

ActivePrinter Property

Applies To   **Application** Object.

Description   Returns or sets the name of the active printer. Read-write. The name is a string.

Remarks   This property cannot be set on the Apple Macintosh.

Example   This example displays the name of the active printer.

```
MsgBox "The name of the active printer is " & Application.ActivePrinter
```

ActiveSheet Property

Applies To   **Application** Object, **Window** Object, **Workbook** Object.

Description   Accessor. Returns an object that represents the active sheet (the sheet on top) in the active workbook or in the specified window or workbook. Returns **Nothing** if no sheet is active. Read-only.

The object type returned by the **ActiveSheet** property depends on the active sheet, as shown in the following table.

Active sheet	Object type returned
Worksheet	**Worksheet**
Visual Basic module	**Module**
Chart	**Chart**
Dialog sheet	**DialogSheet**

Remarks

If you do not specify an object qualifier, this property returns the active sheet in the active workbook.

If a workbook appears in more than one window, the **ActiveSheet** property may be different in different windows.

See Also   **Activate** Method, **Select** Method.

Example   This example displays the name (**Name** property) of the active sheet.

```
MsgBox "The name of the active sheet is " & ActiveSheet.Name
```

ActiveWindow Property

Applies To   **Application** Object.

Description   Accessor. Returns a **Window** object that represents the active window (the window on top). Read-only. Returns **Nothing** if no windows are open.

See Also   **Activate** Method, **Select** Method.

Example   This example displays the name (**Caption** property) of the active window.

```
MsgBox "The name of the active window is " & ActiveWindow.Caption
```

ActiveWorkbook Property

Applies To   **Application** Object.

Description   Accessor. Returns a **Workbook** object that represents the workbook in the active window (the window on top). Read-only. Returns **Nothing** if no windows are open or if the active window is the Info window or the Clipboard window.

Example

This example displays the name (**Name** property) of the active workbook.

```
MsgBox "The name of the active workbook is " & ActiveWorkbook.Name
```

Add Method (AddIns Collection)

Applies To

AddIns Collection.

Description

Adds a new add-in file to the list of add-ins. Returns an **AddIn** object.

Syntax

object.**Add**(*fileName*, *copyFile*)

object
Required. The **AddIns** object.

fileName
Required. The name of the file containing the add-in you wish to add to the list in the add-in manager.

copyFile
Optional. Ignored if the add-in file is on a hard disk. If **True** and the add-in is on removable media (a floppy disk or CD-ROM), the add-in will be copied to your hard disk. If **False**, the add-in will remain on the removable media. If this argument is omitted, Microsoft Excel displays a dialog box and asks you to choose.

Remarks

This method does not install the new add-in. You must set the **Installed** property to install the add-in.

See Also

Installed Property.

Example

This example inserts the add-in MYADDIN.XLA from drive A. When you run this example, Microsoft Excel copies the file A:\MYADDIN.XLA to the LIBRARY folder on your hard disk and adds the add-in title to the list in the Add-Ins dialog box.

```
Set myAddIn = AddIns.Add(filename:="A:\MYADDIN.XLA", _
        copyfile:=True)
MsgBox myAddIn.Title & " has been added to the list"
```

In Microsoft Excel for the Macintosh, this example copies the add-in from the disk labeled Add-In Disk to the Macro Library folder.

```
Set myAddIn = AddIns.Add(filename:="Add-In Disk:My Add-In", _
        copyfile:=True)
MsgBox myAddIn.Title & " has been added to the list"
```

Add Method (Arcs and Lines)

Applies To	**Arcs** Collection, **Lines** Collection.
Description	Creates a new arc or line.
Syntax	*object*.**Add**(*x1*, *y1*, *x2*, *y2*)

object
  Required. The **Arc** or **Line** object.

x1, *y1*
  Required. Specifies the position of the first coordinate of the object, in points (1/72 inch) relative to the top left corner of cell A1 or the upper left corner of the chart.

x2, *y2*
  Required. Specifies the position of the second coordinate of the object, in points relative to the top left corner of cell A1 or the upper left corner of the chart.

See Also	**Add** Method (**Drawings** Collection), **Add** Method (**DropDowns** Collection), **Add** Method (Graphic Objects and Controls), **Duplicate** Method.
Example	This example creates a new line on Sheet1, with the arrowhead pointing to the upper left. Note the order of the points: the arrowhead points to the second coordinate.

```
With Worksheets("Sheet1").Lines.Add(80, 80, 10, 10)
    .ArrowHeadStyle = xlOpen
    .Border.LineStyle = xlDot
End With
```

Add Method (Charts Collection)

Applies To	**Charts** Collection.
Description	Creates a new chart. Returns a **Chart** object.
Syntax	*object*.**Add**(*before*, *after*, *count*)

object
  Required. The **Charts** object.

before
  Optional. Specifies the sheet before which the new sheet is added.

after
  Optional. Specifies the sheet after which the new sheet is added.

       count
          Optional. The number of sheets to add. If omitted, the default is one.

Remarks   If *before* and *after* are omitted, the new chart is inserted before the active sheet.

Example   This example creates an empty chart sheet and inserts it before the active sheet.

```
ActiveWorkbook.Charts.Add
```

Add Method (DialogSheets Collection)

Applies To   **DialogSheets** Collection.

Description   Creates a new dialog sheet. Returns a **DialogSheet** object.

Syntax   *object*.**Add**(*before*, *after*, *count*)

       object
          Required. The **DialogSheets** object.

       before
          Optional. Specifies the sheet before which the new sheet is added.

       after
          Optional. Specifies the sheet after which the new sheet is added.

       count
          Optional. The number of sheets to add. If omitted, the default is one.

Remarks   If *before* and *after* are omitted, the new sheet is inserted before the active sheet.

Example   This example creates a new dialog sheet containing a default dialog frame and buttons. The new sheet is inserted before the active sheet.

```
ActiveWorkbook.DialogSheets.Add
```

Add Method (DocumentProperties Collection)

Applies To   **DocumentProperties** Collection.

Description   Creates a new custom document property. Returns a **DocumentProperty** object.

           To use this method, you should establish a reference to the Microsoft Office 95 Object Library by using the References command (Tools menu).

Syntax   *object*.**Add**(*name*, *linkToContent*, *type*, *value*, *linkSource*)

object

Required. The custom **DocumentProperties** collection object.

name

Required. The name of the property.

linkToContent

Required. Specifies whether the property is linked to the content of the container document. If **True**, the *linkSource* argument is required. If **False**, the *value* argument is required.

type

Required. The data type of the property (can be one of **offPropertyTypeBoolean**, **offPropertyTypeDate**, **offPropertyTypeFloat**, **offPropertyTypeString**, or **offPropertyTypeNumber**).

value

Optional. The value of the property if it's not linked to the content of the container document. The value is converted to match the data type specified by the *type* argument, if possible; otherwise, an error occurs. If *linkToContent* is **True**, this argument is ignored and the new document property has a default value until linked property values are updated by the container application (usually when the document is saved).

linkSource

Optional. Ignored if *linkToContent* is **False**. The source of the linked property. The container application determines what types of source linking are allowed.

Remarks

This method cannot be used with the collection of built-in document properties.

Example

This example adds a new custom document property. You must pass the custom **DocumentProperties** collection to the procedure.

```
Sub AddCustomProperty(dp As DocumentProperties)
    dp.Add name:="Complete", linkToContent:=False, _
        type:=offPropertyTypeBoolean, value:=False
End Sub
```

This example adds a static custom property named "Complete."

```
With ActiveWorkbook.CustomDocumentProperties
    .Add name := "Complete", linkToContent := False, _
        type := offPropertyTypeBoolean, value := False
End With
```

This example adds a property linked to the name "Grand_Total."

```
With ActiveWorkbook.CustomDocumentProperties
    .Add name := "Total Sales", linkToContent := True, _
        linkSource := "Grand_Total"
End With
```

Add Method (Drawings Collection)

Applies To   **Drawings** Collection.

Description   Creates a new drawing using the first two vertices of the polygon as coordinates relative to cell A1 or the upper left corner of the chart. Additional vertices can be added to the first two vertices using the **AddVertex** method.

Syntax   *object*.**Add**(*x1*, *y1*, *x2*, *y2*, *closed*)

object
    Required. The **Drawings** object.

x1, *y1*
    Required. Specifies the position of the first coordinate of the polygon, in points (1/72 inch) relative to the top left corner of cell A1 or the upper left corner of the chart.

x2, *y2*
    Required. Specifies the position of the second coordinate of the polygon, in points relative to the top left corner of cell A1 or the upper left corner of the chart.

closed
    Required. If **True**, the new drawing is closed and the last vertex is always connected to the first vertex. If **False**, the drawing is open and the last vertex is not connected to the first vertex.

See Also   **Add** Method (Arcs and Lines), **Add** Method (**DropDowns** Collection), **Add** Method (Graphic Objects and Controls), **AddVertex** Method, **Reshape** Method, **Vertices** Property.

Example   This example creates a new open trapezoid on Sheet1.

```
With Worksheets("Sheet1").Drawings.Add(100, 100, 200, 100, False)
    .AddVertex 180, 200
    .AddVertex 80, 200
    .AddVertex 100, 100
    .Border.Weight = xlMedium
End With
```

Add Method (DropDowns Collection)

Applies To   **DropDowns** Collection.

Description   Creates a new drop-down list box using rectangular coordinates specified in points (1/72 inch).

Syntax	*object*.**Add**(*left*, *top*, *width*, *height*, *editable*)

object
Required. The **DropDowns** object.

left, *top*, *width*, *height*
Required. Specifies the width, height, and initial coordinates of the upper left corner of the object, in points relative to the top left corner of cell A1 or the upper left corner of the chart.

editable
Optional. True if the drop-down list box can be edited. If this argument is False or omitted, the contents of the list-box editing region can be changed only by selecting from the list.

See Also   **Add** Method (Arcs and Lines), **Add** Method (**Drawings** Collection), **Add** Method (Graphic Objects and Controls), **Duplicate** Method.

Example   This example creates a drop-down list box on Sheet1.

```
With Worksheets("Sheet1").DropDowns.Add(10, 10, 120, 18)
    .DropDownLines = 10
End With
```

Add Method (Graphic Objects and Controls)

Applies To   **Buttons** Collection, **ChartObjects** Collection, **EditBoxes** Collection, **GroupBoxes** Collection, **Labels** Collection, **ListBoxes** Collection, **OptionButtons** Collection, **Ovals** Collection, **Pictures** Collection, **Rectangles** Collection, **ScrollBars** Collection, **Spinners** Collection, **TextBoxes** Collection.

Description   Creates a new graphic object or control using coordinates specified in points (1/72 inch).

The type of the object depends on the collection on which you call **Add**. For example, `Rectangles.Add` creates a new rectangle; `Ovals.Add` creates a new oval.

Syntax   *object*.**Add**(*left*, *top*, *width*, *height*)

object
Required. The object to which this method applies.

left, *top*
Required. Specifies the initial coordinates of the new object, in points (1/72 inch), relative to the top left corner of cell A1 on a worksheet, or to the upper left corner of a chart.

width, height
>   Required. Specifies the initial size of the new object, in points (1/72 inch).

Remarks   The specified coordinates describe the new object's bounding rectangle. The object fills the bounding rectangle.

See Also   **Add** Method (Arcs and Lines), **Add** Method (**Drawings** Collection), **Add** Method (**DropDowns** Collection), **Duplicate** Method.

Example   This example creates a new oval on Sheet1. The oval is aligned with and the same size as cell D3.

```
Set myCell = ActiveWorkbook.Worksheets("Sheet1").Range("D3")
ActiveWorkbook.Worksheets("Sheet1").Ovals.Add _
    Top:=myCell.Top, Left:=myCell.Left, _
    Height:=myCell.Height, Width:=myCell.Width
```

Add Method (MenuBars Collection)

Applies To   **MenuBars** Collection.

Description   Creates a new menu bar. Returns a **MenuBar** object.

Syntax   *object*.**Add(***name***)**

object
>   Required. The **MenuBars** object.

name
>   Optional. The name for the new menu bar.

Remarks   The name of the menu bar is the same as its caption.

Example   The following example adds a new menu bar and then activates it. After running the example, you can use `MenuBars(xlModule).Activate` to restore the Visual Basic Module menu.

```
With MenuBars.Add("Stock Chart")
    With .Menus.Add("File")
        .MenuItems.Add "Update", "UpdateProc"
        .MenuItems.Add "Print", "PrintProc"
    End With
End With
MenuBars("Stock Chart").Activate
```

Add Method (MenuItems Collection)

Applies To   **MenuItems** Collection.

Description   Adds a new menu item to the specified menu. Can also be used to restore a built-in menu item in Microsoft Excel that has been deleted. Returns a **MenuItem** object. Use the **AddMenu** method to add a submenu caption.

Syntax   *object*.**Add**(*caption*, *onAction*, *shortcutKey*, *before*, *restore*, *statusBar*, *helpContextID*, *helpFile*)

object
Required. The **MenuItems** object.

caption
Required. The text of the menu item (sets the initial value of the **Caption** property for the new menu item). Use an ampersand (&) before the command underline. Use a single hyphen ("-") for the caption to create a separator bar.

onAction
Optional. Specifies the name of the macro that runs when the new menu item is selected.

shortcutKey
Optional. Used only on the Apple Macintosh. Specifies the shortcut key for the menu item as text.

before
Optional. Specifies the menu item before which the new item will be added. Can be either a number (1 to insert at the top of the menu, for example) or a caption of another, existing menu item (in the language of the macro, without the ampersand), or a reference to the menu item.

restore
Optional. If **True**, Microsoft Excel will restore the previously deleted built-in menu item named *caption*. If **False** or omitted, Microsoft Excel will add a new menu item. The restored menu item is placed at the end of the menu unless you use the *before* argument to specify the location.

statusBar
Optional. Specifies help text to display in the status bar when the menu item is selected or browsed by the user. If omitted the default status bar text assigned to the macro is used.

helpContextID
Optional. Specifies the context ID for the custom help topic of the menu item. If omitted the default help context ID assigned to the macro is used.

helpFile
Optional. Specifies the help file name containing the custom help topic of the menu item. If omitted the default help file name assigned to the macro is used.

Remarks   The settings specified for the *statusBar*, *helpContextID*, and *helpFile* arguments
override any per-macro options set by the macro specified by the *onAction*
argument.

However, changing the macro options after the menu item has been added overrides
the custom help arguments used with the **Add** method.

See Also   **AddMenu** Method, **Checked** Property, **Enabled** Property, **MacroOptions**
Method, **OnAction** Property.

Example   This example adds a new menu item at the top of the Help menu on each menu bar.

```
For Each mb in MenuBars
    mb.Menus("Help").MenuItems.Add _
        caption:="Read Me First", _
        onAction:="Read_Me_First", _
        before:=1
Next mb
```

Add Method (Menus Collection)

Applies To   **Menus** Collection.

Description   Adds a new menu. Can also be used to restore a built-in menu in Microsoft Excel
that has been deleted. Returns a **Menu** object.

Syntax   *object*.**Add**(*caption*, *before*, *restore*)

object
    Required. The **Menus** object.

caption
    Required. The text of the menu (sets the initial value of the **Caption** property for
    the new menu). Use an ampersand (&) before the command underline.

before
    Optional. Specifies the menu before which the new menu will be added. Can be
    either a number (one to insert at the beginning of the menu bar, for example) or
    a caption of another, existing menu (in the language of the macro, without the
    ampersand), or a reference to the menu. If this argument is omitted, the new
    menu is added to the left of the Window menu.

restore
    Optional. If **True**, Microsoft Excel will restore the previously deleted built-in
    menu named *caption*. If **False** or omitted, Microsoft Excel will add a new menu.
    The restored menu is placed at the end of the menu bar unless you use the *before*
    argument to specify the location.

Remarks   On the Apple Macintosh, this method returns an error if there is not enough room to create the new menu. You should always check the return value to ensure that the new menu was added successfully.

In Windows, the menu bar will wrap if necessary to fit the new menu.

You cannot create a new shortcut menu; you can only modify a built-in shortcut menu.

Example   This example adds a new menu to the worksheet menu bar.

```
MenuBars(xlWorksheet).Menus.Add caption:="More Help"
```

Add Method (Modules Collection)

Applies To   **Modules** Collection.

Description   Creates a new Visual Basic module. Returns a **Module** object.

Syntax   *object*.**Add**(*before*, *after*, *count*)

object
   Required. The **Modules** object.

before
   Optional. Specifies the sheet before which the new module is added.

after
   Optional. Specifies the sheet after which the new module is added.

count
   Optional. The number of sheets to add. If omitted, the default is one.

Remarks   If *before* and *after* are omitted, the module is inserted before the active sheet.

Example   This example inserts a new Visual Basic module before the active sheet.

```
ActiveWorkbook.Modules.Add
```

Add Method (Names Collection)

Applies To   **Names** Collection.

Description   Defines a new name. Returns a **Name** object.

Syntax   *object*.**Add**(*name*, *refersTo*, *visible*, *macroType*, *shortcutKey*, *category*,
                          nameLocal, *refersToLocal*, *categoryLocal*, *refersToR1C1*, *refersToR1C1Local*)

object
> Required. The **Names** object.

name
> Required (unless *nameLocal* is specified). The text to use as the name (in the
> language of the macro). Names cannot include spaces and cannot look like cell
> references.

refersTo
> Required (unless one of the other *refersTo* arguments is specified). Describes
> what the name refers to (in the language of the macro, using A1-style notation).

visible
> Optional. If **True** or omitted, Microsoft Excel defines the name normally. If
> **False**, the name is defined as a hidden name (it does not appear in the Define
> Name, Paste Name, or Goto dialog boxes).

macroType
> Optional. Specifies the macro type, as shown in the following table.

Value	Meaning
1	User-defined function (**Function** procedure)
2	Macro (also known as **Sub** procedure)
3 or omitted	None (that is, the name does not refer to a user-defined function or macro)

shortcutKey
> Optional. Specifies the macro shortcut key. Must be a single letter, such as "z"
> or "Z". Applies only for command macros.

category
> Specifies the category of the macro or function if *macroType* is 1 or 2. The
> category is used in the Function Wizard. Existing categories can be referred to
> by number (starting at one), or by name (in the language of the macro).
> Microsoft Excel creates a new category if the specified category does not
> already exist.

nameLocal
> Required if *name* is not specified. The text to use as the name (in the language
> of the user). Names cannot include spaces, and cannot look like cell references.

refersToLocal
> Required (unless one of the other *refersTo* arguments is specified). Describes
> what the name refers to (in the language of the user, using A1-style notation).

categoryLocal
> Required if *category* is not specified. Text identifying the category of a custom
> function in the language of the user.

refersToR1C1

Required (unless one of the other *refersTo* arguments is specified). Describes what the name refers to (in the language of the macro, using R1C1-style notation).

refersToR1C1Local

Required (unless one of the other *refersTo* arguments is specified). Describes what the name refers to (in the language of the user, using R1C1-style notation).

Example

This example defines a new name for the range A1:D3 on Sheet1.

```
ActiveWorkbook.Names.Add _
    name:="tempRange", _
    refersTo:="=Sheet1!$A$1:$D$3"
```

Add Method (OLEObjects Collection)

Applies To

OLEObjects Collection.

Description

Adds a new OLE object to the current sheet. Returns an **OLEObject** object.

Syntax

object.**Add**(*classType*, *fileName*, *link*, *displayAsIcon*, *iconFileName*, *iconIndex*, *iconLabel*)

object

Required. The **OLEObjects** collection.

classType

Optional (you must specify either *classType* or *fileName*). A string containing the OLE long class name for the object that is to be created. If *classType* is specified, *fileName* and *link* are ignored.

fileName

Optional (you must specify either *classType* or *fileName*). A string specifying the file from which the OLE object is to be created.

link

Optional. **True** if the new OLE object based on *fileName* should be linked to that file. If it is not linked, the file is created as a copy of the file. **False** if omitted.

displayAsIcon

Optional. **True** if the new OLE object is displayed as an icon, or as its regular picture. If **True**, the *iconFileName* and *iconIndex* can be used to specify an icon.

> ### iconFileName
> Optional. A string that specifies the file that contains the icon to be displayed. This is used only if **displayAsIcon** is **True**. If not specified or the file contains no icons, the default icon for the OLE Class is used.
>
> ### iconIndex
> Optional. The number of the icon within the **iconFileName**. This is used only if **displayAsIcon** is **True** and **iconFileName** refers to a valid file containing icons. If an icon with the given index does not exist in the file specified in **iconFileName**, the first one in the file is used.
>
> ### iconLabel
> Optional. A string specifying a label to display beneath the icon. This is used only if **displayAsIcon** is **True**. If this argument is omitted or the string is empty (""), then no caption is displayed.

Example   This example creates a new Microsoft Word OLE object on Sheet1.

```
ActiveWorkbook.Worksheets("Sheet1").OLEObjects.Add _
    classType:="Word.Document.6"
```

Add Method (Scenarios Collection)

Applies To   **Scenarios** Collection.

Description   Creates a new scenario and adds it to the list of scenarios available for the current worksheet. Returns a **Scenario** object.

Syntax   *object*.**Add**(*name*, *changingCells*, *values*, *comment*, *locked*, *hidden*)

> ### object
> Required. The **Scenarios** object.
>
> ### name
> Required. A string specifying the name for the new scenario.
>
> ### changingCells
> Required. A range giving the changing cells for the scenario.
>
> ### values
> Optional. An array containing the scenario values for the cells in **changingCells**. If omitted, the scenario values are assumed to be the current values in the cells of **changingCells**.
>
> ### comment
> Optional. A string specifying comment text for the scenario. When a new scenario is added, author name and date are automatically added at the beginning of the comment text.

locked

Optional. **True** if the scenario is locked to prevent changes. If this argument is omitted, the scenario is locked.

hidden

Optional. **True** if the scenario is hidden. If this argument is omitted, the scenario is not hidden.

Remarks   A scenario name must be unique; Microsoft Excel generates an error if you try to create a scenario with a name already in use.

Example   This example adds a new scenario to Sheet1.

```
Worksheets("Sheet1").Scenarios.Add Name:="Best Case", _
    ChangingCells:=Worksheets("Sheet1").Range("A1:A4"), _
    Values:=Array(23, 5, 6, 21), _
    Comment:="Most favorable outcome."
```

Add Method (SeriesCollection Collection)

Applies To   **SeriesCollection** Collection.

Description   Adds one or more new series to the **SeriesCollection** collection.

Syntax   *object*.**Add**(*source*, *rowcol*, *seriesLabels*, *categoryLabels*, *replace*)

object

Required. The **SeriesCollection** object.

source

Required. Specifies the new data, either as a **Range** or an array of data points.

rowcol

Optional. Specifies whether the new values are in the rows (**xlRows**) or columns (**xlColumns**) of the specified range. The default value is **xlColumns**.

seriesLabels

Optional. Ignored if *source* is an array. **True** if the first row or column contains the name of the data series. **False** if the first row or column contains the first data point of the series. If this argument is omitted, Microsoft Excel attempts to determine the series name location from the contents of the first row or column.

categoryLabels

Optional. Ignored if *source* is an array. **True** if the first row or column contains the name of the category labels. **False** if the first row or column contains the first data point of the series. If this argument is omitted, Microsoft Excel attempts to determine the category label location from the contents of the first row or column.

replace
> Optional. If *categoryLabels* is **True** and *replace* is **True**, the specified categories replace the categories that currently exist for the series. If this argument is **False** or omitted, the existing categories will not be replaced.

See Also   **Extend** Method.

Example   This example creates a new series in Chart1. The data source for the new series is range B1:B10 on Sheet1.

```
Charts("Chart1").SeriesCollection.Add _
    source:=ActiveWorkbook.Worksheets("Sheet1").Range("B1:B10")
```

This is the same as the preceding example, except that the chart is an embedded chart on Sheet1.

```
Worksheets("Sheet1").ChartObjects(1).Activate
ActiveChart.SeriesCollection.Add _
    source:=Worksheets("Sheet1").Range("B1:B10")
```

Add Method (Sheets Collection)

Applies To   **Sheets** Collection.

Description   Creates a new worksheet, chart, module, dialog sheet or macro sheet.

Syntax   *object*.**Add**(*before*, *after*, *count*, *type*)

object
> Required. The **Sheets** object.

before
> Optional. Specifies the sheet before which the new sheet is added. Must be an object, for example `ActiveWorkbook.Worksheets("Sheet1")`.

after
> Optional. Specifies the sheet after which the new sheet is added. Must be an object, for example `ActiveWorkbook.ActiveSheet`.

count
> Optional. The number of sheets to add. If omitted, the default is one.

type
> Optional. The type of sheet to add. Must be one of **xlWorksheet**, **xlChart**, **xlModule**, **xlDialogSheet**, **xlExcel4MacroSheet**, or **xlExcel4IntlMacroSheet**. If omitted, the default is **xlWorksheet**.

Remarks   If *before* and *after* are omitted, the new sheet is inserted before the active sheet.

Example

This example inserts a new worksheet before the active sheet.

```
ActiveWorkbook.Sheets.Add before:=ActiveWorkbook.ActiveSheet
```

This example adds two new dialog sheets after Module1.

```
ActiveWorkbook.Sheets.Add after:=ActiveWorkbook.Sheets("Module1"), _
    type:=xlDialogSheet, count:=2
```

Add Method (Styles Collection)

Applies To

Styles Collection.

Description

Creates a new style and adds it to the list of styles available for the current workbook. Returns a **Style** object.

Syntax

object.**Add**(*name*, *basedOn*)

object
Required. The **Styles** object.

name
Required. A string specifying the name for the new style.

basedOn
Optional. A reference to a cell that will be used as the basis for the new style. If specified, the newly created style will be given a style based on that cell. If omitted, the newly created style will be based on the Normal style.

Remarks

If a style with the specified name already exists, this method redefines the style based on the cell specified in *basedOn*. The following example redefines the Normal style based on the active cell:

```
ActiveWorkbook.Styles.Add name:="Normal", _
    basedOn:=ActiveCell
```

Example

This example defines a new style based on cell A1 on Sheet1.

```
Worksheets("Sheet1").Activate
ActiveWorkbook.Styles.Add name:="myNewStyle", _
    basedOn:=ActiveSheet.Range("A1")
```

This example defines a new style that includes only the **Font** property.

```
With ActiveWorkbook.Styles.Add(name:="theNewStyle")
    .IncludeNumber = False
    .IncludeFont = True
    .IncludeAlignment = False
    .IncludeBorder = False
    .IncludePatterns = False
    .IncludeProtection = False
    .Font.Name = "Arial"
    .Font.Size = 18
End With
```

Add Method (ToolbarButtons Collection)

Applies To **ToolbarButtons** Collection.

Description Adds a new button to an existing toolbar. Returns a **ToolbarButton** object.

Syntax *object*.**Add**(*button*, *before*, *onAction*, *pushed*, *enabled*, *statusBar*, *helpContextID*, *helpFile*)

object
Required. The **ToolbarButtons** object.

button
Optional. The button ID number, as an integer. If this argument is omitted, a gap is inserted in the toolbar. You can only insert a gap between two toolbar buttons (you cannot insert a gap at the beginning or at the end of the toolbar). To insert a button followed by a gap at the beginning of the toolbar, insert the new button first, and then insert the gap after the new button. For a complete list of button IDs available to Visual Basic, see Toolbar Button ID Values.

before
Optional. Specifies the new button position. The new button will be inserted before the button at this position. If this argument is omitted, the button is inserted at the end of the toolbar. Remember that gaps count as toolbar buttons; you cannot simply count buttons to get the button position. For example, if there is a gap between the first and second buttons on the toolbar, you must specify 3 for the *before* argument to insert a new button after the gap.

onAction

Optional. Specifies an initial value for the **OnAction** property, which is the name of the macro that runs when the button is clicked. If omitted with a built-in button, the button will have its built-in behavior. If omitted with a custom button, the Assign Macro dialog box is displayed when the button is first clicked.

pushed

Optional. Specifies an initial value for the **Pushed** property (**True** if the button appears pressed).

enabled

Optional. Specifies an initial value for the **Enabled** property (**True** if the button is enabled).

statusBar

Optional. Specifies help text to display in the status bar when the mouse cursor is positioned over the toolbar button. If omitted the default status bar text assigned to the macro is used.

helpContextID

Optional. Specifies the context ID for the custom help topic of the toolbar button. If omitted the default help context ID assigned to the macro is used.

helpFile

Optional. Specifies the help file name containing the custom help topic of the toolbar button. If omitted the default help file name assigned to the macro is used.

Remarks

The settings specified for the *statusBar*, *helpContextID*, and *helpFile* arguments override any per-macro options set by the macro specified by the *onAction* argument.

However, changing the macro options after the toolbar button has been added overrides the custom help arguments used with the **Add** method.

See Also

Enabled Property, **MacroOptions** Method, **OnAction** Property, **Pushed** Property.

Example

This example creates a new toolbar, adds the Camera button (button index number 228) to it, and then displays the new toolbar.

```
Set myNewToolbar = Toolbars.Add(Name:="My New Toolbar")
myNewToolbar.ToolbarButtons.Add Button:=228
myNewToolbar.Visible = True
```

Add Method (Toolbars Collection)

Applies To   **Toolbars** Collection.

Description	Creates a new toolbar. Returns a **Toolbar** object.
Syntax	*object*.**Add**(*name*)

object
 Required. The **Toolbars** object.

name
 Optional. A string that specifies a name for the new toolbar. If omitted, Microsoft Excel uses a default name (such as "Toolbar 1").

Example   This example creates a new toolbar, adds the Camera button (button index number 228) to it, and then displays the new toolbar.

```
Set myNewToolbar = Toolbars.Add(Name:="My New Toolbar")
myNewToolbar.ToolbarButtons.Add Button:=228
myNewToolbar.Visible = True
```

Add Method (Trendlines Collection)

Applies To   **Trendlines** Collection.

Description   Creates a new **Trendline**.

Syntax   *object*.**Add**(*type*, *order*, *period*, *forward*, *backward*, *intercept*, *displayEquation*, *displayRSquared*, *name*)

object
 Required. The **Trendlines** object.

type
 Optional. Specifies the trendline type (one of **xlLinear**, **xlLogarithmic**, **xlExponential**, **xlPolynomial**, **xlMovingAvg**, or **xlPower**). If omitted, the default is **xlLinear**.

order
 Required if *type* is **xlPolynomial**. Specifies the trendline order. Must be an integer from two to six, inclusive.

period
 Required if *type* is **xlMovingAvg**. Specifies the trendline period. Must be an integer greater than one and less than the number of data points in the series you are adding a trendline to.

forward
 Optional. Sets the number of periods (or units on a scatter chart) that the trendline extends forward.

backward
> Optional. Sets the number of periods (or units on a scatter chart) that the trendline extends backward.

intercept
> Optional. Sets the trendline intercept. If omitted, the intercept is automatically set by the regression.

displayEquation
> Optional. **True** if the equation of the trendline is displayed on the chart (in the same data label as the R-squared value).

displayRSquared
> Optional. **True** if the R-squared value of the trendline is displayed on the chart (in the same data label as the equation).

name
> Optional. Specifies the name of the trendline as text. If this argument is omitted, an automatically generated name is used.

See Also   **Backward** Property, **DisplayEquation** Property, **DisplayRSquared** Property, **Forward** Property, **Intercept** Property, **Order** Property, **Period** Property.

Example   This example creates a new linear trendline in Chart1.

```
ActiveWorkbook.Charts("Chart1").SeriesCollection(1).Trendlines.Add
```

Add Method (Workbooks Collection)

Applies To   **Workbooks** Collection.

Description   Creates a new workbook. The new workbook becomes the active workbook. Returns a **Workbook** object.

Syntax   *object*.**Add**(*template*)

object
> Required. The **Workbooks** object.

template
> Optional. Determines how the new workbook is created. If this argument is a string specifying the name of an existing Microsoft Excel file, the new workbook is created using the specified file as a template. If this argument is a constant (one of **xlWorksheet**, **xlChart**, **xlExcel4MacroSheet**, or **xlExcel4IntlMacroSheet**), the new workbook contains a single sheet of the specified type. If this argument is omitted, Microsoft Excel creates a new workbook with a number of blank sheets (the number of sheets is set by the **SheetsInNewWorkbook** property).

Remarks	If the *template* argument specifies a file, the filename may include a path.
See Also	**ActiveWorkbook** Property, **SheetsInNewWorkbook** Property.
Example	This example creates a new workbook.

```
Workbooks.Add
```

Add Method (Worksheets Collection)

Applies To	**Worksheets** Collection.
Description	Creates a new worksheet. The new worksheet becomes the active sheet. Returns a **Worksheet** object.
Syntax	*object*.**Add**(*before*, *after*, *count*, *type*)

object
    Required. The **Worksheets** object.

before
    Optional. Specifies the sheet before which the new sheet is added.

after
    Optional. Specifies the sheet after which the new sheet is added.

count
    Optional. The number of sheets to add. One if omitted.

type
    Optional. Specifies the worksheet type (one of **xlWorksheet**, **xlExcel4MacroSheet**, or **xlExcel4IntlMacroSheet**). If omitted, the default is **xlWorksheet**.

Remarks	If *before* and *after* are omitted, the new sheet is inserted before the active sheet.
Example	This example creates a new worksheet and inserts it before the active sheet.

```
ActiveWorkbook.Worksheets.Add
```

This example adds a new worksheet after the last worksheet in the active workbook.

```
Worksheets.Add.Move after:=Worksheets(Worksheets.Count)
```

AddChartAutoFormat Method

Applies To	**Application** Object.
Description	Adds a custom chart autoformat to the list of available chart autoformats.
Syntax	*object*.**AddChartAutoFormat**(*chart*, *name*, *description*)

object
  Required. The **Application** object.

chart
  Required. A Chart object that contains the format that will be applied when the new chart autoformat is applied.

name
  Required. A string that represents the name of the autoformat.

description
  Optional. A string that describes the custom autoformat.

See Also	**DeleteChartAutoFormat** Method, **SetDefaultChart** Method.
Example	This example adds a new autoformat based on Chart1.

```
Application.AddChartAutoFormat _
    chart:=Charts("Chart1"), name:="Presentation Chart"
```

AddCustomList Method

Applies To	**Application** Object.
Description	Adds a custom list for custom autofill and/or custom sort.
Syntax	*object*.**AddCustomList**(*listArray*, *byRow*)

object
  Required. The **Application** object.

listArray
  Required. An array of strings, or a Range.

byRow
> Optional. Only used if *listArray* is a **Range**. If **True**, Microsoft Excel creates a custom list from each row in the range. If **False**, Microsoft Excel creates a custom list from each column in the range. If this argument is omitted and there are more rows than columns (or an equal number of rows and columns) in the range, then Microsoft Excel creates a custom list from each column in the range. If this argument is omitted and there are more columns than rows in the range, then Microsoft Excel creates a custom list from each row in the range.

Remarks   If the list you are trying to add already exists, this method does nothing.

See Also   **CustomListCount** Property, **DeleteCustomList** Method, **GetCustomListContents** Method, **GetCustomListNum** Method.

Example   This example adds an array of strings as a custom list.

```
Application.AddCustomList Array("cogs", "sprockets", _
    "widgets", "gizmos")
```

AddFields Method

Applies To   **PivotTable** Object.

Description   Adds row, column and page fields to the PivotTable.

Syntax   *object*.**AddFields**(*rowFields*, *columnFields*, *pageFields*, *addToTable*)

object
> Required. The **PivotTable** object.

rowFields
> Optional. Specifies a pivot field name (or an array of pivot field names) to be added as rows.

columnFields
> Optional. Specifies a pivot field name (or an array of pivot field names) to be added as columns.

pageFields
> Optional. Specifies a pivot field name (or an array of pivot field names) to be added as pages.

addToTable
> Optional. If **True**, the fields are added to the PivotTable (none of the existing fields are replaced). If **False**, the new fields replace existing fields. The default is **False** if this argument is not specified.

Remarks   You must specify one of the field arguments.

See Also   **ColumnFields** Method, **DataFields** Method, **HiddenFields** Method, **PageFields** Method, **RowFields** Method, **VisibleFields** Method.

Example   This example replaces the existing column fields in PivotTable one on Sheet1 with the Status and Closed_By fields.

```
Worksheets("Sheet1").PivotTables(1).AddFields _
    ColumnFields:=Array("Status", "Closed_By")
```

AddIn Object

Description   Represents a single add-in, either installed or not installed.

Accessors   The **AddIn** object is a member of the **AddIns** collection. The **AddIns** collection contains a list of all the add-ins available to Microsoft Excel, regardless of whether they are installed. This list corresponds to the list of add-ins displayed in the Add-Ins dialog box (Tools menu). To access a single member of the collection, use the **AddIns** method with the add-in title or index number as an argument. Do not confuse the add-in title, which appears in the Add-Ins dialog box, with the add-in name, which is the filename of the add-in.

Use the **Title** property to return the title of the add-in (this property is read-only for add-ins). You must exactly match the spelling, but not the capitalization, of the title as it is shown in the Add-Ins dialog box. The following example installs the Analysis Toolpak add-in.

```
AddIns("analysis toolpak").Installed = True
```

The index number represents the position of the add-in in the list of add-ins shown in the Add-Ins dialog box. The following example creates a list on the worksheet named "Sheet1." The list contains specified properties of the available add-ins.

```
Sub EnumerateAddIns()
    Worksheets("sheet1").Rows(1).Font.Bold = True
    Worksheets("sheet1").Range("a1:d1").Value = _
        Array("Name", "Full Name", "Title", "Installed")
    For i = 1 To AddIns.Count
        Worksheets("sheet1").Cells(i + 1, 1) = AddIns(i).Name
        Worksheets("sheet1").Cells(i + 1, 2) = AddIns(i).FullName
        Worksheets("sheet1").Cells(i + 1, 3) = AddIns(i).Title
        Worksheets("sheet1").Cells(i + 1, 4) = AddIns(i).Installed
    Next
    Worksheets("sheet1").Range("a1").CurrentRegion.Columns.AutoFit
End Sub
```

Remarks   The **Add** method adds an add-in to the list of available add-ins but does not install the add-in. Set the **Installed** property of the add-in to **True** to install it. To install an add-in not shown in the list of available add-ins, you must first use the **Add** method and then set the **Installed** property. This can be done in a single step, as shown in the following example (note that you use the name of the add-in, not the title, with the **Add** method):

```
AddIns.Add("generic.xll").Installed = True
```

Use the **Workbooks** method with the add-in filename (not title) to return a reference to the workbook corresponding to a loaded add-in. You must use the filename because loaded add-ins do not normally appear in the **Workbooks** collection. The following example sets the wb variable to the workbook for MYADDIN.XLA.

```
Set wb = Workbooks("myaddin.xla")
```

The following example sets the wb variable to the workbook for the Analysis Toolpak add-in.

```
Set wb = Workbooks(AddIns("analysis toolpak").Name)
```

If the **Installed** property returns **True**, but calls to functions in the add-in still fail, the add-in may not actually be loaded. This is because the **Addin** object represents the existence and installed state of the add-in but doesn't represent the actual contents of the add-in workbook (the add-in dialog sheets, worksheets, and so on).To guarantee that an installed add-in is loaded, you should open the add-in workbook. The following example opens the workbook for the add-in named "My Addin" if the add-in is not already present in the **Workbooks** collection.

```
On Error Resume Next  ' turn off error checking
Set wbMyAddin = Workbooks(Addins("My Addin").Name)
lastError = Err
On Error Goto 0       ' restore error checking
If lastError <> 0 Then
    ' the add-in workbook isn't currently open. Manually open it.
    Set wbMyAddin = Workbooks.Open(Addins("My Addin").FullName)
End If
```

While in a Visual Basic module, you create an add-in by clicking the Make Add-In command on the Tools menu. The **AddIn** object provides a programming interface to the Add-In Manager; it doesn't actually create an add-in.

Properties   **Application** Property, **Author** Property, **Comments** Property, **Creator** Property, **FullName** Property, **Installed** Property, **Keywords** Property, **Name** Property, **Parent** Property, **Path** Property, **Subject** Property, **Title** Property.

AddIndent Property

Applies To **Button** Object, **Buttons** Collection, **DrawingObjects** Collection, **GroupObject** Object, **GroupObjects** Collection, **Range** Object, **Style** Object, **TextBox** Object, **TextBoxes** Collection.

Description **True** if text with the distributed text alignment style has extra space added at the beginning and end of each line. Read-write.

Remarks This property is available only in Far East versions of Microsoft Excel, and only works for text with the **xlDistributed** alignment style in the direction of the text (indent is added if the text **Orientation** is **xlVertical** and the **VerticalAlignment** is **xlDistributed**, or if the text **Orientation** is **xlHorizontal** and the **HorizontalAlignment** is **xlDistributed**).

See Also **HorizontalAlignment** Property, **Orientation** Property, **VerticalAlignment** Property.

Example This example sets cell A1 on Sheet1 to use distributed horizontal alignment with extra space at the beginning and the end.

```
With Worksheets("Sheet1").Range("A1")
    .HorizontalAlignment = xlDistributed
    .AddIndent = True
End With
```

AddIns Collection Object

Description A collection of **AddIn** objects representing all the add-ins available to Microsoft Excel, regardless of whether they are installed. This list corresponds to the list of add-ins displayed in the Add-Ins dialog box (Tools menu).

Accessors Use the **Add** method to add an add-in to the list of available add-ins.

Use the **AddIns** method with an argument to access a single member of the collection or without an argument to access the entire collection at once.

The following example creates a list on the worksheet named "Sheet1" of the names and installed states of all the available add-ins.

```
Sub DisplayAddIns()
    Worksheets("Sheet1").Activate
    rw = 1
    For Each ad In Application.AddIns
        Worksheets("Sheet1").Cells(rw, 1) = ad.Name
        Worksheets("Sheet1").Cells(rw, 2) = ad.Installed
        rw = rw + 1
    Next
End Sub
```

Properties   **Application** Property, **Count** Property, **Creator** Property, **Parent** Property.

Methods   **Add** Method (AddIns Collection), **Item** Method.

AddIns Method

Applies To   **Application** Object.

Description   Accessor. Returns an object that represents a single add-in (an **AddIn** object, Syntax 1) or the collection of add-ins (an **AddIns** object, Syntax 2) listed in the Add-Ins dialog box. Read-only.

Syntax 1   *object*.**AddIns**(*index*)

Syntax 2   *object*.**AddIns**

object
    Optional. The **Application** object.

index
    Required for Syntax 1. The number of the add-in, or the title of the add-in, as a string.

Example   This example displays the status of the Analysis ToolPak add-in. Note that the string used as the index to the **AddIns** method is the **Title** property of the **AddIn** object.

```
If AddIns("Analysis ToolPak").Installed = True Then
    MsgBox "Analysis ToolPak add-in is installed"
Else
    MsgBox "Analysis ToolPak add-in is not installed"
End If
```

AddItem Method

Applies To   **DrawingObjects** Collection, **DropDown** Object, **DropDowns** Collection, **ListBox** Object, **ListBoxes** Collection.

Description   Adds an item to a list box or drop-down list box.

Syntax   *object*.**AddItem**(*text*, *index*)

object
　　Required. The object to which this method applies.

text
　　Required. Specifies the text string to add.

index
　　Optional. Specifies the position at which to add the new entry. If the list has fewer entries than the specified index, blank items are added from the end of the list to the specified position. If this argument is omitted, the item is appended to the existing list.

Remarks   Using this method clears any range specified by the **ListFillRange** property.

See Also   **List** Property, **RemoveItem** Method.

Example   This example replaces the existing contents of list box one on Dialog1 with the letters A through M.

```
DialogSheets("Dialog1").ListBoxes(1).RemoveAllItems
For i = 65 To 77
    DialogSheets("Dialog1").ListBoxes(1).AddItem Text:=Chr(i)
Next i
```

AddMenu Method

Applies To   **MenuItems** Collection.

Description   Adds a new submenu to the menu. This method can also be used to restore a built-in submenu that was previously deleted, by setting the *restore* argument to **True**.

Syntax   *object*.**AddMenu**(*caption*, *before*, *restore*)

object
　　Required. The **MenuItems** object.

caption
　　Required. The caption to use for the new submenu. To create an access key, put an ampersand (&) before the access-key letter.

before
> Optional. If this argument is present, specifies the menu item before which this submenu should be inserted. May be a string containing the caption of the menu item (without the ampersand), a number indicating the position of the menu item, or a reference to the menu item.

restore
> Optional. If this argument is **True**, Microsoft Excel will restore the previously deleted built-in submenu named by the *caption* argument. If **False** or omitted, Microsoft Excel will add a new submenu. The restored submenu is placed at the end of the menu unless you use the *before* argument to specify the location.

See Also   **Add** Method (**MenuItems** Collection).

Example   This example adds a new submenu to the Help menu on the Worksheet menu bar and then adds a submenu item to it.

```
Set newSubMenu = MenuBars(xlWorksheet).Menus("Help"). _
        MenuItems.AddMenu(Caption:="More")
newSubMenu.MenuItems.Add Caption:="More Help"
```

AddReplacement Method

Applies To   **AutoCorrect** Object.

Description   Adds an entry to the array of AutoCorrect replacements. This method is available only in Microsoft Excel for Windows 95.

Syntax   *object*.**AddReplacement**(*what*, *replacement*)

object
> Required. The **AutoCorrect** object.

what
> Required. A string specifying the text to be replaced. If this string already exists in the array of AutoCorrect replacements, the existing substitute text is replaced by the new text.

replacement
> Required. A string specifying the text to be substituted.

See Also   **DeleteReplacement** Method, **ReplacementList** Property.

Example   This example substitutes the word "Temp." for the word "Temperature" in the array of AutoCorrect replacements.

```
With Application.AutoCorrect
    .AddReplacement "Temperature", "Temp."
End With
```

Address Method

Applies To	**Range** Object.
Description	Returns the range reference, as a string in the language of the macro.
Syntax	*object*.**Address(***rowAbsolute*, *columnAbsolute*, *referenceStyle*, *external*, *relativeTo*)

object
> Required. Returns a reference to this range.

rowAbsolute
> Optional. If **True** or omitted, the row part of the reference is returned as an absolute reference.

columnAbsolute
> Optional. If **True** or omitted, the column part of the reference is returned as an absolute reference.

referenceStyle
> Optional. If **xlA1** or omitted, the method returns an A1-style reference. If **xlR1C1**, the method returns an R1C1-style reference.

external
> Optional. If **True**, the method returns an external reference. If **False**, the method returns a local reference. The default is **False**.

relativeTo
> Optional. If *rowAbsolute* and *columnAbsolute* are **False**, and *referenceStyle* is **xlR1C1**, you must include a starting point for the relative reference. This argument is a **Range** object that defines the starting point.

Remarks	If the reference contains more than one cell, *rowAbsolute* and *columnAbsolute* apply to all rows and columns.
See Also	**AddressLocal** Method, **Offset** Method.
Example	The following example displays four different address representations of the same cell address. The comments in the example are the addresses displayed in the message boxes.

```
Set mc = Worksheets("Sheet1").Cells(1, 1)
MsgBox mc.Address()                                    ' $A$1
MsgBox mc.Address(rowAbsolute:=False)                  ' $A1
MsgBox mc.Address(referenceStyle:=xlR1C1)              ' R1C1
MsgBox mc.Address(referenceStyle:=xlR1C1, _
    rowAbsolute:=False,        _
    columnAbsolute:=False,  _
    relativeTo:=Worksheets(1).Cells(3, 3))             ' R[-2]C[-2]
```

AddressLocal Method

Applies To   **Range** Object.

Description   Returns the range reference, as a string in the language of the user.

Syntax   *object*.**AddressLocal**(*rowAbsolute*, *columnAbsolute*, *referenceStyle*, *external*, *relativeTo*)

object
　　Required. Returns a reference to this range.

rowAbsolute
　　Optional. If **True** or omitted, the row part of the reference is returned as an absolute reference.

columnAbsolute
　　Optional. If **True** or omitted, the column part of the reference is returned as an absolute reference.

referenceStyle
　　Optional. If **xlA1** or omitted, the method returns an A1-style reference. If **xlR1C1**, the method returns an R1C1-style reference.

external
　　Optional. If **True**, the method returns an external reference. If **False**, the method returns a local reference.

relativeTo
　　Optional. If *rowAbsolute* and *columnAbsolute* are **False**, and **referenceStyle** is **xlR1C1**, then you must include a starting point for the relative reference. This argument is a **Range** object type that defines the starting point.

Remarks   If the reference contains more than one cell, *rowAbsolute* and *columnAbsolute* apply to all rows and columns.

See Also   **Address** Method, **Offset** Method.

Example   Assume that the following example was created in the American English version of Microsoft Excel and was then run in the German version. The example displays the text shown in the comments.

```
Set mc = Worksheets(1).Cells(1, 1)
MsgBox mc.AddressLocal()                          ' $A$1
MsgBox mc.AddressLocal(rowAbsolute:=False)        ' $A1
MsgBox mc.AddressLocal(ReferenceStyle:=xlR1C1)    ' Z1S1
MsgBox mc.AddressLocal(ReferenceStyle:=xlR1C1, _
    rowAbsolute:=False, _
    columnAbsolute:=False, _
    relativeTo:=Worksheets(1).Cells(3, 3))        ' Z(-2)S(-2)
```

AddVertex Method

Applies To	**Drawing** Object.
Description	Adds a vertex to the end of the drawing.
Syntax	*object*.**AddVertex(***left*, *top***)**

object
Required. The **Drawing** object.

left
Required. The left position of the new vertex in points (1/72 inch), relative to the upper left corner of the sheet.

top
Required. The top position of the new vertex in points, relative to the upper left corner of the sheet.

See Also	**Add** Method (**Drawings** Collection), **Reshape** Method.
Example	This example creates a new open trapezoid on Sheet1.

```
With Worksheets("Sheet1").Drawings.Add(100, 100, 200, 100, False)
    .AddVertex 180, 200
    .AddVertex 80, 200
    .AddVertex 100, 100
    .Border.Weight = xlMedium
End With
```

AdvancedFilter Method

Applies To	**Range** Object.
Description	Filters or copies from a list based on a criteria range. If the initial selection is a single cell, its current region is used.
Syntax	*object*.**AdvancedFilter(***action*, *criteriaRange*, *copyToRange*, *unique***)**

object
Required. The **Range** object.

action
Required. Specifies the operation (either **xlFilterInPlace** or **xlFilterCopy**).

criteriaRange
Optional. The criteria range. If omitted, there are no criteria.

copyToRange
Required if *action* is **xlFilterCopy**, ignored otherwise. The destination range for the copied rows.

unique
Optional. **True** means unique records only, **False** means all records that meet the criteria. If omitted, assumed **False**.

See Also   **AutoFilter** Method, **FilterMode** Property, **ShowAllData** Method.

Example   This example filters a database (named "Database") based on a criteria range named "Criteria."

```
Range("Database").AdvancedFilter _
    action:=xlFilterInPlace, _
    criteriaRange:=Range("Criteria")
```

AlertBeforeOverwriting Property

Applies To   **Application** Object.

Description   **True** if Microsoft Excel displays a message before overwriting non-blank cells during a drag and drop editing operation. Read-write.

Example   This example causes an alert to be displayed before nonblank cells are overwritten during drag-and-drop editing.

```
Application.AlertBeforeOverwriting = True
```

AltStartupPath Property

Applies To   **Application** Object.

Description   Returns or sets a string that names the alternate startup folder. Read-write.

Example   This example sets the alternate startup folder.

```
Application.AltStartupPath = "C:\EXCEL\MACROS"
```

This is the same example in Microsoft Excel for the Macintosh.

```
Application.AltStartupPath = "HD:Excel:My Macros"
```

And Operator

Description   Used to perform a logical conjunction on two expressions.

Syntax   *result* = *expression1* **And** *expression2*

The **And** operator syntax has these parts:

Part	Description
result	Any numeric variable.
expression1	Any expression.
expression2	Any expression.

Remarks   If, and only if, both expressions evaluate **True**, *result* is **True**. If either expression evaluates **False**, *result* is **False**. The following table illustrates how *result* is determined:

If expression1 is	And expression2 is	The result is
True	True	True
True	False	False
True	Null	Null
False	True	False
False	False	False
False	Null	False
Null	True	Null
Null	False	False
Null	Null	Null

The **And** operator also performs a bit-wise comparison of identically positioned bits in two numeric expressions and sets the corresponding bit in *result* according to the following truth table:

If bit in expression1 is	And bit in expression2 is	The result is
0	0	0
0	1	0
1	0	0
1	1	1

See Also   Operator Precedence.

Example

This example uses the **And** operator to perform a logical conjunction on two expressions.

```
A = 10: B = 8: C = 6 : D = Null      ' Initialize variables.
MyCheck = A > B And B > C            ' Returns True.
MyCheck = B > A And B > C            ' Returns False.
MyCheck = A > B And B > D            ' Returns Null.
MyCheck = A And B                         ' Returns 8 (bit-wise
comparison).
```

AppActivate Statement

Description

Activates an application window.

Syntax

AppActivate *title* [,*wait*]

The **AppActivate** statement syntax has these named-argument parts:

Part	Description
title	In Microsoft Windows, the *title* argument is the string in the title bar of the application window you want to activate.
	On the Macintosh (System 7.0 or later), the *title* argument is the application name. You can use the **MacID** function to specify an application's signature instead of the application name. For example,
	`AppActivate MacID("MSWD")`
	In addition, the task ID returned by the **Shell** function can be used, in place of *title*, to activate an application.
wait	Boolean value specifying whether the calling application has the focus before activating another. If **False** (default), the specified application is immediately activated, even if the calling application does not have the focus. If **True**, the calling application waits until it has the focus, then activates the specified application.

Remarks

The **AppActivate** statement changes the focus to the named application or window but does not affect whether it is maximized or minimized. Focus moves from the activated application window when the user takes some action to change the focus or close the window. Use the **Shell** function to start an application and set the window style.

In trying to find the application to activate, a comparison is made to try to find an application whose title string is an exact match with *title*. If unsuccessful, any application's title string that begins with *title* is activated. In Microsoft Windows, if there is more than one instance of the application named by *title*, one is arbitrarily activated.

If you use the **MacID** function with **AppActivate** in Microsoft Windows, an error occurs.

See Also   **MacID** Function, **SendKeys** Statement, **Shell** Function.

Example   This example illustrates various uses of the **AppActivate** statement to activate an application window. On the Macintosh, you can use the **MacID** function to specify the application's signature instead of the application's name. The **AppActivate** statement is available with Macintosh System 7.0 or later.

```
' In Microsoft Windows.
AppActivate "Microsoft Word"                    ' Activate Word.
' AppActivate can also use the return value of the Shell function.
MyAppID = Shell("C:\WORD\WINWORD.EXE", 1)       ' Run Microsoft Word.
AppActivate MyAppID                             ' Activate Microsoft
    ' Word.

' On the Macintosh.
AppActivate "Microsoft Word"                    ' Activate Microsoft
    ' Word.
' MacID("MSWD") returns signature for Microsoft Word.
AppActivate MacID("MSWD")                        ' Activate Microsoft
    ' Word.
' You can also use the return value of the Shell function.
ReturnValue = Shell("Microsoft Excel")          ' Run Microsoft Excel.
AppActivate ReturnValue                          ' Activate Microsoft
    ' Excel.
```

Application Object

Description   Represents the entire Microsoft Excel application. The **Application** object contains:

- Application-wide settings and options (many of the options in the Tools Options dialog box, for example).
- Built-in worksheet functions such as SUM, AVERAGE, and COUNTA.
- Methods that return top-level objects such as **ActiveCell**, **ActiveSheet**, and so on.

Accessors   In Microsoft Excel, you can always access the **Application** object using the word "Application." The following example applies the **Windows** method to the **Application** object.

```
Application.Windows("book1.xls").Activate
```

For all Microsoft Excel objects, the **Application** property returns the Microsoft Excel **Application** object. This can be useful when you are using OLE Automation to access Microsoft Excel objects in another application. The following example creates a Microsoft Excel worksheet object in another application and then opens a workbook in Microsoft Excel.

```
Set xl = CreateObject("Excel.Sheet")
xl.Application.Workbooks.Open "newbook.xls"
```

Remarks

Many of the properties and methods that return the most common user-interface objects, such as the active cell (**ActiveCell** property) can be used without the **Application** object qualifier. For example, instead of writing `Application.ActiveCell.Font.Bold = True`, you can write `ActiveCell.Font.Bold = True`.

Properties

ActiveCell Property, **ActiveChart** Property, **ActiveDialog** Property, **ActiveMenuBar** Property, **ActivePrinter** Property, **ActiveSheet** Property, **ActiveWindow** Property, **ActiveWorkbook** Property, **AlertBeforeOverwriting** Property, **AltStartupPath** Property, **Application** Property, **AskToUpdateLinks** Property, **AutoCorrect** Property, **CalculateBeforeSave** Property, **Calculation** Property, **Caller** Property, **CanPlaySounds** Property, **CanRecordSounds** Property, **Caption** Property, **CellDragAndDrop** Property, **ClipboardFormats** Property, **ColorButtons** Property, **CommandUnderlines** Property, **ConstrainNumeric** Property, **CopyObjectsWithCells** Property, **Creator** Property, **Cursor** Property, **CustomListCount** Property, **CutCopyMode** Property, **DataEntryMode** Property, **DDEAppReturnCode** Property, **DefaultFilePath** Property, **DisplayAlerts** Property, **DisplayClipboardWindow** Property, **DisplayExcel4Menus** Property, **DisplayFormulaBar** Property, **DisplayFullScreen** Property, **DisplayInfoWindow** Property, **DisplayNoteIndicator** Property, **DisplayRecentFiles** Property, **DisplayScrollBars** Property, **DisplayStatusBar** Property, **EditDirectlyInCell** Property, **EnableAnimations** Property, **EnableAutoComplete** Property, **EnableCancelKey** Property, **EnableTipWizard** Property, **FileConverters** Property, **FixedDecimal** Property, **FixedDecimalPlaces** Property, **Height** Property, **IgnoreRemoteRequests** Property, **Interactive** Property, **International** Property, **Iteration** Property, **LargeButtons** Property, **Left** Property, **LibraryPath** Property, **MailSession** Property, **MailSystem** Property, **MathCoprocessorAvailable** Property, **MaxChange** Property, **MaxIterations** Property, **MemoryFree** Property, **MemoryTotal** Property, **MemoryUsed** Property, **MouseAvailable** Property, **MoveAfterReturn** Property, **MoveAfterReturnDirection** Property, **Name** Property, **NetworkTemplatesPath** Property, **OnCalculate** Property, **OnData** Property, **OnDoubleClick** Property, **OnEntry** Property, **OnSheetActivate** Property, **OnSheetDeactivate** Property, **OnWindow** Property, **OperatingSystem** Property, **OrganizationName** Property, **Parent** Property, **Path** Property, **PathSeparator** Property, **PreviousSelections** Property, **PromptForSummaryInfo** Property, **RecordRelative** Property,

ReferenceStyle Property, **RegisteredFunctions** Property, **ScreenUpdating** Property, **Selection** Property, **SheetsInNewWorkbook** Property, **ShowToolTips** Property, **StandardFont** Property, **StandardFontSize** Property, **StartupPath** Property, **StatusBar** Property, **TemplatesPath** Property, **ThisWorkbook** Property, **Top** Property, **TransitionMenuKey** Property, **TransitionMenuKeyAction** Property, **TransitionNavigKeys** Property, **UsableHeight** Property, **UsableWidth** Property, **UserName** Property, **Value** Property, **Version** Property, **Visible** Property, **Width** Property, **WindowsForPens** Property, **WindowState** Property.

Methods   **ActivateMicrosoftApp** Method, **AddChartAutoFormat** Method, **AddCustomList** Method, **AddIns** Method, **Calculate** Method, **Cells** Method, **CentimetersToPoints** Method, **Charts** Method, **CheckSpelling** Method, **Columns** Method, **ConvertFormula** Method, **DDEExecute** Method, **DDEInitiate** Method, **DDEPoke** Method, **DDERequest** Method, **DDETerminate** Method, **DeleteChartAutoFormat** Method, **DeleteCustomList** Method, **Dialogs** Method, **DialogSheets** Method, **DoubleClick** Method, **Evaluate** Method, **Excel4IntlMacroSheets** Method, **Excel4MacroSheets** Method, **ExecuteExcel4Macro** Method, **FindFile** Method, **GetCustomListContents** Method, **GetCustomListNum** Method, **GetOpenFilename** Method, **GetSaveAsFilename** Method, **Goto** Method, **Help** Method, **InchesToPoints** Method, **InputBox** Method, **Intersect** Method, **MacroOptions** Method, **MailLogoff** Method, **MailLogon** Method, **MenuBars** Method, **Modules** Method, **Names** Method, **NextLetter** Method, **OnKey** Method, **OnRepeat** Method, **OnTime** Method, **OnUndo** Method, **Quit** Method, **Range** Method, **RecordMacro** Method, **RegisterXLL** Method, **Repeat** Method, **ResetTipWizard** Method, **Rows** Method, **Run** Method, **Save** Method, **SendKeys** Method, **SetDefaultChart** Method, **Sheets** Method, **ShortcutMenus** Method, **Toolbars** Method, **Undo** Method, **Union** Method, **Volatile** Method, **Wait** Method, **Windows** Method, **Workbooks** Method, **Worksheets** Method.

Application Property

Applies To   All objects.

Description   Accessor. Used without an object qualifier, this property returns an **Application** object that represents the Microsoft Excel application. Used with an object qualifier, this property returns an **Application** object that represents the creator of the specified object (you can use this property with an OLE Automation object to return the automation object's application). Read-only.

See Also   **Creator** Property.

Example   This example displays a message about the application that created `myObject`.

```
Set myObject = ActiveWorkbook
If myObject.Application.Value = "Microsoft Excel" Then
    MsgBox "This is a Microsoft Excel object"
Else
    MsgBox "This is not a Microsoft Excel object"
End If
```

ApplyDataLabels Method

Applies To   **Chart** Object, **Point** Object, **Series** Object.

Description   Applies data labels to the point, the series, or to all series on the chart.

Syntax   *object*.**ApplyDataLabels**(*type*, *legendKey*)

object
    Required. The **Chart**, **Point**, or **Series** object.

type
    Optional. The type of data label, as shown in the following table.

Value	Meaning
xlNone	No data labels.
xlShowValue	Value for the point (assumed if this argument is not specified).
xlShowPercent	Percentage of the total. Only available for pie and doughnut charts.
xlShowLabel	Category for the point.
xlShowLabelAndPercent	Percentage of the total and category for the point. Only available for pie and doughnut charts.

legendKey
    Optional. If **True**, Microsoft Excel shows the legend key next to the point.

See Also   **DataLabel** Property, **HasDataLabel** Property, **HasDataLabels** Property.

Example   This example applies category labels to series one in Chart1.

```
Charts("Chart1").SeriesCollection(1).ApplyDataLabels type:=xlShowLabel
```

ApplyNames Method

Applies To   **Range** Object.

Description   Applies names to the cells in the range.

Syntax   *object*.**ApplyNames**(*names*, *ignoreRelativeAbsolute*, *useRowColumnNames*, *omitColumn*, *omitRow*, *order*, *appendLast*)

object
Required. The range where names will be applied.

names
Optional. Contains an array of the names to apply. If omitted, all names on the sheet are applied to the range.

ignoreRelativeAbsolute
Optional. If **True** or omitted, replaces references with names regardless of the reference types of either the names or references. If **False**, replaces absolute references only with absolute names, relative references only with relative names, and mixed references only with mixed names.

useRowColumnNames
Optional. If **True** or omitted, Microsoft Excel uses the names of row and column ranges containing the specified range if names for the range cannot be found. If **False**, the *omitColumn* and *omitRow* arguments are ignored.

omitColumn
Optional. If **True** or omitted, Microsoft Excel replaces the reference with the row-oriented name without including a column-oriented name if the referenced cell is in the same column as the formula and within a row-oriented named range.

omitRow
Optional. If **True** or omitted, Microsoft Excel replaces the reference with the column-oriented name without including a row-oriented name if the referenced cell is in the same row as the formula within a column-oriented named range.

order
Optional. Determines which range name is listed first when a cell reference is replaced by a row-oriented and column-oriented range name (either **xlRowThenColumn** or **xlColumnThenRow**).

appendLast
Optional. If **True**, Microsoft Excel replaces the definitions of the names in *names* and also replaces the definitions of the last names defined. If *appendLast* is **False** or omitted, Microsoft Excel replaces the definitions of the names in *names* only.

Remarks	You can use the **Array** function to create the list of names for the *names* argument.
	If you want to apply names to the entire sheet, use **Cells**.**ApplyNames**.
	You cannot "unapply" names; to delete names, use the **Delete** method.
See Also	**Add** Method (**Names** Collection), **Delete** Method.
Example	This example applies names to the entire sheet.

```
Cells.ApplyNames names:=Array("Sales", "Profits")
```

ApplyOutlineStyles Method

Applies To	**Range** Object.
Description	Applies outlining styles to the range.
Syntax	*object*.**ApplyOutlineStyles**
	object Required. The range where outlining styles will be applied.
Example	The following example applies automatic outlining styles to the selection. The selection must include the entire outline range on a worksheet.

```
Selection.ApplyOutlineStyles
```

Arc Object

Description	Represents an arc graphic object on a chart sheet, dialog sheet, or worksheet. An arc always describes a quarter of a circle or oval.
Accessors	The **Arc** object is a member of the **Arcs** collection. Use the **Add** method to create a new arc and add it to the collection. To access a single member of the collection, use the **Arcs** method with the index number or name of the arc as an argument.
	The following example sets the interior color for arc one.

```
Worksheets("sheet1").Activate
ActiveSheet.Arcs(1).Interior.Color = RGB(0, 255, 255)
```

The arc name is shown in the Name Box when the arc is selected. Use the **Name** property to set and return the arc name.

The following example selects the arc named "Arc 1" on the active sheet and then sets the arc border color.

```
Worksheets("sheet1").Activate
ActiveSheet.Arcs("arc 1").Select
Selection.Border.Color = RGB(255, 0, 0)
```

Properties

Application Property, **Border** Property, **BottomRightCell** Property, **Creator** Property, **Enabled** Property, **Height** Property, **Index** Property, **Interior** Property, **Left** Property, **Locked** Property, **Name** Property, **OnAction** Property, **Parent** Property, **Placement** Property, **PrintObject** Property, **Top** Property, **TopLeftCell** Property, **Visible** Property, **Width** Property, **ZOrder** Property.

Methods

BringToFront Method, **Copy** Method, **CopyPicture** Method, **Cut** Method, **Delete** Method, **Duplicate** Method, **Select** Method, **SendToBack** Method.

Arcs Collection Object

Description

A collection of all the **Arc** objects on the specified chart sheet, dialog sheet or worksheet

Accessors

Use the **Add** method to create a new arc and add it to the collection. The following example draws an arc starting at the upper-left corner of cell C3 and ending at the upper-left corner of cell D9.

```
Worksheets("sheet1").Activate
Set r1 = Range("c3")
Set r2 = Range("d9")
ActiveSheet.Arcs.Add r1.Left, r1.Top, r2.Left, r2.Top
```

Use the **Arcs** method with an argument to access a single member of the collection or without an argument to access the entire collection at once. The following example deletes all of the arcs on the worksheet named "Sheet1."

```
Worksheets("sheet1").Arcs.Delete
```

Properties

Application Property, **Border** Property, **Count** Property, **Creator** Property, **Enabled** Property, **Height** Property, **Interior** Property, **Left** Property, **Locked** Property, **OnAction** Property, **Parent** Property, **Placement** Property, **PrintObject** Property, **Top** Property, **Visible** Property, **Width** Property, **ZOrder** Property.

Methods

Add Method (Arcs and Lines), **BringToFront** Method, **Copy** Method, **CopyPicture** Method, **Cut** Method, **Delete** Method, **Duplicate** Method, **Group** Method, **Item** Method, **Select** Method, **SendToBack** Method.

Arcs Method

Applies To   **Chart** Object, **DialogSheet** Object, **Worksheet** Object.

Description   Accessor. Returns an object that represents a single arc (an **Arc** object, Syntax 1) or a collection of arcs (an **Arcs** object, Syntax 2) on the sheet. Read-only.

Syntax 1   *object*.**Arcs**(*index*)

Syntax 2   *object*.**Arcs**

object
   Required. The object to which this method applies.

index
   Required for Syntax 1. The name or number of the arc.

Example   This example deletes every arc on Sheet1.

```
Worksheets("Sheet1").Arcs.Delete
```

This example changes the color of arc one on Sheet1 to red.

```
Worksheets("Sheet1").Arcs(1).Border.ColorIndex = 3
```

Area3DGroup Property

Applies To   **Chart** Object.

Description   Accessor. Returns a **ChartGroup** object that represents the area chart group on a 3-D chart. Read-only.

See Also   **AreaGroups** Method.

Example   This example sets the subtype for the 3-D area chart group in Chart1. The example should be run on a 3-D area chart that has more than one series.

```
Charts("Chart1").Area3DGroup.SubType = 1
```

AreaGroups Method

Applies To   **Chart** Object.

Description	Accessor. On a 2-D chart, returns an object that represents a single area chart group (a **ChartGroup** object, Syntax 1), or a collection of the area chart groups (a **ChartGroups** collection, Syntax 2).
Syntax 1	*object*.**AreaGroups(*index*)**
Syntax 2	*object*.**AreaGroups**

object
    Required. The **Chart** object.

index
Required for Syntax 1. Specifies the chart group.

See Also	**Area3DGroup** Property.
Example	This example sets the subtype for area chart group one. The example should be run on a 2-D chart that has an area group and a line group.

```
Charts("Chart1").AreaGroups(1).SubType = 1
```

Areas Collection Object

Description
A collection of the areas, or contiguous blocks of cells, within a selection. There is no singular Area object; individual members of the **Areas** collection are **Range** objects. The **Areas** collection contains one **Range** object for each discrete, contiguous range of cells within the selection. If the selection contains only one area, the **Areas** collection contains a single **Range** object that corresponds to that selection.

Accessors
Use the **Areas** method without an argument to return the entire collection. The following example clears the current selection if the selection contains more than one area.

```
If Selection.Areas.Count <> 1 Then Selection.Clear
```

Use the **Areas** method with an area index number as an argument to return a single area in the collection. The index numbers correspond to the order in which the areas were selected. The following example clears the first area in the current selection if the selection contains more than one area.

```
If Selection.Areas.Count <> 1 Then
        Selection.Areas(1).Clear
End If
```

Some operations cannot be performed on more than one area in a selection at once; you must loop through the individual areas in the selection and perform the operations on each area separately. The following example performs the operation named "myOperation" on the selected range if the selection contains only one area; if the selection contains multiple areas, the example performs myOperation on each individual area in the selection.

```
Set rangeToUse = Selection
If rangeToUse.Areas.Count = 1 Then
    myOperation rangeToUse
Else
    For Each singleArea in rangeToUse.Areas
        myOperation singleArea
    Next
End If
```

Properties   **Application** Property, **Creator** Property, **Count** Property, **Parent** Property.

Methods   **Item** Method.

Areas Method

Applies To   **Range** Object.

Description   Accessor. Returns an object that represents a single range (a **Range** object, Syntax 1), or a collection of all ranges (an **Areas** object, Syntax 2) in a multiple selection.

Syntax 1   *object*.**Areas**(*index*)

Syntax 2   *object*.**Areas**

object
   Required. The multiple-selection range.

index
   Required for Syntax 1. The number of the range within the multiple selection.

Remarks   For a single selection, the **Areas** method returns a collection of one object, the original **Range** object itself. For a multiple selection, the **Areas** method returns a collection that contains one object for each selection.

See Also   **Union** Method.

Example

This example displays a message if the user tries to carry out a command when more than one area is selected. This example must be run from a worksheet.

```
If Selection.Areas.Count > 1 Then
    MsgBox "Cannot do this to a multi-area selection."
End If
```

Arrange Method

Description

Arranges the windows on the screen.

Syntax

object.**Arrange**(*arrangeStyle*, *activeWorkbook*, *syncHorizontal*, *syncVertical*)

object
Required. The **Windows** object.

arrangeStyle
Optional. Arrange windows in this style. Can have one of the following values:

Value	Meaning
xlTiled	Windows are tiled (the default value, used if *arrangeStyle* is omitted).
xlCascade	Windows are cascaded.
xlHorizontal	Windows are arranged horizontally.
xlVertical	Windows are arranged vertically.
xlIcons	Arranges the icons (not available on the Apple Macintosh).

activeWorkbook
Optional. If **True**, arranges only the visible windows of the active workbook, instead of all the windows in Microsoft Excel. If **False** or omitted, arranges all the windows.

syncHorizontal
Optional. Ignored if *activeWorkbook* is **False** or omitted. If **True**, the windows of the active workbook are synchronized when scrolling horizontally. If **False** or omitted, the windows are not synchronized.

syncVertical
Optional. Ignored if *activeWorkbook* is **False** or omitted. If **True**, the windows of the active workbook are synchronized when scrolling vertically. If **False** or omitted, the windows are not synchronized.

Example

This example tiles all the windows in the application.

```
Application.Windows.Arrange arrangeStyle:=xlTiled
```

Array Function

Description   Returns a **Variant** containing an array.

Syntax   **Array**(*arglist*)

The *arglist* consists of a comma-delimited list of an arbitrary number of values that are assigned to the elements of the array contained within the **Variant**. If no arguments are specified, an array of zero-length is created.

Remarks   Although a **Variant** containing an array is conceptually different from an array whose elements are of type **Variant**, the way the array elements are accessed is the same. The notation used to refer to any element of an array consists of the variable name followed by parentheses containing an index number to the desired element. In the following example, the first statement creates a variable A as a **Variant**. The second statement assigns an array to the variable A. The final statement illustrates how to assign the value contained in the second array element to another variable.

```
Dim A As Variant
A = Array(10,20,30)
B = A(2)
```

The lower bound of an array created using the **Array** function is determined by the lower bound specified with the **Option Base** statement.

See Also   **Deftype** Statements, **Dim** Statement, **Let** Statement, **Option Base** Statement.

Example   This example uses the **Array** function to return a **Variant** containing an array.

```
MyWeek = Array("Mon", "Tue", "Wed", "Thu", "Fri", "Sat", "Sun")
' Return values assume lower bound equals 1 (using Option Base).
MyDay = MyWeek(2)                    ' Returns "Tue".
MyDay = MyWeek(4)                    ' Returns "Thu".
```

This example fills the range A1:C5 on Sheet1, Sheet5, and Sheet7 with the contents of the same range on Sheet1.

```
x = Array("Sheet1", "Sheet5", "Sheet7")
Sheets(x).FillAcrossSheets _
    Worksheets("Sheet1").Range("A1:C5")
```

This example consolidates data from Sheet2 and Sheet3 onto Sheet1, using the SUM function.

```
Worksheets("Sheet1").Range("A1").Consolidate _
    sources:=Array("Sheet2!R1C1:R37C6", "Sheet3!R1C1:R37C6"), _
    Function:=xlSum
```

This example adds an array of strings as a custom list.

```
Application.AddCustomList Array("cogs", "sprockets", _
    "widgets", "gizmos")
```

This example hides Chart1, Chart3, and Chart5. Note that in this example, the **Charts** method returns a **Sheets** object instead of a **Charts** object.

```
Charts(Array("Chart1", "Chart3", "Chart5")).Visible = False
```

This example sets the entries in list box one on Dialog1.

```
DialogSheets("Dialog1").ListBoxes(1).List = _
    Array("cogs", "widgets", "sprockets", "gizmos")
```

This example creates a group from drawing objects one, three, and five on Sheet1.

```
Set myGroup = Worksheets("Sheet1").DrawingObjects(Array(1, 3, 5)).Group
Worksheets("Sheet1").Activate
myGroup.Select
```

ArrowHeadLength Property

Applies To   **DrawingObjects** Collection, **GroupObject** Object, **GroupObjects** Collection, **Line** Object, **Lines** Collection.

Description   Returns or sets the length of the arrow head (one of **xlShort**, **xlMedium**, or **xlLong**). Read-write.

See Also   **ArrowHeadStyle** Property, **ArrowHeadWidth** Property.

Example   This example creates a new line on Sheet1 and then sets the arrowhead length, width, and style.

```
Set newLine = Worksheets("Sheet1").Lines.Add(72, 72, 144, 144)
With newLine
    .ArrowHeadLength = xlShort
    .ArrowHeadWidth = xlNarrow
    .ArrowHeadStyle = xlOpen
End With
```

ArrowHeadStyle Property

Applies To   **DrawingObjects** Collection, **GroupObject** Object, **GroupObjects** Collection, **Line** Object, **Lines** Collection.

Description   Returns or sets the arrow head type (one of **xlNone**, **xlOpen**, **xlClosed**, **xlDoubleOpen**, or **xlDoubleClosed**). Read-write.

See Also   **ArrowHeadLength** Property, **ArrowHeadWidth** Property.

Example   This example creates a new line on Sheet1 and then sets the arrowhead length, width, and style.

```
Set newLine = Worksheets("Sheet1").Lines.Add(72, 72, 144, 144)
With newLine
    .ArrowHeadLength = xlShort
    .ArrowHeadWidth = xlNarrow
    .ArrowHeadStyle = xlOpen
End With
```

ArrowHeadWidth Property

Applies To   **DrawingObjects** Collection, **GroupObject** Object, **GroupObjects** Collection, **Line** Object, **Lines** Collection.

Description   Returns or sets the arrow head width (one of **xlNarrow**, **xlMedium**, **xlWide**). Read-write.

See Also   **ArrowHeadLength** Property, **ArrowHeadStyle** Property.

Example   This example creates a new line on Sheet1 and then sets the arrowhead length, width, and style.

```
Set newLine = Worksheets("Sheet1").Lines.Add(72, 72, 144, 144)
With newLine
    .ArrowHeadLength = xlShort
    .ArrowHeadWidth = xlNarrow
    .ArrowHeadStyle = xlOpen
End With
```

Asc Function

Description   Returns the character code corresponding to the first letter in a string.

Syntax   **Asc(*string*)**

The ***string*** named argument is any valid string expression. If the ***string*** contains no characters, and run-time error occurs.

See Also   **Chr** Function.

Example   This example uses the **Asc** function to return and character code corresponding to the first letter in the string.

```
MyNumber = Asc ("A")            ' Returns 65.
MyNumber = Asc ("a")            ' Returns 97.
MyNumber = Asc ("Apple")        ' Returns 65.
```

AskToUpdateLinks Property

Applies To   **Application** Object.

Description   **True** if Microsoft Excel asks the user to update links when opening files with links, or **False** if links are automatically updated with no dialog. Read-write.

Example   This example causes Microsoft Excel to ask the user to update links when a file that contains links is opened.

```
Application.AskToUpdateLinks = True
```

Atn Function

Description   Returns the arctangent of a number.

Syntax   **Atn(*number*)**

The ***number*** named argument can be any valid numeric expression.

Remarks   The **Atn** function takes the ratio of two sides of a right triangle (***number***) and returns the corresponding angle in radians. The ratio is the length of the side opposite the angle divided by the length of the side adjacent to the angle.

The range of the result is -pi/2 to pi/2 radians.

To convert degrees to radians, multiply degrees by pi/180. To convert radians to degrees, multiply radians by 180/pi.

Note **Atn** is the inverse trigonometric function of **Tan**, which takes an angle as its argument and returns the ratio of two sides of a right triangle. Do not confuse **Atn** with the cotangent, which is the simple inverse of a tangent (1/tangent).

See Also   **Cos** Function, Derived Math Functions, **Sin** Function, **Tan** Function.

Example   This example uses the **Atn** function to return the arctangent of a number.

```
Pi = 4 * Atn(1)                    ' Calculate the value of pi.
```

Author Property

Applies To   **AddIn** Object, **Workbook** Object.

Description   Returns or sets the author of the object, as a string. Read-only for **AddIn**, read-write for **Workbook**.

Remarks   In Microsoft Excel for Windows 95, this property has been replaced by a built-in OLE document property. For more information about OLE document properties, see **BuiltinDocumentProperties**.

You cannot use this property with an **AddIn** object that represents an XLL file or an add-in that was created with the Microsoft Excel 4.0 macro language.

See Also   **Comments** Property, **Keywords** Property, **Subject** Property, **Title** Property.

Example   This example displays the author and name of the Solver add-in.

```
Set a = AddIns("Solver Add-In")
MsgBox a.Author & " authored the add-in " & a.Name
```

This example sets the author of the active workbook.

```
ActiveWorkbook.Author = "Anonymous"
```

AutoComplete Method

Applies To   **Range** Object.

Description	Returns an AutoComplete match from the list. If there's no AutoComplete match or if more than one entry in the list matches the string to complete, the method returns an empty string. This method is available only in Microsoft Excel for Windows 95.
Syntax	*object*.**AutoComplete**(*string*)

object
> Required. The **Range** object (must be a single cell).

string
> Required. The string to complete.

Remarks	This method works whether or not the AutoComplete feature is disabled.
Example	This example returns the AutoComplete match for the string segment "Ap." An AutoComplete match is made if the column immediately above or below cell A5 (or the column containing cell A5) contains a contiguous list and one of the entries in the list contains a match for the string.

```
s = Worksheets(1).Range("A5").AutoComplete("Ap")
If Len(s) > 0 Then
    MsgBox "Completes to " & s
Else
    MsgBox "Has no completion"
End If
```

This example returns the AutoComplete match for the string segment "Ap." An AutoComplete match is made if the column immediately above or below cell A5 (or the column containing cell A5) contains a contiguous list and one of the entries in the list contains a match for the string.

```
s = Worksheets(1).Range("A5").AutoComplete("Ap")
If Len(s) > 0 Then
    MsgBox "Completes to " & s
Else
    MsgBox "Has no completion"
End If
```

AutoCorrect Object

Description	Contains Microsoft Excel AutoCorrect attributes (capitalization of names of days, correction of two initial capital letters, automatic correction list, and so on) This object is available only in Microsoft Excel for Windows 95.

Accessors   The **AutoCorrect** property returns the **AutoCorrect** object. The AutoCorrect attributes are properties of the **AutoCorrect** object. The following example sets Microsoft Excel to correct words that begin with two initial capital letters.

```
With Application.AutoCorrect
    .TwoInitialCapitals = True
    .ReplaceText = True
End With
```

Properties   **Application** Property, **Parent** Property, **TwoInitialCapitals** Property, **CapitalizeNamesOfDays** Property, **ReplacementList** Property, **Creator** Property, **ReplaceText** Property.

Methods   **AddReplacement** Method, **DeleteReplacement** Method.

AutoCorrect Property

Applies To   **Application** Object.

Description   Accessor. Returns an **AutoCorrect** object that represents the Microsoft Excel AutoCorrect attributes. This property is available only in Microsoft Excel for Windows 95. Read-only.

See Also   **AddReplacement** Method, **CapitalizeNamesOfDays** Property, **DeleteReplacement** Method, **ReplacementList** Property, **ReplaceText** Property, **TwoInitialCapitals** Property.

Example   This example substitutes the word "Temp." for the word "Temperature" in the array of AutoCorrect replacements.

```
With Application.AutoCorrect
    .AddReplacement "Temperature", "Temp."
End With
```

AutoFill Method

Applies To   **Range** Object.

Description   Performs an autofill on the cells in the range.

Syntax   *object*.**AutoFill**(*destination*, *type*)

object
>   Required. The source range.

destination
>   Required. A **Range** object that represents the cells to fill. The object must include the source range.

type
>   Optional. Can be one of **xlFillDefault, xlFillSeries, xlFillCopy, xlFillFormats, xlFillValues, xlFillDays, xlFillWeekdays, xlFillMonths, xlFillYears, xlLinearTrend, xlGrowthTrend**. If **xlFillDefault** or omitted, the method selects the most appropriate type based on the source range.

Example

This example performs an autofill on cells A1:A20 on Sheet1, based on the source range of A1:A2 on Sheet1. Before running this example, type **1** in cell A1 and type **2** in cell A2.

```
Set sourceRange = Worksheets("Sheet1").Range("A1:A2")
Set fillRange = Worksheets("Sheet1").Range("A1:A20")
sourceRange.AutoFill destination:=fillRange
```

AutoFilter Method

Applies To   **Range** Object.

Description   Syntax 1: Displays or hides the AutoFilter drop-down arrows.

Syntax 2: Filters a list using the AutoFilter.

Syntax 1   *object*.**AutoFilter**

Syntax 2   *object*.**AutoFilter**(*field*, *criteria1*, *operator*, *criteria2*)

object
>   Required. The **Range** object.

field
>   Required. The integer offset of the field on which to base the filter (from the left of the list—the leftmost field is field one).

criteria1
>   Optional. The criteria (a string; for example "101"). Use "=" to find blank fields, "<>" to find non-blank fields. If this argument is omitted, the criteria is **All**. If *operator* is **xlTop10Items**, *criteria1* specifies the number of items (for example "10").

operator
> Optional. Used with *criteria1* and *criteria2* to construct compound criteria. Can be either **xlAnd** or **xlOr**. If omitted, **xlAnd** is used. Specify **xlTop10Items** to use the Top 10 AutoFilter.

criteria2
> Optional. The second criteria (a string). Used with *criteria1* and *operator* to construct compound criteria.

See Also
AdvancedFilter Method, **AutoFilterMode** Property, **FilterMode** Property, **ShowAllData** Method.

Example
This example filters a list starting in cell A1 on Sheet1 to show only the entries in which field one is equal to the string "Otis".

```
Worksheets("Sheet1").Range("A1").AutoFilter _
    field:=1, _
    criteria1:="Otis"
```

AutoFilterMode Property

Applies To
Worksheet Object.

Description
True if the drop-down arrows for AutoFilter are currently displayed on the sheet. This property is independent of the **FilterMode** property. Read-write.

Remarks
This property will be **True** if the drop-down arrows are currently displayed. You can set this property to **False** to remove the arrows, but you cannot set it to **True**. Use the **AutoFilter** method to filter a list and display the drop-down arrows.

See Also
AutoFilter Method, **FilterMode** Property.

Example
This example displays the current state of the **AutoFilterMode** property on Sheet1.

```
If Worksheets("Sheet1").AutoFilterMode Then
    isOn = "On"
Else
    isOn = "Off"
End If
MsgBox "AutoFilterMode is " & isOn
```

AutoFit Method

Applies To	**Range** Object.
Description	Changes the width of the columns in the range or the height of the rows in the range for the best fit.
Syntax	*object*.**AutoFit**

object
> Required. The range to apply the best fit to. Must be a row or a range of rows, or a column or a range of columns. Otherwise, this method generates an error.

Remarks	One unit of column width is equal to the width of one character of the Normal style.
See Also	**ColumnWidth** Property, **RowHeight** Property.
Example	This example changes the width of columns A through I on Sheet1 for the best fit.

```
Worksheets("Sheet1").Columns("A:I").AutoFit
```

This example changes the width of columns A through E on Sheet1 for the best fit, based only on the contents of cells A1:E1.

```
Worksheets("Sheet1").Range("A1:E1").Columns.AutoFit
```

AutoFormat Method (Chart object)

Applies To	**Chart** Object.
Description	Applies a built-in or custom autoformat to the specified chart.
Syntax	*object*.**AutoFormat**(*gallery*, *format*)

object
> Required. The **Chart** object.

gallery
> Required. Specifies the built-in gallery. Can be one of **xl3DArea**, **xl3DBar**, **xl3DColumn**, **xl3DLine**, **xl3DPie**, **xl3DSurface**, **xlArea**, **xlBar**, **xlColumn**, **xlCombination**, **xlCustom**, **xlDefaultAutoFormat**, **xlDoughnut**, **xlLine**, **xlPie**, **xlRadar**, or **xlXYScatter**.

format
> Optional. Specifies the option number for the built-in autoformats or a string containing the name of the custom autoformat if *gallery* is **xlCustom**.

See Also	**AutoFormat** Method (**Range object**).

Example

This example applies the third radar autoformat to Chart1.

```
Charts("Chart1").AutoFormat xlRadar, 3
```

This example applies the "Monthly Sales" custom autoformat to Chart1.

```
Charts("Chart1").AutoFormat xlCustom, "Monthly Sales"
```

AutoFormat Method (Range object)

Applies To

Range Object.

Description

Automatically formats a range of cells using a predefined format.

Syntax

object.**AutoFormat**(*format*, *number*, *font*, *alignment*, *border*, *pattern*, *width*)

object
    Required. The range to format.

format
    Optional. The name or number of the format to apply (one of **xlClassic1**, **xlClassic2**, **xlClassic3**, **xlAccounting1**, **xlAccounting2**, **xlAccounting3**, **xlAccounting4**, **xlColor1**, **xlColor2**, **xlColor3**, **xlList1**, **xlList2**, **xlList3**, **xl3DEffects1**, **xl3DEffects2**, **xlSimple**, or **xlNone**). If this argument is omitted, the default value is **xlClassic1**.

number
    Optional. Corresponds to the Number check box in the AutoFormat dialog box. Can be **True** or **False** (**True** if omitted).

font
    Optional. Corresponds to the Font check box in the AutoFormat dialog box. Can be **True** or **False** (**True** if omitted).

alignment
    Optional. Corresponds to the Alignment check box in the AutoFormat dialog box. Can be **True** or **False** (**True** if omitted).

border
    Optional. Corresponds to the Border check box in the AutoFormat dialog box. Can be **True** or **False** (**True** if omitted).

pattern
    Optional. Corresponds to the Pattern check box in the AutoFormat dialog box. Can be **True** or **False** (**True** if omitted).

width
    Optional. Corresponds to the Column Width/Row Height check box in the AutoFormat dialog box. Can be **True** or **False** (**True** if omitted).

Remarks	If the range is a single cell, this method also formats the current region around the cell. In other words, the **AutoFormat** method performs **CurrentRegion**.**AutoFormat** on the single cell.
	In Japanese Microsoft Excel, the following additional formats are available: **xlLocalFormat1** and **xlLocalFormat2**.
See Also	**AutoFormat** Method (**Chart object**), **CurrentRegion** Property, **Style** Property.
Example	This example formats cells A1:D8 on Sheet1, using a predefined format.

```
Worksheets("Sheet1").Range("A1:D8").AutoFormat format:=xlClassic1
```

AutoLoad Property

Applies To	**OLEObject** Object.
Description	**True** if the OLE object is automatically loaded when the workbook that contains the object is opened. This property is available only in Microsoft Excel for Windows 95. Read-write.
Remarks	For most OLE object types, this property should not be set to **True**. By default, the **AutoLoad** property is set to **False** for new OLE objects; this saves time and memory when Microsoft Excel is loading workbooks. The benefit of automatically loading OLE objects is that, for objects that represent volatile data, links to source data can be reestablished immediately and the objects can be rendered again, if necessary.
Example	This example sets the **AutoLoad** property for OLE object one.

```
ActiveSheet.OLEObjects(1).AutoLoad = True
```

AutomaticStyles Property

Applies To	**Outline** Object.
Description	**True** if the outline uses automatic styles. Read-write.
Example	This example sets the outline on Sheet1 to use automatic styles.

```
Worksheets("Sheet1").Outline.AutomaticStyles = True
```

AutoOutline Method

Applies To   **Range** Object.

Description   Automatically creates an outline for the specified range. If the range is a single cell, Microsoft Excel creates an outline for the entire sheet. The new outline replaces any existing outline.

Syntax   *object*.**AutoOutline**

object
　　Required. The **Range** object.

See Also   **ApplyOutlineStyles** Method, **ClearOutline** Method.

Example   This example creates an outline for the range A1:G37 on Sheet1. The range must contain either a summary row or a summary column.

```
Worksheets("Sheet1").Range("A1:G37").AutoOutline
```

AutoScaling Property

Applies To   **Chart** Object.

Description   If **True**, Microsoft Excel scales a 3-D chart so that it is closer in size to the equivalent 2-D chart. The **RightAngleAxes** property must be **True**. Read-write.

Example   This example automatically scales Chart1. The example should be run on a 3-D chart.

```
With Charts("Chart1")
    .RightAngleAxes = True
    .AutoScaling = True
End With
```

AutoSize Property

Applies To   **Button** Object, **Buttons** Collection, **DrawingObjects** Collection, **GroupObject** Object, **GroupObjects** Collection, **TextBox** Object, **TextBoxes** Collection.

Description   **True** if the object will be automatically resized to fit the text it contains. Read-write.

Remarks   This property is set to **False** if the object is resized manually (by the user or by the **Height** or **Width** properties).

Example   This example sets button one on Sheet1 to automatically size to fit the text it contains.

```
Worksheets("Sheet1").Buttons(1).AutoSize = True
```

AutoText Property

Applies To   **DataLabel** Object, **DataLabels** Collection.

Description   **True** if the object automatically generates appropriate text based on context. Read-write.

Example   This example sets the data labels for series one in Chart1 to automatically generate appropriate text.

```
Charts("Chart1").SeriesCollection(1).DataLabels.AutoText = True
```

AutoUpdate Property

Applies To   **OLEObject** Object.

Description   **True** if the OLE object updates automatically when the source changes. Valid only if the object is linked (its **OLEType** property must be **xlOLELink**). Read-only.

Example   This example displays the status of automatic updating for all OLE objects on Sheet1.

```
Worksheets("Sheet1").Activate
Range("A1").Value = "Name"
Range("B1").Value = "Link Status"
Range("C1").Value = "AutoUpdate Status"
i = 2
For Each obj In ActiveSheet.OLEObjects
    Cells(i, 1) = obj.Name
    If obj.OLEType = xlOLELink Then
        Cells(i, 2) = "Linked"
        Cells(i, 3) = obj.AutoUpdate
    Else
        Cells(i, 2) = "Embedded"
    End If
    i = i + 1
Next
```

Axes Collection Object

Description   A collection of all the **Axis** objects in the specified chart.

Accessors   Use the **Axes** method with an argument to access a single member of the collection or without an argument to access the entire collection at once. Unlike most collections, the **Axes** collection is indexed using constants. Secondary axes, if present, are accessed using an additional argument. For more information, see the **Axes** method.

The following example uses the **Axes** method with an argument to set the category axis title text on the chart sheet named "Chart1."

```
With Charts("chart1").Axes(xlCategory)
    .HasTitle = True
    .AxisTitle.Caption = "1994"
End With
```

Properties   **Application** Property, **Count** Property, **Creator** Property, **Parent** Property.

Methods   **Item** Method.

Axes Method

Applies To   **Chart** Object.

Description   Accessor. Returns an object that represents a single axis (an **Axis** object, Syntax 1) or a collection of the axes on the chart (an **Axes** object, Syntax 2).

Syntax 1   *object*.**Axes**(*type*, *axisGroup*)

Syntax 2   *object*.**Axes**

object
   Required. The **Chart** object.

type
   Required for Syntax 1. Specifies the axis to return. Can be one of **xlValue**, **xlCategory**, or **xlSeries** (**xlSeries** is only valid for 3-D charts).

axisGroup
   Optional. Specifies the axis group (either **xlPrimary** or **xlSecondary**). If this argument is omitted, the primary group is used. 3-D charts have only one axis group.

Example   This example adds an axis label to the category axis in Chart1.

```
With Charts("Chart1").Axes(xlCategory)
    .HasTitle = True
    .AxisTitle.Text = "July Sales"
End With
```

This example turns off major gridlines for the category axis in Chart1.

```
Charts("Chart1").Axes(xlCategory).HasMajorGridlines = False
```

This example turns off all gridlines for all axes in Chart1.

```
For Each a In Charts("Chart1").Axes
    a.HasMajorGridlines = False
    a.HasMinorGridlines = False
Next a
```

Axis Object

Description   Represents a single axis in a chart.

Accessors   The **Axis** object is a member of the **Axes** collection. An individual member of the collection can be accessed with the **Axes** method by specifying the axis type (**xlCategory**, **xlValue**, or **xlSeries**) and optionally the axis group (**xlPrimary** or **xlSecondary**). Only 3-D charts have a series axis, and only 2-D charts can have a secondary axis group.

The following example sets the category axis title text on the chart sheet named "Chart1."

```
With Charts("chart1").Axes(xlCategory)
    .HasTitle = True
    .AxisTitle.Caption = "1995"
End With
```

Properties   **Application** Property, **AxisBetweenCategories** Property, **AxisGroup** Property, **AxisTitle** Property, **Border** Property, **CategoryNames** Property, **Creator** Property, **Crosses** Property, **CrossesAt** Property, **HasMajorGridlines** Property, **HasMinorGridlines** Property, **HasTitle** Property, **MajorGridlines** Property, **MajorTickMark** Property, **MajorUnit** Property, **MajorUnitIsAuto** Property, **MaximumScale** Property, **MaximumScaleIsAuto** Property, **MinimumScale** Property, **MinimumScaleIsAuto** Property, **MinorGridlines** Property, **MinorTickMark** Property, **MinorUnit** Property, **MinorUnitIsAuto** Property, **Parent** Property, **ReversePlotOrder** Property, **ScaleType** Property, **TickLabelPosition** Property, **TickLabels** Property, **TickLabelSpacing** Property, **TickMarkSpacing** Property, **Type** Property.

Methods   **Delete** Method, **Select** Method.

AxisBetweenCategories Property

Applies To   **Axis** Object.

Description   **True** if the value axis crosses the category axis between categories.

Remarks   This property only applies to category axes, and does not apply to 3-D charts.

Example   This example causes the value axis in Chart1 to cross the category axis between categories.

```
Charts("Chart1").Axes(xlCategory).AxisBetweenCategories = True
```

AxisGroup Property

Applies To   **Axis** Object, **ChartGroup** Object, **Series** Object.

Description   Returns the group (either **xlPrimary** or **xlSecondary**) for the specified axis, chart group, or series. Read-write for **Series**; read-only for **Axis** and **ChartGroup**.

Remarks   For 3-D charts, only **xlPrimary** is valid.

Example   This example deletes the value axis in Chart1 if it is in the secondary group.

```
With Charts("Chart1").Axes(xlValue)
    If .AxisGroup = xlSecondary Then .Delete
End With
```

AxisTitle Object

Description   Represents an axis title in a chart.

Accessors   The **AxisTitle** property returns the axis title for the specified axis. The following example activates embedded chart one on the worksheet named "Sheet1," sets the value axis title text, sets the font to Bookman 10 point, and sets the word "millions" to italics.

```
Worksheets("sheet1").ChartObjects(1).Activate
With ActiveChart.Axes(xlValue)
    .HasTitle = True
    With .AxisTitle
        .Caption = "Revenue (millions)"
        .Font.Name = "bookman"
        .Font.Size = 10
        .Characters(10, 8).Font.Italic = True
    End With
End With
```

Remarks   The **AxisTitle** object does not exist and cannot be accessed unless the **HasTitle** property for the axis is **True**.

Properties   **Application** Property, **Border** Property, **Caption** Property, **Creator** Property, **Font** Property, **HorizontalAlignment** Property, **Interior** Property, **Left** Property, **Name** Property, **Orientation** Property, **Parent** Property, **Shadow** Property, **Text** Property, **Top** Property, **VerticalAlignment** Property.

Methods   **Characters** Method, **Delete** Method, **Select** Method.

AxisTitle Property

Applies To   **Axis** Object.

Description   Accessor. Returns an **AxisTitle** object that represents the title of the specified axis. Read-only.

See Also   **ChartTitle** Property, **HasTitle** Property, **Title** Property.

Example   This example adds an axis label to the category axis in Chart1.

```
With Charts("Chart1").Axes(xlCategory)
    .HasTitle = True
    .AxisTitle.Text = "July Sales"
End With
```

Background Property

Applies To   **Font** Object.

Description   Returns or sets the text background type (can be one of **xlAutomatic**, **xlOpaque**, or **xlTransparent**). This property is only used for text on charts. Read-write.

Example   This example adds a chart title to embedded chart one on Sheet1 and then sets the font size and background type of the title.

```
With Worksheets("Sheet1").ChartObjects(1).Chart
    .HasTitle = True
    .ChartTitle.Text = "1995 Rainfall Totals by Month"
    With .ChartTitle.Font
        .Size = 10
        .Background = xlTransparent
    End With
End With
```

Backward Property

Applies To   **Trendline** Object.

Description   Returns or sets the number of periods (or units on a scatter chart) that the trendline extends backward. Read-write.

See Also   **Forward** Property.

Example   This example sets the number of units the trendline on Chart1 extends forward and backward. The example should be run on a 2-D column chart that contains a single series with a trendline.

```
With Charts("Chart1").SeriesCollection(1).Trendlines(1)
    .Forward = 5
    .Backward = .5
End With
```

Bar3DGroup Property

Applies To   **Chart** Object.

Description	Accessor. Returns a **ChartGroup** object that represents the bar chart group on a 3-D chart. Read-only.
See Also	**BarGroups** Method.
Example	This example sets the subtype for the 3-D bar chart group in Chart1. The example should be run on a 3-D bar chart that has more than one series.

```
Charts("Chart1").Bar3DGroup.SubType = 1
```

BarGroups Method

Applies To	**Chart** Object.
Description	Accessor. On a 2-D chart, returns an object that represents a single bar chart group (a **ChartGroup** object, Syntax 1), or a collection of the bar chart groups (a **ChartGroups** collection, Syntax 2).
Syntax 1	*object*.**BarGroups(*index*)**
Syntax 2	*object*.**BarGroups**

object
   Required. The **Chart** object.

index
   Required for Syntax 1. Specifies the chart group.

See Also	**Bar3DGroup** Property.
Example	This example sets the subtype for bar chart group one. The example should be run on a 2-D chart that has a bar group and a line group.

```
Charts("Chart1").BarGroups(1).SubType = 1
```

BaseField Property

Applies To	**PivotField** Object.
Description	Returns or sets the base field for the custom calculation. Valid only for data fields. Read-write.

Example   This example sets the data field in the PivotTable on Sheet1 to calculate the difference from the base field, sets the base field to the field named "ORDER_DATE," and sets the base item to the item named "5/16/89."

```
Worksheets("Sheet1").Range("A3").PivotField.Calculation = _
    xlDifferenceFrom
Worksheets("Sheet1").Range("A3").PivotField.BaseField = "ORDER_DATE"
Worksheets("Sheet1").Range("A3").PivotField.BaseItem = "5/16/89"
```

BaseItem Property

Applies To   **PivotField** Object.

Description   Returns or sets the item in the base field for the custom calculation. Valid only for data fields. Read-write.

Example   This example sets the data field in the PivotTable on Sheet1 to calculate the difference from the base field, sets the base field to the field named "ORDER_DATE," and sets the base item to the item named "5/16/89."

```
Worksheets("Sheet1").Range("A3").PivotField.Calculation = _
    xlDifferenceFrom
Worksheets("Sheet1").Range("A3").PivotField.BaseField = "ORDER_DATE"
Worksheets("Sheet1").Range("A3").PivotField.BaseItem = "5/16/89"
```

BCCRecipients Property

Applies To   **Mailer** Object.

Description   Returns or sets the blind carbon copy recipients of the mailer. Available only in Microsoft Excel for the Apple Macintosh with the PowerTalk mail system extension installed. Read-write.

Remarks   This property is an array of strings specifying the address, in one of the following formats:

- A record in the Preferred Personal Catalog. These names are one level deep ("Fred" or "June").
- A full path specifying either a record in a personal catalog ("HD:Excel Folder:My Catalog:Barney") or a plain record ("HD:Folder:Martin").

- A relative path from the current working folder specifying either a personal catalog record ("My Catalog:Barney") or a plain record ("Martin").

- A path in a PowerShare catalog tree of the form "CATALOG_NAME:<node>:RECORD_NAME" where <node> is a path to a PowerShare catalog. An example of a complete path is "AppleTalk:North Building Zone:George's Mac".

See Also

CCRecipients Property, **Enclosures** Property, **Mailer** Property, **Received** Property, **SendDateTime** Property, **Sender** Property, **SendMailer** Method, **Subject** Property, **ToRecipients** Property.

Example

This example sets up the **Mailer** object for workbook one and then sends the workbook.

```
With Workbooks(1)
    .HasMailer = True
    With .Mailer
        .Subject = "Here is the workbook"
        .ToRecipients = Array("Jean")
        .CCRecipients = Array("Adam", "Bernard")
        .BCCRecipients = Array("Chris")
        .Enclosures = Array("TestFile")
    End With
    .SendMailer
End With
```

Beep Statement

Description

Sounds a tone through the computer's speaker.

Syntax

Beep

Remarks

The frequency and duration of the beep depends on hardware, which may vary among computers.

Example

This example uses the **Beep** statement to sound three consecutive tones through the computer's speaker.

```
For I = 1 to 3                    ' Loop 3 times.
   Beep                          ' Sound a tone.
Next I
```

BlackAndWhite Property

Applies To	**PageSetup** Object.
Description	**True** if elements of the document will be printed in black and white. Read-write.
Remarks	This property applies only to worksheet pages.
Example	This example causes Sheet1 to print in black and white.

```
Worksheets("Sheet1").PageSetup.BlackAndWhite = True
```

Bold Property

Applies To	**Font** Object.
Description	**True** if the font is bold. Read-write.
Example	This example sets the font to bold for the range A1:A5 on Sheet1.

```
Worksheets("Sheet1").Range("A1:A5").Font.Bold = True
```

Boolean Data Type

Description	**Boolean** variables are stored as 16-bit (2-byte) numbers, but they can only be **True** or **False**. **Boolean** variables display as either True or False (when **Print** is used) or `#TRUE#` or `#FALSE#` (when **Write #** is used). Use the keywords **True** and **False** to assign one of the two states to **Boolean** variables.
When other numeric data types are converted to **Boolean** values, 0 becomes **False** while all other values become **True**. When **Boolean** values are converted to other data types, **False** becomes 0 while **True** becomes -1.
See Also	**CBool** Function, Data Type Summary, **Def**_type_ Statements, **Integer** Data Type.

Border Object

Description	Represents the border of an object.

Accessors   Most bordered objects (all except the **Range** and **Style** objects) have a border that is treated as a single entity, regardless of how many sides it has. The entire border must be accessed at once. Use the **Border** property to return the border of this kind of object. The following example activates the chart sheet named "Chart1," places a dashed border around the chart area for the active chart and a dotted border around the plot area.

```
Charts("chart1").Activate
With ActiveChart
    .ChartArea.Border.LineStyle = xlDash
    .PlotArea.Border.LineStyle = xlDot
End With
```

The appearance of line-like objects (such as lines, error bars, and arcs) is controlled by setting properties of the **Border** object for the line-like object. Setting the **Border** property for a line, for example, changes the way the line itself is drawn. The following example activates the worksheet named "Sheet1" and then sets the line style and color for a line on the active sheet.

```
Worksheets("sheet1").Activate
With ActiveSheet.Lines(1).Border
    .LineStyle = xlDashDot
    .Color = RGB(255, 0, 0)
End With
```

Range and **Style** objects have four discrete borders—left, right, top, and bottom—which can be accessed individually or as a group. Use the **Borders** method with an argument to return a single **Border** object. The following example sets the bottom border of cells A1:G1 to a double line.

```
Worksheets("Sheet1").Range("a1:g1"). _
    Borders(xlBottom).LineStyle = xlDouble
```

To change all four borders of a **Range** or **Style** object, use the **Borders** method with no arguments to access the entire **Borders** collection at once.

Properties   **Application** Property, **Color** Property, **ColorIndex** Property, **Creator** Property, **LineStyle** Property, **Parent** Property, **Weight** Property.

Border Property

Applies To   **Arc** Object, **Arcs** Collection, **Axis** Object, **AxisTitle** Object, **ChartArea** Object, **ChartObject** Object, **ChartObjects** Collection, **ChartTitle** Object, **CheckBox** Object, **DataLabel** Object, **DataLabels** Collection, **DownBars** Object, **Drawing** Object, **DrawingObjects** Collection, **Drawings** Collection, **DropLines** Object, **ErrorBars** Object, **Floor** Object, **Gridlines** Object, **GroupObject** Object, **GroupObjects** Collection, **HiLoLines** Object, **Legend** Object, **LegendKey** Object, **Line** Object, **Lines** Collection, **OLEObject** Object, **OLEObjects** Collection, **OptionButton** Object, **OptionButtons** Collection, **Oval** Object, **Ovals** Collection, **Picture** Object, **Pictures** Collection, **PlotArea** Object, **Point** Object, **Rectangle** Object, **Rectangles** Collection, **Series** Object, **SeriesLines** Object, **TextBox** Object, **TextBoxes** Collection, **Trendline** Object, **UpBars** Object, **Walls** Object.

Description   Accessor. Returns a **Border** object that represents the border of the object. Read-only.

Example   This example sets the color of the chart area border of Chart1 to red.

```
Charts("Chart1").ChartArea.Border.ColorIndex = 3
```

This example creates a new rectangle on Sheet1 and then sets the border color to red.

```
Set newRect = Worksheets("Sheet1").Rectangles.Add(72, 72, 72, 144)
newRect.Border.ColorIndex = 3
```

BorderAround Method

Applies To   **Range** Object.

Description   Adds a border to a range and sets the **Color**, **LineStyle**, and **Weight** properties for the new border.

Syntax   *object*.**BorderAround**(*lineStyle*, *weight*, *colorIndex*, *color*)

object
Required. The **Range** object.

lineStyle
Optional. Specifies the border line style. Can be one of **xlContinuous**, **xlDash**, **xlDot**, or **xlDouble**.

weight
> Optional. Specifies the border weight. Can be one of **xlHairline**, **xlThin**, **xlMedium**, or **xlThick**. If omitted, **xlThin** is assumed.

colorIndex
> Optional. Specifies the border color as a color index into the current color palette. Can be a number from 1 to 56, or the special constant **xlAutomatic** to use the window text color.

color
> Optional. Specifies the border color as an RGB value.

Remarks   You can specify either *colorIndex* or *color*, but not both. If you do not specify either argument, Microsoft Excel uses the **xlAutomatic** color index.

Similarly, you can specify either *lineStyle* or *weight*, but not both. If you do not specify either argument, Microsoft Excel creates a default border.

This method outlines the entire range without filling it in. To set the borders of all the cells, you must set the **Color**, **LineStyle**, and **Weight** properties for the **Borders** collection. To clear the border, you must set the **LineStyle** property to **xlNone** for all the cells in the range.

Example   This example adds a thick red border around the range A1:D4 on Sheet1.

```
Worksheets("Sheet1").Range("A1:D4").BorderAround _
        ColorIndex:=3, Weight:=xlThick
```

Borders Collection Object

Description   A collection of four **Border** objects representing the four borders of a **Range** or **Style** object.

Accessors   Use the **Borders** method with an argument to access a single member of the collection. The following example sets the bottom border of cells A1:G1 to a double line.

```
Worksheets("Sheet1").Range("a1:g1"). _
    Borders(xlBottom).LineStyle = xlDouble
```

Use the **Borders** method with no arguments to access all four borders at once. The following example puts a double blue border around cell C5:

```
With Worksheets("sheet1").Range("c5").Borders
    .LineStyle = xlDouble
    .Color = RGB(0, 0, 255)
End With
```

Remarks   You can set border properties for an individual border only with **Range** and **Style** objects. Other bordered objects, such as check boxes or chart areas, have a border that is treated as a single entity, regardless of how many sides it has. For these objects, you must access and set properties for the entire border at once. See the **Border** object for more information.

Properties   **Application** Property, **Color** Property, **ColorIndex** Property, **Count** Property, **Creator** Property, **LineStyle** Property, **Parent** Property, **Value** Property, **Weight** Property.

Methods   **Item** Method.

Borders Method

Applies To   **Range** Object, **Style** Object.

Description   Accessor. Returns an object that represents a single border (a **Border** object, Syntax 1) or a collection of borders (a **Borders** object, Syntax 2). Read-write.

Syntax 1   *object*.**Borders**(*index*)

Syntax 2   *object*.**Borders**

                   object
                   Required. The **Range** or **Style** object.

                   index
                   Required for Syntax 1. Specifies the border (one of **xlTop**, **xlBottom**, **xlLeft**, or **xlRight**).

Example   This example sets the color of the bottom border of cell B2 on Sheet1 to red.

```
With Worksheets("Sheet1").Range("B2").Borders(xlBottom)
    .LineStyle = xlContinuous
    .ColorIndex = 3
End With
```

                   This example sets the color of all four borders of cell B2 on Sheet1 to red.

```
With Worksheets("Sheet1").Range("B2").Borders
    .LineStyle = xlContinuous
    .ColorIndex = 3
End With
```

BottomMargin Property

Applies To   **PageSetup** Object.

Description   Returns or sets the size of the bottom margin, in points (1/72 inch). Read-write.

Remarks   Margins are set or returned in points. Use the **InchesToPoints** or **CentimetersToPoints** function to convert.

See Also   **LeftMargin** Property, **RightMargin** Property, **TopMargin** Property.

Example   These two examples set the bottom margin of Sheet1 to 0.5 inch (36 points).

```
Worksheets("Sheet1").PageSetup.BottomMargin = _
        Application.InchesToPoints(0.5)


Worksheets("Sheet1").PageSetup.BottomMargin = 36
```

This example displays the current bottom margin setting for Sheet1.

```
marginInches = Worksheets("Sheet1").PageSetup.BottomMargin / _
    Application.InchesToPoints(1)
MsgBox "The current bottom margin is " & marginInches & " inches"
```

BottomRightCell Property

Applies To   **Arc** Object, **Button** Object, **ChartObject** Object, **CheckBox** Object, **Drawing** Object, **DropDown** Object, **EditBox** Object, **GroupBox** Object, **GroupObject** Object, **Label** Object, **Line** Object, **ListBox** Object, **OLEObject** Object, **OptionButton** Object, **Oval** Object, **Picture** Object, **Rectangle** Object, **ScrollBar** Object, **Spinner** Object, **TextBox** Object.

Description   Accessor. Returns a **Range** object that represents the cell that lies under the bottom right corner of the object. For drawing objects, this property applies only when the drawing object is on a worksheet. Read-only.

See Also   **TopLeftCell** Property.

Example   This example displays the address of the cell beneath the lower-right corner of rectangle one on Sheet1.

```
MsgBox "The bottom right corner is over cell " & _
    Worksheets("Sheet1").Rectangles(1).BottomRightCell.Address
```

BringToFront Method

Applies To	**Arc** Object, **Arcs** Collection, **Button** Object, **Buttons** Collection, **ChartObject** Object, **ChartObjects** Collection, **CheckBox** Object, **Drawing** Object, **DrawingObjects** Collection, **Drawings** Collection, **DropDown** Object, **DropDowns** Collection, **EditBox** Object, **EditBoxes** Collection, **GroupBox** Object, **GroupBoxes** Collection, **GroupObject** Object, **GroupObjects** Collection, **Label** Object, **Labels** Collection, **Line** Object, **Lines** Collection, **ListBox** Object, **ListBoxes** Collection, **OLEObject** Object, **OLEObjects** Collection, **OptionButton** Object, **OptionButtons** Collection, **Oval** Object, **Ovals** Collection, **Picture** Object, **Pictures** Collection, **Rectangle** Object, **Rectangles** Collection, **ScrollBar** Object, **ScrollBars** Collection, **Spinner** Object, **Spinners** Collection, **TextBox** Object, **TextBoxes** Collection.

Description Brings the object to the front of the z-order.

Syntax *object*.**BringToFront**

object
    Required. The object to which this method applies.

See Also **SendToBack** Method, **ZOrder** Property.

Example This example brings rectangle one on Sheet1 to the front of the z-order.

```
Worksheets("Sheet1").Rectangles(1).BringToFront
```

BuiltIn Property

Applies To **MenuBar** Object, **Toolbar** Object, **ToolbarButton** Object.

Description **True** if the object is built-in (part of Microsoft Excel, as opposed to a custom object). Read-only.

See Also **BuiltInFace** Property.

Example This example lists the names of all built-in buttons on the Formatting toolbar. The names are placed in the first column on Sheet1.

```
rowNumber = 1
For Each btn In Application.Toolbars("Formatting").ToolbarButtons
    If btn.BuiltIn Then
        Worksheets("Sheet1").Cells(rowNumber, 1).Value = btn.Name
        rowNumber = rowNumber + 1
    End If
Next btn
```

This example resets the face of each built-in button on the Standard toolbar that has a custom face.

```
For Each btn In Application.Toolbars("Standard").ToolbarButtons
    If btn.BuiltIn And Not btn.BuiltInFace Then
        If Not(btn.IsGap) Then   ' don't try to reset the separator gap!
            btn.BuiltInFace = True
        End If
    End If
Next btn
```

BuiltinDocumentProperties Property

Applies To   **Workbook** Object.

Description   Returns a **DocumentProperties** collection object that represents all the built-in document properties for the specified workbook. Read-only.

To use this property, you should establish a reference to the Microsoft Office 95 Object Library by using the References command (Tools menu).

Remarks   This property returns the entire collection of built-in document properties. Use the **Item** method to return a single member of the collection (a **DocumentProperty** object) by specifying either the name of the property or the collection index (as a number). For a list of valid built-in document property names, see the **Item** method.

Because the **Item** method is the default method for the **DocumentProperties** collection object, the following statements are identical:

```
BuiltinDocumentProperties.Item(1)
BuiltinDocumentProperties(1)
```

Use the **CustomDocumentProperties** property to return the collection of custom document properties.

Example   This example displays the names of the built-in document properties as a list on worksheet one.

```
rw = 1
Worksheets(1).Activate
For Each p In ActiveWorkbook.BuiltinDocumentProperties
    Cells(rw, 1).Value = p.Name
    rw = rw + 1
Next
```

BuiltInFace Property

Applies To   **ToolbarButton** Object.

Description   **True** if the button is using its built-in face. **False** if the button has a custom face. Read-write.

Remarks   This property can only be set to **True**, which forces the button to use its built-in face. You cannot set this property to **False**; to use a custom face, use the **CopyFace** and **PasteFace** methods (this sets the **BuiltInFace** property to **False**).

See Also   **BuiltIn** Property, **CopyFace** Method, **PasteFace** Method.

Example   This example resets the face of each built-in button on the Standard toolbar that has a custom face.

```
For Each btn In Application.Toolbars("Standard").ToolbarButtons
    If btn.BuiltIn And Not btn.BuiltInFace Then
        If Not(btn.IsGap) Then  ' don't try to reset the separator gap!
            btn.BuiltInFace = True
        End If
    End If
Next btn
```

Button Object

Description   Represents a custom button graphic object on a chart sheet, dialog sheet, or worksheet. Do not confuse the **Button** object with the **ToolbarButton** object, which is a button on a toolbar.

Accessors   The **Button** object is a member of the **Buttons** collection. The **Buttons** collection contains all the **Button** objects on a single sheet. Use the **Add** method to create a new button and add it to the collection.

To access a single member of the collection, use the **Buttons** method with the index number or name or of the button as an argument.

The following example sets the text for button one on the worksheet named "Sheet1."

```
Worksheets("sheet1").Buttons(1).Text = "Repeat"
```

The button name is shown in the Name Box when the button is selected. Use the **Name** property to set or return the name of the button. The following example positions the button named "go_button" so that it completely cover cell C10. When the button is pressed, the GoButtonTest macro runs.

```
Worksheets("sheet1").Activate
Set r = ActiveSheet.Range("c10")
With ActiveSheet.Buttons("go_button")
    .Caption = "Go"
    .Left = r.Left
    .Top = r.Top
    .Width = r.Width
    .Height = r.Height
    .OnAction = "GoButtonTest"
End With
```

Properties

Accelerator Property, **AddIndent** Property, **Application** Property, **AutoSize** Property, **BottomRightCell** Property, **CancelButton** Property, **Caption** Property, **Creator** Property, **DefaultButton** Property, **DismissButton** Property, **Enabled** Property, **Font** Property, **Formula** Property, **Height** Property, **HelpButton** Property, **HorizontalAlignment** Property, **Index** Property, **Left** Property, **Locked** Property, **LockedText** Property, **Name** Property, **OnAction** Property, **Orientation** Property, **Parent** Property, **PhoneticAccelerator** Property, **Placement** Property, **PrintObject** Property, **Text** Property, **Top** Property, **TopLeftCell** Property, **VerticalAlignment** Property, **Visible** Property, **Width** Property, **ZOrder** Property.

Methods

BringToFront Method, **Characters** Method, **CheckSpelling** Method, **Copy** Method, **CopyPicture** Method, **Cut** Method, **Delete** Method, **Duplicate** Method, **Select** Method, **SendToBack** Method.

Buttons Collection Object

Description

A collection of all the **Button** objects on the specified chart sheet, dialog sheet, or worksheet.

Accessors

Use the **Add** method to create a new button and add it to the collection. The following example activates worksheet one and then adds a new button to the active sheet. The new button is positioned over cells C5 and D5.

```
Worksheets(1).Activate
Set r = ActiveSheet.Range("c5:d5")
Set newButton = ActiveSheet.Buttons.Add(r.Left, r.Top, _
    r.Width, r.Height)
```

Use the **Buttons** method with an argument to access a single member of the collection or without an argument to access the entire collection at once.

Properties   **Accelerator** Property, **AddIndent** Property, **Application** Property, **AutoSize** Property, **CancelButton** Property, **Caption** Property, **Count** Property, **Creator** Property, **DefaultButton** Property, **DismissButton** Property, **Enabled** Property, **Font** Property, **Formula** Property, **Height** Property, **HelpButton** Property, **HorizontalAlignment** Property, **Left** Property, **Locked** Property, **LockedText** Property, **OnAction** Property, **Orientation** Property, **Parent** Property, **PhoneticAccelerator** Property, **Placement** Property, **PrintObject** Property, **Text** Property, **Top** Property, **VerticalAlignment** Property, **Visible** Property, **Width** Property, **ZOrder** Property.

Methods   **Add** Method (Graphic Objects and Controls), **BringToFront** Method, **Characters** Method, **CheckSpelling** Method, **Copy** Method, **CopyPicture** Method, **Cut** Method, **Delete** Method, **Duplicate** Method, **Group** Method, **Item** Method, **Select** Method, **SendToBack** Method.

Buttons Method

Applies To   **Chart** Object, **DialogSheet** Object, **Worksheet** Object.

Description   Accessor. Returns an object that represents a single button (a **Button** object, Syntax 1) or a collection of buttons (a **Buttons** object, Syntax 2) on the sheet. Read-only.

Syntax 1   *object*.**Buttons**(*index*)

Syntax 2   *object*.**Buttons**

object
　　Required. The object to which this method applies.

index
　　Required for Syntax 1. The name or number of the button.

Example   This example deletes every button on Sheet1.

```
Worksheets("Sheet1").Buttons.Delete
```

This example changes the text on button one on Sheet1.

```
Worksheets("Sheet1").Buttons(1).Text = "New Button Name"
```

Calculate Method

Applies To   **Application** Object, **Range** Object, **Worksheet** Object.

Description   Calculates all open workbooks, a specific worksheet in a workbook, or a specified range of cells in a sheet, as shown in the following table.

To calculate	Example
All open workbooks	Application.Calculate (or just Calculate)
A specific worksheet	Worksheets(1).Calculate
A specified range	Worksheets(1).Rows(2).Calculate

Syntax   *object*.**Calculate**

object
> Optional for **Application**, required for **Worksheet** and **Range**. Specifies where the calculation will occur.

Example   This example calculates the formulas in columns A, B, and C in the used range on Sheet1.

```
Worksheets("Sheet1").UsedRange.Columns("A:C").Calculate
```

CalculateBeforeSave Property

Applies To   **Application** Object.

Description   **True** if workbooks are calculated before they are saved to disk (if the **Calculation** property is set to **xlManual**). This property is preserved even if you change the **Calculation** property. Read-write.

Example   This example causes workbooks to be calculated before they are saved to disk.

```
Application.Calculation = xlManual
Application.CalculateBeforeSave = True
```

Calculation Property

Applies To   **Application** Object, **PivotField** Object.

Description	For the **Application** object, returns or sets the calculation mode, as shown in the following table. Read-write.

Value	Meaning
xlAutomatic	Recalculate automatically.
xlManual	Recalculate only at user's request.
xlSemiautomatic	Recalculate automatically, except for data tables.

For the **PivotField** object, returns or sets the type of calculation done by the specified pivot field (one of **xlDifferenceFrom**, **xlIndex**, **xlNormal**, **xlPercentDifferenceFrom**, **xlPercentOf**, **xlPercentOfColumn**, **xlPercentOfRow**, **xlPercentOfTotal**, or **xlRunningTotal**). Valid only for data fields. Read-write.

See Also

CalculateBeforeSave Property.

Example

This example causes Microsoft Excel to calculate workbooks before they are saved to disk.

```
Application.Calculation = xlManual
Application.CalculateBeforeSave = True
```

This example sets the data field in the PivotTable on Sheet1 to calculate the difference from the base field, sets the base field to the field named "ORDER_DATE," and sets the base item to the item named "5/16/89."

```
Worksheets("Sheet1").Range("A3").PivotField.Calculation = _
    xlDifferenceFrom
Worksheets("Sheet1").Range("A3").PivotField.BaseField = "ORDER_DATE"
Worksheets("Sheet1").Range("A3").PivotField.BaseItem = "5/16/89"
```

Call Statement

Description

Transfers control to a **Sub** procedure, **Function** procedure, dynamic-link library (DLL) procedure, or a Macintosh code resource procedure.

Syntax

[**Call**] *name* [*argumentlist*]

The **Call** statement syntax has these parts:

Part	Description
Call	Optional keyword; if specified, you must enclose *argumentlist* in parentheses. For example:
	`Call MyProc(0)`
name	Name of the procedure to call.
argumentlist	Comma-delimited list of variables, arrays, or expressions to pass to the procedure. Components of *argumentlist* may include the keywords **ByVal** or **ByRef** to describe how the arguments are to be treated by the called procedure. However, **ByVal** and **ByRef** can be used with **Call** only when making a call to a DLL procedure or a Macintosh code resource.

Remarks

You are never required to use the **Call** keyword when calling a procedure. However, if you use the **Call** keyword to call a procedure that requires arguments, *argumentlist* must be enclosed in parentheses. If you omit the **Call** keyword, you also must omit the parentheses around *argumentlist*. If you use either **Call** syntax to call any intrinsic or user-defined function, the function's return value is discarded.

To pass a whole array to a procedure, use the array name followed by empty parentheses.

See Also

Declare Statement.

Example

This example illustrates how the **Call** statement is used to transfer control to a **Sub** procedure, an intrinsic function, a dynamic-link library (DLL) procedure and a procedure in a Macintosh code resource.

```
' Call a Sub procedure.
Call PrintToDebugWindow("Hello World")
' The above statement causes control to be passed to the following
' Sub procedure.
Sub PrintToDebugWindow(AnyString)
    Debug.Print AnyString            ' Print to Debug window.
End Sub


' Call an intrinsic function. The return value of the function is
' discarded.
Call Shell(AppName, 1)               ' AppName contains the path of the
        ' executable.
' Call a Microsoft Windows DLL procedure.
Declare Sub MessageBeep Lib "User" (ByVal N As Integer)
Sub CallMyDll()
    Call MessageBeep(0)              ' Call Windows DLL procedure.
    MessageBeep 0                    ' Call again without Call keyword.
End Sub
```

```
' Call a Macintosh Code Resource.
Declare Sub MessageAlert Lib "MyHd:MyAlert" Alias "MyAlert" (ByVal N _
As Integer)
Sub CallMyCodeResource()
    Call MessageAlert(0)            ' Call Macintosh code resource.
    MessageAlert 0                  ' Call again without Call keyword.
End Sub
```

Caller Property

Applies To   **Application** Object.

Description   Returns information about how Visual Basic was called (see the Remarks section for details). Read-only.

Remarks   This property returns information about how Visual Basic was called, as shown in the following table.

Caller	Return
A custom function entered in a single cell	A **Range** specifying that cell
A custom function, part of an array formula in a range of cells	A **Range** specifying that range of cells
An Auto_Open, Auto_Close, Auto_Activate, or Auto_Deactivate macro	The name of the document as text
A command on a menu	An array of three elements specifying the command's position number, the menu number, and the menu bar number
A drawing object	The specifier of that object as a string
A button on a toolbar	An array of two elements specifying the tool position number and the toolbar name as text
A macro set by the **OnDoubleClick** or **OnEntry** properties.	The name of the chart object identifier or cell reference, if applicable, to which the macro applies
The Macro dialog box (Tools menu), or any caller not described above	The #REF! error value

CancelButton Property

Applies To	**Button** Object, **Buttons** Collection, **DrawingObjects** Collection.
Description	Applies only to buttons in a user-defined dialog box. **True** if the button is automatically selected when the ESCAPE key is pressed or when the system menu close box or menu item is selected. When the user presses the ESCAPE key, the Cancel button is selected, and Microsoft Excel runs the macro identified by the button's **OnAction** property.
Remarks	Set this property for a button if you want some code to always run when the dialog box is canceled, even if it is canceled by the ESCAPE key or the system menu.
	Only one button in the dialog box can have the **CancelButton** property set to **True** at any given time. Setting one will reset this property for all other buttons on the dialog sheet.
See Also	**DismissButton** Property.
Example	This example sets the **CancelButton** property for button one on Dialog1.

```
DialogSheets("Dialog1").Buttons(1).CancelButton = True
```

CanPlaySounds Property

Applies To	**Application** Object.
Description	**True** if the computer can play sound notes. Read-only.
See Also	**CanRecordSounds** Property.
Example	This example determines whether the computer can play sound notes. If it can, it plays the sound note in cell A1 on Sheet1.

```
If Application.CanPlaySounds = True Then
    Worksheets("Sheet1").Range("A1").SoundNote.Play
End If
```

CanRecordSounds Property

Applies To	**Application** Object.

Description	**True** if the computer can record sound notes. Read-only.
See Also	**CanPlaySounds** Property.
Example	This example determines whether the computer can record sound notes. If it can, it records a sound note into cell A1 on Sheet1.

```
If Application.CanRecordSounds = True Then
    With Worksheets("Sheet1").Range("A1").SoundNote
        .Delete
        .Record
    End With
End If
```

CapitalizeNamesOfDays Property

Applies To	**AutoCorrect** Object.
Description	**True** if the first letters of the names of days are capitalized automatically. This property is available only in Microsoft Excel for Windows 95. Read-write.
Example	This example sets Microsoft Excel to capitalize the first letters of the names of days.

```
With Application.AutoCorrect
    .CapitalizeNamesOfDays = True
    .ReplaceText = True
End With
```

Caption Property

Applies To	**Application** Object, **AxisTitle** Object, **Button** Object, **Buttons** Collection, **Characters** Object, **ChartTitle** Object, **CheckBox** Object, **DataLabel** Object, **DialogFrame** Object, **DrawingObjects** Collection, **DropDown** Object, **DropDowns** Collection, **EditBox** Object, **EditBoxes** Collection, **GroupBox** Object, **GroupBoxes** Collection, **Label** Object, **Labels** Collection, **Menu** Object, **MenuBar** Object, **MenuItem** Object, **OptionButton** Object, **OptionButtons** Collection, **TextBox** Object, **TextBoxes** Collection, **Window** Object.

Description   The **Caption** property has several different meanings, depending on the object type to which it is applied. The **Caption** property is read-write, except as noted in the following table.

Object type	Meaning
Application	The name that appears in the title bar of the main Microsoft Excel window. If you don't set a name, or if you set the name to **Empty**, then this property returns "Microsoft Excel". Read-only on the Apple Macintosh.
AxisTitle	The axis title text.
Button	The button text.
Characters	The text of this range of characters.
ChartTitle	The chart title text.
Controls	The control text (check box, dialog frame, drop down, edit box, group box, label, and option button).
DataLabel	The data label text.
Menu	The name of the menu. Use an ampersand (&) before the letter that you want to be the command underline (for example, "&File").
MenuBar	The menu bar text. Read-only.
MenuItem	The name of the menu item (command). Use an ampersand (&) before the letter that you want to be the command underline (for example, "E&xit").
TextBox	The text in the text box.
Window	The name that appears in the title bar of the document window. When you set the name, you can use that name as the index to the **Windows** property; see the second example.

See Also   **Text** Property.

Example   This example sets the name that appears in the title bar of the main Microsoft Excel window to be a custom name (this can be done only in Windows; **Application.Caption** is read-only on the Macintosh).

```
Application.Caption = "Blue Sky Airlines Reservation System"
```

This example sets the name of the first window in the workbook to be Consolidated Balance Sheet. This name is then used as the index to the **Windows** method.

```
ActiveWorkbook.Windows(1).Caption = "Consolidated Balance Sheet"
ActiveWorkbook.Windows("Consolidated Balance Sheet") _
    .ActiveSheet.Calculate
```

This example changes the Open command on the File menu to Open Workbook. The example changes every menu bar in the product.

```
For Each mb In MenuBars
    mb.Menus("File").MenuItems(2).Caption = "&Open Workbook"
Next mb
```

Category Property

Applies To   **Name** Object.

Description   If the name refers to a custom function or command, this property returns or sets the category for this name as a string translated to the language of the macro. Read-write.

See Also   **MacroType** Property.

Example   This example assumes that you created a custom function or command on a Microsoft Excel version 4.0 macro sheet. The example displays the function category, in the language of the macro. It assumes that the name of the custom function or command is the only name in the workbook.

```
With ActiveWorkbook.Names(1)
    If .MacroType <> xlNone Then
        MsgBox "The category for this name is " & .Category
    Else
        MsgBox "This name does not refer to" & _
            " a custom function or command."
    End If
End With
```

CategoryLocal Property

Applies To   **Name** Object.

Description   If the name refers to a custom function or command, this property returns or sets the category for this name as a string in the language of the user. Read-write.

See Also   **Category** Property, **MacroType** Property.

Example   This example displays, in the language of the user, the function category of a custom function or command created on a Microsoft Excel version 4.0 macro sheet. The example assumes that the custom function name or command name is the only name in the workbook.

```
With ActiveWorkbook.Names(1)
    If .MacroType <> xlNone Then
        MsgBox "The category for this name is " & .CategoryLocal
    Else
        MsgBox "This name does not refer to" & _
            " a custom function or command."
    End If
End With
```

CategoryNames Property

Applies To   **Axis** Object.

Description   Returns or sets all the category names for the specified axis, as a text array. When you set this property, you can set it to an array or a **Range** object containing the category names. Read-write.

Remarks   Category names are really a property of the "special" series in an axis grouping. Deleting or modifying that special series will change the category names for all series using the axis.

See Also   **Formula** Property, **Values** Property, **XValues** Property.

Example   This example sets the category names for Chart1 to the values in cells B1:B5 on Sheet1.

```
Set Charts("Chart1").Axes(xlCategory).CategoryNames = _
    Worksheets("Sheet1").Range("B1:B5")
```

This example uses an array to set individual category names for Chart1.

```
Charts("Chart1").Axes(xlCategory).CategoryNames = _
    Array ("1985", "1986", "1987", "1988", "1989")
```

CBool Function

Description   Converts an expression to a **Boolean**.

Syntax	**CBool**(*expression*)
	The *expression* argument is any valid numeric expression.
Remarks	If *expression* is zero, **False** is returned; otherwise, **True** is returned. If *expression* can't be interpreted as a numeric value, a run-time error occurs.
See Also	Data Type Summary.
Example	This example uses the **CBool** function to convert an expression to a **Boolean**. If the expression evaluates to a nonzero value, **CBool** returns **True**; otherwise, it returns **False**.

```
A = 5 : B = 5    ' Define variables.
Check = CBool(A = B) ' Check contains True.
A = 0    ' Define variable.
Check = CBool(A) ' Check contains False.
```

CCRecipients Property

Applies To	**Mailer** Object.
Description	Returns or sets the carbon copy (indirect) recipients of the mailer. Available only in Microsoft Excel for the Apple Macintosh with the PowerTalk mail system extension installed. Read-write.
Remarks	This property is an array of strings specifying the address, in one of the following formats:

- A record in the Preferred Personal Catalog. These names are one level deep ("Fred" or "June").

- A full path specifying either a record in a personal catalog ("HD:Excel Folder:My Catalog:Barney") or a plain record ("HD:Folder:Martin").

- A relative path from the current working folder specifying either a personal catalog record ("My Catalog:Barney") or a plain record ("Martin").

- A path in a PowerShare catalog tree of the form "CATALOG_NAME:<node>:RECORD_NAME" where <node> is a path to a PowerShare catalog. An example of a complete path is "AppleTalk:North Building Zone:George's Mac".

See Also	**BCCRecipients** Property, **Enclosures** Property, **Mailer** Property, **Received** Property, **SendDateTime** Property, **Sender** Property, **SendMailer** Method, **ToRecipients** Property.

Example   This example sets up the **Mailer** object for workbook one and then sends the workbook.

```
With Workbooks(1)
    .HasMailer = True
    With .Mailer
        .Subject = "Here is the workbook"
        .ToRecipients = Array("Jean")
        .CCRecipients = Array("Adam", "Bernard")
        .BCCRecipients = Array("Chris")
        .Enclosures = Array("TestFile")
    End With
    .SendMailer
End With
```

CCur Function

Description   Converts an expression to a **Currency**.

Syntax   **CCur**(*expression*)

The *expression* argument is any valid numeric or string expression.

Remarks   In general, you can document your code using the data type conversion functions to show that the result of some operation should be expressed as a particular data type rather than the default data type. For example, use **CCur** to force currency arithmetic in cases where single-precision, double-precision, or integer arithmetic normally would occur.

You should use the **CCur** function instead of **Val** to provide internationally-aware conversions from any other data type to a **Currency**. For example, different decimal separators are properly recognized depending on the locale setting of your computer, as are different thousand separators and various currency options.

If expression lies outside the acceptable range for the **Currency** data type, an error occurs.

See Also   Data Type Summary.

Example   This example uses the **CCur** function to convert an expression to a **Currency**.

```
MyDouble = 543.214588    ' MyDouble is a Double.

MyCurr = CCur(MyDouble * 2) ' Convert result (1086.4292) to
    ' Currency.
```

CDate Function

Description	Converts an expression to a **Date**.
Syntax	**CDate**(*date*)

The *date* argument is any valid date expression.

Remarks

Use the **IsDate** function to determine if *date* can be converted to a date or time. **CDate** recognizes date and time literals as well as some numbers that fall within the range of acceptable dates. When converting a number to a date, the whole number portion is converted to a date. Any fractional part of the number is converted to a time of day, starting at midnight.

CDate recognizes date formats according to the international settings of your system. The correct order of day, month, and year may not be determined if it is provided in a format other than one of the recognized date settings. In addition, a long date format is not recognized if it also contains the day-of-the-week string.

Note A **CVDate** function is also provided for compatibility with previous versions of Visual Basic. However, since there is now an intrinsic **Date** type, there is no further need for **CVDate**. The syntax of the **CVDate** function is identical to the **CDate** function. The difference is that it returns a Variant whose subtype is **Date** instead of an actual **Date** type. The same effect can be achieved by converting an expression to a **Date** and then assigning it to a **Variant**. This technique is consistent with the conversion of all other intrinsic types to their equivalent **Variant** subtypes.

See Also

Data Type Summary, **IsDate** Function.

Example

This example uses the **CDate** function to convert a string to a **Date**. In general, it is bad programming practice to hard code dates/times as strings as shown in this example. Use date literals instead.

```
MyDate = "February 12, 1969" ' Define date.
MyShortDate = CDate(MyDate)  ' Convert to Date data type.
MyTime = "4:35:47 PM"    ' Define time.
MyShortTime = CDate(MyTime)  ' Convert to Date data type.
```

CDbl Function

Description	Converts an expression to a **Double**.
Syntax	**CDbl**(*expression*)

The *expression* argument is any valid numeric or string expression.

Remarks

In general, you can document your code using the data type conversion functions to show that the result of some operation should be expressed as a particular data type rather than the default data type. For example, use **CDbl** or **CSng** to force double- or single-precision arithmetic in cases where currency or integer arithmetic normally would occur.

You should use the **CDbl** function instead of **Val** to provide internationally-aware conversions from any other data type to a **Double**. For example, different decimal separators and thousands separators are properly recognized depending on the locale setting of your system.

See Also

Data Type Summary.

Example

This example uses the **CDbl** function to convert an expression to a **Double**.

```
MyCurr = CCur(234.456784)    ' MyCurr is a Currency.
MyDouble = CDbl(MyCurr * 8.2 * 0.01) ' Convert result to Double.
```

Cell Error Values

You can insert a cell error value into a cell or you can test the value of a cell for an error value using the **CVErr** function. The cell error values have constants assigned to them as shown in the following table.

Constant	Error number	Cell error value
xlErrDiv0	2007	#DIV/0!
xlErrNA	2042	#N/A
xlErrName	2029	#NAME?
xlErrNull	2000	#NULL!
xlErrNum	2036	#NUM!
xlErrRef	2023	#REF!
xlErrValue	2015	#VALUE!

Example

This example inserts the seven cell error values into cells A1:A7 on Sheet1.

```
myArray = Array(xlErrDiv0, xlErrNA, xlErrName, xlErrNull, _
    xlErrNum, xlErrRef, xlErrValue)
For i = 1 To 7
    Worksheets("Sheet1").Cells(i, 1).Value = CVErr(myArray(i - 1))
Next i
```

This example displays a message if the active cell on Sheet1 contains a cell error value. You can use this example as a framework for a cell-error-value error handler.

```
Worksheets("Sheet1").Activate
If IsError(ActiveCell.Value) Then
    errval = ActiveCell.Value
    Select Case errval
        Case CVErr(xlErrDiv0)
            MsgBox "#DIV/0! error"
        Case CVErr(xlErrNA)
            MsgBox "#N/A error"
        Case CVErr(xlErrName)
            MsgBox "#NAME? error"
        Case CVErr(xlErrNull)
            MsgBox "#NULL! error"
        Case CVErr(xlErrNum)
            MsgBox "#NUM! error"
        Case CVErr(xlErrRef)
            MsgBox "#REF! error"
        Case CVErr(xlErrValue)
            MsgBox "#VALUE! error"
        Case Else
            MsgBox "This should never happen!!"
    End Select
End If
```

CellDragAndDrop Property

Applies To   **Application** Object.

Description   **True** if Cell Drag And Drop editing is on. Read-write.

Example   This example turns on the Cell Drag And Drop editing option.

```
Application.CellDragAndDrop = True
```

Cells Method

Applies To   **Application** Object, **Range** Object, **Worksheet** Object.

Description	Accessor. Returns a **Range** object that represents a single cell (Syntax 1 and 2) or a collection of cells (Syntax 3). The action of the **Cells** method depends on the object to which it is applied, as shown in the following table.

Object type	Action
Application	If the active document is a worksheet, `Application.Cells` is equivalent to `ActiveSheet.Cells`, which returns a collection of cells on the active worksheet. Otherwise, the **Cells** method returns an error.
Range	Returns a collection of cells from the range.
Worksheet	Returns a collection of cells from the worksheet.

Syntax 1   *object*.**Cells**(*rowIndex*, *columnIndex*)

Syntax 2   *object*.**Cells**(*rowIndex*)

Syntax 3   *object*.**Cells**

object
   Optional for **Application**, required for **Worksheet** and **Range**. The object that contains the cells. If you specify the **Application** object (or omit the object qualifier), the **Cells** method applies to the active sheet in the active workbook. If the active sheet is not a worksheet, this method fails.

rowIndex
   Required for Syntax 1. The row number of the cell you want to access, starting with 1 for row 1 (for **Application** and **Worksheet**) or the first row in the **Range**.

   Required for Syntax 2. A long integer specifying the index number of the cell you want to access, in row-major order. A1 is `Cells(1)`, A2 is `Cells(257)` for **Application** and **Worksheet**; `Range.Cells(1)` is the top left cell in the **Range**.

columnIndex
   Required for Syntax 1. A number or string indicating the column number of the cell you want to access, starting with 1 or "A" for column A (for **Application** or **Worksheet**) or the first column in the **Range**.

Remarks   Syntax 1 uses a row number and a column number or letter as index arguments. For more information about this syntax, see the **Range** object.

Syntax 2 uses a single number as an index argument. The index is 1 for cell A1, 2 for cell B1, 3 for cell C1, 257 for cell A2, and so on.

The *rowIndex* and *columnIndex* arguments are relative offsets when you apply the **Cells** method to a **Range** object. In other words, specifying a *rowIndex* of 1 returns cells in the first row of the range, not the first row of the worksheet. For example, if the selection is cell C3, then `Selection.Cells(2, 2)` returns cell D4 (you can use the method to index outside the original range).

If you apply Syntax 3 to a **Range**, it returns the same **Range** object (in other words, it does nothing).

If you apply Syntax 3 to a **Worksheet**, it returns a collection of all the cells in the worksheet (all the cells, not just the cells that are currently in use).

See Also   **Range** Method.

Example   This example sets the font size of cell C5 on Sheet1 to 14 points.

```
Worksheets("Sheet1").Cells(5, 3).Font.Size = 14
```

This example clears the formula in cell one on Sheet1.

```
Worksheets("Sheet1").Cells(1).ClearContents
```

This example sets the font for every cell on Sheet1 to 8-point Arial.

```
With Worksheets("Sheet1").Cells.Font
    .Name = "Arial"
    .Size = 8
End With
```

This example loops through cells A1:J4 on Sheet1. If one of the cells has a value less than .001, the example replaces that value with zero (0).

```
For rwIndex = 1 to 4
    For colIndex = 1 to 10
        If Worksheets("Sheet1").Cells(rwIndex, colIndex) < .001 Then
            Worksheets("Sheet1").Cells(rwIndex, colIndex).Value = 0
        End If
    Next colIndex
Next rwIndex
```

This example sets the font of cells A1:C5 on Sheet1 to italic.

```
Worksheets("Sheet1").Activate
Range(Cells(1, 1), Cells(5, 3)).Font.Italic = True
```

This example scans a column of data named myRange. If a cell has the same value as the cell above it, the example displays the address of the cell that contains the duplicate data.

```
Set r = Range("myRange")
For n = 1 To r.Rows.Count
    If r. Cells(n, 1) = r. Cells(n + 1, 1) Then
        MsgBox "Duplicate data in " & r. Cells(n + 1, 1).Address
    End If
Next n
```

CenterFooter Property

Applies To	**PageSetup** Object.
Description	Returns or sets the center part of the footer. Read-write.
Remarks	Special format codes can be used in the footer text.
See Also	**CenterHeader** Property, **LeftFooter** Property, **LeftHeader** Property, **RightFooter** Property, **RightHeader** Property.
Example	This example prints the workbook name and page number at the bottom of each page.

```
Worksheets("Sheet1").PageSetup.CenterFooter = "&F page &P"
```

CenterHeader Property

Applies To	**PageSetup** Object.
Description	Returns or sets the center part of the header. Read-write.
Remarks	Special format codes can be used in the header text.
See Also	**CenterFooter** Property, **LeftFooter** Property, **LeftHeader** Property, **RightFooter** Property, **RightHeader** Property.
Example	This example prints the date and page number at the top of each page.

```
Worksheets("Sheet1").PageSetup.CenterHeader = "&D page &P of &N"
```

CenterHorizontally Property

Applies To	**PageSetup** Object.
Description	**True** if the sheet is centered horizontally on the page. Read-write.
See Also	**CenterVertically** Property.
Example	This example centers Sheet1 horizontally when the worksheet is printed.

```
Worksheets("Sheet1").PageSetup.CenterHorizontally = True
```

CenterVertically Property

Applies To	**PageSetup** Object.
Description	**True** if the sheet is centered vertically on the page. Read-write.
See Also	**CenterHorizontally** Property.
Example	This example centers Sheet1 vertically when the worksheet is printed.

```
Worksheets("Sheet1").PageSetup.CenterVertically = True
```

CentimetersToPoints Method

Applies To	**Application** Object.
Description	Converts a measurement in centimeters into points (0.035 centimeters).
Syntax	*object*.**CentimetersToPoints(*centimeters*)**

object
　　Required. The **Application** object.

centimeters
　　Required. Specifies the centimeter value to convert to points.

See Also	**InchesToPoints** Method.
Example	This example sets the left margin of Sheet1 to 5 centimeters.

```
Worksheets("Sheet1").PageSetup.LeftMargin = _
        Application.CentimetersToPoints(5)
```

ChangeFileAccess Method

Applies To   **Workbook** Object.

Description   Changes the access permissions for the workbook. This may require loading an updated version from the disk.

Syntax   *object*.**ChangeFileAccess(***mode*, *writePassword*, *notify***)**

object
   Required. The **Workbook** object.

mode
   Required. Specifies the new access mode (one of **xlReadWrite** or **xlReadOnly**).

writePassword
   Optional. If the file is write reserved and *mode* is **xlReadWrite**, specifies the write-reserved password. Ignored if there is no password for the file or *mode* is **xlReadOnly**.

notify
   Optional. **True** if you wish to be notified if the file cannot be immediately accessed. Assumed to be **True** if omitted.

Remarks   If you have a file open in read-only mode, you do not have exclusive access to the file. If you change a file from read-only to read-write, Microsoft Excel must load a new copy of the file to ensure that no changes were made while you had the file open as read-only.

Example   This example sets the active workbook to read-only.

```
ActiveWorkbook.ChangeFileAccess Mode:=xlReadOnly
```

ChangeLink Method

Applies To   **Workbook** Object.

Description   Changes a link from one document to another.

Syntax   *object*.**ChangeLink(***name*, *newName*, *type***)**

object
   Required. The **Workbook** object.

name
   Required. Specifies the name of the Microsoft Excel or DDE/OLE link to change, as returned from the **LinkSources** method.

newName
> Required. The new name of the link.

type
> Optional. Specifies the link type (either **xlExcelLinks** or **xlOLELinks**). If omitted, the default is **xlExcelLinks**. Use **xlOLELinks** for both DDE and OLE links.

Example   This example changes a Microsoft Excel link.

```
ActiveWorkbook.ChangeLink "c:\excel\book1.xls", _
    "c:\excel\book2.xls", xlExcelLinks
```

ChangeScenario Method

Applies To   **Scenario** Object.

Description   Changes the scenario to have a new set of changing cells and (optionally) scenario values.

Syntax   *object*.**ChangeScenario**(*changingCells*, *values*)

object
> Required. The **Scenario** object.

changingCells
> Required. A **Range** that specifies the new set of changing cells for the scenario. The changing cells must be on the same sheet as the scenario.

values
> Optional. An array containing the new scenario values for the changing cells. If omitted, the scenario values are assumed to be the current values in the changing cells.

Remarks   If you specify *values*, the array must contain an element for each cell in the *changingCells* range, or Microsoft Excel generates an error.

See Also   **ChangingCells** Property, **Comment** Property.

Example   This example sets the changing cells for scenario one to the range A1:A10 on Sheet1.

```
Worksheets("Sheet1").Scenarios(1).ChangeScenario _
    Worksheets("Sheet1").Range("A1:A10")
```

ChangingCells Property

Applies To   **Scenario** Object.

Description   Accessor. Returns a **Range** object that represents the changing cells for a scenario. Read only.

See Also   **ChangeScenario** Method, **Comment** Property.

Example   This example selects the changing cells for scenario one on Sheet1.

```
Worksheets("Sheet1").Activate
ActiveSheet.Scenarios(1).ChangingCells.Select
```

Characters Method

Applies To   **AxisTitle** Object, **Button** Object, **Buttons** Collection, **ChartTitle** Object, **CheckBox** Object, **DataLabel** Object, **DialogFrame** Object, **DrawingObjects** Collection, **DropDown** Object, **DropDowns** Collection, **EditBox** Object, **EditBoxes** Collection, **GroupBox** Object, **GroupBoxes** Collection, **Label** Object, **Labels** Collection, **OptionButton** Object, **OptionButtons** Collection, **Range** Object, **TextBox** Object, **TextBoxes** Collection.

Description   Accessor. Returns a **Characters** object that represents a range of characters within the object text. This allows you to format characters within a text string.

Syntax   *object*.**Characters(***start*, *length***)**

object
        Required. The object to which this method applies.

start
        Optional. The first character to return. If this argument is one or omitted, this method returns a range of characters starting with the first character.

length
        Optional. The number of characters to return. If this argument is omitted, this method returns the remainder of the string after the *start* character.

Remarks   For a **Range** object, this method will fail if it is used with arguments and the cell does not contain a text value.

Example

This example formats the third character in cell A1 on Sheet1 as bold.

```
With Worksheets("Sheet1").Range("A1")
    .Value = "abcdefg"
    .Characters(3, 1).Font.Bold = True
End With
```

Characters Object

Description

Represents characters in an object containing text. The **Characters** object lets you access any sequence of characters contained in the full text string.

Accessors

Use the **Characters** method to return a subset of sequential characters in the text. The following example adds text to cell B1 on the worksheet named "Sheet1" and then makes the second word bold.

```
With Worksheets("sheet1").Range("b1")
    .Value = "New Title"
    .Characters(5, 5).Font.Bold = True
End With
```

Remarks

The **Characters** method is necessary only when you need to change some of the text contained in an object without affecting the rest (you cannot use the **Characters** method to format a portion of the text if the object does not support rich text). To change all the text at once, you can usually apply the appropriate method or property directly to the object. The following example sets the contents of cell A5 on the worksheet named "Sheet1" to italic.

```
Worksheets("sheet1").Range("a5").Font.Italic = True
```

Properties

Application Property, **Caption** Property, **Count** Property, **Creator** Property, **Font** Property, **Parent** Property, **Text** Property.

Methods

Delete Method, **Insert** Method.

Chart Object

Description

Represents a chart in a workbook, either an embedded chart (contained in a **ChartObject** in a **Worksheet** or **DialogSheet** object) or a separate chart sheet.

Embedded Charts

The **ChartObject**, which represents the container for an embedded chart on a worksheet or dialog sheet, is a member of the **ChartObjects** collection. Use the **Add** method to create a new empty embedded chart and add it to the collection. Use the **Chart** property to access the chart contained in the specified **ChartObject** object. The following example sets the pattern for the chart area in embedded chart one on the worksheet named "Sheet1."

```
Worksheets("sheet1").ChartObjects(1).Chart. _
    ChartArea.Interior.Pattern = xlLightDown
```

Chart Sheets

The **Chart** object, which represents a separate chart sheet, is a member of the **Charts** collection. The **Charts** collection contains all the **Chart** objects that represent chart sheets in a workbook. Use the **Add** method to create a new chart sheet and add it to the collection. To access a single member of the collection, use the **Charts** method with the index number or name of the chart sheet as an argument.

The chart index number represents the position of the chart sheet on the tab bar of the workbook. Charts(1) is the first (leftmost) chart in the workbook; Charts(Charts.Count) is the last. All chart sheets are included in the index count, even if they are hidden.

The following example changes the color of series one on chart sheet one.

```
Charts(1).SeriesCollection(1).Interior.Color = RGB(255, 0, 0)
```

The chart name is shown on the workbook tab for the chart. You can use the **Name** property to set or return the chart name.

The following example moves the chart named "Sales" to the end of the active workbook.

```
Charts("sales").Move after:=Sheets(Sheets.Count)
```

The **Chart** object is also a member of the **Sheets** collection. The **Sheets** collection contains all of the sheets in the workbook (chart sheets, dialog sheets, modules, and worksheets). To access a single member of the collection, use the **Sheets** method with the index number or name of the sheet as an argument.

Using ActiveChart

When a chart is the active object, you can use the **ActiveChart** property to refer to it. A chart sheet is active if the user has selected it or it has been activated with the **Activate** method. The following example activates chart sheet one and then sets the chart type and title.

```
Charts(1).Activate
With ActiveChart
    .Type = xlLine
    .HasTitle = True
    .ChartTitle.Text = "January Sales"
End With
```

An embedded chart is active if the user has selected it or the **ChartObject** object that contains it has been activated with the **Activate** method. The following example activates embedded chart one on worksheet one and then sets the chart type and title. Notice that once the embedded chart has been activated, the code in this example is the same as the previous example. Using the **ActiveChart** property allows you to write Visual Basic code that can refer to either an embedded chart or a chart sheet, whichever is active.

```
Worksheets(1).ChartObjects(1).Activate
ActiveChart.Type = xlLine
ActiveChart.HasTitle = True
ActiveChart.ChartTitle.Text = "January Sales"
```

Using ActiveSheet

When a chart sheet is the active sheet, you can use the **ActiveSheet** property to refer to it. The following example uses the **Activate** method to activate the chart sheet named "Chart1" and then sets the interior color for series one in the chart.

```
Charts("chart1").Activate
ActiveSheet.SeriesCollection(1).Interior.ColorIndex = 5
```

Properties

Application Property, **Area3DGroup** Property, **AutoScaling** Property, **Bar3DGroup** Property, **ChartArea** Property, **ChartTitle** Property, **Column3DGroup** Property, **Corners** Property, **Creator** Property, **DepthPercent** Property, **DisplayBlanksAs** Property, **Elevation** Property, **Floor** Property, **GapDepth** Property, **HasAxis** Property, **HasLegend** Property, **HasTitle** Property, **HeightPercent** Property, **Index** Property, **Legend** Property, **Line3DGroup** Property, **Name** Property, **Next** Property, **OnDoubleClick** Property, **OnSheetActivate** Property, **OnSheetDeactivate** Property, **PageSetup** Property, **Parent** Property, **Perspective** Property, **Pie3DGroup** Property, **PlotArea** Property, **PlotVisibleOnly** Property, **Previous** Property, **ProtectContents** Property, **ProtectDrawingObjects** Property, **RightAngleAxes** Property, **Rotation** Property, **SizeWithWindow** Property, **SubType** Property, **SurfaceGroup** Property, **Type** Property, **Visible** Property, **Walls** Property, **WallsAndGridlines2D** Property.

Methods   **Activate** Method, **ApplyDataLabels** Method, **Arcs** Method, **AreaGroups**
Method, **AutoFormat** Method (**Chart** Object), **Axes** Method, **BarGroups**
Method, **Buttons** Method, **ChartGroups** Method, **ChartObjects** Method,
ChartWizard Method, **CheckBoxes** Method, **CheckSpelling** Method,
ColumnGroups Method, **Copy** Method, **CopyPicture** Method, **CreatePublisher**
Method, **Delete** Method, **Deselect** Method, **DoughnutGroups** Method,
DrawingObjects Method, **Drawings** Method, **DropDowns** Method, **Evaluate**
Method, **GroupBoxes** Method, **GroupObjects** Method, **Labels** Method,
LineGroups Method, **Lines** Method, **ListBoxes** Method, **Move** Method,
OLEObjects Method, **OptionButtons** Method, **Ovals** Method, **Paste** Method
(**Chart** Object), **Pictures** Method, **PieGroups** Method, **PrintOut** Method,
PrintPreview Method, **Protect** Method, **RadarGroups** Method, **Rectangles**
Method, **SaveAs** Method, **ScrollBars** Method, **Select** Method, **SeriesCollection**
Method, **SetBackgroundPicture** Method, **Spinners** Method, **TextBoxes** Method,
Unprotect Method, **XYGroups** Method.

Chart Property

Applies To   **ChartObject** Object.

Description   Accessor. Returns a **Chart** object that represents the chart contained in the object.
Read-only.

Example   This example adds a title to the first embedded chart on Sheet1.

```
With Worksheets("Sheet1").ChartObjects(1).Chart
    .HasTitle = True
    .ChartTitle.Text = "1995 Rainfall Totals by Month"
End With
```

ChartArea Object

Description   Represents the chart area of a chart. The chart area on a 2-D chart contains the
axes, the chart title, axis titles, and the legend. The chart area on a 3-D chart
contains the chart title and the legend. It does not include the plot area (the area
within the chart area where the data is plotted). For information about formatting
the plot area, see the **PlotArea** object.

Accessors   The **ChartArea** property returns the chart area for the specified chart. The following example sets the pattern for the chart area in embedded chart one on the worksheet named "Sheet1."

```
Worksheets("sheet1").ChartObjects(1).Chart. _
    ChartArea.Interior.Pattern = xlLightDown
```

Properties   **Application** Property, **Border** Property, **Creator** Property, **Font** Property, **Height** Property, **Interior** Property, **Left** Property, **Name** Property, **Parent** Property, **Shadow** Property, **Top** Property, **Width** Property.

Methods   **Clear** Method, **ClearContents** Method, **ClearFormats** Method, **Copy** Method, **Select** Method.

ChartArea Property

Applies To   **Chart** Object.

Description   Accessor. Returns a **ChartArea** object that represents the complete chart area for the chart. Read-only.

Example   This example sets the chart area interior color of Chart1 to red and sets the border color to blue.

```
With Charts("Chart1").ChartArea
    .Interior.ColorIndex = 3
    .Border.ColorIndex = 5
End With
```

ChartGroup Object

Description   Represents one or more series plotted in a chart using the same format. A chart contains one or more chart groups, each chart group contains one or more series, and each series contains one or more points. For example, a single chart might contain a line chart group, containing all the series plotted using the line chart format, and a bar chart group, containing all the series plotted using the bar chart format.

Accessors

The **ChartGroup** object is a member of the **ChartGroups** collection. To access a single member of the collection, use the **ChartGroups** method with the chart group index number as an argument. The following example adds drop lines to chart group one.

```
Charts(1).ChartGroups(1).HasDropLines = True
```

If the chart has been activated, you can use the **ActiveChart** property:

```
Charts(1).Activate
ActiveChart.ChartGroups(1).HasDropLines = True
```

The chart group index number for a particular chart group can change if the chart format used for that group is changed. For this reason, it may be easier to use one of the named chart group shortcut methods to access a particular chart group. The **PieGroups** method returns the collection of pie chart groups in a chart, the **LineGroups** method returns the collection of line chart groups, and so on. Each of these methods can be used with an index number to return a single **ChartGroup** object, or without an index to return a **ChartGroups** collection. The following chart group methods are available:

AreaGroups Method, **BarGroups** Method, **ColumnGroups** Method, **DoughnutGroups** Method, **LineGroups** Method, **PieGroups** Method, DownBars, DropLines, HiLoLines, Series, SeriesLines, UpBars

Properties

Application Property, **AxisGroup** Property, **Creator** Property, **DoughnutHoleSize** Property, **DownBars** Property, **DropLines** Property, **FirstSliceAngle** Property, **GapWidth** Property, **HasDropLines** Property, **HasHiLoLines** Property, **HasRadarAxisLabels** Property, **HasSeriesLines** Property, **HasUpDownBars** Property, **HiLoLines** Property, **Overlap** Property, **Parent** Property, **RadarAxisLabels** Property, **SeriesLines** Property, **SubType** Property, **Type** Property, **UpBars** Property, **VaryByCategories** Property.

Methods

SeriesCollection Method.

ChartGroups Collection Object

Description

A collection of all the **ChartGroup** objects in the specified chart. Each **ChartGroup** object represents one or more series plotted in a chart using the same format. A chart contains one or more chart groups, each chart group contains one or more series, and each series contains one or more points. For example, a single chart might contain a line chart group, containing all the series plotted using the line chart format, and a bar chart group, containing all the series plotted using the bar chart format.

Accessors	The **ChartGroups** collection contains all of the chart groups in one chart. Use the **ChartGroups** method with an argument to access a single member of the collection or without an argument to access the entire collection at once. You can also use one of the named chart group shortcut methods to access a particular chart group. The **PieGroups** method returns the collection of pie chart groups in a chart, the **LineGroups** method returns the collection of line chart groups, and so on. Each of these methods can be used with an index number to return a single **ChartGroup** object or without an index to return a **ChartGroups** collection. The following chart group methods are available: **AreaGroups** Method, **BarGroups** Method, **ColumnGroups** Method, **DoughnutGroups** Method, **LineGroups** Method, **PieGroups** Method.
Properties	**Application** Property, **Count** Property, **Creator** Property, **Parent** Property.
Methods	**Item** Method.

ChartGroups Method

Applies To	**Chart** Object.
Description	Accessor. Returns an object that represents a single chart group (a **ChartGroup** object, Syntax 1) or a collection of all the chart groups in the chart (a **ChartGroups** object, Syntax 2). Every type of group is included in the returned collection.
Syntax 1	*object*.**ChartGroups**(*index*)
Syntax 2	*object*.**ChartGroups**

object
    Required. The **Chart** object.

index
    Required for Syntax 1. The number of the chart group.

Example	This example turns on up and down bars for chart group one on Chart1 and then sets their colors. The example should be run on a 2-D line chart containing two series that cross each other at one or more data points.

```
With Charts("Chart1").ChartGroups(1)
    .HasUpDownBars = True
    .DownBars.Interior.ColorIndex = 3
    .UpBars.Interior.ColorIndex = 5
End With
```

ChartObject Object

Description   Represents an embedded chart on a sheet. The **ChartObject** object acts as a container for a **Chart** object. Properties and methods for the **ChartObject** object control the appearance and size of the embedded chart on the sheet.

Accessors   The **ChartObject** object is a member of the **ChartObjects** collection. The **ChartObjects** collection contains all the embedded charts on a single sheet. Use the **Add** method to create a new empty embedded chart and add it to the collection. Use the **ChartWizard** method to add data and format the new empty chart. Use the **Chart** property to access the embedded chart contained in the **ChartObject** object.

To access a single member of the collection, use the **ChartObjects** method with the index number or name of the embedded chart as an argument.

The following example sets the pattern for the chart area in embedded chart one on the worksheet named "Sheet1."

```
Worksheets("Sheet1").ChartObjects(1).Chart. _
    ChartArea.Interior.Pattern = xlLightDown
```

The embedded chart name is shown in the Name Box when the embedded chart is selected. Use the **Name** property to set or return the name of the **ChartObject** object. The following example puts rounded corners on the embedded chart named "Chart 1" on the worksheet named "Sheet1."

```
Worksheets("sheet1").ChartObjects("chart 1").RoundedCorners = True
```

Properties   **Application** Property, **Border** Property, **BottomRightCell** Property, **Chart** Property, **Creator** Property, **Enabled** Property, **Height** Property, **Index** Property, **Interior** Property, **Left** Property, **Locked** Property, **Name** Property, **OnAction** Property, **Parent** Property, **Placement** Property, **PrintObject** Property, **RoundedCorners** Property, **Shadow** Property, **Top** Property, **TopLeftCell** Property, **Visible** Property, **Width** Property, **ZOrder** Property.

Methods   **Activate** Method, **BringToFront** Method, **Copy** Method, **CopyPicture** Method, **Cut** Method, **Delete** Method, **Duplicate** Method, **Select** Method, **SendToBack** Method.

ChartObjects Collection Object

Description

A collection of all the **ChartObject** objects on the specified chart sheet, dialog sheet, or worksheet. Each **ChartObject** object represents an embedded chart. The **ChartObject** object acts as a container for a **Chart** object. Properties and methods for the **ChartObject** object control the appearance and size of the embedded chart on the sheet.

Accessors

The **ChartObjects** collection contains all the embedded charts on a single sheet. Use the **Add** method to create a new empty embedded chart and add it to the collection. Use the **ChartWizard** method to add data and format the new empty chart. The following example creates a new embedded chart on the worksheet named "Sheet1" and then adds the data from cells A1:A20 as a line chart.

```
Dim ch As ChartObject
Set ch = Worksheets("sheet1").ChartObjects.Add(100, 30, 400, 250)
ch.Chart.ChartWizard source:=Worksheets("sheet1").Range("a1:a20"), _
    gallery:=xlLine, title:="New Chart"
```

Use the **ChartObjects** method with an argument to access a single member of the collection or without an argument to access the entire collection at once. The following example deletes all of the embedded charts on the worksheet named "Sheet1."

```
Worksheets("sheet1").ChartObjects.Delete
```

Properties

Application Property, **Border** Property, **Count** Property, **Creator** Property, **Enabled** Property, **Height** Property, **Interior** Property, **Left** Property, **Locked** Property, **OnAction** Property, **Parent** Property, **Placement** Property, **PrintObject** Property, **RoundedCorners** Property, **Shadow** Property, **Top** Property, **Visible** Property, **Width** Property, **ZOrder** Property.

Methods

Add Method (Graphic Objects and Controls), **BringToFront** Method, **Copy** Method, **CopyPicture** Method, **Cut** Method, **Delete** Method, **Duplicate** Method, **Group** Method, **Item** Method, **Select** Method, **SendToBack** Method.

ChartObjects Method

Applies To

Chart Object, **DialogSheet** Object, **Worksheet** Object.

Description

Accessor. Returns an object that represents a single embedded chart (a **ChartObject** object, Syntax 1) or a collection of all the embedded charts (a **ChartObjects** object, Syntax 2) on the sheet.

Syntax 1	*object*.**ChartObjects**(*index*)
Syntax 2	*object*.**ChartObjects**

object
> Required. The object to which this method applies. If you specify a **Chart** object, it must be a chart sheet (it cannot be an embedded chart).

index
> Required for Syntax 1. The name or number of the chart (can be an array to specify more than one).

Remarks

This method is not equivalent to the **Charts** method. This method returns embedded charts; the **Charts** method returns chart sheets. Use the **Chart** property to return the chart sheet for an embedded chart object.

See Also

Charts Method.

Example

This example adds a title to embedded chart one on Sheet1.

```
With Worksheets("Sheet1").ChartObjects(1).Chart
    .HasTitle = True
    .ChartTitle.Text = "1995 Rainfall Totals by Month"
End With
```

This example creates a new series in embedded chart one on Sheet1. The data source for the new series is the range B1:B10 on Sheet1.

```
Worksheets("Sheet1").ChartObjects(1).Activate
ActiveChart.SeriesCollection.Add _
    source:=Worksheets("Sheet1").Range("B1:B10")
```

This example clears the formatting of embedded chart one on Sheet1.

```
Worksheets("Sheet1").ChartObjects(1).Chart.ChartArea.ClearFormats
```

Charts Collection Object

Description

A collection of all the chart sheets in the specified or active workbook. This does not include charts embedded on worksheets or dialog sheets. For information about embedded charts, see the **Chart** or **ChartObject** objects.

Accessors

Use the **Add** method to create a new chart sheet and add it to the workbook. The following example adds a new chart sheet to the active workbook and places the new chart sheet after the worksheet named "Sheet1."

```
Charts.Add after:=Worksheets("sheet1")
```

You can combine the **Add** method with the **ChartWizard** method to add a new chart containing data from a worksheet. The following example adds a new line chart based on data in cells A1:A20 on the worksheet named "Sheet1."

```
With Charts.Add
    .ChartWizard source:=Worksheets("sheet1").Range("a1:a20"), _
        gallery:=xlLine, title:="February Data"
End With
```

Use the **Charts** method with an argument to access a single member of the collection or without an argument to access the entire collection at once.

The **Sheets** collection contains all of the sheets in the workbook (chart sheets, dialog sheets, modules, and worksheets). Use the **Sheets** method with an argument to access a single member of the collection or without an argument to access the entire collection at once.

Properties **Application** Property, **Count** Property, **Creator** Property, **Parent** Property, **Visible** Property.

Methods **Add** Method (**Charts** Collection), **Copy** Method, **Delete** Method, **Item** Method, **Move** Method, **PrintOut** Method, **PrintPreview** Method, **Select** Method.

Charts Method

Applies To **Application** Object, **Workbook** Object.

Description Accessor. Returns an object that represents a single chart (a **Chart** object, Syntax 1) or a collection of the charts (a **Charts** object, Syntax 2) in the workbook.

Syntax 1 *object*.**Charts**(*index*)

Syntax 2 *object*.**Charts**

object
Optional for **Application**, required for **Workbook**. The object to which this method applies.

index
Required for Syntax 1. The name or number of the chart (can be an array to specify more than one).

Remarks Using this method with no object qualifier is equivalent to `ActiveWorkbook.Charts`.

See Also **ChartObjects** Method.

Example   This example sets the text for the title of Chart1.

```
With Charts("Chart1")
    .HasTitle = True
    .ChartTitle.Text = "First Quarter Sales"
End With
```

This example deletes every chart sheet in the active workbook.

```
ActiveWorkbook.Charts.Delete
```

This example hides Chart1, Chart3, and Chart5. Note that in this example (and the previous one), the **Charts** method returns a **Sheets** object instead of a **Charts** object.

```
Charts(Array("Chart1", "Chart3", "Chart5")).Visible = False
```

ChartSize Property

Applies To   **PageSetup** Object.

Description   Returns or sets the method used when scaling a chart to fit on a page, as shown in the following table. Read-write.

Value	Meaning
xlScreenSize	Print the chart the same size as it appears on the screen.
xlFitToPage	Print the chart as large as possible, while retaining the chart's height-to-width ratio as shown on the screen.
xlFullPage	Print the chart to fit the page, adjusting the height-to-width ratio as necessary.

Remarks   This property applies only to chart sheets (it cannot be used with embedded charts).

Example   This example scales the first chart in the active workbook to fit a full page.

```
ActiveWorkbook.Charts(1).PageSetup.ChartSize = xlFullPage
```

ChartTitle Object

Description   Represents the title in a chart.

Accessors	Use the **ChartTitle** property to return the title of the specified chart. The following example adds a title to embedded chart one on the worksheet named "Sheet1."

```
With Worksheets("sheet1").ChartObjects(1).Chart
    .HasTitle = True
    .ChartTitle.Text = "February Sales"
End With
```

Remarks	The **ChartTitle** object does not exist and cannot be accessed unless the **HasTitle** property for the chart is **True**.
Properties	**Application** Property, **Border** Property, **Caption** Property, **Creator** Property, **Font** Property, **HorizontalAlignment** Property, **Interior** Property, **Left** Property, **Name** Property, **Orientation** Property, **Parent** Property, **Shadow** Property, **Text** Property, **Top** Property, **VerticalAlignment** Property.
Methods	**Characters** Method, **Delete** Method, **Select** Method.

ChartTitle Property

Applies To	**Chart** Object.
Description	Accessor. Returns a **ChartTitle** object that represents the title of the specified chart. Read-only.
See Also	**AxisTitle** Property, **HasTitle** Property, **Title** Property.
Example	This example sets the text for the title of Chart1.

```
With Charts("Chart1")
    .HasTitle = True
    .ChartTitle.Text = "First Quarter Sales"
End With
```

ChartWizard Method

Applies To	**Chart** Object.
Description	Modifies the properties of the given chart. Allows a chart to be quickly formatted without setting all the individual properties. This method is non-interactive, and changes only the specified properties.

Syntax   *object*.**ChartWizard**(*source*, *gallery*, *format*, *plotBy*, *categoryLabels*, *seriesLabels*, *hasLegend*, *title*, *categoryTitle*, *valueTitle*, *extraTitle*)

object
Required. The **Chart** object.

source
Required if you are creating a chart; the range that contains the source data for the chart. Optional if you are editing an existing chart; the active chart sheet is edited, or the selected chart on the active worksheet is edited.

gallery
Optional. Specifies the chart type (one of **xlArea**, **xlBar**, **xlColumn**, **xlLine**, **xlPie**, **xlRadar**, **xlXYScatter**, **xlCombination**, **xl3DArea**, **xl3DBar**, **xl3DColumn**, **xl3DLine**, **xl3DPie**, **xl3DSurface**, or **xlDoughnut**).

format
Optional. Specifies the option number for the built-in autoformats. Can be a number from 1 to 10, depending on the gallery type. If this argument is omitted, Microsoft Excel chooses a default value based on the gallery type and data source.

plotBy
Optional. Specifies whether the data for each series is in rows or columns (either **xlRows** or **xlColumns**).

categoryLabels
Optional. An integer specifying the number of rows or columns within the source range containing category labels. Legal values are from zero to one less than the maximum number of the corresponding categories or series.

seriesLabels
Optional. An integer specifying the number of rows or columns within the source range containing series labels. Legal values are from zero to one less than the maximum number of the corresponding categories or series.

hasLegend
Optional. **True** to include a legend.

title
Optional. Chart title text.

categoryTitle
Optional. Category axis title text.

valueTitle
Optional. Value axis title text.

extraTitle
Optional. Series axis title for 3-D charts, second value axis title for 2-D charts.

Remarks   If *source* is omitted and either the selection is not an embedded chart on the active worksheet or the active sheet is not an existing chart, the method fails and an error occurs.

Example   This example reformats Chart1 as a line chart, adds a legend, and adds category and value axis titles.

```
Charts("Chart1").ChartWizard _
    gallery:=xlLine, _
    hasLegend:=True, categoryTitle:="Year", valueTitle:="Sales"
```

ChDir Statement

Description   Changes the current directory or folder.

Syntax   **ChDir** *path*

The *path* named argument is a string expression that identifies which directory or folder becomes the new default directory or folder—may include drive. If no drive is specified, **ChDir** changes the default directory or folder on the current drive.

Remarks   In Microsoft Windows, the **ChDir** statement changes the default directory but not the default drive. For example, if the default drive is C, the following statement changes the default directory on drive D, but C remains the default drive:

```
ChDir "D:\TMP"
```

On the Macintosh, the default drive always changes to whatever drive is specified in *path*.

See Also   **ChDrive** Statement, **CurDir** Function, **Dir** Function, **MkDir** Statement, **RmDir** Statement.

Example   This example uses the **ChDir** statement to change the current directory or folder.

```
' Change current directory or folder to "MYDIR".
ChDir "MYDIR"

' In Microsoft Windows.
' Assume "C:" is the current drive. The following statement changes
' the default directory on drive "D:". "C:" remains the current drive.
ChDir "D:\WINDOWS\SYSTEM"

' On the Macintosh.
' Changes default folder and default drive.
ChDir "HD:MY FOLDER"
```

ChDrive Statement

Description   Changes the current drive.

Syntax   **ChDrive** *drive*

The *drive* named argument is a string expression that specifies an existing drive. If you supply a zero-length argument (""), the current drive doesn't change. In Microsoft Windows, if the argument *drive* is a multiple-character string, **ChDrive** uses only the first letter. On the Macintosh, **ChDrive** changes the current folder to the root folder of the specifed drive.

See Also   **ChDir** Statement, **CurDir** Function, **MkDir** Statement, **RmDir** Statement.

Example   This example uses the **ChDrive** statement to change the current drive.

```
' In Microsoft Windows.
ChDrive "D"                          ' Make "D" the current drive.

' On the Macintosh.
' Make "MY DRIVE" the current drive
ChDrive "MY DRIVE:"
' Make "MY DRIVE" the current drive and current folder since its the
' root.
ChDrive "MY DRIVE:MY FOLDER"
```

CheckBox Object

Description   Represents a check box control on a chart sheet, dialog sheet, or worksheet. You can set the position and size of a check box. On a worksheet or chart, you can also format the border and background of the check box. The font is fixed.

Accessors   The **CheckBox** object is a member of the **CheckBoxes** collection. The **CheckBoxes** collection contains all the **CheckBox** objects on a single sheet. Use the **Add** method to create a new check box and add it to the collection.

To access a single member of the collection, use the **CheckBoxes** method with the index number or name of the check box as an argument.

The following example links check box one on dialog sheet one to cell A1 on the worksheet named "Sheet1." When the value of cell A1 is TRUE, the check box is turned on, and vice versa.

```
DialogSheets("sheet1").CheckBoxes(1).LinkedCell = "=sheet1!a1"
```

The check box name is shown in the Name Box when the check box is selected. Use the **Name** property to set or return the check box name. The following example turns on the check box named "Check Box 5."

```
DialogSheets(1).CheckBoxes("check box 5").Value = True
```

Properties   **Accelerator** Property, **Application** Property, **Border** Property, **BottomRightCell** Property, **Caption** Property, **Creator** Property, **Display3DShading** Property, **Enabled** Property, **Height** Property, **Index** Property, **Interior** Property, **Left** Property, **LinkedCell** Property, **Locked** Property, **LockedText** Property, **Name** Property, **OnAction** Property, **Parent** Property, **PhoneticAccelerator** Property, **Placement** Property, **PrintObject** Property, **Text** Property, **Top** Property, **TopLeftCell** Property, **Value** Property, **Visible** Property, **Width** Property, **ZOrder** Property.

Methods   **BringToFront** Method, **Characters** Method, **CheckSpelling** Method, **Copy** Method, **CopyPicture** Method, **Cut** Method, **Delete** Method, **Duplicate** Method, **Select** Method, **SendToBack** Method.

CheckBoxes Collection Object

Description   A collection of all the **CheckBox** objects on the specified chart sheet, dialog sheet, or worksheet. You can set the position and size of a check box. On a worksheet or chart, you can also format the border and background of the check box. The font is fixed.

Accessors   Use the **Add** method to create a new check box and add it to the collection. The following example adds a new check box to the dialog sheet named "Dialog1." The new check box is positioned inside the dialog frame.

```
Dim df as DialogFrame
DialogSheets("dialog1").Activate
Set df = ActiveSheet.DialogFrame
ActiveSheet.CheckBoxes.Add df.Left + 10, df.Top + 10, 100, 10
```

Use the **CheckBoxes** method with an argument to access a single member of the collection or without an argument to access the entire collection at once. The following example turns off (clears) all of the check boxes on the dialog sheet named "Dialog1."

```
DialogSheets("dialog1").CheckBoxes.Value = xlOff
```

Properties   **Accelerator** Property, **Application** Property, **Border** Property, **Caption** Property, **Count** Property, **Creator** Property, **Display3DShading** Property, **Enabled** Property, **Height** Property, **Interior** Property, **Left** Property, **LinkedCell** Property, **Locked** Property, **LockedText** Property, **OnAction** Property, **Parent** Property, **PhoneticAccelerator** Property, **Placement** Property, **PrintObject** Property, **Text** Property, **Top** Property, **Value** Property, **Visible** Property, **Width** Property, **ZOrder** Property.

Methods   **Add** Method (Graphic Objects and Controls), **BringToFront** Method, **Characters** Method, **CheckSpelling** Method, **Copy** Method, **CopyPicture** Method, **Cut** Method, **Delete** Method, **Duplicate** Method, **Group** Method, **Item** Method, **Select** Method, **SendToBack** Method.

CheckBoxes Method

Applies To   **Chart** Object, **DialogSheet** Object, **Worksheet** Object.

Description   Accessor. Returns an object that represents a single check box (a **CheckBox** object, Syntax 1) or a collection of check boxes (a **CheckBoxes** object, Syntax 2) on the sheet.

Syntax 1   *object*.**CheckBoxes**(*index*)

Syntax 2   *object*.**CheckBoxes**

object
   Required. The **Chart**, **DialogSheet**, or **Worksheet** object.

index
   Required for Syntax 1. Specifies the name or number of the check box (can be an array to specify more than one).

Example   This example sets check box one on Dialog1 to be gray and then displays the dialog box.

```
With DialogSheets("Dialog1")
    .CheckBoxes(1).Value = xlMixed
    .Show
End With
```

Checked Property

Applies To   **MenuItem** Object.

Description   **True** if the menu item is checked. Read-write.

Example   This example adds a check mark to the first menu item on the first menu on the
active menu bar (which is usually the New command on the File menu).

```
ActiveMenuBar.Menus(1).MenuItems(1).Checked = True
```

CheckSpelling Method

Applies To   **Application** Object, **Button** Object, **Buttons** Collection, **Chart** Object,
CheckBox Object, **DialogFrame** Object, **DialogSheet** Object, **DrawingObjects**
Collection, **GroupBox** Object, **GroupBoxes** Collection, **GroupObject** Object,
GroupObjects Collection, **Label** Object, **Labels** Collection, **OptionButton**
Object, **OptionButtons** Collection, **Range** Object, **TextBox** Object, **TextBoxes**
Collection, **Worksheet** Object.

Description   Syntax 1: Checks the spelling of an object. This form has no return value; Microsoft
Excel displays the Spelling dialog box.

Syntax 2: Checks the spelling of a single word. Returns **True** if the word is found
in one of the dictionaries, **False** if it is not.

Syntax 1   *object*.**CheckSpelling**(*customDictionary*, *ignoreUppercase*, *alwaysSuggest*)

Syntax 2   *object*.**CheckSpelling**(*word*, *customDictionary*, *ignoreUppercase*)

object
    Required. The object to which this method applies. Use the **Application** object
    to check a single word (Syntax 2).

customDictionary
    Optional. A string indicating the filename of the custom dictionary to examine if
    the word is not found in the main dictionary. If omitted, the currently specified
    dictionary is used.

ignoreUppercase
    Optional. If **True**, Microsoft Excel will ignore words that are in all uppercase.
    If **False**, Microsoft Excel will check words that are in all uppercase. If omitted,
    the current setting will be used.

alwaysSuggest
> Optional. If **True**, Microsoft Excel will display a list of suggested alternate spellings when an incorrect spelling is found. If **False**, Microsoft Excel will wait for you to input the correct spelling. If omitted, the current setting will be used.

word
> Required (used with **Application** object only). The word you want to check.

Remarks   To check headers, footers, and objects, use `Worksheet.CheckSpelling`.

To check only cells and notes, use `Worksheet.Cells.CheckSpelling`.

Example   This example checks the spelling on Sheet1.

```
Worksheets("Sheet1").CheckSpelling
```

ChildField Property

Applies To   **PivotField** Object.

Description   Accessor. Returns a **PivotField** object that represents the child pivot field for the specified field (if the field is grouped and has a child field). Read-only.

Remarks   If the specified field has no child field, this property causes an error.

Example   This example displays the name of the child field for the field named "REGION2."

```
Set pvtTable = Worksheets("Sheet1").Range("A3").PivotTable
MsgBox "The name of the child field is " & _
    pvtTable.PivotFields("REGION2").ChildField.Name
```

ChildItems Method

Applies To   **PivotField** Object, **PivotItem** Object.

Description   Accessor. Returns an object that represents one pivot item (a **PivotItem** object, Syntax 1) or a collection of all the pivot items (a **PivotItems** object, Syntax 2) that are group children in the specified field, or children of the specified item. Read-only.

Syntax 1   *object*.**ChildItems**(*index*)

Syntax 2   *object*.**ChildItems**

object
>Required. The **PivotField** or **PivotItem** object.

index
>Required for Syntax 1. The number or name of the pivot item to return (can be an array to specify more than one).

Example

This example adds the names of all the child items of the item named "Northwest" to a list box. The list box appears on Sheet1.

```
Set pvtTable = Worksheets("Sheet1").Range("A3").PivotTable
Set newListBox = Worksheets("Sheet1").ListBoxes.Add _
    (Left:=10, Top:=72, Width:=144, Height:=144)
Set pvtField = pvtTable.PivotFields("REGION2")
For Each pvtItem In pvtField.PivotItems("Northwest").ChildItems
    newListBox.AddItem (pvtItem.Name)
Next pvtItem
Worksheets("Sheet1").Activate
```

Chr Function

Description

Returns the character associated with the specified character code.

Syntax

Chr(*charcode*)

The *charcode* named argument is a number in the range 0 to 255, inclusive, that identifies a character.

Remarks

Numbers from 0 to 31 are the same as standard, nonprintable ASCII codes. For example, **Chr(10)** returns a linefeed character.

See Also

Asc Function, **Str** Function.

Example

This example uses the **Chr** function to return the character associated with the specified character code.

```
MyChar = Chr(65)                    ' Returns A.
MyChar = Chr(97)                    ' Returns a.
MyChar = Chr(62)                    ' Returns >.
MyChar = Chr(37)                    ' Returns %.
```

This example fills list box one on Dialog1 with the letters A through Z.

```
For i = 65 To 90
    DialogSheets("Dialog1").ListBoxes(1).AddItem Text:=Chr(i)
Next i
```

This example creates a line break in a message box by using the **Chr** function.

```
msgText = "The current folder is:" & Chr(13) & CurDir()
MsgBox msgText
```

CInt Function

Description   Converts an expression to an **Integer**.

Syntax   **CInt**(*expression*)

The *expression* argument is any valid numeric or string expression.

Remarks   In general, you can document your code using the data type conversion functions to show that the result of some operation should be expressed as a particular data type rather than the default data type. For example, use **CInt** or **CLng** to force integer arithmetic in cases where currency, single-precision, or double-precision arithmetic normally would occur.

You should use the **CInt** function instead of **Val** to provide internationally-aware conversions from any other data type to an **Integer**. For example, different decimal separators are properly recognized depending on the locale setting of your system, as are different thousand separators.

If *expression* lies outside the acceptable range for the **Integer** data type, an error occurs.

Note   **CInt** differs from the **Fix** and **Int** functions that truncate, rather than round, the fractional part of a number. When the fractional part is exactly 0.5, the **CInt** function always rounds it to the nearest even number. For example, 0.5 rounds to 0, and 1.5 rounds to 2.

See Also   Data Type Summary, **Int** Function.

Example   This example uses the **CInt** function to convert a value to an **Integer**.

```
MyDouble = 2345.5678 ' MyDouble is a Double.
MyInt = CInt(MyDouble)   ' MyInt contains 2346.
```

CircularReference Property

Applies To	**Worksheet** Object.
Description	Accessor. Returns a **Range** object that represents the range containing the first circular reference on the sheet, or **Nothing** if there is no circular reference present. The circular reference must be removed before calculation can proceed. Read-only.
Example	This example selects the first cell in the first circular reference on Sheet1.

```
Worksheets("Sheet1").CircularReference.Select
```

Clear Method

Applies To	**ChartArea** Object, **Range** Object.
Description	Clears the entire range or chart area.
Syntax	*object*.**Clear**

object
> Required. The **ChartArea** or **Range** object.

See Also	**ClearContents** Method, **ClearFormats** Method.
Example	This example clears the formulas and formatting in A1:G37 on Sheet1.

```
Worksheets("Sheet1").Range("A1:G37").Clear
```

This example clears the chart area (the chart data and formatting) of Chart1.

```
Charts("Chart1").ChartArea.Clear
```

ClearArrows Method

Applies To	**Worksheet** Object.
Description	Clears the tracer arrows on the worksheet. Tracer arrows are added by the auditing feature.
Syntax	*object*.**ClearArrows**

object
> Required. The **Worksheet** object.

See Also

See Also   **ShowDependents** Method, **ShowErrors** Method, **ShowPrecedents** Method.

Example   This example clears tracer arrows on Sheet1.

```
Worksheets("Sheet1").ClearArrows
```

ClearContents Method

Applies To   **ChartArea** Object, **Range** Object.

Description   Clears the formulas from the range. Clears the data from a chart but leaves the
                    formatting.

Syntax   *object*.**ClearContents**

                    object
                        Required. The **Chart** or **Range** object.

Example   This example clears the formulas from cells A1:G37 on Sheet1 but leaves the
                    formatting intact.

```
Worksheets("Sheet1").Range("A1:G37").ClearContents
```

                    This example clears the chart data from Chart1 but leaves the formatting intact.

```
Charts("Chart1").ChartArea.ClearContents
```

ClearFormats Method

Applies To   **ChartArea** Object, **ErrorBars** Object, **Floor** Object, **LegendKey** Object,
                    PlotArea Object, **Point** Object, **Range** Object, **Series** Object, **Trendline** Object,
                    Walls Object.

Description   Clears the formatting of the object.

Syntax   *object*.**ClearFormats**

                    object
                        Required. The object to which this method applies.

See Also   **Clear** Method, **ClearContents** Method.

Example   This example clears all formatting from cells A1:G37 on Sheet1.

```
Worksheets("Sheet1").Range("A1:G37").ClearFormats
```

This example clears the formatting of embedded chart one on Sheet1.

```
Worksheets("Sheet1").ChartObjects(1).Chart.ChartArea.ClearFormats
```

ClearNotes Method

Applies To   **Range** Object.

Description   Clears the note and the sound notes from all the cells in the range.

Syntax   *object*.**ClearNotes**

object
     Required. Clear notes and sound notes from this **Range**.

See Also   **NoteText** Method, **SoundNote** Property.

Example   This example clears all notes and sound notes in columns A through C on Sheet1.

```
Worksheets("Sheet1").Columns("A:C").ClearNotes
```

ClearOutline Method

Applies To   **Range** Object.

Description   Clears the outline for the specified range.

Syntax   *object*.**ClearOutline**

object
     Required. The **Range** object.

See Also   **AutoOutline** Method.

Example   This example clears the outline for the range A1:G37 on Sheet1.

```
Worksheets("Sheet1").Range("A1:G37").ClearOutline
```

ClipboardFormats Property

Applies To   **Application** Object.

Description   Returns the formats currently on the Clipboard, as an array of numeric values. To determine if a particular format is present, compare each element in the array with the appropriate constant shown in the table below. Read-only.

Remarks   This property is available in Microsoft Windows and on the Apple Macintosh. Some formats may be available only on the Apple Macintosh, or only in Microsoft Windows.

This property returns an array of numeric values. To determine if a particular clipboard format is present, compare each element of the array to one of the constants below.

xlClipboardFormatBIFF	**xlClipboardFormatObjectDesc**
xlClipboardFormatBIFF2	**xlClipboardFormatObjectLink**
xlClipboardFormatBIFF3	**xlClipboardFormatOwnerLink**
xlClipboardFormatBIFF4	**xlClipboardFormatPICT**
xlClipboardFormatBinary	**xlClipboardFormatPrintPICT**
xlClipboardFormatBitmap	**xlClipboardFormatRTF**
xlClipboardFormatCGM	**xlClipboardFormatScreenPICT**
xlClipboardFormatCSV	**xlClipboardFormatStandardFont**
xlClipboardFormatDIF	**xlClipboardFormatStandardScale**
xlClipboardFormatDspText	**xlClipboardFormatSYLK**
xlClipboardFormatEmbeddedObject	**xlClipboardFormatTable**
xlClipboardFormatEmbedSource	**xlClipboardFormatText**
xlClipboardFormatLink	**xlClipboardFormatToolFace**
xlClipboardFormatLinkSource	**xlClipboardFormatToolFacePICT**
xlClipboardFormatLinkSourceDesc	**xlClipboardFormatVALU**
xlClipboardFormatMovie	**xlClipboardFormatWK1**
xlClipboardFormatNative	

Example   This example displays a message box if the Clipboard contains a rich-text format (RTF) object. You can create an RTF object by copying text from a Word document.

```
aFmts = Application.ClipboardFormats
For Each fmt In aFmts
    If fmt = xlClipboardFormatRTF Then
        MsgBox "Clipboard contains rich text"
    End If
Next
```

CLng Function

Description   Converts an expression to a **Long**.

Syntax   **CLng**(*expression*)

The *expression* argument is any valid numeric or string expression.

Remarks   In general, you can document your code using the data type conversion functions to show that the result of some operation should be expressed as a particular data type rather than the default data type. For example, use **CInt** or **CLng** to force integer arithmetic in cases where currency, single-precision, or double-precision arithmetic normally would occur.

You should use the **CLng** function instead of **Val** to provide internationally-aware conversions from any other data type to a **Long**. For example, different decimal separators are properly recognized depending on the locale setting of your system, as are different thousand separators.

If *expression* lies outside the acceptable range for the **Long** data type, an error occurs.

Note **CLng** differs from the **Fix** and **Int** functions that truncate, rather than round, the fractional part of a number. When the fractional part is exactly 0.5, the **CLng** function always rounds it to the nearest even number. For example, 0.5 rounds to 0, and 1.5 rounds to 2.

See Also   Data Type Summary, **Int** Function.

Example   This example uses the **CLng** function to convert a value to a **Long**.

```
MyVal1 = 25427.45 : MyVal2 = 25427.55   ' MyVal1, MyVal2 are Doubles.
MyLong1 = CLng(MyVal1)  ' MyLong1 contains 25427.
MyLong2 = CLng(MyVal2)  ' MyLong2 contains 25428.
```

Close Method

Applies To   **Window** Object, **Workbook** Object, **Workbooks** Collection.

Description   Closes the object. The **Workbooks** collection uses Syntax 1. **Window** and **Workbook** objects use Syntax 2.

Syntax 1   *object*.**Close**

Syntax 2	*object*.**Close**(*saveChanges*, *fileName*, *routeWorkbook*)

object
Required. The object to close.

saveChanges
Optional. If there are no changes to the workbook in the window, this argument is ignored. If there are changes to the workbook, and there are other windows open on the workbook, this argument is ignored. If there are changes to the workbook, and there are no other windows open on the workbook, this argument takes the specified action, as shown in the following table.

Value	Action
True	Saves the changes to the workbook. If there is not yet a filename associated with the workbook, then *fileName* is used. If *fileName* is omitted, the user is asked to supply a filename.
False	Does not save the changes to this file.
Omitted	Displays a dialog box asking the user whether or not to save changes.

fileName
Optional. Save changes under this filename.

routeWorkbook
Optional. If the workbook does not need to be routed to the next recipient (has no routing slip, or is already routed), this argument is ignored. Otherwise, Microsoft Excel routes the workbook as shown in the following table.

Value	Meaning
True	Sends the workbook to the next recipient.
False	Does not send the workbook.
Omitted	Displays a dialog box asking the user if the workbook should be sent.

Remarks

Closing a workbook from Visual Basic does not run any Auto_Close macros in the workbook. Use the **RunAutoMacros** method to run the auto close macros.

You cannot close a workbook while a dialog box is displayed. This means that you cannot call this method from an event handler for a dialog-box control. You can use the following steps to close the workbook when the user chooses a button control:

1. Set the **DismissButton** property for the button to **True**.
2. Create a module-level status variable
3. Set the status variable to 0 (zero) before you display the dialog box

4. Set the status variable to 1 when the user chooses the control. Choosing the control dismisses the dialog box.

5. Test the status variable. If it is equal to 1, close the workbook.

Example

This example closes BOOK1.XLS and discards any changes.

```
Workbooks("BOOK1.XLS").Close saveChanges:=False
```

This example closes all open workbooks. If there are changes in any workbook, Microsoft Excel displays the appropriate prompts and dialog boxes to save changes.

```
Workbooks.Close
```

Close Statement

Description

Concludes input/output (I/O) to a file opened using the **Open** statement.

Syntax

Close [*filenumberlist*]

The *filenumberlist* argument can be one or more file numbers using the following syntax, where *filenumber* is any valid file number:

[#]*filenumber*][,[#]*filenumber*] . . .

Remarks

If you omit *filenumberlist*, all active files opened by the **Open** statement are closed.

When you close files that were opened for **Output** or **Append**, the final buffer of output is written to the operating system buffer for that file. All buffer space associated with the closed file is released.

When the **Close** statement executes, the association of a file with its file number ends.

See Also

End Statement, **Open** Statement, **Reset** Statement, **Stop** Statement.

Example

This example uses the **Close** statement to close all three files opened for **Output**.

```
For I = 1 To 3                      ' Loop 3 times.
    FileName = "TEST" & I           ' Create file name.
    Open FileName For Output As #I  ' Open file.
    Print #I, "This is a test."     ' Write string to file.
Next I
Close                               ' Close all 3 open files.
```

Color Property

Applies To   **Border** Object, **Borders** Collection, **Font** Object, **Interior** Object.

Description   Returns or sets the primary color of the object, as shown in the following table. The color is a long integer, created with the **RGB** function. Read-write.

Object	Color
Border	The color of the border.
Borders	The color of all four borders of a range. If they are not the same, returns **Null**.
Font	The color of the font.
Interior	The cell shading color or drawing object fill color.

Remarks   If the color is Automatic, the **Color** property returns the automatic color as an RGB value (a long integer). Use the **ColorIndex** property to determine if the color is Automatic.

Example   This example sets the color of the tick labels on the value axis in Chart1.

```
Charts("Chart1").Axes(xlValue).TickLabels.Font.Color = RGB(0, 255, 0)
```

ColorButtons Property

Applies To   **Application** Object.

Description   **True** if toolbars are displayed using colored faces. Read-write.

See Also   **LargeButtons** Property.

Example   This example turns off colored toolbar buttons.

```
Application.ColorButtons = False
```

ColorIndex Property

Applies To   **Border** Object, **Borders** Collection, **Font** Object, **Interior** Object.

Description

Returns or sets the color of the border, font, or interior, as shown in the following table. The color is specified as an index value into the current color palette, or the special constant **xlAutomatic** to use the automatic fill style. Read-write.

Object	ColorIndex
Border	Color of the border.
Borders	Color of all four borders. Returns **Null** if all four colors are not the same.
Font	Color of the font. Specify **xlAutomatic** to use the automatic color.
Interior	Color of the interior fill. Set this property to **xlNone** to specify no fill. Set this property to **xlAutomatic** to specify the automatic fill (for drawing objects).

Remarks

This property specifies a color as an index into the workbook color palette. You can use the **Colors** property to return the current color palette.

See Also

Color Property, **Colors** Property, **PatternColor** Property.

Example

The following examples assume that you are using the default color palette.

This example changes the font color in cell A1 on Sheet1 to red.

```
Worksheets("Sheet1").Range("A1").Font.ColorIndex = 3
```

This example sets the color of the major gridlines for the value axis in Chart1.

```
With Charts("Chart1").Axes(xlValue)
    If .HasMajorGridlines Then
        .MajorGridlines.Border.ColorIndex = 5    'set color to blue
    End If
End With
```

This example sets the chart area interior color of Chart1 to red and sets the border color to blue.

```
With Charts("Chart1").ChartArea
    .Interior.ColorIndex = 3
    .Border.ColorIndex = 5
End With
```

This example sets the border color of every graphic object on Sheet1 to cyan.

```
For Each d In Worksheets("Sheet1").DrawingObjects
    d.Border.ColorIndex = 8
Next d
```

Colors Property

Applies To	**Workbook** Object.
Description	Returns or sets an array of colors (from 1 to 56) in the palette for the workbook. Read-write.
See Also	**ColorIndex** Property.
Example	This example sets the color palette for the active workbook to be the same as the palette for BOOK2.XLS.

```
ActiveWorkbook.Colors = Workbooks("BOOK2.XLS").Colors
```

Column Property

Applies To	**Range** Object.
Description	Returns the first column of the first area in the range, as a number. Read-only.
Remarks	Column A returns 1, column B returns 2, and so on.
	To return the number of the last column in the range, use the following example.

```
myRange.Columns(myRange.Columns.Count).Column
```

See Also	**Columns** Method, **Row** Property, **Rows** Method.
Example	This example sets the column width of every other column on Sheet1 to 4 points.

```
For Each col In Worksheets("Sheet1").Columns
    If col.Column Mod 2 = 0 Then
        col.ColumnWidth = 4
    End If
Next col
```

Column3DGroup Property

Applies To	**Chart** Object.
Description	Accessor. Returns a **ChartGroup** object that represents the column chart group on a 3-D chart. Read-only.

See Also   **ColumnGroups** Method.

Example   This example sets the subtype for the 3-D column chart group in Chart1.

```
Charts("Chart1").Column3DGroup.SubType = 4
```

ColumnDifferences Method

Applies To   **Range** Object.

Description   Accessor. Returns a **Range** object that represents all the cells whose contents are different than the comparison cell in each column. The comparison cell is the one in the same row as *comparison*.

Syntax   *object*.**ColumnDifferences**(*comparison*)

object
Required. The range containing the cells to compare.

comparison
Required. A cell in the comparison row.

See Also   **RowDifferences** Method.

Example   This example selects the cells in column A on Sheet1 whose contents are different from cell A4.

```
Worksheets("Sheet1").Activate
Set r1 = ActiveSheet.Columns("A").ColumnDifferences( _
    comparison:=ActiveSheet.Range("A4"))
r1.Select
```

ColumnFields Method

Applies To   **PivotTable** Object.

Description   Accessor. Returns an object that represents a single pivot field (a **PivotField** object, Syntax 1) or a collection of the pivot fields (a **PivotFields** object, Syntax 2) that are currently showing as column fields. Read-only.

Syntax 1   *object*.**ColumnFields**(*index*)

Syntax 2   *object*.**ColumnFields**

object
> Required. The **PivotTable** object.

index
> Required for Syntax 1. The name or number of the pivot field to return (can be an array to specify more than one).

See Also   **DataFields** Method, **HiddenFields** Method, **PageFields** Method, **PivotFields** Method, **RowFields** Method, **VisibleFields** Method.

Example   This example adds the PivotTable column field names to a list box. The list box appears on Sheet1.

```
Set pvtTable = Worksheets("Sheet1").Range("A3").PivotTable
Set newListBox = Worksheets("Sheet1").ListBoxes.Add _
    (Left:=10, Top:=72, Width:=144, Height:=144)
For Each clmField In pvtTable.ColumnFields
    newListBox.AddItem (clmField.Name)
Next clmField
Worksheets("Sheet1").Activate
```

ColumnGrand Property

Applies To   **PivotTable** Object.

Description   **True** if the PivotTable shows column grand totals. Read-write.

See Also   **RowGrand** Property.

Example   This example sets the PivotTable to show column grand totals.

```
Set pvtTable = Worksheets("Sheet1").Range("A3").PivotTable
pvtTable.ColumnGrand = True
```

ColumnGroups Method

Applies To   **Chart** Object.

Description   Accessor. On a 2-D chart, returns an object that represents a single column chart group (a **ChartGroup** object, Syntax 1), or a collection of the column chart groups (a **ChartGroups** collection, Syntax 2).

Syntax 1   *object*.**ColumnGroups(*index*)**

Syntax 2	*object*.**ColumnGroups**

object
    Required. The **Chart** object.

index
    Required for Syntax 1. Specifies the chart group.

See Also	**Column3DGroup** Property.
Example	This example sets the subtype for column chart group one in Chart1.

```
Charts("Chart1").ColumnGroups(1).SubType = 3
```

ColumnRange Property

Applies To	**PivotTable** Object.
Description	Accessor. Returns a **Range** object that represents the range that contains the PivotTable column area. Read-only.
See Also	**DataBodyRange** Property, **DataLabelRange** Property, **PageRange** Property, **RowRange** Property.
Example	This example selects the column headers for the PivotTable.

```
Worksheets("Sheet1").Activate
Range("A3").Select
ActiveCell.PivotTable.ColumnRange.Select
```

Columns Method

Applies To	**Application** Object, **Range** Object, **Worksheet** Object.
Description	Accessor. Returns a **Range** object that represents a single column (Syntax 1) or a collection of columns (Syntax 2).
Syntax 1	*object*.**Columns**(*index*)
Syntax 2	*object*.**Columns**

object

Optional for **Application**, required for **Range** and **Worksheet**. The object that contains the columns. If you specify the **Application** object (or omit the object qualifier), this method applies to the active sheet in the active workbook. If the active sheet is not a worksheet, this method fails.

index

Required for Syntax 1. The name or number of the column.

Remarks

When applied to a **Range** object that is a multiple selection, this method returns columns from the first area of the range only. For example, if the **Range** object is a multiple selection with two areas, A1:B2 and C3:D4, Selection.Columns.Count returns 2, not 4. To use this method on a range that may contain a multiple selection, test Areas.Count to determine if the range is a multiple selection, and if it is, then loop over each area in the range; see the third example.

See Also

Range Method, **Rows** Method.

Example

This example formats the font of column one (column A) on Sheet1 as bold.

```
Worksheets("Sheet1").Columns(1).Font.Bold = True
```

This example sets the value of every cell in column one in the range named myRange to zero (0).

```
Range("myRange").Columns(1).Value = 0
```

This example displays the number of columns in the selection on Sheet1. If more than one area is selected, the example loops through each area.

```
Worksheets("Sheet1").Activate
areaCount = Selection.Areas.Count
If areaCount <= 1 Then
    MsgBox "The selection contains " & _
        Selection.Columns.Count & " columns."
Else
    For i = 1 To areaCount
        MsgBox "Area " & i & " of the selection contains " & _
            Selection.Areas(i).Columns.Count & " columns."
    Next i
End If
```

ColumnWidth Property

Applies To   **Range** Object.

Description	Returns or sets the width of all columns in the range. Read-write.
Remarks	One unit of column width is equal to the width of a character of the Normal style. For proportional fonts, the width of the character 0 (zero) is used.
	Use the **Width** property to return the width of a column in points.
	If all columns in the range have the same width, the **ColumnWidth** property returns the width. If columns in the range have different widths, the property returns **Null**.
See Also	**RowHeight** Property.
Example	This example doubles the width of column A on Sheet1.

```
With Worksheets("Sheet1").Columns("A")
    .ColumnWidth = .ColumnWidth * 2
End With
```

CommandUnderlines Property

Applies To	**Application** Object.
Description	Returns or sets the state of the command underlines, as shown in the following table.

Value	Meaning
xlOn	Command underlines are on.
xlOff	Command underlines are off.
xlAutomatic	Command underlines appear when you activate the menus.

Remarks	In Microsoft Excel for Windows, reading this property always returns **xlOn**, and setting this property to anything but **xlOn** is an error.
Example	This example turns off command underlines in Microsoft Excel for the Macintosh.

```
Application.CommandUnderlines = xlOff
```

Comment Property

Applies To	**Scenario** Object.

Description	Returns or sets the comment associated with the scenario. The comment text cannot exceed 255 characters. Read-write.
See Also	**ChangeScenario** Method, **ChangingCells** Property.
Example	This example sets the comment for scenario one on Sheet1.

```
Worksheets("Sheet1").Scenarios(1).Comment = _
    "Worst case July 1993 sales"
```

Comments Property

Applies To	**AddIn** Object, **Workbook** Object.
Description	Returns or sets the comments for the object, as a string. Read-only for **AddIn**, read-write for **Workbook**.
Remarks	In Microsoft Excel for Windows 95, this property has been replaced by a built-in OLE document property. For more information about OLE document properties, see **BuiltinDocumentProperties**.
	You cannot use this property with an **AddIn** object that represents an XLL file or an add-in that was created with the Microsoft Excel 4.0 macro language.
See Also	**Author** Property, **Keywords** Property, **Subject** Property, **Title** Property.
Example	This example displays the name and comments of the Solver add-in. Note that you can use **Chr(13)** to create a line break in a message box.

```
Set a = AddIns("Solver Add-In")
MsgBox a.Name & " description:" & Chr(13) & a.Comments
```

This example sets the comments for the active workbook.

```
ActiveWorkbook.Comments = "This workbook has been reviewed."
```

Comparison Operators

Description	Used to compare expressions.
Syntax	*result = expression1 comparisonoperator expression2*
	result = object1 **Is** *object2*
	result = string **Like** *pattern*

Comparison operators have these parts:

Part	Description
result	Any numeric variable.
expression	Any expression.
comparisonoperator	Any comparison operator.
object	Any object name.
string	Any string expression.
pattern	Any string expression or range of characters.

Remarks

The **Is** and **Like** operators have specific comparison functionality that differs from the operators in the following table. The following table contains a list of the comparison operators and the conditions that determine whether *result* is **True**, **False**, or **Null**:

Operator	Description	True if	False if	Null if
<	Less than	*expression1* < *expression2*	*expression1* >= *expression2*	*expression1* or *expression2* = **Null**
<=	Less than or equal to	*expression1* <= *expression2*	*expression1* > *expression2*	*expression1* or *expression2* = **Null**
>	Greater than	*expression1* > *expression2*	*expression1* <= *expression2*	*expression1* or *expression2* = **Null**
>=	Greater than or equal to	*expression1* >= *expression2*	*expression1* < *expression2*	*expression1* or *expression2* = **Null**
=	Equal to	*expression1* = *expression2*	*expression1* <> *expression2*	*expression1* or *expression2* = **Null**
<>	Not equal to	*expression1* <> *expression2*	*expression1* = *expression2*	*expression1* or *expression2* = **Null**

When comparing two expressions, you may not be able to easily determine whether the expressions are being compared as numbers or as strings. The following table shows how the expressions are compared or what results when either expression is not a **Variant**:

If	Then
Both expressions are numeric data types (**Integer**, **Long**, **Single**, **Double**, or **Currency**)	Perform a numeric comparison.
Both expressions are **String**	Perform a string comparison.
One expression is a numeric data type and the other is a **Variant** that is, or can be, a number	Perform a numeric comparison.
One expression is a numeric data type and the other is a string **Variant** that can't be converted to a number	A `Type Mismatch` error occurs.
One expression is a **String** and the other is any **Variant** (except a **Null**)	Perform a string comparison.
One expression is **Empty** and the other is a numeric data type	Perform a numeric comparison, using 0 as the **Empty** expression.
One expression is **Empty** and the other is a **String**	Perform a string comparison, using a zero-length string as the **Empty** expression.

If *expression1* and *expression2* are both **Variant** expressions, their underlying type determines how they are compared. The following table shows how the expressions are compared or what results from the comparison, depending on the underlying type of the **Variant**:

If	Then
Both **Variant** expressions are numeric	Perform a numeric comparison.
Both **Variant** expressions are strings	Perform a string comparison.
One **Variant** expression is numeric and the other is a string	The numeric expression is less than the string expression.
One **Variant** expression is **Empty** and the other is numeric	Perform a numeric comparison, using 0 as the **Empty** expression.
One **Variant** expression is **Empty** and the other is a string	Perform a string comparison, using a zero-length string as the **Empty** expression.
Both **Variant** expressions are **Empty**	The expressions are equal.

Note If a **Currency** is compared with a **Single** or **Double**, the **Single** or **Double** is converted to a **Currency**. This causes any fractional part of the **Single** or **Double** value less than 0.0001 to be lost and may cause two values to compare as equal when they are not. When a **Single** is compared to a **Double**, the **Double** is rounded to the precision of the **Single**.

See Also   **Is** Operator, **Like** Operator, Operator Precedence, **Option Compare** Statement.

Example   This example shows various uses of comparison operators, which you use to compare expressions.

```
MyResult = (45 < 35)          ' Returns False.
MyResult = (45 = 45)          ' Returns True.
MyResult = (4 <> 3)           ' Returns True.
MyResult = ("5" > "4")        ' Returns True.
Var1 = "5" : Var2 = 4         ' Initialize variables.
MyResult = (Var1 > Var2)      ' Returns True.
Var1 = 5 : Var2 = Empty
MyResult = (Var1 > Var2)      ' Returns True.
Var1 = 0 : Var2 = Empty
MyResult = (Var1 = Var2)      ' Returns True.
```

Consolidate Method

Applies To   **Range** Object.

Description   Consolidates data from multiple ranges on multiple worksheets into a single range on a single worksheet.

Syntax   *object*.**Consolidate**(*sources*, *function*, *topRow*, *leftColumn*, *createLinks*)

object
    Required. The destination range.

sources
    Optional. Specifies the sources of the consolidation as an array of text reference strings in R1C1-style notation. The references must include the full path of sheets to consolidate.

function
    Optional. The consolidation function (one of **xlAverage**, **xlCount**, **xlCountNums**, **xlMax**, **xlMin**, **xlProduct**, **xlStDev**, **xlStDevP**, **xlSum**, **xlVar**, or **xlVarP**).

> *topRow*
> Optional. If True, data is consolidated based on column header titles in the top row of the consolidation ranges. If False or omitted, data is consolidated by position.
>
> *leftColumn*
> Optional. If True, data is consolidated based on row titles in the left column of the consolidation ranges. If False or omitted, data is consolidated by position.
>
> *createLinks*
> Optional. If **True**, the consolidation uses worksheet links. If **False**, the consolidation copies the data.

See Also   **ConsolidationFunction** Property, **ConsolidationOptions** Property, **ConsolidationSources** Property, **Style** Property.

Example   This example consolidates data from Sheet2 and Sheet3 onto Sheet1, using the SUM function.

```
Worksheets("Sheet1").Range("A1").Consolidate _
    sources:=Array("Sheet2!R1C1:R37C6", "Sheet3!R1C1:R37C6"), _
    Function:=xlSum
```

ConsolidationFunction Property

Applies To   **Worksheet** Object.

Description   Returns the function code used for the current consolidation (one of **xlAverage**, **xlCount**, **xlCountNums**, **xlMax**, **xlMin**, **xlProduct**, **xlStDev**, **xlStDevP**, **xlSum**, **xlVar**, or **xlVarP**). Read-only.

See Also   **Consolidate** Method, **ConsolidationOptions** Property, **ConsolidationSources** Property.

Example   This example displays a message box if the current consolidation is using the SUM function.

```
If Worksheets("Sheet1").ConsolidationFunction = xlSum Then
    MsgBox "Sheet1 uses the SUM function for consolidation."
End If
```

ConsolidationOptions Property

Applies To   **Worksheet** Object.

Description   Returns a three-element array of consolidation options, as shown in the following table. If the element is **True**, that option is set. Read-only.

Element	Meaning
1	Labels in top row.
2	Labels in left column.
3	Create links for data.

See Also   **Consolidate** Method, **ConsolidationFunction** Property, **ConsolidationSources** Property.

Example   This example displays the consolidation options for Sheet1. The list appears on a new worksheet created by the example.

```
Set newSheet = Worksheets.Add
aOptions = Worksheets("Sheet1").ConsolidationOptions
newSheet.Range("A1").Value = "Labels in top row"
newSheet.Range("A2").Value = "Labels in left column"
newSheet.Range("A3").Value = "Create links for data"
For i = 1 To 3
    If aOptions(i) = True Then
        newSheet.Cells(i, 2).Value = "True"
    Else
        newSheet.Cells(i, 2).Value = "False"
    End If
Next i
newSheet.Columns("A:B").AutoFit
```

ConsolidationSources Property

Applies To   **Worksheet** Object.

Description   Returns an array of string values that name the source sheets for the worksheet's current consolidation. Returns **Empty** if there is no consolidation on the sheet. Read-only.

See Also   **Consolidate** Method, **ConsolidationFunction** Property, **ConsolidationOptions** Property.

Example

This example displays the names of the source ranges for the consolidation on Sheet1. The list appears on a new worksheet created by the example.

```
Set newSheet = Worksheets.Add
newSheet.Range("A1").Value = "Consolidation Sources"
aSources = Worksheets("Sheet10").ConsolidationSources
If IsEmpty(aSources) Then
    newSheet.Range("A2").Value = "none"
Else
    For i = 1 To UBound(aSources)
        newSheet.Cells(i + 1, 1).Value = aSources(i)
    Next i
End If
newSheet.Columns("A:B").AutoFit
```

Const Statement

Description

Declares constants for use in place of literal values.

Syntax

[**Public** | **Private**] **Const** *constname* [**As** *type*] = *expression*

The **Const** statement syntax has these parts:

Part	Description
Public	Used at module level to declare constants that are available to all procedures in all modules. Not allowed in procedures.
Private	Used at module level to declare constants that are available only within the module where the declaration is made. Not allowed in procedures.
constname	Name of the constant; follows standard variable naming conventions.
type	Data type of the constant; may be **Boolean**, **Integer**, **Long**, **Currency**, **Single**, **Double**, **Date**, **String**, or **Variant**. Use a separate **As** *type* clause for each constant being declared.
expression	Literal, other constant, or any combination including arithmetic or logical operators except **Is**.

Remarks

If not explicitly specified using either **Public** or **Private**, constants are **Private** by default.

Several constant declarations can be combined on the same line by separating each constant assignment with a comma. If constant declarations are combined in this way, the **Public** or **Private** keywords, if used, apply to all of them.

You can't use string concatenation, variables, user-defined or intrinsic functions (such as **Chr**) in expressions assigned to constants.

If you don't explicitly declare the constant type (using **As** *type*), the constant is given a data type that is most appropriate for the expression provided.

Constants declared in **Sub**, **Function**, or **Property** procedures are local to that procedure. A constant declared outside a procedure is defined throughout the module in which it is declared. You can use constants anywhere you would use an expression.

See Also   **Deftype** Statements, **Let** Statement.

Example   This example uses the **Const** statement to declare constants for use in place of literal values.

```
' Constants are Private by default.
Const MyVar = 459

' Declare Public constant.
Public Const MyString = "HELP"

' Declare Private Integer constant.
Private Const MyInt As Integer = 5

' Declare multiple constants on same line.
Const MyStr = "Hello", MyDouble As Double = 3.4567
```

ConstrainNumeric Property

Applies To   **Application** Object.

Description   **True** if handwriting recognition is limited to numbers and punctuation only. Read-write. This property is available only if you are using Microsoft Windows for Pen Computing. If you try to set this property under any other operating system, an error occurs.

Example   This example limits handwriting recognition to numbers and punctuation only if Microsoft Windows for Pen Computing is running.

```
If Application.WindowsForPens Then
    Application.ConstrainNumeric = True
End If
```

Container Property

Applies To   **Workbook** Object.

Description   Accessor. Returns the object containing the specified embedded workbook. This property is available only in Microsoft Excel for Windows 95. Read-only.

Remarks   Use this property with a contained workbook to return the container object. If the container doesn't support OLE Automation or the workbook isn't embedded, this property fails.

Example   This example hides the second section in the binder that contains the active Microsoft Excel workbook and then sets the value of cell A1 to 345.67. In this example, the binder is Binder1.obd.

```
Set myBinder = GetObject("Binder1.obd", "Office.Binder")
Set myWorkbook = myBinder.Sections(1).Object
With myWorkbook
    .Container.Sections(2).Visible = False
    .Sheets(1).Cells(1, 1).Value = 345.67
End With
```

ConvertFormula Method

Applies To   **Application** Object.

Description   Converts cell references in a formula between the A1 and R1C1 reference styles, between relative and absolute references, or both.

Syntax   *object*.**ConvertFormula**(*formula*, *fromReferenceStyle*, *toReferenceStyle*, *toAbsolute*, *relativeTo*)

object
    Required. The **Application** object.

formula
    Required. A string containing the formula that you want to convert. This must be a valid formula and it must begin with an equal sign.

fromReferenceStyle
    Required. The reference style of the formula. May be either **xlA1** or **xlR1C1**.

toReferenceStyle
    Optional. The reference style you want returned. May be either **xlA1** or **xlR1C1**. If omitted, the reference style is not changed (the formula stays in the style specified by *fromReferenceStyle*).

toAbsolute

> Optional. Specifies the converted reference type (one of **xlAbsolute**, **xlAbsRowRelColumn**, **xlRelRowAbsColumn**, or **xlRelative**). If this argument is omitted, the reference type is not changed.

relativeTo

> Optional. A **Range** object that contains one cell. This object determines the cell to which relative references relate.

Example

This example converts a SUM formula that contains R1C1-style references to an equivalent formula that contains A1-style references and then displays the result.

```
inputFormula = "=SUM(R10C2:R15C2)"
MsgBox Application.ConvertFormula( _
    formula:=inputFormula, _
    fromReferenceStyle:=xlR1C1, _
    toReferenceStyle:=xlA1)
```

Copy Method

Applies To

Arc Object, **Arcs** Collection, **Button** Object, **Buttons** Collection, **Chart** Object, **ChartArea** Object, **ChartObject** Object, **ChartObjects** Collection, **Charts** Collection, **CheckBox** Object, **DialogSheet** Object, **DialogSheets** Collection, **Drawing** Object, **DrawingObjects** Collection, **Drawings** Collection, **DropDown** Object, **DropDowns** Collection, **EditBox** Object, **EditBoxes** Collection, **GroupBox** Object, **GroupBoxes** Collection, **GroupObject** Object, **GroupObjects** Collection, **Label** Object, **Labels** Collection, **Line** Object, **Lines** Collection, **ListBox** Object, **ListBoxes** Collection, **Module** Object, **Modules** Collection, **OLEObject** Object, **OLEObjects** Collection, **OptionButton** Object, **OptionButtons** Collection, **Oval** Object, **Ovals** Collection, **Picture** Object, **Pictures** Collection, **Point** Object, **Range** Object, **Rectangle** Object, **Rectangles** Collection, **ScrollBar** Object, **ScrollBars** Collection, **Series** Object, **Sheets** Collection, **Spinner** Object, **Spinners** Collection, **TextBox** Object, **TextBoxes** Collection, **ToolbarButton** Object, **Worksheet** Object, **Worksheets** Collection.

Description

Syntax 1: Copies the control or drawing object to the Clipboard. Copies a picture of the point or series to the Clipboard.

Syntax 2: Copies the **Range** to the specified range or to the Clipboard.

Syntax 3: Copies the sheet to another location in the workbook.

Syntax 4: Copies a toolbar button to another position, either on the same toolbar or to another toolbar.

Syntax 1

object.**Copy**

Syntax 2	*object*.**Copy**(*destination*)
Syntax 3	*object*.**Copy**(*before*, *after*)
Syntax 4	*object*.**Copy**(*toolbar*, *before*)

object
> Required. The object to which this method applies. Copying a **Chart** object uses Syntax 3, and copies the entire chart sheet. To copy only the chart area, use Syntax 1 with the **ChartArea** object.

destination
> Optional. Specifies the new range where the specified range will be copied. If this argument is omitted, Microsoft Excel copies the range to the clipboard.

before
> Syntax 3: Optional. The sheet before which this sheet will be copied. You cannot specify *before* if you specify *after*.

> Syntax 4: Required. Specifies the new button position as a number from one to the number of existing buttons + one. Gaps count as one position. Buttons to the right of this position are moved right (or down) to make room for the copied button.

after
> Optional. The sheet after which this sheet will be copied. You cannot specify *after* if you specify *before*.

toolbar
> Required for Syntax 4. Specifies the toolbar object to copy the button to.

Remarks
If you do not specify either *before* or *after*, Microsoft Excel creates a new workbook containing the copied sheet.

To copy a button and insert a gap before the copied button, first insert a gap on the destination toolbar using the **ToolbarButtons Add** method, then copy the button to the position after the new gap.

See Also
Move Method, **Paste** Method.

Example
This example copies button one on Sheet1 to the Clipboard.

```
Worksheets("Sheet1").Buttons(1).Copy
```

This example copies Sheet1, placing the copy after Sheet3.

```
Worksheets("Sheet1").Copy after := Worksheets("Sheet3")
```

This example copies the used range of Sheet1, creates a new worksheet, and then pastes the values of the copied range into the new worksheet.

```
Worksheets("Sheet1").UsedRange.Copy
Set newSheet = Worksheets.Add
newSheet.Range("A1").PasteSpecial Paste:=xlValues
```

This example copies the formulas in cells A1:D4 on Sheet1 to cells E5:H8 on Sheet2.

```
Worksheets("Sheet1").Range("A1:D4").Copy _
    destination:=Worksheets("Sheet2").Range("E5")
```

CopyFace Method

Applies To   **ToolbarButton** Object.

Description   Copies the specified button face to the Clipboard. This method copies only the bitmap button face, not the button itself.

Syntax   *object*.**CopyFace**

object
    Required. The **ToolbarButton** object.

Remarks   This method cannot be used with a toolbar button that is a gap or that has a palette or list attached (such as the Font or Style buttons).

See Also   **BuiltIn** Property, **BuiltInFace** Property, **PasteFace** Method.

Example   This example copies the bitmap face of button one (the New Workbook button) on the Standard toolbar and pastes it onto button three (the Save button).

```
With Toolbars("Standard")
    .ToolbarButtons(1).CopyFace
    .ToolbarButtons(3).PasteFace
End With
```

CopyFromRecordset Method

Applies To   **Range** Object.

Description   Copies the contents of a DAO **Recordset** object onto a worksheet, beginning at the upper-left corner of the specified range. If the **Recordset** object contains fields with OLE objects, this method fails. This method is available only in Microsoft Excel for Windows 95.

Syntax   *object*.**CopyFromRecordset**(*data*, *maxRows*, *maxColumns*)

object
> Required. The destination **Range** object.

data
> Required. The **Recordset** object to copy into the range.

maxRows
> Optional. The maximum number of records to copy onto the worksheet. If omitted, all records in the **Recordset** object are copied.

maxColumns
> Optional. The maximum number of fields to copy onto the worksheet. If omitted, all fields in the **Recordset** object are copied.

Remarks   Copying begins at the current row of the **Recordset** object. After copying is completed, the **EOF** property of the **Recordset** object is **True**.

Example   This example copies the field names from a DAO **Recordset** object into the first row of a worksheet and formats the names as bold. The example then copies the recordset onto the worksheet, beginning at cell A2.

```
For iCols = 0 to rs.Fields.Count - 1
    ws.Cells(1, iCols + 1).Value = rs.Fields(iCols).Name
Next
ws.Range(ws.Cells(1, 1), _
    ws.Cells(1, rs.Fields.Count)).Font.Bold = True
ws.Range("A2").CopyFromRecordset rs
```

CopyObjectsWithCells Property

Applies To   **Application** Object.

Description   **True** if drawing objects are cut, copied, extracted, and sorted with cells. Read-write.

Example   This example causes Microsoft Excel to cut, copy, extract, and sort drawing objects with cells.

```
Application.CopyObjectsWithCells = True
```

CopyPicture Method

Applies To   Arc Object, **Arcs** Collection, **Button** Object, **Buttons** Collection, **Chart** Object, **ChartObject** Object, **ChartObjects** Collection, **CheckBox** Object, **DialogFrame** Object, **Drawing** Object, **DrawingObjects** Collection, **Drawings** Collection, **DropDown** Object, **DropDowns** Collection, **EditBox** Object, **EditBoxes** Collection, **GroupBox** Object, **GroupBoxes** Collection, **GroupObject** Object, **GroupObjects** Collection, **Label** Object, **Labels** Collection, **Line** Object, **Lines** Collection, **ListBox** Object, **ListBoxes** Collection, **OLEObject** Object, **OLEObjects** Collection, **OptionButton** Object, **OptionButtons** Collection, **Oval** Object, **Ovals** Collection, **Picture** Object, **Pictures** Collection, **Range** Object, **Rectangle** Object, **Rectangles** Collection, **ScrollBar** Object, **ScrollBars** Collection, **Spinner** Object, **Spinners** Collection, **TextBox** Object, **TextBoxes** Collection.

Description   Copies the object to the Clipboard as a **Picture**. Syntax 2 is used for the Chart object. Syntax 1 is used for all other objects.

Syntax 1   *object*.CopyPicture(*appearance, format*)

Syntax 2   *object*.**CopyPicture**(*appearance*, *format*, *size*)

object
   Required. The object to copy.

appearance
   Optional. Specifies how the picture should be copied. If **xlScreen** or omitted, the picture is copied as closely as possible to the picture displayed on the screen. If **xlPrinter**, the picture is copied as it would be printed.

format
   Optional. Specifies the format of the picture (one of **xlPicture** or **xlBitmap**). If omitted, picture format is used.

size
   Optional. Specifies the size of the copied picture when the object is a chart that is on a chart sheet (not embedded on a worksheet). If **xlPrinter** or omitted, the picture is copied as closely as possible to the printed size. If **xlScreen**, the picture is copied as closely as possible to the size as displayed on the screen.

Remarks   This method creates a **Picture** object on the Clipboard, regardless of the copied object.

   If you copy a range, it must be made up of adjacent cells.

See Also   **Copy** Method, **Paste** Method.

Example   This example copies a screen image of cells A1:D4 on Sheet1 to the Clipboard, and then it pastes the bitmap in another location on Sheet1.

```
Worksheets("Sheet1").Range("A1:D4").CopyPicture xlScreen, xlBitmap
Worksheets("Sheet1").Paste _
    destination:=Worksheets("Sheet1").Range("E6")
```

Corners Object

Description   Represents the corners of a 3-D chart. The **Corners** object supports only the **Select** method. The macro recorder uses this object and method to record selecting the corners of a 3-D chart when you drag the corners to set the chart elevation and rotation. Because you can set these properties directly in Visual Basic, you will not need to use the **Corners** object. You can delete the line containing this object without affecting the functionality of the code.

Properties   **Application** Property, **Creator** Property, **Name** Property, **Parent** Property.

Methods   **Select** Method.

Corners Property

Applies To   **Chart** Object.

Description   Accessor. Returns a **Corners** object that represents the corners of a 3-D chart. The corners cannot be formatted; this property can be used only to select the corners of the chart. Read-only.

Example   This example selects the corners of Chart1. The example should be run on a 3-D chart (the **Select** method fails on any other chart type).

```
With Charts("Chart1")
    .Activate
    .Corners.Select
End With
```

Cos Function

Description Returns the cosine of an angle.

Syntax **Cos(*number*)**

The *number* named argument can be any valid numeric expression that expresses an angle in radians.

Remarks The **Cos** function takes an angle and returns the ratio of two sides of a right triangle. The ratio is the length of the side adjacent to the angle divided by the length of the hypotenuse.

The result lies in the range -1 to 1.

To convert degrees to radians, multiply degrees by pi/180. To convert radians to degrees, multiply radians by 180/pi.

See Also **Atn** Function, Derived Math Functions, **Sin** Function, **Tan** Function.

Example This example uses the **Cos** function to return the cosine of an angle.

```
MyAngle = 1.3                     ' Define angle in radians.
MySecant = 1 / Cos(MyAngle)       ' Calculate secant.
```

Count Property

Applies To All collections.

Description Returns the number of items in the collection. Read-only.

For help about using the **Count** worksheet function in Visual Basic, see "Using Worksheet Functions in Visual Basic" in online Help.

Example This example displays the number of menus on the active menu bar.

```
MsgBox "The active menu bar contains " & _
    ActiveMenuBar.Menus.Count & " menus."
```

This example displays the number of columns in the selection on Sheet1. The code also tests for a multi-area selection; if one exists, the code loops on the areas of the multi-area selection.

```
Worksheets("Sheet1").Activate
areaCount = Selection.Areas.Count
If areaCount <= 1 Then
    MsgBox "The selection contains " & _
        Selection.Columns.Count & " columns."
Else
    For i = 1 To areaCount
        MsgBox "Area " & i & " of the selection contains " & _
            Selection.Areas(i).Columns.Count & " columns."
    Next i
End If
```

This example makes the last character in cell A1 a superscript.

```
n = Worksheets("Sheet1").Range("A1").Characters.Count
Worksheets("Sheet1").Range("A1").Characters(n, 1).Font.Superscript = _
            True
```

Count Property (DocumentProperties Collection)

Applies To   **DocumentProperties** Collection.

Description   Returns the number of document properties in the **DocumentProperties** collection. Read-only.

To use this property, you should establish a reference to the Microsoft Office 95 Object Library by using the References command (Tools menu).

Example   This example displays the number of document properties in a collection. You must pass a **DocumentProperties** collection to the procedure.

```
Sub CountDocumentProperties(dp As DocumentProperties)
    MsgBox "There are " & dp.Count & " properties in the collection."
End Sub
```

This example displays the number of custom document properties in the active workbook.

```
MsgBox ActiveWorkbook.CustomDocumentProperties.Count
```

CreateBackup Property

Applies To	**Workbook** Object.
Description	**True** if a backup will be created when this file is saved. Read-only.
Example	This example displays a message if a backup is created when the active workbook is saved.

```
If ActiveWorkbook.CreateBackup = True Then
    MsgBox "Remember, there is a backup copy of this workbook"
End If
```

CreateNames Method

Applies To	**Range** Object.
Description	Creates names in the given range based on text labels in the sheet.
Syntax	*object*.**CreateNames**(*top*, *left*, *bottom*, *right*)

object
　　Required. Create names in this range.

top
　　Optional. Corresponds to the Top Row check box in the Create dialog box. Can be **True** or **False**.

left
　　Optional. Corresponds to the Left Column check box in the Create dialog box. Can be **True** or **False**.

bottom
　　Optional. Corresponds to the Bottom Row check box in the Create dialog box. Can be **True** or **False**.

right
　　Optional. Corresponds to the Right Column check box in the Create dialog box. Can be **True** or **False**.

Remarks	If you do not specify one of *top*, *left*, *bottom*, or *right*, Microsoft Excel guesses the location of the text labels based on the shape of the specified range.
See Also	**Add** Method (**Names** Collection), **Delete** Method.

Example

This example creates names for cells B1:B3 based on the text in cells A1:A3. Note that you must include the cells that contain the names in the range, even though the names are created only for cells B1:B3.

```
Set rangeToName = Worksheets("Sheet1").Range("A1:B3")
rangeToName.CreateNames left:=True
```

CreateObject Function

Description

Creates an OLE Automation object.

Syntax

CreateObject(*class*)

The *class* named argument uses the syntax: *"appname.objecttype"* and has these parts:

Part	Description
appname	The name of the application providing the object.
objecttype	The type or class of object to create.

Remarks

Note If an application that supports OLE Automation exposes an object library, it is preferable to use the functions defined within the library for object creation rather than use **CreateObject**.

Each application that supports OLE Automation provides at least one type of object. For example, a word processing application may provide an application object, a document object, and a toolbar object.

Use this function to create an OLE Automation object and assign the object to an object variable. To do this, use the **Set** statement to assign the object returned by **CreateObject** to the object variable. For example:

```
Set WordBasicObject = CreateObject("Word.Basic")
```

When this code is executed, the application creating the object is started, if it is not already running (Microsoft Word in this example), and an object of the specified type is created. Once an object is created, you reference it in code using the object variable you defined. In the above example, you access properties and methods of the new object using the object variable, WordBasicObject. For example:

```
WordBasicObject.Insert "Hello, world."
WordBasicObject.FilePrint
WordBasicObject.FileSaveAs "C:\DOCS\TEST.DOC"
```

See Also   **GetObject** Function, **Set** Statement.

CreatePublisher Method

Applies To   **Chart** Object, **Range** Object.

Description   Creates a publisher based on a **Chart** or a **Range**. Available only on the Apple Macintosh with System 7 or later.

Syntax   *object*.**CreatePublisher**(*edition, appearance, size, containsPICT, containsBIFF, containsRTF, containsVALU*)

object
  Required. The **Chart** or **Range** object.

edition
  Optional. The filename of the edition to be created. If omitted, a default of <Document Name> Edition #*n* is used.

appearance
  Optional. One of **xlPrinter** or **xlScreen**.

size
  Optional (used only with **Chart** objects). One of **xlPrinter** or **xlScreen**.

containsPICT
  Optional. **True** if the publisher should include PICT format. Assumed **True** if not specified.

containsBIFF
  Optional. **True** if the publisher should include BIFF format. Assumed **True** if not specified for a **Range**, **False** for a **Chart**.

containsRTF
  Optional. **True** if the publisher should include RTF format. Assumed **True** if not specified for a **Range**, **False** for a **Chart**.

containsVALU
  Optional. **True** if the publisher should include VALU format. Assumed **True** if not specified for a **Range**, **False** for a **Chart**.

Example   This example creates a publisher based on cells A1:A20 on Sheet1.

```
Worksheets("Sheet1").Range("A1:A20").CreatePublisher "stock data"
```

CreateSummary Method

Description   Creates a new worksheet containing a summary report for the scenarios on the specified worksheet.

Syntax   *object*.**CreateSummary**(*reportType*, *resultCells*)

object
Required. The **Scenarios** collection object.

reportType
Optional. Specifies the report type (either **xlStandardSummary** or **xlPivotTable**). If this argument is omitted, a standard report is created.

resultCells
Optional. A range containing the result cells on the specified worksheet. Normally, this range refers to one or more cells containing the formulas that depend on the changing cell values for your model—that is, the cells that show the results of a particular scenario. If this argument is omitted, no result cells are included in the report.

Example   This example creates a summary of the scenarios on Sheet1, with result cells in the range C4:C9 on Sheet1.

```
Worksheets("Sheet1").Scenarios.CreateSummary _
    resultCells := Worksheets("Sheet1").Range("C4:C9")
```

Creator Property

Applies To   All objects.

Description   Returns the application that created this object, as a 32-bit integer. If the object was created by Microsoft Excel, this property returns the string XCEL, which is the hexadecimal number 5843454C. Read-only.

Remarks   The **Creator** property is designed to be used in Microsoft Excel for the Apple Macintosh, where each application has a four-character creator code. For example, Microsoft Excel has the creator code XCEL.

See Also   **Application** Property.

Example   This example displays a message about the creator of `myObject`.

```
Set myObject = ActiveWorkbook
If myObject.Creator = &h5843454c Then
    MsgBox "This is a Microsoft Excel object"
Else
    MsgBox "This is not a Microsoft Excel object"
End If
```

Crosses Property

Applies To   **Axis** Object.

Description   Returns or sets the point on the specified axis where the other axis crosses, as shown in the following table. Read-write.

Value	Meaning
xlAutomatic	Microsoft Excel sets the axis crossing.
xlMinimum	The axis crosses at the minimum value.
xlMaximum	The axis crosses at the maximum value.
xlCustom	The **CrossesAt** property specifies the crossing point.

Remarks   This property is not available for 3-D charts or radar charts.

This property can be used for both category and value axes. On the category axis, **xlMinimum** sets the value axis to cross at the first category, and **xlMaximum** sets the value axis to cross at the last category.

xlMinimum and **xlMaximum** can have different meanings, depending on the axis.

See Also   **CrossesAt** Property.

Example   This example sets the value axis in Chart1 to cross the category axis at the maximum x value.

```
Charts("Chart1").Axes(xlCategory).Crosses = xlMaximum
```

CrossesAt Property

Applies To   **Axis** Object.

Description	Returns or sets the point on the value axis where the category axis crosses. Applies only to the value axis. Read-write.
Remarks	Setting this property causes the **Crosses** property to change to **xlCustom**.
	This property is not available for 3-D charts or radar charts.
See Also	**Crosses** Property.
Example	This example sets the category axis in Chart1 to cross the value axis at value 3.

```
With Charts("Chart1").Axes(xlValue)
    .Crosses = xlCustom
    .CrossesAt = 3
End With
```

CSng Function

Description	Converts an expression to a **Single**.
Syntax	**CSng**(*expression*)
	The *expression* argument is any valid numeric or string expression.
Remarks	In general, you can document your code using the data type conversion functions to show that the result of some operation should be expressed as a particular data type rather than the default data type. For example, use **CDbl** or **CSng** to force double- or single-precision arithmetic in cases where currency or integer arithmetic normally would occur.
	You should use the **CSng** function instead of **Val** to provide internationally-aware conversions from any other data type to a **Single**. For example, different decimal separators are properly recognized depending on the locale setting of your system, as are different thousand separators.
	If *expression* lies outside the acceptable range for the **Single** data type, an error occurs.
See Also	Data Type Summary.
Example	This example uses the **CSng** function to convert a value to a **Single**.

```
' MyDouble1, MyDouble2 are Doubles.
MyDouble1 = 75.3421115 : MyDouble2 = 75.3421555
MySingle1 = CSng(MyDouble1)  ' MySingle1 contains 75.34211.
MySingle2 = CSng(MyDouble2)  ' MySingle2 contains 75.34216.
```

CStr Function

Description

Converts an expression to a **String**.

Syntax

CStr(*expression*)

The *expression* argument is any valid numeric or string expression.

Remarks

In general, you can document your code using the data type conversion functions to show that the result of some operation should be expressed as a particular data type rather than the default data type. For example, use **CStr** to force the result to be expressed as a **String**.

You should use the **CStr** function instead of **Str** to provide internationally-aware conversions from any other data type to a **String**. For example, different decimal separators are properly recognized depending on the locale setting of your system.

The data in *expression* determines what is returned according to the following table:

If *expression* is	CStr returns
Boolean	**String** containing **True** or **False** (translated as appropriate for locale).
Date	**String** containing a date in the short-date format of your system.
Null	A run-time error.
Empty	A zero-length **String** ("").
Error	A **String** containing the word **Error** (translated as appropriate for locale) followed by the error number.
Other Numeric	A **String** containing the number.

See Also

Data Type Summary, **Str** Function.

Example

This example uses the **CStr** function to convert a numeric value to a **String**.

```
MyDouble = 437.324   ' MyDouble is a Double.
MyString = CStr(MyDouble)   ' MyString contains "437.324".
```

CurDir Function

Description

Returns the current path.

Syntax

CurDir[(*drive*)]

The *drive* argument is a string expression that specifies an existing drive. In Microsoft Windows, if no drive is specified or if *drive* is zero-length (""), **CurDir** returns the path for the current drive. On the Macintosh, **CurDir** ignores any *drive* specified and simply returns the path for the current drive.

See Also   **ChDir** Statement, **ChDrive** Statement, **MkDir** Statement, **RmDir** Statement.

Example   This example uses the **CurDir** function to return the current path.

```
' In Microsoft Windows.
' Assume current path on C Drive is  "C:\WINDOWS\SYSTEM".
' Assume current path on D Drive is "D:\EXCEL".
' Assume C is the current drive.
MyPath = CurDir                    ' Returns "C:\WINDOWS\SYSTEM".
MyPath = CurDir("C")               ' Returns "C:\WINDOWS\SYSTEM".
MyPath = CurDir("D")               ' Returns "D:\EXCEL".

' On the Macintosh.
' Drive letters are ignored. Path for current drive is returned.
' Assume current path on HD Drive is  "HD:MY FOLDER".
' Assume HD is the current drive. Drive MD also exists on the machine.
MyPath = CurDir                    ' Returns "HD:MY FOLDER".
MyPath = CurDir("HD")              ' Returns "HD:MY FOLDER".
MyPath = CurDir("MD")              ' Returns "HD:MY FOLDER".
```

Currency Data Type

Description   **Currency** variables are stored as 64-bit (8-byte) numbers in an integer format, scaled by 10,000 to give a fixed-point number with 15 digits to the left of the decimal point and 4 digits to the right. This representation provides a range of -922,337,203,685,477.5808 to 922,337,203,685,477.5807. The type-declaration character for **Currency** is @ (character code 64).

The **Currency** data type is useful for calculations involving money and for fixed-point calculations in which accuracy is particularly important.

See Also   **CCur** Function, Data Type Summary, **Def***type* Statements, **Long** Data Type.

CurrentArray Property

Applies To   **Range** Object.

Description   Accessor. If the specified cell is part of an array, returns a **Range** object that represents the entire array. Read-only.

See Also   **CurrentRegion** Property, **HasArray** Property.

Example   This example assumes that the active cell is A1 on Sheet1 and that the active cell is part of an array that includes cells A1:A10. The example selects cells A1:A10 on Sheet1.

```
ActiveCell.CurrentArray.Select
```

CurrentPage Property

Applies To   **PivotField** Object.

Description   Returns or sets the current page showing for the page field (only valid for page fields). Read-write.

Remarks   To set this property, set it to the name of the page. Set it to "All" to set all pages showing.

Example   This example sets the current page for the PivotTable on Sheet1 to the page named "Canada."

```
Set pvtTable = Worksheets("Sheet1").Range("A3").PivotTable
pvtTable.PivotFields("Country").CurrentPage = "Canada"
```

CurrentRegion Property

Applies To   **Range** Object.

Description   Accessor. Returns a **Range** object that represents the current region. The current region is a range bounded by any combination of blank rows and blank columns. Read-only.

Remarks   This property is useful for many operations that automatically expand the selection to include the entire current region, such as the **AutoFormat** method.

See Also   **CurrentArray** Property.

Example   This example selects the current region on Sheet1.

```
Worksheets("Sheet1").Activate
ActiveCell.CurrentRegion.Select
```

This example assumes that you have a table on Sheet1 that has a header row. The example selects the table, without selecting the header row. The active cell must be somewhere in the table before you run the example.

```
Set tbl = ActiveCell.CurrentRegion
tbl.Offset(1, 0).Resize(tbl.Rows.Count - 1, tbl.Columns.Count).Select
```

Cursor Property

Applies To   **Application** Object.

Description   Returns or sets the appearance of the mouse pointer in Microsoft Excel, as listed in the following table. This property is available only in Microsoft Excel for Windows 95. Read-write.

Value	Meaning
xlNormal	The default pointer
xlWait	The hourglass pointer
xlNorthwestArrow	The northwest-arrow pointer
xlIBeam	The I-beam pointer

Remarks   The **Cursor** property isn't reset automatically when the macro stops running. You should reset the mouse pointer to **xlNormal** before your macro stops.

Example   This example changes the mouse pointer to an I-beam, pauses, and then changes the pointer to the default pointer.

```
Sub ChangeCursor()
    Application.Cursor = xlIBeam
    For x = 1 To 1000
        For y = 1 to 1000
        Next y
    Next x
    Application.Cursor = xlNormal
End Sub
```

CustomDocumentProperties Property

Applies To   **Workbook** Object.

Description   Returns a **DocumentProperties** collection object that represents all the custom document properties for the specified workbook. Read-only.

To use this object, you should establish a reference to the Microsoft Office 95 Object Library by using the References command (Tools menu).

Remarks   This property returns the entire collection of custom document properties. Use the **Item** method to return a single member of the collection (a **DocumentProperty** object) by specifying either the name of the property or the collection index as a number.

Because the **Item** method is the default method for the **DocumentProperties** collection object, the following statements are identical:

```
CustomDocumentProperties.Item("Title")
CustomDocumentProperties("Title")
```

Use the **BuiltinDocumentProperties** property to return the collection of built-in document properties.

Example   This example displays the names and values of the custom document properties as a list on worksheet one.

```
rw = 1
Worksheets(1).Activate
For Each p In ActiveWorkbook.CustomDocumentProperties
    Cells(rw, 1).Value = p.Name
    Cells(rw, 2).Value = p.Value
    rw = rw + 1
Next
```

CustomListCount Property

Applies To   **Application** Object.

Description   Returns the number of defined custom lists (including built-in lists). Read-only.

See Also   **AddCustomList** Method, **DeleteCustomList** Method, **GetCustomListContents** Method, **GetCustomListNum** Method.

Example   This example displays the number of custom lists currently defined.

```
MsgBox "There are currently " & Application.CustomListCount & _
    " defined custom lists."
```

Cut Method

Applies To   **Arc** Object, **Arcs** Collection, **Button** Object, **Buttons** Collection, **ChartObject** Object, **ChartObjects** Collection, **CheckBox** Object, **Drawing** Object, **DrawingObjects** Collection, **Drawings** Collection, **DropDown** Object, **DropDowns** Collection, **EditBox** Object, **EditBoxes** Collection, **GroupBox** Object, **GroupBoxes** Collection, **GroupObject** Object, **GroupObjects** Collection, **Label** Object, **Labels** Collection, **Line** Object, **Lines** Collection, **ListBox** Object, **ListBoxes** Collection, **OLEObject** Object, **OLEObjects** Collection, **OptionButton** Object, **OptionButtons** Collection, **Oval** Object, **Ovals** Collection, **Picture** Object, **Pictures** Collection, **Range** Object, **Rectangle** Object, **Rectangles** Collection, **ScrollBar** Object, **ScrollBars** Collection, **Spinner** Object, **Spinners** Collection, **TextBox** Object, **TextBoxes** Collection.

Description   Cuts the object to the Clipboard or to a specified destination.

Syntax   *object*.**Cut**(*destination*)

object
   Required. The object to cut.

destination
   Optional (used only with **Range** objects). Specifies the range where the object should be pasted. If omitted, the object is cut to the Clipboard. The destination range must be a single cell or an enlarged multiple of the range to be cut.

Remarks   The cut range must be made up of adjacent cells.

Only embedded charts can be cut.

See Also   **Copy** Method, **Paste** Method.

Example   This example cuts the range A1:G37 on Sheet1 and places it on the Clipboard.

```
Worksheets("Sheet1").Range("A1:G37").Cut
```

CutCopyMode Property

Applies To

Application Object.

Description

Returns or sets the Cut or Copy mode status, as shown in the following tables. Read-write.

Return value	Description
False	Not in Cut or Copy mode
xlCopy	In Copy mode
xlCut	In Cut mode

Set value	Description
False	Cancels Cut or Copy mode and removes the moving border.
True	Cancels Cut or Copy mode and removes the moving border. On the Macintosh, this also places the contents of the selection in the Macintosh clipboard.

Example

This example uses a message box to display the Cut or Copy mode status.

```
Select Case Application.CutCopyMode
    Case Is = False
        MsgBox "Not in Cut or Copy mode"
    Case Is = xlCopy
        MsgBox "In Copy mode"
    Case Is = xlCut
        MsgBox "In Cut mode"
End Select
```

CVar Function

Description

Converts an expression to a **Variant**.

Syntax

CVar(*expression*)

The *expression* argument is any valid numeric or string expression.

Remarks

In general, you can document your code using the data type conversion functions to show that the result of some operation should be expressed as a particular data type rather than the default data type. For example, use **CVar** to force the result to be expressed as a **Variant**.

See Also   Data Type Summary.

Example   This example uses the **CVar** function to convert an expression to a **Variant**.

```
MyInt = 4534' MyInt is an Integer.
MyVar = CVar(MyInt & "000")  ' MyVar contains 4534000.
```

CVErr Function

Description   Returns a **Variant** of subtype **Error** containing an error number specified by the user.

Syntax   **CVErr**(*errornumber*)

The *errornumber* argument is any valid error number.

Remarks   Use the **CVErr** function to create user-defined errors in user-created procedures. For example, if you create a function that accepts several arguments and normally returns a string, you can have your function evaluate the input arguments to ensure they are within acceptable range. If they are not, it is likely that your function will not return what you expect. In this event, **CVErr** allows you to return an error number that tells you what action to take.

Note that implicit conversion of an **Error** is not allowed. For example, you can't directly assign the return value of **CVErr** to a non-**Variant** variable. However, you can perform an explicit conversion (using **CInt**, **CDbl**, and so on) of the value returned by **CVErr** and assign that to a variable of the appropriate data type.

See Also   Data Type Summary, **IsError** Function.

Example   This example uses the **CVErr** function to return an **Error Variant**. The user-defined function CalculateDouble returns an error if the argument passed to it isn't a number. **CVErr** is useful for returning user-defined errors from user-defined procedures. Use the **IsError** function to test if the value is an error.

```
' Define CalculateDouble Function procedure.
Function CalculateDouble(Number)
    If IsNumeric(Number) Then
        CalculateDouble = Number * 2 ' Return result.
    Else
        CalculateDouble = CVErr(2001)    ' Return a user-defined error
    End If   ' number.
End Function
```

This example inserts the seven cell error values into cells A1:A7 on Sheet1.

```
myArray = Array(xlErrDiv0, xlErrNA, xlErrName, xlErrNull, _
    xlErrNum, xlErrRef, xlErrValue)
For i = 1 To 7
    Worksheets("Sheet1").Cells(i, 1).Value = CVErr(myArray(i - 1))
Next i
```

This example displays a message if the active cell on Sheet1 contains a cell error value. You can use this example as a framework for a cell-error-value error handler.

```
Worksheets("Sheet1").Activate
If IsError(ActiveCell.Value) Then
    errval = ActiveCell.Value
    Select Case errval
        Case CVErr(xlErrDiv0)
            MsgBox "#DIV/0! error"
        Case CVErr(xlErrNA)
            MsgBox "#N/A error"
        Case CVErr(xlErrName)
            MsgBox "#NAME? error"
        Case CVErr(xlErrNull)
            MsgBox "#NULL! error"
        Case CVErr(xlErrNum)
            MsgBox "#NUM! error"
        Case CVErr(xlErrRef)
            MsgBox "#REF! error"
        Case CVErr(xlErrValue)
            MsgBox "#VALUE! error"
        Case Else
            MsgBox "This should never happen!!"
    End Select
End If
```

Data Type Summary

The following table shows the supported data types, including their storage sizes and ranges.

Data type	Storage size	Range
Boolean	2 bytes	**True** or **False**.
Integer	2 bytes	-32,768 to 32,767.
Long (long integer)	4 bytes	-2,147,483,648 to 2,147,483,647.

Data type	Storage size	Range
Single (single-precision floating-point)	4 bytes	-3.402823E38 to -1.401298E-45 for negative values; 1.401298E-45 to 3.402823E38 for positive values.
Double (double-precision floating-point)	8 bytes	-1.79769313486232E308 to -4.94065645841247E-324 for negative values; 4.94065645841247E-324 to 1.79769313486232E308 for positive values.
Currency (scaled integer)	8 bytes	-922,337,203,685,477.5808 to 922,337,203,685,477.5807.
Date	8 bytes	January 1, 100 to December 31, 9999.
Object	4 bytes	Any **Object** reference.
String	1 byte per character	0 to approximately 2 billion (approximately 65,535 for Microsoft Windows version 3.1 and earlier).
Variant	16 bytes + 1 byte for each character	Any numeric value up to the range of a **Double** or any character text.
User-defined (using **Type**)	Number required by elements	The range of each element is the same as the range of its data type.

See Also   **Boolean** Data Type, **Currency** Data Type, **Date** Data Type, **Def***type* Statements, **Double** Data Type, **Integer** Data Type, **Long** Data Type, **Object** Data Type, **Single** Data Type, **String** Data Type, **Type** Statement, **Variant** Data Type.

DataBodyRange Property

Applies To   **PivotTable** Object.

Description   Accessor. Returns a **Range** object that represents the range that contains the PivotTable data area. Read-only.

See Also   **ColumnRange** Property, **DataLabelRange** Property, **PageRange** Property, **RowRange** Property.

Example   This example selects the active PivotTable data.

```
Worksheets("Sheet1").Activate
Range("A3").Select
ActiveCell.PivotTable.DataBodyRange.Select
```

DataEntryMode Property

Applies To   **Application** Object.

Description   Returns or sets Data Entry mode, as shown in the following table. When in Data Entry mode, you can enter data only in the unlocked cells of the currently selected range. Read-write.

Value	Meaning
xlOn	Data Entry mode on.
xlOff	Data Entry mode off.
xlStrict	Data Entry mode on, and ESC will not exit the Data Entry mode.

Example   This example turns the Data Entry mode off if it is on.

```
If (Application.DataEntryMode = xlOn) Or _
    (Application.DataEntryMode = xlStrict) Then
        Application.DataEntryMode = xlOff
End If
```

DataFields Method

Applies To   **PivotTable** Object.

Description   Accessor. Returns an object that represents a single pivot field (a **PivotField** object, Syntax 1) or a collection of the pivot fields (a **PivotFields** object, Syntax 2) which are currently showing as data fields. Read-only.

Syntax 1   *object*.**DataFields**(*index*)

Syntax 2   *object*.**DataFields**

object
    Required. The **PivotTable** object.

index
    Required for Syntax 1. The name or number of the pivot field to return (can be an array to specify more than one).

See Also   **ColumnFields** Method, **HiddenFields** Method, **PageFields** Method, **PivotFields** Method, **RowFields** Method, **VisibleFields** Method.

Example   This example adds the PivotTable data field names to a list box. The list box appears on Sheet1.

```
Set pvtTable = Worksheets("Sheet1").Range("A3").PivotTable
Set newListBox = Worksheets("Sheet1").ListBoxes.Add _
    (Left:=10, Top:=72, Width:=144, Height:=144)
For Each dtaField In pvtTable.DataFields
    newListBox.AddItem (dtaField.Name)
Next dtaField
Worksheets("Sheet1").Activate
```

DataLabel Object

Description   Represents the data label on a chart point or trendline.

Accessors   For a series, the data labels for all points on the series are contained in a **DataLabels** collection. For a series without definable points (such as an area series), the **DataLabels** collection contains a single data label. To access a single member of the collection, use the **DataLabels** method with the data label index number as an argument. The following example sets the number format for data label five of series one in embedded chart one on worksheet one.

```
Worksheets(1).ChartObjects(1).Chart _
    .SeriesCollection(1).DataLabels(5).NumberFormat = "0.000"
```

The **DataLabel** property returns the data label for a single point. The following example turns on the data label for point two on series one on the chart sheet named "Chart1" and sets the data label text to "Saturday".

```
With Charts("chart1")
    With .SeriesCollection(1).Points(2)
        .HasDataLabel = True
        .DataLabel.Text = "Saturday"
    End With
End With
```

On a trendline, the **DataLabel** property returns the text shown with the trendline. This can be the equation, the R-squared value, or both (if both are showing). The following example sets the trendline text to show only the equation and then places the data label text in cell A1 on the worksheet named "Sheet1."

```
With Charts("chart1").SeriesCollection(1).Trendlines(1)
    .DisplayRSquared = False
    .DisplayEquation = True
    Worksheets("sheet1").Range("a1").Value = .DataLabel.Text
End With
```

Properties	**Application** Property, **AutoText** Property, **Border** Property, **Caption** Property, **Creator** Property, **Font** Property, **HorizontalAlignment** Property, **Interior** Property, **Left** Property, **Name** Property, **NumberFormat** Property, **NumberFormatLinked** Property, **Orientation** Property, **Parent** Property, **Shadow** Property, **ShowLegendKey** Property, **Text** Property, **Top** Property, **Type** Property, **VerticalAlignment** Property.
Methods	**Characters** Method, **Delete** Method, **Select** Method.

DataLabel Property

Applies To	**Point** Object, **Trendline** Object.
Description	Accessor. Returns a **DataLabel** object that represents the data label associated with the point or trendline. Read-only.
See Also	**ApplyDataLabels** Method, **HasDataLabel** Property.
Example	This example turns on the data label for point seven in series three in Chart1, and then it sets the data label color to blue.

```
With Charts("Chart1").SeriesCollection(3).Points(7)
    .HasDataLabel = True
    .ApplyDataLabels type:=xlValue
    .DataLabel.Font.ColorIndex = 5
End With
```

DataLabelRange Property

Applies To	**PivotTable** Object.
Description	Accessor. Returns a **Range** object that represents the range that contains the PivotTable data field labels. Read-only.
See Also	**ColumnRange** Property, **DataBodyRange** Property, **PageRange** Property, **RowRange** Property.
Example	This example selects the data field labels in the PivotTable.

```
Worksheets("Sheet1").Activate
Range("A3").Select
ActiveCell.PivotTable.DataLabelRange.Select
```

DataLabels Collection Object

Description   A collection of all the **DataLabel** objects for the specified series. Each **DataLabel** object represents a data label for a point or trendline. For a series without definable points (such as an area series), the **DataLabels** collection contains a single data label.

Accessors   Use the **DataLabels** method with an argument to access a single member of the collection or without an argument to access the entire collection at once. The following example sets the number format for all data labels on series one.

```
With Worksheets("sheet5").ChartObjects(1).Chart.SeriesCollection(1)
    .HasDataLabels = True
    .DataLabels.NumberFormat = "0.00"
End With
```

Properties   **Application** Property, **AutoText** Property, **Border** Property, **Count** Property, **Creator** Property, **Font** Property, **HorizontalAlignment** Property, **Interior** Property, **Name** Property, **NumberFormat** Property, **NumberFormatLinked** Property, **Orientation** Property, **Parent** Property, **Shadow** Property, **ShowLegendKey** Property, **Type** Property, **VerticalAlignment** Property.

Methods   **Delete** Method, **Item** Method, **Select** Method.

DataLabels Method

Applies To   **Series** Object.

Description   Accessor. Returns an object that represents a single data label (a **DataLabel** object, Syntax 1) or a collection of all data labels for the series (a **DataLabels** collection, Syntax 2).

Syntax 1   *object*.**DataLabels**(*index*)

Syntax 2   *object*.**DataLabels**

object
    Required. The **Series** object.

index
    Required for Syntax 1. The number of the data label.

Remarks   If the series has the Show Value option on for the data labels, the returned collection can contain up to one label for each point. Data labels can be turned on or off for individual points in the series.

If the series is on an area chart and has the Show Label option on for the data labels, the returned collection contains only a single label, which is the label for the area series.

See Also   **DataLabel** Property.

Example   This example sets the data labels for series one in Chart1 to show their key, assuming that their values are showing when the example runs.

```
With Charts("Chart1").SeriesCollection(1)
    .HasDataLabels = True
    With .DataLabels
        .ShowLegendKey = True
        .Type = xlValue
    End With
End With
```

DataRange Property

Applies To   **PivotField** Object, **PivotItem** Object.

Description   Accessor. Returns a **Range** object as shown in the following table. Read-only.

Object	DataRange
Data field	Data contained in the field
Row, Column, or Page field	Items in the field
Item	Data qualified by the item

Example   This example selects the pivot items in the field named "REGION."

```
Set pvtTable = Worksheets("Sheet1").Range("A3").PivotTable
Worksheets("Sheet1").Activate
pvtTable.PivotFields("REGION").DataRange.Select
```

DataSeries Method

Applies To   **Range** Object.

Description   Creates a data series in the range.

Syntax	*object*.**DataSeries**(*rowcol*, *type*, *date*, *step*, *stop*, *trend*)

object
> Required. The range where the data series will be created.

rowcol
> Optional. Can be **xlRows** or **xlColumns** to enter the data series in rows or columns, respectively. If omitted, the size and shape of the range is used.

type
> Optional. Can be **xlLinear**, **xlGrowth**, **xlChronological**, or **xlAutoFill**. If omitted, it is **xlLinear**.

date
> Optional. If the *type* argument is **xlChronological**, this indicates the date unit by which to step, either **xlDay**, **xlWeekday**, **xlMonth**, or **xlYear**. If omitted, it is **xlDay**.

step
> Optional. The step value for the series. If omitted, it is assumed to be 1.

stop
> Optional. The stop value for the series. If omitted, the method fills to the end of the range.

trend
> Optional. If **True**, the method creates a linear or growth type of trend. If **False** or omitted, the method creates a standard data series.

Example   This example creates a series of 12 dates. The series contains the last day of every month in 1996 and is created in the range A1:A12 on Sheet1.

```
Set dateRange = Worksheets("Sheet1").Range("A1:A12")
Worksheets("Sheet1").Range("A1").Formula = "31-JAN-1996"
dateRange.DataSeries Type:=xlChronological, Date:=xlMonth
```

DataType Property

Applies To   **PivotField** Object.

Description   Returns a constant describing the type of data in the pivot field. Can be **xlText**, **xlNumber**, or **xlDate**. Read-only.

Example   This example displays the data type of the field named "ORDER_DATE."

```
Set pvtTable = Worksheets("Sheet1").Range("A3").PivotTable
Select Case pvtTable.PivotFields("ORDER_DATE").DataType
    Case Is = xlText
        MsgBox "The field contains text data"
    Case Is = xlNumber
        MsgBox "The field contains numeric data"
    Case Is = xlDate
        MsgBox "The field contains date data"
End Select
```

Date Data Type

Description   **Date** variables are stored as 64-bit (8-byte) numbers that represent dates ranging from 1 January 100 to 31 December 9999 and times from 0:00:00 to 23:59:59. Any recognizable literal date values can be assigned to **Date** variables. Literal dates must be enclosed within number sign characters (#). For example, `#January 1, 1993#` or `#1 Jan 93#`.

Date variables display dates according to the short date format recognized by your computer. Times display according to the time format (either 12- or 24-hour) recognized by your computer.

When other numeric data types are converted to **Date**, values to the left of the decimal represent date information while values to the right of the decimal represent time. Midnight is 0 and midday is .5. Negative whole numbers represent dates before 30 December 1899. When **Date** variables are converted to other numeric data types, they appear only as numbers.

See Also   **CDate** Function, Data Type Summary, **Def***type* Statements, **Double** Data Type, **Variant** Data Type.

Date Function

Description   Returns the current system date.

Syntax   **Date**

Remarks   To set the system date, use the **Date** statement.

See Also　CDate Function, **Date** Statement, **Format** Function, **Now** Function, **Time** Function, **Time** Statement.

Example　This example uses the **Date** function to return the current system date.

```
MyDate = Date                  ' MyDate contains current system date.
```

Date Statement

Description　Sets the current system date.

Syntax　**Date** = *date*

For MS-DOS computers, the *date* argument must be a date from January 1, 1980 through December 31, 2099, or an error occurs. For the Macintosh, *date* must be a date from January 1, 1904 through December 31, 2040. For all other systems, *date* is limited to dates from January 1, 100 through December 31, 9999.

Remarks

Note　If you use the **Date** statement to set the date on computers using versions of MS-DOS earlier than version 3.3, the change remains in effect only until you change it again or turn off your computer. Many computers have a battery-powered CMOS RAM that retains date and time information when the computer is turned off. However, to permanently change the date on computers running earlier versions of MS-DOS, you may have to use your Setup disk or perform some equivalent action. Refer to the documentation for your particular system.

See Also　**Date** Function, **Time** Function, **Time** Statement.

Example　This example uses the **Date** statement to set the computer system date.

```
' In the development environment, the date literal will display in short
' format using the locale settings of your code.
MyDate = #February 12, 1985#      ' Assign a date.
Date = MyDate                     ' Change system date.
```

Date1904 Property

Applies To　**Workbook** Object.

Description　True if this workbook uses the 1904 date system. Read-write.

Example   This example causes Microsoft Excel to use the 1904 date system for the active workbook.

```
ActiveWorkbook.Date1904 = True
```

DateSerial Function

Description   Returns a date for a specified year, month, and day.

Syntax   DateSerial(*year,month,day*)

The **DateSerial** function syntax has these named-argument parts:

Part	Description
year	Number between 100 and 9999, inclusive, or a numeric expression.
month	Number between 1 and 12, inclusive, or a numeric expression.
day	Number between 1 and 31, inclusive, or a numeric expression.

Remarks   To specify a date, such as December 31, 1991, the range of numbers for each **DateSerial** argument should be in the normally accepted range for the unit; that is; 1-31 for days and 1-12 for months. However, you can also specify relative dates for each argument using any numeric expression that represents some number of days, months, or years before or after a certain date.

The following example uses numeric expressions instead of absolute date numbers. Here the **DateSerial** function returns a date that is the day before the first day (1 - 1) of two months before August (8 - 2) of 10 years before 1990 (1990 - 10); in other words, May, 31, 1980.

```
DateSerial(1990 - 10, 8 - 2, 1 - 1)
```

For the *year* argument, values between 0 and 99, inclusive, are interpreted as the years 1900-1999. For all other *year* arguments, use a complete four-digit year (for example, 1800).

If the date specified by the three arguments, either directly or by expression, falls outside the acceptable range of dates, an error occurs.

See Also   **Date** Function, **Date** Statement, **DateValue** Function, **Day** Function, **Month** Function, **Now** Function, **TimeSerial** Function, **TimeValue** Function, **Weekday** Function, **Year** Function.

Example   This example uses the **DateSerial** function to return the date for the specified year, month and day.

```
' MyDate contains the date for February 12, 1969.
MyDate = DateSerial(1969, 2, 12)    ' Return a date.
```

DateValue Function

Description   Returns a date.

Syntax   **DateValue(*date*)**

The ***date*** named argument is normally a string expression representing a date from January 1, 100 through December 31, 9999. However, ***date*** can also be any expression that can represent a date, a time, or both a date and time, in that range.

Remarks   If the ***date*** argument includes time information, **DateValue** doesn't return it. However, if ***date*** includes invalid time information (such as "89:98"), an error occurs.

If ***date*** is a string that includes only numbers separated by valid date separators, **DateValue** recognizes the order for month, day, and year according to the Short Date format you specified for your system. **DateValue** also recognizes unambiguous dates that contain month names, either in long or abbreviated form. For example, in addition to recognizing 12/30/1991 and 12/30/91, **DateValue** also recognizes December 30, 1991 and Dec 30, 1991.

If the year part of ***date*** is omitted, **DateValue** uses the current year from your computer's system date.

See Also   **CDate** Function, **Date** Function, **Date** Statement, **DateSerial** Function, **Day** Function, **Month** Function, **Now** Function, **TimeSerial** Function, **TimeValue** Function, **Weekday** Function, **Year** Function.

Example   This example uses the **DateValue** function to convert a string to a date. In general, it is bad programming practice to hard code dates/times as strings as shown in this example. Use date literals instead.

```
MyDate = DateValue("February 12, 1969")    ' Return a date.
```

Day Function

Description   Returns a whole number between 1 and 31, inclusive, representing the day of the month.

Syntax   **Day**(*date*)

The *date* named argument is limited to a date or numbers and strings, in any combination, that can represent a date. If *date* contains no valid data, **Null** is returned.

See Also   **Date** Function, **Date** Statement, **Hour** Function, **Minute** Function, **Month** Function, **Now** Function, **Second** Function, **Weekday** Function, **Year** Function.

Example   This example uses the **Day** function to obtain the day of the month from a specified date.

```
' In the development environment, the date literal will display in short
' format using the locale settings of your code.
MyDate = #February 12, 1969#        ' Assign a date.
MyDay = Day(MyDate)                 ' MyDay contains 12.
```

DDEAppReturnCode Property

Applies To   **Application** Object.

Description   Returns the application-specific DDE return code that was contained in the last DDE acknowledge message received by Microsoft Excel. Read-only.

Example   This example sets the variable `appErrorCode` to the DDE return code.

```
appErrorCode = Application.DDEAppReturnCode
```

DDEExecute Method

Applies To   **Application** Object.

Description   Runs a command or takes other actions in another application via the specified DDE channel.

Syntax

object.**DDEExecute**(*channel*, *string*)

object

Optional. The **Application** object.

channel

Required. The channel number returned by the **DDEInitiate** method.

string

Required. The message defined in the receiving application.

Remarks

The **DDEExecute** method is designed to send commands to another application. You can also use it to send keystrokes to an application, although the **SendKeys** method is the preferred way to send keystrokes. The *string* argument can specify any single key; any key combined with ALT, CTRL, or SHIFT, or any combination of those keys (in Windows); or any key combined with COMMAND, CTRL, OPTION, or SHIFT or any combination of those keys (on the Macintosh). Each key is represented by one or more characters, such as "a" for the character a, or "{ENTER}" for the ENTER key.

To specify characters that aren't displayed when you press the key, such as ENTER or TAB, use the codes shown in the following table. Each code in the table represents one key on the keyboard.

Key	Code
BACKSPACE	"{BACKSPACE}" or "{BS}"
BREAK	"{BREAK}"
CAPS LOCK	"{CAPSLOCK}"
CLEAR	"{CLEAR}"
DELETE or DEL	"{DELETE}" or "{DEL}"
DOWN ARROW	"{DOWN}"
END	"{END}"
ENTER (numeric keypad)	"{ENTER}"
ENTER	"~" (tilde)
ESC	"{ESCAPE} or {ESC}"
HELP	"{HELP}"
HOME	"{HOME}"
INS	"{INSERT}"
LEFT ARROW	"{LEFT}"
NUM LOCK	"{NUMLOCK}"
PAGE DOWN	"{PGDN}"
PAGE UP	"{PGUP}"
RETURN	"{RETURN}"

Key	Code
RIGHT ARROW	"{RIGHT}"
SCROLL LOCK	"{SCROLLLOCK}"
TAB	"{TAB}"
UP ARROW	"{UP}"
F1 through F15	"{F1}" through "{F15}"

In Windows, you can also specify keys combined with SHIFT and/or CTRL and/or ALT. On the Macintosh, you can also specify keys combined with SHIFT and/or CTRL and/or OPTION and/or COMMAND. To specify a key combined with another key or keys, use the following table.

To combine with	Precede the key code by
SHIFT	"+" (plus sign)
CTRL	"^" (caret)
ALT or OPTION	"%" (percent sign)
COMMAND	"*" (asterisk)

Example

This example opens a channel to Word 6.0 for Windows, opens the Word document FORMLETR.DOC, and then sends the FilePrint command to WordBasic.

```
channelNumber = Application.DDEInitiate( _
    app:="WinWord", _
    topic:="C:\WINWORD\FORMLETR.DOC")
Application.DDEExecute channelNumber, "[FILEPRINT]"
Application.DDETerminate channelNumber
```

This example opens a channel to Word 6.0 for the Macintosh, opens the Word document Form Letter, and then sends the FilePrint command to WordBasic. On the Macintosh, you must use the **Shell** function to start Word, because the **DDEInitiate** method does not automatically start Word as it does in Windows. Also, because the **Shell** function is asynchronous, the macro may call the **DDEInitiate** method before Word has started. This example demonstrates how you can program around this by putting the **DDEInitiate** method call in a loop, testing channelNumber until it is no longer an error.

```
Shell "HD:Form Letter", 6
Do
    channelNumber = Application.DDEInitiate( _
        app:="MSWord", _
        topic:="HD:Form Letter")
Loop Until TypeName(channelNumber) <> "Error"
Application.DDEExecute channelNumber, "[FILEPRINT]"
Application.DDETerminate channelNumber
```

DDEInitiate Method

Applies To   **Application** Object.

Description   Opens a DDE channel to an application.

Syntax   *object*.**DDEInitiate**(*app*, *topic*)

object
Optional. The **Application** object.

app
Required. A string containing the application name.

topic
Required. A string that describes something in the application to which you are
opening a channel, usually a document of that application.

Remarks   If successful, the **DDEInitiate** method returns the number of the open channel. All
subsequent DDE functions use this number to specify the channel.

Example   This example opens a channel to Word 6.0 for Windows, opens the Word document
FORMLETR.DOC, and then sends the FilePrint command to WordBasic.

```
channelNumber = Application.DDEInitiate( _
    app:="WinWord", _
    topic:="C:\WINWORD\FORMLETR.DOC")
Application.DDEExecute channelNumber, "[FILEPRINT]"
Application.DDETerminate channelNumber
```

This example opens a channel to Word 6.0 for the Macintosh, opens the Word
document Form Letter, and then sends the FilePrint command to WordBasic. On the
Macintosh, you must use the **Shell** function to start Word, because the **DDEInitiate**
method does not automatically start Word as it does in Windows. Also, because the
Shell function is asynchronous, the macro may call the **DDEInitiate** method before
Word has started. This example demonstrates how you can program around this by
putting the **DDEInitiate** method call in a loop, testing channelNumber until it is
no longer an error.

```
Shell "HD:Form Letter", 6
Do
    channelNumber = Application.DDEInitiate( _
        app:="MSWord", _
        topic:="HD:Form Letter")
Loop Until TypeName(channelNumber) <> "Error"
Application.DDEExecute channelNumber, "[FILEPRINT]"
Application.DDETerminate channelNumber
```

DDEPoke Method

Applies To   **Application** Object.

Description   Sends data to an application.

Syntax   *object*.**DDEPoke**(*channel*, *item*, *data*)

object
    Optional. The **Application** object.

channel
    Required. The channel number returned by the **DDEInitiate** method.

item
    Required. The item to which the data is to be sent.

data
    Required. The data to send to the application.

Remarks   An error occurs if the method call is not successful.

Example   This example opens a channel to Word 6.0 for Windows, opens the Word document
                        SALES.DOC, and then inserts the contents of cell A1 (on Sheet1) at the beginning
                        of the document.

```
channelNumber = Application.DDEInitiate( _
    app:="WinWord", _
    topic:="C:\WINWORD\SALES.DOC")
Set rangeToPoke = Worksheets("Sheet1").Range("A1")
Application.DDEPoke channelNumber, "\StartOfDoc", rangeToPoke
Application.DDETerminate channelNumber
```

This example opens a channel to Word 6.0 for the Macintosh, opens the Word
document Sales Report, and then inserts the contents of cell A1 (on Sheet1) at the
beginning of the document. On the Macintosh, you must use the **Shell** function to
start Word, because the **DDEInitiate** method does not automatically start Word as
it does in Windows. Also, because the **Shell** function is asynchronous, the macro
may call the **DDEInitiate** method before Word has started. This example
demonstrates how you can program around this by putting the **DDEInitiate** method
call in a loop, testing channelNumber until it is no longer an error.

```
Shell "HD:Sales Report", 6
Do
    channelNumber = Application.DDEInitiate( _
        app:="WinWord", _
        topic:="HD:Sales Report")
Loop Until TypeName(channelNumber) <> "Error"
Set rangeToPoke = Worksheets("Sheet1").Range("A1")
Application.DDEPoke channelNumber, "\StartOfDoc", rangeToPoke
Application.DDETerminate channelNumber
```

DDERequest Method

Applies To   **Application** Object.

Description   Requests information from the specified application. This method always returns an
array; for more information, see the example.

Syntax   *object*.**DDERequest**(*channel*, *item*)

object
> Optional. The **Application** object.

channel
> Required. The channel number returned by the **DDEInitiate** method.

item
> Required. The item to request.

Example   This example opens a channel to the System topic in Word 6.0 for Windows and
then uses the Topics item to return a list of all open documents. The list is returned
in column A on Sheet1.

```
channelNumber = Application.DDEInitiate( _
    app:="WinWord", _
    topic:="System")
returnList = Application.DDERequest(channelNumber, "Topics")
For i = LBound(returnList) To UBound(returnList)
    Worksheets("Sheet1").Cells(i, 1).Formula = returnList(i)
Next i
Application.DDETerminate channelNumber
```

This example opens a channel to the System topic in Word 6.0 for the Macintosh
and then uses the Topics item to return a list of all open documents. The list is
returned in column A on Sheet1. On the Macintosh, you must use the **Shell** function
to start Word, because the **DDEInitiate** method does not automatically start Word
as it does in Windows. Also, because the **Shell** function is asynchronous, the macro
may call the **DDEInitiate** method before Word has started. This example
demonstrates how you can program around this by putting the **DDEInitiate** method
call in a loop, testing channelNumber until it is no longer an error.

```
Shell MacID("MSWD"), 6
Do
    channelNumber = Application.DDEInitiate( _
        app:="MSWord", _
        topic:="System")
Loop Until TypeName(channelNumber) <> "Error"
returnList = Application.DDERequest(channelNumber, "Topics")
For i = LBound(returnList) To UBound(returnList)
    Worksheets("Sheet1").Cells(i, 1).Formula = returnList(i)
Next i
Application.DDETerminate channelNumber
```

DDETerminate Method

Applies To   **Application** Object.

Description   Closes a channel to another application.

Syntax   *object*.**DDETerminate**(*channel*)

object
    Optional. The **Application** object.

channel
    Required. The channel number returned by the **DDEInitiate** method.

Example   This example opens a channel to Word 6.0 for Windows, opens the Word document
                        FORMLETR.DOC, and then sends the FilePrint command to WordBasic.

```
channelNumber = Application.DDEInitiate( _
    app:="WinWord", _
    topic:="C:\WINWORD\FORMLETR.DOC")
Application.DDEExecute channelNumber, "[FILEPRINT]"
Application.DDETerminate channelNumber
```

This example opens a channel to Word 6.0 for the Macintosh, opens the Word
document Form Letter, and then sends the FilePrint command to WordBasic. On the
Macintosh, you must use the **Shell** function to start Word, because the **DDEInitiate**
method does not automatically start Word as it does in Windows. Also, because the
Shell function is asynchronous, the macro may call the **DDEInitiate** method before
Word has started. This example demonstrates how you can program around this by
putting the **DDEInitiate** method call in a loop, testing channelNumber until it is
no longer an error.

```
Shell "HD:Form Letter", 6
Do
    channelNumber = Application.DDEInitiate( _
        app:="MSWord", _
        topic:="HD:Form Letter")
Loop Until TypeName(channelNumber) <> "Error"
Application.DDEExecute channelNumber, "[FILEPRINT]"
Application.DDETerminate channelNumber
```

Debug Object

Description   The **Debug** object is accessed with the keyword **Debug**, and is used to send output
                        to the Debug window at run time.

Methods   **Print** Method

Declare Statement

Description   Used at module level to declare references to external procedures in a dynamic-link
                    library (DLL) or Macintosh code resource.

Syntax 1   [**Public** | **Private**] **Declare Sub** *name* [**CDecl**] **Lib** *"libname"* [**Alias**
                    "aliasname"][([*arglist*])]

Syntax 2   [**Public** | **Private**] **Declare Function** *name* [**CDecl**] **Lib** *"libname"* [**Alias**
                    "aliasname"] [([*arglist*])][**As** *type*]

                    The **Declare** statement syntax has these parts:

Part	Description
Public	Used to declare procedures that are available to all other procedures in all modules.
Private	Used to declare procedures that are available only within the module where the declaration is made.
Sub	Indicates that the procedure doesn't return a value.
Function	Indicates that the procedure returns a value that can be used in an expression.
name	Any valid procedure name.
CDecl	For the Macintosh only. Indicates that the procedure uses C language argument order, naming conventions, and calling conventions.
Lib	Indicates that a DLL or code resource contains the procedure being declared. The **Lib** clause is required for all declarations.
libname	Name of the DLL or code resource that contains the declared procedure.
Alias	Indicates that the procedure being called has another name in the DLL or is in a Macintosh code resource. This is useful when the external procedure name is the same as a keyword. You can also use **Alias** when a DLL procedure has the same name as a **Public** variable or constant or any other procedure in the same scope. **Alias** is also useful if any characters in the DLL procedure name aren't allowed in names.

Part	Description
aliasname	Name of the procedure in the DLL or code resource.
	In Microsoft Windows, if the first character is not a #, *aliasname* is the name of the procedure's entry point in the DLL. If # is the first character, all characters that follow must indicate the ordinal number of the procedure's entry point.
	On the Macintosh, the syntax to specify the code resource type is as follows:
	"[*resourcetype*]$[*resourcename*]"
	The *resourcetype* is any valid 4-character constant. If omitted, the default *resourcetype* is CODE. The *resourcename* is the procedure name in the code resource. If *resourcename* is omitted, it is assumed to be the same as *name*.
arglist	List of variables representing arguments that are passed to the procedure when it is called.
type	Data type of the value returned by a **Function** procedure; may be **Boolean**, **Integer**, **Long**, **Currency**, **Single**, **Double**, **Date**, **String** (variable length only), **Object**, **Variant**, a user-defined type, or an object type.

The *arglist* argument has the following syntax and parts:

[Optional][ByVal | ByRef][ParamArray] *varname*[( )][**As** *type*]

Part	Description
Optional	Indicates that an argument is not required. If used, all subsequent arguments in *arglist* must also be optional and declared using the **Optional** keyword. All **Optional** arguments must be **Variant**. **Optional** can't be used for any argument if **ParamArray** is used.
ByVal	Indicates that the argument is passed by value.
ByRef	Indicates that the argument is passed by reference.
ParamArray	Used only as the last argument in *arglist* to indicate that the final argument is an **Optional** array of **Variant** elements. The **ParamArray** keyword allows you to provide an arbitrary number of arguments. May not be used with **ByVal**, **ByRef**, or **Optional**.
varname	Name of the variable representing the argument being passed to the procedure; follows standard variable naming conventions.
type	Data type of the argument passed to the procedure; may be **Boolean**, **Integer**, **Long**, **Currency**, **Single**, **Double**, **Date**, **String** (variable length only), **Object**, **Variant**, a user-defined type, or an object type.

Remarks

For **Function** procedures, the data type of the procedure determines the data type it returns. You can use an **As** clause following the *arglist* to specify the return type of the function. Within *arglist* you can use an **As** clause to specify the data type of any of the arguments passed to the procedure. In addition to specifying any of the standard data types, you can specify **As Any** in the *arglist* to inhibit type checking and allow any data type to be passed to the procedure.

Empty parentheses indicate that the **Sub** or **Function** procedure has no arguments and that arguments should be checked to ensure that none are passed. In the following example, First takes no arguments. If you use arguments in a call to First, an error occurs:

```
Declare Sub First Lib "MyLib" ()
```

If you include an argument list, the number and type of arguments are checked each time the procedure is called. In the following example, First takes one **Long** argument:

```
Declare Sub First Lib "MyLib" (X As Long)
```

Note You can't have fixed-length strings in the argument list of a **Declare** statement because only variable-length strings can be passed to procedures. Fixed-length strings can appear as procedure arguments, but they are converted to variable-length strings before being passed.

See Also

Call Statement.

Example

This example shows how the **Declare** statement is used at the module level to declare a reference to an external procedure in a dynamic-link library (DLL) or Macintosh code resource.

```
' In Microsoft Windows.
Declare Sub MessageBeep Lib "User" (ByVal N As Integer)

' On the Macintosh.
Declare Sub MessageAlert Lib "MyHd:MyAlert" Alias "MyAlert" (ByVal N _
As Integer)
```

DefaultButton Property

Applies To

Button Object, **Buttons** Collection, **DialogSheet** Object, **DrawingObjects** Collection.

Description	For **Button** objects, this property is **True** if the button is the default button for a user-defined dialog box. When the user presses the ENTER key, the default button is selected, and Microsoft Excel runs the macro identified by the button's **OnAction** property. Applies only to buttons on a dialog sheet. Read-write.

For **DialogSheet** objects, this property is the name of the button that is the default button while a dialog box is running. Read-write.

Remarks	When the dialog box is not displayed, this property can be used with the **Button** object to return or set the initial default button (the default button when the dialog is first displayed). Only one button on the dialog box can be the default button. Setting this property resets the property for all other buttons on the dialog sheet.

While the dialog box is running, use this property in an event procedure to return or set the current default button. In this case, the property is the button ID as a string, and the property is applied to the **DialogSheet** object. You cannot apply this property to a **Button** object while the dialog box is running.

See Also	**CancelButton** Property.

Example	This example sets button four to be the initial default button for Dialog1. You can only set the initial default button when the dialog box is not running.

```
DialogSheets("Dialog1").Buttons(4).DefaultButton = True
```

This example sets button five to be the current default button on Dialog1. You can only set the current default button while the dialog box is running (which means that this example must be in an event procedure for another control on Dialog1).

```
With DialogSheets("Dialog1")
    .DefaultButton = .Buttons(5).Name
End With
```

DefaultFilePath Property

Applies To	**Application** Object.

Description	Returns or sets the default path Microsoft Excel uses when it opens files. Read-write.

Example	This example displays the current default file path.

```
MsgBox "The current default file path is " & _
    Application.DefaultFilePath
```

Def*type* Statements

Description   Used at module level to set the default data type for variables and **Function** procedures whose names start with the specified characters.

Syntax   **DefBool** *letterrange*[,*letterrange*] . . .

DefInt *letterrange*[,*letterrange*] . . .

DefLng *letterrange*[,*letterrange*] . . .

DefCur *letterrange*[,*letterrange*] . . .

DefSng *letterrange*[,*letterrange*] . . .

DefDbl *letterrange*[,*letterrange*] . . .

DefDate *letterrange*[,*letterrange*] . . .

DefStr *letterrange*[,*letterrange*] . . .

DefObj *letterrange*[,*letterrange*] . . .

DefVar *letterrange*[,*letterrange*] . . .

The argument *letterrange* has the following syntax:

letter1[-*letter2*]

The arguments letter1 and letter2 specify the name range for which you can set a default data type. Each argument represents the first letter of the variable or **Function** procedure name and can be any letter of the alphabet. The case of letters in letterrange isn't significant.

Remarks   The statement name determines the data type:

Statement	Data Type
DefBool	**Boolean**
DefInt	**Integer**
DefLng	**Long**
DefCur	**Currency**
DefSng	**Single**
DefDbl	**Double**
DefDate	**Date**
DefStr	**String**
DefObj	**Object**
DefVar	**Variant**

For example, in the following program fragment, `Message` is a string variable:

```
DefStr A-Q
. . .
Message = "Out of stack space."
```

A **Def***type* statement affects only the module where it is used. For example, a **DefInt** statement in one module affects only the default data type of variables and **Function** procedures declared in that module; the default data type of variables in other modules is unaffected. If not explicitly declared with a **Def***type* statement, the default data type for all variables and all **Function** procedures is **Variant**.

When you specify a letter range, it usually defines the data type for variables that begin with letters in the lower 128 characters of the character set. However, when you specify the letter range A-Z, you set the default to the specified data type for all variables, including any that begin with international characters from the extended part of the character set (128-255).

Once the range A-Z has been specified, you can't further redefine any subranges of variables using **Def***type* statements. In fact, once a range has been specified, if you include a previously defined letter in another **Def***type* statement, an error occurs. However, you can explicitly specify the data type of any variable, defined or not, using a **Dim** statement with an **As** *type* clause. For example, you can use the following code at module level to define a variable as a **Double** even though the default data type is **Integer**:

```
DefInt A-Z
Dim TaxRate As Double
```

Def*type* statements don't affect elements of user-defined types since they must be explicitly declared.

See Also   **Let** Statement.

Example   This example shows various uses of the **Def***type* statements to set default data types of variables and function procedures whose names start with specified characters. The default data type can be overridden only by explicit assignment using the **Dim** statement. **Def***type* statements can only be used at the module-level.

```
' Variable names beginning with A through K default to Integer.
DefInt A-K
' Variable names beginning with L through Z default to String.
DefStr L-Z
CalcVar = 4                    ' Initialize Integer.
StringVar = "Hello there"      ' Initialize String.
AnyVar = "Hello"               ' Causes "Type mismatch" error.
Dim Calc As Double             ' Explicitly set the type to Double.
Calc = 2.3455                  ' Assign a Double.
```

```
' Deftype statements also apply to function procedures.
CalcNum = ATestFunction(4)          ' Call user-defined function.

' ATestFunction function procedure definition.
Function ATestFunction(INumber)
    ATestFunction = INumber * 2      ' Return value is an integer.
End Function
```

Delete Method

Applies To   **Arc** Object, **Arcs** Collection, **Axis** Object, **AxisTitle** Object, **Button** Object, **Buttons** Collection, **Characters** Object, **Chart** Object, **ChartObject** Object, **ChartObjects** Collection, **Charts** Collection, **ChartTitle** Object, **CheckBox** Object, **DataLabel** Object, **DataLabels** Collection, **DialogSheet** Object, **DialogSheets** Collection, **DownBars** Object, **Drawing** Object, **DrawingObjects** Collection, **Drawings** Collection, **DropDown** Object, **DropDowns** Collection, **DropLines** Object, **EditBox** Object, **EditBoxes** Collection, **ErrorBars** Object, **Gridlines** Object, **GroupBox** Object, **GroupBoxes** Collection, **GroupObject** Object, **GroupObjects** Collection, **HiLoLines** Object, **Label** Object, **Labels** Collection, **Legend** Object, **LegendEntry** Object, **LegendKey** Object, **Line** Object, **Lines** Collection, **ListBox** Object, **ListBoxes** Collection, **Menu** Object, **MenuBar** Object, **MenuItem** Object, **Module** Object, **Modules** Collection, **Name** Object, **OLEObject** Object, **OLEObjects** Collection, **OptionButton** Object, **OptionButtons** Collection, **Oval** Object, **Ovals** Collection, **Picture** Object, **Pictures** Collection, **Point** Object, **Range** Object, **Rectangle** Object, **Rectangles** Collection, **Scenario** Object, **ScrollBar** Object, **ScrollBars** Collection, **Series** Object, **SeriesLines** Object, **Sheets** Collection, **SoundNote** Object, **Spinner** Object, **Spinners** Collection, **Style** Object, **TextBox** Object, **TextBoxes** Collection, **TickLabels** Object, **Toolbar** Object, **ToolbarButton** Object, **Trendline** Object, **UpBars** Object, **Worksheet** Object, **Worksheets** Collection.

Description   Deletes the object. Syntax 2 applies only to **Range** objects.

Syntax 1   *object*.Delete

Syntax 2   *object*.**Delete**(*shift*)

object
   Required. The object to which this method applies. Syntax 2 applies only to **Range** objects.

shift
> Optional. Specifies how to shift cells to replace the deleted cells (either **xlToLeft**, or **xlUp**). If this argument is omitted, Microsoft Excel selects a default based on the shape of the range.

Remarks

Attempts to delete a built-in **Toolbar** or **MenuBar** object will fail, but will not cause an error. This allows you to use a **For Each** loop to delete all custom tool bars or menu bars.

Deleting a **Point** or **LegendKey** deletes the entire series.

You can delete custom document properties, but you cannot delete a built-in document property.

Example

This example deletes cells A1:D10 on Sheet1, and shifts remaining cells to the left.

```
Worksheets("Sheet1").Range("A1:D10").Delete shift:=xlToLeft
```

This example deletes oval one on Sheet1.

```
Worksheets("Sheet1").Ovals(1).Delete
```

This example deletes all graphic objects and controls (check boxes, buttons, and so on) on Sheet1.

```
Worksheets("Sheet1").DrawingObjects.Delete
```

This example deletes every worksheet in the active workbook without displaying the confirmation dialog box.

```
Application.DisplayAlerts = False
For Each w In Worksheets
    w.Delete
Next w
Application.DisplayAlerts = True
```

This example sorts the data in the first column on Sheet1 and then deletes rows that contain duplicate data.

```
Worksheets("Sheet1").Range("A1").Sort _
        key1:=Worksheets("Sheet1").Range("A1")
Set currentCell = Worksheets("Sheet1").Range("A1")
Do While Not IsEmpty(currentCell)
    Set nextCell = currentCell.Offset(1, 0)
    If nextCell.Value = currentCell.Value Then
        currentCell.EntireRow.Delete
    End If
    Set currentCell = nextCell
Loop
```

Delete Method (DocumentProperty Object)

Applies To	**DocumentProperty** Object.
Description	Deletes a custom document property (you cannot delete a built-in document property).
	To use this method, you should establish a reference to the Microsoft Office 95 Object Library by using the References command (Tools menu).
Example	This example deletes a custom document property. You must pass a **DocumentProperty** object to the procedure.

```
Sub DeleteCustomDocumentProperty(dp As DocumentProperty)
    dp.Delete
End Sub
```

This example deletes the "Total Sales" custom document property

```
ActiveWorkbook.CustomDocumentProperties("Total Sales").Delete
```

DeleteChartAutoFormat Method

Applies To	**Application** Object.
Description	Removes a custom chart autoformat from the list of available chart autoformats.
Syntax	*object*.**DeleteChartAutoFormat(*name*)**
	object Required. The **Application** object.
	name Required. Specifies the name of the custom autoformat to remove.
See Also	**AddChartAutoFormat** Method, **SetDefaultChart** Method.
Example	This example deletes the custom autoformat named "Presentation Chart".

```
Application.DeleteChartAutoFormat name:="Presentation Chart"
```

DeleteCustomList Method

Applies To   **Application** Object.

Description   Deletes a custom list.

Syntax   *object*.**DeleteCustomList**(*listNum*)

                        object
                        Required. The **Application** object.

                        listNum
                        Required. The custom list number. This number must be greater than or equal to five (Microsoft Excel has four built-in custom lists that cannot be deleted).

Remarks   This method generates an error if the list number is less than five or a matching custom list does not exist.

See Also   **AddCustomList** Method, **CustomListCount** Property, **GetCustomListContents** Method, **GetCustomListNum** Method.

Example   This example deletes a custom list.

```
n = Application.GetCustomListNum(Array("cogs", "sprockets", _
    "widgets", "gizmos"))
Application.DeleteCustomList n
```

DeleteNumberFormat Method

Applies To   **Workbook** Object.

Description   Deletes a custom number format from the workbook.

Syntax   *object*.**DeleteNumberFormat**(*numberFormat*)

                        object
                        Required. The **Workbook** object.

                        numberFormat
                        Required. A string that names the number format to delete.

Example   This example deletes the number format "000-00-0000" from the active workbook.

```
ActiveWorkbook.DeleteNumberFormat("000-00-0000")
```

DeleteReplacement Method

Applies To   **AutoCorrect** Object.

Description   Deletes an entry from the array of AutoCorrect replacements. This method is available only in Microsoft Excel for Windows 95.

Syntax   *object*.**DeleteReplacement(***what***)**

object
    Required. The **AutoCorrect** object.

what
    Required. A string specifying the text to be replaced, as it appears in the row to be deleted from the array of AutoCorrect replacements. If this string doesn't exist in the array of AutoCorrect replacements, the method fails.

See Also   **AddReplacement** Method, **ReplacementList** Property.

Example   This example removes the word "Temperature" from the array of AutoCorrect replacements.

```
With Application.AutoCorrect
    .DeleteReplacement "Temperature"
End With
```

Delivery Property

Applies To   **RoutingSlip** Object.

Description   Returns or sets the delivery method used when routing (one of **xlOneAfterAnother** or **xlAllAtOnce**). Read-write before routing starts, read-only once routing is in progress.

Example   This example sends BOOK1.XLS to three recipients, one after the other.

```
Workbooks("BOOK1.XLS").HasRoutingSlip = True
With Workbooks("BOOK1.XLS").RoutingSlip
    .Delivery = xlOneAfterAnother
    .Recipients = Array("Adam Bendel", "Jean Selva", "Bernard Gabor")
    .Subject = "Here is BOOK1.XLS"
    .Message = "Here is the workbook. What do you think?"
End With
Workbooks("BOOK1.XLS").Route
```

Dependents Property

Applies To   **Range** Object.

Description   Accessor. Returns a **Range** object that represents the range that contains all of the dependents of a cell. This may be a multiple selection (a union of **Range** objects) if there is more than one dependent. Read-only.

See Also   **DirectDependents** Property, **DirectPrecedents** Property, **Precedents** Property, **ShowDependents** Method.

Example   This example selects the dependents of cell A1 on Sheet1.

```
Worksheets("Sheet1").Activate
Range("A1").Dependents.Select
```

DepthPercent Property

Applies To   **Chart** Object.

Description   Returns or sets the depth of a 3-D chart as a percentage of the chart width (between 20 and 2000 percent). Read-write.

See Also   **HeightPercent** Property.

Example   This example sets the chart depth of Chart1 to be 50 percent of its width. The example should be run on a 3-D chart.

```
Charts("Chart1").DepthPercent = 50
```

Derived Math Functions

The following is a list of nonintrinsic math functions that can be derived from the intrinsic math functions:

Function	Derived equivalents
Secant	Sec(X) = 1 / Cos(X)
Cosecant	Cosec(X) = 1 / Sin(X)
Cotangent	Cotan((X) = 1 / Tan(X)
Inverse Sine	Arcsin(X) = Atn(X / Sqr(-X * X + 1))

Function	Derived equivalents
Inverse Cosine	Arccos(X) = Atn(-X / Sqr(-X * X + 1)) + 1.5708
Inverse Secant	Arcsec(X) = Atn(X / Sqr(X * X - 1)) + Sgn((X) -1) * 1.5708
Inverse Cosecant	Arccosec(X) = Atn(X / Sqr(X * X - 1)) + (Sgn(X) - 1) * 1.5708
Inverse Cotangent	Arccotan(X) = Atn(X) + 1.5708
Hyperbolic Sine	HSin(X) = (Exp(X) - Exp(-X)) / 2
Hyperbolic Cosine	HCos(X) = (Exp(X) + Exp(-X)) / 2
Hyperbolic Tangent	HTan(X) = (Exp(X) - Exp(-X)) / (Exp(X) + Exp(-X))
Hyperbolic Secant	HSec(X) = 2 / (Exp(X) + Exp(-X))
Hyperbolic Cosecant	HCosec(X) = 2 / (Exp(X) - Exp(-X))
Hyperbolic Cotangent	HCotan(X) = (Exp(X) + Exp(-X)) / (Exp(X) - Exp(-X))
Inverse Hyperbolic Sine	HArcsin(X) = Log(X + Sqr(X * X + 1))
Inverse Hyperbolic Cosine	HArccos(X) = Log(X + Sqr(X * X - 1))
Inverse Hyperbolic Tangent	HArctan(X) = Log((1 + X) / (1 - X)) / 2
Inverse Hyperbolic Secant	HArcsec(X) = Log((Sqr(-X * X + 1) + 1) / X)
Inverse Hyperbolic Cosecant	HArccosec(X) = Log((Sgn(X) * Sqr(X * X + 1) +1) / X)
Inverse Hyperbolic Cotangent	HArccotan(X) = Log((X + 1) / (X - 1)) / 2
Logarithm to base N	LogN(X) = Log(X) / Log(N)

See Also   **Atn** Function, **Cos** Function, **Exp** Function, **Log** Function, **Sin** Function, **Sqr** Function, **Tan** Function.

Deselect Method

Applies To   **Chart** Object.

Description   Cancels the selection for the specified chart.

Syntax   *object*.**Deselect**

object
    Required. The **Chart** object.

See Also   **Select** Method, **Selection** Property.

Example   This example is equivalent to pressing ESC in the active chart. The example should be run on a chart that has a component (such as an axis) selected.

```
ActiveChart.Deselect
```

Dialog Object

Description   Represents a built-in Microsoft Excel dialog box. The only useful thing you can do with a **Dialog** object is use it with the **Show** method to display the dialog box. Do not confuse the **Dialog** object with the **DialogSheet** object, which represents a custom dialog sheet, or the **DialogFrame** object, which represents the boundaries of the custom dialog box on a dialog sheet.

Accessors   The **Dialog** object is a member of the **Dialogs** collection. The **Dialogs** collection contains all Microsoft Excel built-in dialog boxes. You cannot create a new built-in dialog box or add one to the collection.

To access a single member of the collection, use the **Dialogs** method with an argument. The following example runs the built-in File Open dialog box. The **Show** method returns **True** if Microsoft Excel successfully opens a file, or **False** if the user cancels the dialog box.

```
dlgAnswer = Application.Dialogs(xlDialogOpen).Show
```

The Microsoft Excel Visual Basic object library includes built-in constants for many of the built-in dialog boxes. Each constant is formed from the prefix "xlDialog" followed by the name of the dialog box. For example, the Apply Names dialog box constant is **xlDialogApplyNames**, and the Find File dialog box constant is **xlDialogFindFile**. To see a list of the available constants using the Object Browser, select the Constants module in the Excel library, and scroll down the Methods/Properties list until you see the constants beginning with "xlDialog."

Properties   **Application** Property, **Creator** Property, **Parent** Property.

Methods   **Show** Method.

DialogBox Method

Applies To   **Range** Object.

Description   Displays a dialog box defined by a dialog-box definition table on a Microsoft Excel version 4.0 macro sheet. Returns the number of the chosen control, or **False** if the user chooses the Cancel button.

Syntax   *object*.**DialogBox**

object
    Required. A range on a Microsoft Excel 4.0 macro sheet that contains a dialog-box definition table.

Remarks   This method is included for backward compatibility with the Microsoft Excel version 4.0 macro language.

Example   This example runs a Microsoft Excel version 4.0 dialog box and then displays the return value in a message box. The `dialogRange` variable refers to the dialog box definition table on the Microsoft Excel version 4.0 macro sheet Macro1.

```
Set dialogRange = Excel4MacroSheets("Macro1").Range("myDialogBox")
result = dialogRange.DialogBox
MsgBox result
```

DialogFrame Object

Description   Represents the dialog frame. The dialog frame provides the backdrop for user-defined dialog boxes. It has no formatting properties, only a position, a size, and a caption. Only one dialog frame exists per dialog sheet, and it cannot be deleted or moved in front of any other graphic object. Dialog frames do not exist on worksheets.

Accessors   The **DialogFrame** property returns the dialog frame for the dialog sheet. The following example adds a new check box to the dialog sheet named "Dialog1." The new check box is positioned relative to the upper-left corner of the dialog frame.

```
Dim df as DialogFrame
DialogSheets("dialog1").Activate
Set df = ActiveSheet.DialogFrame
ActiveSheet.CheckBoxes.Add df.Left + 10, df.Top + 10, 100, 10
```

Remarks   When a dialog sheet is first shown, Microsoft Excel runs any procedure assigned to the **OnAction** property for the dialog frame.

The position of the dialog frame on the dialog sheet does not affect where the custom dialog is positioned when it is shown in a modal window. There is no way to set a custom position for the running dialog frame.

Properties	**Application** Property, **Caption** Property, **Creator** Property, **Height** Property, **Left** Property, **Locked** Property, **LockedText** Property, **Name** Property, **OnAction** Property, **Parent** Property, **Text** Property, **Top** Property, **Width** Property.
Methods	**Characters** Method, **CheckSpelling** Method, **CopyPicture** Method, **Select** Method.

DialogFrame Property

Applies To	**DialogSheet** Object.
Description	Accessor. Returns a **DialogFrame** object that represents the dialog frame on the specified dialog sheet. Read only.
Example	This example sets the height and width of the dialog box frame for Dialog1.

```
With DialogSheets("Dialog1").DialogFrame
    .Height = 144
    .Width = 196
End With
```

Dialogs Collection Object

Description	A collection of all the **Dialog** objects in the Microsoft Excel application. Each **Dialog** object represents a built-in Microsoft Excel dialog box. The only useful thing you can do with a **Dialog** object is use it with the **Show** method to display the dialog box. Do not confuse the **Dialog** object with the **DialogSheet** object, which represents a custom dialog sheet, or the **DialogFrame** object, which represents the boundaries of the custom dialog box on a dialog sheet. The **Dialogs** collection contains all Microsoft Excel built-in dialog boxes. You cannot create a new built-in dialog box or add one to the collection.
Accessors	Use the **Dialogs** method with an argument to access a single member of the collection or without an argument to access the entire collection at once. The Microsoft Excel Visual Basic object library includes built-in constants for many of the built-in dialog boxes. Each constant is formed from the prefix "xlDialog" followed by the name of the dialog box. For example, the Apply Names dialog box constant is **xlDialogApplyNames**, and the Find File dialog box constant is **xlDialogFindFile**. To see a list of the available constants using the Object Browser, select the Constants module in the Excel library, and scroll down the Methods/Properties list until you see the constants beginning with "xlDialog."

The following example runs the built-in File Open dialog box. The **Show** method returns **True** if Microsoft Excel successfully opens a file, or **False** if the user cancels the dialog box.

```
dlgAnswer = Application.Dialogs(xlDialogOpen).Show
```

Properties   **Application** Property, **Count** Property, **Creator** Property, **Parent** Property.

Methods   **Item** Method.

Dialogs Method

Applies To   **Application** Object.

Description   Accessor. Returns an object that represents a single built-in dialog (a **Dialog** object, Syntax 1) or a collection of all built-in dialogs (a **Dialogs** object, Syntax 2). Read-only.

Syntax 1   *object*.**Dialogs(***index***)**

Syntax 2   *object*.**Dialogs**

object
     Required. The **Application** object.

index
     Required for Syntax 1. A built-in constant. See the following Remarks section for more information.

Remarks   Using the **Dialogs** and **Show** methods, you can display approximately 200 built-in dialog boxes. Each dialog box has a constant assigned to it; these constants all begin with "xlDialog."

For a table of the available constants and their corresponding argument lists, see "Built-In Dialog Box Argument Lists" in online help.

You can also use the Object Browser to browse the list of dialog box constants. On the View menu, click Object Browser. In the Object Browser, select the Microsoft Excel library, and then select the Constants object. Scroll through the list in the Methods/Properties box until you find the constants that begin with "xlDialog." The constants correspond to dialog box names; for example, the constant for the Find File dialog box is **xlDialogFindFile**.

The **Dialogs** method may fail if you try to show a dialog box in an incorrect context. For example, to display the Format Data Labels dialog box (using the Visual Basic expression `Application.Dialogs(xlDialogDataLabel).Show`), the active sheet must be a chart, otherwise the method fails.

See Also   **Show** Method.

Example   This example displays the dialog box for the Open command on the File menu.

```
Application.Dialogs(xlDialogOpen).Show
```

DialogSheet Object

Description   Represents a single dialog sheet in a workbook. Do not confuse a dialog sheet with the **Dialog** object, which represents a built-in Microsoft Excel dialog box, or the **DialogFrame** object, which represents the boundaries of the custom dialog box on a dialog sheet.

Accessors   The **DialogSheet** object is a member of the **DialogSheets** collection. The **DialogSheets** collection contains all the **DialogSheet** objects in a workbook. Use the **Add** method to create a new dialog sheet and add it to the collection. To access a single member of the collection, use the **DialogSheets** method with the index number or name of the dialog sheet as an argument.

The dialog sheet index number represents the position of the dialog sheet on the tab bar of the workbook. DialogSheets(1) is the first (leftmost) dialog sheet in the workbook; DialogSheets(DialogSheets.Count) is the last. All dialog sheets are included in the index count, even if they are hidden. The following example runs dialog sheet one in the active workbook.

```
DialogSheets(1).Show
```

The dialog sheet name is shown on the workbook tab for the dialog sheet. Use the **Name** property to set or return the dialog sheet name. The following example runs the dialog sheet named "Test Dialog."

```
DialogSheets("test dialog").Show
```

The **DialogSheet** object is also a member of the **Sheets** collection. The **Sheets** collection contains all of the sheets in the workbook (chart sheets, dialog sheets, modules, and worksheets). To access a single member of the collection, use the **Sheets** method with the index number or name of the sheet as an argument.

DialogSheets in Add-Ins

When you write code in an add-in to display a dialog sheet that is also contained in the add-in, you must use the **ThisWorkbook** property to return a reference to the add-in workbook. You cannot use **ActiveWorkbook**, and you cannot use **Workbooks("***workbook name***")**. This can be confusing, because all three of these methods will work until you create an add-in from your workbook. Once your code is running in an add-in, however, only **ThisWorkbook** (which returns the workbook where the code is running) can be used to access to add-in workbook.

The following example displays the dialog sheet named "Add-In Dialog" in the running workbook.

```
ThisWorkbook.DialogSheets("add-in dialog").Show
```

Using ActiveSheet

When a dialog sheet is the active sheet, you can use the **ActiveSheet** property to refer to it. The following example uses the **Activate** method to activate dialog sheet one and then runs the dialog sheet.

```
DialogSheets(1).Activate
ActiveSheet.Show
```

Note that after the example activates the dialog sheet, it uses the **ActiveSheet** property, not the **ActiveDialog** property, to return the active dialog sheet. The **ActiveSheet** property returns the active sheet in the workbook, while the **ActiveDialog** property returns the topmost *running* dialog sheet in the workbook. In this example, the dialog sheet is not running and cannot be accessed with the **ActiveDialog** property.

Properties

Application Property, **Creator** Property, **DefaultButton** Property, **DialogFrame** Property, **DisplayAutomaticPageBreaks** Property, **Focus** Property, **Index** Property, **Name** Property, **Next** Property, **OnDoubleClick** Property, **OnSheetActivate** Property, **OnSheetDeactivate** Property, **PageSetup** Property, **Parent** Property, **Previous** Property, **ProtectContents** Property, **ProtectDrawingObjects** Property, **Visible** Property.

Methods   **Activate** Method, **Arcs** Method, **Buttons** Method, **ChartObjects** Method, **CheckBoxes** Method, **CheckSpelling** Method, **Copy** Method, **Delete** Method, **DrawingObjects** Method, **Drawings** Method, **DropDowns** Method, **EditBoxes** Method, **Evaluate** Method, **GroupBoxes** Method, **GroupObjects** Method, **Hide** Method, **Labels** Method, **Lines** Method, **ListBoxes** Method, **Move** Method, **OLEObjects** Method, **OptionButtons** Method, **Ovals** Method, **Paste** Method **(DialogSheet or Worksheet Object)**, **PasteSpecial** Method **(DialogSheet or Worksheet Object)**, **Pictures** Method, **PrintOut** Method, **PrintPreview** Method, **Protect** Method, **Rectangles** Method, **SaveAs** Method, **ScrollBars** Method, **Select** Method, **Show** Method, **Spinners** Method, **TextBoxes** Method, **Unprotect** Method.

DialogSheets Collection Object

Description   A collection of all the **DialogSheet** objects in the specified or active workbook. Do not confuse a dialog sheet with the **Dialog** object, which represents a built-in Microsoft Excel dialog box, or the **DialogFrame** object, which represents the boundaries of the custom dialog box on a dialog sheet.

Accessors   Use the **Add** method to create a new dialog sheet and add it to the workbook. The following example adds a new dialog sheet before sheet one in the active workbook.

```
DialogSheets.Add before:=Sheets(1)
```

Use the **DialogSheets** method with an argument to access a single member of the collection or without an argument to access the entire collection at once. The following example moves all the dialog sheets in the active workbook to the end of the workbook.

```
DialogSheets.Move after:=Sheets(Sheets.Count)
```

The **Sheets** collection contains all of the sheets in the workbook (chart sheets, dialog sheets, modules, and worksheets). Use the **Sheets** method with an argument to access a single member of the collection or without an argument to access the entire collection at once.

Properties   **Application** Property, **Count** Property, **Creator** Property, **Parent** Property, **Visible** Property.

Methods   **Add** Method (DialogSheets Collection), **Copy** Method, **Delete** Method, **Item** Method, **Move** Method, **PrintOut** Method, **PrintPreview** Method, **Select** Method.

See Also   **Charts** Collection, **Modules** Collection, **Sheets** Method, **Worksheets** Collection.

DialogSheets Method

Applies To	**Application** Object, **Workbook** Object.
Description	Accessor. Returns an object that represents a single dialog sheet (a **DialogSheet** object, Syntax 1) or a collection of all dialog sheets (a **DialogSheets** object, Syntax 2) in the workbook. Read-only.
Syntax 1	*object*.**DialogSheets(***index***)**
Syntax 2	*object*.**DialogSheets**

object
> Optional for **Application**, required for **Workbook**. The object that contains dialog sheets.

index
> Required for Syntax 1. The name or number of the dialog sheet to return.

Remarks	Using this method with no object qualifier is a shortcut for **ActiveWorkbook.DialogSheets**.
Example	This example displays the custom dialog box on Dialog1. The loop causes the dialog box to be displayed again if you click the Cancel button.

```
Do
    returnVal = DialogSheets("Dialog1").Show
Loop Until returnVal = True
```

Dim Statement

Description	Declares variables and allocates storage space.
Syntax	**Dim** *varname*[([*subscripts*])][**As** *type*][,*varname*[([*subscripts*])][**As** *type*]] . . .

The **Dim** statement syntax has these parts:

Part	Description
varname	Name of the variable; follows standard variable naming conventions.
subscripts	Dimensions of an array variable; up to 60 multiple dimensions may be declared. The *subscripts* argument uses the following syntax: [*lower* **To**] *upper* [,[*lower* **To**] *upper*] . . .
type	Data type of the variable; may be **Boolean**, **Integer**, **Long**, **Currency**, **Single**, **Double**, **Date**, **String** (for variable-length strings), **String** * *length* (for fixed-length strings), **Object**, **Variant**, a user-defined type, or an object type. Use a separate **As** *type* clause for each variable you declare.

Remarks   Variables declared with **Dim** at the module level are available to all procedures within the module. At the procedure level, variables are available only within the procedure.

Use the **Dim** statement at module or procedure level to declare the data type or object type of a variable. For example, the following statement declares a variable as an **Integer**.

```
Dim NumberOfEmployees As Integer
```

If you do not specify a data type or object type, and there is no **Def***type* statement in the module, the variable is **Variant** by default.

When variables are initialized, a numeric variable is initialized to 0, a variable-length string is initialized to a zero-length string, and a fixed-length string is filled with zeros. **Variant** variables are initialized to **Empty**. Each element of a user-defined type variable is initialized as if it was a separate variable. A variable that refers to an object must be assigned an existing object using the **Set** statement before it can be used. Until it is assigned an object, the declared object variable has the special value **Nothing**, which indicates that it does not refer to any particular instance of an object.

You can also use the **Dim** statement with empty parentheses to declare dynamic arrays. After declaring a dynamic array, use the **ReDim** statement within a procedure to define the number of dimensions and elements in the array. If you try to redeclare a dimension for an array variable whose size was explicitly specified in a **Private**, **Public** or **Dim** statement, an error occurs.

Tip   When you use the **Dim** statement in a procedure, it is a generally accepted programming practice to put the **Dim** statement at the beginning of the procedure.

See Also   **Array** Function, **Option Base** Statement, **Private** Statement, **Public** Statement, **ReDim** Statement, **Set** Statement, **Static** Statement, **Type** Statement.

Example

This example shows various uses of the **Dim** statement to declare variables. The **Dim** statement is also used to declare arrays. The default lower bound for array subscripts is 0 and can be overridden at the module level using the **Option Base** statement.

```
' AnyValue and MyValue are declared as Variant by default with values
' set to Empty.
Dim AnyValue, MyValue

'  Explicitly declare a variable of type Integer.
Dim Number As Integer

' Multiple declarations on a single line. AnotherVar is of type Variant
' since its type is omitted.
Dim AnotherVar, Choice As Boolean, BirthDate As Date

' DayArray is an array of Variants with 51 elements indexed,
' starting at 0 thru 50, assuming Option Base is set to 0 (default) for
' the current module.
Dim DayArray(50)

' Matrix is a two-dimensional array of integers.
Dim Matrix(3,4) As Integer
' MyMatrix is a three-dimensional array of doubles with explicit
' bounds.
Dim MyMatrix(1 To 5,  4 To 9,  3 To 5) As Double

' BirthDay is an array of dates with indexes from 1 to 10.
Dim BirthDay(1 To 10) As Date

' MyArray is a dynamic array.
Dim MyArray()
```

Dir Function

Description

Returns the name of a file, directory, or folder that matches a specified pattern or file attribute, or the volume label of a drive.

Syntax

Dir[(*pathname*[,*attributes*])]

Elements

The **Dir** function syntax has these parts:

Part	Description
pathname	String expression that specifies a file name—may include directory or folder, and drive. **Null** is returned if *pathname* is not found.
attributes	Constant or numeric expression, the sum of which specifies file attributes. If omitted, all normal files are returned that match *pathname*.

The *attributes* argument has these constants and values:

Constant	Value	File Attribute
vbNormal	0	Normal.
vbHidden	2	Hidden.
vbSystem	4	System—not available on the Macintosh.
vbVolume	8	Volume label; if specified, all attributes are ignored—not available on the Macintosh.
vbDirectory	16	Directory or folder.

Note These constants are specified by Visual Basic. As a result, the names can be used anywhere in your code in place of the actual values.

Remarks

Dir supports the use of '*' (multiple character) and '?' (single character) wildcards to specify multiple files. However, on the Macintosh, these characters are treated as valid file name characters and can't be used as wildcards to specify multiple files.

Since the Macintosh does not support wildcards, use the file type to identify groups of files. You can use the **MacID** function to specify file type instead of using the file names. For example, the following statement returns the name of the first "TEXT" file in the current folder:

```
Dir("", MacID("TEXT"))
```

If you use the **MacID** function with **Dir** in Microsoft Windows, an error occurs.

Any *attribute* value greater than 256 is considered a **MacID** value.

You must specify *pathname* the first time you call the **Dir** function, or an error occurs. If you also specify file attributes, *pathname* must be included.

Dir returns the first file name that matches *pathname*. To get any additional file names that match *pathname*, call **Dir** again with no arguments. When no more file names match, **Dir** returns a zero-length string. Once a zero-length string is returned, you must specify *pathname* in subsequent calls or an error occurs. You can change to a new *pathname* without retrieving all of the file names that match the current *pathname*. However, you can't recursively call the **Dir** function.

> **Tip** Because file names are retrieved in no particular order, you may want to store returned file names in an array and then sort the array.

See Also **ChDir** Statement, **CurDir** Function, **MacID** Function.

DirectDependents Property

Applies To **Range** Object.

Description Accessor. Returns a **Range** object that represents the range that contains all of the direct dependents of a cell. This may be a multiple selection (a union of **Range** objects) if there is more than one dependent. Read-only.

See Also **Dependents** Property, **DirectPrecedents** Property, **Precedents** Property, **ShowDependents** Method.

Example This example selects the direct dependents of cell A1 on Sheet1.

```
Worksheets("Sheet1").Activate
Range("A1").DirectDependents.Select
```

DirectPrecedents Property

Applies To **Range** Object.

Description Accessor. Returns a **Range** object that represents the range that contains all of the direct precedents of a cell. This may be a multiple selection (a union of **Range** objects) if there is more than one precedent. Read-only.

See Also **Dependents** Property, **DirectDependents** Property, **Precedents** Property, **ShowPrecedents** Method.

Example This example selects the direct precedents of cell A1 on Sheet1.

```
Worksheets("Sheet1").Activate
Range("A1").DirectPrecedents.Select
```

DismissButton Property

Applies To   **Button** Object, **Buttons** Collection, **DrawingObjects** Collection.

Description   **True** if the button will automatically close a user-defined dialog box when the button is clicked. Any number of buttons on a dialog sheet can have the **DismissButton** property set to **True**. Read-write.

Remarks   When you click a button that has the **DismissButton** property set to **True**, three steps are taken:

1. The button's **OnAction** procedure runs. If you want to do any custom data validation, do it in this procedure. If validation fails, you can set the **DismissButton** property to **False**, in which case the dialog box remains visible. Remember to reset the **DismissButton** property to **True** when validation passes.

2. When the **OnAction** procedure ends, edit boxes in the dialog box are automatically validated to ensure that they contain data of the type specified by their **InputType** properties. If automatic validation fails, Microsoft Excel displays an alert, the offending edit box gets the focus, and the dialog box remains visible.

3. If automatic validation passes, the dialog box closes and the **Show** method that called the dialog sheet returns **True**.

If no button in the dialog box has the **DismissButton** property set to **True**, then you must explicitly call the **Hide** method or cancel the dialog box to close it.

See Also   **CancelButton** Property, **Hide** Method, **InputType** Property, **OnAction** Property, **Show** Method.

Example   This example sets the **DismissButton** property for every button on Dialog1.

```
For Each bt in DialogSheets("Dialog1").Buttons
    bt.DismissButton = True
Next bt
```

Display3DShading Property

Applies To   **CheckBox** Object, **DrawingObjects** Collection, **DropDown** Object, **DropDowns** Collection, **GroupBox** Object, **GroupBoxes** Collection, **ListBox** Object, **ListBoxes** Collection, **OptionButton** Object, **OptionButtons** Collection, **ScrollBar** Object, **ScrollBars** Collection, **Spinner** Object, **Spinners** Collection.

Description   **True** if the control uses 3-D visual effects. This property applies only to controls on worksheets and charts. Read-write.

Example   This example sets check box one on Sheet1 to use 3-D shading.

```
Worksheets("Sheet1").CheckBoxes(1).Display3DShading = True
```

DisplayAlerts Property

Applies To   **Application** Object.

Description   **True** if Microsoft Excel displays certain alerts and messages while a macro is running. Read-write.

Remarks   Defaults to **True**. Set this property to **False** if you do not want to be disturbed by prompts and alert messages while a macro is running, and want Microsoft Excel to choose the default response.

If you set this property to **False**, Microsoft Excel sets it back to **True** when your macro stops running.

This property is not effective from outside Microsoft Excel. For example, you can set this property to **False** from another application (using OLE Automation), but Microsoft Excel will immediately reset it to **True**. Because OLE Automation calls are processed as single-line macros and Microsoft Excel resets this property whenever a macro stops running, the property is reset immediately after you set it.

Example   This example closes the workbook BOOK1.XLS and does not prompt the user to save changes. Any changes to BOOK1.XLS are not saved.

```
Application.DisplayAlerts = False
Workbooks("BOOK1.XLS").Close
Application.DisplayAlerts = True
```

This example suppresses the message that appears when you initiate a DDE channel to an application that is not running.

```
Application.DisplayAlerts = False
channelNumber = Application.DDEInitiate( _
    app:="WinWord", _
    topic:="C:\WINWORD\FORMLETR.DOC")
Application.DisplayAlerts = True
Application.DDEExecute channelNumber, "[FILEPRINT]"
Application.DDETerminate channelNumber
```

DisplayAutomaticPageBreaks Property

Applies To   **DialogSheet** Object, **Worksheet** Object.

Description   **True** if automatic page breaks should be displayed for this sheet. Read-write.

Example   This example causes Sheet1 to display automatic page breaks.

```
Worksheets("Sheet1").DisplayAutomaticPageBreaks = True
```

DisplayBlanksAs Property

Applies To   **Chart** Object.

Description   Returns or sets how blank cells are plotted on a chart (one of **xlNotPlotted**, **xlInterpolated**, or **xlZero**). Read-write.

Example   This example causes Microsoft Excel not to plot blank cells in Chart1.

```
Charts("Chart1").DisplayBlanksAs = xlNotPlotted
```

DisplayClipboardWindow Property

Applies To   **Application** Object.

Description   Apple Macintosh only. **True** if the Clipboard window is displayed. Set this property to **True** to display the Clipboard window. Read-write.

Remarks   In Microsoft Windows, this property retains its value, but does nothing.

Example   This example displays the Clipboard window.

```
Application.DisplayClipboardWindow = True
```

DisplayDrawingObjects Property

Applies To   **Workbook** Object.

Description	Returns or sets how drawing objects are displayed, as shown in the following table. Read-write.

Value	Meaning
xlAll	Show all drawing objects.
xlPlaceholders	Show only placeholders.
xlHide	Hide all drawing objects.

Example	This example hides all the drawing objects in the active workbook.

```
ActiveWorkbook.DisplayDrawingObjects = xlHide
```

DisplayEquation Property

Applies To	**Trendline** Object.
Description	**True** if the equation for the trendline is displayed on the chart (in the same data label as the R-squared value). Setting this property to **True** automatically turns on data labels. Read-write.
See Also	**Add** Method, **DisplayRSquared** Property.
Example	This example displays the R-squared value and equation for trendline one in Chart1. The example should be run on a 2-D column chart that has a trendline for the first series.

```
With Charts("Chart1").SeriesCollection(1).Trendlines(1)
    .DisplayRSquared = True
    .DisplayEquation = True
End With
```

DisplayExcel4Menus Property

Applies To	**Application** Object.
Description	**True** if Microsoft Excel displays version 4.0 menu bars. Read-write.

Example	This example switches to Microsoft Excel version 7.0 menus if version 4.0 menus are currently in use.

```
If Application.DisplayExcel4Menus = True Then
    Application.DisplayExcel4Menus = False
End If
```

DisplayFormulaBar Property

Applies To	**Application** Object.
Description	**True** if the formula bar is displayed. Read-write.
Example	This example hides the formula bar.

```
Application.DisplayFormulaBar = False
```

DisplayFormulas Property

Applies To	**Window** Object.
Description	**True** if the window is displaying formulas, or **False** if the window is displaying values. Read-write.
Remarks	This property applies only to worksheets and macro sheets.
Example	This example changes the active window in BOOK1.XLS to display formulas.

```
Workbooks("BOOK1.XLS").Worksheets("Sheet1").Activate
ActiveWindow.DisplayFormulas = True
```

DisplayFullScreen Property

Applies To	**Application** Object.
Description	**True** if Microsoft Excel is in full-screen mode. Read-write.

Remarks   Full-screen mode maximizes the application window to cover the entire screen and hides the application title bar (in Microsoft Windows). Toolbars, the status bar, and the formula bar maintain separate display settings for full-screen and normal mode.

Example   This example causes Microsoft Excel to display in full-screen mode.

```
Application.DisplayFullScreen = True
```

DisplayGridlines Property

Applies To   **Window** Object.

Description   **True** if gridlines are displayed. Read-write.

Remarks   This property applies only to worksheets and macro sheets.

This property affects only displayed gridlines. Use the **PrintGridlines** property to control gridline printing.

Example   This example toggles the display of gridlines in the active window in BOOK1.XLS.

```
Workbooks("BOOK1.XLS").Worksheets("Sheet1").Activate
ActiveWindow.DisplayGridlines = Not(ActiveWindow.DisplayGridlines)
```

DisplayHeadings Property

Applies To   **Window** Object.

Description   **True** if both row and column headings are displayed, **False** if no headings are displayed. Read-write.

Remarks   This property applies only to worksheets and macro sheets.

This property affects only displayed headings. Use the **PrintHeadings** property to control heading printing.

Example   This example turns off row and column headings in the active window in BOOK1.XLS.

```
Workbooks("BOOK1.XLS").Worksheets("Sheet1").Activate
ActiveWindow.DisplayHeadings = False
```

DisplayHorizontalScrollBar Property

Applies To   **Window** Object.

Description   **True** if the horizontal scroll bar is displayed. Read-write.

See Also   **DisplayScrollBars** Property, **DisplayVerticalScrollBar** Property, **TabRatio** Property.

Example   This example turns on the horizontal scroll bar for the active window.

```
ActiveWindow.DisplayHorizontalScrollBar = True
```

DisplayInfoWindow Property

Applies To   **Application** Object.

Description   **True** if the Info window is displayed. Set this property to **True** to display the Info window. Read-write.

Example   This example displays the Info window.

```
Application.DisplayInfoWindow = True
```

DisplayNoteIndicator Property

Applies To   **Application** Object.

Description   **True** if cells containing notes display cell tips and contain note indicators (small dots in their upper-right corners). Read-write.

Example   This example hides the note indicators.

```
Application.DisplayNoteIndicator = True
```

DisplayOutline Property

Applies To   **Window** Object.

Description   **True** if outline symbols are displayed. Read-write.

Remarks   This property applies only to worksheets and macro sheets.

Example   This example displays outline symbols for the active window in BOOK1.XLS.

```
Workbooks("BOOK1.XLS").Worksheets("Sheet1").Activate
ActiveWindow.DisplayOutline = True
```

DisplayRecentFiles Property

Applies To   **Application** Object.

Description   **True** if the most recently used (MRU) file list is displayed on the File menu. Read-write.

Example   This example turns off the list of most recently used files.

```
Application.DisplayRecentFiles = False
```

DisplayRightToLeft Property

Applies To   **Window** Object.

Description   **True** if the window displays right-to-left instead of left-to-right. Read-write.

Remarks   This property is only available in Arabic and Hebrew Microsoft Excel.

Example   This example sets window one to display right-to-left.

```
ActiveWorkbook.Windows(1).DisplayRightToLeft = True
```

DisplayRSquared Property

Applies To   **Trendline** Object.

Description   **True** if the R-squared value of the trendline is displayed on the chart (in the same data label as the equation). Setting this property to **True** automatically turns on data labels. Read-write.

See Also   **Add** Method, **DisplayEquation** Property.

Example   This example displays the R-squared value and equation for trendline one in Chart1. The example should be run on a 2-D column chart that has a trendline for the first series.

```
With Charts("Chart1").SeriesCollection(1).Trendlines(1)
    .DisplayRSquared = True
    .DisplayEquation = True
End With
```

DisplayScrollBars Property

Applies To   **Application** Object.

Description   **True** if scroll bars are visible for all workbooks. Read-write.

See Also   **DisplayHorizontalScrollBar** Property, **DisplayVerticalScrollBar** Property.

Example   This example turns off scroll bars for all workbooks.

```
Application.DisplayScrollBars = False
```

DisplayStatusBar Property

Applies To   **Application** Object.

Description   **True** if the status bar is displayed. Read-write.

See Also   **StatusBar** Property.

Example   This example saves the current state of the **DisplayStatusBar** property and then sets the property to **True** so the status bar is visible.

```
saveStatusBar = Application.DisplayStatusBar
Application.DisplayStatusBar = True
```

DisplayVerticalScrollBar Property

Applies To	**DrawingObjects** Collection, **EditBox** Object, **EditBoxes** Collection, **Window** Object.
Description	**True** if the vertical scroll bar is displayed. Read-write.
See Also	**DisplayHorizontalScrollBar** Property, **DisplayScrollBars** Property.
Example	This example turns on the vertical scroll bar for the active window.

```
ActiveWindow.DisplayVerticalScrollBar = True
```

DisplayWorkbookTabs Property

Applies To	**Window** Object.
Description	**True** if the workbook tabs are displayed. Read-write.
See Also	**TabRatio** Property.
Example	This example turns on the workbook tabs.

```
ActiveWindow.DisplayWorkbookTabs = True
```

DisplayZeros Property

Applies To	**Window** Object.
Description	**True** if zero values are displayed. Read-write.
Remarks	This property applies only to worksheets and macro sheets.
Example	This example sets the active window in BOOK1.XLS to display zero values.

```
Workbooks("BOOK1.XLS").Worksheets("Sheet1").Activate
ActiveWindow.DisplayZeros = True
```

Do...Loop Statement

Description   Repeats a block of statements while a condition is **True** or until a condition becomes **True**.

Syntax 1   **Do** [{**While** | **Until**} *condition*]
　　　　　　　　[*statements*]
　　　　　　　　[**Exit Do**]
　　　　　　　　[*statements*]
　　　　　　　Loop

Syntax 2   **Do**
　　　　　　　　[*statements*]
　　　　　　　　[**Exit Do**]
　　　　　　　　[*statements*]
　　　　　　　Loop [{**While** | **Until**}*condition*]

The **Do**...**Loop** statement syntax has these parts:

Part	Description
condition	Expression that is **True** or **False**.
statements	One or more statements that are repeated while or until *condition* is **True**.

Remarks   The **Exit Do** can only be used within a **Do**...**Loop** control structure to provide an alternate way to exit a **Do**...**Loop**. Any number of **Exit Do** statements may be placed anywhere in the **Do**...**Loop**. Often used with the evaluation of some condition (for example, **If**...**Then**), **Exit Do** transfers control to the statement immediately following the **Loop**.

When used within nested **Do**...**Loop** statements, **Exit Do** transfers control to the loop that is one nested level above the loop where it occurs.

See Also   **Exit** Statement, **For**...**Next** Statement, **While**...**Wend** Statement.

Example

This example shows how **Do...Loop** statements can be used. The inner **Do...Loop** statement loops 10 times, sets the value of the flag to **False**, and exits prematurely using the **Exit Do** statement. The outer loop exits immediately upon checking the value of the flag.

```
Check = True : Counter = 0          ' Initialize variables.
Do   ' Outer Loop.
    Do While Counter < 20           ' Inner Loop.
        Counter = Counter + 1       ' Increment Counter.
        If Counter = 10 Then        ' If condition is true.
            Check = False           ' Set value of flag to False.
            Exit Do                 ' Exit inner loop.
        End If
    Loop
Loop Until Check = False            ' Exit outer loop immediately.
```

This example sorts the data in the first column on Sheet1 and then deletes rows that contain duplicate data.

```
Worksheets("Sheet1").Range("A1").Sort _
    key1:=Worksheets("Sheet1").Range("A1")
Set currentCell = Worksheets("Sheet1").Range("A1")
Do While Not IsEmpty(currentCell)
    Set nextCell = currentCell.Offset(1, 0)
    If nextCell.Value = currentCell.Value Then
        currentCell.EntireRow.Delete
    End If
    Set currentCell = nextCell
Loop
```

DocumentProperties Collection Object (Microsoft Office 95 Object Library)

Description

Represents a collection of document properties. Each document property is represented by a **DocumentProperty** object.

To use this object, you should establish a reference to the Microsoft Office 95 Object Library by using the References command (Tools menu).

Accessors

Each workbook has a collection of built-in document properties and a collection of custom document properties. Each collection is represented by a **DocumentProperties** object, and each collection contains individual **DocumentProperty** objects.

Use the **BuiltinDocumentProperties** property to return the collection of built-in document properties, and use the **CustomDocumentProperties** property to return the collection of custom document properties.

Use the **Add** method to create a new custom document property and add it to the collection (you cannot create a built-in document property).

The following example creates a list on worksheet one of all the built-in document properties for the active workbook.

```
rw = 1
Worksheets(1).Activate
For Each p In ActiveWorkbook.BuiltinDocumentProperties
    Cells(rw, 1).Value = p.Name
    Cells(rw, 2).Value = p.Value
    rw = rw + 1
Next
```

Properties	**Count** Property (**DocumentProperties** Collection), **Parent** Property (**DocumentProperties** Collection).
Methods	**Add** Method (**DocumentProperties** Collection), **Item** Method (**DocumentProperties** Collection).

DocumentProperty Object (Microsoft Office 95 Object Library)

Description	Represents a single document property. The **DocumentProperty** object is a member of the **DocumentProperties** collection.
	To use this object, you should establish a reference to the Microsoft Office 95 Object Library by using the References command (Tools menu).
Accessors	Each workbook has a collection of built-in document properties and a collection of custom document properties. Each collection is represented by a **DocumentProperties** object, and each collection contains individual **DocumentProperty** objects.
	Use the **BuiltinDocumentProperties** property to return the collection of built-in document properties, and use the **CustomDocumentProperties** property to return the collection of custom document properties. Use the Item method to return a single member of the collection.

The following example sets the value of the built-in document property named "Title."

```
ActiveWorkbook.BuiltinDocumentProperties.Item("Title") _
    .Value = "Year-End Sales Results"
```

Properties   **LinkSource** Property (**DocumentProperty** Object), **LinkToContent** Property (**DocumentProperty** Object), **Name** Property (**DocumentProperty** Object), **Parent** Property (**DocumentProperty** Object), **Type** Property (**DocumentProperty** Object), **Value** Property (**DocumentProperty** Object).

Methods   **Delete** Method (**DocumentProperty** Object).

DoEvents Statement

Description   Yields execution so that the operating system can process other events.

Syntax   **DoEvents**

Remarks   **DoEvents** passes control to the operating system. Control is not returned until the operating system has finished processing the events in its queue and, for Microsoft Windows only, all keys in the **SendKeys** queue have been sent.

If parts of your code take up too much processor time, use **DoEvents** periodically to relinquish control to the operating system so that events, such as keyboard input and mouse clicks, can be processed without significant delay.

Caution   Make sure the procedure that has given up control with **DoEvents** is not executed again from a different part of your code before the first **DoEvents** call returns; this could cause unpredictable results. In addition, do not use **DoEvents** if other applications could possibly interact with your procedure in unforeseen ways during the time you have yielded control.

Example   This example uses the **DoEvents** Statement to cause execution to yield to the operating system once every 1000 iterations of the loop.

```
For I = 1 To 150000              ' Start loop.
    If I Mod 1000 = 0 Then       ' If loop has repeated 1000 times.
        DoEvents                 ' Yield to operating system.
    End If
Next I  ' Increment loop counter.
```

Double Data Type

Description   **Double** (double-precision floating-point) variables are stored as 64-bit (8-byte) numbers ranging in value from -1.79769313486232E308 to -4.94065645841247E-324 for negative values and from 4.94065645841247E-324 to 1.79769313486232E308 for positive values. The type-declaration character for **Double** is # (character code 35).

See Also   **CDbl** Function, Data Type Summary, **Def***type* Statements, **Single** Data Type.

DoubleClick Method

Applies To   **Application** Object.

Description   Equivalent to double-clicking the active cell.

Syntax   *object*.**DoubleClick**

object
        Required. The **Application** object.

See Also   **OnDoubleClick** Property.

Example   This example double-clicks the active cell on Sheet1.

```
Worksheets("Sheet1").Activate
Application.DoubleClick
```

DoughnutGroups Method

Applies To   **Chart** Object.

Description   Accessor. On a 2-D chart, returns an object that represents a single doughnut chart group (a **ChartGroup** object, Syntax 1), or a collection of the doughnut chart groups (a **ChartGroups** collection, Syntax 2).

Syntax 1   *object*.**DoughnutGroups(***index***)**

Syntax 2   *object*.**DoughnutGroups**

object
        Required. The **Chart** object.

index
Required for Syntax 1. Specifies the chart group.

Example This example sets the starting angle for doughnut group one in Chart1.

```
Charts("Chart1").DoughnutGroups(1).FirstSliceAngle = 45
```

DoughnutHoleSize Property

Applies To **ChartGroup** Object.

Description Returns or sets the size of the hole in a doughnut chart group. The hole size is expressed as a percentage of the chart size from 10 to 90 percent. Read-write.

Example This example sets the hole size for doughnut group one in Chart1. The example should be run on a 2-D doughnut chart.

```
Charts("Chart1").DoughnutGroups(1).DoughnutHoleSize = 10
```

DownBars Object

Description Represents the down bars in a chart group. Down bars connect points on series one with lower values on the last series in the chart group (the lines go down from series one). Only 2-D line groups that contain at least two series can have down bars. There is no singular DownBar object; you must turn up bars and down bars on or off for all points in a chart group at once.

Accessors The **DownBars** property returns the down bars for a chart group. The following example turns on up and down bars for chart group one in embedded chart one on the worksheet named "Sheet5." The example then sets the up bar color to blue and the down bar color to red.

```
With Worksheets("sheet5").ChartObjects(1).Chart.ChartGroups(1)
    .HasUpDownBars = True
    .UpBars.Interior.Color = RGB(0, 0, 255)
    .DownBars.Interior.Color = RGB(255, 0, 0)
End With
```

Remarks If the **HasUpDownBars** property is **False**, most properties of the **DownBars** object are disabled.

Properties	**Application** Property, **Border** Property, **Creator** Property, **Interior** Property, **Name** Property, **Parent** Property.
Methods	**Delete** Method, **Select** Method.
See Also	**UpBars** Object.

DownBars Property

Applies To	**ChartGroup** Object.
Description	Accessor. Returns a **DownBars** object that represents the down bars on a line chart. Applies only to line charts. Read-only.
See Also	**HasUpDownBars** Property, **UpBars** Property.
Example	This example turns on up and down bars for chart group one in Chart1 and then sets their colors. The example should be run on a 2-D line chart having two series that cross each other at one or more data points.

```
With Charts("Chart1").ChartGroups(1)
    .HasUpDownBars = True
    .DownBars.Interior.ColorIndex = 3
    .UpBars.Interior.ColorIndex = 5
End With
```

Draft Property

Applies To	**PageSetup** Object.
Description	**True** if the sheet will be printed without graphics. Read-write.
Remarks	Setting this property to **True** makes printing faster (at the expense of not printing graphics).
See Also	**PrintObject** Property.
Example	This example turns off graphics printing for Sheet1.

```
Worksheets("Sheet1").PageSetup.Draft = True
```

Drawing Object

Description   Represents a graphic object created by the Freehand, Freeform, or Filled Freeform buttons.

Accessors   The **Drawing** object is a member of the **Drawings** collection. The **Drawings** collection contains all the **Drawing** objects on a single sheet. Do not confuse the **Drawings** collection with the **DrawingObjects** collection, which contains all the graphic objects and controls on a single sheet. Use the **Add** method to create a new drawing and add it to the collection.

To access a single member of the collection, use the **Drawings** method with the index number or name of the drawing as an argument.

The following example sets the interior color for drawing one on the worksheet named "Sheet1."

```
Worksheets("sheet1").Drawings(1).Interior.Color = RGB(0, 0, 255)
```

The drawing name is shown in the Name Box when the drawing is selected. Use the **Name** property to return or set the name of the drawing. The following example aligns the left edge of the drawing named "Drawing 1" with the left edge of cell C5.

```
Worksheets("sheet1").Drawings("drawing 1").Left = _
    Worksheets("sheet1").Range("c5").Left
```

Properties   **Application** Property, **Border** Property, **BottomRightCell** Property, **Creator** Property, **Enabled** Property, **Height** Property, **Index** Property, **Interior** Property, **Left** Property, **Locked** Property, **Name** Property, **OnAction** Property, **Parent** Property, **Placement** Property, **PrintObject** Property, **Shadow** Property, **Top** Property, **TopLeftCell** Property, **Vertices** Property, **Visible** Property, **Width** Property, **ZOrder** Property.

Methods   **AddVertex** Method, **BringToFront** Method, **Copy** Method, **CopyPicture** Method, **Cut** Method, **Delete** Method, **Duplicate** Method, **Reshape** Method, **Select** Method, **SendToBack** Method.

DrawingObjects Collection Object

Description
The **DrawingObjects** collection contains all the graphic objects, controls, **ChartObject** objects, **Picture** objects, and **OLEObject** objects on a sheet. There is no singular **DrawingObject** object; each member of the **DrawingObjects** collection is an object of a particular type, such as a **CheckBox** object, an **Arc** object, or a **Picture** object.

Accessors
Use the **Add** method for the particular object type (**Arcs.Add**, or **Ovals.Add**, for example) to create a new graphic object or control and add it to the **DrawingObjects** collection. There is no **Add** method for the **DrawingObjects** collection.

While **Picture** objects, **ChartObject** objects, and **OLEObject** objects are all contained in the **DrawingObjects** collection, it is usually easier to use the accessor methods for those individual objects. For more information, see the **Pictures** method, the **ChartObjects** method, and the **OLEObjects** method.

Use the **DrawingObjects** method with no arguments to access the entire collection at once. The following example deletes all **DrawingObject** objects on the dialog sheet named "Dialog1."

```
DialogSheets("dialog1").DrawingObjects.Delete
```

To access a single member of the collection, use the **DrawingObjects** method with the index number or object name as an argument.

The following example deletes **DrawingObject** object one on the worksheet named "Sheet1."

```
Worksheets("sheet1").DrawingObjects(1).Delete
```

The name of the object is shown in the Name Box when the object is selected. Use the **Name** property to set or return the name. The following example activates the dialog sheet named "Dialog1" and then changes the text on the buttons named "Button 2" and "Button 3." Note that the **Buttons** method could have been used where this example uses the **DrawingObjects** method.

```
With DialogSheets("dialog1")
    .DrawingObjects("button 2").Text = "On"
    .DrawingObjects("button 3").Text = "Off"
End With
```

Because the **DrawingObjects** method returns all members of the collection, regardless of object type, it may be more convenient to use the accessor method for a particular object type. For example, use the **Ovals** method to return the collection of ovals on the sheet, or the **OptionButtons** method to return the collection of option buttons. For more information, see the appropriate object topic.

Properties	**Accelerator** Property, **AddIndent** Property, **Application** Property, **ArrowHeadLength** Property, **ArrowHeadStyle** Property, **ArrowHeadWidth** Property, **AutoSize** Property, **Border** Property, **CancelButton** Property, **Caption** Property, **Count** Property, **Creator** Property, **DefaultButton** Property, **DismissButton** Property, **Display3DShading** Property, **DisplayVerticalScrollBar** Property, **DropDownLines** Property, **Enabled** Property, **Font** Property, **Height** Property, **HelpButton** Property, **HorizontalAlignment** Property, **InputType** Property, **Interior** Property, **LargeChange** Property, **Left** Property, **LinkedCell** Property, **List** Property, **ListFillRange** Property, **ListIndex** Property, **Locked** Property, **LockedText** Property, **Max** Property, **Min** Property, **MultiLine** Property, **MultiSelect** Property, **OnAction** Property, **Orientation** Property, **Parent** Property, **PhoneticAccelerator** Property, **Placement** Property, **PrintObject** Property, **RoundedCorners** Property, **Selected** Property, **Shadow** Property, **SmallChange** Property, **Text** Property, **Top** Property, **Value** Property, **VerticalAlignment** Property, **Vertices** Property, **Visible** Property, **Width** Property, **ZOrder** Property.
Methods	**AddItem** Method, **BringToFront** Method, **Characters** Method, **CheckSpelling** Method, **Copy** Method, **CopyPicture** Method, **Cut** Method, **Delete** Method, **Duplicate** Method, **Group** Method, **Item** Method, **LinkCombo** Method, **RemoveAllItems** Method, **RemoveItem** Method, **Reshape** Method, **Select** Method, **SendToBack** Method, **Ungroup** Method.

DrawingObjects Method

Applies To	**Chart** Object, **DialogSheet** Object, **Worksheet** Object.
Description	Accessor. Returns an object that represents a single drawing object (Syntax 1) or a collection of all the drawing objects (Syntax 2) on the sheet. Returns all drawing objects, including graphic objects, pictures, embedded objects, and embedded charts.
Syntax 1	*object*.**DrawingObjects**(*index*)
Syntax 2	*object*.**DrawingObjects**
	object Required. The **Chart**, **DialogSheet**, or **Worksheet** object.
	index Required for Syntax 1. The name or number of the drawing object. Can be an array to return several drawing objects.
See Also	**DrawingObjects** Collection.

Example

This example deletes drawing object three on Sheet1.

```
Worksheets("Sheet1").DrawingObjects(3).Delete
```

This example deletes every drawing object on Sheet1.

```
Worksheets("Sheet1").DrawingObjects.Delete
```

This example adds arrowheads to every graphic object on Sheet1 that has the word "Line" in its name.

```
For Each d In Worksheets("Sheet1").DrawingObjects
    If d.Name Like "*Line*" Then
        d.ArrowHeadLength = xlLong
        d.ArrowHeadStyle = xlOpen
        d.ArrowHeadWidth = xlNarrow
    End If
Next
```

Drawings Collection Object

Description

A collection of all the **Drawing** objects (graphic object created by the Freehand, Freeform, or Filled Freeform buttons) on the specified chart sheet, dialog sheet, or worksheet.

Accessors

Use the **Drawings** method with an argument to access a single member of the collection or without an argument to access the entire collection at once. The following example deletes all of the drawings on worksheet one in the active workbook.

```
Worksheets(1).Drawings.Delete
```

Use the **Add** method to create a new drawing and add it to the collection. You must specify two initial vertices for the drawing. Use the **AddVertex** method to add vertices once the drawing has been created. The following example creates a new drawing.

```
With Worksheets("sheet1").Drawings.Add(10, 10, 100, 100, False)
    .AddVertex 150, 150
    .AddVertex 200, 150
End With
```

You can use the macro recorder to create a more complex example. Turn on the macro recorder (click Record Macro on the Tools menu), and draw a complex freeform drawing. Then turn off the macro recorder, and examine the recorded Visual Basic code.

Properties	**Application** Property, **Border** Property, **Count** Property, **Creator** Property, **Enabled** Property, **Height** Property, **Interior** Property, **Left** Property, **Locked** Property, **OnAction** Property, **Parent** Property, **Placement** Property, **PrintObject** Property, **Shadow** Property, **Top** Property, **Visible** Property, **Width** Property, **ZOrder** Property.
Methods	**Add** Method (**Drawings** Collection), **BringToFront** Method, **Copy** Method, **CopyPicture** Method, **Cut** Method, **Delete** Method, **Duplicate** Method, **Group** Method, **Item** Method, **Reshape** Method, **Select** Method, **SendToBack** Method.

Drawings Method

Applies To   **Chart** Object, **DialogSheet** Object, **Worksheet** Object.

Description   Accessor. Returns an object that represents a single drawing (a **Drawing** object, Syntax 1) or a collection of drawings (a **Drawings** object, Syntax 2) on the sheet. Drawings are created by the Freeform, Freehand, and Filled Freeform buttons on the Drawing toolbar.

Syntax 1   *object*.**Drawings**(*index*)

Syntax 2   *object*.**Drawings**

object
    Required. The **Chart**, **DialogSheet**, or **Worksheet** object.

index
    Required for Syntax 1. The name or number of the drawing to return. More than one index can be specified.

Example   This example brings drawing one to the front of Sheet1.

```
Worksheets("Sheet1").Drawings(1).BringToFront
```

DropDown Object

Description   Represents a drop-down list box on the specified chart sheet, dialog sheet, or worksheet, or a combination drop-down edit box on the specified dialog sheet. A user can click an item in the drop-down list or, in combination drop-down edit boxes, type text in the edit box.

You can fill the drop-down list either by specifying a range of cells that contains list items (using the **ListFillRange** property) or by specifying each item (using the **AddItem** and **RemoveItem** methods or the **List** property).

Accessors

The **DropDown** object is a member of the **DropDowns** collection. The **DropDowns** collection contains all the **DropDown** objects on a single sheet. Use the **Add** method to create a new drop-down list box and add it to the collection. Set the *editable* argument to **True** to create a combination drop-down edit box (you can only create a combination drop-down edit box on a dialog sheet).

To access a single member of the collection, use the **DropDowns** method with the index number or name of the drop-down list box as an argument.

Example

The following example sets the items that appears in the drop-down list box when the dialog sheet runs.

```
DialogSheets(1).DropDowns(1).List = _
    Array("cogs", "widgets", "gadgets", "sprockets")
```

The drop-down list box name is shown in the Name Box when the drop-down list box is selected. Use the **Name** property to set or return the drop-down list box name.

The following example sets the list input range for the drop-down list box named "Drop Down 9." When the dialog sheet runs, the contents of cells A1:A10 on the worksheet named "Sheet1" will appear in the drop-down list box.

```
DialogSheets(1).DropDowns("drop down 9") _
    .ListFillRange = "=sheet1!a1:a10"
```

Properties

Application Property, **BottomRightCell** Property, **Caption** Property, **Creator** Property, **Display3DShading** Property, **DropDownLines** Property, **Enabled** Property, **Height** Property, **Index** Property, **Left** Property, **LinkedCell** Property, **LinkedObject** Property, **List** Property, **ListCount** Property, **ListFillRange** Property, **ListIndex** Property, **Locked** Property, **Name** Property, **OnAction** Property, **Parent** Property, **Placement** Property, **PrintObject** Property, **Text** Property, **Top** Property, **TopLeftCell** Property, **Value** Property, **Visible** Property, **Width** Property, **ZOrder** Property.

Methods

AddItem Method, **BringToFront** Method, **Characters** Method, **Copy** Method, **CopyPicture** Method, **Cut** Method, **Delete** Method, **Duplicate** Method, **RemoveAllItems** Method, **RemoveItem** Method, **Select** Method, **SendToBack** Method.

DropDownLines Property

Applies To   **DrawingObjects** Collection, **DropDown** Object, **DropDowns** Collection.

Description   Returns or sets the number of list lines displayed in the drop-down portion of a drop-down list box. Read-write.

Remarks   This property is ignored on the Apple Macintosh.

Example   This example sets the number of list lines in drop-down list box one on Dialog1.

```
DialogSheets("Dialog1").DropDowns(1).DropDownLines = 10
```

DropDowns Collection Object

Description   A collection of all the **DropDown** objects on the specified chart sheet, dialog sheet, or worksheet. Each **DropDown** object represents a drop-down list box or a combination drop-down edit box. A user can click an item in the drop-down list or, in combination drop-down edit boxes, type text in the edit box.

Accessors   Use the **Add** method to create a drop-down list box and add it to the collection. Set the *editable* argument to **True** to create a combination drop-down edit box (you can only create a combination drop-down edit box on a dialog sheet). The following example adds a new drop-down list box to dialog sheet one. The new drop-down list box is positioned relative to the upper-left corner of the dialog frame.

```
Dim df As DialogFrame
Set df = DialogSheets(1).DialogFrame
DialogSheets(1).DropDowns.Add df.Left + 10, df.Top + 20, 100, 10
```

Use the **DropDowns** method with an argument to access a single member of the collection or without an argument to access the entire collection at once. The following example sets the **Value** property for all the drop-down list boxes on dialog sheet one; each drop-down list box on the sheet will initially display the first item in its list the next time the dialog sheet runs.

```
DialogSheets(1).DropDowns.Value = 1
```

Properties	**Application** Property, **Caption** Property, **Count** Property, **Creator** Property, **Display3DShading** Property, **DropDownLines** Property, **Enabled** Property, **Height** Property, **Left** Property, **LinkedCell** Property, **List** Property, **ListFillRange** Property, **ListIndex** Property, **Locked** Property, **OnAction** Property, **Parent** Property, **Placement** Property, **PrintObject** Property, **Text** Property, **Top** Property, **Value** Property, **Visible** Property, **Width** Property, **ZOrder** Property.
Methods	**Add** Method (**DropDowns** Collection), **AddItem** Method, **BringToFront** Method, **Characters** Method, **Copy** Method, **CopyPicture** Method, **Cut** Method, **Delete** Method, **Duplicate** Method, **Group** Method, **Item** Method, **RemoveAllItems** Method, **RemoveItem** Method, **Select** Method, **SendToBack** Method.

DropDowns Method

Applies To	**Chart** Object, **DialogSheet** Object, **Worksheet** Object.
Description	Accessor. Returns an object that represents a single drop-down list box control (a **DropDown** object, Syntax 1) or a collection of drop-down list box controls (a **DropDowns** object, Syntax 2) on the sheet.
Syntax 1	*object*.**DropDowns**(*index*)
Syntax 2	*object*.**DropDowns**

object
Required. The **Chart**, **DialogSheet**, or **Worksheet** object.

index
Required for Syntax 1. Specifies the name or number of the drop-down list box control (can be an array to specify more than one).

Example	This example sets the number of list lines in drop-down list box one on Dialog1.

```
DialogSheets("Dialog1").DropDowns(1).DropDownLines = 10
```

DropLines Object

Description   Represents the drop lines in a chart group. Drop lines connect the points in the chart with the x-axis. Only line and area chart groups can have drop lines. There is no singular DropLine object; you must turn drop lines on or off for all points in a chart group at once.

Accessors   The **DropLines** property returns the drop lines for a chart group. The following example turns on drop lines for chart group one in embedded chart one on the worksheet named "Sheet1" and then sets the drop line color.

```
Worksheets("sheet1").ChartObjects(1).Activate
ActiveChart.ChartGroups(1).HasDropLines = True
ActiveChart.ChartGroups(1).DropLines.Border.ColorIndex = 3
```

Remarks   If the **HasDropLines** property is **False,** most properties of the **DropLines** object are disabled.

Properties   **Application** Property, **Border** Property, **Creator** Property, **Name** Property, **Parent** Property.

Methods   **Delete** Method, **Select** Method.

DropLines Property

Applies To   **ChartGroup** Object.

Description   Accessor. Returns a **DropLines** object that represents the drop lines for a series on a line or area chart. Applies only to line or area charts. Read-write.

See Also   **HasDropLines** Property.

Example   This example turns on drop lines for chart group one in Chart1 and then sets their line style, weight, and color. The example should be run on a 2-D line chart that has one series.

```
With Charts("Chart1").ChartGroups(1)
    .HasDropLines = True
    With .DropLines.Border
        .LineStyle = xlThin
        .Weight = xlMedium
        .ColorIndex = 3
    End With
End With
```

Duplicate Method

Applies To   **Arc** Object, **Arcs** Collection, **Button** Object, **Buttons** Collection, **ChartObject** Object, **ChartObjects** Collection, **CheckBox** Object, **Drawing** Object, **DrawingObjects** Collection, **Drawings** Collection, **DropDown** Object, **DropDowns** Collection, **EditBox** Object, **EditBoxes** Collection, **GroupBox** Object, **GroupBoxes** Collection, **GroupObject** Object, **GroupObjects** Collection, **Label** Object, **Labels** Collection, **Line** Object, **Lines** Collection, **ListBox** Object, **ListBoxes** Collection, **OLEObject** Object, **OLEObjects** Collection, **OptionButton** Object, **OptionButtons** Collection, **Oval** Object, **Ovals** Collection, **Picture** Object, **Pictures** Collection, **Rectangle** Object, **Rectangles** Collection, **ScrollBar** Object, **ScrollBars** Collection, **Spinner** Object, **Spinners** Collection, **TextBox** Object, **TextBoxes** Collection.

Description   Duplicates the object and returns a reference to the new copy.

Syntax   *object*.**Duplicate**

object
Required. The object to which this method applies.

Example   This example duplicates oval one on Sheet1 and then selects the copy.

```
Set dOval = Worksheets("Sheet1").Ovals(1).Duplicate
dOval.Select
```

Edit Method

Applies To   **ToolbarButton** Object.

Description   Starts the button editor for the specified toolbar button.

Syntax   *object*.**Edit**

object
Required. The **ToolbarButton** object.

Remarks   This method cannot be used with a toolbar button that is a gap or a toolbar button that has a palette or list attached (such as the Font or Style buttons).

Example   This example starts the button editor for the Print button, which is button five on the Standard toolbar.

```
Application.Toolbars("Standard").ToolbarButtons(5).Edit
```

EditBox Object

Description

Represents an edit box on a dialog sheet (edit boxes cannot be used on worksheets). Edit boxes allow the user to enter text or numbers. Unlike other controls, edit boxes do not have a **Value** property or a **LinkedCell** property. An edit box on a dialog sheet can be linked to a list box to form a combination list edit box, using the **LinkCombo** method or the Combination List Edit Box button on the Forms toolbar.

Accessors

The **EditBox** object is a member of the **EditBoxes** collection. The **EditBoxes** collection contains all the **EditBox** objects on a single sheet. Use the **Add** method to create a new edit box and add it to the collection.

To access a single member of the collection, use the **EditBoxes** method with the edit box name or index number as an argument.

The following example sets the text appearing in edit box one on the dialog sheet named "Dialog1."

```
DialogSheets("dialog1").EditBoxes(1).Text = "widgets"
```

The edit box name is shown in the Name Box when the edit box is selected. Use the **Name** property to set or return the edit box name. The following example sets the allowed input type for the edit box named "Edit Box 14" on the dialog sheet named "Dialog1."

```
DialogSheets("dialog1").EditBoxes("edit box 14").InputType = xlInteger
```

Properties

Application Property, **BottomRightCell** Property, **Caption** Property, **Creator** Property, **DisplayVerticalScrollBar** Property, **Enabled** Property, **Height** Property, **Index** Property, **InputType** Property, **Left** Property, **LinkedObject** Property, **Locked** Property, **MultiLine** Property, **Name** Property, **OnAction** Property, **Parent** Property, **PasswordEdit** Property, **Placement** Property, **PrintObject** Property, **Text** Property, **Top** Property, **TopLeftCell** Property, **Visible** Property, **Width** Property, **ZOrder** Property.

Methods

BringToFront Method, **Characters** Method, **Copy** Method, **CopyPicture** Method, **Cut** Method, **Delete** Method, **Duplicate** Method, **Select** Method, **SendToBack** Method.

See Also

TextBox Object

EditBoxes Collection Object

Description

A collection of all the **EditBox** objects on the specified dialog sheet (edit boxes cannot be used on worksheets). Edit boxes allow the user to enter text or numbers. Unlike other controls, edit boxes do not have a **Value** property or a **LinkedCell** property. Edit boxes that are linked to list boxes to form combination list edit boxes are included in the **ListBoxes** collection.

Accessors

Use the **Add** method to create a new edit box and add it to the collection. The following example adds a new edit box to the dialog sheet named "Dialog1." The new edit box is positioned relative to the upper-left corner of the dialog frame.

```
Dim df As DialogFrame
Set df = DialogSheets("dialog1").DialogFrame
DialogSheets("dialog1").EditBoxes.Add df.Left + 10, _
    df.Top + 20, 100, 10
```

Use the **EditBoxes** method with an argument to access a single member of the collection or without an argument to access the entire collection at once. The following example empties all the edit boxes on the dialogsheet named "Dialog1."

```
DialogSheets("dialog1").EditBoxes.Text = ""
```

Properties

Application Property, **Caption** Property, **Count** Property, **Creator** Property, **DisplayVerticalScrollBar** Property, **Enabled** Property, **Height** Property, **InputType** Property, **Left** Property, **Locked** Property, **MultiLine** Property, **OnAction** Property, **Parent** Property, **PasswordEdit** Property, **Placement** Property, **PrintObject** Property, **Text** Property, **Top** Property, **Visible** Property, **Width** Property, **ZOrder** Property.

Methods

Add Method (Graphic Objects and Controls), **BringToFront** Method, **Characters** Method, **Copy** Method, **CopyPicture** Method, **Cut** Method, **Delete** Method, **Duplicate** Method, **Group** Method, **Item** Method, **Select** Method, **ToBack** Method.

EditBoxes Method

Applies To

DialogSheet Object.

Description

Accessor. Returns an object that represents a single edit box control (an **EditBox** object, Syntax 1) or a collection of edit box controls (an **EditBoxes** object, Syntax 2) on the sheet.

Syntax 1

object.**EditBoxes**(*index*)

Syntax 2	*object*.**EditBoxes**

object
Required. The **DialogSheet** object.

index
Required for Syntax 1. Specifies the name or number of the edit box (can be an array to specify me than one).

Example   This example sets the text in edit box one on Dialog1.

```
DialogSheets("Dialog1").EditBoxes(1).Text = "Start here"
```

EditDirectlyInCell Property

Applies To   **Application** Object.

Description   **True** if Microsoft Excel allows editing in cells. Read-write.

Example   This example enables editing in cells.

```
Application.EditDirectlyInCell = True
```

EditionOptions Method

Applies To   **Workbook** Object.

Description   Sets options for publishers and subscribers in the workbook. Available only on the Apple Macintosh running System 7.

Syntax   *object*.**EditionOptions**(*type*, *option*, *name*, *reference*, *appearance*, *chartSize*, *formats*)

object
Required. The **Workbook** object.

type
Required. Specifies the edition type to change (either **xlPublisher** or **xlSubscriber**).

option

Required. Specifies the type of information to set for the edition. If *type* is **xlPublisher**, then *option* can be one of **xlCancel**, **xlSendPublisher**, **xlSelect**, **xlAutomaticUpdate**, **xlManualUpdate**, or **xlChangeAttributes**. If *type* is **xlSubscriber**, then *option* can be one of **xlCancel**, **xlUpdateSubscriber**, **xlOpenSource**, **xlAutomaticUpdate**, or **xlManualUpdate**.

name

Optional. Specifies the name of the edition, as returned from the LinkSources method. If *name* is omitted, *reference* must be specified.

reference

Optional (required if *name* is not specified). Specifies the edition reference as text in R1C1-style form. This argument is required if there is more than one publisher or subscriber with the same edition name in the workbook, or if the *name* argument is omitted.

appearance

Optional. If *option* is **xlChangeAttributes**, specifies whether the edition is published as shown on screen (**xlScreen**) or as shown when printed (**xlPrinter**).

chartSize

Optional. If *option* is **xlChangeAttributes** and the published object is a chart, specifies the size of the edition (either **xlScreen** or **xlPrinter**). If the edition is not a chart, omit this argument.

formats

Optional. If **option** is **xlChangeAttributes**, specifies the format of the published edition. Can be any combination of **xlPICT**, **xlBIFF**, **xlRTF**, or **xlVALU**.

Elevation Property

Applies To   **Chart** Object.

Description   Returns or sets the elevation of the 3-D chart view, in degrees. Read-write.

Remarks   The chart elevation is the height at which you view the chart, in degrees. The default is 15 for most chart types. The value of this property must be between -90 and 90, except for 3-D bar charts, where it must be between 0 and 44.

See Also   **Perspective** Property, **Rotation** Property.

Example   This example sets the chart elevation of Chart1 to 34 degrees. The example should be run on a 3-D chart (the **Elevation** property fails on 2-D charts).

```
Charts("Chart1").Elevation = 34
```

EnableAnimations Property

Applies To   **Application** Object.

Description   **True** if animated insertion and deletion is enabled. When animation is enabled, inserted worksheet rows and columns slowly appear, and deleted worksheet rows and columns slowly disappear. This property is available only in Microsoft Excel for Windows 95. Read-write.

Example   This example turns off animated insertion and deletion.

```
Application.EnableAnimations = False
```

EnableAutoComplete Property

Applies To   **Application** Object.

Description   **True** if the AutoComplete feature is enabled. This property is available only in Microsoft Excel for Windows 95. Read-write.

See Also   **AutoComplete** Method.

Example   This example enables the AutoComplete feature.

```
Application.EnableAutoComplete = True
```

EnableAutoFilter Property

Applies To   **Worksheet** Object.

Description   **True** if AutoFilter arrows are enabled when user-interface-only protection is turned on. This property is available only in Microsoft Excel for Windows 95. Read-write.

See Also   **Protect** Method, **Unprotect** Method.

Remarks   This property applies to each worksheet and isn't saved with the worksheet or session.

Example   This example enables the AutoFilter arrows on a protected worksheet.

```
ActiveSheet.EnableAutoFilter = True
ActiveSheet.Protect contents:=True, userInterfaceOnly:=True
```

EnableCancelKey Property

Applies To

Application Object.

Description

Controls how Microsoft Excel handles CTRL+BREAK (or ESC or COMMAND+PERIOD) user interruptions of the running procedure, as shown in the following table. Read-write.

Value	Meaning
xlDisabled	Cancel key trapping is completely disabled.
xlInterrupt	Interrupt the current procedure and allow the user to debug or end the procedure.
xlErrorHandler	The interrupt is sent to the running procedure as an error, trappable by an error handler setup with an **On Error GoTo** statement. The trappable error code is 18.

Remarks

Use this property very carefully. If you use **xlDisabled**, there is no way to interrupt a runaway loop or other non–self-terminating code. If you use **xlErrorHandler** but your error handler always returns using the **Resume** statement, there is also no way to stop runaway code.

The **EnableCancelKey** property is always reset to **xlInterrupt** whenever Microsoft Excel returns to the idle state and no code is running. To trap or disable cancellation in your procedure you must explicitly change the **EnableCancelKey** property every time the procedure is called.

Example

This example shows how the **EnableCancelKey** property can be used to set up a custom cancellation handler.

```
On Error GoTo handleCancel
Application.EnableCancelKey = xlErrorHandler
MsgBox "This may take a long time: press ESC to cancel"
For x = 1 To 1000000   ' Do something 1,000,000 times (long!)
    ' do something here
Next x

handleCancel:
If Err = 18 Then
    MsgBox "You cancelled"
End If
```

Enabled Property

Applies To   **Arc** Object, **Arcs** Collection, **Button** Object, **Buttons** Collection, **ChartObject** Object, **ChartObjects** Collection, **CheckBox** Object, **Drawing** Object, **DrawingObjects** Collection, **Drawings** Collection, **DropDown** Object, **DropDowns** Collection, **EditBox** Object, **EditBoxes** Collection, **GroupBox** Object, **GroupBoxes** Collection, **GroupObject** Object, **GroupObjects** Collection, **Label** Object, **Labels** Collection, **Line** Object, **Lines** Collection, **ListBox** Object, **ListBoxes** Collection, **Menu** Object, **MenuItem** Object, **OLEObject** Object, **OLEObjects** Collection, **OptionButton** Object, **OptionButtons** Collection, **Oval** Object, **Ovals** Collection, **Picture** Object, **Pictures** Collection, **Rectangle** Object, **Rectangles** Collection, **ScrollBar** Object, **ScrollBars** Collection, **Spinner** Object, **Spinners** Collection, **TextBox** Object, **TextBoxes** Collection, **ToolbarButton** Object.

Description   **True** if the control, drawing object, or menu item is enabled. Read-write, except for **Menu**, which is write-only.

Remarks   A disabled menu item is gray. A disabled toolbar button beeps when it is pressed.

See Also   **Pushed** Property.

Example   This example disables all buttons on the Standard toolbar that have custom images.

```
For Each btn In Application.Toolbars("Standard").ToolbarButtons
    If (Not btn.BuiltInFace And Not btn.IsGap) Then
        btn.Enabled = False
    End If
Next btn
```

EnableOutlining Property

Applies To   **Worksheet** Object.

Description   **True** if outlining symbols are enabled when user-interface-only protection is turned on. This property is available only in Microsoft Excel for Windows 95. Read-write.

Remarks   This property applies to each worksheet and isn't saved with the worksheet or session.

See Also   **Protect** Method, **Unprotect** Method.

Example   This example enables outlining symbols on a protected worksheet.

```
ActiveSheet.EnableOutlining = True
ActiveSheet.Protect contents:=True, userInterfaceOnly:=True
```

EnablePivotTable Property

Applies To   **Worksheet** Object.

Description   **True** if PivotTable controls and actions are enabled when user-interface-only protection is turned on. This property is available only in Microsoft Excel for Windows 95. Read-write.

Remarks   This property applies to each worksheet and isn't saved with the worksheet or session.

There must be a sufficient number of unlocked cells below and to the right of the PivotTable for Microsoft Excel to recalculate and display the PivotTable.

Use the **OnDoubleClick** property to disable double-clicking in the PivotTable.

See Also   **Protect** Method, **Unprotect** Method.

Example   This example enables PivotTable controls on a protected worksheet.

```
ActiveSheet.EnablePivotTable = True
ActiveSheet.Protect contents:=True, userInterfaceOnly:=True
```

EnableTipWizard Property

Applies To   **Application** Object.

Description   **True** if the TipWizard is enabled. Read-write.

Example   This example enables the TipWizard.

```
Application.EnableTipWizard = True
```

Enclosures Property

Applies To   **Mailer** Object.

Description   Returns or sets the enclosed files attached to the workbook mailer, as an array of strings, with each string indicating the path name of a file to attach as an enclosure. Relative paths are allowed, and are assumed to be based on the current folder. Available only in Microsoft Excel for the Apple Macintosh with the PowerTalk mail system extension installed. Read-write.

See Also   **BCCRecipients** Property, **CCRecipients** Property, **Mailer** Property, **Received** Property, **SendDateTime** Property, **Sender** Property, **SendMailer** Method, **Subject** Property, **ToRecipients** Property.

Example   This example sets up the **Mailer** object for workbook one and then sends the workbook.

```
With Workbooks(1)
    .HasMailer = True
    With .Mailer
        .Subject = "Here is the workbook"
        .ToRecipients = Array("Jean")
        .CCRecipients = Array("Adam", "Bernard")
        .BCCRecipients = Array("Chris")
        .Enclosures = Array("TestFile")
    End With
    .SendMailer
End With
```

End Method

Applies To   **Range** Object.

Description   Returns a **Range** object that represents the cell at the end of the region that contains the source range. Equivalent to pressing END+UP ARROW, END+DOWN ARROW, END+LEFT ARROW, or END+RIGHT ARROW.

Syntax   *object*.**End**(*direction*)

object
      Required. A cell in the range.

direction
      Required. Specifies the direction to move. One of **xlToLeft**, **xlToRight**, **xlUp**, or **xlDown**.

Example	This example selects the cell at the top of column B in the region containing cell B4.

```
Range("B4").End(xlUp).Select
```

This example selects the cell at the end of row 4 in the region containing cell B4.

```
Range("B4").End(xlToRight).Select
```

This example extends the selection from cell B4 to the last cell in row four that contains data.

```
Worksheets("Sheet1").Activate
Range("B4", Range("B4").End(xlToRight)).Select
```

End Statement

Description	Ends a procedure or block.
Syntax	**End**
	End Function
	End If
	End Property
	End Select
	End Sub
	End Type
	End With

The **End** statement syntax has these forms:

Statement	Description
End	Terminates procedure execution. Never required by itself but may be placed anywhere in a procedure to close files opened with the **Open** statement and to clear variables.
End Function	Required to end a **Function** statement.
End If	Required to end a block **If...Then...Else** statement.
End Property	Required to end a **Property Let**, **Property Get**, or **Property Set** procedure.
End Select	Required to end a **Select Case** statement.

Statement	Description
End Sub	Required to end a **Sub** statement.
End Type	Required to end a user-defined type definition (**Type** statement).
End With	Required to end a **With** statement.

Remarks

Note When executed, the **End** statement resets all module-level variables and all static local variables in all modules. If you need to preserve the value of these variables, use **Stop** instead. You can then resume execution while preserving the value of those variables.

See Also

Exit Statement, **Function** Statement, **If...Then...Else** Statement, **Property Get** Statement, **Property Let** Statement, **Property Set** Statement, **Select Case** Statement, **Stop** Statement, **Sub** Statement, **Type** Statement, **With** Statement.

Example

This example uses the **End** Statement to end code execution, a **Select Case** block, and a **Sub** procedure.

```
Sub EndStatementDemo()
    For Number = 1 To 2              ' Loop 2 times.
        Select Case Number          ' Evaluate Number.
            Case 1                  ' If Number equals 1.
                Debug.Print Number  ' Print value to Debug window.
            Case Else               ' If Number does not equal 1.
                End                 ' Terminate procedure execution.
        End Select                  ' End of Select Case Statement.
    Next Number
End Sub ' End of Sub procedure.
```

EndStyle Property

Applies To

ErrorBars Object.

Description

Returns or sets the end style for the error bars (either **xlCap** or **xlNoCap**). Read-write.

Example

This example sets the end style for the error bars for series one in Chart1. The example should be run on a 2-D line chart that has Y error bars for the first series.

```
Charts("Chart1").SeriesCollection(1).ErrorBars.EndStyle = xlCap
```

EntireColumn Property

Applies To   **Range** Object.

Description   Accessor. Returns a **Range** object that represents the entire column (or columns) that contain the specified range. Read-only.

See Also   **EntireRow** Property.

Example   This example selects the entire column that contains the active cell. The example must be run from a worksheet.

```
ActiveCell.EntireColumn.Select
```

EntireRow Property

Applies To   **Range** Object.

Description   Accessor. Returns a **Range** object that represents the entire row (or rows) that contain the specified range. Read-only.

See Also   **EntireColumn** Property.

Example   This example selects the entire row that contains the active cell. The example must be run from a worksheet.

```
ActiveCell.EntireRow.Select
```

EOF Function

Description   Returns a value that indicates whether the end of a file has been reached.

Syntax   **EOF(*filenumber*)**

The *filenumber* named argument is any valid file number.

Remarks   Use **EOF** to avoid an error when attempting to get input past the end of a file.

False is returned unless the end of the file has been reached; then **True** is returned. When used with files opened for **Random** or **Binary** access, **EOF** returns **False** unless the last executed **Get** statement is unable to read an entire record; then **True** is returned.

See Also   **Loc** Function, **LOF** Function, **Open** Statement.

Example   This example uses the **EOF** function to detect the end of a file. For purposes of this example, assume that MyFile is a text file with a few lines of text.

```
Open "MyFile" For Input As #1          ' Open file for input.
Do While Not EOF(1)                     ' Check for end of file.
    Line Input #1, InputData           ' Read line of data.
    Debug.Print InputData              ' Print to Debug window.
Loop
Close #1                                ' Close file.
```

Eqv Operator

Description   Used to perform a logical equivalence on two expressions.

Syntax   *result* = *expression1* **Eqv** *expression2*

The **Eqv** operator syntax has these parts:

Part	Description
result	Any numeric variable.
expression1	Any expression.
expression2	Any expression.

Remarks   If either expression is a **Null**, *result* is also a **Null**. When neither expression is a **Null**, *result* is determined according to the following table:

If *expression1* is	And *expression2* is	The *result* is
True	True	True
True	False	False
False	True	False
False	False	True

The **Eqv** operator performs a bit-wise comparison of identically positioned bits in two numeric expressions and sets the corresponding bit in *result* according to the following truth table:

If bit in *expression1* is	And bit in *expression2* is	The *result* is
0	0	1
0	1	0
1	0	0
1	1	1

See Also

Operator Precedence.

Example

This example uses the **Eqv** operator to perform logical equivalence on two expressions.

```
A = 10: B = 8: C = 6 : D = Null      ' Initialize variables.
MyCheck = A > B Eqv B > C             ' Returns True.
MyCheck = B > A Eqv B > C             ' Returns False.
MyCheck = A > B Eqv B > D             ' Returns Null.
MyCheck = A Eqv B                            ' Returns -3 (bit-wise
comparison).
```

Erase Statement

Description

Reinitializes the elements of fixed-size arrays and deallocates dynamic-array storage space.

Syntax

Erase *arraylist*

The *arraylist* argument is one or more comma-delimited array variables to be erased.

Remarks

It is important to know whether an array is fixed-size (ordinary) or dynamic because **Erase** behaves differently depending on the type of array. No memory is recovered for fixed-size arrays. **Erase** sets the elements of a fixed array as follows:

Type of array	Effect of Erase on fixed-array elements
Fixed numeric array	Sets each element to zero.
Fixed string array (variable length)	Sets each element to zero-length ("").
Fixed string array (fixed length)	Sets each element to zero.
Fixed **Variant** array	Sets each element to **Empty**.
Array of user-defined types	Sets each element as if it were a separate variable.
Array of objects	Sets each element to the special value **Nothing**.

Erase frees the memory used by dynamic arrays. Before your program can refer to the dynamic array again, it must redeclare the array variable's dimensions using a **ReDim** statement.

See Also

Array Function, **Dim** Statement, **Private** Statement, **Public** Statement, **ReDim** Statement, **Static** Statement.

Example

This example uses the **Erase** statement to reinitialize the elements of fixed-size arrays and deallocate dynamic-array storage space.

```
' Declare array variables.
Dim NumArray(10) As Integer          ' Integer array.
Dim StrVarArray(10) As String        ' Variable-string array.
Dim StrFixArray(10) As String * 10   ' Fixed-string array.
Dim VarArray(10) As Variant          ' Variant array.
Dim DynamicArray() As Integer        ' Dynamic array.
ReDim DynamicArray(10)               ' Allocate storage space.
Erase NumArray                       ' Each element set to 0.
Erase StrVarArray                    ' Each element set to "".
Erase StrFixArray                    ' Each element set to 0.
Erase VarArray                       ' Each element set to Empty.
Erase DynamicArray                   ' Free memory used by array.
```

Err Statement

Description   Sets **Err** to a specific value.

Syntax   **Err** = *errornumber*

The *errornumber* argument can be any valid error number or 0, which means no run-time error occurred.

Remarks

Err is used to record whether a run-time error has occurred and identifies the error. Use the **Err** statement to set **Err** to a nonzero, whole number to communicate error information between procedures. For example, you might use one of the unassigned run-time error numbers as an application-specific error number. To determine which error numbers are being used, use the **Error** function, the **Error** statement, or both. To avoid conflict with existing error numbers, create user-defined errors by defining your first error at 65,535 and work down from there.

You can also set **Err** to 0 using any form of the **Resume** or **On Error** statement or by executing an **Exit Sub**, **Exit Function** or **Exit Property** statement within an error handler. In addition, the **Error** statement can set **Err** to any value to simulate any run-time error.

See Also

Err Function, **Error** Function, **Error** Statement.

Example

This example shows how the **Err** statement is used to clear an error by setting **Err** to 0. Error number 55 is generated to illustrate its usage.

```
On Error Resume Next ' Enable error handling.
Open "TESTFILE" For Output as #1 ' Open file for output.
Kill "TESTFILE"  ' Attempt to delete open file.
Select Case Err ' Evaluate Error Number.
    Case 55 ' "File already open" error.
        Close #1' Close open file.
        Kill "TESTFILE" ' Delete file.
        Err = 0 ' Reset Err to 0.
    Case Else
        ' Handle other situations here...
End Select
```

Err, Erl Functions

Description   Returns error status.

Syntax   **Err**

          Erl

Remarks   After an error occurs, the **Err** function returns a number that is the run-time error number, identifying the error. The **Erl** function returns a number that is the line number of the line in which the error occurred, or the numbered line most closely preceding it.

Because **Err** and **Erl** return meaningful values only after an error has occurred, they are usually used in error-handling routines to determine the error and corrective action. Both **Err** and **Erl** are reset to 0 after any form of the **Resume** or **On Error** statement and after an **Exit Sub** or **Exit Function** statement within an error-handling routine.

Caution If you set up an error handler using **On Error GoTo** and that error handler calls another procedure, the value of **Err** and **Erl** may be reset to 0. To make sure that the value doesn't change, assign the values of **Err** or **Erl** to variables before calling another procedure or before executing **Resume**, **On Error**, **Exit Sub**, **Exit Function**, or **Exit Property**.

You can directly set the value returned by the **Err** function using the **Err** statement. You can set values for both **Err** and **Erl** indirectly using the **Error** statement.

The **Erl** function returns only a line number, not a line label, located at or before the line producing the error. Line numbers greater than 65,529 are treated as line labels and can't be returned by **Erl**. If your procedure has no line numbers, or if there is no line number before the point at which an error occurs, **Erl** returns 0.

See Also   **Err** Statement, **Error** Function, **Error** Statement, **On Error** Statement, **Resume** Statement.

Example   This example shows an error-handling routine which uses the **Err** and **Erl** functions. If there are no additional errors, **Err** returns error number 11 and **Erl** returns line 1030.

```
Sub ErrDemo()
1010  On Error GoTo ErrorHandler ' Set up an error handler.
1020  B = 1: C = 0   ' Initialize variables.
1030  A = B \ C ' Cause a "Division by zero" error.
1040  Exit Sub
ErrorHandler:    ' Error handler.
    ErrorNumber = Err    ' Get run-time error number.
    ErrorLine = Erl ' Get line number.
    Resume Next ' Resume execution at next line.
End Sub
```

Error Function

Description   Returns the error message that corresponds to a given error number.

Syntax   **Error**[(*errornumber*)]

The *errornumber* argument can be any valid error number. If *errornumber* is not defined, an error occurs. If omitted, the message corresponding to the most recent run-time error is returned. If no run-time error has occurred, **Error** returns a zero-length string ("").

Remarks Use the **Err** function to return the error number for the most recent run-time error.

See Also **Err** Function, **Error** Statement.

Example This example uses the **Error** function to print error messages that correspond to the specified error numbers.

```
For ErrorNumber = 61 To 64   ' Loop through values 61 - 64.
    Debug.Print Error(ErrorNumber)   ' Print error to Debug window.
Next ErrorNumber
```

Error Statement

Description Simulates the occurrence of an error.

Syntax **Error** *errornumber*

The *errornumber* can be any valid error number.

Remarks If *errornumber* is defined, the **Error** statement simulates the occurrence of that error; that is, it sets the value of **Err** to *errornumber*.

To define your own error numbers, use a number greater than any of the standard error numbers. To avoid conflict with existing error numbers, create user-defined errors by defining your first error at 65,535 and work down from there.

If an **Error** statement is executed when no error-handling routine is enabled, an error message is displayed and execution stops. If the **Error** statement specifies an error number that is not used, an error message is displayed.

See Also **Err** Function, **Error** Function, **On Error** Statement, **Resume** Statement.

Example This example uses the **Error** statement to simulate error 11.

```
On Error Resume Next ' Enable error handling.
Error 11' Simulate the "Division by zero" error.
```

ErrorBar Method

Applies To   **Series** Object.

Description   Applies error bars to the series.

Syntax   *object*.**ErrorBar**(*direction*, *include*, *type*, *amount*, *minusValues*)
                          object
                              Required. The **Series** object.

                          direction
                              Optional. Specifies the error bar direction (can be **xlX** or **xlY**; X is only
                              available for scatter charts). If omitted, error bars are applied in the Y direction.

                          include
                              Optional. Specifies the error bar parts to include (one of **xlPlusValues**,
                              xlMinusValues, **xlNone**, or **xlBoth**). If omitted, both error bars are included.

                          type
                              Optional. Specifies the error bar type (one of **xlFixedValue**, **xlPercent**,
                              xlStDev, **xlStError**, or **xlCustom**).

                          amount
                              Optional. The error amount. Used for only the positive error amount when *type*
                              = **xlCustom**.

                          minusValues
                              Optional. The negative error amount when *type* = **xlCustom**.

See Also   **ErrorBars** Property, **HasErrorBars** Property.

Example   This example applies standard error bars in the Y direction for series one in Chart1.
                          The error bars are applied in the positive and negative directions. The example
                          should be run on a 2-D line chart.

```
Charts("Chart1").SeriesCollection(1).ErrorBar _
    direction:=xlY, include:=xlBoth, type:=xlStError
```

ErrorBars Object

Description   Represents the error bars on a chart series. Error bars indicate the degree of
                          uncertainty for chart data. Only series in area, bar, column, line, and scatter groups
                          on a 2-D chart can have error bars. Only series in scatter groups can have x and y
                          error bars. There is no singular ErrorBar object; you must turn x error bars or y
                          error bars on or off for all points on a series at once.

Accessors	The **ErrorBars** property returns the error bars for a chart series. The following example turns on error bars for series one in embedded chart one on the worksheet named "Sheet1" and then sets the end style for the error bars.

```
Worksheets("sheet1").ChartObjects(1).Activate
ActiveChart.SeriesCollection(1).HasErrorBars = True
ActiveChart.SeriesCollection(1).ErrorBars.EndStyle = xlNoCap
```

Remarks	The **ErrorBar** method changes the error bar format and type.
Properties	**Application** Property, **Border** Property, **Creator** Property, **EndStyle** Property, **Name** Property, **Parent** Property.
Methods	**ClearFormats** Method, **Delete** Method, **Select** Method.

ErrorBars Property

Applies To	**Series** Object.
Description	Accessor. Returns an **ErrorBars** object that represents the error bars for the series. Read-only.
See Also	**ErrorBar** Method, **HasErrorBars** Property.
Example	This example sets the error bar color for series one in Chart1. The example should be run on a 2-D line chart that has error bars for series one.

```
With Charts("Chart1").SeriesCollection(1)
    .ErrorBars.Border.ColorIndex = 8
End With
```

Evaluate Method

Applies To	**Application** Object, **Chart** Object, **DialogSheet** Object, **Worksheet** Object.
Description	Converts a Microsoft Excel name to an object or to a value.
Syntax	*object*.**Evaluate**(*name*)

object
    Optional for **Application**, required for **Chart**, **DialogSheet**, and **Worksheet**. Contains the named object.

name
> Required. The name of the object, using the naming convention of Microsoft Excel.

Remarks
The following names in Microsoft Excel may be used with this method:

A1-style references. Any reference to a single cell using A1 notation. All references are considered to be absolute references.

Ranges. You may use the range, intersect, and union operators (colon, space, and comma) with references.

Defined names in the language of the macro.

External references using the ! operator. These references could be to a cell or a name defined in another workbook, for example, `Evaluate("[BOOK1.XLS]Sheet1!A1")`.

Graphic objects using their Microsoft Excel name ("Oval 3", for example). You cannot use the number alone.

Note   Using square brackets (for example, "[A1:C5]") is identical to calling the **Evaluate** method with a string argument. For example, the following expression pairs are equivalent.

```
[a1].Value = 25
Evaluate("A1").Value = 25
trigVariable = [SIN(45)]
trigVariable = Evaluate("SIN(45)")
Set firstCellInSheet = Workbooks("BOOK1.XLS").Sheets(4).[A1]
Set firstCellInSheet = Workbooks("BOOK1.XLS").Sheets(4).Evaluate("A1")
```

The advantage of using square brackets is that it is shorter. The advantage of using **Evaluate** is that the argument is a string, so you can construct the string in your code or use a Visual Basic variable.

Example
This example turns on bold formatting in cell A1 on Sheet1.

```
Worksheets("Sheet1").Activate
boldCell = "A1"
Application.Evaluate(boldCell).Font.Bold = True
```

Excel4IntlMacroSheets Method

Applies To   **Application** Object, **Workbook** Object.

Description   Accessor. Returns an object that represents a Microsoft Excel 4.0 international macro sheet (a **Worksheet** object, Syntax 1) or a collection of all Microsoft Excel 4.0 international macro sheets (a **Worksheets** object, Syntax 2) in the workbook. Read-only.

Syntax 1   *object*.**Excel4IntlMacroSheets**(*index*)

Syntax 2   *object*.**Excel4IntlMacroSheets**

object
　　Optional for **Application**, required for **Workbook**. The object that contains Microsoft Excel 4.0 international macro sheets.

index
　　Required for Syntax 1. The name or number of the Microsoft Excel 4.0 international macro sheet to return.

Remarks   Using this method with no object qualifier is a shortcut for **ActiveWorkbook.Excel4IntlMacroSheets**.

See Also   **Excel4MacroSheets** Method, **Worksheets** Method.

Example   This example displays the number of Microsoft Excel 4.0 international macro sheets in the active workbook.

```
MsgBox "There are " & ActiveWorkbook.Excel4IntlMacroSheets.Count & _
    " Microsoft Excel 4.0 international macro sheets in this workbook."
```

Excel4MacroSheets Method

Applies To   **Application** Object, **Workbook** Object.

Description   Accessor. Returns an object that represents a Microsoft Excel 4.0 macro sheet (a **Worksheet** object, Syntax 1) or a collection of all Microsoft Excel 4.0 macro sheets (a **Worksheets** object, Syntax 2) in the workbook. Read-only.

Syntax 1   *object*.**Excel4MacroSheets**(*index*)

Syntax 2   *object*.**Excel4MacroSheets**

object
　　Optional for **Application**, required for **Workbook**. The object that contains Microsoft Excel 4.0 macro sheets.

index
　　Required for Syntax 1. The name or number of the Microsoft Excel 4.0 macro sheet to return.

Remarks	Using this method with no object qualifier is a shortcut for **ActiveWorkbook.Excel4MacroSheets**.
See Also	**Excel4IntlMacroSheets** Method, **Worksheets** Method.
Example	This example displays the number of Microsoft Excel 4.0 macro sheets in the active workbook.

```
MsgBox "There are " & ActiveWorkbook.Excel4MacroSheets.Count & _
    " Microsoft Excel 4.0 macro sheets in this workbook."
```

ExclusiveAccess Method

Applies To	**Workbook** Object.
Description	Assigns the current user exclusive access to the workbook that's open as a shared list. Returns **True** if the workbook is successfully made an exclusive, nonshared list. This method is available only in Microsoft Excel for Windows 95.
Syntax	*object*.**ExclusiveAccess**
	object Required. The **Workbook** object.
Remarks	The **ExclusiveAccess** method saves any changes you've made to the workbook and requires other users who have the workbook open to save changes to a different file.
	If the specified workbook isn't open as a shared list, **ExclusiveAccess** fails. To determine whether a workbook is open as a shared list, use the **MultiUserEditing** property.
See Also	**MultiUserEditing** Property, **SaveAs** Method.
Example	This example determines whether the active workbook is open as a shared list. If it is, the example assigns the current user exclusive access.

```
If ActiveWorkbook.MultiUserEditing Then
    ActiveWorkbook.ExclusiveAccess
End If
```

ExecuteExcel4Macro Method

Applies To	**Application** Object.

Description	Runs a Microsoft Excel 4.0 macro function and returns the results of the function. Returned type depends on the function. Read-write.
Syntax	*object*.**ExecuteExcel4Macro**(*string*)

object
    Optional. The **Application** object.

string
    Required. A Microsoft Excel 4.0 macro language function without the equal sign. All references must be given as R1C1 strings. If *string* contains embedded double quotation marks, then you must double them. For example, to run the macro function =MID("sometext",1,4), *string* would have to be "MID(""sometext"",1,4)".

Remarks	The Microsoft Excel 4.0 macro is not evaluated in the context of the current workbook or sheet. This means that any references should be external and should specify an explicit workbook name. For example, to run a Microsoft Excel 4.0 macro "My_Macro" in Book1 you must use "Book1!My_Macro()". If you do not specify the workbook name, this method fails.
See Also	**Run** Method.
Example	This example runs the **GET.CELL(42)** macro function on cell C3 on Sheet1 and displays the result in a message box. The **GET.CELL(42)** macro function returns the horizontal distance from the left edge of the active window to the left edge of the active cell. This macro function has no direct Visual Basic equivalent.

```
Worksheets("Sheet1").Activate
Range("C3").Select
MsgBox ExecuteExcel4Macro("GET.CELL(42)")
```

Exit Statement

Description	Exits a block of **Do**...**Loop**, **For**...**Next**, **Function**, **Sub**, or **Property** code.
Syntax	**Exit Do**
	Exit For
	Exit Function
	Exit Property
	Exit Sub

The **Exit** statement syntax has these forms:

Statement	Description
Exit Do	Provides a way to exit a **Do**...**Loop** statement. It can be used only inside a **Do**...**Loop** statement. **Exit Do** transfers control to the statement following the **Loop** statement. When used within nested **Do**...**Loop** statements, **Exit Do** transfers control to the loop that is one nested level above the loop where it occurs.
Exit For	Provides a way to exit a **For** loop. It can be used only in a **For**...**Next** or **For Each**...**Next** loop. **Exit For** transfers control to the statement following the **Next** statement. When used within nested **For** loops, **Exit For** transfers control to the loop that is one nested level above the loop where it occurs.
Exit Function	Immediately exits the **Function** procedure in which it appears. Execution continues with the statement following the statement that called the **Function**.
Exit Property	Immediately exits the **Property** procedure in which it appears. Execution continues with the statement following the statement that called the **Property** procedure.
Exit Sub	Immediately exits the **Sub** procedure in which it appears. Execution continues with the statement following the statement that called the **Sub**.

Remarks

Do not confuse **Exit** statements with **End** statements. **Exit** does not define the end of a structure.

See Also

Do...**Loop** Statement, **End** Statement, **For**...**Next** Statement, **Function** Statement, **Property Get** Statement, **Property Let** Statement, **Property Set** Statement, **Stop** Statement, **Sub** Statement.

Example

This example uses the **Exit** statement to exit a **For**...**Next** loop, a **Do**...**Loop**, and a **Sub** procedure.

```
Sub ExitStatementDemo()
    Do                              ' Set up infinite loop.
    For I = 1 To 1000               ' Loop 1000 times.
    MyNum = Int(Rnd * 1000)         ' Generate random numbers.
    Select Case MyNum               ' Evaluate random number.
    Case 7: Exit For                ' If 7, exit For...Next.
    Case 29: Exit Do                ' If 29, exit Do...Loop.
    Case 54: Exit Sub               ' If 54, exit Sub procedure.
    End Select
    Next I
    Loop
End Sub
```

Exp Function

Description   Returns *e* (the base of natural logarithms) raised to a power.

Syntax   **Exp(*number*)**

The ***number*** named argument can be any valid numeric expression.

Remarks   If the value of ***number*** exceeds 709.782712893, an error occurs. The constant *e* is approximately 2.718282.

Note The **Exp** function complements the action of the **Log** function and is sometimes referred to as the antilogarithm.

See Also   Derived Math Functions, **Log** Function.

Example   This example uses the **Exp** function to return *e* raised to a power.

```
' Define angle in radians.
MyAngle = 1.3
' Calculate hyperbolic sine.
MyHSin = (Exp(MyAngle) - Exp(- 1 * MyAngle)) / 2
```

Explosion Property

Applies To   **Point** Object, **Series** Object.

Description   Returns or sets the percentage of pie-chart or doughnut-chart slice explosion. Zero is no explosion (the tip of the slice is in the center of the pie). Read-write.

Example   This example sets the explosion value for point two in Chart1. The example should be run on a pie chart.

```
Charts("Chart1").SeriesCollection(1).Points(2).Explosion = 20
```

Extend Method

Applies To   **SeriesCollection** Collection.

Description   Adds new data points to an existing series collection.

Syntax   *object*.**Extend**(*source*, *rowcol*, *categoryLabels*)

object
Required. The **SeriesCollection** object.

source
Required. Specifies the new data to be added to the **SeriesCollection** object, either as a **Range** or an array of data points.

rowcol
Optional. Specifies whether the new values are in the rows (**xlRows**) or columns (**xlColumns**) of the given range source. If this argument is omitted, Microsoft Excel attempts to determine where the values are by the size and orientation of the selected range or dimensions of the array. This argument is ignored if the source data is in an array.

categoryLabels
Optional. Ignored if *source* is an array. **True** if the first row or column contains the name of the category labels. **False** if the first row or column contains the first data point of the series. If this argument is omitted, Microsoft Excel attempts to determine the category label location from the contents of the first row or column.

See Also   **Add** Method (**SeriesCollection** Collection).

Example   This example extends the series on Chart1 by adding the data in cells B1:B6 on Sheet1.

```
Charts("Chart1").SeriesCollection.Extend _
        source:=Worksheets("Sheet1").Range("B1:B6")
```

FileAttr Function

Description   Returns file mode or operating system file handle information for files opened using the **Open** statement.

Syntax   **FileAttr**(*filenumber*,*returnType*)
The **FileAttr** function syntax has these named-argument parts:

Part	Description
filenumber	Any valid file number.
returnType	Number indicating the type of information to return: specify **1** to return a value indicating the file mode; specify **2** to return the operating system file handle.

Return Values	When the *returnType* argument is 1, the following return values indicate the file mode:

Value	File Mode
1	Input
2	Output
4	Random
8	Append
32	Binary

See Also   **GetAttr** Function, **Open** Statement, **SetAttr** Statement.

Example   This example uses the **FileAttr** function to return the file mode and file handle of an open file.

```
FileNum = 1                                ' Assign file number.
Open "TESTFILE" For Append As FileNum  ' Open file.
Handle = FileAttr(FileNum, 1)          ' Returns 8 (Append file mode).
Mode = FileAttr(FileNum, 2)            ' Returns file handle.
Close FileNum                          ' Close file.
```

FileConverters Property

Applies To   **Application** Object.

Description   Returns a list of installed file converters as a text array. Each row in the array contains information about a single file converter, as shown in the following table. Returns **Null** if there are no converters installed. Read-only.

Column	Contents
1	The long name of the converter, including the file type search string in Microsoft Windows (for example "Lotus 1-2-3 Files (*.wk*)").
2	The path name of the converter DLL or code resource.
3	The file extension search string in Microsoft Windows or the four-character file type on the Apple Macintosh.

Example

This example displays a message if the Multiplan file converter is installed.

```
installedCvts = Application.FileConverters
foundMultiplan = False
If Not IsNull(installedCvts) Then
    For arrayRow = 1 To UBound(installedCvts, 1)
        If installedCvts(arrayRow, 1) Like "*Multiplan*" Then
            foundMultiplan = True
            Exit For
        End If
    Next arrayRow
End If
If foundMultiplan = True Then
    MsgBox "Multiplan converter is installed"
Else
    MsgBox "Multiplan converter is not installed"
End If
```

FileCopy Statement

Description   Copies a file.

Syntax   **FileCopy** *source*, *destination*

The **FileCopy** statement syntax has these named argument parts:

Part	Description
source	String expression that specifies the name of the file to be copied—may include directory or folder, and drive.
destination	String expression that specifies the target file name—may include directory or folder, and drive.

Remarks   Open files can only be copied for read-only access.

See Also   **Kill** Statement, **Name** Statement.

Example   This example uses the **FileCopy** statement to copy one file to another. For purposes of this example, assume that SRCFILE is a file containing some data.

```
SourceFile = "SRCFILE"              ' Define source file name.
DestinationFile = "DESTFILE"        ' Define target file name.
FileCopy SourceFile, DestinationFile  ' Copy source to target.
```

FileDateTime Function

Description   Returns a date that indicates the date and time when a file was created or last modified .

Syntax   **FileDateTime(*pathname*)**

The ***pathname*** named argument is a string expression that specifies a file name— may include directory or folder, and drive.

See Also   **FileLen** Function, **GetAttr** Function.

Example   This example uses the **FileDateTime** function to get the date and time when a file was created or last modified. The format of the date and time displayed is based on the locale settings of your system.

```
' Assume TESTFILE was last modified on February 12 1993 at 4:35:47 PM.
' Assume United States/English locale settings.
MyStamp = FileDateTime("TESTFILE")  ' Returns "2/12/93 4:35:47 PM".
```

FileFormat Property

Applies To   **Workbook** Object.

Description   Returns the file format and/or type of the workbook, as shown in the following list. Read-only.

xlAddIn	**xlExcel3**	**xlTextMSDOS**
xlCSV	**xlExcel4**	**xlTextWindows**
xlCSVMac	**xlExcel4Workbook**	**xlTextPrinter**
xlCSVMSDOS	**xlIntlAddIn**	**xlWK1**
xlCSVWindows	**xlIntlMacro**	**xlWK3**
xlDBF2	**xlNormal**	**xlWKS**
xlDBF3	**xlSYLK**	**xlWQ1**
xlDBF4	**xlTemplate**	**xlWK3FM3**
xlDIF	**xlText**	**xlWK1FMT**
xlExcel2	**xlTextMac**	**xlWK1ALL**

Remarks   The following additional formats are available in Far East Microsoft Excel: **xlWJ2WD1**, **xlExcel2FarEast**, and **xlWorks2FarEast**.

Example   This example saves the active workbook in Normal file format if its current file format is WK3.

```
If ActiveWorkbook.FileFormat = xlWK3 Then
    ActiveWorkbook.SaveAs fileFormat:=xlNormal
End If
```

FileLen Function

Description   Returns the length of a file in bytes.

Syntax   **FileLen(*pathname*)**

The *pathname* named argument is a string expression that specifies a file name— may include directory or folder, and drive.

Remarks   If the specified file is open when the **FileLen** function is called, the value returned represents the last saved disk size of the file.

To obtain the length of an open file, use the **LOF** function.

See Also   **FileDateTime** Function, **GetAttr** Function, **LOF** Function.

Example   This example uses the **FileLen** function to return the length of a file in bytes. For purposes of this example, assume that TESTFILE is a file containing some data.

```
MySize = FileLen("TESTFILE")         ' Returns file length (bytes).
```

FillAcrossSheets Method

Applies To   **Sheets** Collection, **Worksheets** Collection.

Description   Copies a range to the same area on all other worksheets in a collection.

Syntax   *object*.**FillAcrossSheets(*range*, *type*)**

object
   Required. The **Sheets** or **Worksheets** object.

range
   Required. Specifies the range to fill across the worksheets in the collection. The range must be from a worksheet within the collection.

type
> Optional. Specifies how to copy the range (one of xlAll, xlContents, or xlFormulas). The default is xlAll if this argument is omitted.

Example   This example fills the range A1:C5 on Sheet1, Sheet5, and Sheet7 with the contents of the same range on Sheet1.

```
x = Array("Sheet1", "Sheet5", "Sheet7")
Sheets(x).FillAcrossSheets _
    Worksheets("Sheet1").Range("A1:C5")
```

FillDown Method

Applies To   **Range** Object.

Description   Fills down from the top cell or cells of the range to the bottom. Copies the contents and formats of the cell or cells in the top row of a range into the rest of the rows in the range.

Syntax   *object*.**FillDown**

object
> Required. The range to fill.

See Also   **AutoFill** Method, **FillLeft** Method, **FillRight** Method, **FillUp** Method.

Example   This example fills the range A1:A10 on Sheet1, based on the contents of cell A1.

```
Worksheets("Sheet1").Range("A1:A10").FillDown
```

FillLeft Method

Applies To   **Range** Object.

Description   Fills left from the rightmost cell or cells of the range to the left. Copies the contents and formats of the cell or cells in the right column of a range into the rest of the columns in the range.

Syntax   *object*.**FillLeft**

object
> Required. The range to fill.

See Also   **AutoFill** Method, **FillDown** Method, **FillRight** Method, **FillUp** Method.

Example   This example fills the range A1:M1 on Sheet1, based on the contents of cell M1.

```
Worksheets("Sheet1").Range("A1:M1").FillLeft
```

FillRight Method

Applies To   **Range** Object.

Description   Fills right from the leftmost cell or cells of the range to the right. Copies the
                       contents and formats of the cell or cells in the left column of a range into the rest of
                       the columns in the range.

Syntax   *object*.**FillRight**

                       object
                           Required. The range to fill.

See Also   **AutoFill** Method, **FillDown** Method, **FillLeft** Method, **FillUp** Method.

Example   This example fills the range A1:M1 on Sheet1, based on the contents of cell A1.

```
Worksheets("Sheet1").Range("A1:M1").FillRight
```

FillUp Method

Applies To   **Range** Object.

Description   Fills up from the bottom cell or cells of the range to the top. Copies the contents and
                       formats of the cell or cells in the bottom row of a range into the rest of the rows in
                       the range.

Syntax   *object*.**FillUp**

                       object
                           Required. The range to fill.

See Also   **AutoFill** Method, **FillDown** Method, **FillLeft** Method, **FillRight** Method.

Example   This example fills the range A1:A10 on Sheet1, based on the contents of cell A10.

```
Worksheets("Sheet1").Range("A1:A10").FillUp
```

FilterMode Property

Applies To   **Worksheet** Object.

Description   **True** if the worksheet is in filter mode. Read-only.

Remarks   This property will be **True** if the worksheet contains a filtered list in which there are hidden rows.

See Also   **AdvancedFilter** Method, **AutoFilter** Method, **AutoFilterMode** Property, **ShowAllData** Method.

Example   This example displays the filter status of Sheet1 in a message box.

```
If Worksheets("Sheet1").FilterMode = True Then
    MsgBox "Filter mode is on"
Else
    MsgBox "Filter mode is off"
End If
```

Find Method

Applies To   **Range** Object.

Description   Finds specific information in a range, and returns a **Range** object that represents the first cell where it is found. Returns **Nothing** if no match is found. Does not affect the selection or active cell.

For help about using the **Find** worksheet function in Visual Basic, see "Using Worksheet Functions in Visual Basic" in online Help.

Syntax   *object*.**Find**(*what*, *after*, *lookIn*, *lookAt*, *searchOrder*, *searchDirection*, *matchCase*, *matchByte*)

object
    Required. The range to search.

what
    Required. The contents for which you want to search. May be a string or any Microsoft Excel data type.

after

Optional. The first cell after which you want to search. This corresponds to the position of the active cell when a search is done from the user interface. Note that *after* must be one cell in the range. If this argument is omitted, the top left cell of the range is used as the starting point for the search. Remember that the search begins *after* this cell; the specified cell is not searched until the method wraps back around to this cell.

lookIn

Optional. One of **xlFormulas**, **xlValues**, or **xlNotes**.

lookAt

Optional. May be **xlWhole** or **xlPart**.

searchOrder

Optional. One of **xlByRows** (to search row-major) or **xlByColumns** (to search column-major).

searchDirection

Optional. **xlNext** or **xlPrevious**; if omitted it is **xlNext**.

matchCase

Optional. If **True**, case-sensitive search is performed.

matchByte

Optional. Used only in Far East Microsoft Excel. If **True**, double-byte characters match only double-byte characters. If **False**, double-byte characters can match their single-byte equivalents.

Remarks

The settings for *lookIn*, *lookAt*, *searchOrder*, *matchCase*, and *matchByte* are saved each time you use this method. If you do not specify values for these arguments the next time you call the method, the saved values are used. Setting these arguments changes the settings in the Find dialog box, and changing the settings in the Find dialog box changes the saved values that are used if you omit the arguments. To avoid problems, explicitly set these arguments each time you use this method.

The **FindNext** and **FindPrevious** methods can be used to repeat the search.

When the search reaches the end of the specified search range, it wraps around to the beginning of the range. To stop a search when this wraparound occurs, save the address of the first found cell, and then test each successive found-cell address against this saved address.

To find cells matching more complicated patterns, use **For Each** with the **Like** operator. For example, the following code searches for all cells in the range A1:C5 that use a font starting with the letters "Cour". When it finds a match, it changes the font to Times New Roman:

```
For Each c In [A1:C5]
    If c.Font.Name Like "Cour*" Then
        c.Font.Name = "Times New Roman"
    End If
Next
```

See Also   **FindNext** Method, **FindPrevious** Method, **Replace** Method.

Example   This example finds the first occurrence of the word Phoenix in column B on Sheet1 and then displays the address of the cell that contains this word. If the word is not found, the example diplays a message.

```
Set foundCell = Worksheets("Sheet1").Columns("B").Find("Phoenix")
If foundCell Is Nothing Then
    MsgBox "The word was not found"
Else
    MsgBox "The word was found in cell " & foundCell.Address
End If
```

FindFile Method

Applies To   **Application** Object.

Description   Displays the File Open dialog box.

Syntax   *object*.**FindFile**

object
    Required. The **Application** object.

Remarks   This method displays the File Open dialog box and allows the user to open a file. If a new file is opened successfully, this method returns **True**. If the user cancels the dialog box, this method returns **False**.

Example   This example displays the Open dialog box.

```
Application.FindFile
```

FindNext Method

Applies To	**Range** Object.
Description	Continues a search started with the **Find** method. Finds the next cell matching the same conditions and returns a **Range** object that represents that cell. Does not affect the selection or active cell.
Syntax	*object*.**FindNext**(*after*)

object
> Required. The range to search.

after
> Optional. The first cell after which you want to search. This corresponds to the position of the active cell when a search is done from the user interface. If omitted, the top left cell of the range is used as the starting point for the search. Remember that the search begins *after* this cell; the specified cell is not searched until the method wraps back around to this cell.

Remarks	When the search reaches the end of the specified search range, it wraps around to the beginning of the range. To stop a search when this wraparound occurs, save the address of the first found cell, and then test each successive found-cell address against this saved address.
See Also	**Find** Method, **FindPrevious** Method, **Replace** Method.
Example	This example changes all occurrences of the word Phoenix in column A on Sheet1 to the word Flagstaff.

```
Set foundCell = Worksheets("Sheet1").Columns("A").Find("Phoenix")
Do While Not (foundCell Is Nothing)
    foundCell.Value = "Flagstaff"
    Set foundCell = Worksheets("Sheet1").Columns("A").FindNext
Loop
```

FindPrevious Method

Applies To	**Range** Object.
Description	Continues a search started with the **Find** method. Finds the previous cell matching the same conditions and returns a **Range** object that represents that cell. Does not affect the selection or active cell.
Syntax	*object*.**FindPrevious**(*after*)

object
> Required. The range to search.

after
> Optional. The first cell before which you want to search. This corresponds to the position of the active cell when a search is done from the user interface. If omitted, the top left cell of the range is used as the starting point for the search. Remember that the search begins *before* this cell; the specified cell is not searched until the method wraps back around to this cell.

Remarks   When the search reaches the beginning of the specified search range, it wraps around to the end of the range. To stop a search when this wraparound occurs, save the address of the first found cell, and then test each successive found-cell address against this saved address.

See Also   **Find** Method, **FindNext** Method, **Replace** Method.

Example   This example shows how the **FindPrevious** method is used with the **Find** and **FindNext** methods. Before running this example, make sure that Sheet1 contains at least two occurrences of the word Phoenix in column B.

```
Set fc = Worksheets("Sheet1").Columns("B").Find(what:="Phoenix")
    MsgBox "The first occurrence is in cell " & fc.Address
Set fc = Worksheets("Sheet1").Columns("B").FindNext(after:=fc)
    MsgBox "The next occurrence is in cell " & fc.Address
Set fc = Worksheets("Sheet1").Columns("B").FindPrevious(after:=fc)
    MsgBox "The previous occurrence is in cell " & fc.Address
```

FirstPageNumber Property

Applies To   **PageSetup** Object.

Description   Returns or sets the first page number that will be used for printing this sheet (the default value is **xlAutomatic**). Read-write.

Example   This example sets the first page number of Sheet1 to 100.

```
Worksheets("Sheet1").PageSetup.FirstPageNumber = 100
```

FirstSliceAngle Property

Applies To   **ChartGroup** Object.

Description   Returns or sets the angle of the first pie or doughnut slice for a pie, 3-D pie, or doughnut chart, in degrees clockwise from vertical. Applies only to pie, 3-D pie, and doughnut charts. Read-write.

Example   This example sets the angle for the first slice in chart group one in Chart1. The example should be run on a 2-D pie chart.

```
Charts("Chart1").ChartGroups(1).FirstSliceAngle = 15
```

FitToPagesTall Property

Applies To   **PageSetup** Object.

Description   Returns or sets how many pages tall the worksheet will be scaled to when it is printed. The **Zoom** property must be **False**, or this property is ignored. Read-write.

Remarks   If this property is **False**, Microsoft Excel scales the worksheet according to the **FitToPagesWide** property.

This property applies only to worksheets.

Example   This example causes Sheet1 to print exactly one page wide and tall.

```
With Worksheets("Sheet1").PageSetup
    .Zoom = False
    .FitToPagesTall = 1
    .FitToPagesWide = 1
End With
```

FitToPagesWide Property

Applies To   **PageSetup** Object.

Description   Returns or sets how many pages wide the worksheet will be scaled when it is printed. The **Zoom** property must be **False**, or this property is ignored. Read-write.

Remarks   If this property is **False**, Microsoft Excel scales the worksheet according to the **FitToPagesTall** property.

This property applies only to worksheets.

Example   This example causes Sheet1 to print exactly one page wide and tall.

```
With Worksheets("Sheet1").PageSetup
    .Zoom = False
    .FitToPagesTall = 1
    .FitToPagesWide = 1
End With
```

FixedDecimal Property

Applies To   **Application** Object.

Description   All data entered after this property is set to **True** will be formatted with the number of fixed decimal places set by the **FixedDecimalPlaces** property.

Example   This example sets the **FixedDecimal** property to **True** and then sets the **FixedDecimalPlaces** property to 4. Entering "30000" after running this example produces "3" on the worksheet, and entering "12500" produces "1.25."

```
Application.FixedDecimal = True
Application.FixedDecimalPlaces = 4
```

FixedDecimalPlaces Property

Applies To   **Application** Object.

Description   Returns or sets the number of fixed decimal places used when the **FixedDecimal** property is set to **True**. Read-write.

Example   This example sets the **FixedDecimal** property to **True** and then sets the **FixedDecimalPlaces** property to 4. Entering "30000" after running this example produces "3" on the worksheet, and entering "12500" produces "1.25."

```
Application.FixedDecimal = True
Application.FixedDecimalPlaces = 4
```

Floor Object

Description   Represents the floor of a 3-D chart.

Accessors	The **Floor** property returns the floor for the specified chart. The following example sets the floor color for embedded chart one on the worksheet named "Sheet1." The example will fail if the chart is not a 3-D chart.

```
Worksheets("sheet1").ChartObjects(1).Activate
ActiveChart.Floor.Interior.Color = RGB(0, 255, 255)
```

Properties	**Application** Property, **Border** Property, **Creator** Property, **Interior** Property, **Name** Property, **Parent** Property.
Methods	**ClearFormats** Method, **Select** Method.

Floor Property

Applies To	**Chart** Object.
Description	Returns a **Floor** object that represents the floor of the 3-D chart. Read-only.
	For help about using the **Floor** worksheet function in Visual Basic, see Using Worksheet Functions in Visual Basic.
Example	This example sets the chart floor color of Chart1 to blue. The example should be run on a 3-D chart (the **Floor** property fails on 2-D charts).

```
Charts("Chart1").Floor.Interior.ColorIndex = 5
```

Focus Property

Applies To	**DialogSheet** Object.
Description	Returns or sets the dynamic focus of the running dialog box, as a string containing the ID for the control with the focus. The control with the focus is where user keyboard input is directed, and the focus is visually indicated by a dashed rectangle around the control or around selections within the control. Read-write.
Remarks	Reading and setting this property while the dialog is not running will cause an error. While the dialog is running, setting this property will attempt to change the focus to the specified control. Not all controls will accept the focus, and the dialog manager may refuse to move the focus under certain conditions. Reading this property always returns the ID of the control with the focus.

Example   This example sets the focus to button one in the running dialog box and then displays the button name in a message box. The example should be the event procedure for a control or dialog box frame on a dialog sheet.

```
ActiveDialog.Focus = ActiveDialog.Buttons(1).Name
MsgBox ActiveDialog.Focus
```

Font Object

Description   Contains font attributes (font name, font size, color, and so on) for an object.

Accessors   The **Font** property returns the **Font** object. The font attributes are properties of the **Font** object. The following example makes cells A1:C5 bold on the worksheet named "Sheet1."

```
Worksheets("sheet1").Range("a1:c5").Font.Bold = True
```

If you do not want to format all the text contained in a cell or graphic object at once, use the **Characters** method to return a subset of the text.

Properties   **Application** Property, **Background** Property, **Bold** Property, **Color** Property, **ColorIndex** Property, **Creator** Property, **FontStyle** Property, **Italic** Property, **Name** Property, **OutlineFont** Property, **Parent** Property, **Shadow** Property, **Size** Property, **Strikethrough** Property, **Subscript** Property, **Superscript** Property, **Underline** Property.

Font Property

Applies To   **AxisTitle** Object, **Button** Object, **Buttons** Collection, **Characters** Object, **ChartArea** Object, **ChartTitle** Object, **DataLabel** Object, **DataLabels** Collection, **DrawingObjects** Collection, **GroupObject** Object, **GroupObjects** Collection, **Legend** Object, **LegendEntry** Object, **Range** Object, **Style** Object, **TextBox** Object, **TextBoxes** Collection, **TickLabels** Object.

Description   Accessor. Returns a **Font** object that represents font of the specified object. Read-only.

See Also   **Font** Object.

Example   This example sets the font in cell B5 on Sheet1 to 14-point bold italic.

```
With Worksheets("Sheet1").Range("B5").Font
    .Size = 14
    .Bold = True
    .Italic = True
End With
```

FontStyle Property

Applies To   **Font** Object.

Description   Returns or sets the font style (as a string). Read-write.

Remarks   Changing this property may affect other **Font** properties (such as **Bold** and **Italic**).

See Also   **Background** Property, **Bold** Property, **Color** Property, **ColorIndex** Property, **Font** Object, **Italic** Property, **Name** Property, **OutlineFont** Property, **Shadow** Property, **Size** Property, **Strikethrough** Property, **Subscript** Property, **Superscript** Property, **Underline** Property.

Example   This example sets the font style for cell A1 on Sheet1 to bold and italic.

```
Worksheets("Sheet1").Range("A1").Font.FontStyle = "Bold Italic"
```

FooterMargin Property

Applies To   **PageSetup** Object.

Description   Returns or sets the distance from the bottom of the page to the footer, in points (1/72 inch). Read-write.

See Also   **BottomMargin** Property, **HeaderMargin** Property, **LeftMargin** Property, **RightMargin** Property, **TopMargin** Property.

Example   This example sets the footer margin of Sheet1 to 0.5 inch.

```
Worksheets("Sheet1").PageSetup.FooterMargin = _
            Application.InchesToPoints(0.5)
```

For Each...Next Statement

Description   Repeats a group of statements for each element in an array or collection.

Syntax   **For Each** *element* **In** *group*
    [*statements*]
    [**Exit For**]
    [*statements*]
Next [*element*]

The **For Each**...**Next** statement syntax has these parts:

Part	Description
element	Variable used to iterate through the elements of the collection or array. For collections, *element* can only be a **Variant** variable, a generic **Object** variable, or any specific OLE Automation object variable. For arrays, *element* can only be a **Variant** variable.
group	Name of an object collection or array (except an array of user-defined types).
statements	One or more statements that are executed on each item in *collection*.

Important When using **For Each**... **Next** with arrays, you can only read the value contained in the array elements indicated by the control variable *element*. You cannot set the value by assigning a value to *element*.

Remarks   The **For Each** block is entered if there is at least one element in *group*. Once the loop has been entered, all the statements in the loop are executed for the first element in *group*. Then, as long as there are more elements in *group*, the statements in the loop continue to execute for each element. When there are no more elements in *group*, the loop is exited and execution continues with the statement following the **Next** statement.

The **Exit For** can only be used within a **For Each...Next** or **For...Next** control structure to provide an alternate way to exit. Any number of **Exit For** statements may be placed anywhere in the loop. The **Exit For** is often used with the evaluation of some condition (for example, **If...Then**), and transfers control to the statement immediately following **Next**.

You can nest **For Each**...**Next** loops by placing one **For Each**...**Next** loop within another. However, each loop *element* must be unique.

Note If you omit *element* in a **Next** statement, execution continues as if you had included it. If a **Next** statement is encountered before its corresponding **For** statement, an error occurs.

You can't use the **For Each**...**Next** statement with an array of user-defined types because a **Variant** can't contain a user-defined type.

See Also

Do...**Loop** Statement, **Exit** Statement, **For**...**Next** Statement, **While**...**Wend** Statement.

Example

This example uses the **For Each**...**Next** statement to search the `Text` property of all elements in a collection for the existence of the string "Hello". In the example, `MyObject` is a text-related object and is an element of the collection `MyCollection`. Both are generic names used for illustration purposes only.

```
Found = False                        ' Initialize variable.
For Each MyObject In MyCollection    ' Iterate through each element.
    If MyObject.Text = "Hello" Then  ' If Text equals "Hello".
        Found = True                 ' Set Found to True.
        Exit For                     ' Exit loop.
    End If
Next
```

This example loops on cells A1:D10 on Sheet1. If one of the cells has a value less than 0.001, the code replaces the value with 0 (zero).

```
For Each c in Worksheets("Sheet1").Range("A1:D10")
    If c.Value < .001 Then
        c.Value = 0
    End If
Next c
```

This example loops on the range named "TestRange" and displays the number of empty cells in the range.

```
numBlanks = 0
For Each c In Range("TestRange")
    If c.Value = "" Then
        numBlanks = numBlanks + 1
    End If
Next c
MsgBox "There are " & numBlanks & " empty cells in this range."
```

This example closes and saves changes to all workbooks except the one that is running the example.

```
For Each w In Workbooks
    If w.Name <> ThisWorkbook.Name Then
        w.Close savechanges:=True
    End If
Next w
```

This example deletes every worksheet in the active workbook without displaying the confirmation dialog box.

```
Application.DisplayAlerts = False
For Each w In Worksheets
    w.Delete
Next w
Application.DisplayAlerts = True
```

This example creates a new worksheet and then inserts a list of all names in the active workbook, including their formulas in A1-style notation in the language of the user.

```
Set newSheet = ActiveWorkbook.Worksheets.Add
i = 1
For Each nm In ActiveWorkbook.Names
    newSheet.Cells(i, 1).Value = nm.NameLocal
    newSheet.Cells(i, 2).Value = "'" & nm.RefersToLocal
    i = i + 1
Next nm
```

For...Next Statement

Description   Repeats a group of statements a specified number of times.

Syntax   **For** *counter* = *start* **To** *end* [**Step** *step*]
                   [*statements*]
                   [**Exit For**]
                   [*statements*]
              Next [*counter*]

The **For**...**Next** statement syntax has these parts:

Part	Description
counter	Numeric variable used as a loop counter. The variable can't be any array element or any element of a user-defined type.
start	Initial value of *counter*.
end	Final value of *counter*.
step	Amount *counter* is changed each time through the loop. If not specified, *step* defaults to one.
statements	One or more statements between **For** and **Next** that are executed the specified number of times.

Remarks

The *step* argument can be either positive or negative. The value of the *step* argument determines loop processing as follows:

Value	Loop executes if
Positive or 0	*counter <= end*
Negative	*counter >= end*

Once the loop starts and all statements in the loop have executed, *step* is added to *counter*. At this point, either the statements in the loop execute again (based on the same test that caused the loop to execute initially), or the loop is exited and execution continues with the statement following the **Next** statement.

Tip Changing the value of *counter* while inside a loop can make it more difficult to read and debug.

The **Exit For** can only be used within a **For Each**...**Next** or **For**...**Next** control structure to provide an alternate way to exit. Any number of **Exit For** statements may be placed anywhere in the loop. The **Exit For** is often used with the evaluation of some condition (for example, **If**...**Then**), and transfers control to the statement immediately following **Next**.

You can nest **For**...**Next** loops by placing one **For**...**Next** loop within another. Give each loop a unique variable name as its *counter*. The following construction is correct:

```
For I = 1 To 10
    For J = 1 To 10
        For K = 1 To 10
            . . .
        Next K
    Next J
Next I
```

Note If you omit *counter* in a **Next** statement, execution continues as if you had included it. If a **Next** statement is encountered before its corresponding **For** statement, an error occurs.

See Also

Do...**Loop** Statement, **Exit** Statement, **For Each**...**Next** Statement, **While**...**Wend** Statement.

Example

This example uses the **For**...**Next** statement to create a string that contains 10 instances of the numbers 0 through 9, each string separated from the other by a single space. The outer loop uses a loop counter variable that is decremented each time through the loop.

```
For Words = 10 To 1 Step -1      ' Set up 10 repetitions.
    For Chars = 0 To 9           ' Set up 10 repetitions.
        MyString = MyString & Chars ' Append number to string.
    Next Chars
    MyString = MyString & " "        ' Append a space.
Next Words
```

This example displays the number of columns in the selection on Sheet1. The code also tests for a multiple-area selection; if one exists, the code loops on the areas of the selection.

```
Worksheets("Sheet1").Activate
areaCount = Selection.Areas.Count
If areaCount <= 1 Then
    MsgBox "The selection contains " & _
        Selection.Columns.Count & " columns."
Else
    For i = 1 To areaCount
        MsgBox "Area " & i & " of the selection contains " & _
            Selection.Areas(i).Columns.Count & " columns."
    Next i
End If
```

This example creates a new worksheet and then inserts a list of the active workbook's sheet names in the first column.

```
Set newSheet = Sheets.Add(Type:=xlWorksheet)
For i = 1 To Sheets.Count
    newSheet.Cells(i, 1).Value = Sheets(i).Name
Next i
```

This example selects every other item in list box one on Sheet1.

```
Dim items() As Boolean
Set lbox = Worksheets("Sheet1").ListBoxes(1)
ReDim items(1 To lbox.ListCount)
For i = 1 To lbox.ListCount
    If i Mod 2 = 1 Then
        items(i) = True
    Else
        items(i) = False
    End If
Next
lbox.MultiSelect = xlExtended
lbox.Selected = items
```

Format Function

Description   Formats an expression according to instructions contained in a format expression.

Syntax   **Format**(*expression*[,*format*])

The **Format** function syntax has these parts:

Part	Description
expression	Any valid *expression*.
format	A valid named or user-defined format expression.

Remarks

To Format These	Do This
Numbers	Use predefined named numeric formats or create user-defined numeric formats.
Dates and times	Use predefined named date/time formats or create user-defined date/time formats.
Date and time serial numbers	Use date and time formats or numeric formats.
Strings	Create your own user-defined string formats.

If you try to format a number without specifying *format*, **Format** provides the same functionality as the **Str** function. However, positive numbers formatted as strings using **Format** lack the leading space reserved for displaying the sign of the value; whereas, those converted using **Str** retain the leading space.

Example   This example shows various uses of the **Format** function to format values using both named and user-defined formats. For the date separator (/), time separator (:) and AM/ PM literal, the actual formatted output displayed by your system depends on the settings at the time. When times and dates are listed back in the development environment, the short time and short date formats of the code locale are used. When displayed by running code, the short time and short date formats of the system locale are used, which may be different from the code locale. For this example, English - US is assumed.

```
' MyTime and MyDate will be displayed in the development environment
' using current system short time and short date settings.
MyTime = #17:04:23#
MyDate = #January 27, 1993#

' Returns current system time in the system-defined long time format.
MyStr = Format(Time, "Long Time")

' Returns current system date in the system-defined long date format.
MyStr = Format(Date, "Long Date")
```

```
MyStr = Format(MyTime, "h:m:s")              ' Returns "17:4:23".
MyStr = Format(MyTime, "hh:mm:ss AMPM")      ' Returns "05:04:23 PM".
MyStr = Format(MyDate, "dddd, mmm d yyyy")   ' Returns
    ' "Wednesday, Jan 27 1993".
' If format is not supplied, a string is returned.
MyStr = Format(23)                           ' Returns "23".

' User-defined formats.
MyStr = Format(5459.4, "##,##0.00")          ' Returns "5,459.40".
MyStr = Format(334.9, "###0.00")             ' Returns "334.90".
MyStr = Format(5, "0.00%")                   ' Returns "500.00%".
MyStr = Format("HELLO", "<")                 ' Returns "hello".
MyStr = Format("This is it", ">")            ' Returns "THIS IS IT".
```

Different Formats for Different Numeric Values

A format expression for numbers can have from one to four sections separated by semicolons. (If the *format* argument contains one of the predefined formats, only one section is allowed.)

If you use	The result is
One section only	The format expression applies to all values.
Two sections	The first section applies to positive values and zeros, the second to negative values.
Three sections	The first section applies to positive values, the second to negative values, and the third to zeros.
Four sections	The first section applies to positive values, the second to negative values, the third to zeros, and the fourth to **Null** values.

The following example has two sections: the first defines the format for positive values and zeros; the second section defines the format for negative values.

```
"$#,##0;($#,##0)"
```

If you include semicolons with nothing between them, the missing section is printed using the format of the positive value. For example, the following format displays positive and negative values using the format in the first section and displays "Zero" if the value is zero.

```
"$#,##0;;\Z\e\r\o"
```

Examples   Some sample format expressions for numbers are shown below. (These examples all assume that your system's locale setting is English-US.) The first column contains the format strings. The other columns contain the output that results if the formatted data has the value given in the column headings.

Format (*format*)	Positive 5	Negative 5	Decimal .5	Null
Zero-length string	5	-5	0.5	
0	5	-5	1	
0.00	5.00	-5.00	0.50	
#,##0	5	-5	1	
#,##0.00;;;Nil	5.00	-5.00	0.50	Nil
$#,##0;($#,##0)	$5	($5)	$1	
$#,##0.00;($#,##0.00)	$5.00	($5.00)	$0.50	
0%	500%	-500%	50%	
0.00%	500.00%	-500.00%	50.00%	
0.00E+00	5.00E+00	-5.00E+00	5.00E-01	
0.00E-00	5.00E00	-5.00E00	5.00E-01	

Different Formats for Different String Values

A format expression for strings can have one section, or two sections separated by a semicolon.

If you use	The result is
One section only	The format applies to all string data.
Two sections	The first section applies to string data, the second to **Null** values and zero-length strings.

Named Date/Time Formats

The following table identifies the predefined date and time format names:

Format Name	Description
General Date	Display a date and/or time. For real numbers, display a date and time (for example, 4/3/93 05:34 PM); if there is no fractional part, display only a date (for example, 4/3/93); if there is no integer part, display time only (for example, 05:34 PM). Date display is determined by your system settings.
Long Date	Display a date according to your system's long date format.
Medium Date	Display a date using the medium date format appropriate for the language version of the host application.
Short Date	Display a date using your system's short date format.
Long Time	Display a time using your system's long time format: includes hours, minutes, seconds.

Format Name	Description
Medium Time	Display time in 12-hour format using hours and minutes and the AM/PM designator.
Short Time	Display a time using the 24-hour format (for example, 17:45).

Named Numeric Formats

The following table identifies the predefined numeric format names:

Format name	Description
General Number	Display number as is, with no thousand separators.
Currency	Display number with thousand separator, if appropriate; display negative numbers enclosed in parentheses; display two digits to the right of the decimal separator. Note that output is based on system settings.
Fixed	Display at least one digit to the left and two digits to the right of the decimal separator.
Standard	Display number with thousands separator, at least one digit to the left and two digits to the right of the decimal separator.
Percent	Display number multiplied by 100 with a percent sign (%) appended to the right; always displays two digits to the right of the decimal separator.
Scientific	Use standard scientific notation.
Yes/No	Display No if number is 0; otherwise, display Yes.
True/False	Display **False** if number is 0; otherwise, display **True**.
On/Off	Display Off if number is 0; otherwise, display On.

User-Defined Date/Time Formats

The following table identifies characters you can use to create user-defined date/time formats:

Character	Description
:	Time separator. In some locales, other characters may be used to represent the time separator. The time separator separates hours, minutes, and seconds when time values are formatted. The actual character used as the time separator in formatted output is determined by your system settings.
/	Date separator. In some locales, other characters may be used to represent the date separator. The date separator separates the day, month, and year when date values are formatted. The actual character used as the date separator in formatted output is determined by your system settings.

Character	Description
c	Display the date as ddddd and display the time as t t t t t, in that order. Display only date information if there is no fractional part to the date serial number; display only time information if there is no integer portion.
d	Display the day as a number without a leading zero (1-31).
dd	Display the day as a number with a leading zero (01-31).
ddd	Display the day as an abbreviation (Sun-Sat).
dddd	Display the day as a full name (Sunday-Saturday).
ddddd	Display a date as a complete date (including day, month, and year), formatted according to your system's short date format setting. For Microsoft Windows, the default short date format is m/d/yy.
dddddd	Display a date serial number as a complete date (including day, month, and year) formatted according to the long date setting recognized by your system. For Microsoft Windows, the default long date format is mmmm dd, yyyy.
w	Display the day of the week as a number (1 for Sunday through 7 for Saturday).
ww	Display the week of the year as a number (1-53).
m	Display the month as a number without a leading zero (1-12). If m immediately follows h or hh, the minute rather than the month is displayed.
mm	Display the month as a number with a leading zero (01-12). If m immediately follows h or hh, the minute rather than the month is displayed.
mmm	Display the month as an abbreviation (Jan-Dec).
mmmm	Display the month as a full month name (January-December).
q	Display the quarter of the year as a number (1-4).
y	Display the day of the year as a number (1-366).
yy	Display the year as a 2-digit number (00-99).
yyyy	Display the year as a 4-digit number (100-9999).
h	Display the hour as a number without leading zeros (0-23).
hh	Display the hour as a number with leading zeros (00-23).
n	Display the minute as a number without leading zeros (0-59).
nn	Display the minute as a number with leading zeros (00-59).
s	Display the second as a number without leading zeros (0-59).
ss	Display the second as a number with leading zeros (00-59).

Character	Description
t t t t t	Display a time as a complete time (including hour, minute, and second), formatted using the time separator defined by the time format recognized by your system. A leading zero is displayed if the leading zero option is selected and the time is before 10:00 A.M. or P.M. The default time format is `h:mm:ss`.
AM/PM	Use the 12-hour clock and display an uppercase AM with any hour before noon; display an uppercase PM with any hour between noon and 11:59 P.M.
am/pm	Use the 12-hour clock and display a lowercase AM with any hour before noon; display a lowercase PM with any hour between noon and 11:59 P.M.
A/P	Use the 12-hour clock and display an uppercase A with any hour before noon; display an uppercase P with any hour between noon and 11:59 P.M.
a/p	Use the 12-hour clock and display a lowercase A with any hour before noon; display a lowercase P with any hour between noon and 11:59 P.M.
AMPM	Use the 12-hour clock and display the AM string literal as defined by your system with any hour before noon; display the PM string literal as defined by your system with any hour between noon and 11:59 P.M. AMPM can be either uppercase or lowercase, but the case of the string displayed matches the string as defined by your system settings. For Microsoft Windows, the default format is AM/PM.

Examples

The following are examples of user-defined date and time formats for December 7, 1958:

Format	Display
`m/d/yy`	12/7/58
`d-mm`	7-Dec
`d-mmmm-yy`	7-December-58
`d-mmmm`	7 December
`mmmm-yy`	December 58
`hh:mm AM/PM`	08:50 PM
`h:mm:ss a/p`	8:50:35 p
`h:mm`	20:50
`h:mm:ss`	20:50:35
`m/d/yy h:mm`	12/7/58 20:50

User-Defined Numeric Formats

The following table identifies characters you can use to create user-defined number formats:

Character	Description
None	**No formatting**
	Display the number with no formatting.
0	**Digit placeholder**
	Display a digit or a zero. If the expression has a digit in the position where the 0 appears in the format string, display it; otherwise, display a zero in that position.
	If the number has fewer digits than there are zeros (on either side of the decimal) in the format expression, display leading or trailing zeros. If the number has more digits to the right of the decimal separator than there are zeros to the right of the decimal separator in the format expression, round the number to as many decimal places as there are zeros. If the number has more digits to the left of the decimal separator than there are zeros to the left of the decimal separator in the format expression, display the extra digits without modification.
#	**Digit placeholder**
	Display a digit or nothing. If the expression has a digit in the position where the # appears in the format string, display it; otherwise, display nothing in that position.
	This symbol works like the 0 digit placeholder, except that leading and trailing zeros aren't displayed if the number has the same or fewer digits than there are # characters on either side of the decimal separator in the format expression.
.	**Decimal placeholder**
	In some locales, a comma is used as the decimal separator. The decimal placeholder determines how many digits are displayed to the left and right of the decimal separator. If the format expression contains only number signs to the left of this symbol, numbers smaller than 1 begin with a decimal separator. If you always want a leading zero displayed with fractional numbers, use 0 as the first digit placeholder to the left of the decimal separator instead. The actual character used as a decimal placeholder in the formatted output depends on the Number Format recognized by your system.
%	**Percentage placeholder**
	The expression is multiplied by 100. The percent character (%) is inserted in the position where it appears in the format string.

Character	Description
,	**Thousand separator**
	In some locales, a period is used as a thousand separator. The thousand separator separates thousands from hundreds within a number that has four or more places to the left of the decimal separator. Standard use of the thousand separator is specified if the format contains a thousand separator surrounded by digit placeholders (0 or #). Two adjacent thousand separators or a thousand separator immediately to the left of the decimal separator (whether or not a decimal is specified) means "scale the number by dividing it by 1000, rounding as needed." You can scale large numbers using this technique. For example, you can use the format string "##0,," to represent 100 million as 100. Numbers smaller than 1 million are displayed as 0. Two adjacent thousand separators in any position other than immediately to the left of the decimal separator are treated simply as specifying the use of a thousand separator. The actual character used as the thousand separator in the formatted output depends on the Number Format recognized by your system.
:	**Time separator**
	In some locales, other characters may be used to represent the time separator. The time separator separates hours, minutes, and seconds when time values are formatted. The actual character used as the time separator in formatted output is determined by your system settings.
/	**Date separator**
	In some locales, other characters may be used to represent the date separator. The date separator separates the day, month, and year when date values are formatted. The actual character used as the date separator in formatted output is determined by your system settings.
E- E+ e- e+	**Scientific format**
	If the format expression contains at least one digit placeholder (0 or #) to the right of E-, E+, e-, or e+, the number is displayed in scientific format and E or e is inserted between the number and its exponent. The number of digit placeholders to the right determines the number of digits in the exponent. Use E- or e- to place a minus sign next to negative exponents. Use E+ or e+ to place a minus sign next to negative exponents and a plus sign next to positive exponents.
- + $ ( ) space	**Display a literal character**
	To display a character other than one of those listed, precede it with a backslash (\) or enclose it in double quotation marks (" ").

Character	Description
\	**Display the next character in the format string**
	Many characters in the format expression have a special meaning and can't be displayed as literal characters unless they are preceded by a backslash. The backslash itself isn't displayed. Using a backslash is the same as enclosing the next character in double quotation marks. To display a backslash, use two backslashes (\\).
	Examples of characters that can't be displayed as literal characters are the date- and time-formatting characters (a, c, d, h, m, n, p, q, s, t, w, y, and /:), the numeric-formatting characters (#, 0, %, E, e, comma, and period), and the string-formatting characters (@, &, <, >, and !).
"ABC"	**Display the string inside the double quotation marks**
	To include a string in *format* from within code, you must use **Chr**(34) to enclose the text (34 is the character code for a double quotation mark).

Example

Some sample format expressions for numbers are shown below. (These examples all assume that your system's locale setting is English-US.) The first column contains the format strings. The other columns contain the output that results if the formatted data has the value given in the column headings.

Format (*format*)	Positive 5	Negative 5	Decimal .5	Null
Zero-length string	5	-5	0.5	
0	5	-5	1	
0.00	5.00	-5.00	0.50	
#,##0	5	-5	1	
#,##0.00;;;Nil	5.00	-5.00	0.50	Nil
$#,##0;($#,##0)	$5	($5)	$1	
$#,##0.00;($#,##0.00)	$5.00	($5.00)	$0.50	
0%	500%	-500%	50%	
0.00%	500.00%	-500.00%	50.00%	
0.00E+00	5.00E+00	-5.00E+00	5.00E-01	
0.00E-00	5.00E00	-5.00E00	5.00E-01	

User-Defined String Formats

You can use any of the following characters to create a format expression for strings:

Character	Description
@	**Character placeholder**
	Display a character or a space. If the string has a character in the position where the @ appears in the format string, display it; otherwise, display a space in that position. Placeholders are filled from right to left unless there is an ! character in the format string. See below.
&	**Character placeholder**
	Display a character or nothing. If the string has a character in the position where the & appears, display it; otherwise, display nothing. Placeholders are filled from right to left unless there is an ! character in the format string. See below.
<	**Force lowercase**
	Display all characters in lowercase format.
>	**Force uppercase**
	Display all characters in uppercase format.
!	**Force left to right fill of placeholders**
	The default is to fill from right to left.

Formula Property

Applies To   **Button** Object, **Buttons** Collection, **Picture** Object, **Pictures** Collection, **Range** Object, **Series** Object, **TextBox** Object, **TextBoxes** Collection.

Description   Returns or sets the object's formula, in A1-style notation and the language of the macro. Read-write.

Remarks   If the cell contains a constant, this property returns the constant. If the cell is empty, it returns an empty string. If the cell contains a formula, it returns the formula as a string, in the same format as it would be displayed in the formula bar (including the equal sign).

If you set the value or formula of a cell to a date, Microsoft Excel checks to see if that cell is already formatted with one of the date or time number formats. If not, it changes the number format to the default short date number format.

If the range is a one- or two-dimensional range, you can set the formula to a Visual Basic array of the same dimensions. Similarly, you can put the formula into a Visual Basic array.

Setting the formula of a multi-cell range fills all cells in the range with the formula.

When used with a **Picture** object, the formula must use absolute A1-style notation.

See Also   **FormulaArray** Property, **FormulaLocal** Property, **FormulaR1C1** Property, **FormulaR1C1Local** Property.

Example   This example sets the formula for cell A1 on Sheet1.

```
Worksheets("Sheet1").Range("A1").Formula = "=$A$4+$A$10"
```

FormulaArray Property

Applies To   **Range** Object.

Description   Returns or sets the formula of a range, entered as an array. Returns (or can be set to) a single formula or a Visual Basic array. If the specified range is not array-entered, this property returns **Null**. Read-write.

Remarks   If you use this property to array-enter a formula, the formula must use the R1C1 reference style, not the A1 reference style; see the second example.

See Also   **Formula** Property.

Example   This example enters the number 3 as an array constant in cells A1:C5 on Sheet1.

```
Worksheets("Sheet1").Range("A1:C5").FormulaArray = "=3"
```

This example array-enters the formula =SUM(R1C1:R3C3) in cells E1:E3 on Sheet1.

```
Worksheets("Sheet1").Range("E1:E3").FormulaArray = _
    "=Sum(R1C1:R3C3)"
```

FormulaHidden Property

Applies To   **Range** Object, **Style** Object.

Description	**True** if the formula will be hidden when the workbook or worksheet is protected. Read-write.
Remarks	Do not confuse this property with the **Hidden** property.
See Also	**Locked** Property, **Protect** Method, **Unprotect** Method.
Example	This example hides the formulas in column A on Sheet1 when the worksheet is protected.

```
Worksheets("Sheet1").Columns("A").FormulaHidden = True
```

FormulaLocal Property

Applies To	**Range** Object, **Series** Object.
Description	Returns or sets the formula for the object, using A1-style references in the user's language. Read-write.
Remarks	If the cell contains a constant, this property returns the constant. If the cell is empty, it returns an empty string. If the cell contains a formula, it returns the formula as a string, in the same format as it would be displayed in the formula bar (including the equal sign).
	If you set the value or formula of a cell to a date, Microsoft Excel checks to see if that cell is already formatted with one of the date or time number formats. If not, it changes the number format to the default short date number format.
	If the range is a one- or two-dimensional range, you can set the formula to a Visual Basic array of the same dimensions. Similarly, you can put the formula into a Visual Basic array.
	Setting the formula of a multi-cell range fills all cells in the range with the formula.
See Also	**Formula** Property, **FormulaArray** Property, **FormulaR1C1** Property, **FormulaR1C1Local** Property.
Example	Assume that you enter the formula =SUM(A1:A10) in cell A11 on Sheet1, using the American English version of Microsoft Excel. If you then open the workbook on a computer that is running the German version and run the following example, the example displays the formula =SUMME(A1:A10) in a message box.

```
MsgBox Worksheets(1).Range(A11).FormulaLocal
```

FormulaR1C1 Property

Applies To   **Range** Object, **Series** Object.

Description   Returns or sets the formula for the object, using R1C1-style notation in the language of the macro. Read-write.

Remarks   If the cell contains a constant, this property returns the constant. If the cell is empty, it returns an empty string. If the cell contains a formula, it returns the formula as a string, in the same format as it would be displayed in the formula bar (including the equal sign).

If you set the value or formula of a cell to a date, Microsoft Excel checks to see if that cell is already formatted with one of the date or time number formats. If not, it changes the number format to the default short date number format.

If the range is a one- or two-dimensional range, you can set the formula to a Visual Basic array of the same dimensions. Similarly, you can put the formula into a Visual Basic array.

Setting the formula of a multi-cell range fills all cells in the range with the formula.

See Also   **Formula** Property, **FormulaArray** Property, **FormulaLocal** Property, **FormulaR1C1Local** Property.

Example   This example sets the formula for cell B1 on Sheet1.

```
Worksheets("Sheet1").Range("B1").FormulaR1C1 = "=SQRT(R1C1)"
```

FormulaR1C1Local Property

Applies To   **Range** Object, **Series** Object.

Description   Returns or sets the formula for the object, using R1C1-style notation in the user's language.

Remarks   If the cell contains a constant, this property returns the constant. If the cell is empty, it returns an empty string. If the cell contains a formula, it returns the formula as a string, in the same format as it would be displayed in the formula bar (including the equal sign).

If you set the value or formula of a cell to a date, Microsoft Excel checks to see if that cell is already formatted with one of the date or time number formats. If not, it changes the number format to the default short date number format.

If the range is a one- or two-dimensional range, you can set the formula to a Visual Basic array of the same dimensions. Similarly, you can put the formula into a Visual Basic array.

Setting the formula of a multi-cell range fills all cells in the range with the formula.

See Also **Formula** Property, **FormulaArray** Property, **FormulaLocal** Property, **FormulaR1C1** Property.

Example Assume that you enter the formula =SUM(A1:A10) in cell A11 on Sheet1, using the American English version of Microsoft Excel. If you then open the workbook on a computer that is running the German version and run the following example, the example displays the formula =SUMME(Z1S1:Z10S1) in a message box.

```
MsgBox Worksheets(1).Range("A11").FormulaR1C1Local
```

Forward Property

Applies To **Trendline** Object.

Description Returns or sets the number of periods (or units on a scatter chart) that the trendline extends forward. Read-write.

See Also **Backward** Property, **ForwardMailer** Method.

Example This example sets the number of units the trendline on Chart1 extends forward and backward. The example should be run on a 2-D column chart that contains a single series with a trendline.

```
With Charts("Chart1").SeriesCollection(1).Trendlines(1)
    .Forward = 5
    .Backward = .5
End With
```

ForwardMailer Method

Applies To **Workbook** Object.

Description   Sets up the workbook mailer for forwarding by creating a new mailer that is preset with the subject and enclosures of the existing mailer. Valid only when the workbook has a received mailer attached (you can only forward a workbook you have received). Available only in Microsoft Excel for the Apple Macintosh with the PowerTalk mail system extension installed.

Syntax   *object*.**ForwardMailer**

object
    Required. The **Workbook** object.

Remarks   After you use this method to set up a workbook mailer for forwarding, you can change the mailer settings (if necessary) with the **Mailer** property and then use the **SendMailer** method to forward the workbook.

This method generates an error if it is used in Microsoft Windows.

See Also   **Mailer** Property, **MailSystem** Property, **SendMailer** Method.

Example   This example forwards the active workbook.

```
ActiveWorkbook.ForwardMailer
```

FreeFile Function

Description   Returns the next file number available for use by the **Open** statement.

Syntax   **FreeFile**[(*rangenumber*)]

The *rangenumber* argument specifies the range from which the next free file number is to be returned. Specify a **0** (default) to return a file number in the range 1 to 255, inclusive. Specify a **1** to return a file number in the range 256 to 511.

Remarks   Use **FreeFile** when you need to supply a file number and you want to make sure the file number is not already in use.

See Also   **Open** Statement.

Example

This example uses the **FreeFile** function to return the next available file number. Five files are opened for output within the loop and some sample data is written to each.

```
For MyIndex - 1 to 5                                    ' Loop 5 times.
    FileNumber = FreeFile                               ' Get unused file
    ' number.
    Open "TEST" & MyIndex For Output As #FileNumber     ' Create file
name.
    Write #FileNumber, "This is a sample"               ' Output text.
    Close #FileNumber                                   ' Close file.
Next MyIndex
```

FreezePanes Property

Applies To

Window Object.

Description

True if split panes are frozen. Read-write.

Remarks

It is possible for **FreezePanes** to be **True** and **Split** to be **False**, or vice versa.

This property applies only to worksheets and macro sheets.

Example

This example freezes split panes in the active window in BOOK1.XLS.

```
Workbooks("BOOK1.XLS").Worksheets("Sheet1").Activate
ActiveWindow.FreezePanes = True
```

FullName Property

Applies To

AddIn Object, **Workbook** Object.

Description

Returns the name of the object, including its path on disk, as a string. Read-only.

Remarks

This property is equivalent to the **Path** property, followed by the current file system separator, followed by the **Name** property.

Example

This example displays the path and filename of every add-in.

```
For Each a In AddIns
    MsgBox a.FullName
Next a
```

This example displays the path and filename of the active workbook (assuming that the workbook has been saved).

```
MsgBox ActiveWorkbook.FullName
```

Function Property

Applies To   **PivotField** Object.

Description   Returns or sets the function used to summarize the **PivotField** (data fields only). Can be one of **xlAverage**, **xlCount**, **xlCountNums**, **xlMax**, **xlMin**, **xlProduct**, **xlStDev**, **xlStDevP**, **xlSum**, **xlVar**, or **xlVarP**. Read-write.

Example   This example sets the Sum of 1994 field in PivotTable1 to use the SUM function.

```
ActiveSheet.PivotTables("PivotTable1"). _
    PivotFields("Sum of 1994").Function = xlSum
```

Function Statement

Description   Declares the name, arguments, and code that form the body of a **Function** procedure.

Syntax   [**Public** | **Private**][**Static**] **Function** *name* [(*arglist*)][**As** *type*]
    [*statements*]
    [*name = expression*]
    [**Exit Function**]
    [*statements*]
    [*name = expression*]
End Function

The **Function** statement syntax has these parts:

Part	Description
Public	Indicates that the **Function** procedure is accessible to all other procedures in all modules. If used in a private module (one that contains an **Option Private** statement) the procedure is not available outside the project.
Private	Indicates that the **Function** procedure is accessible only to other procedures in the module where it is declared.

Part	Description
Static	Indicates that the **Function** procedure's local variables are preserved between calls. The **Static** attribute doesn't affect variables that are declared outside the **Function**, even if they are used in the procedure.
name	Name of the **Function**; follows standard variable naming conventions.
arglist	List of variables representing arguments that are passed to the **Function** procedure when it is called. Multiple variables are separated by commas.
type	Data type of the value returned by the **Function** procedure; may be **Boolean**, **Integer**, **Long**, **Currency**, **Single**, **Double**, **Date**, **String** (except fixed length), **Object**, **Variant** or any user-defined type. Arrays of any type can't be returned, but a **Variant** containing an array can.
statements	Any group of statements to be executed within the body of the **Function** procedure.
expression	Return value of the **Function**.

The *arglist* argument has the following syntax and parts:

[Optional][ByVal | ByRef][ParamArray] *varname*[( )][**As** *type*]

Part	Description
Optional	Indicates that an argument is not required. If used, all subsequent arguments in *arglist* must also be optional and declared using the **Optional** keyword. All **Optional** arguments must be **Variant**. **Optional** can't be used for any argument if **ParamArray** is used.
ByVal	Indicates that the argument is passed by value.
ByRef	Indicates that the argument is passed by reference.
ParamArray	Used only as the last argument in *arglist* to indicate that the final argument is an **Optional** array of **Variant** elements. The **ParamArray** keyword allows you to provide an arbitrary number of arguments. May not be used with **ByVal**, **ByRef**, or **Optional**.
varname	Name of the variable representing the argument; follows standard variable naming conventions.
type	Data type of the argument passed to the procedure; may be **Boolean**, **Integer**, **Long**, **Currency**, **Single**, **Double**, **Date**, **String** (variable length only), **Object**, **Variant**, a user-defined type, or an object type.

Remarks

If not explicitly specified using either **Public** or **Private**, **Function** procedures are **Public** by default. If **Static** is not used, the value of local variables is not preserved between calls.

All executable code must be in procedures. You can't define a **Function** procedure inside another **Function**, **Sub**, or **Property** procedure.

The **Exit Function** keywords cause an immediate exit from a **Function** procedure. Program execution continues with the statement following the statement that called the **Function** procedure. Any number of **Exit Function** statements can appear anywhere in a **Function** procedure.

Like a **Sub** procedure, a **Function** procedure is a separate procedure that can take arguments, perform a series of statements, and change the values of its arguments. However, unlike a **Sub** procedure, a **Function** procedure can be used on the right hand side of an expression in the same way you use any intrinsic function, such as **Sqr**, **Cos**, or **Chr**, when you want to use the value returned by the function.

You call a **Function** procedure using the function name, followed by the argument list in parentheses, in an expression. If the function has no arguments, you still must include the parentheses. See the **Call** statement for specific information on how to call **Function** procedures.

Caution   Function procedures can be recursive; that is, they can call themselves to perform a given task. However, recursion can lead to stack overflow. The **Static** keyword is usually not used with recursive **Function** procedures.

To return a value from a function, assign the value to the function name. Any number of such assignments can appear anywhere within the procedure. If no value is assigned to *name*, the procedure returns a default value: a numeric function returns 0, a string function returns a zero-length string (""), and a **Variant** function returns **Empty**. A function that returns an object reference returns **Nothing** if no object reference is assigned to *name* (using **Set**) within the **Function**.

The following example shows how to assign a return value to a function named BinarySearch. In this case, **False** is assigned to the name to indicate that some value was not found.

```
Function BinarySearch(. . .) As Boolean
. . .
    ' Value not found. Return a value of False.
    If lower > upper Then
        BinarySearch = False
        Exit Function
    End If
. . .
End Function
```

Variables used in **Function** procedures fall into two categories: those that are explicitly declared within the procedure and those that are not. Variables that are explicitly declared in a procedure (using **Dim** or the equivalent) are always local to the procedure. Other variables used but not explicitly declared in a procedure are also local unless they are explicitly declared at some higher level outside the procedure.

Caution A procedure can use a variable that is not explicitly declared in the procedure, but a name conflict can occur if anything you have defined at the module level has the same name. If your procedure refers to an undeclared variable that has the same name as another procedure, constant or variable, it is assumed that your procedure is referring to that module-level name. Explicitly declare variables to avoid this kind of conflict. You can use an **Option Explicit** statement to force explicit declaration of variables.

Caution Arithmetic expressions may be rearranged to increase internal efficiency. Avoid using a **Function** procedure in an arithmetic expression when the function changes the value of variables in the same expression.

See Also

Call Statement, **Dim** Statement, **Option Explicit** Statement, **Property Get** Statement, **Property Let** Statement, **Property Set** Statement, **Set** Statement, **Static** Statement, **Sub** Statement.

Example

This example uses the **Function** statement to declare the name, arguments and code that form the body of a **Function** procedure.

```
' The following user-defined function returns the square root of the
' argument passed to it.
Function CalculateSquareRoot(NumberArg As Double) As Double
    If NumberArg < 0 Then                    ' Evaluate argument.
        Exit Function                        ' Exit to calling procedure.
    Else
        CalculateSquareRoot = Sqr(NumberArg) ' Return square root.
    EndIf
End Function

' Using the ParamArray keyword enables a function to accept a variable
' number of arguments. In the following definition, FirstArg is passed
' by value.
Function CalcSum(ByVal FirstArg As Integer, ParamArray OtherArgs())
' If the function is invoked as...
ReturnValue = CalcSum(4,3,2,1)
' Local variables get the following values: FirstArg=4, OtherArgs(1)=3,
' OtherArgs(2) = 2 and so on, assuming default lower bound for
' arrays = 1.

' If a function's arguments are defined as...
Function MyFunc(MyStr As String, Optional MyArg1, Optional MyArg2)
' It can be invoked in the following ways.
RetVal = MyFunc("Hello", 2, "World")    ' All 3 arguments supplied.
RetVal = MyFunc("Test", , 5)            ' Second argument omitted.
RetVal = MyFunc("Test")                 ' First argument only.
```

FunctionWizard Method

Applies To   **Range** Object.

Description   Starts the Function Wizard for the upper left cell of the range.

Syntax   *object*.**FunctionWizard**

object
     Required. The **Range** object.

Example   This example starts the Function Wizard for the active cell on Sheet1.

```
Worksheets("Sheet1").Activate
ActiveCell.FunctionWizard
```

GapDepth Property

Applies To   **Chart** Object.

Description   Returns or sets the distance between the data series in a 3-D chart, as a percentage of the marker width (between 0 and 500). Read-write.

Example   This example sets the distance between the data series in Chart1 to 200 percent of the marker width. The example should be run on a 3-D chart.

```
Charts("Chart1").GapDepth = 200
```

GapWidth Property

Applies To   **ChartGroup** Object.

Description   Returns or sets the space between bar or column clusters as a percentage of the width of a bar or column. This property must be between 0 and 500. Read-write.

See Also   **Overlap** Property.

Example   This example sets the space between column clusters in Chart1 to be 50 percent of the width of a column.

```
Charts("Chart1").ChartGroups(1).GapWidth = 50
```

Get Statement

Description

Reads from an open disk file into a variable.

Syntax

Get [**#**]*filenumber*,[*recnumber*],*varname*

The **Get** statement syntax has these parts:

Part	Description
filenumber	Any valid file number.
recnumber	Record number (**Random** mode files) or byte number (**Binary** mode files) at which reading begins.
varname	Valid variable name into which data is read.

Remarks

The first record/byte in a file is at position 1, the second record/byte is at position 2, and so on. If you omit recnumber, the next record or byte (the one after the last **Get** or **Put** statement or the one pointed to by the last **Seek** function) is read. Delimiting commas must be included, for example:

```
Get #4,,FileBuffer
```

For files opened in **Random** mode, the following rules apply:

- If the length of the data being read is less than the length specified in the **Len** clause of the **Open** statement, **Get** still reads subsequent records on record-length boundaries. The space between the end of one record and the beginning of the next record is padded with the existing contents of the file buffer. Because the amount of padding data can't be determined with any certainty, it is generally a good idea to have the record length match the length of the data being read.

- If the variable being read into is a variable-length string, **Get** reads a 2-byte descriptor containing the string length and then the data that goes into the variable. Therefore, the record length specified by the **Len** clause in the **Open** statement must be at least 2 bytes greater than the actual length of the string.

- If the variable being read into is a **Variant** of numeric type, **Get** reads 2 bytes identifying the **VarType** of the **Variant** and then the data that goes into the variable. For example, when reading a **Variant** of **VarType** 3, **Get** reads 6 bytes: 2 bytes identifying the **Variant** as **VarType** 3 (**Long**) and 4 bytes containing the **Long** data. The record length specified by the **Len** clause in the **Open** statement must be at least 2 bytes greater than the actual number of bytes required to store the variable.

- If the variable being read into is a **String Variant** (**VarType** 8), **Get** reads 2 bytes identifying the **VarType**, 2 bytes indicating the length of the string, and then the string data. The record length specified by the **Len** clause in the **Open** statement must be at least 4 bytes greater than the actual length of the string.

- If the variable being read into is any other type of variable (not a variable-length string or a **Variant**), **Get** reads only the variable data. The record length specified by the **Len** clause in the **Open** statement must be greater than or equal to the length of the data being read.

- **Get** reads elements of user-defined types as if each were being read individually except that there is no padding between elements. The record length specified by the **Len** clause in the **Open** statement must be greater than or equal to the sum of all the bytes required to read the individual elements.

For files opened in **Binary** mode, all of the **Random** rules apply except that:

- In **Binary** mode, the **Len** clause in the **Open** statement has no effect. **Get** reads all variables from disk contiguously; that is, with no padding between records.

- **Get** reads variable-length strings that aren't elements of user-defined types without expecting the 2-byte length descriptor. The number of bytes read equals the number of characters already in the string. For example, the following statements read 10 bytes from file number 1:

```
VarString = String(10," ")
Get #1,,VarString
```

See Also

Open Statement, **Put** Statement, **Type** Statement, **VarType** Function.

Example

This example uses the **Get** statement to read data from a disk file into a variable. For purposes of this example, assume that TESTFILE is a file containing five records of the user-defined type Record.

```
Type Record                          ' Define user-defined type.
    ID As Integer
    Name As String * 20
End Type
Dim MyRecord As Record               ' Declare variable.
' Open sample file for random access.
Open "TESTFILE" For Random As #1 Len = Len(MyRecord)
' Read the sample file using the Get statement.
Position = 3                         ' Define record number.
Get #1, Position, MyRecord           ' Read third record.
Close #1                             ' Close file.
```

GetAttr Function

Description

Returns a number representing the attributes of a file, directory or folder, or volume label.

Syntax

GetAttr(*pathname***)**

The *pathname* named argument is a string expression that specifies a file name—may include directory or folder, and drive.

Return Values

The value returned by **GetAttr** is the sum of the following attribute values:

Value	Constant	File Attribute
0	vbNormal	Normal.
1	vbReadonly	Read-only.
2	vbHidden	Hidden.
4	vbSystem	System file—not available on the Macintosh.
8	vbVolume	Volume label—not available on the Macintosh.
16	vbDirectory	Directory or folder.
32	vbArchive	File has changed since last backup—not available on the Macintosh.

Note These constants are specified by Visual Basic. As a result, the names can be used anywhere in your code in place of the actual values.

Remarks

To determine which attributes are set, use the **And** operator to perform a bit-wise comparison of the value returned by the **GetAttr** function and the value of the individual file attribute you want. If the result is not zero, that attribute is set for the named file. For example, the return value of the following **And** expression is zero if the Archive attribute is not set:

```
Result = GetAttr(FName) And vbArchive
```

A nonzero value is returned if the Archive attribute is set.

See Also

FileAttr Function, **SetAttr** Statement.

Example

This example uses the **GetAttr** statement to determine the attributes of a file and directory or folder.

```
' Assume file TESTFILE has hidden attribute set.
MyAttr = GetAttr("TESTFILE")          ' Returns 2.

' Assume file TESTFILE has hidden and read-only attributes set.
MyAttr = GetAttr("TESTFILE")          ' Returns 3.

' Assume MYDIR is a directory or folder.
MyAttr = GetAttr("MYDIR")             ' Returns 16.
```

GetCustomListContents Method

Applies To **Application** Object.

Description Returns a custom list (an array of strings) for a specified list number.

Syntax *object*.**GetCustomListContents**(*listNum*)

object
  Required. The **Application** object.

listNum
  Required. The list number.

See Also **AddCustomList** Method, **CustomListCount** Property, **DeleteCustomList** Method, **GetCustomListNum** Method.

Example This example writes the elements of the first custom list in column one on Sheet1.

```
Sub foo()
On Error GoTo err_handler
listArray = Application.GetCustomListContents(1)
For i = LBound(listArray, 1) To UBound(listArray, 1)
    Worksheets("sheet1").Cells(i, 1).Value = listArray(i)
Next i
Exit Sub

err_handler:
    MsgBox "Custom list does not exist"
End Sub
```

GetCustomListNum Method

Applies To **Application** Object.

Description Returns the custom list number for an array of strings. Both built-in and custom defined lists can be matched using this method.

Syntax *object*.**GetCustomListNum**(*listArray*)

object
  Required. The **Application** object.

listArray
  Required. An array of strings.

Remarks This method generates an error if a corresponding list does not exist.

See Also   **AddCustomList** Method, **CustomListCount** Property, **DeleteCustomList** Method, **GetCustomListContents** Method.

Example   This example deletes a custom list.

```
n = Application.GetCustomListNum(Array("cogs", "sprockets", _
    "widgets", "gizmos"))
Application.DeleteCustomList n
```

GetObject Function

Description   Retrieves an OLE Automation object from a file.

Syntax   **GetObject**([*pathname*][*,class*])

The **GetObject** function syntax has these named-argument parts:

Part	Description
pathname	The full path and name of the file containing the object to retrieve. If *pathname* is omitted, *class* is required.
class	A string representing the class of the object.

The *class* argument uses the syntax: "*appname.objecttype*" and has these parts:

Part	Description
appname	The name of the application providing the object.
objecttype	The type or class of object to create.

Remarks

Note If an application which supports OLE Automation exposes an object library, it is preferable to use the functions defined within the library for object access rather than use **GetObject**.

Use the **GetObject** function to access an OLE Automation object from a file and assign the object to an object variable. To do this, use the **Set** statement to assign the object returned by **GetObject** to the object variable. For example:

```
Set CADObject = GetObject("C:\CAD\SCHEMA.CAD")
```

When this code is executed, the application associated with the specified file name is started and the object in the specified file is activated.

If *pathname* is a zero-length string (""), **GetObject** returns a new object instance of the specified type. If the *pathname* argument is omitted entirely, **GetObject** returns the currently active object of the specified type. If no object of the specified type exists, an error occurs.

The above example shows how to activate an entire file. However, some applications allow you to activate part of a file. To do this, add an exclamation point (!) to the end of the file name followed by a string that identifies the part of the file you want to activate. For information on how to create this string, see the documentation for the application that created the object.

For example, in a drawing application you might have multiple layers to a drawing stored in a file. You could use the following code to activate a layer within a drawing called SCHEMA.CAD:

```
Set LayerObject = GetObject("C:\CAD\SCHEMA.CAD!Layer3")
```

If you do not specify the object's *class*, the OLE.DLLs determine the application to invoke and the object to activate based on the file name you provide. Some files, however, may support more than one class of object. For example, a drawing might support three different types of objects: an application object, a drawing object, and a toolbar object, all of which are part of the same file. To specify which object in a file you want to activate, use the optional *class* argument. For example:

```
Set MyObject = GetObject("C:\DRAWINGS\SAMPLE.DRW", "FIGMENT.DRAWING")
```

In the above example, FIGMENT is the name of a drawing application and DRAWING is one of the object types it supports.

Once an object is activated, you reference it in code using the object variable you defined. In the above example, you access properties and methods of the new object using the object variable MyObject. For example:

```
MyObject.Line 9, 90
MyObject.InsertText 9, 100, "Hello, world."
MyObject.SaveAs "C:\DRAWINGS\SAMPLE.DRW"
```

See Also   **CreateObject** Function, **Set** Statement.

GetOpenFilename Method

Applies To   **Application** Object.

Description   Displays the standard Open dialog box and gets a filename from the user without actually opening any files.

Syntax   *object*.**GetOpenFilename**(*fileFilter*, *filterIndex*, *title*, *buttonText*, *multiSelect*)

object
Required. The **Application** object.

fileFilter
Optional. A string specifying file filtering criteria.

In Microsoft Windows, this string consists of pairs of file filter strings followed by the MS-DOS wildcard file filter specification, with each part and each pair separated by commas. Each separate pair is listed in the File Type drop-down list box. For example, the following string specifies two file filters—text and addin: "Text Files (*.txt),*.txt,Add-In Files (*.xla),*.xla".

To use multiple MS-DOS wildcard expressions for a single file filter type, separate the wildcard expressions with semicolons. For example: "Visual Basic Files (*.bas; *.txt),*.bas;*.txt".

If omitted on Windows, this argument defaults to "All Files (*.*),*.*".

On the Apple Macintosh, this string is a list of comma-separated file type codes, ("TEXT,XLA,XLS4"). Spaces are significant and should not be inserted before or after the comma separators unless they are part of the file type code. If omitted, this argument defaults to all file types.

filterIndex
Optional. Microsoft Windows only (ignored on the Apple Macintosh). Specifies the index number of the default file filtering criteria from one to the number of filters specified in *fileFilter*. If this argument is omitted or greater than the number of filters present, the first file filter is used.

title
Optional. Microsoft Windows only (ignored on the Apple Macintosh). Specifies the dialog title. If this argument is omitted, the dialog title is "Open".

buttonText
Optional. Apple Macintosh only (ignored in Microsoft Windows). Specifies the text used for the Open button in the dialog box. If this argument is omitted, the button text is "Open".

multiSelect
Optional. If **True**, multiple filenames are allowed. If **False** or omitted, only a single filename can be selected.

Remarks   This method returns the selected filename or the name entered by the user. The returned name may include a path specification. If *multiSelect* is **True**, the return value is an array of the selected filenames (even if only one file name is selected). Returns **False** if the user cancels the dialog box.

This method may change the current drive or directory.

See Also   **GetSaveAsFilename** Method, **Open** Method.

Example

This example displays the Open dialog box, with the file filter set to text files. If the user chooses a filename, the code displays that filename in a message box.

```
fileToOpen = Application.GetOpenFilename("Text Files (*.txt), *.txt")
If fileToOpen <> False Then
    MsgBox "Open " & fileToOpen
End If
```

This is the same example in Microsoft Excel for the Macintosh.

```
fileToOpen = Application.GetOpenFilename("TEXT")
If fileToOpen <> False Then
    MsgBox "Open " & fileToOpen
End If
```

GetSaveAsFilename Method

Applies To   **Application** Object.

Description   Displays the standard Save As dialog box and gets a filename from the user without actually saving any files.

Syntax   *object*.**GetSaveAsFilename**(*initialFilename*, *fileFilter*, *filterIndex*, *title*, *buttonText*)

object
Required. The **Application** object.

initialFilename
Optional. Specifies the suggested filename. If this argument is omitted, Microsoft Excel uses the active workbook's name.

fileFilter
Optional. A string specifying file filtering criteria.

In Microsoft Windows, this string consists of pairs of file filter strings followed by the MS-DOS wildcard file filter specification, with each part and each pair separated by commas. Each separate pair is listed in the File Type drop-down list box. For example, the following string specifies two file filters—text and addin: "Text Files (*.txt), *.txt, Add-In Files (*.xla), *.xla"

To use multiple MS-DOS wildcard expressions for a single file filter type, separate the wildcard expressions with semicolons. For example: "Visual Basic Files (*.bas; *.txt),*.bas;*.txt"

If omitted on Windows, this argument defaults to "All Files (*.*),*.*".

On the Apple Macintosh, this string is a list of comma-separated file type codes, ("TEXT,XLA,XLS4"). Spaces are significant and should not be inserted before or after the comma separators unless they are part of the file type code. If omitted, this argument defaults to all file types.

filterIndex

Optional. Microsoft Windows only (ignored on the Apple Macintosh). Specifies the index number of the default file filtering criteria from one to the number of filters specified in *fileFilter*. If this argument is omitted or greater than the number of filters present, the first file filter is used.

title

Optional. Specifies the dialog title. If this argument is omitted, the default title is used.

buttonText

Optional. Apple Macintosh only (ignored in Microsoft Windows). Specifies the text used for the Save button in the dialog box. If this argument is omitted, the button text is "Save".

Remarks

This method returns the selected filename or the name entered by the user. The returned name may include a path specification. Returns **False** if the user cancels the dialog box.

This method may change the current drive or directory.

See Also

GetOpenFilename Method, **Save** Method, **SaveAs** Method.

Example

This example displays the Save As dialog box, with the file filter set to text files. If the user chooses a filename, the code displays that filename in a message box.

```
fileSaveName = Application.GetSaveAsFilename( _
    fileFilter:="Text Files (*.txt), *.txt")
If fileSaveName <> False Then
    MsgBox "Save as " & fileSaveName
End If
```

This is the same example in Microsoft Excel for the Macintosh.

```
fileSaveName = Application.GetSaveAsFilename( _
    fileFilter:="TEXT")
If fileSaveName <> False Then
    MsgBox "Save as " & FileSaveName
End If
```

GoalSeek Method

Applies To   **Range** Object.

Description   Calculates the values necessary to achieve a specific goal. If the goal is an amount returned by a formula, this calculates a value that, when supplied to your formula, causes the formula to return the number you want. Returns **True** if the goal seek is successful.

Syntax   *object*.**GoalSeek**(*goal*, *changingCell*)

object
    Required. The specified range must be a single cell.

goal
    Required. The value you want returned in this cell.

changingCell
    Required. A **Range** object indicating which cell should be changed to achieve the target value.

Example   This example assumes that Sheet1 has a cell named "Polynomial" containing the formula =(X^3)+(3*X^2)+6 and another cell named "X" that is empty. The example finds a value for X so that Polynomial contains the value 15.

```
Worksheets("Sheet1").Range("Polynomial").GoalSeek _
    goal:=15, _
    changingCell:=Worksheets("Sheet1").Range("X")
```

GoSub...Return Statement

Description   Branch to and return from a subroutine within a procedure.

Syntax   **GoSub** *line*

        . . .
        line

        . . .
        Return
        The *line* argument can be any line label or line number.

Remarks   You can use **GoSub** and **Return** anywhere in a procedure, but **GoSub** and the corresponding **Return** must be in the same procedure. A subroutine can contain more than one **Return** statement, but the first **Return** statement encountered causes the flow of execution to branch back to the statement immediately following the most recently executed **GoSub** statement.

> **Note** You can't enter or exit **Sub** procedures with **GoSub**...**Return**.

> **Tip** Creating separate procedures which you can call may provide a more structured alternative to using **GoSub**...**Return**.

See Also

End Statement; **GoTo** Statement; **On**...**GoSub**, **On**...**GoTo** Statements; **Sub** Statement.

Example

This example uses **GoSub** to call a subroutine within a **Sub** procedure. The **Return** statement causes the execution to resume at the statement immediately following the **Gosub** statement. The **Exit Sub** statement is used to prevent control from accidentally flowing into the subroutine.

```
Sub GosubDemo()
    Num = 10                        ' Initialize variable.
    GoSub MyRoutine                 ' Branch to subroutine.
    Debug.Print Num                 ' Print value upon return.
    Exit Sub                        ' Exit Sub procedure.
MyRoutine:                          ' Start of subroutine.
    Num = Num \ 2                   ' Halve the value.
    Return                          ' Return from subroutine.
End Sub
```

Goto Method

Applies To

Application Object.

Description

Selects any range or Visual Basic procedure in any workbook, and activates that workbook if it is not already active.

Syntax

object.**Goto**(*reference*, *scroll*)

object
Required. The **Application** object.

reference
Optional. Specifies the destination. Can be a **Range** object, a string containing a cell reference in R1C1 notation, or a string containing a Visual Basic procedure name. If this argument is omitted, the destination is the last range you used the **Goto** method to select.

scroll

Optional. If this argument is **True**, Microsoft Excel scrolls the window so that the top left corner of the range appears in the top left corner of the window. If **False** or omitted, Microsoft Excel does not scroll the window.

Remarks   This method differs from the **Select** method in the following ways.

- If you specify a range on a sheet that is not on top, Microsoft Excel will switch to that sheet before selecting. (If you use **Select** with a range on a sheet that is not on top, the range will be selected but the sheet will not be activated).

- This method has a *scroll* argument that lets you scroll the destination window.

- When you use the **Goto** method, the previous selection (before the **Goto** method runs) is added to the array of previous selections (for more information, see the **PreviousSelections** property). You can use this feature to quickly jump between up to four selections.

- The **Select** method has a *replace* argument; the **Goto** method does not.

See Also   **Select** Method.

Example   This example selects cell A154 on Sheet1 and then scrolls through the worksheet to display the range.

```
Application.Goto reference:=Worksheets("Sheet1").Range("A154"), _
    scroll:=True
```

GoTo Statement

Description   Branches unconditionally to a specified line within a procedure.

Syntax   **GoTo** *line*

The *line* argument can be any line label or line number.

Remarks   **GoTo** can branch only to lines within the procedure where it appears.

Note Too many **GoTo** statements can be difficult to read and debug. Use structured control statements (**Do**...**Loop**, **For**...**Next**, **If**...**Then**...**Else**, **Select Case**) whenever possible.

See Also   **Do**...**Loop** Statement, **For**...**Next** Statement, **GoSub**...**Return** Statement, **If**...**Then**...**Else** Statement, **Select Case** Statement.

Example   This example uses the **GoTo** statement to branch to line labels within a procedure.

```
Sub GotoStatementDemo()
    Number = 1                          ' Initialize variable.
    ' Evaluate Number and branch to appropriate label.
    If Number = 1 Then GoTo Line1 Else GoTo Line2

Line1:
    MyString = "Number equals 1"
    GoTo LastLine                       ' Go to LastLine.
Line2:
    ' The following statement never gets executed.
    MyString = "Number equals 2"
LastLine:
    Debug.Print MyString                ' Print 1 in Debug window.
End Sub
```

GridlineColor Property

Applies To   **Window** Object.

Description   Returns or sets the gridline color as an RGB value. Read-write.

See Also   **DisplayGridlines** Property, **GridlineColorIndex** Property.

Example   This example sets the gridline color in the active window in BOOK1.XLS to red.

```
Workbooks("BOOK1.XLS").Worksheets("Sheet1").Activate
ActiveWindow.GridlineColor = RGB(255,0,0)
```

GridlineColorIndex Property

Applies To   **Window** Object.

Description   Returns or sets the gridline color as an index into the current color palette. Read-write.

Remarks   Set this property to **xlAutomatic** to specify the automatic color.

See Also   **Colors** Property, **DisplayGridlines** Property, **GridlineColor** Property.

Example   This example sets the active window gridline color to blue.

```
ActiveWindow.GridlineColorIndex = 5
```

Gridlines Object

Description   Represents major gridlines or minor gridlines on a chart axis. Gridlines extend the tick marks on a chart axis to make it easier to see the values associated with the data markers. There is no singular GridLine object; you must turn all gridlines for an axis on or off at once.

Accessors   The **MajorGridlines** property returns the major gridlines for the axis. The **MinorGridlines** property returns the minor gridlines. There is no GridLines property or collection; you must access the major and minor gridlines separately.

The following example turns on major gridlines for the category axis on the chart sheet named "Chart1" and then formats the gridlines to be blue dashed lines.

```
Charts("chart1").Axes(xlCategory).HasMajorGridlines = True
Charts("chart1").Axes(xlCategory).MajorGridlines.Border.Color = _
    RGB(0, 0, 255)
Charts("chart1").Axes(xlCategory).MajorGridlines.Border.LineStyle = _
    xlDash
```

Properties   **Application** Property, **Border** Property, **Creator** Property, **Name** Property, **Parent** Property.

Methods   **Delete** Method, **Select** Method.

Group Method

Applies To   **Arcs** Collection, **Buttons** Collection, **ChartObjects** Collection, **DrawingObjects** Collection, **Drawings** Collection, **DropDowns** Collection, **EditBoxes** Collection, **GroupBoxes** Collection, **GroupObjects** Collection, **Labels** Collection, **Lines** Collection, **ListBoxes** Collection, **OLEObjects** Collection, **OptionButtons** Collection, **Ovals** Collection, **Pictures** Collection, **Range** Object, **Rectangles** Collection, **ScrollBars** Collection, **Spinners** Collection, **TextBoxes** Collection.

Description   Syntax 1: Demotes a range in an outline (in other words, increases its outline level). The range should be an entire row or column, or a range of rows or columns.

Groups a discontinuous range in a PivotTable.

Groups multiple controls or drawing objects together; returns a new **GroupObject** object.

Syntax 2: Performs numeric or date grouping in a pivot field.

Syntax 1   *object*.**Group**

Syntax 2

object.**Group**(*start*, *end*, *by*, *periods*)

object

Required. The object to which this method applies. For syntax 2, the **Range** object must be a single cell in the data range of the pivot field. The method will fail (without displaying any error message) if you attempt to apply the method to more than one cell. To see how to use the **Group** method in this way, see the second example.

start

Optional. The first value to be grouped. If omitted or **True**, the first value in the field is used.

end

Optional. The last value to be grouped. If omitted or **True**, the last value in the field is used.

by

Optional. If the field is numeric, specifies the size of each group.

If the field is a date, specifies the number of days in each group if element four of the *periods* array is **True**. Otherwise *by* is ignored.

If this argument is omitted, a default group size is automatically chosen.

periods

Optional. An array of Boolean values specifying the period for the group, as shown in the following table.

Array element	Period
1	Seconds
2	Minutes
3	Hours
4	Days
5	Months
6	Quarters
7	Years

If an element of the array is **True**, a group is created for the corresponding time. If the element is **False**, no group is created. This argument is ignored if the field is not a date field.

See Also

OutlineLevel Property, **Ungroup** Method.

Example

This example creates a group from drawing objects one, three, and five on Sheet1.

```
Set myGroup = Worksheets("Sheet1").DrawingObjects(Array(1, 3, 5)).Group
Worksheets("Sheet1").Activate
myGroup.Select
```

This example groups the field named "ORDER_DATE" by 10-day periods.

```
Set pvtTable = Worksheets("Sheet1").Range("A3").PivotTable
Set groupRange = pvtTable.PivotFields("ORDER_DATE").DataRange
groupRange.Cells(1).Group by:=10, periods:=Array(False, False, False,
True, False, False, False)
```

GroupBox Object

Description   Represents a static frame used to label and group sets of option buttons (**OptionButton** objects) and other controls on a chart sheet, dialog sheet, or worksheet. Group boxes control how option buttons select and clear. All option buttons with an upper-left corner contained within the group box boundaries are considered to be part of a group, and only one option button within that group can be turned on at any given time.

Group boxes have no font or background formatting, but group boxes on dialog sheets do have an accelerator key. Group boxes can be positioned and sized.

Do not confuse **GroupBox** objects, which group option buttons on a dialog sheet, with **GroupObject** objects, which combine objects into a single logical collection but do not affect dialog sheet behavior.

Accessors   The **GroupBox** object is a member of the **GroupBoxes** collection. The **GroupBoxes** collection contains all the **GroupBox** objects on a single sheet. Use the **Add** method to create a new group box and add it to the collection.

To access a single member of the collection, use the **GroupBoxes** method with the index number or name of the group box as an argument.

The following example sets the caption for group box one on the dialog sheet named "Dialog1."

```
DialogSheets("dialog1").GroupBoxes(1).Caption = "Test Group"
```

The group box name is shown in the Name Box when the group box is selected. Use the **Name** property to set or return the group box name. The following example hides the group box named "Group Box 14" on dialog sheet one.

```
DialogSheets(1).GroupBoxes("group box 14").Visible = False
```

Properties   **Accelerator** Property, **Application** Property, **BottomRightCell** Property, **Caption** Property, **Creator** Property, **Display3DShading** Property, **Enabled** Property, **Height** Property, **Index** Property, **Left** Property, **Locked** Property, **LockedText** Property, **Name** Property, **OnAction** Property, **Parent** Property, **PhoneticAccelerator** Property, **Placement** Property, **PrintObject** Property, **Text** Property, **Top** Property, **TopLeftCell** Property, **Visible** Property, **Width** Property, **ZOrder** Property.

Methods   **BringToFront** Method, **Characters** Method, **CheckSpelling** Method, **Copy** Method, **CopyPicture** Method, **Cut** Method, **Delete** Method, **Duplicate** Method, **Select** Method, **SendToBack** Method.

GroupBoxes Collection Object

Description   A collection of all the **GroupBox** objects on the specified chart sheet, dialog sheet, or worksheet. Each **GroupBox** object represents a static frame used to label and group sets of option buttons (**OptionButton** objects) and other controls. Group boxes control how option buttons select and clear. All option buttons with an upper-left corner contained within the group box boundaries are considered to be part of a group, and only one option button within that group can be turned on at any given time.

Do not confuse **GroupBox** objects, which group option buttons on a dialog sheet, with **GroupObject** objects, which combine objects into a single logical collection but do not affect dialog sheet behavior.

Accessors   Use the **Add** method to create a new group box and add it to the collection. The following example creates a new group box on dialog sheet one.

```
DialogSheets(1).GroupBoxes.Add 77, 44, 82, 63
```

Use the **GroupBoxes** method with an argument to access a single member of the collection or without an argument to access the entire collection at once. The following example deletes all of the group boxes on the worksheet named "Sheet1."

```
Sheets("sheet1").GroupBoxes.Delete
```

Properties   **Accelerator** Property, **Application** Property, **Caption** Property, **Count** Property, **Creator** Property, **Display3DShading** Property, **Enabled** Property, **Height** Property, **Left** Property, **Locked** Property, **LockedText** Property, **OnAction** Property, **Parent** Property, **PhoneticAccelerator** Property, **Placement** Property, **PrintObject** Property, **Text** Property, **Top** Property, **Visible** Property, **Width** Property, **ZOrder** Property.

Methods   **Add** Method (Graphic Objects and Controls), **BringToFront** Method, **Characters** Method, **CheckSpelling** Method, **Copy** Method, **CopyPicture** Method, **Cut** Method, **Delete** Method, **Duplicate** Method, **Group** Method, **Item** Method, **Select** Method, **SendToBack** Method.

GroupBoxes Method

Applies To   **Chart** Object, **DialogSheet** Object, **Worksheet** Object.

Description   Accessor. Returns an object that represents a single group box control (a **GroupBox** object, Syntax 1) or a collection of group box controls (a **GroupBoxes** object, Syntax 2) on the sheet.

Syntax 1   *object*.**GroupBoxes(*index*)**

Syntax 2   *object*.**GroupBoxes**

object
   Required. The **Chart**, **DialogSheet**, or **Worksheet** object.

index
   Required for Syntax 1. Specifies the name or number of the group box (can be an array to specify more than one).

Example   This example sets the title for group box one on Dialog1.

```
DialogSheets("Dialog1").GroupBoxes.Text = "Choose one"
```

GroupLevel Property

Applies To   **PivotField** Object.

Description   Returns the placement of the specified field within a group of fields (if the field is a member of a grouped set of fields). Read-only.

Remarks   The highest-level parent field (leftmost parent field) is **GroupLevel** one, its child is **GroupLevel** two, and so on.

Example
This example displays a message box if the field that contains the active cell is the highest-level parent field.

```
Worksheets("Sheet1").Activate
If ActiveCell.PivotField.GroupLevel = 1 Then
    MsgBox "This is the highest-level parent field."
End If
```

GroupObject Object

Description
Represents a group of graphic objects and controls. A group is created using either the **Group** method or the Group Objects button on the Drawing toolbar.

Do not confuse **GroupObject** objects, which combine objects into a single logical collection but do not affect dialog sheet behavior, with **GroupBox** objects, which group option buttons on a dialog sheet.

Accessors
The **GroupObject** object is a member of the **GroupObjects** collection. The **GroupObjects** collection contains all the **GroupObject** objects on a single sheet. Use the **Group** method to create a new group and add it to the collection. The following example creates a group containing all of the rectangles on worksheet one and then sets the position of the group.

```
Dim g As GroupObject
Set g = Worksheets(1).Rectangles.Group
g.Left = Worksheets(1).Range("c1").Left
g.Top = Worksheets(1).Range("c1").Top
```

To access a single member of the collection, use the **GroupObjects** method with the index number or name of the group as an argument.

The following example sets the interior color for all objects in group one on worksheet one.

```
Worksheets(1).GroupObjects(1).Interior.Color = RGB(0, 255, 0)
```

The group name is shown in the Name Box when the group is selected. Use the **Name** property to set or return the group name. The following example sets the border style for all objects in the group named "Group 24."

```
Worksheets(1).GroupObjects("group 24").Border.LineStyle = xlDashDot
```

Properties   **AddIndent** Property, **Application** Property, **ArrowHeadLength** Property, **ArrowHeadStyle** Property, **ArrowHeadWidth** Property, **AutoSize** Property, **Border** Property, **BottomRightCell** Property, **Creator** Property, **Enabled** Property, **Font** Property, **Height** Property, **HorizontalAlignment** Property, **Index** Property, **Interior** Property, **Left** Property, **Locked** Property, **Name** Property, **OnAction** Property, **Orientation** Property, **Parent** Property, **Placement** Property, **PrintObject** Property, **RoundedCorners** Property, **Shadow** Property, **Top** Property, **TopLeftCell** Property, **VerticalAlignment** Property, **Visible** Property, **Width** Property, **ZOrder** Property.

Methods   **BringToFront** Method, **CheckSpelling** Method, **Copy** Method, **CopyPicture** Method, **Cut** Method, **Delete** Method, **Duplicate** Method, **Select** Method, **SendToBack** Method, **Ungroup** Method.

GroupObjects Collection Object

Description   A collection of all the **GroupObject** objects on the specified chart sheet, dialog sheet, or worksheet. Each **GroupObject** represents a group of graphic objects and controls. Unlike other collection objects, the **GroupObjects** object has no **Add** method. Groups are created and added to the collection using either the **Group** method or the Group Objects button on the Drawing toolbar.

Do not confuse **GroupObject** objects, which combine objects into a single logical collection but do not affect dialog sheet behavior, with **GroupBox** objects, which group option buttons on a dialog sheet.

Accessors   Use the **GroupObjects** method with an argument to access a single member of the collection or without an argument to access the entire collection at once. The following example ungroups all of the graphic object groups on the worksheet named "Sheet1."

```
Worksheets("sheet1").GroupObjects.Ungroup
```

Properties   **AddIndent** Property, **Application** Property, **ArrowHeadLength** Property, **ArrowHeadStyle** Property, **ArrowHeadWidth** Property, **AutoSize** Property, **Border** Property, **Count** Property, **Creator** Property, **Enabled** Property, **Font** Property, **Height** Property, **HorizontalAlignment** Property, **Interior** Property, **Left** Property, **Locked** Property, **OnAction** Property, **Orientation** Property, **Parent** Property, **Placement** Property, **PrintObject** Property, **RoundedCorners** Property, **Shadow** Property, **Top** Property, **VerticalAlignment** Property, **Visible** Property, **Width** Property, **ZOrder** Property.

Methods	**BringToFront** Method, **CheckSpelling** Method, **Copy** Method, **CopyPicture** Method, **Cut** Method, **Delete** Method, **Duplicate** Method, **Group** Method, **Item** Method, **Select** Method, **SendToBack** Method, **Ungroup** Method.

GroupObjects Method

Applies To	**Chart** Object, **DialogSheet** Object, **Worksheet** Object.
Description	Accessor. Returns an object that represents a single group (a **GroupObject** object, Syntax 1) or a collection of all the groups (a **GroupObjects** object, Syntax 2) on the sheet.
Syntax 1	*object*.**GroupObjects**(*index*)
Syntax	*object*.**GroupObjects**

object
> Required. The **Chart**, **DialogSheet** or **Worksheet** object.

index
> Required for Syntax 1. The name or number of the group (can be an array to specify more than one).

Example	This example ungroups the graphic objects in group one on Sheet1.

```
Worksheets("Sheet1").GroupObjects(1).Ungroup
```

HasArray Property

Applies To	**Range** Object.
Description	**True** if the specified cell is a part of an array. Read-only.
See Also	**CurrentArray** Property.
Example	This example displays a message if the active cell on Sheet1 is part of an array.

```
Worksheets("Sheet1").Activate
If ActiveCell.HasArray =True Then
    MsgBox "The active cell is part of an array"
End If
```

HasAutoFormat Property

Applies To   **PivotTable** Object.

Description   **True** if the PivotTable is automatically formatted when it is refreshed or when
fields are moved. Read-write.

Example   This example causes the PivotTable to be automatically reformatted when it is
refreshed or when fields are moved.

```
Set pvtTable = Worksheets("Sheet1").Range("A3").PivotTable
pvtTable.HasAutoFormat = True
```

HasAxis Property

Applies To   **Chart** Object.

Description   Indicates which axes exist on the chart, as a two-dimensional array of Boolean
values. Read-write.

The first array dimension indicates the axis (one of **xlCategory**, **xlValue**, or
xlSeries). Series axes apply only to 3-D charts.

The second array dimension indicates the axis group (**xlPrimary** or **xlSecondary**).
Read-write. 3-D charts have only one set of axes.

Remarks   Microsoft Excel may create or delete axes if you change the chart type or change
the **AxisGroup** property.

See Also   **Axes** Collection.

Example   This example turns on the primary value axis for Chart1.

```
Charts("Chart1").HasAxis(xlValue, xlPrimary) = True
```

HasDataLabel Property

Applies To   **Point** Object.

Description   **True** if the point has a data label. Read-write.

See Also   **ApplyDataLabels** Method, **DataLabel** Property, **HasDataLabels** Property.

Example

This example turns on the data label for point seven in series three in Chart1, and then it sets the data label color to blue.

```
With Charts("Chart1").SeriesCollection(3).Points(7)
    .HasDataLabel = True
    .ApplyDataLabels type:=xlValue
    .DataLabel.Font.ColorIndex = 5
End With
```

HasDataLabels Property

Applies To   **Series** Object.

Description   **True** if the series has data labels. Read-write.

See Also   **ApplyDataLabels** Method, **DataLabel** Property, **HasDataLabel** Property.

Example   This example turns on data labels for series three in Chart1.

```
With Charts("Chart1").SeriesCollection(3)
    .HasDataLabels = True
    .ApplyDataLabels type:=xlValue
End With
```

HasDropLines Property

Applies To   **ChartGroup** Object.

Description   **True** if the line or area chart has drop lines. Applies only to line and area charts. Read-write.

See Also   **DropLines** Property.

Example   This example turns on drop lines for chart group one in Chart1 and then sets their line style, weight, and color. The example should be run on a 2-D line chart that has one series.

```
With Charts("Chart1").ChartGroups(1)
    .HasDropLines = True
    With .DropLines.Border
        .LineStyle = xlThin
        .Weight = xlMedium
        .ColorIndex = 3
    End With
End With
```

HasErrorBars Property

Applies To   **Series** Object.

Description   **True** if the series has error bars. This property is not available on 3-D charts. Read-write.

See Also   **ErrorBar** Method, **ErrorBars** Property.

Example   This example removes error bars for series one in Chart1. The example should be run on a 2-D line chart that has error bars for series one.

```
Charts("Chart1").SeriesCollection(1).HasErrorBars = False
```

HasFormula Property

Applies To   **Range** Object.

Description   **True** if all cells in the range contain formulas; **False** if no cell in the range contains a formula; **Null** otherwise. Read-only.

Example   This example prompts the user to select a range on Sheet1. If every cell in the selected range contains a formula, the example displays a message.

```
Worksheets("Sheet1").Activate
Set rr = Application.InputBox( _
    prompt:="Select a range on this worksheet", _
    Type:=8)
If rr.HasFormula = True Then
    MsgBox "Every cell in the selection contains a formula"
End If
```

HasHiLoLines Property

Applies To   **ChartGroup** Object.

Description   True if the line chart has high-low lines. Applies only to line charts. Read-write.

See Also   **HiLoLines** Property.

Example   This example turns on high-low lines for chart group one in Chart1 and then sets line style, weight, and color. The example should be run on a 2-D line chart that has three series of stock-quote-like data (high-low-close).

```
With Charts("Chart1").ChartGroups(1)
    .HasHiLoLines = True
    With .HiLoLines.Border
        .LineStyle = xlThin
        .Weight = xlMedium
        .ColorIndex = 3
    End With
End With
```

HasLegend Property

Applies To   **Chart** Object.

Description   **True** if the chart has a legend. Read-write.

See Also   **Legend** Property.

Example   This example turns on the legend for Chart1 and then sets the legend font color to blue.

```
Charts("Chart1").HasLegend = True
Charts("Chart1").Legend.Font.ColorIndex = 5
```

HasMailer Property

Applies To   **Workbook** Object.

Description   **True** if the workbook has a mailer. Available only in Microsoft Excel for the Apple Macintosh with the PowerTalk mail system extension installed. Read-write.

See Also   **Mailer** Property, **MailSystem** Property, **SendMailer** Method.

Example   This example replies to the sender of the active workbook.

```
Set original = ActiveWorkbook
If original.HasMailer Then
    original.Reply
    original.Mailer.Subject = "Here's my reply"
    ActiveWorkbook.SendMailer
End If
```

HasMajorGridlines Property

Applies To   **Axis** Object.

Description   **True** if the axis has major gridlines. Only axes in the primary axis group can have gridlines. Read-write.

See Also   **AxisGroup** Property, **HasMinorGridlines** Property, **MajorGridlines** Property, **MinorGridlines** Property.

Example   This example sets the color of the major gridlines for the value axis in Chart1.

```
With Charts("Chart1").Axes(xlValue)
    If .HasMajorGridlines Then
        .MajorGridlines.Border.ColorIndex = 3 'set color to red
    End If
End With
```

HasMinorGridlines Property

Applies To   **Axis** Object.

Description   **True** if the axis has minor gridlines. Only axes in the primary axis group can have gridlines. Read-write.

See Also   **AxisGroup** Property, **HasMajorGridlines** Property, **MajorGridlines** Property, **MinorGridlines** Property.

Example   This example sets the color of the minor gridlines for the value axis in Chart1.

```
With Charts("Chart1").Axes(xlValue)
    If .HasMinorGridlines Then
        .MinorGridlines.Border.ColorIndex = 4 'set color to green
    End If
End With
```

HasPassword Property

Applies To   **Workbook** Object.

Description   **True** if the workbook has a protection password. Read-only.

Remarks   You can assign a protection password to a workbook with the **SaveAs** method.

Example   This example displays a message if the active workbook has a protection password.

```
If ActiveWorkbook.HasPassword = True Then
    MsgBox "Remember to obtain the workbook password" & Chr(13) & _
        " from the Network Administrator."
End If
```

HasRadarAxisLabels Property

Applies To   **ChartGroup** Object.

Description   **True** if a radar chart has axis labels. Applies only to radar charts. Read-write.

See Also   **RadarAxisLabels** Property.

Example

This example turns on radar axis labels for chart group one in Chart1 and sets their color. The example should be run on a radar chart.

```
With Charts("Chart1").ChartGroups(1)
    .HasRadarAxisLabels = True
    .RadarAxisLabels.Font.ColorIndex = 3
End With
```

HasRoutingSlip Property

Applies To   **Workbook** Object.

Description   **True** if the workbook has a **RoutingSlip**. Read-write.

Remarks   Setting this property to **True** creates a routing slip with default values. Setting the property to **False** deletes the routing slip.

See Also   **RoutingSlip** Property.

Example   This example creates a routing slip for BOOK1.XLS and then sends the workbook to three recipients, one after another.

```
Workbooks("BOOK1.XLS").HasRoutingSlip = True
With Workbooks("BOOK1.XLS").RoutingSlip
    .Delivery = xlOneAfterAnother
    .Recipients = Array("Adam Bendel", "Jean Selva", "Bernard Gabor")
    .Subject = "Here is BOOK1.XLS"
    .Message = "Here is the workbook. What do you think?"
End With
Workbooks("BOOK1.XLS").Route
```

HasSeriesLines Property

Applies To   **ChartGroup** Object.

Description   True if a stacked column or bar chart has series lines. Applies only to stacked column and bar charts. Read-write.

See Also   **SeriesLines** Property.

Example   This example turns on series lines for chart group one in Chart1 and then sets their line style, weight, and color. The example should be run on a 2-D stacked column chart that has two or more series.

```
With Charts("Chart1").ChartGroups(1)
    .HasSeriesLines = True
    With .SeriesLines.Border
        .LineStyle = xlThin
        .Weight = xlMedium
        .ColorIndex = 3
    End With
End With
```

HasTitle Property

Applies To   **Axis** Object, **Chart** Object.

Description   True if the axis or chart has a visible title. Read-write.

Remarks   An axis title is an **AxisTitle** object.

A chart title is a **ChartTitle** object.

Example   This example adds an axis label to the category axis in Chart1.

```
With Charts("Chart1").Axes(xlCategory)
    .HasTitle = True
    .AxisTitle.Text = "July Sales"
End With
```

HasUpDownBars Property

Applies To   **ChartGroup** Object.

Description   **True** if a line chart has up and down bars. Applies only to line charts. Read-write.

See Also   **DownBars** Property, **UpBars** Property.

Example   This example turns on up and down bars for chart group one in Chart1 and then sets their colors. The example should be run on a 2-D line chart containing two series that cross each other at one or more data points.

```
With Charts("Chart1").ChartGroups(1)
    .HasUpDownBars = True
    .DownBars.Interior.ColorIndex = 3
    .UpBars.Interior.ColorIndex = 5
End With
```

HeaderMargin Property

Applies To   **PageSetup** Object.

Description   Returns or sets the distance from the top of the page to the header, in points (1/72 inch). Read-write.

See Also   **BottomMargin** Property, **FooterMargin** Property, **LeftMargin** Property, **RightMargin** Property, **TopMargin** Property.

Example   This example sets the header margin of Sheet1 to 0.5 inch.

```
Worksheets("Sheet1").PageSetup.HeaderMargin = _
        Application.InchesToPoints(0.5)
```

Height Property

Applies To   **Application** Object, **Arc** Object, **Arcs** Collection, **Button** Object, **Buttons** Collection, **ChartArea** Object, **ChartObject** Object, **ChartObjects** Collection, **CheckBox** Object, **DialogFrame** Object, **Drawing** Object, **DrawingObjects** Collection, **Drawings** Collection, **DropDown** Object, **DropDowns** Collection, **EditBox** Object, **EditBoxes** Collection, **GroupBox** Object, **GroupBoxes** Collection, **GroupObject** Object, **GroupObjects** Collection, **Label** Object, **Labels** Collection, **Legend** Object, **Line** Object, **Lines** Collection, **ListBox** Object, **ListBoxes** Collection, **OLEObject** Object, **OLEObjects** Collection, **OptionButton** Object, **OptionButtons** Collection, **Oval** Object, **Ovals** Collection, **Picture** Object, **Pictures** Collection, **PlotArea** Object, **Range** Object, **Rectangle** Object, **Rectangles** Collection, **ScrollBar** Object, **ScrollBars** Collection, **Spinner** Object, **Spinners** Collection, **TextBox** Object, **TextBoxes** Collection, **Toolbar** Object, **Window** Object.

Description   Returns or sets the height of an object, in points (1/72 inch).

Remarks   The height set or returned depends on the specified object.

Object type	Height
Application	Height of the main Application window. On the Apple Macintosh this is always equal to the total height of the screen, in points. Setting this value to something else on the Macintosh will have no effect. In Windows, if the window is minimized, this property is read-only and refers to the height of the icon. If the window is maximized, this property cannot be set. Use the **WindowState** property to determine the window state.
Range	Height of the range. Read-only.
Toolbar	Height of the toolbar. Returns the exact height of the toolbar in points. Use the **Width** property to change the size of the toolbar. Read-only.
Window	Height of the window. Use the **UsableHeight** property to determine the maximum size for the window.
	You cannot set this property if the window is maximized or minimized. Use the **WindowState** property to determine the window state.
Arc, Button, ChartArea, ChartObject, CheckBox, DialogFrame, Drawing, DrawingObjects, DropDown, EditBox, GroupBox, GroupObject, Label, Legend, Line, ListBox, OLEObject, OptionButton, Oval, Picture, PlotArea, Rectangle, ScrollBar, Spinner, TextBox	Height of the object. If you set the height for an entire collection of objects (using `Ovals.Height = 100`, for example), the height of each object changes in proportion to its existing height (this mimics the behavior of selecting all the objects and then dragging a handle to change the height of the selection). This means that the height of each object changes, but they are *not* all set to the same height. To set every object in the collection to the same height, you must iterate the collection and set the height of each individual object.

You can use negative numbers to set the **Height** and **Width** properties of the following drawing objects: **Arc, Button, CheckBox, Drawing, DropDown, EditBox, GroupBox, GroupObject, Label, Line, ListBox, OLEObject, OptionButton, Oval, Picture, Rectangle, ScrollBar, Spinner**, and **TextBox**. This causes the object to reflect or translate (the behavior depends on the object), after which the **Top** and **Left** properties change to describe the new position. The **Height** and **Width** properties always return positive numbers.

See Also   **Left** Property, **Top** Property, **Width** Property.

Example   This example sets the height of oval one on Sheet1 to 1 inch (72 points).

```
Worksheets("Sheet1").Ovals(1).Height = 72
```

This example sets the height of every button on Sheet1 to 18 points.

```
For Each b In Worksheets("Sheet1").Buttons
    b.Height = 18
Next b
```

HeightPercent Property

Applies To   **Chart** Object.

Description   Returns or sets the height of a 3-D chart as a percentage of the chart width (between 5 and 500 percent). Read-write.

See Also   **DepthPercent** Property.

Example   This example sets the height of Chart1 to 80 percent of its width. The example should be run on a 3-D chart.

```
Charts("Chart1").HeightPercent = 80
```

Help Method

Applies To   **Application** Object.

Description   Displays a Help topic.

Syntax   *object*.**Help(***helpFile*, *helpContextID***)**

object
   Required. The **Application** object.

helpFile
   Optional. The name of the online Help file you wish to display. If this argument is not specified, Microsoft Excel's Help file is used.

helpContextID
   Optional. Specifies the context ID for the Help topic. If this argument is not specified, the Help Topics dialog box is displayed.

Example   This example displays the contents screen for the Help file OTISAPP.HLP.

```
Application.Help "OTISAPP.HLP"
```

HelpButton Property

Applies To   **Button** Object, **Buttons** Collection, **DrawingObjects** Collection.

Description   Applies only to buttons in a user-defined dialog box. If **True**, then pressing the Help key runs the macro identified by the button's **OnAction** property. If **False**, pressing the Help key does nothing. The Help key is F1 in Windows and COMMAND+? on the Macintosh. Read-write.

Remarks   Only one button in the dialog box can have the **HelpButton** property set to **True** at any given time; setting the property resets it for all other buttons in the dialog box.

If the user presses the Help key in a dialog box that has no Help button, nothing happens.

See Also   **Help** Method.

Example   This example displays the name of the Help button in Dialog1.

```
For Each b In DialogSheets("Dialog1").Buttons
    If b.HelpButton = True Then
        MsgBox "Help button is " & b.Name
    End If
Next b
```

HelpContextID Property

Applies To   **MenuItem** Object, **ToolbarButton** Object.

Description   Returns or sets the Help context ID (a number) for the Help topic attached to the menu item or toolbar button. Read-write. Microsoft Windows only.

Remarks   To use this property, you must also set the **HelpFile** property.

See Also   **HelpFile** Property, **StatusBar** Property.

Example   This example adds a new menu item to the Help menu on the Visual Basic Module menu bar, and then it sets the status bar text, the Help filename, and the Help context ID for the new menu item (note that the **HelpFile** and **HelpContextId** properties are Windows-only properties).

```
Set menuObj = MenuBars(xlModule).Menus("Help")
Set newMenuItem = menuObj.MenuItems.Add(Caption:="&Read Me First", _
                OnAction:="readmeMacro", _
                Before:=1)
newMenuItem.StatusBar = "Read this topic before you begin"
newMenuItem.HelpFile = "C:\xl5\vba_xl.hlp"
newMenuItem.HelpContextID = 65535
```

HelpFile Property

Applies To   **MenuItem** Object, **ToolbarButton** Object.

Description   Returns or sets the Help filename, as a string, for the Help topic attached to the menu item or toolbar button. Read-write. Microsoft Windows only.

Remarks   To use this property, you must also set the **HelpContextID** property.

See Also   **HelpContextID** Property, **StatusBar** Property.

Example   This example adds a new menu item to the Help menu on the Visual Basic Module menu bar, and then it sets the status bar text, the Help filename, and the Help context ID for the new menu item (note that the **HelpFile** and **HelpContextId** properties are Windows-only properties).

```
Set menuObj = MenuBars(xlModule).Menus("Help")
Set newMenuItem = menuObj.MenuItems.Add(Caption:="&Read Me First", _
                OnAction:="readmeMacro", _
                Before:=1)
newMenuItem.StatusBar = "Read this topic before you begin"
newMenuItem.HelpFile = "C:\xl5\vba_xl.hlp"
newMenuItem.HelpContextID = 65535
```

Hex Function

Description   Returns a string representing the hexadecimal value of a number.

Syntax   **Hex(*number*)**

The *number* named argument is any valid numeric expression.

Remarks   If *number* is not already a whole number, it is rounded to the nearest whole number before being evaluated.

If *number* is	Hex returns
Null	An error.
Empty	Zero (0).
Any other number	Up to eight hexadecimal characters.

You can represent hexadecimal numbers directly by preceding numbers in the proper range with `&H`. For example, `&H10` represents decimal 16 in hexadecimal notation.

See Also   **Oct** Function.

Example   This example uses the **Hex** function to return the hexadecimal value of a number.

```
MyHex = Hex(5)                    ' Returns 5.
MyHex = Hex(10)                   ' Returns A.
MyHex = Hex(459)' Returns 1CB.
```

Hidden Property

Applies To   **Range** Object, **Scenario** Object.

Description   **Range** object: **True** if the rows or columns are hidden. The specified range must span an entire column or row. Read-write.

Scenario object: **True** if the scenario is hidden. The default value is **False**. Read-write.

Remarks   Do not confuse this property with the **FormulaHidden** property.

Example   This example hides column C on Sheet1.

```
Worksheets("Sheet1").Columns("C").Hidden = True
```

HiddenFields Method

Applies To   **PivotTable** Object.

Description	Accessor. Returns an object that represents a single pivot field (a **PivotField** object, Syntax 1) or a collection of the pivot fields (a **PivotFields** object, Syntax 2) that are currently not showing as row, column, page or data fields. Read-only.
Syntax 1	*object*.**HiddenFields**(*index*)
Syntax 2	*object*.**HiddenFields**

object
> Required. The **PivotTable** object.

index
> Required for Syntax 1. The name or number of the pivot field to return (can be an array to specify more than one).

See Also	**ColumnFields** Method, **DataFields** Method, **PageFields** Method, **PivotFields** Method, **RowFields** Method, **VisibleFields** Method.
Example	This example adds the hidden field names to a list box. The list box appears on Sheet1.

```
Set pvtTable = Worksheets("Sheet1").Range("A3").PivotTable
Set newListBox = Worksheets("Sheet1").ListBoxes.Add _
    (Left:=10, Top:=72, Width:=144, Height:=144)
For Each hdnField In pvtTable.HiddenFields
    newListBox.AddItem (hdnField.Name)
Next hdnField
Worksheets("Sheet1").Activate
```

HiddenItems Method

Applies To	**PivotField** Object.
Description	Accessor. Returns an object that represents one hidden pivot item (a **PivotItem** object, Syntax 1) or a collection of all the hidden pivot items (a **PivotItems** object, Syntax 2) in the specified field. Read-only.
Syntax 1	*object*.**HiddenItems**(*index*)
Syntax 2	*object*.**HiddenItems**

object
> Required. The **PivotField** object.

index
> Required for Syntax 1. The number or name of the pivot item to return (can be an array to specify more than one).

See Also	**ChildItems** Method, **ParentItems** Method, **PivotItems** Method, **VisibleItems** Method.
Example	This example adds the names of all the hidden items in the field named "ORDER_DATE" to a list box. The list box appears on Sheet1.

```
Set pvtTable = Worksheets("Sheet1").Range("A3").PivotTable
Set newListBox = Worksheets("Sheet1").ListBoxes.Add _
    (Left:=10, Top:=72, Width:=144, Height:=144)
Set pvtField = pvtTable.PivotFields("ORDER_DATE")
For Each pvtItem In pvtField.HiddenItems
    newListBox.AddItem (pvtItem.Name)
Next pvtItem
Worksheets("Sheet1").Activate
```

Hide Method

Applies To	**DialogSheet** Object.
Description	Hides a dialog box. If the dialog box is not currently displayed, an error occurs.
Syntax	*object*.**Hide**(*cancel*)
	object
	Required. The **DialogSheet** object.
	cancel
	Optional. If **True**, the dialog box is canceled without validating edit-box contents. If **False** or omitted, edit box contents are validated before returning. No macros assigned to Cancel or OK buttons are run in either case.
Remarks	If *cancel* is **False** and edit fields in the dialog box could not be validated then this method returns **False**, and the dialog box does not exit. Otherwise, this method returns **True**.
Example	This example hides the active dialog box.

```
ActiveDialog.Hide
```

HiLoLines Object

Description   Represents the high-low lines in a chart group. High-low lines connect the highest point with the lowest point for every category in the chart group. Only 2-D line groups can have high-low lines. There is no singular HiLoLine object; you must turn high-low lines on or off for all points in a chart group at once.

Accessors   The **HiLoLines** property returns the high-low lines for a chart group. The following example uses the **AutoFormat** method to create a high-low-close stock chart in embedded chart one (the chart must contain three series). The example then makes the high-low lines blue.

```
Worksheets(1).ChartObjects(1).Activate
ActiveChart.AutoFormat gallery:=xlLine, format:=8
ActiveChart.ChartGroups(1).HiLoLines.Border.Color = RGB(0, 0, 255)
```

Remarks   If the **HasHiLoLines** property is **False**, most properties of the **HiLoLines** object are disabled.

Properties   **Application** Property, **Border** Property, **Creator** Property, **Name** Property, **Parent** Property.

Methods   **Delete** Method, **Select** Method.

HiLoLines Property

Applies To   **ChartGroup** Object.

Description   Accessor. Returns a **HiLoLines** object that represents the high-low lines for a series on a line chart. Applies only to line charts. Read-only.

See Also   **HasHiLoLines** Property.

Example   This example turns on high-low lines for chart group one in Chart1 and then sets their line style, weight, and color. The example should be run on a 2-D line chart that has three series of stock-quote-like data (high-low-close).

```
With Charts("Chart1").ChartGroups(1)
    .HasHiLoLines = True
    With .HiLoLines.Border
        .LineStyle = xlThin
        .Weight = xlMedium
        .ColorIndex = 3
    End With
End With
```

HorizontalAlignment Property

Applies To	**AxisTitle** Object, **Button** Object, **Buttons** Collection, **ChartTitle** Object, **DataLabel** Object, **DataLabels** Collection, **DrawingObjects** Collection, **GroupObject** Object, **GroupObjects** Collection, **Range** Object, **Style** Object, **TextBox** Object, **TextBoxes** Collection.
Description	Returns or sets the horizontal alignment for the object. Can be one of **xlCenter**, **xlDistributed**, **xlJustify**, **xlLeft**, or **xlRight** for all objects. In addition, the **Range** or **Style** object can be set to **xlCenterAcrossSelection**, **xlFill**, or **xlGeneral**. Read-write.
Remarks	The **xlDistributed** alignment style works only in Far East versions of Microsoft Excel.
See Also	**AddIndent** Property, **VerticalAlignment** Property.
Example	This example applies left alignment to the range A1:A5 on Sheet1.

```
Worksheets("Sheet1").Range("A1:A5").HorizontalAlignment = xlLeft
```

Hour Function

Description	Returns a whole number between 0 and 23, inclusive, representing the hour of the day.
Syntax	**Hour**(*time*)
	The *time* named argument is limited to a time or numbers and strings, in any combination, that can represent a time. If *time* contains no valid data, **Null** is returned.
See Also	**Day** Function, **Minute** Function, **Now** Function, **Second** Function, **Time** Function, **Time** Statement.
Example	This example uses the **Hour** function to obtain the hour from a specified time.

```
' In the development environment, the time (date literal) will display
' in short format using the locale settings of your code.
MyTime = #4:35:17 PM#              ' Assign a time.
MyHour = Hour(MyTime)    ' MyHour contains 16.
```

Id Property

Applies To	**ToolbarButton** Object.
Description	The button identification number of the button (built-in buttons only). Read-only.
Example	This example displays the button ID number for button one on the Formatting toolbar.

```
buttonId = Toolbars("Formatting").ToolbarButtons(1).Id
MsgBox "This button's ID number is " & buttonId
```

This example creates a two-column list of the button names and button ID numbers for the Standard toolbar. The list is placed in the first two columns on worksheet one.

```
i = 1
For Each btn In Toolbars("Standard").ToolbarButtons
    If btn.IsGap = False Then
        Worksheets(1).Cells(i, 1) = btn.Name
        Worksheets(1).Cells(i, 2) = btn.Id
        i = i + 1
    End If
Next btn
```

If...Then...Else Statement

Description	Conditionally executes a group of statements, depending on the value of an expression.
Syntax 1	**If** *condition* **Then** *statements* [**Else** *elsestatements*]

Syntax 2	**If** *condition* **Then**
	    [*statements*]
	[**ElseIf** *condition-n* **Then**
	    [*elseifstatements*]] . . .
	[**Else**
	    [*elsestatements*]]
	End If

Syntax 1 has these parts:

Part	Description
condition	Numeric or string expression that evaluates **True** or **False**.
statements	One or more statements separated by colons; executed if *condition* is **True**.
elsestatements	One or more statements separated by colons; executed if *condition* is **False**.

Syntax 2 has these parts:

Part	Description
condition	Expression that is **True** or **False**.
statements	One or more statements executed if *condition* is **True**.
condition-n	Numeric or string expression that evaluates **True** or **False**.
elseifstatements	One or more statements executed if associated *condition-n* is **True**.
elsestatements	One or more statements executed if no previous *condition-n* expressions are **True**.

Remarks

You can use the single-line form (Syntax 1) for short, simple tests. However, the block form (Syntax 2) provides more structure and flexibility than the single-line form and is usually easier to read, maintain, and debug.

Note With Syntax 1 it is possible to have multiple statements executed as the result of an **If**...**Then** decision, but they must all be on the same line and separated by colons, as in the following statement:

If A > 10 Then A = A + 1 : B = B + A : C = C + B

When executing a block **If** (Syntax 2), *condition* is tested. If *condition* is **True**, the statements following **Then** are executed. If *condition* is **False**, each **ElseIf** condition (if any) is evaluated in turn. When a **True** condition is found, the statements immediately following the associated **Then** are executed. If none of the **ElseIf** conditions are **True** (or if there are no **ElseIf** clauses), the statements following **Else** are executed. After executing the statements following **Then** or **Else**, execution continues with the statement following **End If**.

The **Else** and **ElseIf** clauses are both optional. You can have as many **ElseIf** clauses as you want in a block **If**, but none can appear after an **Else** clause. Block **If** statements can be nested; that is, contained within one another.

What follows the **Then** keyword is examined to determine whether or not a statement is a block **If**. If anything other than a comment appears after **Then** on the same line, the statement is treated as a single-line **If** statement.

A block **If** statement must be the first statement on a line. The **Else**, **ElseIf**, and **End If** parts of the statement can have only a line number or line label preceding them. The block **If** must end with an **End If** statement.

Tip **Select Case** may be more useful when evaluating a single expression that has several possible actions.

See Also   **Select Case** Statement.

Example   This example shows uses of the **If**...**Then**...**Else** statement.

```
Number = 53                          ' Initialize variable.
If Number < 10 Then
    Digits = 1
ElseIf Number < 100 Then
' Condition evaluates to True so the next statement is executed.
    Digits = 2
Else
    Digits = 3
End If
' Assign a value using the single line form of syntax.
If Digits = 1 Then MyString = "One" Else MyString = "More than one"
```

This example loops on cells A1:D10 on Sheet1. If one of the cells has a value less than 0.001, the code replaces the value with 0 (zero).

```
For Each c in Worksheets("Sheet1").Range("A1:D10")
    If c.Value < .001 Then
        c.Value = 0
    End If
Next c
```

This example loops on the range named "TestRange" and displays the number of empty cells in the range.

```
numBlanks = 0
For Each c In Range("TestRange")
    If c.Value = "" Then
        numBlanks = numBlanks + 1
    End If
Next c
MsgBox "There are " & numBlanks & " empty cells in this range."
```

This example sets the standard font to Arial (in Windows) or Geneva (on the Macintosh).

```
If Application.OperatingSystem Like "*Macintosh*" Then
    Application.StandardFont = "Geneva"
Else
    Application.StandardFont = "Arial"
End If
```

IgnoreRemoteRequests Property

Applies To   **Application** Object.

Description   **True** if remote DDE requests are ignored. Read-write.

Example   This example sets the **IgnoreRemoteRequests** property to **True** so that remote DDE requests are ignored.

```
Application.IgnoreRemoteRequests = True
```

Imp Operator

Description   Used to perform a logical implication on two expressions.

Syntax   *result* = *expression1* **Imp** *expression2*

The **Imp** operator syntax has these parts:

Part	Description
result	Any numeric variable.
expression1	Any expression.
expression2	Any expression.

Remarks   The following table illustrates how *result* is determined:

If *expression1* is	And *expression2* is	The *result* is
True	True	True
True	False	False
True	Null	Null
False	True	True

If *expression1* is	And *expression2* is	The *result* is
False	False	True
False	Null	True
Null	True	True
Null	False	Null
Null	Null	Null

The **Imp** operator performs a bit-wise comparison of identically positioned bits in two numeric expressions and sets the corresponding bit in *result* according to the following truth table:

If bit in *expression1* is	And bit in *expression2* is	The *result* is
0	0	1
0	1	1
1	0	0
1	1	1

See Also   Operator Precedence.

Example   This example uses the **Imp** Operator to perform logical implication on two expressions.

```
A = 10: B = 8: C = 6 : D = Null     ' Initialize variables.
MyCheck = A > B Imp B > C           ' Returns True.
MyCheck = A > B Imp C > B           ' Returns False.
MyCheck = B > A Imp C > B           ' Returns True.
MyCheck = B > A Imp C > D           ' Returns True.
MyCheck = C > D Imp B > A           ' Returns Null.
MyCheck = B Imp A    ' Returns -1 (bit-wise comparison).
```

Import Method

Applies To   **SoundNote** Object.

Description   Imports a sound note from a file.

Syntax   *object*.**Import**(*file*, *resource*)

object
> Required. The **SoundNote** object.

file
> Required. The name of the file containing sounds.

resource
> Required for the Apple Macintosh (not used with Microsoft Windows). The name or number of the sound resource in the file to import.

See Also   **Play** Method, **Record** Method.

Example   This example adds a sound note to cell A1 on Sheet1.

```
Worksheets("Sheet1").Range("A1").SoundNote.Import "C:\SOUNDS\CHIMES.WAV"
```

This is the same example in Microsoft Excel for the Macintosh.

```
Worksheets("Sheet1").Range("A1").SoundNote.Import "HD:Sounds:Sound Note
1"
```

InchesToPoints Method

Applies To   **Application** Object.

Description   Converts a measurement in inches into points (1/72 inch).

Syntax   *object*.**InchesToPoints**(*inches*)

object
> Required. The **Application** object.

inches
> Required. Specifies the inch value to convert to points.

See Also   **CentimetersToPoints** Method.

Example   This example sets the left margin of Sheet1 to 2.5 inches.

```
Worksheets("Sheet1").PageSetup.LeftMargin = _
          Application.InchesToPoints(2.5)
```

IncludeAlignment Property

Applies To   **Style** Object.

Description   **True** if the style includes the **AddIndent**, **HorizontalAlignment**, **VerticalAlignment**, **WrapText**, and **Orientation** properties. Read-write.

See Also	**IncludeBorder** Property, **IncludeFont** Property, **IncludeNumber** Property, **IncludePatterns** Property, **IncludeProtection** Property.
Example	This example sets the style attached to cell A1 on Sheet1 to include alignment format.

```
Worksheets("Sheet1").Range("A1").Style.IncludeAlignment = True
```

IncludeBorder Property

Applies To	**Style** Object.
Description	**True** if the style includes the **Borders** properties. Read-write.
See Also	**IncludeAlignment** Property, **IncludeFont** Property, **IncludeNumber** Property, **IncludePatterns** Property, **IncludeProtection** Property.
Example	This example sets the style attached to cell A1 on Sheet1 to include border format.

```
Worksheets("Sheet1").Range("A1").Style.IncludeBorder = True
```

IncludeFont Property

Applies To	**Style** Object.
Description	**True** if the style includes the **Font** property. Read-write.
See Also	**IncludeAlignment** Property, **IncludeBorder** Property, **IncludeNumber** Property, **IncludePatterns** Property, **IncludeProtection** Property.
Example	This example sets the style attached to cell A1 on Sheet1 to include font format.

```
Worksheets("Sheet1").Range("A1").Style.IncludeFont = True
```

IncludeNumber Property

Applies To	**Style** Object.
Description	**True** if the style includes the **NumberFormat** property. Read-write.

| **See Also** | **IncludeAlignment** Property, **IncludeBorder** Property, **IncludeFont** Property, **IncludePatterns** Property, **IncludeProtection** Property. |
| **Example** | This example sets the style attached to cell A1 on Sheet1 to include number format. |

```
Worksheets("Sheet1").Range("A1").Style.IncludeNumber = True
```

IncludePatterns Property

Applies To	**Style** Object.
Description	**True** if the style includes the **Interior** properties. Read-write.
See Also	**IncludeAlignment** Property, **IncludeBorder** Property, **IncludeFont** Property, **IncludeNumber** Property, **IncludeProtection** Property.
Example	This example sets the style attached to cell A1 on Sheet1 to include pattern format.

```
Worksheets("Sheet1").Range("A1").Style.IncludePatterns = True
```

IncludeProtection Property

Applies To	**Style** Object.
Description	**True** if the style includes the **FormulaHidden** and **Locked** protection properties. Read-write.
See Also	**IncludeAlignment** Property, **IncludeBorder** Property, **IncludeFont** Property, **IncludeNumber** Property, **IncludePatterns** Property.
Example	This example sets the style attached to cell A1 on Sheet1 to include protection format.

```
Worksheets("Sheet1").Range("A1").Style.IncludeProtection = True
```

Index Property

Applies To   **Arc** Object, **Button** Object, **Chart** Object, **ChartObject** Object, **CheckBox** Object, **DialogSheet** Object, **Drawing** Object, **DropDown** Object, **EditBox** Object, **GroupBox** Object, **GroupObject** Object, **Label** Object, **LegendEntry** Object, **Line** Object, **ListBox** Object, **Menu** Object, **MenuBar** Object, **MenuItem** Object, **Module** Object, **Name** Object, **OLEObject** Object, **OptionButton** Object, **Oval** Object, **Pane** Object, **Picture** Object, **Rectangle** Object, **Scenario** Object, **ScrollBar** Object, **Spinner** Object, **TextBox** Object, **Trendline** Object, **Window** Object, **Worksheet** Object.

Description   Returns the index number of the object within the collection of similar objects. Read-only.

For help about using the **Index** worksheet function in Visual Basic, see "Using Worksheet Functions in Visual Basic" in online Help.

Example   This example displays the tab number of the sheet name that you type. For example, if Chart1 is the third tab in the active workbook, the example displays the number 3 in a message box.

```
sheetname = InputBox("Type a sheet name, such as Sheet12 or Module1")
MsgBox "This sheet is tab number " & Sheets(sheetname).Index
```

InnerDetail Property

Applies To   **PivotTable** Object.

Description   Returns or sets the name of the field which will be shown as detail when the **ShowDetail** property is **True** for the innermost row or column field. Read-write.

See Also   **ShowDetail** Property.

Example   This example displays the name of the field that will be shown as detail when the **ShowDetail** property is **True** for the innermost row field or column field.

```
Set pvtTable = Worksheets("Sheet1").Range("A3").PivotTable
MsgBox pvtTable.InnerDetail
```

Input # Statement

Description

Reads data from an open sequential file and assigns the data to variables.

Syntax

Input #*filenumber,varlist*

The **Input #** statement syntax has these parts:

Part	Description
filenumber	Any valid file number.
varlist	Comma-delimited list of variables that are assigned values read from the file: can't be an array or object variable. However, variables that describe an element of an array or user-defined type may be used.

Remarks

When read, standard string or numeric data is assigned to variables as is. The following table illustrates how other input data is treated:

Data	Value assigned to variable
Delimiting comma or blank line	**Empty**.
#NULL#	**Null**.
#TRUE# or #FALSE#	**True** or **False**.
#*yyyy-mm-dd hh:mm:ss*#	The date and/or time represented by the expression.
#ERROR *errornumber*#	*errornumber* (variable is a **Variant** tagged as an error).

Double quotation marks (") within input data are ignored.

Data items in a file must appear in the same order as the variables in *varlist* and be matched with variables of the same data type. If a variable is numeric and the data is not, zero is assigned to the variable.

If the end of the file is reached while a data item is being input, the input is terminated and an error occurs.

Note In order to correctly read data from a file into variables, you should always use the **Write #** statement instead of the **Print #** statement to write the data to the files. Using **Write #** ensures that each separate data field is properly delimited.

See Also

Input Function, **Write #** Statement.

Example   This example uses the **Input #** statement to read data from a file into two variables. For purposes of this example, assume that TESTFILE is a file with a few lines of data written to it using the **Write #** statement; that is, each line contains a string in quotations and a number separated by a comma, for example, ("Hello", 234).

```
Open "TESTFILE" For Input As #1      ' Open file for input.
Do While Not EOF(1)                  ' Loop until end of file.
    Input #1, MyString, MyNumber     ' Read data into variables.
    Debug.Print MyString, MyNumber   ' Print data to Debug window.
Loop
Close #1' Close file.
```

Input Function

Description   Returns characters (bytes) from an open sequential file.

Syntax   **Input**(*number*,[#]*filenumber*)

The **Input** function syntax has these parts:

Part	Description
number	Any valid numeric expression specifying the number of characters to return.
filenumber	Any valid file number.

Remarks   Use this function only with files opened in **Input** or **Binary** mode.

Unlike the **Input #** statement, the **Input** function returns all of the characters it reads including commas, carriage returns, linefeeds, quotation marks, and leading spaces.

Note   Another function (**InputB**) is provided for use with the double-byte character sets (DBCS) used in some Asian locales. Instead of specifying the number of characters to return, *number* specifies the number of bytes. In areas where DBCS is not used, **InputB** behaves the same as **Input**.

See Also   **Input #** Statement.

Example   This example uses the **Input** function to read one character at a time from a file and print it to the Debug window. For purposes of this example, assume that TESTFILE is a text file with a few lines of sample data.

```
Open "TESTFILE" For Input As #1      ' Open file.
Do While Not EOF(1)                   ' Loop until end of file.
    MyChar = Input(1, #1)            ' Get one character.
    Debug.Print MyChar               ' Print to Debug window.
Loop
Close #1' Close file.
```

InputBox Function

Description

Displays a prompt in a dialog box, waits for the user to input text or choose a button, and returns the contents of the text box.

Syntax

InputBox(*prompt*[,*title*][,*default*][,*xpos*][,*ypos*][,*helpfile*,*context*])

The **InputBox** function syntax has these named-argument parts:

Part	Description
prompt	String expression displayed as the message in the dialog box. The maximum length of *prompt* is approximately 1024 characters, depending on the width of the characters used. If *prompt* consists of more than one line, be sure to include a carriage return (character code 13), or carriage return linefeed (character code 10) between each line.
title	String expression displayed in the title bar of the dialog box. If you omit *title*, nothing is placed in the title bar.
default	String expression displayed in the text box as the default response if no other input is provided. If you omit *default*, the text box is displayed empty.
xpos	Numeric expression that specifies, in twips, the horizontal distance of the left edge of the dialog box from the left edge of the screen. If *xpos* is omitted, the dialog box is horizontally centered.
ypos	Numeric expression that specifies, in twips, the vertical distance of the upper edge of the dialog box from the top of the screen. If *ypos* is omitted, the dialog box is vertically positioned approximately one-third of the way down the screen.
helpfile	String expression that identifies the Help file to use to provide context-sensitive Help for the dialog box. If *helpfile* is provided, *context* must also be provided.
context	Numeric expression that is the Help context number the Help author assigned to the appropriate Help topic. If *context* is provided, *helpfile* must also be provided.

Remarks	When both *helpfile* and *context* are supplied, a Help button is automatically added to the dialog box.
	If the user chooses OK or presses Enter, the **InputBox** function returns whatever is in the text box. If the user chooses Cancel, the function returns a zero-length string (" ").
	In Microsoft Excel, the *prompt* string cannot contain more than 256 characters.
See Also	**MsgBox** Function.
Example	This example shows various ways to use the **InputBox** function to prompt the user to enter a value. If the x and y positions are omitted, the dialog is automatically centered for the respective axes. The variable MyValue contains the value entered by the user if the user chooses OK or presses ENTER. If the user chooses Cancel, a zero-length string is returned.

```
Message = "Enter a value between 1 and 3"  ' Set prompt.
Title = "InputBox Demo"                     ' Set title.
Default = "1"                               ' Set default.
' Display message, title, and default value.
MyValue = InputBox(Message, Title, Default)

' Use helpfile and context. The help button is added automatically.
MyValue = InputBox(Message, Title, , , , "DEMO.HLP", 10)

' Display dialog at position 100,100
MyValue = InputBox(Message, Title, Default, 100, 100)
```

InputBox Method

Applies To	**Application** Object.
Description	Displays a dialog box for user input. Returns the information entered in the dialog box.
Syntax	*object*.**InputBox**(*prompt*, *title*, *default*, *left*, *top*, *helpFile*, *helpContextID*, *type*)

object
    Required. The **Application** object.

prompt
    Required. The message to be displayed in the dialog box. This may be a string, a number, a date, or a Boolean value.

title

Optional. The title for the input box. If this argument is omitted, the default title is "Input".

default

Optional. Specifies a value to be put in the edit box when the dialog box is initially displayed. If this argument is omitted, the edit box is left empty. This value may be a **Range** object.

left

Optional. Specifies an x position for the dialog box, in points, from the top left of the screen. One point is 1/72 inch.

top

Optional. Specifies a y position for the dialog box, in points, from the top left of the screen.

helpFile

Optional. The name of the online Help file for this input box. If the *helpFile* and *helpContextID* arguments are present, a Help button will appear in the dialog.

helpContextID

Optional. The context ID of the Help topic in *helpFile*.

type

Optional. Specifies the return data type. If this argument is omitted, the dialog box returns text. May have one of the following values:

Value	Meaning
0	A formula
1	A number
2	Text (a string)
4	A logical value (**True** or **False**)
8	A cell reference, as a **Range** object
16	An error value, such as #N/A
64	An array of values

You can use the sum of the allowable values for *type*. For example, for an input box that can accept text or numbers, set *type* equal to 1 + 2.

Remarks

Use **InputBox** to display a simple dialog box so you can enter information to be used in a macro. The dialog box has an OK and a Cancel button. If you choose the OK button, **InputBox** returns the value entered in the dialog box. If you choose the Cancel button, **InputBox** returns **False**.

If *type* = 0, **InputBox** returns the formula in the form of text, for example, "=2*PI()/360". If there are any references in the formula, they are returned as A1-style references. (Use **ConvertFormula** to convert between reference styles.)

If *type* = 8, **InputBox** returns a **Range** object. You must use the **Set** statement to assign the result to a **Range** object, as shown in the following example.

```
Set myRange = Application.InputBox(prompt := "Sample", type := 8)
```

If you do not use the **Set** statement, the variable is set to the value in the **Range**, rather than the **Range** itself.

If you use the **InputBox** method to ask the user for a formula, you must use the **FormulaLocal** property to assign the formula to a **Range** object. The input formula will be in the user's language. The **InputBox** method differs from the **InputBox** function because it allows selective validation of the user's input, and it can be used with Microsoft Excel objects, error values and formulas. Note that `Application.InputBox` calls the **InputBox** method; `InputBox` with no object qualifier calls the **InputBox** function.

Example   This example prompts the user for a number.

```
myNum = Application.InputBox("Enter a number")
```

This example prompts the user to select a cell on Sheet1. The example uses the *type* argument to ensure that the return value is a valid cell reference (a **Range** object).

```
Worksheets("Sheet1").Activate
Set myCell = Application.InputBox( _
    prompt:="Select a cell", Type:=8)
```

InputType Property

Applies To   **DrawingObjects** Collection, **EditBox** Object, **EditBoxes** Collection.

Description   Returns or sets what type of input validation is applied to the contents of an edit box (one of **xlFormula**, **xlInteger**, **xlNumber**, **xlReference**, or **xlText**). Read-write.

Example   This example sets edit box one on Dialog1 to require an integer.

```
DialogSheets("Dialog1").EditBoxes(1).InputType = xlInteger
```

Insert Method

Applies To   **Characters** Object, **Pictures** Collection, **Range** Object.

Description	Syntax 1 (**Range** object): Inserts a cell or a range of cells into the worksheet or macro sheet and shifts other cells away to make space.
	Syntax 2 (**Characters** object): Inserts a string before the selected characters.
	Syntax 3 (**Pictures** objcct): Inserts the specified file as a picture.
Syntax 1	*object*.**Insert**(*shift*)
Syntax 2	*object*.**Insert**(*string*)
Syntax 3	*object*.**Insert**(*filename*, *converter*)

object
> Required. Insert cells at this range (Syntax 1) or insert string before this character (Syntax 2).

shift
> Optional. Specifies which way to shift the cells, either **xlToRight** or **xlDown**. If omitted, a default is used based on the shape of the range.

string
> Required. The string to insert.

filename
> Required. Specifies the file to insert.

converter
> Required. Specifies the picture converter to use when loading the file. Can be one of **xlBMP**, **xlWMF**, **xlPLT**, **xlCGM**, **xlHGL**, **xlPIC**, **xlEPS**, **xlDRW**, **xlTIF**, **xlWPG**, **xlDXF**, **xlPCX**, or **xlPCT**.

Example

This example inserts a new row before row four on Sheet1.

```
Worksheets("Sheet1").Rows(4).Insert
```

This example inserts new cells at the range A1:C5 on Sheet1 and shifts cells down.

```
Worksheets("Sheet1").Range("A1:C5").Insert shift:=xlDown
```

This example inserts a new row at the active cell. The example must be run from a worksheet.

```
ActiveCell.EntireRow.Insert
```

This example replaces the first three characters in text box one on Sheet1 with the string "New" formatted as bold.

```
With Worksheets("Sheet1").TextBoxes(1).Characters(1, 3)
    .Insert "New"
    .Font.Bold = True
End With
```

This example adds the string "Done" to the end of text box one on Sheet1 by inserting the new string after the last character in the text box.

```
With Worksheets("Sheet1").TextBoxes(1)
    .Characters(.Characters.Count + 1).Insert String:="Done"
End With
```

InsertFile Method

Applies To **Module** Object.

Description Adds text from a file to the end of the module.

Syntax *object*.**InsertFile**(*fileName*, *merge*)

object
Required. The **Module** object.

fileName
Required. The name of the file containing the text that you wish to insert.

merge
Optional. If **True**, the new file is merged, so that all declarations are at the top of the module and all procedures are below the declarations. If **False** or omitted, the new file is inserted at the insertion point.

Remarks You cannot insert text into a running code module. This applies both to running procedures as well as modules containing code that is stacked waiting to run after the current procedure returns.

Example This example adds text from a file to Module2. Note that you cannot use the **InsertFile** method to add text to the module that contains the running example. Run the example from Module1 after inserting a new macro module (Module2).

```
Modules("Module2").InsertFile fileName:="MYMACRO.TXT"
```

Installed Property

Applies To **AddIn** Object.

Description **True** if the add-in is installed. Read-write.

Remarks	Setting this property to **True** installs the add-in and calls its Auto_Add functions. Setting this property to **False** removes the add-in and calls its Auto_Remove functions.
Example	This example uses a message box to display the installation status of the Solver add-in.

```
Set a = AddIns("Solver Add-In")
If a.Installed = True Then
    MsgBox "The Solver add-in is installed"
Else
    MsgBox "The Solver add-in is not installed"
End If
```

InStr Function

Description   Returns the position of the first occurrence of one string within another.

Syntax   **InStr**([*start,*]*string1,string2*[*,compare*])

The **InStr** function syntax has these parts:

Part	Description
start	Numeric expression that sets the starting position for each search. If omitted, search begins at the first character position. If *start* contains no valid data, an error occurs. *Start* is required if *compare* is specified.
string1	String expression being searched. If *string1* contains no valid data, **Null** is returned.
string2	String expression sought. If *string2* contains no valid data, **Null** is returned.
compare	Number specifying the type of string comparison. Specify **1** to perform a textual case-insensitive comparison. Specify **0** (default) to perform a binary comparison. If *compare* is **Null**, an error occurs. *Start* is required if *compare* is specified. If *compare* is omitted, the setting of **Option Compare** is used to determine the type of comparison.

Return Values

Value	Description
0	*string1* is zero-length.
start	*string2* is zero-length.

Value	Description
0	*string2* not found.
Position at which match is found	*string2* is found within *string1*.
0	*start > string2*.

Remarks

Note When **Option Compare Text** is specified, comparisons are textual and case-insensitive. When **Option Compare Binary** is specified, comparisons are strictly binary.

Note Another function (**InStrB**) is provided for use with the double-byte character sets (DBCS) used in some Asian locales. Instead of returning the character position of the first occurrence of one string within another, **InStrB** returns the byte position. In areas where DBCS is not used, **InStrB** behaves the same as **InStr**.

See Also

Option Compare Statement.

Example

This example uses the **InStr** function to return the position of the first occurrence of one string within another.

```
SearchString ="XXpXXpXXPXXP"          ' String to search in.
SearchChar = "P"                      ' Search for "P".

' A textual comparison starting at position 4. Returns 6.
MyPos = InStr(4, SearchString, SearchChar, 1)

' A binary comparison starting at position 1. Returns 9.
MyPos = InStr(1, SearchString, SearchChar, 0)

' Comparison is binary by default (if last argument is omitted).
MyPos = InStr(SearchString, SearchChar) ' Returns 9.

MyPos = InStr(1, SearchString, "W")  ' Returns 0.
```

Int Function, Fix Function

Description

Returns the integer portion of a number.

Syntax

Int(*number*)
Fix(*number*)

The *number* argument can be any valid numeric expression. If *number* contains no valid data, **Null** is returned.

Remarks   Both **Int** and **Fix** remove the fractional part of *number* and return the resulting integer value.

The difference between **Int** and **Fix** is that if *number* is negative, **Int** returns the first negative integer less than or equal to *number,* whereas **Fix** returns the first negative integer greater than or equal to *number.* For example, **Int** converts -8.4 to -9, and **Fix** converts -8.4 to -8.

Fix(*number*) is equivalent to:

```
Sgn(number) * Int(Abs(number))
```

See Also   **CInt** Function.

Example   This example illustrates how the **Int** and **Fix** functions return integer portions of numbers. In the case of a negative number argument, the **Int** function returns the first negative integer less than or equal to the number; whereas, the **Fix** function returns the first negative integer greater than or equal to the number.

```
MyNumber = Int(99.8)                  ' Returns 99.
MyNumber = Fix(99.2)                  ' Returns 99.
MyNumber = Int(-99.8)                 ' Returns -100.
MyNumber = Fix(-99.8)                 ' Returns -99.
MyNumber = Int(-99.2)                 ' Returns -100.
MyNumber = Fix(-99.2)    ' Returns -99.
```

Integer Data Type

Description   **Integer** variables are stored as 16-bit (2-byte) numbers ranging in value from -32,768 to 32,767. The type-declaration character for **Integer** is % (character code 37).

You can also use **Integer** variables to represent enumerated values. An enumerated value can contain a finite set of unique whole numbers, each of which has special meaning in the context in which it is used. Enumerated values provide a convenient way to select among a known number of choices. For example, when asking the user to select a color from a list, you could have 0 = black, 1 = white, and so on. It is good programming practice to define constants using the **Const** statement for each enumerated value.

See Also   **CInt** Function, Data Type Summary, **Def**type Statements, **Long** Data Type, **Variant** Data Type.

Interactive Property

Applies To   **Application** Object.

Description   **True** if Microsoft Excel is in interactive mode; this property is usually **True**. If you set it to **False**, Microsoft Excel will block all input from the keyboard and mouse (except input to dialog boxes that are displayed by your code). Blocking user input will prevent the user from interfering with the macro as it moves or activates Microsoft Excel objects. Read-write.

Remarks   This property is useful if you are using DDE, AppleEvents, or OLE Automation to communicate with Microsoft Excel from another application.

If you set this property to **False**, don't forget to set it back to **True**. Microsoft Excel will not set this property back to **True** when your macro stops running.

Example   This example sets the **Interactive** property to **False** while it is using DDE in Windows and then sets this property back to **True** when it is done. This prevents the user from interfering with the macro.

```
Application.Interactive = False
Application.DisplayAlerts = False
channelNumber = Application.DDEInitiate( _
    app:="WinWord", _
    topic:="C:\WINWORD\FORMLETR.DOC")
Application.DDEExecute channelNumber, "[FILEPRINT]"
Application.DDETerminate channelNumber
Application.DisplayAlerts = True
Application.Interactive = True
```

Intercept Property

Applies To   **Trendline** Object.

Description   Returns or sets the point where the trendline crosses the value axis. Read-write.

For help about using the **Intercept** worksheet function in Visual Basic, see "Using Worksheet Functions in Visual Basic" in online Help.

Remarks   Setting this property causes the **InterceptIsAuto** property to be set to **False**.

See Also   **InterceptIsAuto** Property.

Example   This example causes trendline one in Chart1 to cross the value axis at 5. The example should be run on a 2-D column chart that contains a single series with a trendline.

```
Charts("Chart1").SeriesCollection(1).Trendlines(1).Intercept = 5
```

InterceptIsAuto Property

Applies To   **Trendline** Object.

Description   **True** if the point where the trendline crosses the value axis is automatically determined by the regression. Read-write.

Remarks   Setting the **Intercept** property causes this property to be set to **False**.

See Also   **Intercept** Property.

Example   This example causes Microsoft Excel to automatically determine the trendline intercept point for Chart1. The example should be run on a 2-D column chart that contains a single series with a trendline.

```
Charts("Chart1").SeriesCollection(1).Trendlines(1).InterceptIsAuto = _
        True
```

Interior Object

Description   Represents the interior of an object. Both cells (**Range** objects) and graphic objects use the **Interior** object.

Accessors   The **Interior** property returns the interior of an object. The following example sets the interior color for all the ovals on the worksheet named "Sheet1."

```
Worksheets("sheet1").Ovals.Interior.ColorIndex = 3
```

Properties   **Application** Property, **Color** Property, **ColorIndex** Property, **Creator** Property, **Parent** Property, **Pattern** Property, **PatternColor** Property, **PatternColorIndex** Property.

Interior Property

Applies To

Arc Object, **Arcs** Collection, **AxisTitle** Object, **ChartArea** Object, **ChartObject** Object, **ChartObjects** Collection, **ChartTitle** Object, **CheckBox** Object, **DataLabel** Object, **DataLabels** Collection, **DownBars** Object, **Drawing** Object, **DrawingObjects** Collection, **Drawings** Collection, **Floor** Object, **GroupObject** Object, **GroupObjects** Collection, **Legend** Object, **LegendKey** Object, **OLEObject** Object, **OLEObjects** Collection, **OptionButton** Object, **OptionButtons** Collection, **Oval** Object, **Ovals** Collection, **Picture** Object, **Pictures** Collection, **PlotArea** Object, **Point** Object, **Range** Object, **Rectangle** Object, **Rectangles** Collection, **Series** Object, **Style** Object, **TextBox** Object, **TextBoxes** Collection, **UpBars** Object, **Walls** Object.

Description

Accessor. Returns an **Interior** object that represents the interior of the specified object. Read-only.

Example

This example sets the interior color for cell A1 onSheet1 to cyan.

```
Worksheets("Sheet1").Range("A1").Interior.ColorIndex = 8
```

International Property

Applies To

Application Object.

Description

Returns a 45-element array containing information about the current country and international settings. Read-only.

Syntax

object.**International**(*index*)

object
Required. The **Application** object.

index
Optional. Specifies a single setting to return, as shown in the following table.

Index	Built-in constant	Type	Meaning
1	**xlCountryCode**	number	Country version of Microsoft Excel.
2	**xlCountrySetting**	number	Current country setting in the Microsoft Windows Control Panel or the country number as determined by your Apple system software.
3	**xlDecimalSeparator**	text	Decimal separator.

Index	Built-in constant	Type	Meaning
4	**xlThousandsSeparator**	text	Zero or thousands separator.
5	**xlListSeparator**	text	List separator.
6	**xlUpperCaseRowLetter**	text	Uppercase Row letter (for R1C1 references).
7	**xlUpperCaseColumnLetter**	text	Uppercase Column letter.
8	**xlLowerCaseRowLetter**	text	Lowercase Row letter.
9	**xlLowerCaseColumnLetter**	text	Lowercase Column letter.
10	**xlLeftBracket**	text	Character used instead of the left bracket ([) in R1C1 relative references.
11	**xlRightBracket**	text	Character used instead of the right bracket (]).
12	**xlLeftBrace**	text	Character used instead of the left brace ({) in array literals.
13	**xlRightBrace**	text	Character used instead of the right brace (}).
14	**xlColumnSeparator**	text	Character used to separate columns in array literals.
15	**xlRowSeparator**	text	Character used to separate rows.
16	**xlAlternateArraySeparator**	text	Alternate array item separator to use if the current array separator is the same as the decimal separator.
17	**xlDateSeparator**	text	Date separator (/ in US).
18	**xlTimeSeparator**	text	Time separator (: in US).
19	**xlYearCode**	text	Year symbol in number formats (y in US).
20	**xlMonthCode**	text	Month symbol (m).
21	**xlDayCode**	text	Day symbol (d).
22	**xlHourCode**	text	Hour symbol (h).
23	**xlMinuteCode**	text	Minute symbol (m).
24	**xlSecondCode**	text	Second symbol (s).
25	**xlCurrencyCode**	text	Currency symbol ($).
26	**xlGeneralFormatName**	text	Name of the General number format.
27	**xlCurrencyDigits**	number	Number of decimal digits to use in currency formats.

Index	Built-in constant	Type	Meaning
28	**xlCurrencyNegative**	number	Indicates the currency format for negative currencies: 0 = ($x) or (x$) 1 = -$x or -x$ 2 = $-x or x-$ 3 = $x- or x$- Note: The position of the currency symbol is determined by 37.
29	**xlNoncurrencyDigits**	number	Number of decimal digits to use in non-currency formats.
30	**xlMonthNameChars**	number	Number of characters to use in month names.
31	**xlWeekdayNameChars**	number	Number of characters to use in weekday names.
32	**xlDateOrder**	number	Indicates the date order: 0 = month-day-year 1 = day-month-year 2 = year-month-day
33	**xl24HourClock**	Boolean	**True** if using 24-hour time; **False** if using 12-hour time.
34	**xlNonEnglishFunctions**	Boolean	**True** if not displaying functions in English.
35	**xlMetric**	Boolean	**True** if using the metric system; **False** if using the English measurement system.
36	**xlCurrencySpaceBefore**	Boolean	**True** if adding a space before the currency symbol.
37	**xlCurrencyBefore**	Boolean	**True** if the currency symbol precedes the currency values; **False** if it goes after.
38	**xlCurrencyMinusSign**	Boolean	**True** if using a minus sign for negative numbers; **False** if using parentheses.
39	**xlCurrencyTrailingZeros**	Boolean	**True** if trailing zeros are displayed for zero currency values.
40	**xlCurrencyLeadingZeros**	Boolean	**True** if leading zeros are displayed for zero currency values.

Index	Built-in constant	Type	Meaning
41	**xlMonthLeadingZero**	Boolean	**True** if a leading zero is displayed in months when months are displayed as numbers.
42	**xlDayLeadingZero**	Boolean	**True** if a leading zero is displayed in days.
43	**xl4DigitYears**	Boolean	**True** if using 4-digit years; **False** if using 2-digit years.
44	**xlMDY**	Boolean	**True** if the date order is Month-Day-Year when dates are displayed in the long form; **False** if the date order is Day-Month-Year.
45	**xlTimeLeadingZero**	Boolean	**True** if the leading zero is shown in the time.

Example   This example displays the international decimal separator.

```
MsgBox "The decimal separator is " & _
    Application.International(xlDecimalSeparator)
```

Intersect Method

Applies To   **Application** Object.

Description   Returns the rectangular intersection of two or more ranges.

Syntax   *object*.**Intersect**(*arg1*, *arg2*, ...)

object
   Optional. The **Application** object.

arg1, *arg2*, ...
   Required. The intersecting ranges. At least two **Range** objects must be specified.

See Also   **Union** Method.

Example

This example selects the intersection of two named ranges, rg1 and rg2, on Sheet1. If the ranges do not intersect, the example displays a message.

```
Worksheets("Sheet1").Activate
Set isect = Application.Intersect(Range("rg1"), Range("rg2"))
If isect Is Nothing Then
    MsgBox "Ranges do not intersect"
Else
    isect.Select
End If
```

InvertIfNegative Property

Applies To

LegendKey Object, **Point** Object, **Series** Object.

Description

True if Microsoft Excel inverts the pattern in the item when it corresponds to a negative number. Read-write.

Example

This example inverts the pattern for negative values in series one in Chart1. The example should be run on a 2-D column chart.

```
Charts("Chart1").SeriesCollection(1).InvertIfNegative = True
```

Is Operator

Description

Used to compare two object reference variables.

Syntax

result = *object1* **Is** *object2*

The **Is** operator syntax has these parts:

Part	Description
result	Any numeric variable.
object1	Any object name.
object2	Any object name.

Remarks

If *object1* and *object2* both refer to the same object, *result* is **True**; if they do not, *result* is **False**. Two variables can be made to refer to the same object in several ways.

In the following example, A has been set to refer to the same object as B:

```
Set A = B
```

The following example makes A and B refer to the same object as C:

```
Set A = C
Set B = C
```

See Also

Comparison Operators, Operator Precedence, **Set** Statement.

Example

This example uses the **Is** operator to compare two object references. All the object variables used here are generic names and for illustration purposes only.

```
Set YourObject = MyObject          ' Assign object references.
Set ThisObject = MyObject
Set ThatObject = OtherObject
MyCheck = YourObject Is ThisObject  ' Returns True.
MyCheck = ThatObject Is ThisObject  ' Returns False.
' Assume MyObject <> OtherObject
MyCheck = MyObject Is ThatObject    ' Returns False.
```

This example selects the intersection of two named ranges, rg1 and rg2, on Sheet1. If the ranges do not intersect, the example displays a message.

```
Worksheets("Sheet1").Activate
Set isect = Application.Intersect(Range("rg1"), Range("rg2"))
If isect Is Nothing Then
    MsgBox "Ranges do not intersect"
Else
    isect.Select
End If
```

This example finds the first occurrence of the word "Phoenix" in column B on Sheet1 and then displays the address of the cell that contains this word. If the word is not found, the example diplays a message.

```
Set foundCell = Worksheets("Sheet1").Columns("B").Find("Phoenix")
If foundCell Is Nothing Then
    MsgBox "The word was not found"
Else
    MsgBox "The word was found in cell " & foundCell.Address
End If
```

IsArray Function

Description   Returns a value indicating whether a variable is an array.

Syntax   **IsArray(*varname*)**

The ***varname*** named argument can be any variable.

Remarks   **IsArray** returns **True** if the variable is an array; otherwise, it returns **False**.

See Also   **Array** Function, **IsDate** Function, **IsEmpty** Function, **IsError** Function, **IsMissing** Function, **IsNull** Function, **IsNumeric** Function, **IsObject** Function, **TypeName** Function, **Variant Data** Type, **VarType** Function.

Example   This example uses the **IsArray** function to check if a variable is an array.

```
Dim MyArray(1 To 5) As Integer    ' Declare array variable.
YourArray = Array(1, 2, 3)        ' Use Array function.
MyCheck = IsArray(MyArray)        ' Returns True.
MyCheck = IsArray(YourArray) ' Returns True.
```

IsDate Function

Description   Returns a value indicating whether an expression can be converted to a date.

Syntax   **IsDate(*expression*)**

The ***expression*** named argument can be any date or string expression recognizable as a date or time.

Remarks   **IsDate** returns **True** if the expression is a date or can legally be converted to a date; otherwise, it returns **False**. The range of valid dates is January 1, 100 A.D. through December 31, 9999 A.D.

See Also   **CDate** Function, **Date Data** Type, **IsArray** Function, **IsEmpty** Function, **IsError** Function, **IsMissing** Function, **IsNull** Function, **IsNumeric** Function, **IsObject** Function, **TypeName** Function, **Variant Data** Type, **VarType** Function.

Example   This example uses the **IsDate** function to determine if an expression can be converted to a date.

```
MyDate = "February 12, 1969" : YourDate = #2/12/69# : NoDate = "Hello"
MyCheck = IsDate(MyDate)          ' Returns True.
MyCheck = IsDate(YourDate)        ' Returns True.
MyCheck = IsDate(NoDate) ' Returns False.
```

IsEmpty Function

Description   Returns a value indicating whether a variable has been initialized.

Syntax   **IsEmpty(*expression*)**

The *expression* named argument can be any numeric or string expression. However, because **IsEmpty** is used to determine if individual variables are initialized, the *expression* argument is most often a single variable name.

Remarks   **IsEmpty** returns **True** if the variable is **Empty**; otherwise, it returns **False**. **False** is always returned if *expression* contains more than one variable.

See Also   **IsArray** Function, **IsDate** Function, **IsError** Function, **IsMissing** Function, **IsNull** Function, **IsNumeric** Function, **IsObject** Function, **TypeName** Function, **Variant Data** Type, **VarType** Function.

Example   This example uses the **IsEmpty** function to determine whether or not a variable has been initialized.

```
MyCheck = IsEmpty(MyVar)            ' Returns True.
MyVar = Null                        ' Assign Null.
MyCheck = IsEmpty(MyVar)            ' Returns False.
MyVar = Empty                       ' Assign Empty.
MyCheck = IsEmpty(MyVar) ' Returns True.
```

This example sorts the data in the first column on Sheet1 and then deletes rows that contain duplicate data.

```
Worksheets("Sheet1").Range("A1").Sort _
    key1:=Worksheets("Sheet1").Range("A1")
Set currentCell = Worksheets("Sheet1").Range("A1")
Do While Not IsEmpty(currentCell)
    Set nextCell = currentCell.Offset(1, 0)
    If nextCell.Value = currentCell.Value Then
        currentCell.EntireRow.Delete
    End If
    Set currentCell = nextCell
Loop
```

IsError Function

Description   Returns a value indicating whether an expression is an error value.

Syntax	**IsError(***expression***)**

The *expression* named argument can be any numeric expression used to indicate an error value.

Remarks	Error values are created by converting real numbers to error values using the **CVErr** function. The **IsError** function is used to determine if a numeric expression represents an error. **IsError** returns **True** if the *expression* argument indicates an error; otherwise, it returns **False**.

See Also	**CVErr** Function, **IsArray** Function, **IsDate** Function, **IsEmpty** Function, **IsMissing** Function, **IsNull** Function, **IsNumeric** Function, **IsObject** Function, **TypeName** Function, **Variant Data** Type, **VarType** Function.

Example	This example uses the **IsError** function to check if a numeric expression is an error value. The **CVErr** function is used to return an **Error Variant** from a user-defined function.

```
' Assume UserFunction is a user-defined function procedure that returns
' an error value; e.g., return value assigned with the statement
' UserFunction = CVErr(32767) where 32767 is a user-defined number.
ReturnVal = UserFunction()
MyCheck = IsError(ReturnVal) ' Returns True.
```

IsGap Property

Applies To	**ToolbarButton** Object.

Description	**True** if the button is really a gap (an extended space between buttons). Read-only.

Example	This example displays the number of separator gaps on the Standard toolbar.

```
gapCount = 0
For Each btn In Toolbars("Standard").ToolbarButtons
    If btn.IsGap Then
        gapCount = gapCount + 1
    End If
Next btn
MsgBox "There are " & gapCount & " gaps on the Standard toolbar"
```

IsMissing Function

Description   Returns a value indicating whether an optional argument has been passed to a procedure.

Syntax   **IsMissing(*argname*)**

The ***argname*** named argument is the name of an optional procedure argument.

Remarks   The **IsMissing** function is used in a procedure that has optional arguments, including **ParamArray** arguments, to determine whether an argument has been passed to the procedure. **IsMissing** returns **True** if no value has been passed for the specified argument; otherwise, it returns **False**.

See Also   **Function** Statement, **IsArray** Function, **IsDate** Function, **IsEmpty** Function, **IsError** Function, **IsNull** Function, **IsNumeric** Function, **IsObject** Function, **Property Get** Statement, **Property Let** Statement, **Property Set** Statement, **Sub** Statement, **TypeName** Function, **Variant Data** Type, **VarType** Function.

Example   This example uses the **IsMissing** function to check if an optional argument has been passed to a user-defined procedure.

```
' The following statements call the user-defined function procedure.
ReturnValue = ReturnTwice()        ' Returns Null.
ReturnValue = ReturnTwice(2)       ' Returns 4.

' Function procedure definition.
Function ReturnTwice(Optional A)
    If IsMissing(A) Then
        ' If argument is missing, return a Null.
        ReturnTwice = Null
    Else
        ' If argument is present, return twice the value.
        ReturnTwice = A * 2
    End If
End Function
```

IsNull Function

Description   Returns a value that indicates whether an expression contains no valid data (**Null**).

Syntax   **IsNull(*expression*)**

The ***expression*** named argument can be any numeric or string expression.

Remarks

IsNull returns **True** if *expression* is **Null**, that is, it contains no valid data; otherwise, **IsNull** returns **False**. If *expression* consists of more than one variable, **Null** in any variable causes **True** to be returned for the entire expression.

The **Null** value indicates that the **Variant** contains no valid data. **Null** is not the same as **Empty**, which indicates that a variable has not yet been initialized. It is also not the same as a zero-length string, which is sometimes referred to as a null string.

Important Use the **IsNull** function to determine whether an expression contains a **Null** value. Expressions that you might expect to evaluate **True** under some circumstances, such as `If Var = Null` and `If Var <> Null`, are always **False**. This is because any expression containing a **Null** is itself **Null** and therefore **False**.

See Also

IsArray Function, **IsDate** Function, **IsEmpty** Function, **IsError** Function, **IsMissing** Function, **IsNumeric** Function, **IsObject** Function, **TypeName** Function, **Variant Data** Type, **VarType** Function.

Example

This example uses the **IsNull** function to determine if a variable contains a **Null**.

```
MyCheck = IsNull(MyVar)              ' Returns False.
MyVar = ""
MyCheck = IsNull(MyVar)              ' Returns False.
MyVar = Null
MyCheck = IsNull(MyVar)  ' Returns True.
```

This example creates a list of registered functions, placing each registered function in a separate row on Sheet1. Column A contains the full path and filename of the DLL or code resource, column B contains the function name, and column C contains the argument data type code.

```
theArray = Application.RegisteredFunctions
If IsNull(theArray) Then
    MsgBox "No registered functions"
Else
    For i = LBound(theArray) To UBound(theArray)
        For j = 1 To 3
            Worksheets("Sheet1").Cells(i, j).Formula = theArray(i, j)
        Next j
    Next i
End If
```

IsNumeric Function

Description   Returns a value indicating whether an expression can be evaluated as a number.

Syntax   **IsNumeric(*expression*)**

The *expression* named argument can be any numeric or string expression.

Remarks   **IsNumeric** returns **True** if the entire *expression* is recognized as a number; otherwise, it returns **False**.

IsNumeric returns **False** if *expression* is a date expression.

See Also   **IsArray** Function, **IsDate** Function, **IsEmpty** Function, **IsError** Function, **IsMissing** Function, **IsNull** Function, **IsObject** Function, **TypeName** Function, **Variant Data** Type, **VarType** Function.

Example   This example uses the **IsNumeric** function to determine if a variable can be evaluated as a number.

```
MyVar = "53"                          ' Assign value.
MyCheck = IsNumeric(MyVar)            ' Returns True.
MyVar = "459.95"                      ' Assign value.
MyCheck = IsNumeric(MyVar)            ' Returns True.
MyVar = "45 Help"                     ' Assign value.
MyCheck = IsNumeric(MyVar)    ' Returns False.
```

IsObject Function

Description   Returns a value indicating whether an expression references a valid OLE Automation object.

Syntax   **IsObject(*expression*)**

The *expression* named argument can be any expression.

Remarks   **IsObject** returns **True** if *expression* is a valid reference to an actual object; otherwise, it returns **False**.

See Also   **IsArray** Function, **IsDate** Function, **IsEmpty** Function, **IsError** Function, **IsMissing** Function, **IsNull** Function, **IsNumeric** Function, **Object Data** Type, **Set** Statement, **TypeName** Function, **Variant Data** Type, **VarType** Function.

Example   This example uses the **IsObject** function to determine if a variable references a valid object. `MyObject` and `YourObject` are object variables of the same type. They are generic names used here for illustration purposes only.

```
Dim MyInt As Integer              ' Declare variable.
Set YourObject = MyObject         ' Assign an object reference.
MyCheck = IsObject(YourObject)    ' Returns True.
MyCheck = IsObject(MyInt)    ' Returns False.
```

Italic Property

Applies To   **Font** Object.

Description   **True** if the font is italic. Read-write.

Example   This example sets the font to italic for the range A1:A5 on Sheet1.

```
Worksheets("Sheet1").Range("A1:A5").Font.Italic = True
```

Item Method

Applies To   All collections.

Description   Accessor. Returns part of a collection. The **Item** method works like the accessor method for a collection. For example, the following two lines of code are equivalent.

```
ActiveWorkbook.Worksheets.Item(1)
ActiveWorkbook.Worksheets(1)
```

For more information about accessing an individual member of a collection, see the accessor method or property listed in the following table.

AddIns	**EditBoxes**	**PivotItems**
Arcs	**Excel4IntlMacroSheets**	**PivotTables**
AreaGroups	**Excel4MacroSheets**	**Points**
Axes	**GroupBoxes**	**RadarGroups**
BarGroups	**GroupObjects**	**Range**
Borders	**HiddenFields**	**Rectangles**
BuiltinDocumentProperties	**HiddenItems**	**RowFields**

Buttons	Labels	Rows
Cells	LegendEntries	Scenarios
Characters	LineGroups	ScrollBars
ChartGroups	Lines	SeriesCollection
ChartObjects	ListBoxes	Sheets
Charts	MenuBars	ShortcutMenus
CheckBoxes	MenuItems	Spinners
ChildItems	Menus	Styles
ColumnFields	Modules	TextBoxes
ColumnGroups	Names	ToolbarButtons
Columns	OLEObjects	Toolbars
CustomDocumentProperties	OptionButtons	Trendlines
DataFields	Ovals	VisibleFields
DialogSheets	PageFields	VisibleItems
Dialogs	Panes	Windows
DoughnutGroups	ParentItems	Workbooks
DrawingObjects	Pictures	Worksheets
Drawings	PieGroups	XYGroups
DropDowns	PivotFields	

Item Method (DocumentProperties Collection)

Applies To   **DocumentProperties** Collection.

Description   Accessor. Returns a single **DocumentProperty** object from the collection of document properties.

To use this method, you should establish a reference to the Microsoft Office 95 Object Library by using the References command (Tools menu).

Remarks   Because the **Item** method is the default method for the **DocumentProperties** collection object, the following statements are identical.

```
CustomDocumentProperties.Item(1)
CustomDocumentProperties(1)
```

You can refer to document properties either by index value or by name. The following list shows the available built-in document property names:

Title, Subject, Author, Keywords, Comments, Template, Last Author, Revision Number, Application Name, Last Print Date, Creation Date, Last Save Time, Total Editing Time, Number of Pages, Number of Words, Number of Characters, Security, Category, Format, Manager, Company, Number of Bytes, Number of Lines, Number of Paragraphs, Number of Slides, Number of Notes, Number of Hidden Slides, Number of Multimedia Clips

Container applications aren't required to define values for every built-in document property. If the application doesn't define a value for one of the built-in document properties, reading the **Value** property for that document property causes an error.

Example   This example displays the names of the document properties in a collection. You must pass a **DocumentProperties** collection to the procedure.

```
Sub DisplayPropertyNames(dp As DocumentProperties)
    Dim i As Integer
    For i = 1 To dp.Count
        MsgBox dp.Item(i).Name
    Next
End Sub
```

This example creates a list containing the names of the built-in document properties in the active workbook.

```
Set wk = Worksheets(1)
Set builtinProps = ActiveWorkbook.BuiltinDocumentProperties
For i = 1 To builtinProps.Count
    wk.Cells(i, 1).Value = builtinProps.Item(i).Name
Next
```

Iteration Property

Applies To   **Application** Object.

Description   **True** if Microsoft Excel will use iteration to resolve circular references. Read-write.

See Also   **MaxChange** Property, **MaxIterations** Property.

Example   This example sets the **Iteration** property to **True**, so that circular references are resolved by iteration.

```
Application.Iteration = True
```

Justify Method

Applies To	**Range** Object.
Description	Rearranges the text in a range so that it fills the range evenly.
Syntax	*object*.**Justify**

object
> Required. The range to justify.

Remarks	If the range is not large enough, Microsoft Excel displays a message that text will extend below the range. If you choose the OK button, justified text will replace the contents in cells extending beyond the selected range. To prevent this message from appearing, set the **DisplayAlerts** property to **False**, in which case the text will always replace the contents in cells below the range.
Example	This example justifies text in cell A1 on Sheet1.

```
Worksheets("Sheet1").Range("A1").Justify
```

Keywords Property

Applies To	**AddIn** Object, **Workbook** Object.
Description	Returns or sets the keywords for the object, as a string. Read-only for **AddIn**, read-write for **Workbook**.
Remarks	In Microsoft Excel for Windows 95, this property has been replaced by a built-in OLE document property. For more information about OLE document properties, see **BuiltinDocumentProperties**.
	You cannot use this property with an **AddIn** object that represents an XLL file or an add-in that was created with the Microsoft Excel 4.0 macro language.
See Also	**Author** Property, **Comments** Property, **Subject** Property, **Title** Property.
Example	This example sets the keywords for the active workbook.

```
ActiveWorkbook.Keywords = "Sales, West Region, 1995"
```

Kill Statement

Description   Deletes files from a disk.

Syntax   **Kill** *pathname*

The *pathname* named argument is a string expression that specifies one or more file names to be deleted—may include directory or folder, and drive.

Remarks   **Kill** supports the use of '*****' (multiple character) and '**?**' (single character) wildcards to specify multiple files. However, on the Macintosh, these characters are treated as valid file name characters and can't be used as wildcards to specify multiple files.

Since the Macintosh does not support wildcards, use the file type to identify groups of files to delete. You can use the **MacID** function to specify file type instead of repeating the command with separate file names. For example, the following statement deletes all 'TEXT' files in the current folder.

```
Kill MacID("TEXT")
```

If you use the **MacID** function with **Kill** in Microsoft Windows, an error occurs.

An error occurs if you try to use **Kill** to delete an open file.

To delete directories, use the **RmDir** statement.

See Also   **MacID** Function, **RmDir** Statement.

Example   This example uses the **Kill** statement to delete a file from a disk. Since the Macintosh does not support wildcards, you can use the **MacID** function to specify the file type instead of the file name.

```
' Assume TESTFILE is a file containing some data.
Kill "TestFile"                    ' Delete file.

' In Microsoft Windows.
' Delete all *.txt files in current directory.
Kill "*.txt"

' On the Macintosh.
' Use the MacID function to delete all PICT files in current folder
Kill MacID("PICT")
```

Label Object

Description   Represents a static text object on a chart sheet, dialog sheet, or worksheet. Labels have no font or background formatting, but labels on dialog sheets do have an accelerator key. Labels can be positioned and sized.

Accessors   The **Label** object is a member of the **Labels** collection. The **Labels** collection contains all the **Label** objects on a single sheet. Use the **Add** method to create a new label and add it to the collection.

To access a single member of the collection, use the **Labels** method with the index number or name of the label as an argument.

The following example sets the text in label one on the dialog sheet named "Dialog1."

```
DialogSheets("dialog1").Labels(1).Text = "Options"
```

The label name is shown in the Name Box when the label is selected. Use the **Name** property to set or return the label name. The following example hides the label named "Option Label" on the dialog sheet named "Dialog1."

```
DialogSheets("dialog1").Labels("option label").Visible = False
```

Properties   **Accelerator** Property, **Application** Property, **BottomRightCell** Property, **Caption** Property, **Creator** Property, **Enabled** Property, **Height** Property, **Index** Property, **Left** Property, **Locked** Property, **LockedText** Property, **Name** Property, **OnAction** Property, **Parent** Property, **PhoneticAccelerator** Property, **Placement** Property, **PrintObject** Property, **Text** Property, **Top** Property, **TopLeftCell** Property, **Visible** Property, **Width** Property, **ZOrder** Property.

Methods   **BringToFront** Method, **Characters** Method, **CheckSpelling** Method, **Copy** Method, **CopyPicture** Method, **Cut** Method, **Delete** Method, **Duplicate** Method, **Select** Method, **SendToBack** Method.

LabelRange Property

Applies To   **PivotField** Object, **PivotItem** Object.

Description   Accessor. **PivotField**: Returns a **Range** object that represents the cell (or cells) that contain the field label. **PivotItem**: Returns a **Range** object that represents all the PivotTable cells that contain the item. Read-only.

Example This example selects the field button for the field named "ORDER_DATE."

```
Set pvtTable = Worksheets("Sheet1").Range("A3").PivotTable
Set pvtField = pvtTable.PivotFields("ORDER_DATE")
Worksheets("Sheet1").Activate
pvtField.LabelRange.Select
```

Labels Collection Object

Description A collection of all the **Label** objects on the specified chart sheet, dialog sheet, or worksheet. Labels have no font or background formatting, but labels on dialog sheets do have an accelerator key. Labels can be positioned and sized.

Accessors Use the **Add** method to create a new label and add it to the collection. The following example adds a new label to dialog sheet one. The upper-left corner of the new label is positioned 10 points from the left and 20 points from the bottom of the dialog frame.

```
Dim df As DialogFrame
Set df = DialogSheets(1).DialogFrame
DialogSheets(1).Labels.Add df.Left + 10, _
    df.Top + df.Height - 20, 100, 10
```

Use the **Labels** method with an argument to access a single member of the collection or without an argument to access the entire collection at once. The following example deletes all the labels on the dialog sheet named "Dialog1."

```
DialogSheets("dialog1").Labels.Delete
```

Properties **Accelerator** Property, **Application** Property, **Caption** Property, **Count** Property, **Creator** Property, **Enabled** Property, **Height** Property, **Left** Property, **Locked** Property, **LockedText** Property, **OnAction** Property, **Parent** Property, **PhoneticAccelerator** Property, **Placement** Property, **PrintObject** Property, **Text** Property, **Top** Property, **Visible** Property, **Width** Property, **ZOrder** Property.

Methods **Add** Method (Graphic Objects and Controls), **BringToFront** Method, **Characters** Method, **CheckSpelling** Method, **Copy** Method, **CopyPicture** Method, **Cut** Method, **Delete** Method, **Duplicate** Method, **Group** Method, **Item** Method, **Select** Method, **SendToBack** Method.

Labels Method

Applies To	**Chart** Object, **DialogSheet** Object, **Worksheet** Object.
Description	Accessor. Returns an object that represents a single label (a **Label** object, Syntax 1) or a collection of labels (a **Labels** object, Syntax 2) on the sheet.
Syntax 1	*object*.**Labels**(*index*)
Syntax 2	*object*.**Labels**

object
  Required. The **Chart**, **DialogSheet** or **Worksheet** object.

index
  Required for Syntax 1. Specifies the name or number of the label (can be an array to specify more than one).

Example	This example sets the text for label one on Dialog1.

```
DialogSheets("Sheet1").Labels(1).Text = "Search results"
```

LargeButtons Property

Applies To	**Application** Object.
Description	**True** if Microsoft Excel is using large toolbar buttons. **False** if Microsoft Excel is using standard toolbar buttons. Read-write.
See Also	**ColorButtons** Property.
Example	This example displays the large toolbar buttons.

```
Application.LargeButtons = True
```

LargeChange Property

Applies To	**DrawingObjects** Collection, **ScrollBar** Object, **ScrollBars** Collection.
Description	Returns or sets the amount that the scroll box increments or decrements for a page scroll (when the user clicks in the scroll bar body region). Read-write.
See Also	**SmallChange** Property.

Example   This example sets scroll bar one on Dialog1 to move two units for each line scroll and 20 units for each page scroll.

```
With DialogSheets("Dialog1").ScrollBars(1)
    .SmallChange = 2
    .LargeChange = 20
End With
```

LargeScroll Method

Applies To   **Pane** Object, **Window** Object.

Description   Scrolls the window by pages.

Syntax   *object*.**LargeScroll**(*down*, *up*, *toRight*, *toLeft*)

object
    Required. The window to scroll.

down
    Optional. The number of pages to scroll the window down.

up
    Optional. The number of pages to scroll the window up.

toRight
    Optional. The number of pages to scroll the window right.

toLeft
    Optional. The number of pages to scroll the window left.

Remarks   If *down* and *up* are both specified, the window is scrolled by the difference of the arguments. For example, if *down* is three and *up* is six, the window is scrolled up three pages.

If *toLeft* and *toRight* are both specified, the window is scrolled by the difference of the arguments. For example, if *toLeft* is three and *toRight* is six, the window is scrolled right three pages.

Any of the arguments can be a negative number.

See Also   **SmallScroll** Method.

Example   This example scrolls the active window of Sheet1 down three pages.

```
Worksheets("Sheet1").Activate
ActiveWindow.LargeScroll down:=3
```

LBound Function

Description   Returns the smallest available subscript for the indicated dimension of an array.

Syntax   **LBound**(*arrayname*[*,dimension*])

The **LBound** statement syntax has these parts:

Part	Description
arrayname	Name of the array variable; follows standard variable naming conventions.
dimension	Whole number indicating which dimension's lower bound is returned. Use 1 for the first dimension, 2 for the second, and so on. If *dimension* is omitted, 1 is assumed.

Remarks   The **LBound** function is used with the **UBound** function to determine the size of an array. Use the **UBound** function to find the upper limit of an array dimension.

LBound returns the values listed in the table below for an array with the following dimensions:

```
Dim A(1 To 100, 0 To 3, -3 To 4)
```

Statement	Return Value
LBound(A, 1)	1
LBound(A, 2)	0
LBound(A, 3)	-3

The default lower bound for any dimension is either 0 or 1, depending on the setting of the **Option Base** statement.

Arrays for which dimensions are set using the **To** clause in a **Dim**, **Private**, **Public**, **ReDim**, or **Static** statement can have any integer value as a lower bound.

See Also   **Dim** Statement, **Option Base** Statement, **Private** Statement, **Public** Statement, **ReDim** Statement, **Static** Statement, **UBound** Function.

Example   This example uses the **LBound** function to determine the smallest available subscript for the indicated dimension of an array. Use the **Option Base** statement to override the default base array subscript value of 0.

```
Dim MyArray(1 To 10, 5 To 15, 10 To 20)    ' Declare array variables.
Dim AnyArray(10)
Lower = LBound(MyArray, 1)                  ' Returns 1.
Lower = LBound(MyArray, 3)                  ' Returns 10.
Lower = LBound(AnyArray)                    ' Returns 0 or 1, depending on
    ' setting of Option Base.
```

This example writes the elements of the first custom list in column one on Sheet1.

```
Sub foo()
On Error GoTo err_handler
listArray = Application.GetCustomListContents(1)
For i = LBound(listArray, 1) To UBound(listArray, 1)
    Worksheets("sheet1").Cells(i, 1).Value = listArray(i)
Next i
Exit Sub

err_handler:
    MsgBox "Custom list does not exist"
End Sub
```

This example assumes that you used an external data source to create a PivotTable on Sheet1. The example inserts the SQL connection string and query string into a new worksheet.

```
Set newSheet = ActiveWorkbook.Worksheets.Add
sdArray = Worksheets("Sheet1").UsedRange.PivotTable.SourceData
For i = LBound(sdArray) To UBound(sdArray)
    newSheet.Cells(i, 1) = sdArray(i)
Next i
```

LCase Function

Description   Returns a string that has been converted to lowercase.

Syntax   **LCase(*string*)**

The *string* named argument is any valid string expression. If *string* contains no valid data, **Null** is returned.

Remarks   Only uppercase letters are converted to lowercase; all lowercase letters and nonletter characters remain unchanged.

See Also   **UCase** Function.

Example   This example uses the **LCase** function to return a lowercase version of a string.

```
Uppercase = "Hello World 1234"      ' String to convert.
Lowercase = LCase(UpperCase) ' Returns "hello world 1234".
```

Left Function

Description

Returns a specified number of characters from the left side of a string.

Syntax

Left(*string*,*length*)

The **Left** function syntax has these named-argument parts:

Part	Description
string	String expression from which the leftmost characters are returned. If *string* contains no valid data, **Null** is returned.
length	Numeric expression indicating how many characters to return. If 0, a zero-length string is returned. If greater than or equal to the number of characters in *string*, the entire string is returned.

Remarks

To determine the number of characters in *string*, use the **Len** function.

Note   Another function (**LeftB**) is provided for use with the double-byte character sets (DBCS) used in some Asian locales. Instead of specifying the number of characters to return, *length* specifies the number of bytes. In areas where DBCS is not used, **LeftB** behaves the same as **Left**.

See Also

Len Function, **Mid** Function, **Right** Function.

Example

This example uses the **Left** function to return a specified number of characters from the left side of a string.

```
AnyString = "Hello World"          ' Define string.
MyStr = Left(AnyString, 1)         ' Returns "H".
MyStr = Left(AnyString, 7)         ' Returns "Hello W".
MyStr = Left(AnyString, 20) ' Returns "Hello World".
```

Left Property

Applies To   **Application** Object, **Arc** Object, **Arcs** Collection, **AxisTitle** Object, **Button** Object, **Buttons** Collection, **ChartArea** Object, **ChartObject** Object, **ChartObjects** Collection, **ChartTitle** Object, **CheckBox** Object, **DataLabel** Object, **DialogFrame** Object, **Drawing** Object, **DrawingObjects** Collection, **Drawings** Collection, **DropDown** Object, **DropDowns** Collection, **EditBox** Object, **EditBoxes** Collection, **GroupBox** Object, **GroupBoxes** Collection, **GroupObject** Object, **GroupObjects** Collection, **Label** Object, **Labels** Collection, **Legend** Object, **Line** Object, **Lines** Collection, **ListBox** Object, **ListBoxes** Collection, **OLEObject** Object, **OLEObjects** Collection, **OptionButton** Object, **OptionButtons** Collection, **Oval** Object, **Ovals** Collection, **Picture** Object, **Pictures** Collection, **PlotArea** Object, **Range** Object, **Rectangle** Object, **Rectangles** Collection, **ScrollBar** Object, **ScrollBars** Collection, **Spinner** Object, **Spinners** Collection, **TextBox** Object, **TextBoxes** Collection, **Toolbar** Object, **Window** Object.

Description   Returns or sets the position of the specified object, in points (1/72 inch). Read-write, except for the **Range** object.

Remarks   The **Left** property has several different meanings, depending on the object it is applied to.

Object	Meaning
Application	The distance from the left edge of the physical screen to the left edge of the main Microsoft Excel window, in points.
ClipboardWindow	Macintosh only. The left position of the window, in points, measured from the left edge of the usable area (below the menus, left-docked toolbars, and/or the formula bar).
Range	The distance from the left edge of column A to the left edge of the range, in points. If the range is discontinuous, the first area is used. If the range is more than one column wide, the leftmost column in the range is used. Read-only.
Toolbar	If the toolbar is docked (its **Position** property is not **xlFloating**), the number of points from the left edge of the toolbar to the left edge of the toolbar's docking area.
	If the toolbar is floating, the number of points from the left edge of the toolbar to the left edge of the Microsoft Excel workspace.

Object	Meaning
Window	The left position of the window, in points, measured from the left edge of the usable area.
Arc, AxisTitle, Button, ChartArea, ChartTitle, CheckBox, DataLabel, DialogFrame, Drawing, DrawingObjects, DropDown, EditBox, GroupObject, GroupBox, Label, Legend, Line, ListBox, OLEObject, OptionButton, Oval, Picture, PlotArea, Rectangle, ScrollBar, Spinner, TextBox	The left position of the object, in points, measured from the left edge of column A (on a worksheet) or the upper left of the chart area (on a chart).

If the window is maximized, the **Application.Left** property returns a negative number that varies based on the width of the window border. Setting **Application.Left** to zero will make the window a tiny bit smaller than it would if the application window were maximized. In other words, if **Application.Left** is zero, the left border of the main Microsoft Excel window will just be visible on screen.

On the Apple Macintosh, **Application.Left** is always zero. Setting this value to something else on the Macintosh will have no effect.

With Microsoft Windows, if the Microsoft Excel window is minimized, **Application.Left** controls the position of the icon.

See Also   **Height** Property, **Top** Property, **Width** Property.

Example   This example moves oval one on Sheet1 so that it is aligned with the left edge of column B.

```
Worksheets("Sheet1").Ovals(1).Left = _
    Worksheets("Sheet1").Columns("B").Left
```

This example aligns the left edge of every button on Sheet1 to the left edge of column B.

```
leftEdge = Worksheets("Sheet1").Columns("B").Left
For Each b In Worksheets("Sheet1").Buttons
    b.Left = leftEdge
Next b
```

LeftFooter Property

Applies To	**PageSetup** Object.
Description	Returns or sets the left part of the footer. Read-write.
Remarks	Special format codes can be used in the footer text.
See Also	**CenterFooter** Property, **CenterHeader** Property, **LeftHeader** Property, **RightFooter** Property, **RightHeader** Property.
Example	This example prints the page number in the lower-left corner of every page.

```
Worksheets("Sheet1").PageSetup.LeftFooter = "&P"
```

LeftHeader Property

Applies To	**PageSetup** Object.
Description	Returns or sets the left part of the header. Read-write.
Remarks	Special format codes can be used in the header text.
See Also	**CenterFooter** Property, **CenterHeader** Property, **LeftFooter** Property, **RightFooter** Property, **RightHeader** Property.
Example	This example prints the date in the upper-left corner of every page.

```
Worksheets("Sheet1").PageSetup.LeftHeader = "&D"
```

LeftMargin Property

Applies To	**PageSetup** Object.
Description	Returns or sets the size of the left margin, in points (1/72 inch). Read-write.
Remarks	Margins are set or returned in points. Use the **InchesToPoints** or **CentimetersToPoints** function to convert.
See Also	**BottomMargin** Property, **RightMargin** Property, **TopMargin** Property.

Example	This example sets the left margin of Sheet1 to 1.5 inches.

```
Worksheets("Sheet1").PageSetup.LeftMargin = _
       Application.InchesToPoints(1.5)
```

This example sets the left margin of Sheet1 to 2 centimeters.

```
Worksheets("Sheet1").PageSetup.LeftMargin = _
       Application.CentimetersToPoints(2)
```

This example displays the current left margin setting for Sheet1.

```
marginInches = Worksheets("Sheet1").PageSetup.LeftMargin / _
    Application.InchesToPoints(1)
MsgBox "The current left margin is " & marginInches & " inches"
```

Legend Object

Description	Represents the legend in a chart. The **Legend** object contains one or more **LegendEntry** objects; each **LegendEntry** object contains a **LegendKey** object. There is no Legends collection because each chart can have only one legend.
Accessors	The **Legend** property returns the chart legend. The following example sets the font for the legend in embedded chart one on worksheet one.

```
Worksheets(1).ChartObjects(1).Chart.Legend.Font.Bold = True
```

Remarks	The chart legend is not visible unless the **HasLegend** property is **True**. If this property is **False**, properties and methods of the **Legend** object will fail.
Properties	**Application** Property, **Border** Property, **Creator** Property, **Font** Property, **Height** Property, **Interior** Property, **Left** Property, **Name** Property, **Parent** Property, **Position** Property, **Shadow** Property, **Top** Property, **Width** Property.
Methods	**Delete** Method, **LegendEntries** Method, **Select** Method.

Legend Property

Applies To	**Chart** Object.
Description	Accessor. Returns a **Legend** object that represents the legend for the chart. Read-only.

See Also   **HasLegend** Property.

Example   This example turns on the legend for Chart1 and then sets the legend font color to blue.

```
Charts("Chart1").HasLegend = True
Charts("Chart1").Legend.Font.ColorIndex = 5
```

LegendEntries Collection Object

Description   A collection of all the **LegendEntry** objects in the specified chart legend. Each legend entry has two parts: the text of the entry, which is the name of the series or trendline associated with the legend entry; and an entry marker, which visually links the legend entry with its associated series or trendline in the chart. Formatting properties for the entry marker and its associated series or trendline are contained in the **LegendKey** object.

Accessors   Use the **LegendEntries** method with an argument to access a single member of the collection or without an argument to access the entire collection at once. The following example loops through the collection of legend entries and changes the color of their fonts.

```
With Worksheets("sheet1").ChartObjects(1).Chart.Legend
    For i = 1 To .LegendEntries.Count
        .LegendEntries(i).Font.ColorIndex = 5
    Next
End With
```

Properties   **Application** Property, **Count** Property, **Creator** Property, **Parent** Property.

Methods   **Item** Method.

LegendEntries Method

Applies To   **Legend** Object.

Description   Accessor. Returns an object that represents a single legend entry (a **LegendEntry** object, Syntax 1) or a collection of legend entries (a **LegendEntries** object, Syntax 2) for the legend.

Syntax 1   *object*.**LegendEntries**(*index*)

Syntax 2	*object*.**LegendEntries**

object
> Required. The **Legend** object.

index
> Required for Syntax 1. Specifies the number of the legend entry.

Example   This example sets the font for legend entry one on Chart1.

```
Charts("Chart1").Legend.LegendEntries(1).Font.Name = "Arial"
```

LegendEntry Object

Description   Represents a legend entry in a chart legend.

Each legend entry has two parts: the text of the entry, which is the name of the series associated with the legend entry; and an entry marker, which visually links the legend entry with its associated series or trendline in the chart. Formatting properties for the entry marker and its associated series or trendline are contained in the **LegendKey** object.

The text of a legend entry cannot be changed. **LegendEntry** objects support font formatting, and they can be deleted. No pattern formatting is supported for legend entries. The position and size of entries is fixed.

Accessors   The **LegendEntry** object is a member of the **LegendEntries** collection. The **LegendEntries** collection contains all the **LegendEntry** objects in the legend.

To access a single member of the collection, use the **LegendEntries** method with the index number of the legend entry as an argument. You cannot access legend entries by name.

The index number represents the position of the legend entry in the legend. LegendEntries(1) is at the top of the legend; LegendEntries(LegendEntries.Count) is at the bottom. The following example changes the font for the text of the legend entry at the top of the legend (this is usually the legend for series one).

```
Worksheets("sheet1").ChartObjects(1).Chart _
    .Legend.LegendEntries(1).Font.Italic = True
```

Remarks   There is no direct way to access the series or trendline corresponding to the legend entry.

Once legend entries have been deleted, the only way to restore them is to remove and recreate the legend that contained them by setting the **HasLegend** property for the chart to **False** and then back to **True**.

Properties	**Application** Property, **Creator** Property, **Font** Property, **Index** Property, **LegendKey** Property, **Parent** Property.
Methods	**Delete** Method, **Select** Method.

LegendKey Object

Description   Represents a legend key in a chart legend. Each legend key is a graphic that visually links a legend entry with its associated series or trendline in the chart. The legend key is linked to its associated series or trendline is such a way that changing the formatting of one simultaneously changes the formatting of the other.

Accessors   The **LegendKey** property returns the legend key for a **LegendEntry** object. The following example changes the marker background color for the legend entry at the top of the legend for the embedded chart. This simultaneously changes the format of every point in the series associated with this legend entry. The associated series must support data markers.

```
Worksheets("sheet1").ChartObjects(1).chart _
    .Legend.LegendEntries(1).LegendKey.MarkerBackgroundColorIndex = 5
```

Properties   **Application** Property, **Border** Property, **Creator** Property, **Interior** Property, **InvertIfNegative** Property, **MarkerBackgroundColor** Property, **MarkerBackgroundColorIndex** Property, **MarkerForegroundColor** Property, **MarkerForegroundColorIndex** Property, **MarkerStyle** Property, **Parent** Property, **Smooth** Property.

Methods   **ClearFormats** Method, **Delete** Method, **Select** Method.

LegendKey Property

Applies To   **LegendEntry** Object.

Description   Accessor. Returns a **LegendKey** object that represents the legend key associated with the entry.

Example   This example sets the legend key for legend entry one on Chart1 to be a triangle. The example should be run on a 2-D line chart.

```
Charts("Chart1").Legend.LegendEntries(1).LegendKey.MarkerStyle = _
        xlTriangle
```

Len Function

Description   Returns the number of characters in a string or the number of bytes required to store a variable.

Syntax   **Len**(*string* | *varname*)

The **Len** function syntax has these parts:

Part	Description
string	Any valid string expression. If *string* contains no valid data, **Null** is returned.
varname	Any valid variable name. If *varname* contains no valid data, **Null** is returned.

Remarks

Caution **Len** may not be able to determine the actual number of storage bytes required when used with user-defined data types.

Note Another function (**LenB**) is provided for use with the double-byte character sets (DBCS) used in some Asian locales. Instead of returning the number of characters in a string, **LenB** returns the number of bytes used to represent that string. In areas where DBCS is not used, **LenB** behaves the same as **Len**.

See Also   **InStr** Function.

Example   This example uses the **Len** function to return the number of characters in a string or the number of bytes required to store a variable.

```
Type CustomerRecord                 ' Define user-defined type.
    ID As Integer
    Name As String * 10
    Address As String * 30
End Type
Dim Customer As CustomerRecord      ' Declare variables.
Dim MyInt As Integer, MyCur As Currency
MyString = "Hello World"            ' Initialize.
MyLen = Len(MyInt)                  ' Returns 2.
MyLen = Len(Customer)               ' Returns 42.
MyLen = Len(MyString)               ' Returns 11.
MyLen = Len(MyCur)   ' Returns 8.
```

Let Statement

Description   Assigns the value of an expression to a variable or property.

Syntax   [**Let**] *varname* = *expression*

The **Let** statement syntax has these parts:

Part	Description
varname	Name of the variable or property; follows standard variable naming conventions.
expression	Value assigned to the variable.

Remarks   In order to simplify Basic code, the optional **Let** keyword is most often omitted.

A value expression can be assigned to a variable only if it is of a data type that is compatible with the variable. You can't assign string expressions to numeric variables, and you can't assign numeric expressions to string variables. If you do, an error occurs at compile time.

Variant variables can be assigned either string or numeric expressions. However, the reverse is not always true. Any **Variant** except a **Null** can be assigned to a string variable, but only a **Variant** whose value can be interpreted as a number can be assigned to a numeric variable. Use the **IsNumeric** function to determine if the **Variant** can be converted to a number.

Caution   Assigning an expression of one numeric data type to a variable of a different numeric data type coerces the value of the expression into the data type of the resulting variable.

Let statements can be used to assign one record variable to another only when both variables are of the same user-defined type. Use the **LSet** statement to assign record variables of different user-defined types. Use the **Set** statement to assign object references to variables.

See Also   **Const** Statement, **Data Type** Summary, **IsNumeric** Function, **LSet** Statement, **Set** Statement, **Variant Data** Type.

Example

This example uses statements with and without the **Let** statement to assign the value of an expression to a variable.

```
' The following variable assignments use the Let statement.
Let MyStr = "Hello World"
Let MyInt = 5
' The following are the same assignments without the Let statement.
MyStr = "Hello World"
MyInt = 5
```

LibraryPath Property

Applies To

Application Object.

Description

Returns the path to the LIBRARY directory, not including the final separator. Read-only.

Example

This example opens the file OSCAR.XLA in the LIBRARY folder (the Macro Library folder on the Macintosh).

```
pathSep = Application.PathSeparator
f = Application.LibraryPath & pathSep & "OSCAR.XLA"
Workbooks.Open filename:=f
```

Like Operator

Description

Used to compare two strings.

Syntax

result = *string* **Like** *pattern*

The **Like** operator syntax has these parts:

Part	Description
result	Any numeric variable.
string	Any string expression.
pattern	Any string expression conforming to the pattern-matching conventions described in the following section.

Remarks

If *string* matches *pattern*, *result* is **True**; if there is no match, *result* is **False**; and if either *string* or *pattern* is a **Null**, *result* is also a **Null**.

The behavior of the **Like** operator depends on the **Option Compare** statement. Unless otherwise specified, the default string-comparison method for each module is **Option Compare Binary**.

Option Compare Binary results in string comparisons based on a sort order derived from the internal binary representations of the characters. In Microsoft Windows, sort order is determined by the code page. On the Macintosh, sort order is determined by the character set. In the following example, a typical binary sort order is shown:

$$A < B < E < Z < a < b < e \ < z < À < Ê < Ø < à < ê < ø$$

Option Compare Text results in string comparisons based on a case-insensitive textual sort order determined by your system's locale. The same characters shown above, when sorted using **Option Compare Text**, produce the following text sort order:

$$(A{=}a) \ < (\ À{=}à) < (B{=}b) < (E{=}e) < (Ê{=}ê) < (Z{=}z) < (Ø{=}ø)$$

Built-in pattern matching provides a versatile tool for string comparisons. The pattern-matching features allow you to use wildcard characters, character lists, or character ranges, in any combination, to match strings. The following table shows the characters allowed in *pattern* and what they match:

Character(s) in *pattern*	Matches in *string*
?	Any single character.
*	Zero or more characters.
#	Any single digit (0-9).
[*charlist*]	Any single character in *charlist*.
[!*charlist*]	Any single character not in *charlist*.

A group of one or more characters (*charlist*) enclosed in brackets ([ ]) can be used to match any single character in *string* and can include almost any character code, including digits.

Note The special characters left bracket ([), question mark (?), number sign (#), and asterisk (*) can be used to match themselves directly only by enclosing them in brackets. The right bracket (]) can't be used within a group to match itself, but it can be used outside a group as an individual character.

In addition to a simple list of characters enclosed in brackets, *charlist* can specify a range of characters by using a hyphen (-) to separate the upper and lower bounds of the range. For example, [A-Z] in *pattern* results in a match if the corresponding character position in *string* contains any of the uppercase letters in the range A through Z. Multiple ranges are included within the brackets without any delimiters.

The meaning of a specified range depends on the character ordering valid at run time (as determined by **Option Compare** and the locale setting of the system the code is running on). Using the same example shown above with **Option Compare Binary**, the range [A-E] matches A, B and E. With **Option Compare Text**, [A-E] matches A, a, À, à, B, b, E, e. Note that it does not match Ê or ê because accented characters fall after unaccented characters in the sort order.

Other important rules for pattern matching include the following:

- An exclamation point (**!**) at the beginning of *charlist* means that a match is made if any character except the ones in *charlist* are found in *string*. When used outside brackets, the exclamation point matches itself.

- The hyphen (**-**) can appear either at the beginning (after an exclamation mark if one is used) or at the end of *charlist* to match itself. In any other location, the hyphen is used to identify a range of characters.

- When a range of characters is specified, they must appear in ascending sort order (from lowest to highest). [A-Z] is a valid pattern, but [Z-A] is not.

- The character sequence [] is ignored; it is considered a zero-length string.

See Also

Comparison Operators, **InStr** Function, Operator Precedence, **Option Compare** Statement, **StrComp** Function.

Example

This example uses the **Like** operator to compare a string to a pattern.

```
MyCheck = "aBBBa" Like "a*a"          ' Returns True.
MyCheck = "F" Like "[A-Z]"            ' Returns True.
MyCheck = "F" Like "[!A-Z]"           ' Returns False.
MyCheck = "a2a" Like "a#a"            ' Returns True.
MyCheck = "aM5b" Like "a[L-P]#[!c-e]" ' Returns True.
MyCheck = "BAT123khg" Like "B?T*"     ' Returns True.
MyCheck = "CAT123khg" Like "B?T*"     ' Returns False.
```

This example deletes every defined name that contains "temp" in the name. The Option Compare Text statement must be included at the top of any module that contains this example.

```
For Each nm In ActiveWorkbook.Names
    If nm.Name Like "*temp*" Then
        nm.Delete
    End If
Next nm
```

This example adds an arrowhead to every graphic object on Sheet1 that has the word "Line" in its name.

```
For Each d In Worksheets("Sheet1").DrawingObjects
    If d.Name Like "*Line*" Then
        d.ArrowHeadLength = xlLong
        d.ArrowHeadStyle = xlOpen
        d.ArrowHeadWidth = xlNarrow
    End If
Next
```

Line Input # Statement

Description   Reads a line from an open sequential file and assigns it to a string variable.

Syntax   **Line Input #***filenumber,varname*

The **Line Input #** statement syntax has these parts:

Part	Description
filenumber	Any valid file number.
varname	Valid string variable name.

Remarks   The **Line Input #** statement reads from a file one character at a time until it encounters a carriage return (**Chr**(13)) or carriage return-linefeed sequence. Carriage return-linefeed sequences are skipped rather than appended to the character string.

See Also   **Input #** Statement.

Example   This example uses the **Line Input #** statement to read a line from a sequential file and assign it to a variable. For purposes of this example, assume that TESTFILE is a text file with a few lines of sample data.

```
Open "TESTFILE" For Input As #1    ' Open file.
Do While Not EOF(1)                ' Loop until end of file.
    Line Input #1, TextLine        ' Read line into variable.
    Debug.Print TextLine           ' Print to Debug window.
Loop
Close #1' Close file.
```

Line Object

Description   Represents a line graphic object on a chart sheet, dialog sheet, or worksheet. An arrow is a line with its **ArrowHeadStyle** property set to something other than **xlNone**.

Accessors   The **Line** object is a member of the **Lines** collection. The **Lines** collection contains all the **Line** objects on a single sheet. Use the **Add** method to create a new line and add it to the collection. To access a single member of the collection, use the **Lines** method with the index number or name of the line as an argument.

The following example sets the line color for line one on the worksheet named "Sheet1."

```
Worksheets("sheet1").Lines(1).Border.Color = RGB(0, 255, 0)
```

The line name is shown in the Name Box when the line is selected. Use the **Name** property to set or return the name of the line. The following example adds an open arrowhead to the end of the line named "Line 1."

```
Worksheets("sheet1").Lines("line 1").ArrowHeadStyle = xlOpen
```

Properties   **Application** Property, **ArrowHeadLength** Property, **ArrowHeadStyle** Property, **ArrowHeadWidth** Property, **Border** Property, **BottomRightCell** Property, **Creator** Property, **Enabled** Property, **Height** Property, **Index** Property, **Left** Property, **Locked** Property, **Name** Property, **OnAction** Property, **Parent** Property, **Placement** Property, **PrintObject** Property, **Top** Property, **TopLeftCell** Property, **Visible** Property, **Width** Property, **ZOrder** Property.

Methods   **BringToFront** Method, **Copy** Method, **CopyPicture** Method, **Cut** Method, **Delete** Method, **Duplicate** Method, **Select** Method, **SendToBack** Method.

Line3DGroup Property

Applies To   **Chart** Object.

Description   Accessor. Returns a **ChartGroup** object that represents the line chart group on a 3-D chart. Read-only.

See Also   **LineGroups** Method.

Example   This example changes the 3-D line group in Chart1 to an area group. The example should be run on a 3-D chart.

```
Charts("Chart1").Line3DGroup.Type = xl3DArea
```

LineGroups Method

Applies To   **Chart** Object.

Description   Accessor. On a 2-D chart, returns an object that represents a single line chart group (a **ChartGroup** object, Syntax 1), or a collection of the line chart groups (a **ChartGroups** collection, Syntax 2).

Syntax 1   *object*.**LineGroups**(*index*)

Syntax 2   *object*.**LineGroups**

                      object
                          Required. The **Chart** object.

                      index
                          Required for Syntax 1. Specifies the chart group.

See Also   **Line3DGroup** Property.

Example   This example sets the subtype for line group one in Chart1. The example should be run on a 2-D chart.

```
Charts("Chart1").LineGroups(1).SubType = 2
```

Lines Collection Object

Description   A collection of all the **Line** objects on the specified chart sheet, dialog sheet, or worksheet.

Accessors   Use the **Add** method to create a new line and add it to the collection. The following example creates a new line on worksheet one. The new line starts at the upper-left corner of cell B10 and ends at the upper-left corner of cell C20.

```
Dim rStart As Range, rEnd As Range
Set rStart = Worksheets(1).Range("b10")
Set rEnd = Worksheets(1).Range("c20")
Worksheets(1).Lines.Add rStart.Left, rStart.Top, _
    rEnd.Left, rEnd.Top
```

Use the **Lines** method with an argument to access a single member of the collection or without an argument to access the entire collection at once. The following example sets the arrowhead style for all of the lines on worksheet one in the active workbook.

```
Worksheets(1).Lines.ArrowHeadStyle = xlClosed
```

Properties	**Application** Property, **ArrowHeadLength** Property, **ArrowHeadStyle** Property, **ArrowHeadWidth** Property, **Border** Property, **Count** Property, **Creator** Property, **Enabled** Property, **Height** Property, **Left** Property, **Locked** Property, **OnAction** Property, **Parent** Property, **Placement** Property, **PrintObject** Property, **Top** Property, **Visible** Property, **Width** Property, **ZOrder** Property.
Methods	**Add** Method (Arcs and Lines), **BringToFront** Method, **Copy** Method, **CopyPicture** Method, **Cut** Method, **Delete** Method, **Duplicate** Method, **Group** Method, **Item** Method, **Select** Method, **SendToBack** Method.

Lines Method

Applies To	**Chart** Object, **DialogSheet** Object, **Worksheet** Object.
Description	Accessor. Returns an object that represents a single line (a **Line** object, Syntax 1) or a collection of lines (a **Lines** object, Syntax 2) on the sheet. Read-only.
Syntax 1	*object*.**Lines**(*index*)
Syntax 2	*object*.**Lines**

object
   Required. The object to which this method applies.

index
   Required for Syntax 1. The name or number of the line.

Remarks	This property returns both lines and arrows. The only difference between a line and an arrow is the **ArrowHeadStyle** property.
Example	This example deletes line three on Sheet1.

```
Worksheets("Sheet1").Lines(3).Delete
```

This example formats every line on Sheet1 as red.

```
For Each l In Worksheets("Sheet1").Lines
    l.Border.ColorIndex = 3
Next l
```

LineStyle Property

Applies To	**Border** Object, **Borders** Collection.

Description

Returns or sets the line style of the border. Read-write.

For **Range** object borders, this property can have one of the following values: **xlContinuous**, **xlDash**, **xlDot**, **xlDouble**, **xlNone**.

For drawing object borders, this property can have one of the following values: **xlAutomatic**, **xlContinuous**, **xlDash**, **xlDashDot**, **xlDashDotDot**, **xlDot**, **xlGray25**, **xlGray50**, **xlGray75**, **xlNone**.

Example

This example sets the line style of oval one on Sheet1 to 50 percent gray.

```
Worksheets("Sheet1").Ovals(1).Border.LineStyle = xlGray50
```

This example creates a rectangle on Sheet1 and then gives the rectangle a dashed border.

```
Set myRect = Worksheets("Sheet1").Rectangles.Add(Left:=72, _
            Top:=72, Width:=144, Height:=36)
myRect.Border.LineStyle = xlDash
```

LinkCombo Method

Applies To

DrawingObjects Collection.

Description

Creates a combination list-edit box from a list box and an edit box. The edit box and list box to be linked must be the only two objects in the **DrawingObjects** collection.

Syntax

object.**LinkCombo**(*link*)

object
Required. The **DrawingObjects** collection.

link
Optional. If omitted or **True**, the objects are linked so that the edit box text is always updated to the current selection in the list box whenever the user selects a new list box item. If **False**, the link between the objects is broken.

Remarks

This function is only useful on a dialog sheet, because edit boxes are not allowed on a worksheet or chart. To see how to use the **LinkCombo** method, use the macro recorder to record creating a Combination List-Edit control on a dialog sheet.

See Also

DrawingObjects Method, **EditBox** Object, **LinkedObject** Property, **ListBox** Object.

Example   This example links list box one and edit box two on Dialog1.

```
DialogSheets("Dialog1").DrawingObjects( _
    Array("List Box 1", "Edit Box 2")).LinkCombo
```

LinkedCell Property

Applies To   **CheckBox** Object, **DrawingObjects** Collection, **DropDown** Object, **DropDowns** Collection, **ListBox** Object, **ListBoxes** Collection, **OptionButton** Object, **OptionButtons** Collection, **ScrollBar** Object, **ScrollBars** Collection, **Spinner** Object, **Spinners** Collection.

Description   Returns or sets the cell or cells (as a string reference) linked to the control's value. When a value is placed in the cell, the control takes this value. Likewise, if the value of the control changes, that value is also placed in the cell.

Remarks   This property cannot be used with multi-select list boxes.

Example   This example sets the fill range and the cell link for list box one on Sheet1.

```
Worksheets("Sheet1").ListBoxes(1).ListFillRange = "Sheet1!A1:A8"
Worksheets("Sheet1").ListBoxes(1).LinkedCell = "Sheet1!B1"
```

LinkedObject Property

Applies To   **DropDown** Object, **EditBox** Object, **ListBox** Object.

Description   Returns the name of the object linked to an edit box, list box, or drop-down control. For a **DropDown** object, returns the name of the drop-down control if it can be edited, or **False** if it is not editable. Read-only.

See Also   **LinkCombo** Method.

Example   This example displays the name of the list box that is linked to edit box one on dialog sheet one. The example should be run on a dialog sheet that contains a combination list-edit control.

```
MsgBox DialogSheets(1).EditBoxes(1).LinkedObject
```

LinkInfo Method

Applies To	**Workbook** Object.
Description	Returns information on link date and update state.
Syntax	*object*.**LinkInfo**(*name*, *linkInfo*, *type*, *editionRef*)

object
Required. The **Workbook** object.

name
Required. Specifies the name of the link, as returned from the LinkSources method.

linkInfo
Required. Specifies the type of information to be returned about the link (either **xlUpdateState** or **xlEditionDate**). **xlEditionDate** applies only to editions. For **xlUpdateState**, this method returns 1 if the link updates automatically, or 2 if the link must be updated manually.

type
Optional. Specifies the type of link to return. Can be one of **xlOLELinks** (also handles DDE links), **xlPublishers**, or **xlSubscribers**.

editionRef
Optional. If the link is an edition, this argument specifies the edition reference as a string in R1C1-style form. This argument is required if there are more than one publisher or subscriber with the same name in the workbook.

Example

This example displays a message box if the link updates automatically.

```
If ActiveWorkbook.LinkInfo( _
        "Word.Document.6|Document1!'!DDE_LINK1", xlUpdateState, _
        xlOLELinks) = 1 Then
    MsgBox "Link updates automatically"
End If
```

LinkSource Property (DocumentProperty Object)

Applies To	**DocumentProperty** Object.
Description	Returns or sets the source of a linked custom document property. Read-write.

To use this property, you should establish a reference to the Microsoft Office 95 Object Library by using the References command (Tools menu).

Remarks   The source of a link is defined by the container application. For Microsoft Excel, the source is the name in the workbook.

This property cannot be used with built-in document properties.

Setting the **LinkSource** property sets the **LinkToContent** property to **True**.

Example   This example displays the linked status of a custom document property. You must pass a **DocumentProperty** object to the procedure.

```
Sub DisplayLinkStatus(dp As DocumentProperty)
    Dim stat As String, tf As String
    If dp.LinkToContent Then
        tf = ""
    Else
        tf = "not "
    End If
    stat = "This property is " & tf & "linked"
    If dp.LinkToContent Then
        stat = stat + Chr(13) & "The link source is " & dp.LinkSource
    End If
    MsgBox stat
End Sub
```

This example links the custom document property named "TotalSales" to the named range "SalesNumbers" in the active workbook.

```
ActiveWorkbook.CustomDocumentProperties _
    .Item("TotalSales").LinkSource = "SalesNumbers"
```

LinkSources Method

Applies To   **Workbook** Object.

Description   Returns an array of links in the workbook. The names in the array are the names of the linked documents, editions, or DDE or OLE servers. Returns **Empty** if there are no links.

Syntax   *object*.**LinkSources(***type***)**

object
    Required. The **Workbook** object.

type
    Optional. Specifies the type of link to return. Can be one of **xlExcelLinks**, **xlOLELinks** (also handles DDE links), **xlPublishers**, or **xlSubscribers**.

Remarks   The format of the array is a single-dimensional array for all types but publisher and subscriber. The returned strings contain the name of the link source in the notation appropriate for the link type. For example, DDE links use the "Server|Document!Item" syntax.

For publisher and subscriber links, the returned array is two-dimensional. The first column of the array contains the names of the edition, and the second column contains the references of the editions as text.

Example   This example displays a list of OLE and DDE links in the active workbook. The example should be run on a workbook that contains one or more linked Microsoft Word objects.

```
aLinks = ActiveWorkbook.LinkSources(xlOLELinks)
If Not IsEmpty(aLinks) Then
    For i = 1 To UBound(aLinks)
        MsgBox "Link " & i & ":" & Chr(13) & aLinks(i)
    Next i
End If
```

LinkToContent Property (DocumentProperty Object)

Applies To   **DocumentProperty** Object.

Description   **True** if the value of a custom document property is linked to the content of the container document; **False** if the value is static. Read-write.

To use this property, you should establish a reference to the Microsoft Office 95 Object Library by using the References command (Tools menu).

Remarks   This property applies only to custom document properties. For built-in document properties, this property is always **False**.

Use the **LinkSource** property to set the source for the linked property. Setting the **LinkSource** property sets the **LinkToContent** property to **True**.

Example

This example displays the linked status of a custom document property. You must pass a **DocumentProperty** object to the procedure.

```
Sub DisplayLinkStatus(dp As DocumentProperty)
    Dim stat As String, tf As String
    If dp.LinkToContent Then
        tf = ""
    Else
        tf = "not "
    End If
    stat = "This property is " & tf & "linked"
    If dp.LinkToContent Then
        stat = stat + Chr(13) & "The link source is " & dp.LinkSource
    End If
    MsgBox stat
End Sub
```

This example displays the linked status for each custom document property as a list on worksheet one.

```
rw = 1
With Worksheets(1)
    For Each pro In ActiveWorkbook.CustomDocumentProperties
        .Cells(rw, 1) = pro.Name
        .Cells(rw, 2) = pro.LinkToContent
        If pro.LinkToContent Then
            .Cells(rw, 3) = pro.LinkSource
        End If
        rw = rw + 1
    Next
End With
```

List Property

Applies To

DrawingObjects Collection, **DropDown** Object, **DropDowns** Collection, **ListBox** Object, **ListBoxes** Collection.

Description

Returns or sets the text entries in a list box or drop-down list box, as an array of strings (Syntax 1), or returns or sets a single text entry (Syntax 2). Returns an error if there are no entries in the list. Read-write.

Syntax 1

object.**List**

Syntax 2

object.**List**(*index*)

Remarks

Setting this property clears any range specified by the **ListFillRange** property.

See Also   **AddItem** Method, **ListCount** Property, **RemoveItem** Method.

Example   This example sets the entries in list box one on Dialog1.

```
DialogSheets("Dialog1").ListBoxes(1).List = _
    Array("cogs", "widgets", "sprockets", "gizmos")
```

This example sets entry four in list box one on Dialog1.

```
DialogSheets("Dialog1").ListBoxes(1).List(4) = "gadgets"
```

ListBox Object

Description   Represents a scrollable list box on the specified chart sheet, dialog sheet, or worksheet. There are three list-box types: single select, simple multi-select, and extended multi-select. The list-box type specifies whether more than one item can be selected from the list, and how multiple items can be selected. For more information, see the **MultiSelect** property.

You can fill the list either by specifying a range of cells that contains list items (using the **ListFillRange** property) or by specifying each item (using the **AddItem** and **RemoveItem** methods or the **List** property).

Accessors   The **ListBox** object is a member of the **ListBoxes** collection. The **ListBoxes** collection contains all the **ListBox** objects on a single sheet. Use the **Add** method to create a new list box and add it to the collection.

To access a single member of the collection, use the **ListBoxes** method with the index number or name of the list box as an argument.

The following example sets the list input range for list box two on the worksheet named "Sheet2." When the dialog sheet runs, the contents of cells D1:D15 on the worksheet named "Sheet2" will appear as items in the list box.

```
Worksheets("sheet2").ListBoxes(2).ListFillRange = "=sheet2!d1:d15"
```

The list box name is shown in the Name Box when the list box is selected. Use the **Name** property to set or return the list box name. The following example adds an item to the list shown in the list box named "List Box 2."

```
Worksheets(1).ListBoxes("list box 2").AddItem "end"
```

Remarks   On dialog sheets, the **LinkCombo** method can be used to link a list box and an edit box to create a combination list edit box. For information about combination drop-down edit boxes, see the **DropDown** object.

Properties	**Application** Property, **BottomRightCell** Property, **Creator** Property, **Display3DShading** Property, **Enabled** Property, **Height** Property, **Index** Property, **Left** Property, **LinkedCell** Property, **LinkedObject** Property, **List** Property, **ListCount** Property, **ListFillRange** Property, **ListIndex** Property, **Locked** Property, **MultiSelect** Property, **Name** Property, **OnAction** Property, **Parent** Property, **Placement** Property, **PrintObject** Property, **Selected** Property, **Top** Property, **TopLeftCell** Property, **Value** Property, **Visible** Property, **Width** Property, **ZOrder** Property.
Methods	**AddItem** Method, **BringToFront** Method, **Copy** Method, **CopyPicture** Method, **Cut** Method, **Delete** Method, **Duplicate** Method, **RemoveAllItems** Method, **RemoveItem** Method, **Select** Method, **SendToBack** Method.

ListBoxes Collection Object

Description

A collection of all the **ListBox** objects on the specified chart sheet, dialog sheet, or worksheet. List boxes that are linked to edit boxes to form combination list edit boxes are included in the **ListBoxes** collection.

Accessors

Use the **Add** method to create a new list box and add it to the collection. The following example adds a new list box to the dialog sheet named "Dialog1." The new list box is positioned relative to the upper-left corner of the dialog frame.

```
Dim df As DialogFrame
Set df = DialogSheets("dialog1").DialogFrame
DialogSheets("dialog1").ListBoxes.Add df.Left + 10, _
    df.Top + 20, 100, 100
```

Use the **ListBoxes** method with an argument to access a single member of the collection or without an argument to access the entire collection at once. The following example deletes all of the list boxes on the dialog sheet named "Dialog1."

```
DialogSheets("dialog1").ListBoxes.Delete
```

Properties

Application Property, **Count** Property, **Creator** Property, **Display3DShading** Property, **Enabled** Property, **Height** Property, **Left** Property, **LinkedCell** Property, **List** Property, **ListFillRange** Property, **ListIndex** Property, **Locked** Property, **MultiSelect** Property, **OnAction** Property, **Parent** Property, **Placement** Property, **PrintObject** Property, **Selected** Property, **Top** Property, **Value** Property, **Visible** Property, **Width** Property, **ZOrder** Property.

Methods	**Add** Method (Graphic Objects and Controls), **AddItem** Method, **BringToFront** Method, **Copy** Method, **CopyPicture** Method, **Cut** Method, **Delete** Method, **Duplicate** Method, **Group** Method, **Item** Method, **RemoveAllItems** Method, **RemoveItem** Method, **Select** Method, **SendToBack** Method.

ListBoxes Method

Applies To	**Chart** Object, **DialogSheet** Object, **Worksheet** Object.
Description	Accessor. Returns an object that represents a single list-box control (a **ListBox** object, Syntax 1) or a collection of list-box controls (a **ListBoxes** object, Syntax 2) on the sheet.
Syntax 1	*object*.**ListBoxes**(*index*)
Syntax 2	*object*.**ListBoxes**

object
    Required. The **Chart**, **DialogSheet**, or **Worksheet** object.

index
    Required for Syntax 1. Specifies the name or number of the list box (can be an array to specify more than one).

Example	This example fills list box one on Dialog1 with the letters A through Z.

```
For i = 65 To 90
    DialogSheets("Dialog1").ListBoxes(1).AddItem Text:=Chr(i)
Next i
```

ListCount Property

Applies To	**DropDown** Object, **ListBox** Object.
Description	Returns the number of entries in a list box or drop-down list box. Returns zero if there are no entries in the list. Read-only.
See Also	**List** Property.
Example	This example displays the number of entries in list box one on Dialog1.

```
cEntries = DialogSheets("Dialog1").ListBoxes(1).ListCount
MsgBox "There are " & cEntries & " entries in list box one."
```

ListFillRange Property

Applies To   **DrawingObjects** Collection, **DropDown** Object, **DropDowns** Collection, **ListBox** Object, **ListBoxes** Collection.

Description   Returns or sets the worksheet range used to fill the list box, as a string. Setting this property destroys any existing list in the list box. Read-write.

Remarks   Microsoft Excel reads the contents of every cell in the range and puts it into the list box. The list will track changes in the range cells.

    If the list in the list box was created with the **AddItem** method, this property returns an empty string ("").

See Also   **AddItem** Method, **List** Property, **RemoveItem** Method.

Example   This example fills list box one with the range A1:A10 on Sheet1.

```
DialogSheets("Dialog1").Listboxes(1).ListFillRange = _
    "Sheet1!A1:A10"
```

ListHeaderRows Property

Applies To   **Range** Object.

Description   Returns the number of header rows for the specified range. This property is available only in Microsoft Excel for Windows 95. Read-only.

Remarks   Before you use this property, use the **CurrentRegion** property to find the boundaries of the range.

Example   This example sets the rTbl variable to the range represented by the current region for the active cell, not including any header rows.

```
Set rTbl = ActiveCell.CurrentRegion
' remove the headers from the range
iHdrRows = rTbl.ListHeaderRows
If iHdrRows > 0 Then
    ' resize the range minus n rows
    Set rTbl = rTbl.Resize(rTbl.Rows.Count - iHdrRows)
    ' and then move the resized range down to
    ' get to the first non-header row
    Set rTbl = rTbl.Offset(iHdrRows)
End If
```

ListIndex Property

Applies To	**DrawingObjects** Collection, **DropDown** Object, **DropDowns** Collection, **ListBox** Object, **ListBoxes** Collection.
Description	Returns or sets the index of the currently selected item in a list box or drop-down list box. Read-write.
Remarks	This property cannot be used with multi-select list boxes. Use the **Selected** property instead.
See Also	**MultiSelect** Property, **Selected** Property, **Value** Property.
Example	This example selects item four in list box one on Dialog1.

```
DialogSheets("Dialog1").ListBoxes(1).ListIndex = 4
```

ListNames Method

Applies To	**Range** Object.
Description	Pastes a list of all non-hidden names on the worksheet, beginning at the first cell of the range.
Syntax	*object*.**ListNames**
	object Required. Identifies the worksheet for which to list names, and the start of the range where the names will be listed.
Remarks	Use the **Names** method to return a collection of all the names on a worksheet.
Example	This example pastes a list of defined names into cell A1 on Sheet1. The example pastes workbook-level names and sheet-level names defined on Sheet1.

```
Worksheets("Sheet1").Range("A1").ListNames
```

Loc Function

Description   Returns the current read/write position within an open file.

Syntax   **Loc**(*filenumber*)

The *filenumber* named argument is any valid file number.

Remarks   The following describes the return value for each file access mode:

File Access	Return Value
Random	Number of the last record read from or written to the file.
Sequential	Current byte position in the file divided by 128.
Binary	Position of the last byte read or written.

See Also   **EOF** Function, **LOF** Function, **Open** Statement.

Example   This example uses the **Loc** function to return the current read/write position within an open file. For purposes of this example, assume that TESTFILE is a text file with a few lines of sample data.

```
Open "TESTFILE" For Input As #1      ' Open file just created.
Do While Not EOF(1)                   ' Loop until end of file.
    Line Input #1, MyLine             ' Read line into variable.
    MyLocation = Loc(1)               ' Get current position within file.
    ' Print to Debug window.
    Debug.Print MyLine; Tab; MyLocation
Loop
```

LocationInTable Property

Applies To   **Range** Object.

Description   Returns a constant that describes the part of the **PivotTable** which contains the top left corner of the specified range. Can be one of **xlRowHeader**, **xlColumnHeader**, **xlPageHeader**, **xlDataHeader**, **xlRowItem**, **xlColumnItem**, **xlPageItem**, **xlDataItem**, or **xlTableBody**. Read-only.

Example

This example displays a message box that describes the location of the active cell within the PivotTable.

```
Worksheets("Sheet1").Activate
Select Case ActiveCell.LocationInTable
Case Is = xlRowHeader
    MsgBox "Active cell is part of a row header"
Case Is = xlColumnHeader
    MsgBox "Active cell is part of a column header"
Case Is = xlPageHeader
    MsgBox "Active cell is part of a page header"
Case Is = xlDataHeader
    MsgBox "Active cell is part of a data header"
Case Is = xlRowItem
    MsgBox "Active cell is part of a row item"
Case Is = xlColumnItem
    MsgBox "Active cell is part of a column item"
Case Is = xlPageItem
    MsgBox "Active cell is part of a page item"
Case Is = xlDataItem
    MsgBox "Active cell is part of a data item"
Case Is = xlTableBody
    MsgBox "Active cell is part of the table body"
End Select
```

Lock...Unlock Statements

Description

Controls access by other processes to all or part of a file opened using the **Open** statement.

Syntax

Lock [#]*filenumber*[,*recordrange*]

. . .

Unlock [#]*filenumber*[,*recordrange*]

The **Lock** and **Unlock** statement syntax has these parts:

Part	Description
filenumber	Any valid file number.
recordrange	The range of records to lock or unlock.

The *recordrange* argument has the following syntax and parts:

recnumber | [start] **To** end

Part	Description
recnumber	Record number (**Random** mode files) or byte number (**Binary** mode files) at which locking or unlocking begins.
start	Number of the first record or byte to lock or unlock.
end	Number of the last record or byte to lock or unlock.

Remarks

The **Lock** and **Unlock** statements are used in environments where several processes might need access to the same file.

Lock and **Unlock** statements are always used in pairs. The arguments to **Lock** and **Unlock** must match exactly.

The first record/byte in a file is at position 1, the second record/byte is at position 2, and so on. If you specify just one record, then only that record is locked or unlocked. If you specify a range of records and omit a starting record (*start*), all records from the first record to the end of the range (*end*) are locked or unlocked. Using **Lock** without *recnumber* locks the entire file; using **Unlock** without *recnumber* unlocks the entire file.

If the file has been opened for sequential input or output, **Lock** and **Unlock** affect the entire file, regardless of the range specified by *start* and *end*.

Caution Be sure to remove all locks with an **Unlock** statement before closing a file or terminating your program. Failure to remove locks produces unpredictable results.

See Also

Open Statement.

Example

This example illustrates the use of the **Lock** and **Unlock** statements. While a record is being modified, access by other processes to the record is denied. For purposes of this example, assume that TESTFILE is a file containing five records of the user-defined type Record.

```
Type Record                          ' Define user-defined type.
    ID As Integer
    Name As String * 20
End Type
Dim MyRecord As Record               ' Declare variable.
' Open sample file for random access.
Open "TESTFILE" For Random Shared As #1 Len = Len(MyRecord)
RecordNumber = 4                     ' Define record number.
Lock #1, RecordNumber                ' Lock record.
Get #1, RecordNumber, MyRecord       ' Read record.
MyRecord.ID = 234                    ' Modify record.
MyRecord.Name = "John Smith"
Put #1, RecordNumber, MyRecord       ' Write modified record.
Unlock #1, RecordNumber              ' Unlock current record.
Close #1' Close file.
```

Locked Property

Applies To

Arc Object, **Arcs** Collection, **Button** Object, **Buttons** Collection, **ChartObject** Object, **ChartObjects** Collection, **CheckBox** Object, **DialogFrame** Object, **Drawing** Object, **DrawingObjects** Collection, **Drawings** Collection, **DropDown** Object, **DropDowns** Collection, **EditBox** Object, **EditBoxes** Collection, **GroupBox** Object, **GroupBoxes** Collection, **GroupObject** Object, **GroupObjects** Collection, **Label** Object, **Labels** Collection, **Line** Object, **Lines** Collection, **ListBox** Object, **ListBoxes** Collection, **OLEObject** Object, **OLEObjects** Collection, **OptionButton** Object, **OptionButtons** Collection, **Oval** Object, **Ovals** Collection, **Picture** Object, **Pictures** Collection, **Range** Object, **Rectangle** Object, **Rectangles** Collection, **Scenario** Object, **ScrollBar** Object, **ScrollBars** Collection, **Spinner** Object, **Spinners** Collection, **Style** Object, **TextBox** Object, **TextBoxes** Collection.

Description

False if the object can be modified when the sheet is protected. Read-write.

See Also

FormulaHidden Property, **Protect** Method, **Unprotect** Method.

Example

This example unlocks cells A1:G37 on Sheet1 so that they can be modified when the sheet is protected.

```
Worksheets("Sheet1").Range("A1:G37").Locked = False
Worksheets("Sheet1").Protect
```

LockedText Property

Applies To   **Button** Object, **Buttons** Collection, **CheckBox** Object, **DialogFrame** Object, **DrawingObjects** Collection, **GroupBox** Object, **GroupBoxes** Collection, **Label** Object, **Labels** Collection, **OptionButton** Object, **OptionButtons** Collection, **TextBox** Object, **TextBoxes** Collection.

Description   **True** if the text in the object will be locked to prevent changes when the document is protected. Read-write.

See Also   **Protect** Method, **ProtectContents** Property.

Example   This example locks the text on button one on Sheet1.

```
Worksheets("Sheet1").Buttons(1).LockedText = True
```

LOF Function

Description   Returns the size, in bytes, of a file opened using the **Open** statement.

Syntax   **LOF(*filenumber*)**

The *filenumber* named argument is any valid file number.

Remarks   To obtain the length of a file that is not open, use the **FileLen** function.

See Also   **EOF** Function, **FileLen** Function, **Loc** Function, **Open** Statement.

Example   This example uses the **LOF** function to determine the size of an open disk file. For purposes of this example, assume that TESTFILE is a text file containing sample data.

```
Open "TESTFILE" For Input As #1     ' Open file.
FileLength = LOF(1)                 ' Get length of file.
Close #1' Close file.
```

Log Function

Description   Returns the natural logarithm of a number.

Syntax   **Log(*number*)**

The *number* named argument can be any valid numeric expression greater than 0.

Remarks

The natural logarithm is the logarithm to the base *e*. The constant *e* is approximately 2.718282.

You can calculate base-*n* logarithms for any number *x* by dividing the natural logarithm of *x* by the natural logarithm of *n* as follows:

Log*n(x)* = **Log**(*x*) / **Log**(*n*)

The following example illustrates a custom **Function** that calculates base-10 logarithms:

```
Static Function Log10(X)
    Log10 = Log(X) / Log(10#)
End Function
```

See Also

Derived Math Functions, **Exp** Function.

Example

This example uses the **Log** function to return the natural logarithm of a number.

```
' Define angle in radians.
MyAngle = 1.3
' Calculate inverse hyperbolic sine.
MyLog = Log(MyAngle + Sqr(MyAngle * MyAngle + 1))
```

Long Data Type

Description

Long (long integer) variables are stored as signed 32-bit (4-byte) numbers ranging in value from -2,147,483,648 to 2,147,483,647. The type-declaration character for **Long** is **&** (character code 38).

See Also

CLng Function, Data Type Summary, **Def***type* Statements, **Integer** Data Type.

LSet Statement

Description

Left aligns a string within a string variable, or copies a variable of one user-defined type to another variable of a different user-defined type.

Syntax

LSet *stringvar* = *string*

LSet *varname1* = *varname2*

The **LSet** statement syntax has these parts:

Part	Description
stringvar	Name of string variable.
string	String expression to be left aligned within *stringvar*.
varname1	Variable name of the user-defined type being copied to.
varname2	Variable name of the user-defined type being copied from.

Remarks

LSet replaces any leftover characters in *stringvar* with spaces.

If *string* is longer than *stringvar*, **LSet** places only the leftmost characters, up to the length of the *stringvar,* in *stringvar*.

Only user-defined types containing **Integer**, **Long**, **Double**, **Single**, **String** (fixed-length), or **Currency** types may be copied. The following example copies the contents of RecTwo (a user-defined type variable) to RecOne (a variable of another user-defined type):

```
Type TwoString
    StrFld As String * 2
End Type
Type ThreeString
    StrFld As String * 3
End Type
Dim RecOne As TwoString, RecTwo As ThreeString
LSet RecOne = RecTwo
```

Because RecOne is 2 bytes long, only 2 bytes are copied from RecTwo. **LSet** copies only the number of bytes in the shorter of the two user-defined type variables.

See Also

RSet Statement.

Example   This example uses the **LSet** statement to left align a string within a string variable and to copy a variable of one user-defined type to another variable of a different user-defined type.

```
MyString = "0123456789"            ' Initialize string.
LSet MyString = "<-Left"           ' MyString contains "<-Left     ".

' LSet is also used to copy a variable of one user-defined type to
' another variable of a different user-defined type.
' Module level.
Type AType                         ' Define types.
    AName As String * 10
    AAdd As String * 10
End Type
Type BType
    BName As String * 5
    BAdd As String * 5
End Type

' Procedure level.
Dim AVar As AType, BVar As BType     ' Declare variables.
AVar.AName = "John Smith"           ' Define fields.
AVar.AAdd = "Rodeo Drv."
LSet BVar = AVar                    ' Copy variables.
' After copying, values are truncated.
Debug.Print BVar.BName              ' Prints "John ".
Debug.Print BVar.BAdd     ' Prints "Smith".
```

LTrim, RTrim, and Trim Functions

Description   Returns a copy of a string without leading spaces (**LTrim**), trailing spaces (**RTrim**), or both leading and trailing spaces (**Trim**).

Syntax   **LTrim**(*string*)

RTrim(*string*)

Trim(*string*)

The *string* named argument is any valid string expression. If *string* contains no valid data, **Null** is returned.

See Also   **Left** Function, **Right** Function.

Example   This example uses the **LTrim** and **RTrim** functions to strip leading and trailing spaces from a string variable. Using the **Trim** function alone achieves the same result.

```
MyString = "  <-Trim->  "                ' Initialize.
TrimString = LTrim(MyString)            ' TrimString = "<-Trim->  ".
TrimString = RTrim(MyString)            ' TrimString = "  <-Trim->".
TrimString = LTrim(RTrim(MyString))     ' TrimString = "<-Trim->".
' Using the Trim function alone achieves the same result.
TrimString = Trim(MyString)  ' TrimString = "<-Trim->".
```

MacID Function

Description   Used only on the Macintosh to convert a four-character constant to a value that may be used by **Dir**, **Kill**, **Shell**, and **AppActivate**.

Syntax   **MacID(*constant*)**

The ***constant*** named argument consists of four-characters used to specify a resource type, file type, application signature, or Apple Event. For example, TEXT, OBIN, MSWD (Microsoft Word), XCEL (Microsoft Excel), and so on.

Remarks   **MacID** is used with **Dir** and **Kill** to specify a Macintosh file type. Since the Macintosh does not support '*' and '?' as wildcards, you can use a four-character constant instead to identify groups of files. For example, the following statement returns 'TEXT' type files from the current folder:

```
Dir("", MacID("TEXT"))
```

MacID is used with **Shell** and **AppActivate** to specify an application using the application's unique signature.

See Also   **AppActivate** Statement, **Dir** Function, **Kill** Statement, **Shell** Function.

Example   This example shows various uses of the **MacID** function. The **MacID** function is not available in Microsoft Windows.

```
' Return the first text file in folder HD:My Folder.
FileName = Dir("HD:My Folder:", MacID("TEXT"))

' Deletes all "TEXT" files in the current folder.
Kill MacID("TEXT")
```

```
' Run Microsoft Excel.
ReturnValue = Shell(MacID("XCEL"))

' Activate Microsoft Word.
AppActivate MacID("MSWD")
```

MacroOptions Method

Applies To   **Application** Object.

Description   Corresponds to options in the Macro Options dialog box.

Syntax   *object*.**MacroOptions**(*macro*, *description*, *hasMenu*, *menuText*,
                      hasShortcutKey, *shortcutKey*, *category*, *statusBar*, *helpContextID*, *helpFile*)

object
   Required. The **Application** object.

macro
   Required. The name of the macro to set options for, as a string.

description
   Optional. The description of the macro, as a string.

hasMenu
   Optional. If **True**, then a menu item is automatically added to the Tools menu
   for this macro. If **True**, then *menuText* must also be specified. If **False** or
   omitted, no menu item is added for the macro. If the macro already has a menu
   item created for it, setting this argument to **False** will remove the menu item.

menuText
   Required if *hasMenu* is **True**; ignored otherwise. The text of the menu item, as
   a string.

hasShortcutKey
   Optional. If **True**, a shortcut key is assigned to the macro. If **True**, then
   shortcutKey must also be specified. If **False** or omitted, no shortcut key is
   assigned to the macro. If the macro already has a shortcut key, setting this
   argument to **False** will remove the shortcut key.

shortcutKey
   Required if *hasShortcutKey* is **True**; ignored otherwise. The shortcut key (first
   character only) as a string.

category
   Optional. The function category (Financial, Date & Time, User Defined, and so
   on) that the macro appears in, as an integer.

statusBar
> Optional. The status bar text for the macro, as a string.

helpContextId
> Optional. The context ID for the Help topic assigned to the macro, as an integer. The context ID also applies to any menu items and/or toolbar buttons assigned to the macro.

helpFile
> Optional. The name of the Help file that contains the Help topic defined by **helpContextId**, as a string.

MacroType Property

Applies To   **Name** Object.

Description   Returns or sets what the name refers to, as shown in the following table. Read-write.

Value	Meaning
xlCommand	Name is a user-defined macro.
xlFunction	Name is a user-defined function.
xlNone	Name is not a function or macro.

See Also   **Category** Property.

Example   This example assumes that you created a custom function or command on a Microsoft Excel version 4.0 macro sheet. The example displays the function category, in the language of the macro. It assumes that the name of the custom function or command is the only name in the workbook.

```
With ActiveWorkbook.Names(1)
    If .MacroType <> xlNone Then
        MsgBox "The category for this name is " & .Category
    Else
        MsgBox "This name does not refer to" & _
            " a custom function or command."
    End If
End With
```

MacScript Statement

Description   Executes an AppleScript script; available on the Macintosh using System 7.0 or later.

Syntax   **MacScript** *script*

The *script* named argument is a string expression specifying the name of an AppleScript script.

Remarks   Multiline scripts may be created by embedding carriage return characters (**Chr**(13)).

See Also   **MacID** Function.

Mailer Object

Description   Represents the PowerTalk Mailer for a workbook. This object is available only on the Apple Macintosh with the PowerTalk system extension installed.

Accessors   The **Mailer** property returns the mailer for the workbook when the **HasMailer** property is **True**. The following example sets the **Subject** property for the mailer attached to the active workbook.

```
ActiveWorkbook.HasMailer = True
ActiveWorkbook.Mailer.Subject = "Here is the workbook."
```

Properties   **Application** Property, **BCCRecipients** Property, **CCRecipients** Property, **Creator** Property, **Enclosures** Property, **Parent** Property, **Received** Property, **SendDateTime** Property, **Sender** Property, **Subject** Property, **ToRecipients** Property.

See Also   **SendMailer** Method.

Mailer Property

Applies To   **Workbook** Object.

Description   Accessor. Returns a **Mailer** object that represents the PowerTalk mailer attached to the workbook. Available only in Microsoft Excel for the Apple Macintosh with the PowerTalk mail system extension installed. Read-only.

Remarks   The **Mailer** object contains the properties needed to mail workbooks with PowerTalk. To mail a workbook, turn on the mailer with the **HasMailer** property, set the mailer properties, and then send the workbook and mailer with the **SendMailer** method.

See Also   **BCCRecipients** Property, **CCRecipients** Property, **Enclosures** Property, **HasMailer** Property, **Received** Property, **SendDateTime** Property, **Sender** Property, **SendMailer** Method, **Subject** Property, **ToRecipients** Property.

Example   This example sets up the **Mailer** object for workbook one and then sends the workbook.

```
With Workbooks(1)
    .HasMailer = True
    With .Mailer
        .Subject = "Here is the workbook"
        .ToRecipients = Array("Jean")
        .CCRecipients = Array("Adam", "Bernard")
        .BCCRecipients = Array("Chris")
        .Enclosures = Array("TestFile")
    End With
    .SendMailer
End With
```

MailLogoff Method

Applies To   **Application** Object.

Description   Closes a MAPI mail session established by Microsoft Excel.

Syntax   *object*.**MailLogoff**

object
    Required. The **Application** object.

Remarks   This method cannot be used to close or log off Microsoft Mail.

See Also   **MailLogon** Method, **MailSession** Property, **SendMail** Method.

Example   This example closes the established mail session if there is one.

```
If Not IsNull(Application.MailSession) Then Application.MailLogoff
```

MailLogon Method

Applies To   **Application** Object.

Description   Logs into MAPI Mail or Microsoft Exchange and establishes a mail session. If Microsoft Mail is not already running, you must use this method to establish a mail session before mail or document routing functions can be used.

Syntax   *object*.**MailLogon**(*name*, *password*, *downloadNewMail*)

object
    Required. The **Application** object.

name
    Optional. The mail account name or Microsoft Exchange profile name. If omitted, the default mail account name is used.

password
    Optional. The mail account password. This argument is ignored in Microsoft Exchange.

downloadNewMail
    Optional. If **True**, new mail is downloaded immediately.

Remarks   Mail sessions previously established by Microsoft Excel are logged off before an attempt is made to establish the new session.

Omit both the name and password parameters to piggyback on the system default mail session.

See Also   **MailLogoff** Method, **MailSession** Property, **SendMail** Method.

Example   This example logs into mail and downloads any new mail immediately.

```
If IsNull(Application.MailSession) Then
    Application.MailLogon "oscarx", "mypassword", True
End If
```

MailSession Property

Applies To   **Application** Object.

Description   Returns the MAPI mail session number as a hexadecimal string (if there is an active session), or **Null** if there is no session. Read-only.

Remarks   This property applies only to mail sessions created by Microsoft Excel (it does not return a mail session number for Microsoft Mail).

This property is not used on PowerTalk mail systems.

See Also   **MailLogoff** Method, **MailLogon** Method, **MailSystem** Property, **SendMail** Method.

Example   This example closes the established mail session if there is one.

```
If Not IsNull(Application.MailSession) Then Application.MailLogoff
```

MailSystem Property

Applies To   **Application** Object.

Description   Returns the mail system installed on the host machine (one of **xlNoMailSystem**, **xlMAPI**, or **xlPowerTalk**). Read-only.

See Also   **MailLogoff** Method, **MailLogon** Method, **MailSession** Property, **SendMail** Method.

Example   This example displays the name of the mail system installed on the computer.

```
Sub foo()
Select Case Application.MailSystem
    Case Is = xlMAPI
        MsgBox "Mail system is Microsoft Mail"
    Case Is = xlPowerTalk
        MsgBox "Mail system is PowerTalk"
    Case Is = xlNoMailSystem
        MsgBox "No mail system installed"
End Select
End Sub
```

MajorGridlines Property

Applies To   **Axis** Object.

Description   Accessor. Returns a **Gridlines** object that represents the major gridlines for the specified axis. Only axes in the primary axis group can have gridlines. Read-only.

See Also   **AxisGroup** Property, **HasMajorGridlines** Property, **HasMinorGridlines** Property, **MinorGridlines** Property.

Example   This example sets the color of the major gridlines for the value axis in Chart1.

```
With Charts("Chart1").Axes(xlValue)
    If .HasMajorGridlines Then
        .MajorGridlines.Border.ColorIndex = 5    '' 273.'set color to
blue
    End If
End With
```

MajorTickMark Property

Applies To   **Axis** Object.

Description   Returns or sets the type of major tick mark for the specified axis (one of **xlNone**, **xlInside**, **xlOutside**, or **xlCross**). Read-write.

See Also   **MinorTickMark** Property.

Example   This example sets the major tick marks for the value axis in Chart1 to be outside the axis.

```
Charts("Chart1").Axes(xlValue).MajorTickMark = xlOutside
```

MajorUnit Property

Applies To   **Axis** Object.

Description   Returns or sets the major units for the value axis. Applies only to the value axis. Read-write.

Remarks   Setting this property sets the MajorUnitIsAuto property to False.

Use the **TickMarkSpacing** property to set tick mark spacing on the category axis.

See Also   **MajorUnitIsAuto** Property, **MinorUnit** Property, **MinorUnitIsAuto** Property, **TickMarkSpacing** Property.

Example   This example sets the major and minor units for the value axis in Chart1.

```
With Charts("Chart1").Axes(xlValue)
    .MajorUnit = 100
    .MinorUnit = 20
End With
```

MajorUnitIsAuto Property

Applies To   **Axis** Object.

Description   **True** if Microsoft Excel calculates major units for the value axis. Applies only to the value axis. Read-write.

Remarks   Setting the **MajorUnit** property sets this property to **False**.

See Also   **MajorUnit** Property, **MinorUnit** Property, **MinorUnitIsAuto** Property.

Example   This example automatically sets major and minor units for the value axis in Chart1.

```
With Charts("Chart1").Axes(xlValue)
    .MajorUnitIsAuto = True
    .MinorUnitIsAuto = True
End With
```

MarkerBackgroundColor Property

Applies To   **LegendKey** Object, **Point** Object, **Series** Object.

Description   Returns or sets the marker background color as an RGB value. Line, scatter and radar charts only. Read-write.

See Also   **MarkerBackgroundColorIndex** Property, **MarkerForegroundColor** Property, **MarkerStyle** Property.

Example   This example sets the marker background and foreground colors for the second point in series one in Chart1.

```
With Charts("Chart1").SeriesCollection(1).Points(2)
    .MarkerBackgroundColor = RGB(0,255,0) ' green
    .MarkerForegroundColor = RGB(255,0,0) ' red
End With
```

MarkerBackgroundColorIndex Property

Applies To   **LegendKey** Object, **Point** Object, **Series** Object.

Description   Returns or sets the marker background color as an index into the current color palette (a value from one to 56, or **xlNone** if there is no background color). Line, scatter and radar charts only. Read-write.

See Also   **Colors** Property, **MarkerBackgroundColor** Property,
MarkerForegroundColorIndex Property, **MarkerStyle** Property.

Example   This example sets the marker background and foreground color for the second point
in series one in Chart1.

```
With Charts("Chart1").SeriesCollection(1).Points(2)
    .MarkerBackgroundColorIndex = 4 'green
    .MarkerForegroundColorIndex = 3 'red
End With
```

MarkerForegroundColor Property

Applies To   **LegendKey** Object, **Point** Object, **Series** Object.

Description   Returns or sets the foreground color of the marker, specified as an RGB value.
Line, scatter and radar charts only. Read-write.

See Also   **MarkerBackgroundColor** Property, **MarkerForegroundColorIndex** Property,
MarkerStyle Property.

Example   This example sets the marker background and foreground colors for the second
point in series one in Chart1.

```
With Charts("Chart1").SeriesCollection(1).Points(2)
    .MarkerBackgroundColor = RGB(0,255,0) ' green
    .MarkerForegroundColor = RGB(255,0,0) ' red
End With
```

MarkerForegroundColorIndex Property

Applies To   **LegendKey** Object, **Point** Object, **Series** Object.

Description   Returns or sets the marker foreground color as an index into the current color
palette (a value from one to 56, or **xlNone** if there is no foreground color). Line,
scatter and radar charts only. Read-write.

See Also   **Colors** Property, **MarkerBackgroundColorIndex** Property,
MarkerForegroundColor Property, **MarkerStyle** Property.

Example

This example sets the marker background and foreground colors for the second point in series one in Chart1.

```
With Charts("Chart1").SeriesCollection(1).Points(2)
    .MarkerBackgroundColorIndex = 4 'green
    .MarkerForegroundColorIndex = 3 'red
End With
```

MarkerStyle Property

Applies To

LegendKey Object, **Point** Object, **Series** Object.

Description

Returns or sets the marker style for a point or series on a line chart, a scatter chart, or a radar chart. Read-write.

Remarks

This property can have one of the following values.

Value	Meaning
xlNone	No markers.
xlAutomatic	Automatic markers.
xlSquare	Square markers.
xlDiamond	Diamond-shaped markers.
xlTriangle	Triangular markers.
xlX	Square markers with an X.
xlStar	Square markers with an asterisk.
xlDot	Short bar markers.
xlDash	Long bar markers.
xlCircle	Circular markers.
xlPlus	Square markers with a plus sign.
xlPicture	Picture markers.

Example

This example sets the marker style for series one in Chart1. The example should be run on a 2-D line chart.

```
Charts("Chart1").SeriesCollection(1).MarkerStyle = xlCircle
```

MathCoprocessorAvailable Property

Applies To	**Application** Object.
Description	**True** if a math coprocessor is available. Read-only.
Example	This example displays a message box if a math coprocessor is not available.

```
If Not Application.MathCoprocessorAvailable Then
    MsgBox "This macro requires a math coprocessor"
End If
```

Max Property

Applies To	**DrawingObjects** Collection, **ScrollBar** Object, **ScrollBars** Collection, **Spinner** Object, **Spinners** Collection.
Description	Returns or sets the maximum value of a scroll bar or spinner range. The scroll bar or spinner will not take on values above this maximum value. Read-write.
	For help about using the **Max** worksheet function in Visual Basic, see "Using Worksheet Functions in Visual Basic" in online Help.
Remarks	The value of the **Max** property must be greater than the value of the **Min** property.
See Also	**Min** Property.
Example	This example sets the minimum and maximum values for scroll bar one on Dialog1.

```
With DialogSheets("Dialog1").ScrollBars(1)
    .Min = 20
    .Max = 50
End With
```

MaxChange Property

Applies To	**Application** Object.
Description	Returns or sets the maximum amount of change that is used in each iteration as Microsoft Excel tries to resolve circular references. Read-write.

Remarks	The **MaxIterations** property sets the maximum number of iterations used when resolving circular references.
See Also	**Iteration** Property, **MaxIterations** Property.
Example	This example sets the maximum change for each iteration to 0.1.

```
Application.MaxChange = 0.1
```

MaximumScale Property

Applies To	**Axis** Object.
Description	Returns or sets the maximum value on the value axis. Applies only to the value axis. Read-write.
Remarks	Setting this property sets the **MaximumScaleIsAuto** property to **False**.
See Also	**MaximumScaleIsAuto** Property, **MinimumScale** Property, **MinimumScaleIsAuto** Property.
Example	This example sets the maximum and minimum values for the value axis in Chart1.

```
With Charts("Chart1").Axes(xlValue)
    .MinimumScale = 10
    .MaximumScale = 120
End With
```

MaximumScaleIsAuto Property

Applies To	**Axis** Object.
Description	**True** if Microsoft Excel calculates the maximum value for the value axis. Applies only to the value axis. Read-write.
Remarks	Setting the **MaximumScale** property sets this property to **False**.
See Also	**MaximumScale** Property, **MinimumScale** Property, **MinimumScaleIsAuto** Property.

Example   This example automatically calculates the maximum scale and minimum scale for the value axis in Chart1.

```
With Charts("Chart1").Axes(xlValue)
    .MinimumScaleIsAuto = True
    .MaximumScaleIsAuto = True
End With
```

MaxIterations Property

Applies To   **Application** Object.

Description   Returns or sets the maximum number of iterations that will be allowed to resolve a circular reference. Read-write.

Remarks   The **MaxChange** property sets the maximum amount of change used in each iteration when resolving circular references.

See Also   **Iteration** Property, **MaxChange** Property.

Example   This example sets the maximum number of iterations to 1000.

```
Application.MaxIterations = 1000
```

MemoryFree Property

Applies To   **Application** Object.

Description   Returns the amount of memory that is still available for Microsoft Excel to use, in bytes. Read-only.

See Also   **MemoryTotal** Property, **MemoryUsed** Property.

Example   This example displays a message box showing the number of free bytes.

```
MsgBox "Microsoft Excel has " & Application.MemoryFree & " bytes free"
```

MemoryTotal Property

Applies To   **Application** Object.

Description   Returns the total amount of memory that is available to Microsoft Excel, including memory already in use, in bytes. Read-only.

Remarks   **MemoryTotal** is equal to **MemoryUsed + MemoryFree**.

See Also   **MemoryFree** Property, **MemoryUsed** Property.

Example   This example displays a message box showing the total number of available bytes.

```
MsgBox "Microsoft Excel has " & Application.MemoryTotal & _
    " total bytes available"
```

MemoryUsed Property

Applies To   **Application** Object.

Description   Returns the amount of memory that is currently in use by Microsoft Excel, in bytes. Read-only.

See Also   **MemoryFree** Property, **MemoryTotal** Property.

Example   This example displays a message box showing the number of bytes currently being used.

```
MsgBox "Microsoft Excel is currently using " & _
    Application.MemoryUsed & " bytes"
```

Menu Object

Description   Represents a drop-down menu, shortcut menu, or submenu.

Accessors   The **Menu** object is a member of the **Menus** collection. The **Menus** collection contains all of the menus on a menu bar. Use the **Add** method to create a new menu and add it to the specified menu bar. To access a single member of the collection, use the **Menus** method with the menu caption or index number as an argument.

The index number indicates the position of the menu on the menu bar. The following example adds a new menu item to the bottom of the File menu on the Worksheet menu bar.

```
MenuBars("worksheet").Menus(1).MenuItems.Add "Search"
```

The menu caption is the text that appears in the menu bar. Use the **Caption** property to set or return the menu caption. The following example changes the caption for the Help menu on the Visual Basic Module menu bar.

```
MenuBars(xlModule).Menus("help").Caption = "HELP!"
```

The following example creates a table on worksheet one that contains the captions of all the menus on all the menu bars in the application. The column headings are the menu bar captions, and the column entries under each heading are the menu captions on that menu bar.

```
Sub EnumerateMenuBars()
    Worksheets(1).Activate
    c = 1
    For Each mb In MenuBars
        Cells(1, c) = mb.Caption
        i = 2
        For Each mn In mb.Menus
            Cells(i, c) = mn.Caption
            i = i + 1
        Next
        c = c + 1
    Next
End Sub
```

The **MenuItems** method returns a **Menu** object when the specified menu item is a submenu. The following example sets the **Checked** property for the mySubMenuItem submenu item on the mySubMenu submenu.

```
MenuBars(xlModule).Menus("myMenu").MenuItems("mySubMenu") _
    .MenuItems("mySubMenuItem").Checked = True
```

Remarks

You should use the menu name instead of its index number so your code will not depend on the current menu layout. Other Visual Basic procedures may change the menu layout, and the layout may change in future versions of Microsoft Excel. It is safer to use **Menubars(xlWorksheet).Menus("File")** than to rely on the File menu being the first menu on the menubar and use **Menubars(xlWorksheet).Menus(1)**.

Properties

Application Property, **Caption** Property, **Creator** Property, **Enabled** Property, **Index** Property, **Parent** Property.

Methods

Delete Method, **MenuItems** Method.

MenuBar Object

Description Represents a built-in or custom menu bar.

Accessors The **MenuBar** object is a member of the **MenuBars** collection. The **MenuBars** collection contains all of the menu bars available to Microsoft Excel. Use the **Add** method to create a new menu bar and add it to the collection. Use the **Activate** method to display a menu bar. To access a single member of the collection, use the **MenuBars** method with the menu bar caption or index number as an argument.

Several built-in constants are available for the menu bar index number, as shown in the following list.

Constant	Description
xlWorksheet	Worksheet, macro sheet, and dialog sheet.
xlChart	Chart
xlModule	Visual Basic module
xlNoDocuments	No documents open
xlInfo	Info Window
xlWorksheetShort	Short Worksheet menu (for Microsoft Excel version 3 compatibility)
xlChartShort	Short Chart menu (for Microsoft Excel version 3 compatibility)
xlWorksheet4	Old worksheet menu bar (for Microsoft Excel version 4 compatibility)
xlChart4	Old chart menu bar (for Microsoft Excel version 4 compatibility)

Microsoft Excel automatically displays the built-in menu bar appropriate to the active sheet. When the active sheet type changes, Microsoft Excel changes the menu bar. If you create a custom menu bar and display it using Visual Basic code, Microsoft Excel stops changing the menu bar to fit the active sheet, and your code must activate and deactivate the menu bar (if necessary) when the sheet type changes.

The following example adds a new menu item to the bottom of the File menu on the Visual Basic Module menu bar.

```
MenuBars(xlModule).Menus("file").MenuItems.Add "S&earch"
```

The following example creates a table on worksheet one. The table contains the captions of all the menus on all the menu bars in the application. The column headings are the menu bar captions, and the column entries under each heading are the menu captions on that menu bar.

```
Sub EnumerateMenuBars()
    Worksheets(1).Activate
    c = 1
    For Each mb In MenuBars
        Cells(1, c) = mb.Caption
        i = 2
        For Each mn In mb.Menus
            Cells(i, c) = mn.Caption
            i = i + 1
        Next
        c = c + 1
    Next
End Sub
```

Properties

Application Property, **BuiltIn** Property, **Caption** Property, **Creator** Property, **Index** Property, **Parent** Property.

Methods

Activate Method, **Delete** Method, **Menus** Method, **Reset** Method.

MenuBars Collection Object

Description

A collection of all the **MenuBar** objects in the Microsoft Excel application. Each **MenuBar** object represents a built-in or custom menu bar.

Accessors

Use the **Add** method to add a new menu bar to the application. The following example adds a new menu bar and then activates it.

```
With MenuBars.Add("Stock Chart")
    With .Menus.Add("File")
        .MenuItems.Add "Update", "UpdateProc"
        .MenuItems.Add "Print", "PrintProc"
    End With
End With
MenuBars("stock chart").Activate
```

After running the example, you can use `MenuBars(xlModule).Activate` to restore the Visual Basic Module menu.

Use the **MenuBars** method with an argument to access a single member of the collection or without an argument to access the entire collection at once.

Properties	**Application** Property, **Count** Property, **Creator** Property, **Parent** Property.
Methods	**Add** Method (**MenuBars** Collection), **Item** Method.

MenuBars Method

Applies To	**Application** Object.
Description	Accessor. Returns an object that represents a single menu bar (a **MenuBar** object, Syntax 1) or a collection of the top-level menu bars (the **MenuBars** object, Syntax 2). Read-only.
Syntax 1	*object*.**MenuBars**(*index*)
Syntax 2	*object*.**MenuBars**

object
Optional. The **Application** object.

index
Required for Syntax 1. The name or number of the menu bar. Several predefined constants are available, as shown in the following table.

Constant	Description
xlWorksheet	Worksheet, macro sheet and dialog sheet.
xlChart	Chart
xlModule	Visual Basic module
xlNoDocuments	No documents open
xlInfo	Info Window
xlWorksheetShort	Short Worksheet menu (for Microsoft Excel version 3 compatibility)
xlChartShort	Short Chart menu (for Microsoft Excel version 3 compatibility)
xlWorksheet4	Old worksheet menu bar (for Microsoft Excel version 4 compatibility)
xlChart4	Old chart menu bar (for Microsoft Excel version 4 compatibility)

Example	This example resets all menu bars in Microsoft Excel.

```
For Each mb In MenuBars
    mb.Reset
Next mb
```

This example adds a new menu to the module menu bar.

```
MenuBars(xlModule).Menus.Add Caption:="&More Help"
```

Menultem Object

Description   Represents an item on a menu (either a command or a separator bar).

Accessors   The **MenuItem** object is a member of the **MenuItems** collection. The **MenuItems** collection contains all of the menu items (the commands and command separators) on a menu. Use the **Add** method to create a new menu item and add it to a menu. Use the **AddMenu** method to add a submenu. To access a single member of the collection, use the **MenuItems** method with the index number or caption of the menu item as an argument.

The menu item index number indicates its position on the menu. MenuItems(1) is the item at the top of the menu; MenuItems(MenuItems.Count) is at the bottom. Remember that menu item separators (lines across the menu) are included in the collection of menu items. The following example adds a check mark to the left of menu item one on the Help menu of the Visual Basic Module menu bar.

```
MenuBars(xlModule).Menus("help").MenuItems(1).Checked = True
```

Use the **Caption** property to set or return the menu item caption. The following example adds a new menu item to the Help menu of the Visual Basic Module menu bar and then disables the menu item.

```
MenuBars(xlModule).Menus("help").MenuItems.Add "More Help"
MenuBars(xlModule).Menus("help").MenuItems("More Help").Enabled = False
```

The following example creates a table on worksheet one that contains the captions of all the menu items on all the menus on the Worksheet menu bar. The column headings are the menu captions, and the column entries under each heading are the menu item captions on that menu.

```
Sub EnumerateMenuItems()
    Worksheets(1).Activate
    c = 1
    For Each mn In MenuBars(xlWorksheet).Menus
        r = 1
        Cells(r, c) = mn.Caption
        r = r + 1
        For Each mi In mn.MenuItems
            Cells(r, c) = mi.Caption
            r = r + 1
        Next
        c = c + 1
    Next
End Sub
```

Properties   **Application** Property, **Caption** Property, **Checked** Property, **Creator** Property, **Enabled** Property, **HelpContextID** Property, **HelpFile** Property, **Index** Property, **OnAction** Property, **Parent** Property, **StatusBar** Property.

Methods   **Delete** Method.

MenuItems Collection Object

Description   A collection of all the **MenuItem** objects on the specified menu.

Accessors   Use the **Add** method to add a new menu item to a menu. Use the **AddMenu** method to add a submenu. The following example adds a new menu item to the Help menu on the Visual Basic Module menu bar.

```
MenuBars(xlModule).Menus("help").MenuItems.Add "More Help"
```

Use the **MenuItems** method with an argument to access a single member of the collection or without an argument to access the entire collection at once. The following example creates a list on worksheet one that contains the menu items in the File menu on the Visual Basic Module menu bar.

```
Sub EnumerateFileMenu()
    Worksheets(1).Activate
    For r = 1 To MenuBars(xlModule).Menus("file").MenuItems.Count
        Worksheets(1).Cells(r, 1) = MenuBars(xlModule). _
            Menus("file").MenuItems(r).Caption
    Next
End Sub
```

Properties   **Application** Property, **Count** Property, **Creator** Property, **Parent** Property.

Methods   **Add** Method (**MenuItems** Collection), **AddMenu** Method, **Item** Method.

MenuItems Method

Applies To   **Menu** Object.

Description   Accessor. Returns an object that represents a single menu item (a **MenuItem** object or **Menu** object, Syntax 1), or a collection of the menu items (a **MenuItems** object, Syntax 2) on the menu. Read-only.

This method returns a **MenuItem** object when the menu item is a command or separator bar, and it returns a **Menu** object when the menu item is a submenu caption.

Syntax 1   *object*.**MenuItems(*index*)**

Syntax 2   *object*.**MenuItems**

object
    Required. The **Menu** object.

index
    Required for Syntax 1. The name or number of the menu item.

Remarks   You must apply the **MenuItems** method twice to return an item on a submenu. The following example sets the **Checked** property for the mySubMenuItem submenu item on the mySubMenu submenu.

```
MenuBars(xlModule).Menus("myMenu").MenuItems("mySubMenu") _
    .MenuItems("mySubMenuItem").Checked = True
```

See Also   **Menus** Method.

Example   This example adds a menu item to the Help menu on the active menu bar.

```
With ActiveMenuBar.Menus("Help")
    Set mi = .MenuItems.Add("&More Help", "my_Help_Macro")
End With
```

This example changes the Open command on the File menu to Open Workbook. The example makes this change to every menu bar in the product.

```
For Each mb In MenuBars
    mb.Menus("File").MenuItems(2).Caption = "&Open Workbook"
Next mb
```

Menus Collection Object

Description   A collection of all the **Menu** objects on the specified menu bar. Each **Menu** object represents a drop-down menu, shortcut menu, or submenu.

Accessors   Use the **Add** method to add a new menu to a menu bar. The following example adds a menu to the Visual Basic Module menu bar.

```
MenuBars(xlModule).Menus.Add "&Debug"
```

Use the **Menus** method with an argument to access a single member of the collection or without an argument to access the entire collection at once.

Properties   **Application** Property, **Count** Property, **Creator** Property, **Parent** Property.

Methods   **Add** Method (**Menus** Collection), **Item** Method.

Menus Method

Applies To   **MenuBar** Object.

Description   Accessor. Returns a single menu (a **Menu** object, Syntax 1), or a collection of the menus (a **Menus** object, Syntax 2) on the menu bar. Read-only.

Syntax 1   *object*.**Menus(*index*)**

Syntax 2   *object*.**Menus**

object
    Required. The **MenuBar** object.

index
> Required for Syntax 1. The name of the menu as a string, or the number of the menu. For example, on the worksheet menu bar, you return the Help menu with `Menus("Help")` or with `Menus(8)`.

See Also   **MenuItems** Method.

Example   This example adds a new menu to the active menu bar. The menu is added immediately to the left of the Help menu.

```
ActiveMenuBar.Menus.Add caption:="&MyMenu", before:="Help"
```

This example changes the Open command on the File menu to Open Workbook. The example makes this change to every menu bar in the product.

```
For Each mb In MenuBars
    mb.Menus("File").MenuItems(2).Caption = "&Open Workbook"
Next mb
```

Merge Method

Applies To   **Styles** Collection.

Description   Syntax 1: Merges the scenarios from another sheet into the collection of scenarios.

Syntax 2: Merges the styles from another workbook into the collection of styles.

Syntax 1   *object*.**Merge**(*source*)

Syntax 2   *object*.**Merge**(*workbook*)

object
> Required. The **Scenarios** or **Styles** object.

source
> Required for Syntax 1. The **Worksheet** object, or name of the sheet containing scenarios to merge.

workbook
> Required for Syntax 2. The **Workbook** object containing styles to merge.

Example   This example merges the styles from the workbook TEMPLATE.XLS into the active workbook.

```
ActiveWorkbook.Styles.Merge Workbook:=Workbooks("TEMPLATE.XLS")
```

Message Property

Applies To

RoutingSlip Object.

Description

Returns or sets the message text of the routing slip. This text is used as the body text of mail messages used to route the workbook. Read-write.

See Also

Subject Property.

Example

This example sends BOOK1.XLS to three recipients, one after the other.

```
Workbooks("BOOK1.XLS").HasRoutingSlip = True
With Workbooks("BOOK1.XLS").RoutingSlip
    .Delivery = xlOneAfterAnother
    .Recipients = Array("Adam Bendel", "Jean Selva", "Bernard Gabor")
    .Subject = "Here is BOOK1.XLS"
    .Message = "Here is the workbook. What do you think?"
End With
Workbooks("BOOK1.XLS").Route
```

Mid Function

Description

Returns a specified number of characters from a string.

Syntax

Mid(*string*,*start*[,*length*])

The **Mid** function syntax has these parts:

Part	Description
string	String expression from which characters are returned. If *string* contains no valid data, **Null** is returned.
start	Character position in *string* at which the part to be taken begins. If *start* is greater than the number of characters in *string*, **Mid** returns a zero-length string.
length	Number of characters to return. If omitted or if there are fewer than *length* characters in the text (including the character at *start*), all characters from the *start* position to the end of the string are returned.

Remarks   To determine the number of characters in *string*, use the **Len** function.

Note Another function (**MidB**) is provided for use with the double-byte character sets (DBCS) used in some Asian locales. Instead of specifying the number of characters to return, *length* specifies the number of bytes. In areas where DBCS is not used, **MidB** behaves the same as **Mid**.

See Also   **Left** Function; **Len** Function; **LTrim**, **RTrim**, and **Trim** Functions; **Mid** Statement; **Right** Function.

Example   This example uses the **Mid** function to return a specified number of characters from a string.

```
MyString = "Mid Function Demo"     ' Create text string.
FirstWord = Mid(MyString, 1, 3)    ' Returns "Mid".
LastWord = Mid(MyString, 14, 4)    ' Returns "Demo".
MidWords = Mid(MyString, 5) ' Returns "Function Demo".
```

Mid Statement

Description   Replaces a specified number of characters in a string variable with characters from another string.

Syntax   **Mid**(*stringvar*,*start*[,*length*])*=string*

The **Mid** statement syntax has these parts:

Part	Description
stringvar	Name of string variable to modify.
start	Character position in *stringvar* where the replacement of text begins.
length	Number of characters to replace. If omitted, all of *string* is used.
string	String expression that replaces part of *stringvar*.

Remarks   The number of characters replaced is always less than or equal to the number of characters in *stringvar*.

See Also   **Mid** Function.

Example

This example uses the **Mid** statement to replace a specified number of characters in a string variable with characters from another string.

```
MyString = "The dog jumps"              ' Initialize string.
Mid(MyString, 5, 3) = "fox"             ' MyString = "The fox jumps".
Mid(MyString, 5) = "cow"                ' MyString = "The cow jumps".
Mid(MyString, 5) = "cow jumped over"    ' MyString = "The cow jumpe".
Mid(MyString, 5, 3) = "duck" ' MyString = "The duc jumps".
```

Min Property

Applies To

DrawingObjects Collection, **ScrollBar** Object, **ScrollBars** Collection, **Spinner** Object, **Spinners** Collection.

Description

Returns or sets the minimum value of a scroll bar or spinner range. The scroll bar or spinner will not take on values below this minimum value. Read-write.

For help about using the **Min** worksheet function in Visual Basic, see "Using Worksheet Functions in Visual Basic" in online Help.

Remarks

The value of the **Min** property must be less than the value of the **Max** property.

See Also

Max Property.

Example

This example sets the minimum and maximum values for scroll bar one on Dialog1.

```
With DialogSheets("Dialog1").ScrollBars(1)
    .Min = 20
    .Max = 50
End With
```

MinimumScale Property

Applies To

Axis Object.

Description

Returns or sets the minimum value on the value axis. Applies only to the value axis. Read-write.

Remarks

Setting this property sets the **MinimumScaleIsAuto** property to **False**.

See Also

MaximumScale Property, **MaximumScaleIsAuto** Property, **MinimumScaleIsAuto** Property.

Example   This example sets the maximum and minimum values for the value axis in Chart1.

```
With Charts("Chart1").Axes(xlValue)
    .MinimumScale = 10
    .MaximumScale = 120
End With
```

MinimumScaleIsAuto Property

Applies To   **Axis** Object.

Description   **True** if Microsoft Excel calculates the minimum value for the value axis. Applies only to the value axis. Read-write.

Remarks   Setting the **MinimumScale** property sets this property to **False**.

See Also   **MaximumScale** Property, **MaximumScaleIsAuto** Property, **MinimumScale** Property.

Example   This example automatically calculates the maximum scale and minimum scale for the value axis in Chart1.

```
With Charts("Chart1").Axes(xlValue)
    .MinimumScaleIsAuto = True
    .MaximumScaleIsAuto = True
End With
```

MinorGridlines Property

Applies To   **Axis** Object.

Description   Accessor. Returns a **Gridlines** object that represents the minor gridlines for the specified axis. Only axes in the primary axis group can have gridlines. Read-only.

See Also   **AxisGroup** Property, **HasMajorGridlines** Property, **HasMinorGridlines** Property, **MajorGridlines** Property.

Example   This example sets the color of the minor gridlines for the value axis in Chart1.

```
With Charts("Chart1").Axes(xlValue)
    If .HasMinorGridlines Then
        .MinorGridlines.Border.ColorIndex = 5    '' 273.'set color to
blue
    End If
End With
```

MinorTickMark Property

Applies To	**Axis** Object.
Description	Returns or sets the type of minor tick mark for the specified axis (one of **xlNone**, **xlInside**, **xlOutside**, or **xlCross**). Read-write.
See Also	**MajorTickMark** Property.
Example	This example sets the minor tick marks for the value axis in Chart1 to be inside the axis.

```
Charts("Chart1").Axes(xlValue).MinorTickMark = xlInside
```

MinorUnit Property

Applies To	**Axis** Object.
Description	Returns or sets the minor units on the value axis. Applies only to the value axis. Read-write.
Remarks	Setting this property sets the **MinorUnitIsAuto** property to **False**.
	Use the **TickMarkSpacing** property to set tick mark spacing on the category axis.
See Also	**MajorUnit** Property, **MajorUnitIsAuto** Property, **MinorUnitIsAuto** Property, **TickMarkSpacing** Property.
Example	This example sets the major and minor units for the value axis in Chart1.

```
With Charts("Chart1").Axes(xlValue)
    .MajorUnit = 100
    .MinorUnit = 20
End With
```

MinorUnitIsAuto Property

Applies To	**Axis** Object.
Description	**True** if Microsoft Excel calculates minor units for the value axis. Applies only to the value axis. Read-write.
Remarks	Setting the **MinorUnit** property sets this property to **False**.

See Also   **MajorUnit** Property, **MajorUnitIsAuto** Property, **MinorUnit** Property.

Example   This example automatically calculates major and minor units for the value axis in Chart1.

```
With Charts("Chart1").Axes(xlValue)
    .MajorUnitIsAuto = True
    .MinorUnitIsAuto = True
End With
```

Minute Function

Description   Returns a whole number between 0 and 59, inclusive, representing the minute of the hour.

Syntax   **Minute(*time*)**

The *time* named argument is limited to a time or numbers and strings, in any combination, that can represent a time. If *time* contains no valid data, **Null** is returned.

See Also   **Day** Function, **Hour** Function, **Now** Function, **Second** Function, **Time** Function, **Time** Statement.

Example   This example uses the **Minute** function to obtain the minute of the hour from a specified time.

```
' In the development environment, the time (date literal) will display
' in short format using the locale settings of your code.
MyTime = #4:35:17 PM#              ' Assign a time.
MyMinute = Minute(MyTime)    ' MyMinute contains 35.
```

MkDir Statement

Description   Creates a new directory or folder.

Syntax   **MkDir *path***

The *path* named argument is a string expression that identifies the directory or folder to be created—may include drive. If no drive is specified, **MkDir** creates the new directory or folder on the current drive.

Remarks	In Microsoft Windows, if you use **MkDir** to create a directory whose name contains an embedded space, you may be able to access it with some applications, but you can't remove it using standard operating system commands. To remove such a directory, use the **RmDir** statement.
See Also	**ChDir** Statement, **CurDir** Function, **RmDir** Statement.
Example	This example uses the **MkDir** statement to create a directory or folder. If the drive is not specified, the new directory or folder is created on the current drive.

```
MkDir "MYDIR"    ' Make new directory or folder.
```

Mod Operator

Description	Divides two numbers and returns only the remainder.
Syntax	*result* = *number1* **Mod** *number2*

The **Mod** operator syntax has these parts:

Part	Description
result	Any numeric variable.
number1	Any numeric expression.
number2	Any numeric expression.

Remarks	The modulus, or remainder, operator divides *number1* by *number2* (rounding floating-point numbers to integers) and returns only the remainder as *result*. For example, in the following expression, A (which is *result*) equals 5.

```
A = 19 Mod 6.7
```

Usually, the data type of *result* is an **Integer**, **Integer** variant, **Long**, or **Variant** containing a **Long**, regardless of whether or not *result* is a whole number. Any fractional portion is truncated. However, if any expression is a **Null**, *result* is also a **Null**. Any expression that is **Empty** is treated as 0.

See Also	Operator Precedence.

Example

This example uses the **Mod** operator to divide two numbers and return only the remainder. If either number is a floating-point number, it is first rounded to an integer.

```
MyResult = 10 Mod 5              ' Returns 0.
MyResult = 10 Mod 3              ' Returns 1.
MyResult = 12 Mod 4.3           ' Returns 0.
MyResult = 12.6 Mod 5    ' Returns 3.
```

This example sets the column width of every other column on Sheet1 to 4 points.

```
For Each col In Worksheets("Sheet1").Columns
    If col.Column Mod 2 = 0 Then
        col.ColumnWidth = 4
    End If
Next col
```

This example sets the row height of every other row on Sheet1 to 4 points.

```
For Each rw In Worksheets("Sheet1").Rows
    If rw.Row Mod 2 = 0 Then
        rw.RowHeight = 4
    End If
Next rw
```

This example selects every other item in list box one on Sheet1.

```
Dim items() As Boolean
Set lbox = Worksheets("Sheet1").ListBoxes(1)
ReDim items(1 To lbox.ListCount)
For i = 1 To lbox.ListCount
    If i Mod 2 = 1 Then
        items(i) = True
    Else
        items(i) = False
    End If
Next
lbox.MultiSelect = xlExtended
lbox.Selected = items
```

Module Object

Description

Represents a Visual Basic module in a workbook.

Accessors

The **Module** object is a member of the **Modules** collection. The **Modules** collection contains all the **Module** objects in a workbook. Use the **Add** method to create a new module and add it to the collection. To access a single member of the collection, use the **Modules** method with the index number or name of the module as an argument.

The module index number represents the position of the module on the tab bar of the workbook. Modules(1) is the first (leftmost) module in the workbook; Modules(Modules.Count) is the last. All modules are included in the index count, even if they are hidden.

The following example hides module two in the active workbook.

```
Modules(2).Visible = False
```

The module name is shown on the workbook tab for the module. Use the **Name** property to set or return the module name (you cannot change the name of the module where the Visual Basic code is running, however). The following example protects the Visual Basic code on the module named "Sample Code."

```
Modules("sample code").Protect password:="drowssap", contents:=True
```

The **Module** object is also a member of the **Sheets** collection. The **Sheets** collection contains all of the sheets in the workbook (chart sheets, dialog sheets, modules, and worksheets). To access a single member of the collection, use the **Sheets** method with the index number or name of the sheet as an argument.

Using ActiveSheet

When a module is the active sheet, you can use the **ActiveSheet** property to refer to it. The following example uses the **Activate** method to activate the module named "Module1" and then protects the module.

```
Modules("module1").Activate
ActiveSheet.Protect
```

Properties

Application Property, **Creator** Property, **Index** Property, **Name** Property, **Next** Property, **OnDoubleClick** Property, **OnSheetActivate** Property, **OnSheetDeactivate** Property, **PageSetup** Property, **Parent** Property, **Previous** Property, **ProtectContents** Property, **Visible** Property.

Methods

Activate Method, **Copy** Method, **Delete** Method, **InsertFile** Method, **Move** Method, **PrintOut** Method, **Protect** Method, **SaveAs** Method, **Select** Method, **Unprotect** Method.

Modules Collection Object

Description   A collection of all the **Module** objects in the specified or active workbook.

Accessors   Use the **Add** method to create a new module and add it to the collection. The following example adds a new module before sheet one in the active workbook.

```
Modules.Add before:=Sheets(1)
```

Use the **Modules** method to with an argument to access a single member of the collection or without an argument to access the entire collection at once. The following example moves all the modules in the active workbook to the end of the workbook.

```
Modules.Move after:=Sheets(Sheets.Count)
```

The **Sheets** collection contains all of the sheets in the workbook (chart sheets, dialog sheets, modules, and worksheets). Use the **Sheets** method with an argument to access a single member of the collection or without an argument to access the entire collection at once.

Properties   **Application** Property, **Count** Property, **Creator** Property, **Parent** Property, **Visible** Property.

Methods   **Add** Method (**Modules Collection**), **Copy** Method, **Delete** Method, **Item** Method, **Move** Method, **PrintOut** Method, **Select** Method.

Modules Method

Applies To   **Application** Object, **Workbook** Object.

Description   Accessor. Returns an object that represents a module (a **Module** object, Syntax 1) or a collection of all modules (a **Modules** object, Syntax 2) in the workbook. Read-only.

Syntax 1   *object*.**Modules**(*index*)

Syntax 2   *object*.**Modules**

object
    Required. The **Workbook** object.
index
    Required for Syntax 1. The name or number of the module to return.

Example	This example creates a new Visual Basic module in the active workbook and then inserts the file TESTCODE.TXT into the new module.

```
Set newModule = Modules.Add
newModule.InsertFile fileName:="testcode.txt"
```

Month Function

Description	Returns a whole number between 1 and 12, inclusive, representing the month of the year.
Syntax	**Month(*date*)**
	The ***date*** named argument is limited to a date or numbers and strings, in any combination, that can represent a date. If ***date*** contains no valid data, **Null** is returned.
See Also	**Date** Function, **Date** Statement, **Day** Function, **Now** Function, **Weekday** Function, **Year** Function.
Example	This example uses the **Month** function to obtain the month from a specified date.

```
' In the development environment, the date literal will display in short
' format using the locale settings of your code.
MyDate = #February 12, 1969#        ' Assign a date.
MyMonth = Month(MyDate) ' MyMonth contains 2.
```

MouseAvailable Property

Applies To	**Application** Object.
Description	**True** if a mouse is available (always **True** on the Macintosh). Read-only.
Example	This example displays a message if a mouse is not available.

```
If Application.MouseAvailable = False Then
    MsgBox "Your system does not have a mouse"
End If
```

Move Method

Applies To   **Chart** Object, **Charts** Collection, **DialogSheet** Object, **DialogSheets** Collection, **Module** Object, **Modules** Collection, **Sheets** Collection, **ToolbarButton** Object, **Worksheet** Object, **Worksheets** Collection.

Description   Syntax 1: Moves the sheet to another location in the workbook.

Syntax 2: Moves a toolbar button to another position, either on the same toolbar or to another toolbar.

Syntax 1   *object*.**Move**(*before*, *after*)
Syntax 2   *object*.**Move**(*toolbar*, *before*)
   object
      Required. The object to which this method applies.

   before
      Syntax 1: Optional. The sheet before which this sheet will be moved. You cannot specify *before* if you specify *after*.

      Syntax 2: Required. Specifies the new button position as a number from 1 to the number of existing buttons + 1. Gaps count as one position. Buttons to the right of this position are moved right (or down) to make room for the moved button.

   after
      Optional. The sheet after which this sheet will be moved. You cannot specify *after* if you specify *before*.

   toolbar
      Required for Syntax 2. Specifies the toolbar object to move the button to.

Remarks   If you do not specify either *before* or *after*, Microsoft Excel creates a new workbook containing the moved sheet.

See Also   **Copy** Method.

Example   This example moves Sheet1 after Sheet3 in the active workbook.

```
Worksheets("Sheet1").Move _
    after:=Worksheets("Sheet3")
```

MoveAfterReturn Property

Applies To   **Application** Object.

Description   **True** if the active cell will be moved as soon as the ENTER (RETURN) key is pressed. Read-write.

Remarks	Use the **MoveAfterReturnDirection** property to specify the direction in which the active cell is moved.
See Also	**MoveAfterReturnDirection** Property.
Example	This example sets the **MoveAfterReturn** property to **True**.

```
Application.MoveAfterReturn = True
```

MoveAfterReturnDirection Property

Applies To	**Application** Object.
Description	Returns or sets how the active cell is moved after the user presses ENTER (one of **xlToLeft**, **xlToRight**, **xlUp**, or **xlDown**). This property is available only in Microsoft Excel for Windows 95. Read-write.
Remarks	If the **MoveAfterReturn** property is **False**, the selection doesn't move at all, regardless of how the **MoveAfterReturnDirection** property is set.
See Also	**MoveAfterReturn** Property.
Example	This example causes the active cell to move to the right when the user presses ENTER.

```
Application.MoveAfterReturn = True
Application.MoveAfterReturnDirection = xlToRight

Application.MoveAfterReturnDirection = xlToRight
```

MsgBox Function

Description	Displays a message in a dialog box, waits for the user to choose a button, and returns a value indicating which button the user has chosen.

Syntax

MsgBox(*prompt*[,*buttons*][,*title*][,*helpfile*,*context*])

The **MsgBox** function syntax has these named-argument parts:

Part	Description
prompt	String expression displayed as the message in the dialog box. The maximum length of *prompt* is approximately 1024 characters, depending on the width of the characters used. If *prompt* consists of more than one line, be sure to include a carriage return (character code 13) or carriage return linefeed (character code 10) between each line.
buttons	Numeric expression that is the sum of values specifying the number and type of buttons to display, the icon style to use, the identity of the default button, and the modality. If omitted, the default value for *buttons* is 0.
title	String expression displayed in the title bar of the dialog box. If you omit *title*, nothing is placed in the title bar.
helpfile	String expression that identifies the Help file to use to provide context-sensitive Help for the dialog box. If *helpfile* is provided, *context* must also be provided.
context	Numeric expression that is the Help context number the Help author assigned to the appropriate Help topic. If *context* is provided, *helpfile* must also be provided.

The *buttons* named argument has these values:

Constant	Value	Description
vbOKOnly	0	Display OK button only.
vbOKCancel	1	Display OK and Cancel buttons.
vbAbortRetryIgnore	2	Display Abort, Retry, and Ignore buttons.
vbYesNoCancel	3	Display Yes, No, and Cancel buttons.
vbYesNo	4	Display Yes and No buttons.
vbRetryCancel	5	Display Retry and Cancel buttons.
vbCritical	16	Display Critical Message icon.
vbQuestion	32	Display Warning Query icon.
vbExclamation	48	Display Warning Message icon.
vbInformation	64	Display Information Message icon.

Constant	Value	Description
vbDefaultButton1	0	First button is default.
vbDefaultButton2	256	Second button is default.
vbDefaultButton3	512	Third button is default.
vbApplicationModal	0	Application modal; the user must respond to the message box before continuing work in the current application.
vbSystemModal	4096	System modal; all applications are suspended until the user responds to the message box.

The first group of values (0-5) describes the number and type of buttons displayed in the dialog box; the second group (16, 32, 48, 64) describes the icon style; the third group (0, 256, 512) determines which button is the default, and the fourth group (0, 4096) determines the modality of the message box. When adding numbers to create a final value for the argument *buttons*, use only one number from each group.

Note These constants are specified by Visual Basic. As a result, the names can be used anywhere in your code in place of the actual values.

Return Values

Constant	Value	Button Selected
vbOK	1	OK
vbCancel	2	Cancel
vbAbort	3	Abort
vbRetry	4	Retry
vbIgnore	5	Ignore
vbYes	6	Yes
vbNo	7	No

Remarks

When both *helpfile* and *context* are provided, a Help button is automatically added to the dialog box.

If the dialog box displays a Cancel button, pressing the ESC key has the same effect as choosing Cancel. If the dialog box contains a Help button, context-sensitive Help is provided for the dialog box. However, no value is returned until one of the other buttons is chosen.

In Microsoft Excel, the *prompt* string cannot contain more than 256 characters.

See Also

InputBox Function.

Example
The example uses the **MsgBox** function to display a critical-error message in a dialog box with Yes and No buttons. The No button is specified as the default response. The value returned by the **MsgBox** function depends on the button chosen by the user. For purposes of this example, assume that DEMO.HLP is a Help file that contains a topic with context number equal to 1000.

```
Msg = "Do you want to continue ?"              ' Define message.
Style = vbYesNo + vbCritical + vbDefaultButton2  ' Define buttons.
Title = "MsgBox Demonstration"                 ' Define title.
Help = "DEMO.HLP"                              ' Define help file.
Ctxt = 1000                                    ' Define topic
    ' context.
' Display message.
Response = MsgBox(Msg, Style, Title, Help, Ctxt)
If Response = vbYES Then                       ' User chose Yes
    ' button.
    MyString = "Yes"                           ' Perform some action.
Else                                           ' User chose No
    ' button.
    MyString = "No"                            ' Perform some action.
End If
```

MultiLine Property

Applies To   **DrawingObjects** Collection, **EditBox** Object, **EditBoxes** Collection.

Description   **True** if the edit box is multi-line enabled. Read-write.

Example   This example enables multiline input for edit box one on Dialog1.

```
DialogSheets("Dialog1").EditBoxes(1).MultiLine = True
```

MultiSelect Property

Applies To   **DrawingObjects** Collection, **ListBox** Object, **ListBoxes** Collection.

Description   Returns or sets the selection mode of the list box (or collection of list boxes). Can be one of **xlNone**, **xlSimple**, or **xlExtended**. Read-write.

Remarks   **Single select** (**xlNone**) allows only one item at a time to be selected. Any click or spacebar press deselects the currently selected item and selects the clicked-upon item.

Simple multi-select (**xlSimple**) toggles the selection on an item in the list when it is selected with the mouse or the spacebar is pressed when the focus is on the item. This mode is appropriate for pick lists where multiple items are often selected.

Extended multi-select (**xlExtended**) normally acts like a single-selection list box, so that mouse clicks on an item cancel all other selected items. When you hold down SHIFT while clicking the mouse or pressing an ARROW key, items are sequentially selected from the current item as the user navigates. When you hold down CTRL while clicking the mouse, single items are added to the list selection. This mode is appropriate when multiple items are allowed but not often used.

You can use the **Value** or **ListIndex** properties to get and set the selected item in a single-select list box. You must use the **Selected** property to get and set the selected items in a multi-select list box.

Multi-select list boxes cannot be linked to cells with the **LinkedCell** property.

See Also   **ListIndex** Property, **Selected** Property, **Value** Property.

Example   This example sets list box one on Dialog1 to allow extended multiple selections.

```
DialogSheets("Dialog1").ListBoxes(1).MultiSelect = xlExtended
```

MultiUserEditing Property

Applies To   **Workbook** Object.

Description   **True** if the workbook is open as a shared list. This property is available only in Microsoft Excel for Windows 95. Read-only.

Remarks   To save a workbook as a shared list, use the **SaveAs** method. To change the workbook from shared mode to exclusive mode, use the **ExclusiveAccess** method.

See Also   **ExclusiveAccess** Method, **SaveAs** Method, **UserStatus** Property.

Example   This example determines whether the active workbook is open as a shared list. If it is, the example notifies the user that the macros in the active workbook cannot be modified.

```
If ActiveWorkbook.MultiUserEditing Then
    MsgBox "Cannot modify Visual Basic modules in this workbook."
End If
```

This example determines whether the active workbook is open in exclusive mode. If it is, the example saves it as a shared list.

```
If Not ActiveWorkbook.MultiUserEditing Then
    ActiveWorkbook.SaveAs accessMode := xlShared
End If
```

Name Object

Description

Represents a defined name for a range of cells. Names can be built-in, such as Database, Print_Area, and Auto_Open, or they can be custom names.

Application, Workbook, and Worksheet Objects

The **Name** object is a member of the **Names** collection for the **Application**, **Workbook**, and **Worksheet** objects. Use the **Add** method to create a new name and add it to the collection. To access a single member of the collection, use the **Names** method with the index number or name of the defined name as an argument.

The index number indicates the position of the name within the collection. Names are placed in alphabetical order from a to z and are not case-sensitive (this is the same order as is displayed in the Define Name and Apply Names dialog boxes, accessed by clicking the Name command on the Insert menu). The following example displays the cell reference for name one in the application collection.

```
MsgBox Names(1).RefersTo
```

Use the **Name** property on a **Name** object to return or set the text of the name itself. The following example changes the name of the first **Name** object in the active workbook.

```
Names(1).Name = "stock_values"
```

The following example deletes the name "mySortRange" from the active workbook.

```
ActiveWorkbook.Names("mySortRange").Delete
```

Range Objects

While a **Range** object can have more than one name, there is no **Names** collection for the **Range** object. The **Name** property of the **Range** object returns the first name (sorted alphabetically) assigned to the range. The following sets the **Visible** property for the first name assigned to cells A1:B1 on worksheet one.

```
Worksheets(1).Range("a1:b1").Name.Visible = False
```

Properties	**Application** Property, **Category** Property, **CategoryLocal** Property, **Creator** Property, **Index** Property, **MacroType** Property, **Name** Property, **NameLocal** Property, **Parent** Property, **RefersTo** Property, **RefersToLocal** Property, **RefersToR1C1** Property, **RefersToR1C1Local** Property, **RefersToRange** Property, **ShortcutKey** Property, **Value** Property, **Visible** Property.
Methods	**Delete** Method.

Name Property

Applies To	**AddIn** Object, **Application** Object, **Arc** Object, **AxisTitle** Object, **Button** Object, **Chart** Object, **ChartArea** Object, **ChartObject** Object, **ChartTitle** Object, **CheckBox** Object, **Corners** Object, **DataLabel** Object, **DataLabels** Collection, **DialogFrame** Object, **DialogSheet** Object, **DownBars** Object, **Drawing** Object, **DropDown** Object, **DropLines** Object, **EditBox** Object, **ErrorBars** Object, **Floor** Object, **Font** Object, **Gridlines** Object, **GroupBox** Object, **GroupObject** Object, **HiLoLines** Object, **Label** Object, **Legend** Object, **Line** Object, **ListBox** Object, **Module** Object, **Name** Object, **OLEObject** Object, **OptionButton** Object, **Oval** Object, **Picture** Object, **PivotField** Object, **PivotItem** Object, **PivotTable** Object, **PlotArea** Object, **Range** Object, **Rectangle** Object, **Scenario** Object, **ScrollBar** Object, **Series** Object, **SeriesLines** Object, **Spinner** Object, **Style** Object, **TextBox** Object, **TickLabels** Object, **Toolbar** Object, **ToolbarButton** Object, **Trendline** Object, **UpBars** Object, **Walls** Object, **Workbook** Object, **Worksheet** Object.
Description	Returns or sets the name of the object. See the Remarks section for details.
Remarks	The meaning of this property depends on the object, as shown in the following table. The name of a **Range** object is a **Name** object. For every other object, the name is a string.

Object	Name
AddIn	The filename of the add-in, not including its path on disk. Read-only.
Application	The name of the application. Read-only.
Chart	If the chart is a page in the workbook, this is the name of that page as shown on the tab. If the chart is an embedded object, it is the name of the object. Read-write.
Control or drawing object	The name of the control or drawing object, in the language of the macro. Read-write.
DataLabel	The name of the data label. Read-only.

Object	Name
DialogSheet, **Module**, **Worksheet**	The name of the sheet, as shown on the tab. Read-write.
Font	The name of the font.
Legend	The name of the legend. Read-only.
Name	The name itself. If it is one of the built-in names it will be translated to the language of the macro. Read-write.
OLEObject	The name of the object. Read-write.
PivotField	The name of the field in the PivotTable. Read-write.
PivotItem	The name of the item in the PivotTable field. Read-write.
PivotTable	The name of the PivotTable. Read-write.
Range	The name of the range (this is a **Name** object). Assign to this property to define a name. If the range has multiple names, returns the first one. Read-write.
Scenario	The name of the scenario. Read-write.
Series	The name of the series. Read-write.
Style	The name of the style. If the style is a built-in style, this will return the name of the style in the language of the macro. Read only.
Toolbar	The name of the toolbar, as a string. If the toolbar is built-in, returns the name in the language of the user. Read only.
ToolbarButton	The name of the button, as a string. Read-write.
Trendline	The name of the trendline as it will appear in the legend. Read-write.
Workbook	The name of the workbook, not including its path on disk. Read-only .

See Also   **NameLocal** Property.

Example   This example displays the name and localized name of style one in the active workbook.

```
With ActiveWorkbook.Styles(1)
    MsgBox "The name of the style is " & .Name
    MsgBox "The localized name of the style is " & .NameLocal
End With
```

Name Property (DocumentProperty Object)

Applies To   **DocumentProperty** Object.

Description	Returns or sets the name of the document property. Read-only for built-in document properties; read-write for custom document properties.

To use this property, you should establish a reference to the Microsoft Office 95 Object Library by using the References command (Tools menu).

For a list of valid built-in document property names, see the **Item** method.

Example	This example displays the name, type, and value of a document property. You must pass a **DocumentProperty** object to the procedure.

```
Sub DisplayPropertyInfo(dp As DocumentProperty)
    MsgBox "value = " & dp.Value & Chr(13) & _
        "type = " & dp.Type & Chr(13) & _
        "name = " & dp.Name
End Sub
```

This example displays the name of custom document property one in the active workbook.

```
MsgBox ActiveWorkbook.CustomDocumentProperties(1).Name
```

Name Statement

Description	Renames a disk file, directory, or folder.
Syntax	**Name** *oldpathname* **As** *newpathname*

The **Name** statement syntax has these parts:

Part	Description
oldpathname	String expression that specifies the existing file name and location—may include directory or folder, and drive.
newpathname	String expression that specifies the new file name and location—may include directory or folder, and drive. The file specified by *newpathname* can't already exist.

Remarks	Both *newpathname* and *oldpathname* must be on the same drive. If the path in *newpathname* exists and is different from the path in *oldpathname*, the **Name** statement moves the file to the new directory or folder and renames the file, if necessary. If *newpathname* and *oldpathname* have different paths and the same file name, **Name** moves the file to the new location and leaves the file name unchanged. Using **Name**, you can move a file from one directory or folder to another, but you can't move a directory or folder.

Name supports the use of '*' (multiple character) and '?' (single character) wildcards. However, on the Macintosh, these characters are treated as valid file name characters and can't be used as wildcards to specify multiple files.

Using **Name** on an open file produces an error. You must close an open file before renaming it.

See Also   **Kill** Statement.

Example   This example uses the **Name** statement to rename a file. For purposes of this example, assume that the directories or folders that are specified already exist.

```
OldName = "OLDFILE" : NewName = "NEWFILE"  ' Define file names.
Name OldName As NewName                    ' Rename file.

' In Microsoft Windows.
OldName = "C:\MYDIR\OLDFILE" : NewName = "C:\YOURDIR\NEWFILE"
Name OldName As NewName                    ' Move and rename file.

' On the Macintosh.
OldName = "HD:MY FOLDER:OLDFILE" : NewName = "HD:YOUR FOLDER:NEWFILE"
Name OldName As NewName  ' Move and rename file.
```

NamelsAuto Property

Applies To   **Trendline** Object.

Description   **True** if Microsoft Excel automatically determines the name of the trendline. Read-write.

Example   This example causes Microsoft Excel to automatically determine the name for trendline one in Chart1. The example should be run on a 2-D column chart that contains a single series with a trendline.

```
Charts("Chart1").SeriesCollection(1).Trendlines(1).NameIsAuto = True
```

NameLocal Property

Applies To   **Name** Object, **Style** Object.

Description   Returns or sets the name of the object, in the language of the user. Read-write for **Name**, read-only for **Style**.

Remarks	If the style is a built-in style, this property returns the name of the style in the language of the current locale.
See Also	**Name** Property.
Example	This example displays the name and localized name of style one in the active workbook.

```
With ActiveWorkbook.Styles(1)
    MsgBox "The name of the style is " & .Name
    MsgBox "The localized name of the style is " & .NameLocal
End With
```

Names Collection Object

Description	A collection of all the **Name** objects in the specified or active workbook. Each **Name** object represents a defined name for a range of cells. Names can be built-in, such as Database, Print_Area, and Auto_Open, or they can be custom names.
Accessors	Use the **Names** method with an argument to access a single member of the collection or without an argument to access the entire collection at once.
	Use the **Add** method to create a name and add it to the collection. The *refersTo* argument must be specified in A1-style notation, including dollar signs ($) where appropriate. For example, if cell A10 is selected on sheet1, and you define a name using the *refersTo* argument "=sheet1!A1:B1", the new name actually refers to cells A10:B10 (because you specified a relative reference). To specify an absolute reference, use "=sheet1!$A$1:$B$1".
	The following example creates a new name that refers to cells A1:C20 on the worksheet named "Sheet1."

```
Names.Add "test", "=sheet1!$a$1:$c$20"
```

Properties	**Application** Property, **Count** Property, **Creator** Property, **Parent** Property.
Methods	**Add** Method (**Names** Collection), **Item** Method.

Names Method

Applies To	**Application** Object, **Workbook** Object, **Worksheet** Object.

Description	Accessor. Returns an object that represents a single name (a **Name** object, Syntax 1) or a collection of names (the **Names** object, Syntax 2). Read-only.
Syntax 1	*object*.**Names**(*index*, *indexLocal*, *refersTo*)
Syntax 2	*object*.**Names**

object

 Optional for **Application**, required for **Workbook** and **Worksheet**. Specifies the object containing names to return.

index

 Optional (Syntax 1 requires one of the three arguments). The name or number of the defined name to return.

indexLocal

 Optional (Syntax 1 requires one of the three arguments). The name of the defined name, in the language of the user. No names will be translated if you use this argument.

refersTo

 Optional (Syntax 1 requires one of the three arguments). What the name refers to. This allows you to get a name by what it refers to.

Remarks	For Syntax 1, you must specify one (and only one) of the three arguments.

This method returns worksheet-specific names (names defined with the "WorksheetName!" prefix) for the **Worksheet** object.

This method returns names in the specified workbook (including all worksheet-specific names) for the **Workbook** object, and names in the active workbook for the **Application** object.

Example	This example defines the name myName for cell A1 on Sheet1.

```
ActiveWorkbook.Names.Add Name:="myName", RefersToR1C1:= _
    "=Sheet1!R1C1"
```

This example deletes every defined name that contains "temp" in the name. The `Option Compare Text` statement must be included at the top of any module that contains this example.

```
For Each nm In ActiveWorkbook.Names
    If nm.Name Like "*temp*" Then
        nm.Delete
    End If
Next nm
```

NavigateArrow Method

Applies To   **Range** Object.

Description   Navigates a tracer arrow for the specified range to the precedent, dependent, or error-causing cell or cells. Selects the precedent, dependent, or error cell and returns a **Range** object that represents the new selection. This method causes an error if applied to a cell without visible tracer arrows.

Syntax   *object*.**NavigateArrow**(*towardPrecedent*, *arrowNumber*, *linkNumber*)

object
Required. The **Range** object.

towardPrecedent
Required. Specifies the direction to navigate (**True** to navigate toward precedents or **False** to navigate toward dependents).

arrowNumber
Required. Specifies the arrow number to navigate, corresponding to the numbered reference in the cell's formula.

linkNumber
Optional. If the arrow is an external reference arrow, this argument indicates which external reference to follow. If this argument is omitted, the first external reference is followed.

Example   This example navigates along the first tracer arrow from cell A1 on Sheet1 toward the precedent cell. The example should be run on a worksheet containing a formula in cell A1 that uses cells D1, D2, and D3 (for example, the formula =D1*D2*D3). Before running the example, display the auditing toolbar, select cell A1, and choose the Trace Precedents button.

```
Worksheets("Sheet1").Activate
Range("A1").Select
ActiveCell.NavigateArrow True, 1
```

NetworkTemplatesPath Property

Applies To   **Application** Object.

Description   Returns the network path where templates are stored. If the network path doesn't exist, the property returns an empty string. This property is available only in Microsoft Excel for Windows 95. Read-only.

Example   This example displays the network path where templates are stored.

```
Msgbox Application.NetworkTemplatesPath
```

NewWindow Method

Applies To	**Window** Object, **Workbook** Object.
Description	Creates a new window for the workbook, or a copy of the specified window.
Syntax	*object*.**NewWindow**
	object Required. The **Window** or **Workbook** object.
Example	This example creates a new window for the active workbook.

```
ActiveWorkbook.NewWindow
```

Next Property

Applies To	**Chart** Object, **DialogSheet** Object, **Module** Object, **Range** Object, **Worksheet** Object.
Description	Accessor. Returns a **Chart**, **DialogSheet**, **Module**, **Range** or **Worksheet** object that represents the next sheet or cell. Read-only.
Remarks	If the object is a range, this property emulates the TAB key, although the property returns the next cell without selecting it.
	On a protected sheet, this property returns the next unlocked cell. On an unprotected sheet, this property always returns the cell to the right of the specified cell.
See Also	**ActivateNext** Method, **Previous** Property.
Example	This example selects the next unlocked cell on Sheet1. If Sheet1 is unprotected, this is the cell immediately to the right of the active cell.

```
Worksheets("Sheet1").Activate
ActiveCell.Next.Select
```

NextLetter Method

Applies To	**Application** Object.
Description	Opens the oldest unread Microsoft Excel letter from the In Tray. Available only in Microsoft Excel for the Apple Macintosh with the PowerTalk mail system extension installed.
Syntax	*object*.**NextLetter**

object
   Required. The **Application** object.

Remarks	This method returns a Workbook object for the newly opened workbook, or **Null** if there are no more workbooks to open.

This method generates an error if it is used in Microsoft Windows.

See Also	**MailSystem** Property, **SendMail** Method.
Example	This example opens the oldest unread Microsoft Excel letter from the In Tray.

```
If Application.MailSystem = xlPowerTalk Then _
    Application.NextLetter
```

Not Operator

Description	Used to perform logical negation on an expression.
Syntax	*result* = **Not** *expression*

The **Not** operator syntax has these parts:

Part	Description
result	Any numeric variable.
expression	Any expression.

Remarks The following table illustrates how *result* is determined:

If *expression* is	Then *result* is
True	**False**
False	**True**
Null	**Null**

In addition, the **Not** operator inverts the bit values of any variable and sets the corresponding bit in *result* according to the following truth table:

Bit in *expression*	Bit in *result*
0	1
1	0

See Also   Operator Precedence.

Example   This example uses the **Not** operator to perform logical negation on an expression.

```
A = 10: B = 8: C = 6 : D = Null     ' Initialize variables.
MyCheck = Not(A > B)                 ' Returns False.
MyCheck = Not(B > A)                 ' Returns True.
MyCheck = Not(C > D)                 ' Returns Null.
MyCheck = Not A ' Returns -11 (bit-wise comparison).
```

NoteText Method

Applies To   **Range** Object.

Description   Returns or sets the cell note associated with the upper-left cell in this range. Read-write.

Syntax   *object*.**NoteText**(*text*, *start*, *length*)

object
    Required. The range to which this property applies.

text
    Optional. If specified, contains the text to add to the note (up to 255 characters). The text is inserted starting at position *start*, replacing *length* characters of the existing note. If this argument is omitted, this method returns the current text of the note starting at position *start*, for *length* characters.

start
    Optional. Specifies the starting position for the set or returned text. If omitted, this method starts at the first character. This argument is omitted if there is no existing note. Specify a number larger than the number of characters in the existing note to append text to the note.

length
    Optional. Specifies the number of characters to set or return. If this argument is omitted, Microsoft Excel sets or returns characters from the start position to the end of the note (up to 255 characters) If there are more than 255 characters from *start* to the end of the note, this method returns only 255 characters.

Remarks	To add a note containing more than 255 characters, use this method once to specify the first 255 characters, then append the remainder of the note 255 characters at a time.
See Also	**ClearNotes** Method.
Example	This example sets the cell note text for cell A1 on Sheet1.

```
Worksheets("Sheet1").Range("A1").NoteText "This may change!"
```

Now Function

Description	Returns the current date and time according to the setting of your computer's system date and time.
Syntax	**Now**
Remarks	**Note** When displayed directly, the **Now** function's return value is displayed as a string using the short date and time formats you specified for your system.
See Also	**Date** Function, **Date** Statement, **Day** Function, **Hour** Function, **Minute** Function, **Month** Function, **Second** Function, **Time** Function, **Time** Statement, **Weekday** Function, **Year** Function.
Example	This example uses the **Now** function to return the current system date and time.

```
Today = Now ' Get current system date and time.
```

NumberFormat Property

Applies To	**DataLabel** Object, **DataLabels** Collection, **PivotField** Object, **Range** Object, **Style** Object, **TickLabels** Object.
Description	Returns or sets the format code for the object (as a string). Read-write.
Remarks	For the **PivotField** object, the **NumberFormat** property can be set only for a data field.
	The format code is the same string as the Format Codes option in the Format Cells dialog box. The **Format** function uses different format code strings than the **NumberFormat** and **NumberFormatLocal** properties.

See Also   **NumberFormatLinked** Property, **NumberFormatLocal** Property.

Example   These examples set the number format for cell A17, row one, and column C on Sheet1.

```
Worksheets("Sheet1").Range("A17").NumberFormat = "General"
Worksheets("Sheet1").Rows(1).NumberFormat = "hh:mm:ss"
Worksheets("Sheet1").Columns("C").NumberFormat = _
    "$#,##0.00_);[Red]($#,##0.00)"
```

NumberFormatLinked Property

Applies To   **DataLabel** Object, **DataLabels** Collection, **TickLabels** Object.

Description   **True** if the number format is linked to the cells (so that the number format changes in the labels when it changes in the cells). Read-write.

Example   This example links the tick label number format to its cells for the value axis in Chart1.

```
Charts("Chart1").Axes(xlValue).TickLabels.NumberFormatLinked = True
```

NumberFormatLocal Property

Applies To   **Range** Object, **Style** Object.

Description   Returns or sets the format code for the object as a string, in the language of the user (not the language of the macro writer). Read-write.

Remarks   The **Format** function uses different format code strings than the **NumberFormat** and **NumberFormatLocal** properties.

See Also   **NumberFormat** Property.

Example   This example displays the number format for cell A1 on Sheet1, in the language of the user.

```
MsgBox "The number format for cell A1 is " & _
    Worksheets("Sheet1").Range("A1").NumberFormatLocal
```

Object Data Type

Description   **Object** variables are stored as 32-bit (4-byte) addresses that refer to objects within an application. A variable declared as an **Object** is one that can subsequently be assigned (using the **Set** statement) to refer to any object produced by the application.

See Also   Data Type Summary, **Def***type* Statements, **IsObject** Function, **Variant** Data Type.

Object Property

Applies To   **OLEObject** Object.

Description   Returns the OLE Automation object associated with this OLE object. Read-only.

Example   This example inserts text at the beginning of an embedded Microsoft Word document object on Sheet1. Note that the three statements in the **With** control structure are WordBasic statements.

```
Set wordObj = Worksheets("Sheet1").OLEObjects(1)
wordObj.Activate
With wordObj.Object.Application.WordBasic
    .StartOfDocument
    .Insert "This is the beginning"
    .InsertPara
End With
```

Oct Function

Description   Returns a string representing the octal value of a number.

Syntax   **Oct(***number***)**

The ***number*** named argument is any valid numeric expression.

Remarks

If *number* is not already a whole number, it is rounded to the nearest whole number before being evaluated.

If *number* is	Oct returns
Null	An error.
Empty	Zero (0).
Any other number	Up to 11 octal characters.

You can represent octal numbers directly by preceding numbers in the proper range with &O. For example, &O10 is the octal notation for decimal 8.

See Also

Hex Function.

Example

This example uses the **Oct** function to return the octal value of a number.

```
MyOct = Oct(4)              ' Returns 4.
MyOct = Oct(8)              ' Returns 10.
MyOct = Oct(459)' Returns 713.
```

Offset Method

Applies To

Range Object.

Description

Accessor. Returns a **Range** object that represents a range at an offset to the specified range.

Syntax

object.**Offset**(*rowOffset*, *columnOffset*)

object
> Required. Return a range offset to this one.

rowOffset
> Optional. Number of rows (positive, negative, or zero) by which to offset the range. If omitted, zero is assumed.

columnOffset
> Optional. Number of columns (positive, negative, or zero) by which to offset the range. If omitted, zero is assumed.

See Also

Address Method.

Example

This example activates the cell three columns to the right of and three rows down from the active cell on Sheet1.

```
Worksheets("Sheet1").Activate
ActiveCell.Offset(rowOffset:=3, columnOffset:=3).Activate
```

This example assumes that you have a table on Sheet1 that has a header row. The example selects the table, without selecting the header row. The active cell must be somewhere in the table before you run the example.

```
Set tbl = ActiveCell.CurrentRegion
tbl.Offset(1, 0).Resize(tbl.Rows.Count - 1, tbl.Columns.Count).Select
```

OLEObject Object

Description   Represents a linked or embedded OLE object on a chart sheet, dialog sheet, or worksheet. You add an OLE object to a sheet by clicking the Object command on the Insert menu or by using the **Add** method.

Accessors   The **OLEObject** object is a member of the **OLEObjects** collection. The **OLEObjects** collection contains all of the OLE objects on a single sheet. Use the **Add** method to create a new OLE object and add it to the collection. To access a single member of the collection, use the **OLEObjects** method with the index number or name of the OLE object as an argument.

The following example deletes OLE object one on the worksheet named "Sheet1."

```
Worksheets("sheet1").OLEObjects(1).Delete
```

The OLE object name is shown in the Name Box when the object is selected. Use the **Name** property to set or return the object name. The following example lines up the left edge of the OLE object named "Picture 8" with the left edge of column B on the worksheet named "Sheet1."

```
Worksheets("sheet1").OLEObjects("picture 8").Left = _
    Worksheets("sheet1").Columns("b").Left
```

Properties   **Application** Property, **AutoLoad** Property, **AutoUpdate** Property, **Border** Property, **BottomRightCell** Property, **Creator** Property, **Enabled** Property, **Height** Property, **Index** Property, **Interior** Property, **Left** Property, **Locked** Property, **Name** Property, **Object** Property, **OLEType** Property, **OnAction** Property, **Parent** Property, **Placement** Property, **PrintObject** Property, **Shadow** Property, **Top** Property, **TopLeftCell** Property, **Visible** Property, **Width** Property, **ZOrder** Property.

Methods   **Activate** Method, **BringToFront** Method, **Copy** Method, **CopyPicture** Method, **Cut** Method, **Delete** Method, **Duplicate** Method, **Select** Method, **SendToBack** Method, **Update** Method, **Verb** Method.

OLEObjects Collection Object

Description   A collection of all the **OLEObject** objects on the specified chart sheet, dialog sheet, or worksheet.

Accessors   Use the **OLEObjects** method with an argument to access a single member of the collection or without an argument to access the entire collection at once. Use the **Add** method to create a new OLE object and add it to the collection. The following example creates a new OLE object representing the bitmap file ARCADE.BMP and adds it to worksheet one.

```
Worksheets(1).OLEObjects.Add fileName:="arcade.bmp"
```

Properties   **Application** Property, **Border** Property, **Count** Property, **Creator** Property, **Enabled** Property, **Height** Property, **Interior** Property, **Left** Property, **Locked** Property, **OnAction** Property, **Parent** Property, **Placement** Property, **PrintObject** Property, **Shadow** Property, **Top** Property, **Visible** Property, **Width** Property, **ZOrder** Property.

Methods   **Add** Method (**OLEObjects** Collection), **BringToFront** Method, **Copy** Method, **CopyPicture** Method, **Cut** Method, **Delete** Method, **Duplicate** Method, **Group** Method, **Item** Method, **Select** Method, **SendToBack** Method.

OLEObjects Method

Applies To   **Chart** Object, **DialogSheet** Object, **Worksheet** Object.

Description   Accessor. Returns an object that represents a single OLE Object (an **OLEObject**, Syntax 1) or a collection of all OLE objects (an **OLEObjects** collection, Syntax 2) on the chart or sheet. Read-only.

Syntax 1   *object*.**OLEObjects**(*index*)

Syntax 2   *object*.**OLEObjects**

object
    Required. The **Chart**, **DialogSheet**, or **Worksheet** object.

index
    Required for Syntax 1. The name or number of the OLE object.

See Also   **Charts** Method, **OLEType** Property.

Example

This example creates a list of link types for OLE objects on Sheet1. The list appears on a new worksheet created by the example.

```
Set newSheet = Worksheets.Add
i = 2
newSheet.Range("A1").Value = "Name"
newSheet.Range("B1").Value = "Link Type"
For Each obj In Worksheets("Sheet1").OLEObjects
    newSheet.Cells(i, 1).Value = obj.Name
    If obj.OLEType = xlOLELink Then
        newSheet.Cells(i, 2) = "Linked"
    Else
        newSheet.Cells(i, 2) = "Embedded"
    End If
    i = i + 1
Next
```

OLEType Property

Applies To   **OLEObject** Object.

Description   Returns **xlOLELink** if the object is linked (exists outside of the file), or **xlOLEEmbed** if the object is embedded (is entirely contained within the file). Read-only.

See Also   **OLEObjects** Method.

Example   This example creates a list of link types for OLE objects on Sheet1. The list appears on a new worksheet created by the example.

```
Set newSheet = Worksheets.Add
i = 2
newSheet.Range("A1").Value = "Name"
newSheet.Range("B1").Value = "Link Type"
For Each obj In Worksheets("Sheet1").OLEObjects
    newSheet.Cells(i, 1).Value = obj.Name
    If obj.OLEType = xlOLELink Then
        newSheet.Cells(i, 2) = "Linked"
    Else
        newSheet.Cells(i, 2) = "Embedded"
    End If
    i = i + 1
Next
```

On...GoSub, On...GoTo Statements

Description   Branch to one of several specified lines, depending on the value of an expression.

Syntax   **On** *expression* **GoSub** *destinationlist*

On *expression* **GoTo** *destinationlist*

The **On...GoSub** and **On...GoTo** statement syntax has these parts:

Part	Description
expression	Any numeric expression that evaluates to a whole number between 0 and 255, inclusive. If *expression* is any number other than a whole number, it is rounded before it is evaluated.
destinationlist	List of line numbers or line labels separated by commas.

Remarks   The value of *expression* determines which line in *destinationlist* is branched to. If the value of *expression* is less than 1 or greater than the number of items in the list, one of the following results occurs:

If expression is:	Then
Equal to 0	Control drops to the statement following **On**...**GoSub** or **On**...**GoTo**.
Greater than number of items in list	Control drops to the statement following **On**...**GoSub** or **On**...**GoTo**.
Negative	An error occurs.
Greater than 255	An error occurs.

You can mix line numbers and line labels in the same list. There is no practical limit to the number of line labels and line numbers you can use with **On**...**GoSub** and **On**...**GoTo**. However, if you use more labels or numbers than will fit on a single line, you must use the line-continuation character to continue the logical line onto the next physical line.

Tip **Select Case** provides a more structured and flexible way to perform multiple branching.

See Also   **GoSub**...**Return** Statement, **GoTo** Statement, **Select Case** Statement.

Example
This example uses the **On**...**GoSub** and **On**...**GoTo** statements to branch to subroutines and line labels respectively.

```
Sub OnGosubGotoDemo()
    Number = 2                        ' Initialize variable.
    ' Branch to Sub2.
    On Number GoSub Sub1, Sub2       ' Execution resumes here after
    ' On...GoSub.
    On Number GoTo Line1, Line2      ' Branch to Line2.
    ' Execution does not resume here after On...GoTo.
    Exit Sub
Sub1:
    MyString = "In Sub1" : Return
Sub2:
    MyString = "In Sub2" : Return
Line1:
    MyString = "In Line1"
Line2:
    MyString = "In Line2"
End Sub
```

OnAction Property

Applies To
Arc Object, **Arcs** Collection, **Button** Object, **Buttons** Collection, **ChartObject** Object, **ChartObjects** Collection, **CheckBox** Object, **DialogFrame** Object, **Drawing** Object, **DrawingObjects** Collection, **Drawings** Collection, **DropDown** Object, **DropDowns** Collection, **EditBox** Object, **EditBoxes** Collection, **GroupBox** Object, **GroupBoxes** Collection, **GroupObject** Object, **GroupObjects** Collection, **Label** Object, **Labels** Collection, **Line** Object, **Lines** Collection, **ListBox** Object, **ListBoxes** Collection, **MenuItem** Object, **OLEObject** Object, **OLEObjects** Collection, **OptionButton** Object, **OptionButtons** Collection, **Oval** Object, **Ovals** Collection, **Picture** Object, **Pictures** Collection, **Rectangle** Object, **Rectangles** Collection, **ScrollBar** Object, **ScrollBars** Collection, **Spinner** Object, **Spinners** Collection, **TextBox** Object, **TextBoxes** Collection, **ToolbarButton** Object.

Description
Returns or sets the name of a macro that runs when the object is clicked. Read-write.

Remarks
Setting this property for a menu item overrides any custom help information set up for the menu item with the information set up for the assigned macro.

This property cannot be used with a toolbar button that is a gap or that has a palette or list attached (such as the Font or Style buttons).

See Also
Add Method, **Help** Method, **MacroOptions** Method, **StatusBar** Property.

Example   This example replaces the built-in function of the Print button (button five on the Standard toolbar) with the my_Print_Macro procedure.

```
ToolBars("Standard").ToolbarButtons(5).OnAction = "my_Print_Macro"
```

This example restores the built-in function of the Print button (button five on the Standard toolbar).

```
ToolBars("Standard").ToolbarButtons(5).OnAction = ""
```

OnCalculate Property

Applies To   **Application** Object, **Worksheet** Object.

Description   Returns or sets the name of the macro that runs whenever you recalculate the worksheet. Read-write.

Remarks   Setting this property for a worksheet overrides any macro that may be set for the application.

Set this property to empty text ("") to remove the macro.

A macro set to run by the **OnCalculate** property is not run by actions taken by other macros. For example, a macro set by **OnCalculate** will not run if a macro calls the **Calculate** method, but will be run if you change data in a sheet set to calculate automatically or choose the Calc Now button.

Example   This example causes "my_Recalc_Macro" to run when you recalculate Sheet1.

```
Worksheets("Sheet1").OnCalculate = "my_Recalc_Macro"
```

This example disables the **OnCalculate** macro for Sheet1.

```
Worksheets("Sheet1").OnCalculate = ""
```

OnData Property

Applies To	**Application** Object, **Worksheet** Object.
Description	Returns or sets the name of the procedure that runs when DDE- or OLE-linked data arrives in Microsoft Excel. The specified procedure runs only when data arrives from another application. Read-write.
Remarks	Set this property to empty text ("") to remove the procedure.
Example	This example runs my_Worksheet_Data_Handler if data arrives on Sheet1.

```
Worksheets("Sheet1").OnData = "my_Worksheet_Data_Handler"
```

This example disables the **OnData** procedure for Sheet1.

```
Worksheets("Sheet1").OnData = ""
```

OnDoubleClick Property

Applies To	**Application** Object, **Chart** Object, **DialogSheet** Object, **Module** Object, **Worksheet** Object.
Description	Returns or sets the name of the macro that runs whenever you double-click anywhere on the sheet. Read-write.
Remarks	Setting this property has no effect on a module.
	Setting this property for a sheet overrides any macro that may be set for the application.
	On a dialog sheet, you must double-click the border of a selected drawing object or control to call the macro assigned by this property.
	This property overrides normal double-click behavior in Microsoft Excel, such as editing data in a cell or displaying a formatting dialog box.
	Set this property to empty text ("") to remove the macro.
See Also	**DoubleClick** Method.
Example	This example causes Microsoft Excel to run the macro named "my_DblClick_Macro" when you double-click anywhere on Sheet1.

```
Worksheets("Sheet1").OnDoubleClick = "my_DblClick_Macro"
```

This example removes the **OnDoubleClick** macro.

```
Worksheets("Sheet1").OnDoubleClick = ""
```

OnEntry Property

Applies To	**Application** Object, **Worksheet** Object.
Description	Returns or sets the name of the procedure that runs when you enter data using the formula bar or when you edit data in a cell. Read-write.
Remarks	The procedure does not run when you use edit commands or macro functions.
	Set this property to empty text ("") to remove the procedure.
	To determine which cell had data entered in it, use the **Caller** property.
Example	This example runs my_Worksheet_Entry_Procedure when data is entered on Sheet1.

```
Worksheets("Sheet1").OnEntry = "my_Worksheet_Entry_Procedure"
```

This example disables the **OnEntry** procedure for Sheet1.

```
Worksheets("Sheet1").OnEntry = ""
```

On Error Statement

Description	Enables an error-handling routine and specifies the location of the routine within a procedure; can also be used to disable an error-handling routine.
Syntax	**On Error GoTo** *line*
	On Error Resume Next
	On Error GoTo 0

The **On Error** statement syntax can have any of the following forms:

Statement	Description
On Error GoTo *line*	Enables the error-handling routine that starts at *line*, which is any line label or line number. Thereafter, if a run-time error occurs, control branches to *line*. The specified *line* must be in the same procedure as the **On Error** statement. If it isn't, a compile-time error occurs.
On Error Resume Next	Specifies that when a run-time error occurs, control goes to the statement immediately following the statement where the error occurred. In other words, execution continues.
On Error GoTo 0	Disables any enabled error handler in the current procedure.

Remarks

If you don't use an **On Error** statement, any run-time error that occurs is fatal; that is, an error message is generated and execution stops.

If an error occurs while an error handler is active (between the occurrence of the error and a **Resume**, **Exit Sub**, **Exit Function**, or **Exit Property** statement), the current procedure's error handler can't handle the error. If the calling procedure has an enabled error handler, control is returned to the calling procedure and its error handler is activated to handle the error. If the calling procedure's error handler is also active, control is passed back through any previous calling procedures until an inactive error handler is found. If no inactive error handler is found, the error is fatal at the point at which it actually occurred. Each time the error handler passes control back to the calling procedure, that procedure becomes the current procedure. Once an error is handled by an error handler in any procedure, execution resumes in the current procedure at the point designated by the **Resume** statement.

Notice that an error-handling routine is not a **Sub** or **Function** procedure. It is a block of code marked by a line label or line number.

Error-handling routines rely on the value in **Err** to determine the cause of the error. The error-handling routine should test or save this value before any other error can occur or before a procedure that could cause an error is called. The value in **Err** reflects only the most recent error. You can use the **Error** function to return the error message associated with any given run-time error number returned by **Err**.

On Error Resume Next causes execution to continue with the statement immediately following the statement that caused the run-time error, or with the statement immediately following the most recent call out of the procedure containing the error-handling routine. This allows execution to continue despite a run-time error. You can then build the error-handling routine in line with the procedure rather than transferring control to another location within the procedure.

On Error GoTo 0 disables error handling in the current procedure. It doesn't specify line 0 as the start of the error-handling code, even if the procedure contains a line numbered 0. Without an **On Error GoTo 0** statement, an error handler is automatically disabled when a procedure is exited.

To prevent error-handling code from running when no error has occurred, place an **Exit Sub**, **Exit Function**, or **Exit Property** statement, as appropriate, immediately ahead of the error-handling routine, as in the following example:

```
Sub InitializeMatrix(Var1, Var2, Var3, Var4)
    On Error GoTo ErrorHandler
    . . .
    Exit Sub
ErrorHandler:
    . . .
    Resume Next
End Sub
```

Here, the error-handling code follows the **Exit Sub** statement and precedes the **End Sub** statement to separate it from the normal procedure flow. This is only one possible solution; error-handling code can be placed anywhere in a procedure.

See Also   **Err** Function, **Error** Function, **Resume** Statement.

Example   This example uses the **On Error GoTo** statement to specify the location of an error-handling routine within a procedure. Attempting to delete an open file generates error number 55. The error is handled in the error-handling routine and control is then returned to the statement that caused it.

```
Sub OnErrorStatementDemo()
    On Error GoTo ErrorHandler  ' Enable error-handling routine.
    Open "TESTFILE" For Output as #1 ' Open file for output.
    Kill "TESTFILE" ' Attempt to delete open file.
    Exit Sub' Exit Sub before error handler.
ErrorHandler:    ' Error-handling routine.
    Select Case Err ' Evaluate Error Number.
        Case 55 ' "File already open" error.
            Close #1' Close open file.
        Case Else
            ' Handle other situations here...
    End Select
    Resume   ' Resume execution at same line
             ' that caused the error.
End Sub
```

OnKey Method

Applies To	**Application** Object.
Description	Runs a specified procedure when a particular key or key combination is pressed.
Syntax	*object*.**OnKey**(*key*, *procedure*)

object
> Required. The **Application** object.

key
> Required. A string indicating the keystroke.

procedure
> Optional. A string indicating the name of the procedure. If *procedure* is """
> (empty text), nothing happens when *key* is pressed. This form of **OnKey**
> disables the normal meaning of keystrokes in Microsoft Excel. If *procedure* is
> omitted, *key* reverts to its normal meaning in Microsoft Excel, and any special
> key assignments made with previous **OnKey** methods are cleared.

Remarks

The *key* argument can specify any single key; any key combined with ALT, CTRL,
or SHIFT, or any combination of those keys (in Windows); or COMMAND, CTRL,
OPTION, or SHIFT, or any combination of those keys (on the Macintosh). Each key
is represented by one or more characters, such as "a" for the character a, or
"{ENTER}" for the ENTER key.

To specify characters that aren't displayed when you press the key, such as ENTER
or TAB, use the codes shown in the following table. Each code in the table
represents one key on the keyboard.

Key	Code
BACKSPACE	"{BACKSPACE}" or "{BS}"
BREAK	"{BREAK}"
CAPS LOCK	"{CAPSLOCK}"
CLEAR	"{CLEAR}"
DELETE or DEL	"{DELETE}" or "{DEL}"
DOWN ARROW	"{DOWN}"
END	"{END}"
ENTER (numeric keypad)	"{ENTER}"
ENTER	"~" (tilde)
ESC	"{ESCAPE} or {ESC}"
HELP	"{HELP}"

Key	Code
HOME	"{HOME}"
INS	"{INSERT}"
LEFT ARROW	"{LEFT}"
NUM LOCK	"{NUMLOCK}"
PAGE DOWN	"{PGDN}"
PAGE UP	"{PGUP}"
RETURN	"{RETURN}"
RIGHT ARROW	"{RIGHT}"
SCROLL LOCK	"{SCROLLLOCK}"
TAB	"{TAB}"
UP ARROW	"{UP}"
F1 through F15	"{F1}" through "{F15}"

In Windows, you can also specify keys combined with SHIFT and/or CTRL and/or ALT. On the Macintosh, you can also specify keys combined with SHIFT and/or CTRL and/or OPTION and/or COMMAND. To specify a key combined with another key or keys, use the following table.

To combine with	Precede the key code by
SHIFT	"+" (plus sign)
CTRL	"^" (caret)
ALT or OPTION	"%" (percent sign)
COMMAND	"*" (asterisk)

To assign a procedure to one of the special characters (+, ^, %, and so on), enclose the character in braces. See the example for details.

Example   This example assigns my_InsertItem_Procedure to the key sequence CTRL+PLUS SIGN and assigns my_SpecialPrint_Procedure to the key sequence SHIFT+CTRL+RIGHT ARROW.

```
Application.OnKey "^{+}", "my_InsertItem_Procedure"
Application.OnKey "+^{RIGHT}", "my_SpecialPrint_Procedure"
```

This example returns SHIFT+CTRL+RIGHT ARROW to its normal meaning.

```
Application.OnKey "+^{RIGHT}"
```

This example disables the SHIFT+CTRL+RIGHT ARROW key sequence.

```
Application.OnKey "+^{RIGHT}", ""
```

OnRepeat Method

Applies To	**Application** Object.
Description	Sets the Repeat menu item and the name of the procedure that will run if you choose Repeat from the Edit menu after running the procedure that sets this property.
Syntax	*object*.**OnRepeat**(*text*, *procedure*)

object
Required. The **Application** object.

text
Required. Specifies the text that appears with the Repeat command (Edit menu).

procedure
Required. Specifies the name of the procedure that will run when you choose Repeat from the Edit menu.

Remarks	If a procedure does not use the **OnRepeat** method, the Repeat command repeats the most recently run procedure.
	The procedure must use the **OnRepeat** and **OnUndo** methods last, to prevent the repeat or undo procedures from being overwritten by subsequent actions in the procedure.
See Also	**OnUndo** Method, **Repeat** Method.
Example	This example sets the repeat and undo procedures.

```
Application.OnRepeat "Repeat VB Procedure", _
    "Book1.xls!My_Repeat_Sub"
Application.OnUndo "Undo VB Procedure", _
    "Book1.xls!My_Undo_Sub"
```

OnSave Property

Applies To	**Workbook** Object.
Description	Returns or sets the name of a Visual Basic procedure to run after the user invokes either the Save or Save As command but before the workbook is actually saved. This property is available only in Microsoft Excel for Windows 95. Read-write.
Remarks	The procedure you specify must take one Boolean argument.

Only Visual Basic procedures are supported. Microsoft Excel 4.0 Macro Language procedures aren't supported.

The value of this property isn't saved with the workbook; it must be reset each time the workbook is opened.

This event isn't called if the workbook is saved when a macro or mail command runs, when an embedded workbook is updated, or when an unsaved workbook is saved as part of a workbook that's being closed.

Example

This example displays a message box after the user invokes either the Save or Save As command but before the workbook is saved.

```
' Specifies the procedure to run when the workbook is saved
Sub SetSaveEvent()
    ActiveWorkbook.OnSave = "SaveProcedure"
End Sub

Sub SaveProcedure(s As Boolean)
    MsgBox "Excel will now save your work"
End Sub
```

OnSheetActivate Property

Applies To

Application Object, **Chart** Object, **DialogSheet** Object, **Module** Object, **Workbook** Object, **Worksheet** Object.

Description

Returns or sets the name of the macro that runs when the user activates the specified sheet (**Chart**, **DialogSheet**, **Module**, or **Worksheet** object), any sheet in the specified workbook (**Workbook** object), or any sheet in any open workbook (**Application** object). Read-write.

Remarks

To disable an **OnSheetActivate** macro, set the property to an empty string, as shown in the examples.

See Also

OnSheetDeactivate Property, **OnWindow** Property, **RunAutoMacros** Method.

Example

This example sets the **OnSheetActivate** property to the macro "my_Activate_Sub" in Module1 in the active workbook. This macro will run whenever the user activates a sheet in any workbook.

```
Application.OnSheetActivate = ActiveWorkbook.Name & _
    "!Module1.my_Activate_Sub"
```

This example removes the **OnSheetActivate** macro.

```
Application.OnSheetActivate = ""
```

OnSheetDeactivate Property

Applies To	**Application** Object, **Chart** Object, **DialogSheet** Object, **Module** Object, **Workbook** Object, **Worksheet** Object.
Description	Returns or sets the name of the macro that runs when the user deactivates the specified sheet (**Chart**, **DialogSheet**, **Module**, or **Worksheet** object), any sheet in the specified workbook (**Workbook** object), or any sheet in any open workbook (**Application** object). Read-write.
See Also	**OnSheetActivate** Property, **OnWindow** Property, **RunAutoMacros** Method.
Example	This example sets the **OnSheetDeactivate** property to the macro "my_Deactivate_Sub" in Module1 in the active workbook. This macro will run whenever the user deactivates a sheet in any workbook.

```
Application.OnSheetDeactivate = ActiveWorkbook.Name & _
    "!Module1.my_Deactivate_Sub"
```

This example removes the **OnSheetDeactivate** macro.

```
Application.OnSheetDeactivate = ""
```

OnTime Method

Applies To	**Application** Object.
Description	Schedules a procedure to run at a specified time in the future (either at a specific time of day or after a specific period has passed).
Syntax	*object*.**OnTime**(*earliestTime*, *procedure*, *latestTime*, *schedule*)

object
   Required. The **Application** object.

earliestTime
   Required. The time when you want this procedure to run.

procedure
   Required. The name of the procedure to run.

latestTime
> Optional. The latest time the procedure can be run. For example, if *latestTime* is set to *earliestTime* + 30 and Microsoft Excel is not in Ready, Copy, Cut, or Find mode at *earliestTime* because another procedure is running, Microsoft Excel will wait 30 seconds for the first procedure to complete. If Microsoft Excel is not in Ready mode within 30 seconds, the procedure will not run. If this argument is omitted, Microsoft Excel will wait until the procedure can be run.

schedule
> Optional. **False** to clear a previously set **OnTime** procedure. **True** (or omitted) to schedule a new procedure.

Remarks   Use `Now + TimeValue(time)` to schedule something at a time after the current time. Use `TimeValue(time)` to schedule something at a specific time.

Example   This example runs my_Procedure 15 seconds from now.

```
Application.OnTime Now + TimeValue("00:00:15"), "my_Procedure"
```

This example runs my_Procedure at 5 P.M.

```
Application.OnTime TimeValue("17:00:00"), "my_Procedure"
```

This example cancels the **OnTime** setting from the previous example.

```
Application.OnTime TimeValue("17:00:00"), "my_Procedure",,False
```

OnUndo Method

Applies To   **Application** Object.

Description   Sets the Undo menu item and the name of the procedure that will run if you choose Undo from the Edit menu after running the procedure that sets this property.

Syntax   *object*.**OnUndo**(*text*, *procedure*)

object
> Required. The **Application** object.

text
> Required. Specifies the text that appears with the Undo command (Edit menu).

procedure
> Required. Specifies the name of the procedure that runs when you choose Undo from the Edit menu.

Remarks   If a procedure does not use the **OnUndo** method, the Undo command is disabled.

The procedure must use the **OnRepeat** and **OnUndo** methods last, to prevent the repeat or undo procedures from being overwritten by subsequent actions in the procedure.

See Also   **OnRepeat** Method, **Repeat** Method.

Example   This example sets the repeat and undo procedures.

```
Application.OnRepeat "Repeat VB Procedure", _
    "Book1.xls!My_Repeat_Sub"
Application.OnUndo "Undo VB Procedure", _
    "Book1.xls!My_Undo_Sub"
```

OnWindow Property

Applies To   **Application** Object, **Window** Object.

Description   Returns or sets the name of the procedure that runs whenever you switch to a window. Read-write.

Remarks   The procedure specified by this property does not run when other procedures switch to the window or when a command to switch to a window is received through a DDE channel. Instead, the procedure responds to a user's actions, such as clicking a window with the mouse, choosing the Go To command from the Edit menu, and so on.

If a worksheet or macro sheet has an Auto_Activate or Auto_Deactivate macro defined for it, those macros will be run after the procedure specified by **OnWindow**.

Example   This example runs my_Stock_Procedure when the user switches to the STOCKS.XLS window from another workbook window.

```
Application.Windows("STOCKS.XLS").OnWindow = "my_Stock_Procedure"
```

This example disables the **OnWindow** procedure for the STOCKS.XLS window.

```
Application.Windows("STOCKS.XLS").OnWindow = ""
```

Open Method

Applies To   **Workbooks** Collection.

Description	Opens a workbook.
Syntax	*object*.**Open**(*fileName*, *updateLinks*, *readOnly*, *format*, *password*, *writeResPassword*, *ignoreReadOnlyRecommended*, *origin*, *delimiter*, *editable*, *notify*, *converter*)

object
Required. The **Workbooks** object.

fileName
Required. Specifies the filename of the workbook to open.

updateLinks
Optional. Specifies how links in the file are updated. If this argument is omitted, the user is prompted to determine how to update links. Otherwise, this argument is one of the values shown in the following table.

Value	Meaning
0	No updates
1	Updates external but not remote references
2	Updates remote but not external references
3	Updates both remote and external references

If Microsoft Excel is opening a file in the WKS, WK1, or WK3 format and the *updateLinks* argument is 2, Microsoft Excel generates charts from the graphs attached to the file. If the argument is 0, no charts are created.

readOnly
Optional. If **True**, the workbook is opened in read-only mode.

format
Optional. If Microsoft Excel is opening a text file, this argument specifies the delimiter character, as shown in the following table. If this argument is omitted, the current delimiter is used.

Value	Delimiter
1	Tabs
2	Commas
3	Spaces
4	Semicolons
5	Nothing
6	Custom character, see the *delimiter* argument.

password
Optional. A string containing the password required to open a protected workbook. If omitted and the workbook requires a password, the user is prompted for the password.

writeResPassword

Optional. A string containing the password required to write to a write-reserved workbook. If omitted and the workbook requires a password, the user will be prompted for the password.

ignoreReadOnlyRecommended

Optional. If **True** and the workbook was saved with the Read-Only Recommended option, Microsoft Excel does not display the read-only recommended message.

origin

Optional. If the file is a text file, this indicates where it originated (so that code pages and CR/LF can be mapped correctly). May be one of **xlMacintosh**, **xlWindows**, or **xlMSDOS**. If this argument is omitted, the current operating system is used.

delimiter

Optional. If the file is a text file and the *format* argument is 6, this is a string that specifies the character to use as the delimiter. For example, Chr(9) for tabs, "," for commas, ";" for semicolons, or a custom character. Only the first character of the string is used.

editable

Optional. If the file is a Microsoft Excel 4.0 add-in, using **True** opens the add-in so that it is a visible window. If **False** or omitted, the add-in is opened hidden and it cannot be unhidden. This option does not apply for add-ins created in Microsoft Excel 5.0 or later. If the file is not an add-in, specifying **True** prevents the running of any Auto_Open macros.

notify

Optional. If the file cannot be opened in the read-write mode, specifying **True** adds the file to the file notification list. Microsoft Excel will open the file read-only, poll the file notification list, and then notify the user when the file becomes available. If this argument is **False** or omitted, no notification is requested, and attempts to open an unavailable file will fail.

converter

Optional. Specifies the index of the first file converter to try when opening the file. The specified file converter is tried first, then all other converters are tried if the specified converter does not recognize the file. The converter index is the row number of the converters returned by the **FileConverters** property.

Remarks

If the workbook being opened has any Auto_Open macros in it, they will not be run when you open the file from Visual Basic. If you want to run the Auto_Open macro, you must use the **RunAutoMacros** method.

See Also

Activate Method, **Close** Method, **FileConverters** Property, **OpenText** Method.

Example   This example opens the workbook ANALYSIS.XLS and then runs its Auto_Open macro.

```
Workbooks.Open "ANALYSIS.XLS"
ActiveWorkbook.RunAutoMacros xlAutoOpen
```

Open Statement

Description   Enables input/output (I/O) to a file.

Syntax   **Open** *pathname* [**For** *mode*] [**Access** *access*] [*lock*] **As** [#]*filenumber*
                   [**Len**=*reclength*]

                   The **Open** statement syntax has these parts:

Part	Description
pathname	String expression that specifies a file name—may include directory or folder, and drive.
mode	Keyword specifying the file mode: **Append**, **Binary**, **Input**, **Output**, or **Random**.
access	Keyword specifying the operations permitted on the open file: **Read**, **Write**, or **Read Write**.
lock	Keyword specifying the operations permitted on the open file by other processes: **Shared**, **Lock Read**, **Lock Write**, **Lock Read Write**.
filenumber	A valid file number in the range 1 to 511, inclusive. Use the **FreeFile** function to obtain the next available file number.
reclength	Number less than or equal to 32,767 (bytes). For files opened for random access, this value is the record length. For sequential files, this value is the number of characters buffered.

Remarks   You must open a file before any I/O operation can be performed on it. **Open**
                   allocates a buffer for I/O to the file and determines the mode of access to use with
                   the buffer.

                   If the file specified by *pathname* doesn't exist, it is created when a file is opened for
                   Append, **Binary**, **Output**, or **Random** modes.

                   If the file is already opened by another process and the specified type of access is
                   not allowed, the **Open** operation fails and an error occurs.

The **Len** clause is ignored if *mode* is **Binary**.

Important In **Binary**, **Input**, and **Random** modes, you can open a file using a different file number without first closing the file. In **Append** and **Output** modes, you must close a file before opening it with a different file number.

On the Macintosh, the file mode specified in the **Open** statement determines the initial **Creator** and **Type** property settings:

File mode	Creator	Type
Output	????	TEXT
Append	????	TEXT
Random	????	OBIN
Binary	????	OBIN
Unspecified	????	OBIN

See Also   **Close** Statement, **FreeFile** Function.

Example   This example illustrates various uses of the **Open** statement to enable input/output to a file.

```
' Open in sequential-input mode.
Open "TESTFILE" For Input As #1

' Open in binary-file mode for writing operations only.
Open "TESTFILE" For Binary Access Write As #1

' Open file in random-access mode. The file contains records of the
' user-defined type Record.
Type Record                         ' Define user-defined type.
    ID As Integer
    Name As String * 20
End Type
Dim MyRecord As Record              ' Declare variable.
Open "TESTFILE" For Random As #1 Len = Len(MyRecord)

' Open for sequential output; any process can read/write to file.
Open "TESTFILE" For Output Shared As #1

' Open in binary-file mode for reading; other processes can't read
' file.
Open "TESTFILE" For Binary Access Read Lock Read As #1
```

OpenLinks Method

Applies To   **Workbook** Object.

Description   Opens the supporting documents for a link or links.

Syntax   *object*.**OpenLinks**(*name*, *readOnly*, *type*)

object
Required. The **Workbook** object.

name
Required. Specifies the name of the Microsoft Excel or DDE/OLE link, as returned from the **LinkSources** method (can be an array of names to specify more than one link).

readOnly
Optional. **True** if the documents are opened read-only. **False** if omitted.

type
Optional. Specifies the link type. Can be one of **xlExcelLinks**, **xlOLELinks** (also handles DDE links), **xlPublishers**, or **xlSubscribers**. **xlExcelLinks** if omitted.

Example   This example opens OLE link one in the active workbook.

```
linkArray = ActiveWorkbook.LinkSources(xlOLELinks)
ActiveWorkbook.OpenLinks linkArray(1)
```

This example opens all supporting Microsoft Excel documents for the active workbook.

```
ActiveWorkbook.OpenLinks _
    name:=ActiveWorkbook.LinkSources(xlExcelLinks)
```

OpenText Method

Applies To   **Workbooks** Collection.

Description   Loads and parses a text file as a new workbook with a single sheet containing the parsed text-file data.

Syntax   *object*.**OpenText**(*filename*, *origin*, *startRow*, *dataType*, *textQualifier*, *consecutiveDelimiter*, *tab*, *semicolon*, *comma*, *space*, *other*, *otherChar*, *fieldInfo*)

object
> Required. The **Workbooks** object.

filename
> Required. Specifies the filename of the text file to open and parse.

origin
> Optional. Specifies the origin of the text file (one of **xlMacintosh**, **xlWindows**, or **xlMSDOS**). If this argument is omitted, the method uses the current setting in the File Origin option of the Text Import Wizard.

startRow
> Optional. The row number at which to start parsing text. The first row is 1. If omitted, 1 is assumed.

dataType
> Optional. Specifies the column format of the data within the file (either **xlDelimited** or **xlFixedWidth**). The default is **xlDelimited**.

textQualifier
> Optional. Specifies the text qualifier. Can be one of **xlDoubleQuote**, **xlSingleQuote**, or **xlNone**. The default is **xlDoubleQuote**.

consecutiveDelimiter
> Optional. **True** if consecutive delimiters should be considered as one delimiter. The default is **False**.

tab
> Optional. **True** if *dataType* is **xlDelimited** and the tab character is a delimiter. The default is **False**.

semicolon
> Optional. True if *dataType* is xlDelimited and the semicolon character is a delimiter. The default is False.

comma
> Optional. True if *dataType* is xlDelimited and the comma character is a delimiter. The default is False.

space
> Optional. True if *dataType* is xlDelimited and the space character is a delimiter. The default is False.

other
> Optional. **True** if *dataType* is **xlDelimited** and the character specified by the *otherChar* argument is a delimiter. The default is **False**.

otherChar
> Optional (required if *other* is **True**). Specifies the delimiter character when *other* is True. If more than one character is specified, only the first character of the string is used, remaining characters are ignored.

fieldInfo

Optional. An array containing parse information for the individual columns of data. The interpretation depends on the value of *dataType*.

When the data is delimited, this argument is an array of two-element arrays, with each two-element array specifying the conversion options for a particular column. The first element is the column number (one based), and the second element is one of the following numbers specifying how the column in parsed:

1   General

2   Text

3   MDY date

4   DMY date

5   YMD date

6   MYD date

7   DYM date

8   YDM date

9   Skip the column

The column specifiers may be in any order. If a column specifier is not present for a particular column in the input data, the column is parsed using the General setting. This example causes the third column to be skipped, the first column to be parsed as text, and the remaining columns in the source data to be parsed with the General setting.

```
Array(Array(3, 9), Array(1, 2))
```

If the source data has fixed-width columns, the first element of each two-element array specifies the starting character position in the column (as an integer; character zero is the first character). The second element of the two-element array specifies the parse option for the column as a number from one through nine, as listed above.

The following example parses two columns from a fixed-width text file. The first column includes characters 1 through 10. Characters 11, 12, 13, 14, and 15 are skipped. The second column includes characters 16 through the last character in the line.

```
Array(Array(0, 1), Array(10, 9), Array(15, 1))
```

See Also

Close Method, **Open** Method, **TextToColumns** Method.

Example

This example opens the file DATA.TXT and uses tab delimiters to parse the text file into a worksheet.

```
Workbooks.OpenText filename:="DATA.TXT", _
    dataType:=xlDelimited, tab:=True
```

OperatingSystem Property

Applies To   **Application** Object.

Description   Returns the name and version number of the current operating system. For example, "Windows 3.10" or "Macintosh 7.00". Read-only.

Example   This example displays the name of the operating system.

```
MsgBox "Microsoft Excel is using " & Application.OperatingSystem
```

Operator Precedence

When several operations occur in an expression, each part is evaluated and resolved in a predetermined order. That order is known as operator precedence. Parentheses can be used to override the order of precedence and force some parts of an expression to be evaluated before others. Operations within parentheses are always performed before those outside. Within parentheses, however, normal operator precedence is maintained.

When expressions contain operators from more than one category, arithmetic operators are evaluated first, comparison operators are evaluated next, and logical operators are evaluated last. Comparison operators all have equal precedence; that is, they are evaluated in the left to right order in which they appear. Arithmetic and logical operators are evaluated in the following order of precedence:

Arithmetic	Comparison	Logical
Exponentiation (^)	Equality (=)	**Not**
Negation (-)	Inequality (<>)	**And**
Multiplication and division (*,/)	Less than (<)	**Or**
Integer division (\)	Greater than (>)	**Xor**
Modulo arithmetic (**Mod**)	Less than or Equal to (<=)	**Eqv**
Addition and subtraction (+,-)	Greater than or Equal to (>=)	**Imp**
String concatenation (**&**)	**Like**	**Is**

When multiplication and division occur together in an expression, each operation is evaluated as it occurs from left to right. Likewise, when addition and subtraction occur together in an expression, each operation is evaluated in order of appearance from left to right.

The string concatenation operator (**&**) is not really an arithmetic operator, but in precedence it does fall after all arithmetic operators and before all comparison operators. Similarly, the **Like** operator, while equal in precedence to all comparison operators, is actually a pattern-matching operator. The **Is** operator is an object reference comparison operator. It does not compare objects or their values; it checks only to determine if two object references refer to the same object.

Arithmetic Operators

^ Operator

* Operator

/ Operator

\ Operator

Mod Operator

+ Operator

- Operator

Concatenation Operators

& Operator

+ Operator

Logical Operators

And Operator

Eqv Operator

Imp Operator

Not Operator

Or Operator

Xor Operator

Option Base Statement

Description   Used at module level to declare the default lower bound for array subscripts.

Syntax   **Option Base {0 | 1}**

Remarks   If used, the **Option Base** statement must appear in a module before any statements that declare variables or define constants.

Since the default base is **0**, the **Option Base** statement is never required. However, if used, it can appear only once in a module and must precede array declarations that include dimensions.

The **Option Base** statement has no effect on arrays within user-defined types for which the lower bound is always 0.

Tip The **To** clause in the **Dim**, **Private**, **Public**, **ReDim**, and **Static** statements provides a more flexible way to control the range of an array's subscripts. However, if you don't explicitly set the lower bound with a **To** clause, you can use **Option Base** to change the default lower bound to 1.

The **Option Base** statement only affects the lower bound of arrays in the module where the statement is located.

See Also   **Dim** Statement, **LBound** Function, **Option Compare** Statement, **Option Explicit** Statement, **Option Private** Statement, **Private** Statement, **Public** Statement, **ReDim** Statement, **Static** Statement.

Example   This example uses the **Option Base** statement to override the default base array subscript value of 0. The **LBound** function returns the smallest available subscript for the indicated dimension of an array. The **Option Base** statement is used at the module-level only.

```
' Set default array subscripts to 1.
Option Base 1

Dim MyArray(20), TwoDArray(3,4)     ' Declare array variables.
Dim ZeroArray(0 To 5)               ' Override default base subscript.
' Use LBound function to test lower bounds of arrays.
Lower = LBound(MyArray)             ' Returns 1.
Lower = LBound(TwoDArray, 2)        ' Returns 1.
Lower = LBound(ZeroArray)    ' Returns 0.
```

Option Compare Statement

Description   Used at module level to declare the default comparison mode to use when string data is compared.

Syntax   **Option Compare {Binary | Text}**

Remarks   If used, the **Option Compare** statement must appear in a module before any statements that declare variables or define constants.

The **Option Compare** statement specifies the string comparison method (**Binary** or **Text**) for a module. If a module doesn't include an **Option Compare** statement, the default text comparison method is **Binary**.

Option Compare Binary results in string comparisons based on a sort order derived from the internal binary representations of the characters. In Microsoft Windows, sort order is determined by the code page. On the Macintosh, sort order is determined by the character set. In the following example, a typical binary sort order is shown:

```
A < B < E < Z < a < b < e  < z < À < Ê < Ø < à < ê < ø
```

Option Compare Text results in string comparisons based on a case-insensitive textual sort order determined by your system's locale. The same characters shown above, when sorted using **Option Compare Text**, produce the following text sort order:

```
(A=a) < ( À=à)  < (B=b) < (E=e) < (Ê=ê) < (Z=z) < (Ø=ø)
```

See Also

Comparison Operators, **InStr** Function, **Option Base** Statement, **Option Explicit** Statement, **Option Private** Statement, **StrComp** Function.

Example

This example uses the **Option Compare** statement to set the default string comparison mode. The **Option Compare** statement is used at the module-level only.

```
' Set the string comparison method to Binary.
Option Compare Binary              ' i.e. "AAA" less than "aaa"
' Set the string comparison method to Text.
Option Compare Text ' i.e. "AAA" equal to "aaa".
```

Option Explicit Statement

Description

Used at module level to force explicit declaration of all variables in that module.

Syntax

Option Explicit

Remarks

If used, the **Option Explicit** statement must appear in a module before any statements that declare variables or define constants.

If you don't use the **Option Explicit** statement, all undeclared variables are **Variant** unless the default type is otherwise specified with a **Def***type* statement.

When you use the **Option Explicit** statement, you must explicitly declare all variables using the **Dim**, **Private**, **Public**, **ReDim**, or **Static** statements. If you attempt to use an undeclared variable name, an error occurs at compile time.

Tip Use **Option Explicit** to avoid incorrectly typing the name of an existing variable or to avoid risking confusion in code where the scope of the variable is not clear.

See Also **Const** Statement, **Deftype** Statements, **Dim** Statement, **Function** Statement, **Option Base** Statement, **Option Compare** Statement, **Option Private** Statement, **Private** Statement, **Public** Statement, **ReDim** Statement, **Static** Statement, **Sub** Statement.

Example This example uses the **Option Explicit** statement to force you to explicitly declare all variables. Attempting to use an undeclared variable gives you an error at compile time. The **Option Explicit** statement is used at the module-level only.

```
Option Explicit            ' Force explicit variable declaration.
Dim MyVar                  ' Declare variable.
MyInt = 10                 ' Undeclared variable generates error.
MyVar = 10  ' Will not generate error.
```

Option Private Statement

Description Used at module level to indicate that an entire module is **Private**.

Syntax **Option Private Module**

Remarks If used, the **Option Private** statement must appear in a module before any statements that declare variables or define constants.

The public parts (variables, objects, and user-defined types declared at module level) of modules declared **Private** using the **Option Private** statement are still available within the project containing the module, but they are not available to other applications or projects.

See Also **Option Base** Statement, **Option Compare** Statement, **Option Explicit** Statement, **Private** Statement.

Example This **Option Private** statement is used at the module-level to indicate that the entire module is private.

```
Option Private Module   ' Indicate that module is private.
```

OptionButton Object

Description

Option buttons allow the user to select one of a group of options. Option buttons are usually placed within a group box control (**GroupBox** object). You can set the position and size of an option button. On a worksheet or chart, you can also format the border and background. The font is fixed.

Accessors

The **OptionButton** object is a member of the **OptionButtons** collection. The **OptionButtons** collection contains all the **OptionButton** objects on a single sheet. Use the **Add** method to create a new option button and add it to the collection.

To access a single member of the collection, use the **OptionButtons** method with the index number or name of the option button as an argument. The following example turns on option button one on the worksheet named "Sheet2."

```
Worksheets("sheet2").OptionButtons(1).Value = xlOn
```

The option button name is shown in the Name Box when the option button is selected. Use the **Name** property to set or return the option button name. The following example disables the option button named "Option Button 13" on the worksheet named "Sheet2."

```
Worksheets("sheet2").OptionButtons("option button 13").Enabled = False
```

Properties

Accelerator Property, **Application** Property, **Border** Property, **BottomRightCell** Property, **Caption** Property, **Creator** Property, **Display3DShading** Property, **Enabled** Property, **Height** Property, **Index** Property, **Interior** Property, **Left** Property, **LinkedCell** Property, **Locked** Property, **LockedText** Property, **Name** Property, **OnAction** Property, **Parent** Property, **PhoneticAccelerator** Property, **Placement** Property, **PrintObject** Property, **Text** Property, **Top** Property, **TopLeftCell** Property, **Value** Property, **Visible** Property, **Width** Property, **ZOrder** Property.

Methods

BringToFront Method, **Characters** Method, **CheckSpelling** Method, **Copy** Method, **CopyPicture** Method, **Cut** Method, **Delete** Method, **Duplicate** Method, **Select** Method, **SendToBack** Method.

OptionButtons Collection Object

Description

A collection of all the **OptionButton** objects on the specified chart sheet, dialog sheet, or worksheet. Option buttons allow the user to select one of a group of options. Option buttons are usually placed within a group box control (**GroupBox** object). You can set the position and size of an option button. On a worksheet or chart, you can also format the border and background. The font is fixed.

Accessors

The **OptionButtons** collection contains all of the option buttons on a single sheet. Use the **Add** method to create a new option button and add it to the collection. The following example adds four option buttons to the dialog sheet named "Dialog1." The new option buttons are positioned relative to the upper-left corner of the dialog frame.

```
Dim df As DialogFrame
Set df = DialogSheets("dialog1").DialogFrame
With DialogSheets("dialog1").OptionButtons
    .Add df.Left + 10, df.Top + 20, 100, 10
    .Add df.Left + 10, df.Top + 40, 100, 10
    .Add df.Left + 10, df.Top + 60, 100, 10
    .Add df.Left + 10, df.Top + 80, 100, 10
End With
```

Use the **OptionButtons** method with an argument to access a single member of the collection or without an argument to access the entire collection at once. The following example creates a new group box around all the option buttons on dialog sheet one by first using the **Group** method to create a new **GroupObject** object from all of the option buttons and then using the size of the **GroupObject** object to create the **GroupBox** object.

```
Dim op_btns As GroupObject
Set op_btns = DialogSheets(1).OptionButtons.Group
DialogSheets(1).GroupBoxes.Add op_btns.Left, _
    op_btns.Top - 10, op_btns.Width, op_btns.Height
```

Properties

Accelerator Property, **Application** Property, **Border** Property, **Caption** Property, **Count** Property, **Creator** Property, **Display3DShading** Property, **Enabled** Property, **Height** Property, **Interior** Property, **Left** Property, **LinkedCell** Property, **Locked** Property, **LockedText** Property, **OnAction** Property, **Parent** Property, **PhoneticAccelerator** Property, **Placement** Property, **PrintObject** Property, **Text** Property, **Top** Property, **Value** Property, **Visible** Property, **Width** Property, **ZOrder** Property.

Methods

Add Method (Graphic Objects and Controls), **BringToFront** Method, **Characters** Method, **CheckSpelling** Method, **Copy** Method, **CopyPicture** Method, **Cut** Method, **Delete** Method, **Duplicate** Method, **Group** Method, **Item** Method, **Select** Method, **SendToBack** Method.

OptionButtons Method

Applies To	**Chart** Object, **DialogSheet** Object, **Worksheet** Object.
Description	Accessor. Returns an object that represents a single option button control (an **OptionButton** object, Syntax 1) or a collection of option button controls (an OptionButtons object, Syntax 2) on the sheet.
Syntax 1	*object*.**OptionButtons**(*index*)
Syntax 2	*object*.**OptionButtons**

object
> Required. The **Chart**, **DialogSheet**, or **Worksheet** object.

index
> Required for Syntax 1. Specifies the name or number of the option button (can be an array to specify more than one).

Example	This example sets option button one on Dialog1.

```
Dialogsheets("Dialog1").OptionButtons(1).Value = xlOn
```

Or Operator

Description	Used to perform a logical disjunction on two expressions.
Syntax	*result* = *expression1* **Or** *expression2*

The **Or** operator syntax has these parts:

Part	Description
result	Any numeric variable.
expression1	Any expression.
expression2	Any expression.

Remarks	If either or both expressions evaluate **True**, *result* is **True**. The following table illustrates how *result* is determined:

If *expression1* is	And *expression2* is	The *result* is
True	**True**	**True**
True	**False**	**True**
True	**Null**	**True**
False	**True**	**True**

If *expression1* is	And *expression2* is	The *result* is
False	False	False
False	Null	Null
Null	True	True
Null	False	Null
Null	Null	Null

The **Or** operator also performs a bit-wise comparison of identically positioned bits in two numeric expressions and sets the corresponding bit in *result* according to the following truth table:

If bit in *expression1* is	And bit in *expression2* is	The *result* is
0	0	0
0	1	1
1	0	1
1	1	1

See Also   Operator Precedence.

Example   This example uses the **Or** operator to perform logical disjunction on two expressions.

```
A = 10: B = 8: C = 6 : D = Null      ' Initialize variables.
MyCheck = A > B Or B > C             ' Returns True.
MyCheck = B > A Or B > C             ' Returns True.
MyCheck = A > B Or B > D             ' Returns True.
MyCheck = B > D Or B > A             ' Returns Null.
MyCheck = A Or B' Returns 10 (bit-wise comparison).
```

Order Property

Applies To   **PageSetup** Object, **Trendline** Object.

Description   **PageSetup** object: Returns or sets the order that Microsoft Excel uses to number pages when printing a large worksheet (either **xlDownThenOver** or **xlOverThenDown**). Read-write.

Trendline object: Returns or sets the trendline order (an integer greater than one) when the trendline **Type** is **xlPolynomial**. Read-write.

Remarks   For the **PageSetup** object, this property applies only to worksheets.

Example   This example breaks Sheet1 into pages when the worksheet is printed. Numbering and printing proceed from the first page to the pages to the right, and then move down and continue printing across the sheet.

```
Worksheets("Sheet1").PageSetup.Order = xlOverThenDown
```

OrganizationName Property

Applies To   **Application** Object.

Description   Returns the registered organization name (as a string). Read-only.

See Also   **UserName** Property.

Example   This example displays the registered organization name.

```
MsgBox "The registered organization is " & Application.OrganizationName
```

Orientation Property

Applies To   **AxisTitle** Object, **Button** Object, **Buttons** Collection, **ChartTitle** Object, **DataLabel** Object, **DataLabels** Collection, **DrawingObjects** Collection, **GroupObject** Object, **GroupObjects** Collection, **PageSetup** Object, **PivotField** Object, **Range** Object, **Style** Object, **TextBox** Object, **TextBoxes** Collection, **TickLabels** Object.

Description   Returns or sets the object's orientation, as shown in the following table.

Object	Orientation
PageSetup	Portrait or landscape printing mode. One of **xlPortrait** or **xlLandscape**.
PivotField	Location of the field in the PivotTable. One of **xlHidden**, **xlRowField**, **xlColumnField**, **xlPageField**, or **xlDataField**.
AxisTitle, Button, ChartTitle, DataLabel, DrawingObjects, GroupObject, RadarAxisLabels, Range, Style, TextBox, TickLabels	The text orientation. One of **xlHorizontal**, **xlVertical**, **xlUpward**, or **xlDownward**. Can also be **xlAutomatic** for **TickLabels** only.

Example

This example displays the orientation for the field named "ORDER_DATE."

```
Set pvtTable = Worksheets("Sheet1").Range("A3").PivotTable
Set pvtField = pvtTable.PivotFields("ORDER_DATE")
Select Case pvtField.Orientation
    Case xlHidden
        MsgBox "Hidden field"
    Case xlRowField
        MsgBox "Row field"
    Case xlColumnField
        MsgBox "Column field"
    Case xlPageField
        MsgBox "Page field"
    Case xlDataField
        MsgBox "Data field"
End Select
```

This example sets Sheet1 to print in landscape orientation.

```
Worksheets("Sheet1").PageSetup.Orientation = xlLandscape
```

Outline Object

Description

An outline on a worksheet.

Accessors

The **Outline** property returns the outline for a worksheet. The following example sets the outline on the worksheet named "Sheet4" to show only the first outline level.

```
Worksheets("sheet4").Outline.ShowLevels 1
```

Use the following properties and methods to create and control outlines: **ApplyOutlineStyles** Method, **AutoOutline** Method, **ClearOutline** Method, **DisplayOutline** Property, **Group** Method, **OutlineLevel** Property, **ShowDetail** Property, **Ungroup** Method.

Properties

Application Property, **AutomaticStyles** Property, **Creator** Property, **Parent** Property, **SummaryColumn** Property, **SummaryRow** Property.

Methods

ShowLevels Method.

Outline Property

Applies To   **Worksheet** Object.

Description   Accessor. Returns an **Outline** object that represents the outline for the specified
worksheet.

Example   This example sets the outline on Sheet1 to use automatic styles.

```
Worksheets("Sheet1").Outline.AutomaticStyles = True
```

OutlineFont Property

Applies To   **Font** Object.

Description   **True** if the font is an outline font. Read-write.

Remarks   This property has no effect in Microsoft Windows, but its value is retained (it can
be set and returned).

Example   This example sets the font for cell A1 on Sheet1 to an outline font.

```
Worksheets("Sheet1").Range("A1").Font.OutlineFont = True
```

OutlineLevel Property

Applies To   **Range** Object.

Description   Returns or sets the current row or column outline level of the specified row or
column. Read-write.

Remarks   Level one is the outermost summary level.

See Also   **EntireColumn** Property, **EntireRow** Property.

Example   This example sets the outline level for row two on Sheet1.

```
Worksheets("Sheet1").Rows(2).OutlineLevel = 1
```

Oval Object

Description   Represents an oval graphic object on a chart sheet, dialog sheet, or worksheet.

Accessors   The **Oval** object is a member of the **Ovals** collection. The **Ovals** collection contains all the **Oval** objects on a single sheet. Use the **Add** method (or click the Ellipse or Filled Ellipse button on the Drawing toolbar) to create a new oval and add it to the collection. To access a single member of the collection, use the **Ovals** method with the index number or name of the oval as an argument.

The following example sets the border color for oval one.

```
Worksheets("Sheet1").Activate
ActiveSheet.Ovals(1).Border.Color = RGB(0, 255, 255)
```

The oval name is shown in the Name Box when the oval is selected. Use the **Name** property to set and return the oval name.

The following example selects the oval named "Oval 1" on the active sheet and then sets the oval interior color.

```
Worksheets("sheet1").Activate
ActiveSheet.Ovals("oval 1").Select
Selection.Interior.Color = RGB(255, 0, 0)
```

Properties   **Application** Property, **Border** Property, **BottomRightCell** Property, **Creator** Property, **Enabled** Property, **Height** Property, **Index** Property, **Interior** Property, **Left** Property, **Locked** Property, **Name** Property, **OnAction** Property, **Parent** Property, **Placement** Property, **PrintObject** Property, **Shadow** Property, **Top** Property, **TopLeftCell** Property, **Visible** Property, **Width** Property, **ZOrder** Property.

Methods   **BringToFront** Method, **Copy** Method, **CopyPicture** Method, **Cut** Method, **Delete** Method, **Duplicate** Method, **Select** Method, **SendToBack** Method.

Ovals Collection Object

Description   A collection of all the **Oval** objects on the specified chart sheet, dialog sheet, or worksheet.

Accessors

Use the **Add** method to create a new oval and add it to the collection. The following example creates a new oval aligned with the left and top edges of cell C5 on the worksheet named "Sheet1." The new oval is twice as long and high as the cell, and its interior has a grid pattern.

```
Set r = Worksheets("sheet1").Range("c5")
Set o = Worksheets("sheet1").Ovals.Add(r.Left, _
    r.Top, 2 * r.Width, 2 * r.Height)
o.Interior.Pattern = xlGrid
```

Use the **Ovals** method with an argument to access a single member of the collection or without an argument to access the entire collection at once. The following example sets the interior color for all the ovals on the worksheet named "Sheet1."

```
Worksheets("sheet1").Ovals.Interior.ColorIndex = 3
```

Properties

Application Property, **Border** Property, **Count** Property, **Creator** Property, **Enabled** Property, **Height** Property, **Interior** Property, **Left** Property, **Locked** Property, **OnAction** Property, **Parent** Property, **Placement** Property, **PrintObject** Property, **Shadow** Property, **Top** Property, **Visible** Property, **Width** Property, **ZOrder** Property.

Methods

Add Method (Graphic Objects and Controls), **BringToFront** Method, **Copy** Method, **CopyPicture** Method, **Cut** Method, **Delete** Method, **Duplicate** Method, **Group** Method, **Item** Method, **Select** Method, **SendToBack** Method.

Ovals Method

Applies To

Chart Object, **DialogSheet** Object, **Worksheet** Object.

Description

Accessor. Returns an object that represents a single oval (an **Oval** object, Syntax 1) or a collection of ovals (an **Ovals** object, Syntax 2) on the sheet. Read-only.

Syntax 1

object.**Ovals**(*index*)

Syntax 2

object.**Ovals**

object
   Required. The object containing the ovals.

index
   Required for Syntax 1. The name or number of the oval.

Example

This example deletes every oval on Sheet1.

```
Worksheets("Sheet1").Ovals.Delete
```

This example changes the color of oval one on Sheet1 to red.

```
Worksheets("Sheet1").Ovals(1).Border.ColorIndex = 3
```

Overlap Property

Applies To   **ChartGroup** Object.

Description   Specifies how bars and columns are positioned. Can be a value from -100 to 100. Applies only to 2-D bar and 2-D column charts. Read-write.

Remarks   If this property is set to -100, bars are positioned so that there is one bar width between them. With zero overlap, there is no space between bars (one bar starts immediately after the preceding bar). At 100 overlap, bars are positioned on top of each other.

See Also   **GapWidth** Property.

Example   This example sets the overlap for chart group one to -50. The example should be run on a 2-D column chart that has two or more series.

```
Charts("Chart1").ChartGroups(1).Overlap = -50
```

PageBreak Property

Applies To   **Range** Object.

Description   Returns or sets the location of a page break (one of **xlNone**, **xlManual**, or **xlAutomatic**). Read-write.

Remarks   This property can return the location of either automatic or manual page breaks, but it can only set the location of manual breaks (it can only be set to **xlManual** or **xlNone**).

To remove all manual page breaks on a worksheet, set **Cells.PageBreak** to **xlNone**.

Example   This example sets a manual page break above row 25 on Sheet1.

```
Worksheets("Sheet1").Rows(25).PageBreak = xlManual
```

This example sets a manual page break to the left of column J on Sheet1.

```
Worksheets("Sheet1").Columns("J").PageBreak = xlManual
```

This example deletes the two page breaks that were set in the previous examples.

```
Worksheets("Sheet1").Rows(25).PageBreak = xlNone
Worksheets("Sheet1").Columns("J").PageBreak = xlNone
```

PageFields Method

Applies To   **PivotTable** Object.

Description   Accessor. Returns an object that represents a single pivot field (a **PivotField** object, Syntax 1) or a collection of the pivot fields (a **PivotFields** object, Syntax 2) that are currently showing as page fields. Read-only.

Syntax 1   *object*.**PageFields**(*index*)

Syntax 2   *object*.**PageFields**

object
   Required. The **PivotTable** object.

index
   Required for Syntax 1. The name or number of the pivot field to return (can be an array to specify more than one).

See Also   **ColumnFields** Method, **DataFields** Method, **HiddenFields** Method, **PivotFields** Method, **RowFields** Method, **VisibleFields** Method.

Example   This example adds the page field names to a list box. The list box appears on Sheet1.

```
Set pvtTable = Worksheets("Sheet1").Range("A3").PivotTable
Set newListBox = Worksheets("Sheet1").ListBoxes.Add _
    (Left:=10, Top:=72, Width:=144, Height:=144)
For Each hdnField In pvtTable.PageFields
    newListBox.AddItem (hdnField.Name)
Next hdnField
Worksheets("Sheet1").Activate
```

PageRange Property

Applies To	**PivotTable** Object.
Description	Accessor. Returns a **Range** object that represents the range that contains the PivotTable page area. Read-only.
See Also	**ColumnRange** Property, **DataBodyRange** Property, **DataLabelRange** Property, **RowRange** Property.
Example	This example selects the PivotTable page headers.

```
Worksheets("Sheet1").Activate
Range("A3").Select
ActiveCell.PivotTable.PageRange.Select
```

PageSetup Object

Description	Represents the page setup description. The **PageSetup** object contains all page setup attributes (left margin, bottom margin, paper size, and so on) as properties.
Accessors	The **PageSetup** property returns the **PageSetup** object for a sheet or window. The following example sets the orientation to landscape mode for the module named "Module1" and then prints the module.

```
Modules("module1").PageSetup.Orientation = xlLandscape
Modules("module1").PrintOut
```

The **With** statement makes it easier and faster to set several properties at once. The following example sets all the margins for worksheet one.

```
With Worksheets(1).PageSetup
    .LeftMargin = Application.InchesToPoints(0.5)
    .RightMargin = Application.InchesToPoints(0.75)
    .TopMargin = Application.InchesToPoints(1.5)
    .BottomMargin = Application.InchesToPoints(1)
    .HeaderMargin = Application.InchesToPoints(0.5)
    .FooterMargin = Application.InchesToPoints(0.5)
End With
```

Properties   **Application** Property, **BlackAndWhite** Property, **BottomMargin** Property, **CenterFooter** Property, **CenterHeader** Property, **CenterHorizontally** Property, **CenterVertically** Property, **ChartSize** Property, **Creator** Property, **Draft** Property, **FirstPageNumber** Property, **FitToPagesTall** Property, **FitToPagesWide** Property, **FooterMargin** Property, **HeaderMargin** Property, **LeftFooter** Property, **LeftHeader** Property, **LeftMargin** Property, **Order** Property, **Orientation** Property, **PaperSize** Property, **Parent** Property, **PrintArea** Property, **PrintGridlines** Property, **PrintHeadings** Property, **PrintNotes** Property, **PrintQuality** Property, **PrintTitleColumns** Property, **PrintTitleRows** Property, **RightFooter** Property, **RightHeader** Property, **RightMargin** Property, **TopMargin** Property, **Zoom** Property.

PageSetup Property

Applies To   **Chart** Object, **DialogSheet** Object, **Module** Object, **Window** Object, **Worksheet** Object.

Description   Accessor. Returns a **PageSetup** object that contains all of the page setup settings for the specified object. Read-only.

Example   This example sets the center header text for Chart1.

```
Charts("Chart1").PageSetup.CenterHeader = "December Sales"
```

Pane Object

Description   Represents a pane of a window. **Pane** objects exist only for worksheets and Excel 4.0 macro sheets.

Accessors   The **Pane** object is a member of the **Panes** collection. The **Panes** collection contains all of the panes shown in a single **Window**. To access a single member of the collection, use the **Panes** method with the pane index number as an argument. The following example splits the window showing worksheet one and then scrolls the pane in the lower-left corner to position row five at the top.

```
Worksheets(1).Activate
ActiveWindow.Split = True
ActiveWindow.Panes(3).ScrollRow = 5
```

Properties   **Application** Property, **Creator** Property, **Index** Property, **Parent** Property, **ScrollColumn** Property, **ScrollRow** Property, **VisibleRange** Property.

| Methods | **Activate** Method, **LargeScroll** Method, **SmallScroll** Method. |

Panes Collection Object

| Description | A collection of all the **Pane** objects shown in the specified window. **Pane** objects exist only for worksheets and Excel 4.0 macro sheets. |
| Accessors | Use the **Panes** method with an argument to access a single member of the collection or without an argument to access the entire collection at once. |

The following example scrolls the upper-left pane of the window showing the worksheet named "Sheet1."

```
Worksheets("sheet1").Activate
Windows(1).Panes(1).LargeScroll down:=1
```

| Properties | **Application** Property, **Count** Property, **Creator** Property, **Parent** Property. |
| Methods | **Item** Method. |

Panes Method

Applies To	**Window** Object.
Description	Accessor. Returns an object that represents one pane (a **Pane** object, Syntax 1) or a collection of all the panes (a **Panes** object, Syntax 2) in a window. Read-only.
Syntax 1	*object*.**Panes**(*index*)
Syntax 2	*object*.**Panes**

object
   Required. The **Window** object.

index
   Required for Syntax 1. The name or number of the pane.

| Remarks | This method is only available on a window if its **Split** property can be set to **True**. |
| Example | This example displays the number of panes in the active window in BOOK1.XLS. |

```
Workbooks("BOOK1.XLS").Worksheets("Sheet1").Activate
MsgBox "There are " & ActiveWindow.Panes.Count & _
    " panes in the active window"
```

This example activates the upper-left pane in the active window in BOOK1.XLS.

```
Workbooks("BOOK1.XLS").Worksheets("Sheet1").Activate
ActiveWindow.Panes(1).Activate
```

PaperSize Property

Applies To   **PageSetup** Object.

Description   Windows only. Returns or sets the size of the paper. Read-write.

Remarks   This property may have one of the following values.

Value	Meaning
xlPaperLetter	Letter (8 1/2 x 11 in.)
xlPaperLetterSmall	Letter Small (8 1/2 x 11 in.)
xlPaperTabloid	Tabloid (11 x 17 in.)
xlPaperLedger	Ledger (17 x 11 in.)
xlPaperLegal	Legal (8 1/2 x 14 in.)
xlPaperStatement	Statement (5 1/2 x 8 1/2 in.)
xlPaperExecutive	Executive (7 1/2 x 10 1/2 in.)
xlPaperA3	A3 (297 x 420 mm)
xlPaperA4	A4 (210 x 297 mm)
xlPaperA4Small	A4 Small (210 x 297 mm)
xlPaperA5	A5 (148 x 210 mm)
xlPaperB4	B4 (250 x 354 mm)
xlPaperB5	B5 (182 x 257 mm)
xlPaperFolio	Folio (8 1/2 x 13 in.)
xlPaperQuarto	Quarto (215 x 275 mm)
xlPaper10x14	10 x 14 in.
xlPaper11x17	11 x 17 in.
xlPaperNote	Note (8 1/2 x 11 in.)
xlPaperEnvelope9	Envelope #9 (3 7/8 x 8 7/8 in.)
xlPaperEnvelope10	Envelope #10 (4 1/8 x 9 1/2 in.)
xlPaperEnvelope11	Envelope #11 (4 1/2 x 10 3/8 in.)
xlPaperEnvelope12	Envelope #12 (4 1/2 x 11 in.)
xlPaperEnvelope14	Envelope #14 (5 x 11 1/2 in.)

Value	Meaning
xlPaperCsheet	C size sheet
xlPaperDsheet	D size sheet
xlPaperEsheet	E size sheet
xlPaperEnvelopeDL	Envelope DL (110 x 220 mm)
xlPaperEnvelopeC3	Envelope C3 (324 x 458 mm)
xlPaperEnvelopeC4	Envelope C4 (229 x 324 mm)
xlPaperEnvelopeC5	Envelope C5 (162 x 229 mm)
xlPaperEnvelopeC6	Envelope C6 (114 x 162 mm)
xlPaperEnvelopeC65	Envelope C65 (114 x 229 mm)
xlPaperEnvelopeB4	Envelope B4 (250 x 353 mm)
xlPaperEnvelopeB5	Envelope B5 (176 x 250 mm)
xlPaperEnvelopeB6	Envelope B6 (176 x 125 mm)
xlPaperEnvelopeItaly	Envelope (110 x 230 mm)
xlPaperEnvelopeMonarch	Envelope Monarch (3 7/8 x 7 1/2 in.)
xlPaperEnvelopePersonal	Envelope (3 5/8 x 6 1/2 in.)
xlPaperFanfoldUS	U.S. Standard Fanfold (14 7/8 x 11 in.)
xlPaperFanfoldStdGerman	German Standard Fanfold (8 1/2 x 12 in.)
xlPaperFanfoldLegalGerman	German Legal Fanfold (8 1/2 x 13 in.)
xlPaperUser	User defined

Some printers may not support all paper sizes.

Example   This example sets the paper size of Sheet1 to legal.

```
Worksheets("Sheet1").PageSetup.PaperSize = xlPaperLegal
```

Parent Property

Applies To   All objects.

Description   Accessor. Returns the parent object for the specified object. Read-only.

Example   This example displays the name of the chart that contains `myAxis`.

```
Set myAxis = Charts(1).Axes(xlValue)
MsgBox myAxis.Parent.Name
```

Parent Property (DocumentProperty Object)

Description   Accessor. Returns the parent object for the specified object. Read-only.

To use this property, you should establish a reference to the Microsoft Office 95 Object Library by using the References command (Tools menu).

Example   This example displays the name of the parent for a document property. You must pass a **DocumentProperty** object to the procedure.

```
Sub DisplayParent(dp as DocumentProperty)
    MsgBox dp.Parent.Name
End Sub
```

ParentField Property

Applies To   **PivotField** Object.

Description   Accessor. Returns a **PivotField** object that represents the pivot field that is the group parent of the object. The field must be grouped and have a parent field. Read-only.

Example   This example displays the name of the field that is the group parent of the field that contains the active cell.

```
Worksheets("Sheet1").Activate
MsgBox "The active field is a child of the field " & _
    ActiveCell.PivotField.ParentField.Name
```

ParentItem Property

Applies To   **PivotItem** Object.

Description   Accessor. Returns a **PivotItem** object that represents the parent pivot item in the parent **PivotField** (the field must be grouped so that it has a parent). Read-only.

Example   This example displays the name of the parent item for the item that contains the active cell.

```
Worksheets("Sheet1").Activate
MsgBox "This item is a subitem of " & _
    ActiveCell.PivotItem.ParentItem.Name
```

ParentItems Method

Applies To **PivotField** Object.

Description Accessor. Returns an object that represents one pivot item (a **PivotItem** object, Syntax 1) or a collection of all the pivot items (a **PivotItems** object, Syntax 2) that are group parents in the specified field. The specified field must be a group parent of another field. Read-only.

Syntax 1 *object*.**ParentItems**(*index*)

Syntax 2 *object*.**ParentItems**

object
    Required. The **PivotField** object.

index
    Required for Syntax 1. The number or name of the pivot item to return (can be an array to specify more than one).

See Also **ChildItems** Method, **HiddenItems** Method, **PivotItems** Method, **VisibleItems** Method.

Example This example adds to a list box the names of all the items that are group parents in the field that contains the active cell. The list box appears on Sheet1.

```
Worksheets("Sheet1").Activate
Set newListBox = Worksheets("Sheet1").ListBoxes.Add _
    (Left:=10, Top:=72, Width:=144, Height:=144)
For Each pvtItem In ActiveCell.PivotField.ParentItems
    newListBox.AddItem (pvtItem.Name)
Next pvtItem
```

ParentShowDetail Property

Applies To **PivotItem** Object.

Description **True** if the specified item is showing because one of its parents is showing detail; **False** if the specified item is not showing because one of its parents is hiding detail. This property is only available if the item is grouped. Read-only.

Example

This example displays a message if the pivot item that contains the active cell is visible because its parent item is showing detail.

```
Worksheets("Sheet1").Activate
Set pvtItem = ActiveCell.PivotItem
If pvtItem.ParentShowDetail = True Then
    MsgBox "Parent item is showing detail"
End If
```

Parse Method

Applies To   **Range** Object.

Description   Parses a range of data and breaks it into multiple cells. Distributes the contents of the range to fill several adjacent columns; the range can be no more than one column wide.

Syntax   *object*.**Parse(***parseLine*, *destination***)**

object
    Required. The range to parse.

parseLine
    Optional. The parse line, as a string. This is a string containing left and right brackets to indicate where the cells should be split. For example, "[xxx][xxx]" would put the first three characters into the first column, and the next three characters into the second column of the destination range. If omitted, Microsoft Excel guesses where to split the columns based on the spacing of the top left cell in the range. If you want to use a different range to guess the parse line, use a **Range** as the *parseLine* argument. That range must be one of the cells that is being parsed. The *parseLine* argument cannot be longer than 255 characters, including the brackets and spaces.

destination
    Optional. A range indicating the upper-left corner of the destination for the parsed data. If omitted, Microsoft Excel will parse in place.

Example   This example divides telephone numbers of the form 206-555-1212 into two columns. The first coulmn contains only the area code, and the second column contains the 7-digit telephone number with the embedded hyphen.

```
Worksheets("Sheet1").Columns("A").Parse _
    parseLine:="[xxx] [xxxxxxx]", _
    destination:=Worksheets("Sheet1").Range("B1")
```

PasswordEdit Property

Applies To   **EditBox** Object, **EditBoxes** Collection.

Description   **True** if the edit box displays its contents as a series of asterisks. This property is available only in Microsoft Excel for Windows 95. Read-write.

Example   This example sets edit box one to display asterisks when the user enters data.

```
DialogSheets(1).EditBoxes(1).PasswordEdit = True
```

Paste Method (Chart Object)

Applies To   **Chart** Object.

Description   Pastes chart data from the Clipboard into the specified chart.

Syntax   *object*.**Paste**(*type*)

object
   Required. The **Chart** object.

type
   Optional. If another chart is in the Clipboard, specifies the chart information to paste (one of **xlFormats**, **xlFormulas**, or **xlAll**). The default is **xlAll**. If there is data other than a chart in the Clipboard, this parameter cannot be used.

Remarks   This method changes the current selection.

See Also   **Copy** Method, **Cut** Method, **Paste** Method (**DialogSheet** or **Worksheet** Object).

Example   This example pastes data from the range B1:B5 on Sheet1 into Chart1.

```
Worksheets("Sheet1").Range("B1:B5").Copy
Charts("Chart1").Paste
```

Paste Method (DialogSheet or Worksheet Object)

Applies To   **DialogSheet** Object, **Worksheet** Object.

Description   Pastes the contents of the Clipboard onto the sheet.

Syntax   *object*.**Paste**(*destination*, *link*)

object
> Required. The **DialogSheet** or **Worksheet** object.

destination
> Optional. A **Range** specifying where the Clipboard contents should be placed. If omitted, the current selection is used. This argument can only be specified if the contents of the Clipboard can be pasted into a range—it cannot be used with drawing objects. If this argument is specified, the *link* argument cannot be used.

link
> Optional. If **True**, a link is established to the source of the pasted data. If this argument is specified, the *destination* argument cannot be used.

Remarks

If you do not specify the *destination* argument, you must select the destination range before you use this method.

This method may modify the sheet selection depending on the contents of the Clipboard. For example, pasted drawing objects remain selected.

See Also

Copy Method, **Cut** Method, **Paste** Method (**Chart** Object), **PasteSpecial** Method.

Example

This example copies data from cells C1:C5 on Sheet1 to cells D1:D5 on Sheet1.

```
Worksheets("Sheet1").Range("C1:C5").Copy
ActiveSheet.Paste destination:=Worksheets("Sheet1").Range("D1:D5")
```

Paste Method (Pictures Object)

Applies To

Pictures Collection.

Description

Pastes a picture from the Clipboard to a sheet or chart. The position of the new picture is determined by the current selection.

Syntax

object.**Paste**(*link*)

object
> Required. The **Pictures** object.

link
> Optional. If **True**, a link is established between the pasted picture and the source data. The default is **False**.

See Also

Copy Method, **Cut** Method.

Example

This example pastes a picture from the Clipboard to cell A1 on Sheet1.

```
Worksheets("Sheet1").Range("A1").Select
ActiveSheet.Pictures.Paste
```

Paste Method (Point or Series Object)

Applies To   **Point** Object, **Series** Object.

Description   Pastes a picture from the Clipboard as the marker on the selected point or series. This method can be used on column, bar, line, or radar charts, and it sets the **MarkerStyle** to **xlPicture**.

Syntax   *object*.**Paste**

object
　　Required. The **Point** or **Series** object.

See Also   **Copy** Method, **Cut** Method, **MarkerStyle** Property.

Example   This example copies a picture to the Clipboard and then pastes it into series one in Chart1.

```
Worksheets("Sheet1").Activate
ActiveSheet.Pictures(1).Copy
Charts("Chart1").Activate
ActiveChart.SeriesCollection(1).Paste
```

Paste Method (SeriesCollection Object)

Applies To   **SeriesCollection** Collection.

Description   Pastes data from the Clipboard to the specified series collection.

Syntax   *object*.**Paste**(*rowcol*, *seriesLabels*, *categoryLabels*, *replace*, *newSeries*)

object
　　Required. The **SeriesCollection** object.

rowcol
　　Optional. Specifies whether the values corresponding to a particular data series are in rows (**xlRows**) or columns (**xlColumns**). The default is **xlColumns**.

seriesLabels
　　Optional. If **True**, Microsoft Excel uses the contents of the cell in the first column of each row (or first row of each column) as the name of the data series in that row (or column). If **False** (or omitted), Microsoft Excel uses the contents of the cell in the first column of each row (or first row of each column) as the first data point of the data series.

categoryLabels

Optional. If **True**, Microsoft Excel uses the contents of the first row (or column) of the selection as the categories for the chart. If **False** (or omitted), Microsoft Excel uses the contents of the first row (or column) as the first data series in the chart.

replace

Optional. If **True**, Microsoft Excel applies categories while replacing existing categories with information from the copied cell range. If **False**, Microsoft Excel inserts new categories without replacing any old ones.

newSeries

Optional. Specifies whether the data is to be pasted as new series (**True**) or as new points on existing series (**False**). The default is **True**.

See Also   **Add** Method (**SeriesCollection** Collection), **ChartWizard** Method, **Copy** Method, **Cut** Method, **Extend** Method.

Example   This example copies data to the Clipboard from cells C1:C5 on Sheet1 and then pastes the data into Chart1 as a new series.

```
Worksheets("Sheet1").Range("C1:C5").Copy
Charts("Chart1").SeriesCollection.Paste
```

PasteFace Method

Applies To   **ToolbarButton** Object.

Description   Pastes a bitmap button face from the Clipboard onto the specified button.

Syntax   *object*.**PasteFace**

object
Required. The **ToolbarButton** object.

Remarks   This method cannot be used with a toolbar button that is a gap or that has a palette list attached (such as the Font or Style buttons).

See Also   **BuiltInFace** Property, **CopyFace** Method.

Example   This example copies the bitmap face of button one (the New Workbook button) on the Standard toolbar and pastes it onto button three (the Save button).

```
With Toolbars("Standard")
    .ToolbarButtons(1).CopyFace
    .ToolbarButtons(3).PasteFace
End With
```

PasteSpecial Method (DialogSheet or Worksheet Object)

Applies To   **DialogSheet** Object, **Worksheet** Object.

Description   Pastes the contents of the Clipboard onto the sheet using a specified format. Use this method to paste data from other applications or paste in a specific format.

Syntax   *object*.**PasteSpecial**(*format*, *link*, *displayAsIcon*, *iconFileName*, *iconIndex*, *iconLabel*)

object
   Required. The **DialogSheet** or **Worksheet** object.

format
   Required. Specifies the clipboard format of the data to paste (as text).

link
   Optional. If **True**, a link is established to the source of the pasted data. If the source data is not suitable for linking or the source application doesn't support linking, this parameter is ignored. The default value is **False**.

displayAsIcon
   Optional. If **True**, the pasted data is displayed as an icon. The default value is **False**.

iconFileName
   Optional. The name of the file that contains the icon to use if *displayAsIcon* is **True**.

iconIndex
   Optional. The index number of the icon within the icon file.

iconLabel
   Optional. The text label of the icon.

Remarks   You must select the destination range before you use this method.

This method may modify the sheet selection depending on the contents of the Clipboard. For example, pasted drawing objects remain selected.

See Also   **Copy** Method, **Cut** Method, **Paste** Method (**DialogSheet** or **WorkSheet** Object), **PasteSpecial** Method (**Range** Object).

Example   This example pastes a Microsoft Word version 6.0 document object from the Clipboard to cell D1 on Sheet1.

```
Worksheets("Sheet1").Range("D1").Select
ActiveSheet.PasteSpecial format:="Microsoft Word 6.0 Document Object"
```

This example pastes the same Microsoft Word version 6.0 document object and displays it as an icon.

```
Worksheets("Sheet1").Range("F5").Select
ActiveSheet.PasteSpecial _
        format:="Microsoft Word 6.0 Document Object", _
        displayAsIcon:=True
```

PasteSpecial Method (Range Object)

Applies To   **Range** Object.

Description   Pastes a **Range** from the Clipboard to the specified range.

Syntax   *object*.**PasteSpecial**(*paste*, *operation*, *skipBlanks*, *transpose*)

object
Required. The **Range** object.

paste
Optional. Specifies the part of the range to be pasted (one of **xlAll**, **xlFormulas**, **xlValues**, **xlFormats**, **xlNotes**, or **xlAllExceptBorders**). If omitted, the default is **xlAll**.

operation
Optional. Specifies the paste operation (one of **xlNone**, **xlAdd**, **xlSubtract**, **xlMultiply**, or **xlDivide**). If omitted, the default is **xlNone**.

skipBlanks
Optional. If **True**, blank cells in the **Range** on the Clipboard will not be pasted into the destination. If omitted, the default is **False**.

transpose
Optional. If **True**, rows and columns are transposed when the **Range** is pasted. If omitted, the default is **False**.

See Also   **Copy** Method, **Cut** Method, **Paste** Method, **PasteSpecial** Method (**DialogSheet** or **Worksheet** Object).

Example   This example replaces the data in cells D1:D5 on Sheet1 with the sum of the existing contents and cells C1:C5 on Sheet1.

```
Worksheets("Sheet1").Range("C1:C5").Copy
Worksheets("Sheet1").Range("D1:D5").PasteSpecial operation:=xlAdd
```

Path Property

Applies To   **AddIn** Object, **Application** Object, **Workbook** Object.

Description   Returns the complete path of the object (as a string), without including the final separator and name of the object. Read-only.

Remarks   If you do not specify an object qualifier, this property returns the path to the Microsoft Excel application (it is equivalent to `Application.Path`).

Example   This example displays the complete path to Microsoft Excel.

```
MsgBox "The path is " & Application.Path
```

PathSeparator Property

Applies To   **Application** Object.

Description   Returns the character ":" on the Macintosh; "\" in Windows. Read-only.

Example   This example displays the current path separator.

```
MsgBox "The path separator character is " & Application.PathSeparator
```

Pattern Property

Applies To   **Interior** Object.

Description   Returns or sets the pattern of the interior. Read-write.

Remarks   This property can have one of the these values: **xlAutomatic**, **xlChecker**, **xlCrissCross**, **xlDown**, **xlGray16**, **xlGray25**, **xlGray50**, **xlGray75**, **xlGray8**, **xlGrid**, **xlHorizontal**, **xlLightDown**, **xlLightHorizontal**, **xlLightUp**, **xlLightVertical**, **xlNone**, **xlSemiGray75**, **xlSolid**, **xlUp**, or **xlVertical**.

See Also   **PatternColor** Property.

Example   This example adds a crisscross pattern to the interior of cell A1 on Sheet1.

```
Worksheets("Sheet1").Range("A1").Interior.Pattern = xlCrissCross
```

PatternColor Property

Applies To   **Interior** Object.

Description   Returns or sets the interior pattern color as an RGB value. Read-write.

See Also   **Color** Property, **Pattern** Property, **PatternColorIndex** Property.

Example   This example sets the interior pattern color for rectangle one on Sheet1.

```
With Worksheets("Sheet1").Rectangles(1).Interior
    .Pattern = xlGrid
    .PatternColor = RGB(255,0,0)
End With
```

PatternColorIndex Property

Applies To   **Interior** Object.

Description   Returns or sets the interior pattern color as an index into the current color palette (a value from 1 to 56, or **xlNone** if there is no background color). Read-write.

Remarks   Set this property to **xlAutomatic** to specify the automatic pattern for cells or the automatic fill style for drawing objects. Set this property to **xlNone** to specify no pattern (this is the same as setting **Interior.Pattern** to **xlNone**).

See Also   **Color** Property, **Colors** Property, **Pattern** Property, **PatternColor** Property.

Example   This example sets the interior pattern color for rectangle one on Sheet1.

```
With Worksheets("Sheet1").Rectangles(1).Interior
    .Pattern = xlChecker
    .PatternColorIndex = 5
End With
```

Period Property

Applies To   **Trendline** Object.

Description   Returns or sets the period of the trendline (applies only if this is a moving average trendline; its **Type** property must be **xlMovingAvg**). Read-write.

See Also   **Type** Property.

Example

This example sets the period for trendline one on Chart1, if the trendline is a moving-average trendline. The example should be run on a 2-D column chart with a single series that contains 10 data points and a moving-average trendline.

```
With Charts("Chart1").SeriesCollection(1).Trendlines(1)
    If .Type = xlMovingAvg Then .Period = 5
End With
```

Perspective Property

Applies To

Chart Object.

Description

Returns or sets the perspective for the 3-D chart view. Must be between 0 and 100. This property is ignored if the **RightAngleAxes** property is **True**. Read-write.

See Also

Elevation Property, **RightAngleAxes** Property, **Rotation** Property.

Example

This example sets the perspective of Chart1 to 70. The example should be run on a 3-D chart.

```
Charts("Chart1").RightAngleAxes = False
Charts("Chart1").Perspective = 70
```

PhoneticAccelerator Property

Applies To

Button Object, **Buttons** Collection, **CheckBox** Object, **DrawingObjects** Collection, **GroupBox** Object, **GroupBoxes** Collection, **Label** Object, **Labels** Collection, **OptionButton** Object, **OptionButtons** Collection.

Description

Returns or sets the phonetic keyboard accelerator key character for the control (this property is available only in Far East Microsoft Excel). The phonetic accelerator is used when the system accelerator mode is switched to phonetic characters (as opposed to roman characters, which use the **Accelerator** property). Read-write.

See Also

Accelerator Property.

Example

This example sets the accelerator and phonetic accelerator for button four on Dialog1.

```
With DialogSheets("Dialog1").Buttons(4)
    .Accelerator = "E"
    .PhoneticAccelerator = "l"
End With
```

Picture Object

Description   Represents a graphic (a bitmap, metafile, or image created from some other graphic file) or a linked or embedded OLE object attached to a sheet.

Accessors   The **Picture** object is a member of the **Pictures** collection. The **Pictures** collection includes all of the graphics on the sheet, as well as any linked or embedded OLE objects. Use the **Insert** method or the Picture command on the Insert menu to add a graphic file to a sheet as a graphic and add it to the collection. To access a single member of the collection, use the **Pictures** method with the index number or name of the graphic as an argument. While the **Pictures** collection contains **OLEObject** objects, it is easier to access the **OLEObject** objects using the **OLEObjects** collection and the **OLEObjects** method.

The following example deletes graphic one on worksheet one.

```
Worksheets(1).Pictures(1).Delete
```

The graphic name is shown in the Name Box when the graphic is selected. Use the **Name** property to set or return the graphic name. The following example duplicates the graphic named "Picture 13" and moves the new graphic so that its left edge lines up with the left edge of column H, and its top lines up with the top of row 10.

```
Set px = Worksheets(1).Pictures("picture 13").Duplicate
px.Left = Worksheets(1).Columns("H").Left
px.Top = Worksheets(1).Rows(10).Top
```

Properties   **Application** Property, **Border** Property, **BottomRightCell** Property, **Creator** Property, **Enabled** Property, **Formula** Property, **Height** Property, **Index** Property, **Interior** Property, **Left** Property, **Locked** Property, **Name** Property, **OnAction** Property, **Parent** Property, **Placement** Property, **PrintObject** Property, **Shadow** Property, **Top** Property, **TopLeftCell** Property, **Visible** Property, **Width** Property, **ZOrder** Property.

Methods   **BringToFront** Method, **Copy** Method, **CopyPicture** Method, **Cut** Method, **Delete** Method, **Duplicate** Method, **Select** Method, **SendToBack** Method.

Pictures Collection Object

Description   A collection of all the **Picture** objects on the specified chart sheet, dialog sheet, or worksheet. This collection includes graphics (bitmaps, metafiles, or images created from some other graphic file) and linked or embedded OLE objects.

Accessors

You add a graphic to a sheet by clicking the Picture command on the Insert menu or by using the **Insert** method. The following example adds the file ARCADE.BMP as a new graphic on worksheet one. The upper-left corner of the new graphic fits into the upper-left corner of the active cell.

```
Worksheets(1).Pictures.Insert "arcade.bmp"
```

Use the **Pictures** method with an argument to access a single member of the collection or without an argument to access the entire collection at once. The following example deletes all of the pictures on the worksheet named "Sheet1."

```
Worksheets("sheet1").Pictures.Delete
```

While the **Pictures** collection contains **OLEObject** objects, it is easier to access the **OLEObject** objects using the **OLEObjects** collection and the **OLEObjects** method.

Properties

Application Property, **Border** Property, **Count** Property, **Creator** Property, **Enabled** Property, **Formula** Property, **Height** Property, **Interior** Property, **Left** Property, **Locked** Property, **OnAction** Property, **Parent** Property, **Placement** Property, **PrintObject** Property, **Shadow** Property, **Top** Property, **Visible** Property, **Width** Property, **ZOrder** Property.

Methods

Add Method (Graphic Objects and Controls), **BringToFront** Method, **Copy** Method, **CopyPicture** Method, **Cut** Method, **Delete** Method, **Duplicate** Method, **Group** Method, **Insert** Method, **Item** Method, **Paste** Method (**Pictures** Object), **Select** Method, **SendToBack** Method.

Pictures Method

Applies To

Chart Object, **DialogSheet** Object, **Worksheet** Object.

Description

Accessor. Returns an object that represents a single picture (a **Picture** object, Syntax 1) or a collection of pictures (a **Pictures** object, Syntax 2) on the sheet. Read-only.

Syntax 1

object.**Pictures**(*index*)

Syntax 2

object.**Pictures**

object
    Required. The object containing the pictures.

index
    Required for Syntax 1. The name or number of the picture.

Example   This example deletes every picture on Sheet1.

```
Worksheets("Sheet1").Pictures.Delete
```

This example changes the color of the border of picture one on Sheet1 to red.

```
Worksheets("Sheet1").Pictures(1).Border.ColorIndex = 3
```

PictureType Property

Applies To   **Point** Object, **Series** Object.

Description   Returns or sets how pictures are displayed on a column or bar picture chart, as shown in the following table. Applies only to column and bar picture charts. Read-write.

Value	Meaning
xlStretch	Stretch the picture to reach the necessary value.
xlStack	Stack the pictures to reach the necessary value.
xlScale	Stack the pictures, but use the **PictureUnit** property to determine what unit each picture represents.

See Also   **PictureUnit** Property.

Example   This example sets series one in Chart1 to stretch pictures. The example should be run on a 2-D column chart with picture data markers.

```
Charts("Chart1").SeriesCollection(1).PictureType = xlStretch
```

PictureUnit Property

Applies To   **Point** Object, **Series** Object.

Description   Returns or sets the unit for each picture on a column or bar picture chart if the **PictureType** property is set to **xlScale** (if not, this property is ignored). Read-write.

See Also   **PictureType** Property.

Example   This example sets series one in Chart1 to stack pictures and uses each picture to represent five units. The example should be run on a 2-D column chart with picture data markers.

```
With Charts("Chart1").SeriesCollection(1)
    .PictureType = xlScale
    .PictureUnit = 5
End With
```

Pie3DGroup Property

Applies To   **Chart** Object.

Description   Accessor. Returns a **ChartGroup** object that represents the pie chart group on a 3-D chart. Read-only.

See Also   **PieGroups** Method.

Example   This example converts the 3-D pie group in Chart1 to a 3-D area group. The example should be run on a 3-D chart.

```
Charts("Chart1").Pie3DGroup.Type = xl3DArea
```

PieGroups Method

Applies To   **Chart** Object.

Description   Accessor. On a 2-D chart, returns an object that represents a single pie chart group (a **ChartGroup** object, Syntax 1), or a collection of the pie chart groups (a **ChartGroups** collection, Syntax 2).

Syntax 1   *object*.**PieGroups**(*index*)

Syntax 2   *object*.**PieGroups**

object
     Required. The **Chart** object.

index
     Required for Syntax 1. Specifies the chart group.

See Also   **Pie3DGroup** Property.

Example

This example converts pie group one in Chart1 to an area group. The example should be run on a 2-D chart.

```
Charts("Chart1").PieGroups(1).Type = xlArea
```

PivotField Object

Description   Represents a field in a pivot table.

Accessors   The **PivotField** object is a member of the **PivotFields** collection. The **PivotFields** collection contains all the fields objects in a PivotTable, including hidden fields.

To access a single member of the collection, use the **PivotFields** method with the index number or name of the pivot field as an argument.

Use the **Name** property to set or return the pivot field name. The following example makes the field named "year" a row field.

```
Worksheets("sheet3").PivotTables(1) _
    .PivotFields("year").Orientation = xlRowField
```

In some cases, it may be easier to use one of the methods that returns a subset of the PivotTable fields. The following accessor methods are available: **ColumnFields** method, **DataFields** method, **HiddenFields** method, **PageFields** method, **RowFields** method, **VisibleFields** method.

Properties   **Application** Property, **BaseField** Property, **BaseItem** Property, **Calculation** Property, **ChildField** Property, **Creator** Property, **CurrentPage** Property, **DataRange** Property, **DataType** Property, **Function** Property, **GroupLevel** Property, **LabelRange** Property, **Name** Property, **NumberFormat** Property, **Orientation** Property, **Parent** Property, **ParentField** Property, **Position** Property, **SourceName** Property, **Subtotals** Property, **TotalLevels** Property, **Value** Property.

Methods   **ChildItems** Method, **HiddenItems** Method, **ParentItems** Method, **PivotItems** Method, **VisibleItems** Method.

PivotField Property

Applies To   **Range** Object.

Description   Accessor. Returns a **PivotField** object that represents the pivot field containing the top left corner of the specified range. Read-only.

Example   This example displays the name of the pivot field containing the active cell.

```
Worksheets("Sheet1").Activate
MsgBox "The active cell is in the field " & _
    ActiveCell.PivotField.Name
```

PivotFields Collection Object

Description   A collection of all the **PivotField** objects in a PivotTable.

Accessors   Use the **PivotFields** method with an argument to access a single member of the collection or without an argument to access the entire collection at once. The following example uses the **Count** property of the **PivotFields** collection to set up a loop that enumerates the pivot field names.

```
With Worksheets("sheet3").PivotTables(1)
    For i = 1 To .PivotFields.Count
        MsgBox .PivotFields(i).Name
    Next
End With
```

In some cases, it may be easier to use one of the methods that returns a subset of the pivot fields. The following accessor methods are available: **ColumnFields** method, **DataFields** method, **HiddenFields** method, **PageFields** method, **RowFields** method, **VisibleFields** method.

Properties   **Application** Property, **Count** Property, **Creator** Property, **Parent** Property.

Methods   **Item** Method.

PivotFields Method

Applies To   **PivotTable** Object.

Description   Accessor. Returns an object that represents a single pivot field (a **PivotField** object, Syntax 1) or a collection of the visible and hidden pivot fields (a **PivotFields** object, Syntax 2) in the PivotTable. Read-only.

Syntax 1   *object*.**PivotFields**(*index*)

Syntax 2	*object*.**PivotFields**

object
> Required. The **PivotTable** object.

index
> Required for Syntax 1. The name or number of the pivot field to return (can be an array to specify more than one).

See Also   **ColumnFields** Method, **DataFields** Method, **HiddenFields** Method, **PageFields** Method, **RowFields** Method, **VisibleFields** Method.

Example   This example adds the PivotTable field names to a list box. The list box appears on Sheet1.

```
Set pvtTable = Worksheets("Sheet1").Range("A3").PivotTable
Set newListBox = Worksheets("Sheet1").ListBoxes.Add _
    (Left:=10, Top:=72, Width:=144, Height:=144)
For Each hdnField In pvtTable.PivotFields
    newListBox.AddItem (hdnField.Name)
Next hdnField
Worksheets("Sheet1").Activate
```

PivotItem Object

Description   Represents an item in a pivot field. The items are the individual data entries in a field category.

Accessors   The **PivotItem** object is a member of the **PivotItems** collection. The **PivotItems** collection contains all the items in a **PivotField** object.

To access a single member of the collection, use the **PivotItems** method with the pivot item index number or name as an argument.

Use the **Name** property to set or return the item name. The following example hides the entries containing the value "1998" in the year field.

```
Worksheets("sheet3").PivotTables(1) _
    .PivotFields("year").PivotItems("1998").Visible = False
```

Properties   **Application** Property, **Creator** Property, **DataRange** Property, **LabelRange** Property, **Name** Property, **Parent** Property, **ParentItem** Property, **ParentShowDetail** Property, **Position** Property, **ShowDetail** Property, **SourceName** Property, **Value** Property, **Visible** Property.

Methods   **ChildItems** Method.

PivotItem Property

Applies To   **Range** Object.

Description   Accessor. Returns a **PivotItem** object that represents the pivot item containing the top left corner of the specified range. Read-only.

Example   This example displays the name of the pivot item containing the active cell.

```
Worksheets("Sheet1").Activate
MsgBox "The active cell is in the item " & _
    ActiveCell.PivotItem.Name
```

PivotItems Collection Object

Description   A collection of all the **PivotItem** objects in a pivot field. The items are the individual data entries in a field category.

Accessors   Use the **PivotItems** method with an argument to access a single member of the collection or without an argument to access the entire collection at once. The following example creates an enumerated list of pivot field names and the items contained in those fields. It uses the **Count** method on the **PivotItems** collection to set up the item-enumeration loop.

```
Worksheets("sheet4").Activate
With Worksheets("sheet3").PivotTables(1)
    c = 1
    For i = 1 To .PivotFields.Count
        r = 1
        Cells(r, c) = .PivotFields(i).Name
        r = r + 1
        For x = 1 To .PivotFields(i).PivotItems.Count
            Cells(r, c) = .PivotFields(i).PivotItems(x).Name
            r = r + 1
        Next
        c = c + 1
    Next
End With
```

Properties   **Application** Property, **Count** Property, **Creator** Property, **Parent** Property.

Methods   **Item** Method.

PivotItems Method

Applies To **PivotField** Object.

Description Accessor. Returns an object that represents a single pivot item (a **PivotItem** object, Syntax 1) or a collection of all the visible and hidden pivot items (a **PivotItems** object, Syntax 2) in the specified field. Read-only.

Syntax 1 *object*.**PivotItems**(*index*)

Syntax 2 *object*.**PivotItems**

object
  Required. The **PivotField** object.

index
  Required for Syntax 1. The number or name of the pivot item to return (can be an array to specify more than one).

See Also **ChildItems** Method, **HiddenItems** Method, **ParentItems** Method, **VisibleItems** Method.

Example This example adds the names of all items in the field named "COMPANY" to a list box. The list box appears on Sheet1.

```
Set pvtTable = Worksheets("Sheet1").Range("A3").PivotTable
Set newListBox = Worksheets("Sheet1").ListBoxes.Add _
    (Left:=10, Top:=72, Width:=144, Height:=144)
Set pvtField = pvtTable.PivotFields("COMPANY")
For Each pvtItem In pvtField.PivotItems
    newListBox.AddItem (pvtItem.Name)
Next pvtItem
Worksheets("Sheet1").Activate
```

PivotTable Object

Description Represents a PivotTable on a worksheet.

Accessors The **PivotTable** object is a member of the **PivotTables** collection. The **PivotTables** collection contains all the **PivotTable** objects on a single worksheet. Use the **PivotTableWizard** method to create a new PivotTable and add it to the collection.

To access a single member of the collection, use the **PivotTables** method with the PivotTable index number or name as an argument.

The following example makes the field named "year" a row field in PivotTable one on the worksheet named "Sheet3."

```
Worksheets("sheet3").PivotTables(1) _
    .PivotFields("year").Orientation = xlRowField
```

Use the **Name** property to set or return the PivotTable name. The following example moves the field named "year" on the PivotTable named "PivotTable2."

```
Worksheets("sheet3").PivotTables("pivottable2") _
    .PivotFields("year").Position = 2
```

Because PivotTable programming can be complex, it is generally easier to record PivotTable actions by clicking the Record Macro command on the Tools menu.

Properties	**Application** Property, **ColumnGrand** Property, **ColumnRange** Property, **Creator** Property, **DataBodyRange** Property, **DataLabelRange** Property, **HasAutoFormat** Property, **InnerDetail** Property, **Name** Property, **PageRange** Property, **Parent** Property, **RefreshDate** Property, **RefreshName** Property, **RowGrand** Property, **RowRange** Property, **SaveData** Property, **SourceData** Property, **TableRange1** Property, **TableRange2** Property, **Value** Property.
Methods	**AddFields** Method, **ColumnFields** Method, **DataFields** Method, **HiddenFields** Method, **PageFields** Method, **PivotFields** Method, **RefreshTable** Method, **RowFields** Method, **ShowPages** Method, **VisibleFields** Method.

PivotTable Property

Applies To	**Range** Object.
Description	Accessor. Returns a **PivotTable** object that represents the PivotTable containing the top left corner of the specified range. Read-only.
Example	This example sets the current page for the PivotTable on Sheet1 to the page named "Canada."

```
Set pvtTable = Worksheets("Sheet1").Range("A3").PivotTable
pvtTable.PivotFields("Country").CurrentPage = "Canada"
```

PivotTables Collection Object

Description	A collection of all the **PivotTable** objects on the specified worksheet.

Accessors	Use the **PivotTableWizard** method to create a new PivotTable and add it to the collection.

Use the **PivotTables** method with an argument to access a single member of the collection or without an argument to access the entire collection at once. The following example displays the number of PivotTables on the worksheet named "Sheet3."

```
MsgBox Worksheets("sheet3").PivotTables.Count
```

Properties	**Application** Property, **Count** Property, **Creator** Property, **Parent** Property.
Methods	**Item** Method.

PivotTables Method

Applies To	**Worksheet** Object.
Description	Accessor. Returns an object that represents a single PivotTable (a **PivotTable** object, Syntax 1) or a collection of all the PivotTables (a **PivotTables** object, Syntax 2) in a worksheet. Read-only.
Syntax 1	*object*.**PivotTables**(*index*)
Syntax 2	*object*.**PivotTables**

object
    Required. The **Worksheet** object.

index
    Required for Syntax 1. The name or number of the PivotTable (can be an array to specify more than one).

See Also	**PivotFields** Method, **PivotItems** Method.
Example	This example sets the Sum of 1994 field in PivotTable1 to use the SUM function.

```
ActiveSheet.PivotTables("PivotTable1"). _
    PivotFields("Sum of 1994").Function = xlSum
```

PivotTableWizard Method

Applies To	**Worksheet** Object.

Description	Creates a **PivotTable**. This method does not display the PivotTable Wizard.
Syntax	*object*.**PivotTableWizard**(*sourceType*, *sourceData*, *tableDestination*, *tableName*, *rowGrand*, *columnGrand*, *saveData*, *hasAutoFormat*, *autoPage*)

object
Required. The **Worksheet** object.

sourceType
Optional. Describes the source of the PivotTable data, as shown in the following table. If you specify this argument, you must also specify *sourceData*.

Value	Meaning
xlConsolidation	Multiple consolidation ranges
xlDatabase	Microsoft Excel list or database
xlExternal	Data from another application
xlPivotTable	Same source as another PivotTable

If *sourceType* and *sourceData* are not specified, Microsoft Excel assumes that the source type is **xlDatabase**, and the source data comes from the named range Database. If the named range does not exist, Microsoft Excel uses the current region if the current selection is in a range of more than 10 cells containing data. If this is not true, this method will fail.

sourceData
Optional. The data for the new PivotTable. A **Range**, an array of ranges, or a text constant representing the name of another PivotTable. For an external database, this is a two-element array. The first element is the connection string specifying the ODBC source for the data. The second element is the SQL query string used to get the data. If you specify this argument, you must specify *sourceType*. If the active cell is inside the *sourceData* range, you must specify *tableDestination*.

tableDestination
Optional. A **Range** specifying where the PivotTable should be placed on the worksheet. If this argument is not specified, the PivotTable is placed at the active cell.

tableName
Optional. The name of the PivotTable to be created, given as a string.

rowGrand
Optional. If **True**, the new PivotTable shows row grand totals. If **False**, row grand totals are omitted.

columnGrand
Optional. If **True**, the new PivotTable shows column grand totals. If **False**, column grand totals are omitted.

saveData
> Optional. If **True**, data is saved with the table. If **False**, only the table definition is saved.

hasAutoFormat
> Optional. If **True**, Microsoft Excel automatically formats the PivotTable when it is refreshed or when fields are moved.

autoPage
> Optional. Valid only if *sourceType* is **xlConsolidation**. If **True**, Microsoft Excel creates a page field for the consolidation. If **False**, you must create the page field or fields.

Example

This example creates a new PivotTable from a Microsoft Excel database (contained in the range A1:C100).

```
ActiveSheet.PivotTableWizard xlDatabase, Range("A1:C100")
```

Placement Property

Applies To

Arc Object, **Arcs** Collection, **Button** Object, **Buttons** Collection, **ChartObject** Object, **ChartObjects** Collection, **CheckBox** Object, **Drawing** Object, **DrawingObjects** Collection, **Drawings** Collection, **DropDown** Object, **DropDowns** Collection, **EditBox** Object, **EditBoxes** Collection, **GroupBox** Object, **GroupBoxes** Collection, **GroupObject** Object, **GroupObjects** Collection, **Label** Object, **Labels** Collection, **Line** Object, **Lines** Collection, **ListBox** Object, **ListBoxes** Collection, **OLEObject** Object, **OLEObjects** Collection, **OptionButton** Object, **OptionButtons** Collection, **Oval** Object, **Ovals** Collection, **Picture** Object, **Pictures** Collection, **Rectangle** Object, **Rectangles** Collection, **ScrollBar** Object, **ScrollBars** Collection, **Spinner** Object, **Spinners** Collection, **TextBox** Object, **TextBoxes** Collection.

Description

Returns or sets how the object is attached to the cells below it. Can be one of **xlMoveAndSize**, **xlMove**, or **xlFreeFloating**. Can be used only on objects in a worksheet. Read-write.

Example

This example sets oval one on Sheet1 to be free floating (it neither moves nor is sized with its underlying cells).

```
Worksheets("Sheet1").Ovals(1).Placement = xlFreeFloating
```

Play Method

Applies To	**SoundNote** Object.
Description	Plays the sound note.
Syntax	*object*.**Play**

object
> Required. The **SoundNote** object.

Remarks	To play sounds, you must have sound hardware installed in your computer.
See Also	**Record** Method.
Example	This example deletes the sound note in cell A1 on Sheet1, records a new sound note for the same cell, and then plays the sound note.

```
With Worksheets("Sheet1").Range("A1").SoundNote
    .Delete
    .Record
    .Play
End With
```

PlotArea Object

Description	Represents the plot area of a chart. This is the area in which your chart data is plotted. The plot area on a 2-D chart contains the data markers, gridlines, data labels, trendlines, and optional chart items placed in the chart area. The plot area on a 3-D chart contains all the above items plus the walls, floor, axes, axis titles, and tick-mark labels in the chart.
	The plot area is surrounded by the chart area. The chart area on a 2-D chart contains the axes, the chart title, axis titles, and the legend. The chart area on a 3-D chart contains the chart title and the legend. For information about formatting the chart area, see the **ChartArea** object.
Accessors	The **PlotArea** property returns the plot area for the specified chart. The following example activates the chart sheet named "Chart1," places a dashed border around the chart area for the active chart, and places a dotted border around the plot area.

```
Charts("Chart1").Activate
With ActiveChart
    .ChartArea.Border.LineStyle = xlDash
    .PlotArea.Border.LineStyle = xlDot
End With
```

Properties	**Application** Property, **Border** Property, **Creator** Property, **Height** Property, **Interior** Property, **Left** Property, **Name** Property, **Parent** Property, **Top** Property, **Width** Property.
Methods	**ClearFormats** Method, **Select** Method.

PlotArea Property

Applies To	**Chart** Object.
Description	Accessor. Returns a **PlotArea** object that represents the plot area of a chart. Read-only.
Example	This example sets the color of the plot area interior of Chart1 to cyan.

```
Charts("Chart1").PlotArea.Interior.ColorIndex = 8
```

PlotOrder Property

Applies To	**Series** Object.
Description	Returns or sets the plot order for this series within the chart group. Read-write.
Remarks	Plot order can only be set within a chart group (you cannot set the plot order for the entire chart if you have more than one chart type). A chart group is a collection of series with the same chart type and subtype.
	Changing the plot order of one series will cause the plot orders of the other series on the chart group to adjust as necessary.
Example	This example makes series two in Chart1 appear third in the plot order. The example should be run on a 2-D column chart with three or more series.

```
Charts("Chart1").ChartGroups(1).SeriesCollection(2).PlotOrder = 3
```

PlotVisibleOnly Property

Applies To	**Chart** Object.

Description   **True** if only visible cells are plotted (**False** if both visible and hidden cells are plotted). Read-write.

Example   This example causes Microsoft Excel to plot only visible cells in Chart1.

```
Charts("Chart1").PlotVisibleOnly = True
```

Point Object

Description   Represents a single point in a series in a chart.

Accessors   The **Point** object is a member of the **Points** collection. The **Points** collection contains all of the points in one series. To access a single member of the collection, use the **Points** method with the point index number as an argument. Points are numbered from left to right on the series. Points(1) is the leftmost point; Points(Points.Count) is the rightmost point. The following example sets the marker style for point three in series one in embedded chart one on worksheet one. The specified series must be a 2-D line, scatter, or radar series.

```
Worksheets(1).ChartObjects(1).Chart. _
    SeriesCollection(1).Points(3).MarkerStyle = xlDiamond
```

Properties   **Application** Property, **Border** Property, **Creator** Property, **DataLabel** Property, **Explosion** Property, **HasDataLabel** Property, **Interior** Property, **InvertIfNegative** Property, **MarkerBackgroundColor** Property, **MarkerBackgroundColorIndex** Property, **MarkerForegroundColor** Property, **MarkerForegroundColorIndex** Property, **MarkerStyle** Property, **Parent** Property, **PictureType** Property, **PictureUnit** Property.

Methods   **ApplyDataLabels** Method, **ClearFormats** Method, **Copy** Method, **Delete** Method, **Paste** Method (**Point** or **Series** Object), **Select** Method.

Points Collection Object

Description   A collection of all the **Point** objects in the specified series in a chart.

Accessors   Use the **Points** method with an argument to access a single member of the collection or without an argument to access the entire collection at once. The following example adds a data label to the last point on series one.

```
Dim pts As Points
Set pts = Worksheets(1).ChartObjects(1).Chart. _
    SeriesCollection(1).Points
pts(pts.Count).ApplyDataLabels type:=xlShowValue
```

Properties   **Application** Property, **Count** Property, **Creator** Property, **Parent** Property.

Methods   **Item** Method.

Points Method

Applies To   **Series** Object.

Description   Accessor. Returns an object that represents a single point (a **Point** object, Syntax 1) or a collection of all of the points (a **Points** object, Syntax 2) in the series. Read-only.

Syntax 1   *object*.**Points**(*index*)

Syntax 2   *object*.**Points**

object
    Required. The **Series** object.

index
    Required for Syntax 1. The name or number of the point.

Example   This example applies a data label to point one in series one in Chart1.

```
Charts("Chart1").SeriesCollection(1).Points(1).ApplyDataLabels
```

Position Property

Applies To   **Legend** Object, **PivotField** Object, **PivotItem** Object, **Toolbar** Object.

Description   Returns or sets the position of the specified object, as shown in the following table. Read-write.

Object	Position
Legend	Position of the legend on the chart. One of **xlBottom**, **xlCorner**, **xlTop**, **xlRight**, or **xlLeft**.
PivotField	Position of the field (first, second, third, and so on) among all the fields in its orientation (Rows, Columns, Pages, Data).
PivotItem	Position of the item in its field, if the item is currently showing.
Toolbar	Position of the toolbar. One of **xlTop**, **xlLeft**, **xlRight**, **xlBottom**, or **xlFloating**.

Example   This example sets the pivot field that contains the active cell to position one.

```
Worksheets("Sheet1").Activate
ActiveCell.PivotField.Position = 1
```

This example displays the position number of the pivot item that contains the active cell.

```
Worksheets("Sheet1").Activate
MsgBox "The active item is in position number " & _
    ActiveCell.PivotItem.Position
```

Post Method

Applies To   **Workbook** Object.

Description   Posts the specified workbook to a public folder or a Lotus Notes database. This method is available only in Microsoft Excel for Windows 95.

Syntax   *object*.**Post(***destName***)**

object
    Required. The workbook to post.

destName
    Optional. Specifies the name of the destination public folder or Lotus Notes database. In Microsoft Excel for Windows 95, this argument is ignored. The **Post** method prompts the user to specify the destination for the workbook.

Example   This example posts the active workbook.

```
ActiveWorkbook.Post
```

Precedents Property

Applies To   **Range** Object.

Description   Accessor. Returns a **Range** object that represents all of the precedents of a cell. This may be a multiple selection (a union of **Range** objects) if there is more than one precedent. Read-only.

See Also   **Dependents** Property, **DirectDependents** Property, **DirectPrecedents** Property, **ShowPrecedents** Method.

Example   This example selects the precedents of cell A1 on Sheet1.

```
Worksheets("Sheet1").Activate
Range("A1").Precedents.Select
```

PrecisionAsDisplayed Property

Applies To   **Workbook** Object.

Description   **True** if calculations in this workbook will be done using only the precision of the numbers as they are displayed. Read-write.

Example   This example causes calculations on the active workbook to use only the precision of the numbers as they are displayed.

```
ActiveWorkbook.PrecisionAsDisplayed = True
```

PrefixCharacter Property

Applies To   **Range** Object.

Description   Returns the prefix character for the cell. Read-only.

Remarks   If the **TransitionNavigKeys** property is **False**, this character will be ' for a text
label, or blank. If the **TransitionNavigKeys** property is **True**, this will be ' for a
left-justified label, " for a right-justified label, ^ for a centered label, \ for a
repeated label, or blank.

Example   This example displays the prefix character for cell A1 on Sheet1.

```
MsgBox "The prefix character is " & _
    Worksheets("Sheet1").Range("A1").PrefixCharacter
```

Previous Property

Applies To   **Chart** Object, **DialogSheet** Object, **Module** Object, **Range** Object, **Worksheet**
Object.

Description   Accessor. Returns a **Chart**, **DialogSheet**, **Module**, **Range** or **Worksheet** object
that represents the previous sheet or cell. Read-only.

Remarks   If the object is a range, this property emulates SHIFT+TAB, although the property
returns the previous cell without selecting it.

On a protected sheet, this property returns the previous unlocked cell. On an
unprotected sheet, this property always returns the cell to the left of the specified
cell.

See Also   **ActivatePrevious** Method, **Next** Property.

Example   This example selects the previous unlocked cell on Sheet1. If Sheet1 is unprotected,
this is the cell immediately to the left of the active cell.

```
Worksheets("Sheet1").Activate
ActiveCell.Previous.Select
```

PreviousSelections Property

Applies To   **Application** Object.

Description   Accessor. Returns an array of the four previous ranges or names selected. Each
element in the array is a **Range** object. Read-only. Each time you go to a range or
cell using the name box or Go To command (Edit menu), or a macro calls the **Goto**
method, whatever range was selected before is added to this array as element
number one, and the other items in the array are moved down.

Example

This example displays the cell addresses of all items in the array of previous selections. If there are no previous selections, the **LBound** function returns an error. This error is trapped, and a message box appears.

```
On Error GoTo noSelections
For i = LBound(Application.PreviousSelections) To _
            UBound(Application.PreviousSelections)
    MsgBox Application.PreviousSelections(i).Address
Next i
Exit Sub
On Error GoTo 0

noSelections:
    MsgBox "There are no previous selections"
```

Print # Statement

Description

Writes display-formatted data to a sequential file.

Syntax

Print #*filenumber*,[*outputlist*]

The **Print #** statement syntax has these parts:

Part	Description
filenumber	Any valid file number.
outputlist	Expression or list of expressions to print.

The *outputlist* argument has the following syntax and parts:

[{**Spc**(*n*) | **Tab**[(*n*)]}][*expression*][*charpos*]

Part	Description
Spc(*n*)	Used to insert space characters in the output, where *n* is the number of space characters to insert.
Tab(*n*)	Used to position the insertion point to an absolute column number, where *n* is the column number. Use **Tab** with no argument to position the insertion point at the beginning of the next print zone.
expression	Numeric or string expressions to print.
charpos	Specifies the insertion point for the next character. Use a semicolon to specify the insertion point to be immediately after the last character displayed. Use **Tab**(*n*) to position the insertion point to an absolute column number. Use **Tab** with no argument to position the insertion point at the beginning of the next print zone. If *charpos* is omitted, the next character is printed on the next line.

Remarks

If you omit *outputlist* and include only a list separator after *filenumber*, a blank line prints to the file. Multiple expressions can be separated with either a space or a semicolon. A space has the same effect as a semicolon.

All data written to the file using **Print #** is internationally aware; that is, the data is properly formatted (using the appropriate decimal separator) and the keywords are output in the language appropriate for the international locale specified for your system.

For **Boolean** data, either `True` or `False` is printed. The **True** and **False** keywords are translated, as appropriate, according to the locale setting specified for your system.

Date data is written to the file using the standard short date format recognized by your system. When either the date or the time component is missing or zero, only the provided part gets written to the file.

Nothing is written to the file if *outputlist* data is **Empty**. However, if *outputlist* data is **Null**, `Null` is written to the file. Again, the **Null** keyword is translated, as appropriate.

For error data, the output appears as `Error errorcode`. The **Error** keyword is translated, as appropriate, when written to the file.

Because **Print #** writes an image of the data to the file, you must delimit the data so it prints correctly. If you use **Tab** with no arguments to move the print position to the next print zone, **Print #** also writes the spaces between print fields to the file.

Note If, at some future time, you want to read the data from a file using the **Input #** statement, use the **Write #** statement instead of the **Print #** statement to write the data to the file. Using **Write #** ensures the integrity of each separate data field by properly delimiting it, so that it can be read back in using **Input #**. Using **Write #** also ensures that it can be correctly read in any locale.

See Also

Open Statement, **Print** Method, **Spc** Function, **Tab** Function, **Write #** Statement.

Example

This example uses the **Print #** statement to write data to a file.

```
Open "TESTFILE" For Output As #1        ' Open file for output.
Print #1, "This is a test"              ' Print text to file.
Print #1,                               ' Print blank line to file.
Print #1, "Zone 1"; Tab ; "Zone 2"      ' Print in two print zones.
Print #1, "Hello" ; " " ; "World"       ' Separate strings with space.
Print #1, Spc(5) ; "5 leading spaces "  ' Print 5 leading spaces.
Print #1, Tab(10) ; "Hello"             ' Print word at col 10.
```

```
' Assign Boolean, Date, Null and Error values.
MyBool = False : MyDate = #February 12, 1969# : MyNull = Null
MyError = CVErr(32767)
' True, False, Null and Error are translated using locale settings of
' your system. Date literals are written using standard short date
' format.
Print #1, MyBool ; " is a Boolean value"
Print #1, MyDate ; " is a date"
Print #1, MyNull ; " is a null value"
Print #1, MyError ; " is an error value"
Close #1' Close file.
```

Print Method

Applies To	**Debug** Object.
Description	Prints text in the Immediate pane of the Debug window.
Syntax	[*object.*]**Print** [*outputlist*]

The **Print** method syntax has these parts:

Part	Description
object	Object expression that evaluates to the **Debug** object.
outputlist	Expression or list of expressions to print. If omitted, a blank line is printed.

The *outputlist* argument has the following syntax and parts:

[{**Spc**(*n*) | **Tab**[(*n*)]}][*expression*][*charpos*]

Part	Description
Spc(*n*)	Used to insert space characters in the output, where *n* is the number of space characters to insert.
Tab(*n*)	Used to position the insertion point at an absolute column number where *n* is the column number. Use **Tab** with no argument to position the insertion point at the beginning of the next print zone.
expression	Numeric or string expressions to print.
charpos	Specifies the insertion point for the next character. Use a semicolon to specify the insertion point to immediately follow the last character displayed. Use **Tab**(*n*) to position the insertion point at an absolute column number. Use **Tab** with no argument to position the insertion point at the beginning of the next print zone. If *charpos* is omitted, the next character is printed on the next line.

Remarks

Multiple expressions can be separated with either a space or a semicolon. A space has the same effect as a semicolon.

All data printed to the Immediate pane is internationally aware; that is, the data is properly formatted (using the appropriate decimal separator) and the keywords are output in the language appropriate for the international locale specified for your system.

For **Boolean** data, either `True` or `False` is printed. The **True** and **False** keywords are translated, as appropriate, according to the locale setting specified for your system.

Date data is written using the standard short date format recognized by your system. When either the date or the time component is missing or zero, only the data provided gets written.

Nothing is written if *outputlist* data is **Empty**. However, if *outputlist* data is **Null**, `Null` is output. Again, the **Null** keyword is translated, as appropriate, when output.

For error data, the output appears as `Error errorcode`. The **Error** keyword is translated, as appropriate, when output.

Note Because the **Print** method normally prints with proportionally-spaced characters, it is important to remember that there is no correlation between the number of characters printed and the number of fixed-width columns those characters occupy. For example, a wide letter, such as a "W", occupies more than one fixed-width column, whereas a narrow letter, such as an "i", occupies less. To account for cases where wider than average characters are used, you must ensure that your tabular columns are positioned far enough apart. Alternatively, you can print using a fixed-pitch font (such as Courier) to ensure that each character uses only one column.

See Also

Debug Object, **Print #** Statement, **Spc** Function, **Tab** Function.

Example

This example uses the **Print** method to output text to the **Debug** object; that is, display text in the Debug window.

```
For I = 11 To 20                        ' Loop 10 times.
    ' Print each value on a new line.
    Debug.Print I
Next I

For I = 11 To 20                        ' Loop 10 times.
    ' Print values on the same line, next to each other.
    Debug.Print I;
Next I
```

```
Debug.Print Spc(10) ; "Hello there"      ' Print 10 spaces before.
Debug.Print Tab(20) ; "This is a test" ' Print at column 20.
Debug.Print "Hello"; Tab; Tab; "There"  ' Print 2 print zones apart.
```

PrintArea Property

Applies To   **PageSetup** Object.

Description   Returns or sets the range to print, as a string using A1-style references in the
                        language of the macro. Read-write.

Remarks   Set this property to **False** or to the empty string ("") to set the print area to the
                        entire sheet.

                        This property applies only to worksheet pages.

See Also   **PrintOut** Method.

Example   This example sets the print area to cells A1:C5 on Sheet1.

```
Worksheets("Sheet1").PageSetup.PrintArea = "$A$1:$C$5"
```

                        This example sets the print area to the current region on Sheet1. Note that you use
                        the **Address** method to return an A1-style address.

```
Worksheets("Sheet1").Activate
ActiveSheet.PageSetup.PrintArea = _
        ActiveCell.CurrentRegion.Address
```

PrintGridlines Property

Applies To   **PageSetup** Object.

Description   **True** if cell gridlines are printed on the page. Read-write.

Remarks   This property applies only to worksheets.

See Also   **DisplayGridlines** Property.

Example   This example prints cell gridlines when Sheet1 is printed.

```
Worksheets("Sheet1").PageSetup.PrintGridlines = True
```

PrintHeadings Property

Applies To   **PageSetup** Object.

Description   **True** if row and column headings are printed with this page. Read-write.

Remarks   This property applies only to worksheets.

The **DisplayHeadings** property controls on-screen heading display.

Example   This example turns off heading printing for Sheet1.

```
Worksheets("Sheet1").PageSetup.PrintHeadings = False
```

PrintNotes Property

Applies To   **PageSetup** Object.

Description   **True** if cell notes will be printed along with the sheet. Read-write.

Remarks   This property applies only to worksheet pages.

Example   This example turns off notes printing.

```
Worksheets("Sheet1").PageSetup.PrintNotes = False
```

PrintObject Property

Applies To   **Arc** Object, **Arcs** Collection, **Button** Object, **Buttons** Collection, **ChartObject** Object, **ChartObjects** Collection, **CheckBox** Object, **Drawing** Object, **DrawingObjects** Collection, **Drawings** Collection, **DropDown** Object, **DropDowns** Collection, **EditBox** Object, **EditBoxes** Collection, **GroupBox** Object, **GroupBoxes** Collection, **GroupObject** Object, **GroupObjects** Collection, **Label** Object, **Labels** Collection, **Line** Object, **Lines** Collection, **ListBox** Object, **ListBoxes** Collection, **OLEObject** Object, **OLEObjects** Collection, **OptionButton** Object, **OptionButtons** Collection, **Oval** Object, **Ovals** Collection, **Picture** Object, **Pictures** Collection, **Rectangle** Object, **Rectangles** Collection, **ScrollBar** Object, **ScrollBars** Collection, **Spinner** Object, **Spinners** Collection, **TextBox** Object, **TextBoxes** Collection.

Description   **True** if the object will be printed when the document is printed. Read-write.

See Also

See Also   **PrintOut** Method.

Example   This example sets line one on Sheet1 to print with the worksheet.

```
Worksheets("Sheet1").Lines(1).PrintObject = True
```

PrintOut Method

Applies To   **Chart** Object, **Charts** Collection, **DialogSheet** Object, **DialogSheets** Collection, **Module** Object, **Modules** Collection, **Range** Object, **Sheets** Collection, **Window** Object, **Workbook** Object, **Worksheet** Object, **Worksheets** Collection.

Description   Prints the object.

Syntax   *object*.**PrintOut**(*from*, *to*, *copies*, *preview*, *activePrinter*, *printToFile*, *collate*)

object
Required. The object to print.

from
Optional. The number of the page with which to start printing. If omitted, printing starts at the beginning.

to
Optional. The number of the last page to print. If omitted, printing goes to the last page.

copies
Optional. The number of copies to print. If omitted, one copy is printed.

preview
Optional. If **True**, Microsoft Excel invokes print preview before printing the object. If **False** (or omitted) the object is printed immediately.

activePrinter
Optional. Sets the name of the active printer.

printToFile
Optional. If **True**, printing goes to a file. Microsoft Excel prompts the user to enter the name of the output file. There is no way to specify the output filename from Visual Basic.

collate
Optional. If **True**, multiple copies are collated.

Remarks   "Pages" in the descriptions of *from* and *to* refers to printed pages—not overall pages in the sheet or workbook.

This method applies to the **Window** object only when it is the Info window.

See Also	**PrintArea** Property, **PrintPreview** Method.
Example	This example prints the active sheet.

```
ActiveSheet.PrintOut
```

PrintPreview Method

Applies To	**Chart** Object, **Charts** Collection, **DialogSheet** Object, **DialogSheets** Collection, **Range** Object, **Sheets** Collection, **Window** Object, **Workbook** Object, **Worksheet** Object, **Worksheets** Collection.
Description	Shows a preview of the object as it would be printed.
Syntax	*object*.**PrintPreview**
	object Required. The object to preview.
See Also	**PrintOut** Method.
Example	This example displays a print preview of Sheet1.

```
Worksheets("Sheet1").PrintPreview
```

PrintQuality Property

Applies To	**PageSetup** Object.
Description	Returns or sets the print quality, as a two-element array containing both horizontal and vertical print quality. Some printers may not support vertical print quality. Read-write.
Remarks	This property always returns a two-element array, even if the printer does not support vertical print quality.
Example	This example sets print quality on a printer with nonsquare pixels. The array specifies both horizontal and vertical print quality. This example may cause an error, depending on the printer driver you are using.

```
Worksheets("Sheet1").PageSetup.PrintQuality = Array(240, 140)
```

This example displays the current horizontal print quality setting.

```
MsgBox "Horizontal Print Quality is " & _
    Worksheets("Sheet1").PageSetup.PrintQuality(1)
```

PrintTitleColumns Property

Applies To   **PageSetup** Object.

Description   Returns or sets the columns containing the cells to be repeated on the left of each page, as a string in A1-style notation in the language of the macro. Read-write.

Remarks   If you specify only part of a column or columns, Microsoft Excel expands the range to full columns.

Set this property to **False** or to the empty string ("") to turn off title columns.

This property applies only to worksheet pages.

See Also   **PrintTitleRows** Property.

Example   This example defines row three as the title row, and it defines columns one through three as the title columns.

```
Worksheets("Sheet1").Activate
ActiveSheet.PageSetup.PrintTitleRows = ActiveSheet.Rows(3).Address
ActiveSheet.PageSetup.PrintTitleColumns = _
        ActiveSheet.Columns("A:C").Address
```

PrintTitleRows Property

Applies To   **PageSetup** Object.

Description   Returns or sets the rows containing the cells to be repeated on the top of each page, as a string in A1-style notation in the language of the macro. Read-write.

Remarks   If you specify only part of a row or rows, Microsoft Excel expands the range to full rows.

Set this property to **False** or to the empty string ("") to turn off title rows.

This property applies only to worksheet pages.

See Also   **PrintTitleColumns** Property.

Example   This example defines row three as the title row, and it defines columns one through three as the title columns.

```
Worksheets("Sheet1").Activate
ActiveSheet.PageSetup.PrintTitleRows = ActiveSheet.Rows(3).Address
ActiveSheet.PageSetup.PrintTitleColumns = _
        ActiveSheet.Columns("A:C").Address
```

PromptForSummaryInfo Property

Applies To   **Application** Object.

Description   **True** if Microsoft Excel asks for summary info when files are initially saved. Read-write.

Example   This example displays a prompt that asks for summary information when files are first saved.

```
Application.PromptForSummaryInfo = True
```

Property Get Statement

Description   Declares the name, arguments, and code that form the body of a **Property** procedure, which gets the value of a property.

Syntax   [**Public** | **Private**][**Static**] **Property Get** *name* [(*arglist*)][**As** *type*]
   [*statements*]
   [*name* = *expression*]
   [**Exit Property**]
   [*statements*]
   [*name* = *expression*]
End Property

The **Property Get** statement syntax has these parts:

Part	Description
Public	Indicates that the **Property Get** procedure is accessible to all other procedures in all modules. If used in a private module (one that contains an **Option Private** statement) the procedure is not available outside the project.
Private	Indicates that the **Property Get** procedure is accessible only to other procedures in the module where it is declared.
Static	Indicates that the **Property Get** procedure's local variables are preserved between calls. The **Static** attribute doesn't affect variables that are declared outside the **Property Get** procedure, even if they are used in the procedure.
name	Name of the **Property Get** procedure; follows standard variable naming conventions, except that the name can be the same as a **Property Let** or **Property Set** procedure in the same module.
arglist	List of variables representing arguments that are passed to the **Property Get** procedure when it is called. Multiple variables are separated by commas.
type	Data type of the value returned by the **Property Get** procedure; may be **Boolean**, **Integer**, **Long**, **Currency**, **Single**, **Double**, **Date**, **String** (except fixed length), **Object**, or **Variant**. Arrays of any type can't be returned, but a **Variant** containing an array can.
statements	Any group of statements to be executed within the body of the **Property Get** procedure.
expression	Value of the property returned by the procedure defined by the **Property Get** statement.

The *arglist* argument has the following syntax and parts:

[**Optional**][**ByVal** | **ByRef**] *varname*[( )][**As** *type*]

Part	Description
Optional	Indicates that an argument is not required. If used, all subsequent arguments in *arglist* must also be optional and declared using the **Optional** keyword. All **Optional** arguments must be **Variant**.
ByVal	Indicates that the argument is passed by value.
ByRef	Indicates that the argument is passed by reference.
varname	Name of the variable representing the argument; follows standard variable naming conventions.
type	Data type of the argument passed to the **Property Get** procedure; may be **Boolean**, **Integer**, **Long**, **Currency**, **Single**, **Double**, **Date**, **String** (variable length only), **Object**, **Variant**, a user-defined type, or an object type.

Remarks

If not explicitly specified using either **Public** or **Private**, **Property** procedures are **Public** by default. If **Static** is not used, the value of local variables is not preserved between calls.

All executable code must be in procedures. You can't define a **Property Get** procedure inside another **Sub**, **Function**, or **Property** procedure.

The **Exit Property** keywords cause an immediate exit from a **Property Get** procedure. Program execution continues with the statement following the statement that called the **Property Get** procedure. Any number of **Exit Property** statements can appear anywhere in a **Property Get** procedure.

Like a **Sub** and **Property Let** procedure, a **Property Get** procedure is a separate procedure that can take arguments, perform a series of statements, and change the values of its arguments. However, unlike a **Sub** or **Property Let** procedure, a **Property Get** procedure can be used on the right-hand side of an expression in the same way you use a **Function** or a property name when you want to return the value of a property.

See Also

Function Statement, **Property Let** Statement, **Property Set** Statement, **Sub** Statement.

Example

This example uses the **Property Get** Statement to define a property procedure that gets the value of a property that identifies, as a string, the current color of a pen in a drawing package:

```
Dim CurrentColor As Integer
Const BLACK = 0, RED = 1, GREEN = 2, BLUE = 3

' Returns the current color of the pen as a string
Property Get PenColor() As String
    Select Case CurrentColor
        Case RED
            PenColor = "Red"
        Case GREEN
            PenColor = "Green"
        Case BLUE
            PenColor = "Blue"
    End Select
End Property

' The following line gets the color of the pen
' calling the Property Get procedure.
ColorName = PenColor()
```

Property Let Statement

Description   Declares the name, arguments, and code that form the body of a **Property Let** procedure, which assigns a value to a property.

Syntax   [**Public** | **Private**][**Static**] **Property Let** *name* [(*arglist*)]
    [*statements*]
    [**Exit Property**]
    [*statements*]
End Property

The **Property Let** statement syntax has these parts:

Part	Description
Public	Indicates that the **Property Let** procedure is accessible to all other procedures in all modules. If used in a private module (one that contains an **Option Private** statement), the procedure is not available outside the project.
Private	Indicates that the **Property Let** procedure is accessible only to other procedures in the module where it is declared.
Static	Indicates that the **Property Let** procedure's local variables are preserved between calls. The **Static** attribute doesn't affect variables that are declared outside the **Property Let** procedure, even if they are used in the procedure.
name	Name of the **Property Let** procedure; follows standard variable naming conventions, except that the name can be the same as a **Property Get** or **Property Set** procedure in the same module.
arglist	List of variables representing arguments that are passed to the **Property Let** procedure when it is called. Multiple variables are separated by commas. The last argument is the value assigned to the property on the right-hand side of an expression.
statements	Any group of statements to be executed within the body of the **Property Let** procedure.

The *arglist* argument has the following syntax and parts:

[**ByVal** | **ByRef**] *varname*[( )][**As** *type*]

Part	Description
ByVal	Indicates that the argument is passed by value.
ByRef	Indicates that the argument is passed by reference.
varname	Name of the variable representing the argument; follows standard variable naming conventions.
type	Data type of the argument passed to the **Property Let** procedure; may be **Boolean**, **Integer**, **Long**, **Currency**, **Single**, **Double**, **Date**, **String** (variable length only), **Object**, **Variant**, a user-defined type, or an object type.

Note Every **Property Let** statement must define at least one argument for the procedure it defines. That argument (or the last argument if there is more than one) will contain the actual value to be assigned to the property when the procedure defined by the **Property Let** statement is invoked.

Remarks

If not explicitly specified using either **Public** or **Private**, **Property** procedures are **Public** by default. If **Static** is not used, the value of local variables is not preserved between calls.

All executable code must be in procedures. You can't define a **Property Let** procedure inside another **Sub**, **Function**, or **Property** procedure.

The **Exit Property** keywords cause an immediate exit from a **Property Let** procedure. Program execution continues with the statement following the statement that called the **Property Let** procedure. Any number of **Exit Property** statements can appear anywhere in a **Property Let** procedure.

Like a **Function** and **Property Get** procedure, a **Property Let** procedure is a separate procedure that can take arguments, perform a series of statements, and change the value of its arguments. However, unlike a **Function** and **Property Get** procedure, both of which return a value, a **Property Let** procedure can only be used on the left side of a property assignment expression or **Let** statement.

See Also

Function Statement, **Let** Statement, **Property Get** Statement, **Property Set** Statement, **Sub** Statement.

Example

This example uses the **Property Let** statement to define a procedure that assigns a value to a property that identifies the pen color for a drawing package.

```
Dim CurrentColor As Integer
Const BLACK = 0, RED = 1, GREEN = 2, BLUE = 3


' Sets the pen color property for a Drawing package.
' The module level variable 'CurrentColor' is set to
' a numeric value that identifies the color used for drawing.
Property Let PenColor(ColorName as String)
    Select Case ColorName          ' Check color name string.
        Case "Red"
            CurrentColor = RED     ' Assign value for Red.
        Case "Green"
            CurrentColor = GREEN   ' Assign value for Green.
        Case "Blue"
            CurrentColor = BLUE    ' Assign value for Blue.
        Case Else
            CurrentColor = BLACK   ' Assign default value.
    End Select
End Property


' The following line sets the PenColor property for a drawing package
' by calling the Property Let procedure.

PenColor() = "Red"
```

Property Set Statement

Description

Declares the name, arguments, and code that form the body of a **Property** procedure, which sets a reference to an object.

Syntax

[**Public** | **Private**][**Static**] **Property Set** *name* [(*arglist*)]
    [*statements*]
    [**Exit Property**]
    [*statements*]
End Property

The **Property Set** statement syntax has these parts:

Part	Description
Public	Indicates that the **Property Set** procedure is accessible to all other procedures in all modules. If used in a private module (one that contains an **Option Private** statement), the procedure is not available outside the project.
Private	Indicates that the **Property Set** procedure is accessible only to other procedures in the module where it is declared.
Static	Indicates that the **Property Set** procedure's local variables are preserved between calls. The **Static** attribute doesn't affect variables that are declared outside the **Property Set** procedure, even if they are used in the procedure.
name	Name of the **Property Set** procedure; follows standard variable naming conventions, except that the name can be the same as a **Property Get** or **Property Let** procedure in the same module.
arglist	List of variables representing arguments that are passed to the **Property Set** procedure when it is called. Multiple variables are separated by commas. The last argument is the object reference used on the right-hand side of an object reference assignment.
statements	Any group of statements to be executed within the body of the **Property** procedure.

The *arglist* argument has the following syntax and parts:

[**ByVal** | **ByRef**] *varname*[( )][**As** *type*]

Part	Description
ByVal	Indicates that the argument is passed by value.
ByRef	Indicates that the argument is passed by reference.
varname	Name of the variable representing the argument; follows standard variable naming conventions.
type	Data type of the argument passed to the **Property Set** procedure; may be **Boolean**, **Integer**, **Long**, **Currency**, **Single**, **Double**, **Date**, **String** (variable length only), **Object**, **Variant**, a user-defined type, or an object type.

Note Every **Property Set** statement must define at least one argument for the procedure it defines. That argument (or the last argument if there is more than one) will contain the actual object reference for the property when the procedure defined by the **Property Set** statement is invoked.

Remarks

If not explicitly specified using either **Public** or **Private**, **Property** procedures are **Public** by default. If **Static** is not used, the value of local variables is not preserved between calls.

All executable code must be in procedures. You can't define a **Property Set** procedure inside another **Sub**, **Function**, or **Property** procedure.

The **Exit Property** keywords cause an immediate exit from a **Property Set** procedure. Program execution continues with the statement following the statement that called the **Property Set** procedure. Any number of **Exit Property** statements can appear anywhere in a **Property Set** procedure.

Like a **Function** and **Property Get** procedure, a **Property Set** procedure is a separate procedure that can take arguments, perform a series of statements, and change the value of its arguments. However, unlike a **Function** and **Property Get** procedure, both of which return a value, a **Property Set** procedure can only be used on the left side of an object reference assignment (**Set** statement).

See Also

Function Statement, **Property Get** Statement, **Property Let** Statement, **Sub** Statement.

Example

This example uses the **Property Set** statement to declare a property procedure which sets a reference to an object.

```
' The Pen property may be set to different Pen implementations.
Property Set Pen(P As Object)
    Set CurrentPen = P              ' Assign Pen to object.
End Property
```

Protect Method

Applies To

Chart Object, **DialogSheet** Object, **Module** Object, **Workbook** Object, **Worksheet** Object.

Description

Protects a chart, dialog sheet, Visual Basic module or worksheet (Syntax 1), or a workbook (Syntax 2) so that it cannot be modified.

Syntax 1

object.**Protect**(*password*, *drawingObjects*, *contents*, *scenarios*, *userInterfaceOnly*)

Syntax 2

object.**Protect**(*password*, *structure*, *windows*)

object
   Required. The **Chart**, **DialogSheet**, **Module**, or **Worksheet** (Syntax 1) or **Workbook** object (Syntax 2).

password

Optional. A string that specifies a case-sensitive password for the sheet or workbook. If omitted, you can unprotect the sheet or workbook without a password. If specified, you must specify the password to unprotect the sheet or workbook. If you forget the password, you cannot unprotect the sheet or workbook. It's a good idea to keep a list of your passwords and their corresponding document names in a safe place.

drawingObjects

Optional. **True** to protect the drawing objects on the sheet. For a dialog sheet, this protects the layout of the controls. If this argument is omitted, the drawing objects are not protected. Ignored for Visual Basic modules.

contents

Optional. **True** (or omitted) to protect the contents of the object. For a Visual Basic module, this protects the source code. For a chart, this protects the entire chart. For a dialog sheet, this protects the dialog layout and text of the dialog controls. For a worksheet, this protects the cells.

scenarios

Optional. **True** (or omitted) to protect scenarios. This argument is valid only for worksheets.

structure

Optional. **True** to protect the structure of the workbook (the relative position of the sheets). If this argument is omitted, the structure is not protected.

userInterfaceOnly

Optional. **True** to protect the user interface but not macros. If this argument is omitted, protection applies to macros and the user interface.

windows

Optional. **True** to protect the windows of the sheet or workbook. If omitted, the windows are not protected.

Remarks   Using the **Protect** method causes an error if the workbook is already protected.

See Also   **Locked** Property, **ProtectContents** Property, **ProtectDrawingObjects** Property, **ProtectScenarios** Property, **ProtectStructure** Property, **ProtectWindows** Property, **Unprotect** Method.

Example   This example protects the active workbook.

```
ActiveWorkbook.Protect password := "drowssap"
```

ProtectContents Property

Applies To   **Chart** Object, **DialogSheet** Object, **Module** Object, **Worksheet** Object.

Description	**True** if the contents of a sheet are protected. For a Visual Basic module, this protects the source code. For a chart, this protects the entire chart. For a dialog sheet, this protects the dialog layout and text of the dialog controls. For a worksheet, this protects the cells. Read-only.
See Also	**Locked** Property, **Protect** Method, **ProtectWindows** Property, **Unprotect** Method.
Example	This example displays a message box if the contents of Sheet1 are protected.

```
If Worksheets("Sheet1").ProtectContents = True Then
    MsgBox "The contents of Sheet1 are protected."
End If
```

ProtectDrawingObjects Property

Applies To	**Chart** Object, **DialogSheet** Object, **Worksheet** Object.
Description	**True** if the drawing objects of a sheet are protected. On a dialog sheet, this protects the layout of the controls. Read-only.
See Also	**Locked** Property, **Protect** Method, **ProtectContents** Property, **Unprotect** Method.
Example	This example displays a message box if the drawing objects on the active sheet are protected.

```
If Worksheets("Sheet1").ProtectDrawingObjects = True Then
    MsgBox "The drawing objects on Sheet1 are protected."
End If
```

Protection Property

Applies To	**Toolbar** Object.

Description	Returns or sets how the toolbar is protected from changes by the user, as shown in the following table (in order from minimum to maximum protection). This property is available only in Microsoft Excel for Windows 95. Read-write.

Value	Meaning
xlNormal	Normal toolbar behavior. The toolbar can be moved, resized, and docked. Toolbar buttons can be added, removed, and repositioned.
xlNoButtonChanges	The toolbar can be moved, resized, and docked. Toolbar buttons cannot be added, removed, or repositioned.
xlNoShapeChanges	Same as **xlNoButtonChanges**, but the toolbar cannot be resized. The toolbar can be moved and docked.
xlNoDockingChanges	Same as **xlNoShapeChanges**, but the toolbar cannot be docked or undocked. The toolbar can be moved.
xlNoChanges	Same as **xlNoDockingChanges**, but the toolbar cannot be moved.

Remarks	This property is saved with the toolbar configuration file and recalled for each Microsoft Excel session.
	New toolbars are always created with the protection set to **xlNormal**.
Example	This example sets the protection for My Custom Toolbar. The toolbar can be moved, resized, and docked, but the toolbar buttons cannot be added, removed, or repositioned.

```
Toolbars("My Custom Toolbar").Protection = xlNoButtonChanges
```

ProtectionMode Property

Applies To	**Worksheet** Object.
Description	**True** if user-interface-only protection is turned on. To turn on user interface protection, use the **Protect** method with the *userInterfaceOnly* argument set to **True**. This property is available only in Microsoft Excel for Windows 95. Read-only.
Example	This example displays the state of the **ProtectionMode** property.

```
MsgBox ActiveSheet.ProtectionMode
```

ProtectScenarios Property

Applies To   **Worksheet** Object.

Description   **True** if the worksheet scenarios are protected. Read-only.

See Also   **Protect** Method, **Unprotect** Method.

Example   This example displays a message box if scenarios are protected on Sheet1.

```
If Worksheets("Sheet1").ProtectScenarios Then _
    MsgBox "Scenarios are protected on this worksheet."
```

ProtectStructure Property

Applies To   **Workbook** Object.

Description   **True** if the order of the sheets in the workbook is protected. Read-only.

See Also   **Protect** Method, **ProtectWindows** Property, **Unprotect** Method.

Example   This example displays a message if the structure of the active workbook is protected.

```
If ActiveWorkbook.ProtectStructure = True Then
    MsgBox "Remember, you cannot delete, add, or change " & Chr(13) & _
        "the location of any sheets in this workbook."
End If
```

ProtectWindows Property

Applies To   **Workbook** Object.

Description   **True** if the windows of the workbook are protected. Read-only.

See Also   **Protect** Method, **ProtectStructure** Property, **Unprotect** Method.

Example   This example displays a message if the windows in the active workbook are protected.

```
If ActiveWorkbook.ProtectWindows = True Then
    MsgBox "Remember, you cannot rearrange any window in this workbook."
End If
```

Public Statement

Description

Used at module level to declare public variables and allocate storage space.

Syntax

Public *varname*[([*subscripts*])][**As** *type*][,*varname*[([*subscripts*])][**As** *type*]] . . .

The **Public** statement syntax has these parts:

Part	Description
varname	Name of the variable; follows standard variable naming conventions.
subscripts	Dimensions of an array variable; up to 60 multiple dimensions may be declared. The argument *subscripts* uses the following syntax:
	[*lower* **To**] *upper* [,[*lower* **To**] *upper*] . . .
type	Data type of the variable; may be **Boolean**, **Integer**, **Long**, **Currency**, **Single**, **Double**, **Date**, **String** (for variable-length strings), **String** * *length* (for fixed-length strings), **Object**, **Variant**, a user-defined type, or an object type. Use a separate **As** *type* clause for each variable being defined.

Remarks

Variables declared using the **Public** statement are available to all procedures in all modules in all applications unless **Option Private Module** is in effect; in which case, the variables are **Public** only within the project in which they reside.

Use the **Public** statement to declare the data type or object type of a variable. For example, the following statement declares a variable as an **Integer**:

```
Public NumberOfEmployees As Integer
```

If you do not specify a data type or object type and there is no **Def***type* statement in the module, the variable is **Variant** by default.

When variables are initialized, a numeric variable is initialized to 0, a variable-length string is initialized to a zero-length string, and a fixed-length string is filled with zeros. **Variant** variables are initialized to **Empty**. Each element of a user-defined type variable is initialized as if it was a separate variable. A variable that refers to an object must be assigned an existing object using the **Set** statement before it can be used. Until it is assigned an object, the declared object variable has the special value **Nothing**, which indicates that it does not refer to any particular instance of an object.

You can also use the **Public** statement with empty parentheses to declare dynamic arrays. After declaring a dynamic array, use the **ReDim** statement within a procedure to define the number of dimensions and elements in the array. If you try to redeclare a dimension for an array variable whose size was explicitly specified in a **Private**, **Public** or **Dim** statement, an error occurs.

See Also	**Array** Function, **Const** Statement, **Dim** Statement, **Option Base** Statement, **Option Private** Statement, **Private** Statement, **ReDim** Statement, **Static** Statement, **Type** Statement.
Example	The **Public** statement is used at the module-level to declare variables as public; that is, they are available to all procedures in all modules in all applications unless **Option Private Module** is in effect.

```
Public Number As Integer                   ' Public integer variable.
Public NameArray(1 To 5) As String         ' Public array variable.
Public MyVar, YourVar, ThisVar As Integer  ' Multiple declarations.
```

Pushed Property

Applies To	**ToolbarButton** Object.
Description	**True** if the button appears pressed down. Read-write.
Remarks	You cannot set this property for a built-in button. You can only set it for a custom button, and then only if the button has a procedure attached to it.
See Also	**Enabled** Property.
Example	This example adds a custom button to the Standard toolbar, attaches the my_Macro procedure to the button, and then makes the button appear pressed.

```
Set btn = Toolbars("Standard").ToolbarButtons.Add _
        (button:=220, before:=3)
btn.OnAction = "my_Macro"
btn.Pushed = True
```

Put Statement

Description	Writes from a variable to a disk file.
Syntax	**Put** [#]*filenumber*,[*recnumber*],*varname*

The **Put** statement syntax has these parts:

Part	Description
filenumber	Any valid file number.
recnumber	Record number (**Random** mode files) or byte number (**Binary** mode files) at which writing begins.
varname	Name of variable containing data to be written to disk.

Remarks

The first record/byte in a file is at position 1, the second record/byte is at position 2, and so on. If you omit *recnumber*, the next record or byte (the one after the last **Get** or **Put** statement or the one pointed to by the last **Seek** function) is written. You must include delimiting commas, for example:

```
Put #4,,FileBuffer
```

For files opened in **Random** mode, the following rules apply:

- If the length of the data being written is less than the length specified in the **Len** clause of the **Open** statement, **Put** still writes subsequent records on record-length boundaries. The space between the end of one record and the beginning of the next record is padded with the existing contents of the file buffer. Because the amount of padding data can't be determined with any certainty, it is generally a good idea to have the record length match the length of the data being written.

- If the variable being written is a variable-length string, **Put** writes a 2-byte descriptor containing the string length and then the variable. The record length specified by the **Len** clause in the **Open** statement must be at least 2 bytes greater than the actual length of the string.

- If the variable being written is a **Variant** of a numeric type, **Put** writes 2 bytes identifying the **VarType** of the **Variant** and then the variable. For example, when writing a **Variant** of **VarType** 3, **Put** writes 6 bytes: 2 bytes identifying the **Variant** as **VarType** 3 (**Long**) and 4 bytes containing the **Long** data. The record length specified by the **Len** clause in the **Open** statement must be at least 2 bytes greater than the actual number of bytes required to store the variable.

- If the variable being written is a **String Variant** (**VarType** 8), **Put** writes 2 bytes identifying the **VarType**, 2 bytes indicating the length of the string, and then the string data. The record length specified by the **Len** clause in the **Open** statement must be at least 4 bytes greater than the actual length of the string.

- If the variable being written is any other type of variable (not a variable-length string and not a **Variant**), **Put** writes only the variable data. The record length specified by the **Len** clause in the **Open** statement must be greater than or equal to the length of the data being written.

- **Put** writes elements of user-defined types as if each were written individually, except there is no padding between elements. The record length specified by the **Len** clause in the **Open** statement must be greater than or equal to the sum of all the bytes required to write the individual elements.

For files opened in **Binary** mode, all of the **Random** rules apply except that:

- The **Len** clause in the **Open** statement has no effect. **Put** writes all variables to disk contiguously; that is, with no padding between records.

- **Put** writes variable-length strings that are not elements of user-defined types without the 2-byte length descriptor. The number of bytes written equals the number of characters in the string. For example, the following statements write 10 bytes to file number 1:

```
VarString$ = String$(10," ")
Put #1,,VarString$
```

See Also   **Get** Statement, **Open** Statement, **VarType** Function.

Example   This example uses the **Put** statement to write data to a disk file. Five records of the user-defined type Record are written to the file.

```
' Define user-defined type.
Type Record
    ID As Integer
    Name As String * 20
End Type
Dim MyRecord As Record                    ' Declare variable.
' Open file for random access.
Open "TESTFILE" For Random As #1 Len = Len(MyRecord)
For RecordNumber = 1 To 5                  ' Loop 5 times.
    MyRecord.ID = RecordNumber             ' Define ID.
    MyRecord.Name = "My Name" & RecordNumber ' Create a string.
    Put #1, RecordNumber, MyRecord         ' Write record to file.
Next RecordNumber
Close #1' Close file.
```

QueryGetData Function

Description   Builds a new query.

This function is contained in the Microsoft Query add-in. Before you use the function, you must establish a reference to the add-in using the References command (Tools menu).

Syntax

QueryGetData(*connectionStr*, *queryText*, *keepQueryDef*, *fieldNames*, *rowNumbers*, *festination*, *execute*)

connectionStr
> Required. A string that contains database connection information, such as the data source name, user ID, and passwords, necessary to make a SQL connection to an external data source. For example, "DSN=Myserver; Server=server1; UID=dbayer; PWD=buyer1; Database=nwind".

queryText
> Required. A string that contains the SQL language query to be run on the data source.

keepQueryDef
> Optional. If **True** or omitted, preserves the query definition. If **False**, the query definition is lost and the data from the query is no longer a data range.

fieldNames
> Optional. If **True** or omitted, places field names from Microsoft Query into the first row of the data range. If **False**, the field names are discarded.

rowNumbers
> Optional. If **True**, places row numbers from Microsoft Query into the first column in the data range. If **False** or omitted, the row numbers are discarded.

destination
> Optional. The destination for the returned data, as a **Range** object. If *destination* is in a data range then that data range is changed to reflect the new SQL query. The default destination is the active cell or the selection.

execute
> Optional. If **True** or omitted, the query is run immediately. If **False**, the query text is added to a buffer and the query is not run until a subsequent **QueryGetData** function call with the *execute* argument set to **True**. When this occurs, Microsoft Query runs all query text in the buffer.

See Also   **QueryGetDataDialog** Function, **QueryRefresh** Function.

QueryGetDataDialog Function

Description   Builds a new query. Equivalent to the Get External Data command (Data menu).

This function is contained in the Microsoft Query add-in. Before you use the function, you must establish a reference to the add-in using the References command (Tools menu).

Syntax

QueryGetDataDialog(*connectionStr*, *queryText*, *keepQueryDef*, *fieldNames*, *rowNumbers*, *destination*, *execute*)

connectionStr
> Required. A string that contains database connection information, such as the data source name, user ID, and passwords, necessary to make a SQL connection to an external data source. For example, "DSN=Myserver; Server=server1; UID=dbayer; PWD=buyer1; Database=nwind".

queryText
> Required. A string that contains the SQL language query to be run on the data source.

keepQueryDef
> Optional. If **True** or omitted, preserves the query definition. If **False**, the query definition is lost and the data from the query is no longer a data range.

fieldNames
> Optional. If **True** or omitted, places field names from Microsoft Query into the first row of the data range. If **False**, the field names are discarded.

rowNumbers
> Optional. If **True**, places row numbers from Microsoft Query into the first column in the data range. If **False** or omitted, the row numbers are discarded.

destination
> Optional. The destination for the returned data, as a **Range** object. If *destination* is in a data range then that data range is changed to reflect the new SQL query. The default destination is the active cell or the selection.

execute
> Optional. If **True** or omitted, the query is run immediately. If **False**, the query text is added to a buffer and the query is not run until a subsequent **QueryGetData** function call with the *execute* argument set to **True**. When this occurs, Microsoft Query runs all query text in the buffer.

See Also

QueryGetData Function, **QueryRefresh** Function.

QueryRefresh Function

Description

Refreshes the data in a data range returned by Microsoft Query.

This function is contained in the Microsoft Query add-in. Before you use the function, you must establish a reference to the add-in using the References command (Tools menu).

Syntax

QueryRefresh(*ref*)

ref
Optional. A single cell, as a **Range** object, that is inside a data range. If *ref* is not in a data range then the function returns the #REF! error value.

See Also

QueryGetData Function, **QueryGetDataDialog** Function.

Quit Method

Applies To

Application Object.

Description

Quits Microsoft Excel. Does not run any Auto_Close macros before quitting.

Syntax

object.**Quit**

object
Required. The **Application** object.

Remarks

If unsaved workbooks are open when you use this method, Microsoft Excel displays a dialog box asking if you want to save the changes. You can prevent this by saving all workbooks before using the **Quit** method or by setting the **DisplayAlerts** property to **False**. When this property is **False**, Microsoft Excel does not display the dialog box when you quit with unsaved workbooks, and it quits without saving them.

If you set the **Saved** property for a workbook to **True** without saving it to the disk, Microsoft Excel will quit without asking you to save the workbook.

Example

This example saves all open workbooks and then closes Microsoft Excel.

```
For Each w In Application.Workbooks
    w.Save
Next w
Application.Quit
```

RadarAxisLabels Property

Applies To

ChartGroup Object.

Description   Accessor. Returns a **TickLabels** object that represents the radar axis labels for the specified chart group. Read-only.

See Also   **HasRadarAxisLabels** Property.

Example   This example turns on radar axis labels for chart group one in Chart1 and then sets their color. The example should be run on a radar chart.

```
With Charts("Chart1").ChartGroups(1)
    .HasRadarAxisLabels = True
    .RadarAxisLabels.Font.ColorIndex = 3
End With
```

RadarGroups Method

Applies To   **Chart** Object.

Description   Accessor. On a 2-D chart, returns an object that represents a single radar chart group (a **ChartGroup** object, Syntax 1), or a collection of the radar chart groups (a **ChartGroups** collection, Syntax 2).

Syntax 1   *object*.**RadarGroups(*index*)**

Syntax 2   *object*.**RadarGroups**

object
    Required. The **Chart** object.

index
    Required for Syntax 1. Specifies the chart group.

Example   This example sets the subtype for radar group one in Chart1. The example should be run on a 2-D chart.

```
Charts("Chart1").RadarGroups(1).SubType = 2
```

Randomize Statement

Description   Initializes the random-number generator.

Syntax   **Randomize [*number*]**

The *number* named argument can be any valid numeric expression.

Remarks	**Randomize** uses *number* to initialize a random-number generator, giving it a new seed value. If you omit *number,* the value returned by the **Timer** function is used as the new seed value.

If **Randomize** is not used, the same initial seed is always used to start the sequence.

Use the **Randomize** statement without an argument to provide a random seed based on the system timer to initialize the random-number generator before **Rnd** is called.

See Also	**Rnd** Function, **Timer** Function.
Example	This example uses the **Randomize** statement to initialize the random-number generator. Because the number argument has been omitted, **Randomize** uses the return value from the **Timer** function as the new seed value.

```
' Initialize random-number generator.
Randomize
' Generate random value between 1 and 6.
MyAngle = Int((6 * Rnd) + 1)
```

Range Method

Applies To	**Application** Object, **Range** Object, **Worksheet** Object.
Description	Accessor. Returns a **Range** object that represents a cell or range of cells.
Syntax 1	*object*.**Range**(*cell1*)
Syntax 2	*object*.**Range**(*cell1*, *cell2*)

object
> Optional for **Application**, required for **Range** and **Worksheet**. The object to which this method applies.

cell1
> Required for Syntax 1. The name of the range. This must be an A1-style reference in the language of the macro. It may include the range operator ':' (colon), the intersection operator ' ' (space), or the union operator ',' (comma). It may include dollar signs, but they are ignored. Any part of the range may use a local defined name. If you use a name, the name is assumed to be in the language of the macro.

cell1, *cell2*
> Required for Syntax 2. The cells at the top left and bottom right of the range. Each one may be a **Range** containing exactly a single cell (or an entire column or entire row), or a string naming a single cell in the language of the macro.

Remarks   When used with no object qualifier, this method is a shortcut for `ActiveSheet.Range` (it returns a range from the active sheet; if the active sheet is not a worksheet, the method fails).

When applied to a **Range** object, the method is relative to the **Range** object. For example, if the selection is cell C3, then `Selection.Range("B1")` returns cell D3 because it is relative to the **Range** object returned by the **Selection** property. On the other hand, the code `ActiveSheet.Range("B1")` always returns cell B1.

See Also   **Cells** Method.

Example   This example sets the value of cell A1 on Sheet1 to 3.14159.

```
Worksheets("Sheet1").Range("A1").Value = 3.14159
```

This example creates a formula in cell A1 on Sheet1.

```
Worksheets("Sheet1").Range("A1").Formula = "=10*RAND()"
```

This example loops on cells A1:D10 on Sheet1. If one of the cells has a value less than 0.001, the code replaces the value with 0 (zero).

```
For Each c in Worksheets("Sheet1").Range("A1:D10")
    If c.Value < .001 Then
        c.Value = 0
    End If
Next c
```

This example loops on the range named "TestRange" and displays the number of empty cells in the range.

```
numBlanks = 0
For Each c In Range("TestRange")
    If c.Value = "" Then
        numBlanks = numBlanks + 1
    End If
Next c
MsgBox "There are " & numBlanks & " empty cells in this range"
```

This example sets the font in cells A1:C5 on Sheet1 to italic. The example uses Syntax 2 of the **Range** method.

```
Worksheets("Sheet1").Activate
Range(Cells(1, 1), Cells(5, 3)).Font.Italic = True
```

Range Object

Description   Represents a cell, a row, a column, a selection of cells containing one or more contiguous blocks of cells, or a 3-D range.

Accessors   Here are several examples of how to use the most important accessor properties and methods of the **Range** object.

Range Method

Use the **Range** method to return a single cell or range of cells. The following example places the value of cell A1 in cell A5.

```
Worksheets("Sheet1").Range("A5").Value = _
    Worksheets("Sheet1").Range("A1").Value
```

The following example fills the range A1:H8 with random numbers by setting the formula for each cell in the range. When it is used without an object qualifier (an object to the left of the period), the **Range** method returns a range on the active sheet. If the active sheet is not a worksheet, the method will fail. Use the **Activate** method to activate a worksheet before you use the **Range** method without an explicit object qualifier.

```
Worksheets("sheet1").Activate
Range("A1:H8").Formula = "=rand()"   'Range is on the active sheet
```

The following example clears the contents of the range named "Criteria."

```
Worksheets(1).Range("criteria").ClearContents
```

If you use a text argument for the range address, you must specify the address in A1-style notation (you cannot use R1C1-style notation).

Cells Method

Use the **Cells** method to return a single cell by specifying the row and column. The following example sets the value of cell A1 to 24.

```
Worksheets(1).Cells(1, 1).Value = 24
```

The following example sets the formula for cell A2.

```
ActiveSheet.Cells(2, 1).Formula = "=sum(b1:b5)"
```

Although you can also use `Range("A1")` to return cell A1, there may be times when the **Cells** method is more convenient because you can use a variable for the row or column. The following example creates column and row headings on the worksheet named "Sheet1." Notice that once the worksheet has been activated, the **Cells** method can be used without an explicit sheet declaration (it returns a cell on the active sheet).

```
Sub SetUpTable()
Worksheets("sheet1").Activate
For theYear = 1 To 5
    Cells(1, theYear + 1).Value = 1990 + theYear
Next theYear
'
For theQuarter = 1 To 4
    Cells(theQuarter + 1, 1).Value = "Q" & theQuarter
Next theQuarter
End Sub
```

Although you could use Visual Basic string functions to alter A1-style references, it's much easier (and much better programming practice) to use the `Cells(1, 1)` notation.

Cells and Range Methods

You can also use the **Cells** method to return part of a range by specifying the row and column relative to the upper-left corner of the range. The following example sets the formula for cell C5.

```
Worksheets(1).Range("c5:c10").cells(1,1).formula = "=rand()"
```

You can also use the **Cells** method inside the **Range** method to specify the start and end cells for the range. The following example sets the border line style for cells A1:J10.

```
With Worksheets(1)
    .Range(.Cells(1, 1), .Cells(10, 10)).Borders.LineStyle = xlThick
End With
```

Notice the period in front of each occurrence of the **Cells** method. The period is required to apply the result of the preceding **With** statement to the **Cells** method— in this case to indicate that the cells are on worksheet one (without the period, the **Cells** method would return cells on the active sheet).

Offset Method

The **Offset** method returns a range at a specified offset to another range. The following example selects the cell three rows down and one column to the right from the upper-left cell of the current selection. You cannot select a cell that is not on the active sheet, so you must first activate the worksheet.

```
Worksheets("sheet1").Activate  'can't select unless the sheet is active
Selection.Offset(3, 1).Range("a1").Select
```

Union Method

Use the **Union** method and **Range** method to return multi-area ranges (ranges composed of two or more contiguous blocks of cells). The following example creates an object called myMultiAreaRange, defines it as the union of ranges A1:B2 and C3:D4, and then selects it.

```
Dim r1, r2, myMultiAreaRange As Range
Worksheets("sheet1").Activate
Set r1 = Range("A1:B2")
Set r2 = Range("C3:D4")
Set myMultiAreaRange = Union(r1, r2)
myMultiAreaRange.Select
```

If you work with selections containing more than one area, the **Areas** method is very useful. It divides a multi-area selection into individual **Range** objects and then returns them as a collection. You can use the **Count** property on the returned collection to check for a selection containing more than one area, as shown in the following example:

```
Sub NoMultiAreaSelection()
    numberOfSelectedAreas = Selection.Areas.Count
    If numberOfSelectedAreas > 1 Then
        MsgBox "You cannot carry out this command " & _
            "on multi-area selections"
    End If
End Sub
```

Properties	**AddIndent** Property, **Application** Property, **Column** Property, **ColumnWidth** Property, **Count** Property, **Creator** Property, **CurrentArray** Property, **CurrentRegion** Property, **Dependents** Property, **DirectDependents** Property, **DirectPrecedents** Property, **EntireColumn** Property, **EntireRow** Property, **Font** Property, **Formula** Property, **FormulaArray** Property, **FormulaHidden** Property, **FormulaLocal** Property, **FormulaR1C1** Property, **FormulaR1C1Local** Property, **HasArray** Property, **HasFormula** Property, **Height** Property, **Hidden** Property, **HorizontalAlignment** Property, **Interior** Property, **Left** Property, **ListHeaderRows** Property, **LocationInTable** Property, **Locked** Property, **Name** Property, **Next** Property, **NumberFormat** Property, **NumberFormatLocal** Property, **Orientation** Property, **OutlineLevel** Property, **PageBreak** Property, **Parent** Property, **PivotField** Property, **PivotItem** Property, **PivotTable** Property, **Precedents** Property, **PrefixCharacter** Property, **Previous** Property, **Row** Property, **RowHeight** Property, **ShowDetail** Property, **SoundNote** Property, **Style** Property, **Summary** Property, **Text** Property, **Top** Property, **UseStandardHeight** Property, **UseStandardWidth** Property, **Value** Property, **VerticalAlignment** Property, **Width** Property, **Worksheet** Property, **WrapText** Property.
Methods	**Activate** Method, **Address** Method, **AddressLocal** Method, **AdvancedFilter** Method, **ApplyNames** Method, **ApplyOutlineStyles** Method, **Areas** Method, **AutoComplete** Method, **AutoFill** Method, **AutoFilter** Method, **AutoFit** Method, **AutoFormat** Method (**Range** Object), **AutoOutline** Method, **BorderAround** Method, **Borders** Method, **Calculate** Method, **Cells** Method, **Characters** Method, **CheckSpelling** Method, **Clear** Method, **ClearContents** Method, **ClearFormats** Method, **ClearNotes** Method, **ClearOutline** Method, **ColumnDifferences** Method, **Columns** Method, **Consolidate** Method, **Copy** Method, **CopyFromRecordset** Method, **CopyPicture** Method, **CreateNames** Method, **CreatePublisher** Method, **Cut** Method, **DataSeries** Method, **Delete** Method, **DialogBox** Method, **End** Method, **FillDown** Method, **FillLeft** Method, **FillRight** Method, **FillUp** Method, **Find** Method, **FindNext** Method, **FindPrevious** Method, **FunctionWizard** Method, **GoalSeek** Method, **Group** Method, **Insert** Method, **Item** Method, **Justify** Method, **ListNames** Method, **NavigateArrow** Method, **NoteText** Method, **Offset** Method, **Parse** Method, **PasteSpecial** Method (**Range** Object), **PrintOut** Method, **PrintPreview** Method, **Range** Method, **RemoveSubtotal** Method, **Replace** Method, **Resize** Method, **RowDifferences** Method, **Rows** Method, **Run** Method, **Select** Method, **Show** Method, **ShowDependents** Method, **ShowErrors** Method, **ShowPrecedents** Method, **Sort** Method, **SortSpecial** Method, **SpecialCells** Method, **SubscribeTo** Method, **Subtotal** Method, **Table** Method, **TextToColumns** Method, **Ungroup** Method.

RangeSelection Property

Applies To	**Window** Object.

Description	Returns a **Range** object that represents the selected cells on the worksheet in the specified window even if a graphic object is active or selected on the worksheet. This property is available only in Microsoft Excel for Windows 95. Read-only.
Remarks	When a graphic object is selected on a worksheet, the **Selection** property returns the graphic object instead of a **Range**; the **RangeSelection** property returns the range of cells that was selected before the graphic object was selected.
	This property and the **Selection** property return identical values when a range (not a graphic object) is selected on the worksheet.
	If a worksheet is not the active sheet in the specified window, this property fails.
Example	This example displays the address of the selected cells on the worksheet in the active window.

```
MsgBox ActiveWindow.RangeSelection.Address
```

ReadOnly Property

Applies To	**Workbook** Object.
Description	**True** if the workbook has been opened as read-only. Read-only.
See Also	**Open** Method, **SaveAs** Method.
Example	If the active workbook is read-only, this example saves it as NEWFILE.XLS.

```
If ActiveWorkbook.ReadOnly Then
    ActiveWorkbook.SaveAs fileName:="NEWFILE.XLS"
End If
```

ReadOnlyRecommended Property

Applies To	**Workbook** Object.
Description	**True** if the workbook was saved as read-only recommended. Read-only.
Remarks	When you open a document that was saved as read-only recommended, Microsoft Excel displays a message recommending that you open the document as read-only.
	Use the **SaveAs** method to change this property.
See Also	**Open** Method, **SaveAs** Method.

Example   This example displays a message if the active workbook is saved as read-only recommended.

```
If ActiveWorkbook.ReadOnlyRecommended = True Then
    MsgBox "This workbook is saved as read-only recommended"
End If
```

Received Property

Applies To   **Mailer** Object.

Description   **True** if the workbook mailer has been received (if it has been sent by another user to the current user) and the current user has not modified the mailer by using the **Reply**, **ReplyAll**, or **ForwardMailer** methods. PowerTalk requires that mailers be received before they can be forwarded or replied to. Available only in Microsoft Excel for the Apple Macintosh with the PowerTalk mail system extension installed. Read-only.

See Also   **BCCRecipients** Property, **CCRecipients** Property, **Enclosures** Property, **ForwardMailer** Method, **Mailer** Property, **Reply** Method, **ReplyAll** Method, **SendDateTime** Property, **Sender** Property, **SendMailer** Method, **Subject** Property, **ToRecipients** Property.

Example   This example displays the current state of the **Received** property.

```
With ActiveWorkbook
    If .HasMailer Then
        If .Mailer.Received Then
            state = "True"
        Else
            state = "False"
        End If
        MsgBox "Received property is " & state
    Else
        MsgBox "The workbook has no mailer"
    End If
End With
```

Recipients Property

Applies To   **RoutingSlip** Object.

Description   Returns or sets the recipients on the routing slip (as an array of strings). Read-write.

Remarks   The order of the recipient list defines the delivery order if the routing delivery option is **xlOneAfterAnother**. If a routing slip is in progress, only those recipients who have not already received and routed the document are returned or set.

Example   This example sends BOOK1.XLS to three recipients, one after the other.

```
Workbooks("BOOK1.XLS").HasRoutingSlip = True
With Workbooks("BOOK1.XLS").RoutingSlip
    .Delivery = xlOneAfterAnother
    .Recipients = Array("Adam Bendel", "Jean Selva", "Bernard Gabor")
    .Subject = "Here is BOOK1.XLS"
    .Message = "Here is the workbook. What do you think?"
    .ReturnWhenDone = True
End With
Workbooks("BOOK1.XLS").Route
```

Record Method

Applies To   **SoundNote** Object.

Description   Displays the Record dialog box so you can record a sound note.

Syntax   *object*.**Record**

object
    Required. The **SoundNote** object.

Remarks   To record sounds, you must have sound hardware installed in your computer. You cannot record a sound note to a cell that already has one; you must delete the existing sound note before recording a new one.

See Also   **Play** Method.

Example

This example deletes the sound note in cell A1 on Sheet1, records a new sound note for the same cell, and then plays the sound note.

```
With Worksheets("Sheet1").Range("A1").SoundNote
    .Delete
    .Record
    .Play
End With
```

RecordMacro Method

Applies To

Application Object.

Description

Records code if the macro recorder is on.

Syntax

object.**RecordMacro**(*basicCode*, *xlmCode*)

object
Required. The **Application** object.

basicCode
Optional. A string that specifies the Visual Basic code that will be recorded if the macro recorder is recording into a Visual Basic module. The string will be recorded on one line. If the string contains a carriage return (ASCII character 10, or Chr$(10) in code), it will be recorded on more than one line.

xlmCode
Optional. A string that specifies the formula that will be recorded if the macro recorder is recording into a Microsoft Excel version 4.0 macro sheet. The string will be recorded into one cell. If the string does not begin with an equal sign, a comment is recorded.

Remarks

The **RecordMacro** method cannot record into the active module (the module in which the **RecordMacro** method exists).

If *basicCode* is omitted, and the application is recording into Visual Basic, Microsoft Excel will record a suitable **Application.Run** statement.
If *xlmCode* is omitted, and the application is recording into Microsoft Excel version 4.0, Microsoft Excel will record a suitable **RUN** macro function.

To prevent recording (for example, if the user cancels your dialog box), call this function with two empty strings.

Example

This example records either Visual Basic code or an XLM formula.

```
Application.RecordMacro basicCode:="Application.Run ""MySub"" ", _
    xlmCode:="=MySub()"
```

RecordRelative Property

Applies To   **Application** Object.

Description   **True** if macros are recorded using relative references; **False** if recording is absolute. Read-only.

Example   This example displays the address of the active cell on Sheet1 in A1 style if **RecordRelative** is **False**; otherwise, it displays the address in R1C1 style.

```
Worksheets("Sheet1").Activate
If Application.RecordRelative = False Then
    MsgBox ActiveCell.Address(ReferenceStyle:=xlA1)
Else
    MsgBox ActiveCell.Address(ReferenceStyle:=xlR1C1)
End If
```

Rectangle Object

Description   Represents a rectangle graphic object on a chart sheet, dialog sheet, or worksheet.

Accessors   The **Rectangle** object is a member of the **Rectangles** collection. The **Rectangles** collection contains all the **Rectangle** objects on a single sheet. Use the **Add** method to create a new rectangle and add it to the collection.

To access a single member of the collection, use the **Rectangles** method with the index number or name of the rectangle as an argument.

The following example sets the interior color for rectangle one on the worksheet named "Sheet1."

```
Worksheets("sheet1").Rectangles(1).Interior.ColorIndex = 5
```

The rectangle name is shown in the Name Box when the rectangle is selected. Use the **Name** property to set or return the rectangle name. The following example sets the border line style for the rectangle named "Rectangle 3."

```
Worksheets("sheet1").Rectangles("rectangle 3"). _
    Border.LineStyle = xlDash
```

Properties
Application Property, **Border** Property, **BottomRightCell** Property, **Creator** Property, **Enabled** Property, **Height** Property, **Index** Property, **Interior** Property, **Left** Property, **Locked** Property, **Name** Property, **OnAction** Property, **Parent** Property, **Placement** Property, **PrintObject** Property, **RoundedCorners** Property, **Shadow** Property, **Top** Property, **TopLeftCell** Property, **Visible** Property, **Width** Property, **ZOrder** Property.

Methods
BringToFront Method, **Copy** Method, **CopyPicture** Method, **Cut** Method, **Delete** Method, **Duplicate** Method, **Select** Method, **SendToBack** Method.

Rectangles Collection Object

Description
A collection of all the **Rectangle** objects on the specified chart sheet, dialog sheet, or worksheet.

Accessors
Use the **Add** method to create a new rectangle and add it to the collection. The following example adds a new rectangle to the worksheet named "Sheet1." The new rectangle is 200 points high and 100 points wide, and its upper-left corner is positioned at the upper-left corner of cell C5.

```
Set r = Worksheets("sheet1").Range("c5")
Worksheets("sheet1").Rectangles.Add r.Left, r.Top, 200, 100
```

Use the **Rectangles** method with an argument to access a single member of the collection or without an argument to access the entire collection at once. The following example deletes all of the rectangles on the worksheet named "Sheet1."

```
Worksheets("sheet1").Rectangles.Delete
```

Properties
Application Property, **Border** Property, **Count** Property, **Creator** Property, **Enabled** Property, **Height** Property, **Interior** Property, **Left** Property, **Locked** Property, **OnAction** Property, **Parent** Property, **Placement** Property, **PrintObject** Property, **RoundedCorners** Property, **Shadow** Property, **Top** Property, **Visible** Property, **Width** Property, **ZOrder** Property.

Methods
Add Method (Graphic Objects and Controls), **BringToFront** Method, **Copy** Method, **CopyPicture** Method, **Cut** Method, **Delete** Method, **Duplicate** Method, **Group** Method, **Item** Method, **Select** Method, **SendToBack** Method.

Rectangles Method

Applies To   **Chart** Object, **DialogSheet** Object, **Worksheet** Object.

Description   Accessor. Returns an object that represents a single rectangle (a **Rectangle** object, Syntax 1) or a collection of rectangles (a **Rectangles** object, Syntax 2) on the sheet. Read-only.

Syntax 1   *object*.**Rectangles**(*index*)

Syntax 2   *object*.**Rectangles**

object
    Required. The object containing the rectangles.

index
    Required for Syntax 1. The name or number of the rectangle.

Example   This example deletes every rectangle on Sheet1.

```
Worksheets("Sheet1").Rectangles.Delete
```

This example changes the color of rectangle one on Sheet1 to red.

```
Worksheets("Sheet1").Rectangles(1).Border.ColorIndex = 3
```

ReDim Statement

Description   Used at the procedure level to declare dynamic-array variables and allocate or reallocate storage space.

Syntax   **ReDim** [**Preserve**] *varname*(*subscripts*) [**As** *type*][,*varname*(*subscripts*) [**As** *type*]] . . .

The **ReDim** statement syntax has these parts:

Part	Description
Preserve	Preserves the data in an existing array when you change the size of the last dimension.
varname	Name of the variable; follows standard variable naming conventions.

Part	Description
subscripts	Dimensions of an array variable; up to 60 multiple dimensions may be declared. The *subscripts* argument uses the following syntax: [*lower* **To**] *upper* [,[*lower* **To**] *upper*] . . .
type	Data type of the variable; may be **Boolean**, **Integer**, **Long**, **Currency**, **Single**, **Double**, **Date**, **String** (for variable-length strings), **String** * *length* (for fixed-length strings), **Object**, **Variant**, a user-defined type, or an object type. Use a separate **As** *type* clause for each variable being defined. For a **Variant** containing an array, *type* describes the type of each element of the array, but does not change the **Variant** to some other type.

Remarks

The **ReDim** statement is usually used to size or resize a dynamic array that has already been formally declared using a **Private**, **Public** or **Dim** statement with empty parentheses (without dimension subscripts).

You can use the **ReDim** statement repeatedly to change the number of elements and dimensions in an array. However, you can't declare an array of one data type and later use **ReDim** to change the array to another data type, unless the array is contained in a **Variant**. If the array is contained in a **Variant**, the type of the elements can be changed using an **As** *type* clause.

If you use the **Preserve** keyword, you can resize only the last array dimension and you can't change the number of dimensions at all. For example, if your array has only one dimension, you can resize that dimension because it is the last and only dimension. However, if your array has two or more dimensions you can only change the size of the last dimension and still preserve the contents of the array. The following example shows how you can increase the size of the last dimension of a dynamic array without erasing any existing data contained in the array.

```
ReDim X(10, 10, 10)
. . .
ReDim Preserve X(10, 10, 15)
```

Caution If you make an array smaller than it was, data in the eliminated elements will be lost.

When variables are initialized, a numeric variable is initialized to 0, a variable-length string is initialized to a zero-length string, and a fixed-length string is filled with zeros. **Variant** variables are initialized to **Empty**. Each element of a user-defined type variable is initialized as if it was a separate variable. A variable that refers to an object must be assigned an existing object using the **Set** statement before it can be used. Until it is assigned an object, the declared object variable has the special value **Nothing**, which indicates that it does not refer to any particular instance of an object.

Note In order to resize an array contained in a **Variant**, you must explicitly declare the **Variant** variable before attempting to resize its array.

See Also

Array Function, **Dim** Statement, **Option Base** Statement, **Private** Statement, **Public** Statement, **Static** Statement.

Example

This example uses the **ReDim** statement to declare dynamic-array variables and then allocate and reallocate storage space.

```
Dim MyArray() As Integer          ' Declare dynamic array.
ReDim MyArray(5)                  ' Allocate 5 elements.
For I = 1 To 5                    ' Loop 5 times.
    MyArray(I) = I               ' Initialize array.
Next I
' The next statement resizes the array and erases the elements.
ReDim MyArray(10)                 ' Resize to 10 elements.
For I = 1 To 10                   ' Loop 10 times.
    MyArray(I) = I               ' Initialize array.
Next I
' The next statement resizes the array but does not erase elements.
ReDim Preserve MyArray(15)   ' Resize to 15 elements.
```

ReferenceStyle Property

Applies To

Application Object.

Description

Returns or sets how Microsoft Excel displays cell references and row and column headings in A1 or R1C1 reference style (either **xlA1** or **xlR1C1**). Read-write.

Example

This example displays the current reference style.

```
If Application.ReferenceStyle = xlR1C1 Then
    MsgBox ("Microsoft Excel is using R1C1 references")
Else
    MsgBox ("Microsoft Excel is using A1 references")
End If
```

RefersTo Property

Applies To

Name Object.

Description   Returns or sets a string containing the formula that the name is defined to refer to, in A1-style notation, in the language of the macro writer, beginning with an equal sign. Read-write.

See Also   **Formula** Property, **RefersToLocal** Property, **RefersToR1C1** Property, **RefersToR1C1Local** Property, **RefersToRange** Property.

Example   This example creates a list of all the names in the active workbook, and it shows their formulas in A1-style notation in the language of the macro. The list appears on a new worksheet created by the example.

```
Set newSheet = Worksheets.Add
i = 1
For Each nm In ActiveWorkbook.Names
    newSheet.Cells(i, 1).Value = nm.Name
    newSheet.Cells(i, 2).Value = "'" & nm.RefersTo
    i = i + 1
Next
newSheet.Columns("A:B").AutoFit
```

RefersToLocal Property

Applies To   **Name** Object.

Description   Returns or sets a string containing the formula that the name is defined to refer to, in A1 notation, in the language of the user, beginning with an equal sign. Read-write.

See Also   **RefersTo** Property, **RefersToR1C1** Property, **RefersToR1C1Local** Property.

Example   This example creates a new worksheet and then inserts a list of all names in the active workbook, including their formulas in A1-style notation in the language of the user.

```
Set newSheet = ActiveWorkbook.Worksheets.Add
i = 1
For Each nm In ActiveWorkbook.Names
    newSheet.Cells(i, 1).Value = nm.NameLocal
    newSheet.Cells(i, 2).Value = "'" & nm.RefersToLocal
    i = i + 1
Next
```

RefersToR1C1 Property

Applies To   **Name** Object.

Description   Returns or sets a string containing the formula that the name is defined to refer to, in R1C1-style notation, in the language of the macro writer, beginning with an equal sign. Read-write.

See Also   **RefersTo** Property, **RefersToLocal** Property, **RefersToR1C1Local** Property, **RefersToRange** Property.

Example   This example creates a new worksheet and then inserts a list of all names in the active workbook, including their formulas in R1C1-style notation in the language of the macro.

```
Set newSheet = ActiveWorkbook.Worksheets.Add
i = 1
For Each nm In ActiveWorkbook.Names
    newSheet.Cells(i, 1).Value = nm.Name
    newSheet.Cells(i, 2).Value = "'" & nm.RefersToR1C1
    i = i + 1
Next
```

RefersToR1C1Local Property

Applies To   **Name** Object.

Description   Returns or sets a string containing the formula that the name is defined to refer to, in R1C1-style notation, in the language of the user, beginning with an equal sign. Read-write.

See Also   **RefersTo** Property, **RefersToLocal** Property, **RefersToR1C1** Property.

Example   This example creates a new worksheet and then inserts a list of all names in the active workbook, including their formulas in R1C1-style notation in the language of the user.

```
Set newSheet = ActiveWorkbook.Worksheets.Add
i = 1
For Each nm In ActiveWorkbook.Names
    newSheet.Cells(i, 1).Value = nm.NameLocal
    newSheet.Cells(i, 2).Value = "'" & nm.RefersToR1C1Local
    i = i + 1
Next
```

RefersToRange Property

Applies To **Name** Object.

Description Returns the **Range** object referred to by a **Name** object. This property is available only in Microsoft Excel for Windows 95. Read-only.

Remarks If the **Name** object doesn't refer to a range (for example, if the **Name** object refers to a constant or a formula), this property fails.

To change the range that a name refers to, use the **RefersTo** property.

See Also **RefersTo** Property, **RefersToR1C1** Property.

Example This example displays the number of rows and columns in the print area on the active worksheet.

```
p = Names("Print_Area").RefersToRange.Value
MsgBox "Print_Area: " & UBound(p, 1) & " rows, " & _
    UBound(p, 2) & " columns"

    UBound(p, 2) & " columns"
```

RefreshDate Property

Applies To **PivotTable** Object.

Description Returns the date when the PivotTable was last refreshed. Read-only.

See Also **RefreshName** Property, **RefreshTable** Method.

Example This example displays the date on which the PivotTable was last refreshed.

```
Set pvtTable = Worksheets("Sheet1").Range("A3").PivotTable
dateString = Format(pvtTable.RefreshDate, "Long Date")
MsgBox "The data was last refreshed on " & dateString
```

RefreshName Property

Applies To **PivotTable** Object.

Description Returns the name of the person who last refreshed the PivotTable data. Read-only.

See Also	**RefreshDate** Property, **RefreshTable** Method.
Example	This example displays the name of the person who last refreshed the PivotTable.

```
Set pvtTable = Worksheets("Sheet1").Range("A3").PivotTable
MsgBox "The data was last refreshed by " & pvtTable.RefreshName
```

RefreshTable Method

Applies To	**PivotTable** Object.
Description	Refreshes the PivotTable from the source data. Returns **True** if it is successful.
Syntax	*object*.**RefreshTable**
	object Required. The **PivotTable** object.
See Also	**RefreshDate** Property, **RefreshName** Property.
Example	This example refreshes the PivotTable.

```
Set pvtTable = Worksheets("Sheet1").Range("A3").PivotTable
pvtTable.RefreshTable
```

RegisteredFunctions Property

Applies To	**Application** Object.
Description	Returns an array containing a list of functions in dynamic-link libraries (DLLs) or code resources that were registered with the REGISTER or REGISTER.ID functions. Read-only. Each row in the array contains information about a single function, as shown in the following table.

Column	Contents
1	The name of the DLL or code resource.
2	The name of the procedure in the DLL or code resource.
3	Strings specifying the data types of the return values, and the number and data types of the arguments.

Remarks	If there are no registered functions, the property returns **Null**. Use the **IsNull** function to test the return value for **Null**.

Example

This example creates a list of registered functions, placing one registered function in each row on Sheet1. Column A contains the full path and filename of the DLL or code resource, column B contains the function name, and column C contains the argument data type code.

```
theArray = Application.RegisteredFunctions
If IsNull(theArray) Then
    MsgBox "No registered functions"
Else
    For i = LBound(theArray) To UBound(theArray)
        For j = 1 To 3
            Worksheets("Sheet1").Cells(i, j).Formula = theArray(i, j)
        Next j
    Next i
End If
```

RegisterXLL Method

Applies To

Application Object.

Description

Loads an XLL code resource and automatically registers the functions and commands that the resource contains.

Syntax

object.**RegisterXLL**(*filename*)

object
    Required. The **Application** object.

filename
    Required. Specifies the name of the XLL to load.

Remarks

This method returns **True** if the code resource is successfully loaded. Otherwise, the method returns **False**.

See Also

RegisteredFunctions Property.

Example

This example loads an XLL file and registers the functions and commands in the file.

```
Application.RegisterXLL "XLMAPI.XLL"
```

Rem Statement

Description

Used to include explanatory remarks in a program.

Syntax 1	**Rem** *comment*
Syntax 2	**'** *comment*

The argument *comment* is the text of any comment you want to include. After the **Rem** keyword, a space before *comment* is required.

Remarks

If you use line numbers or line labels, you can branch from a **GoTo** or **GoSub** statement to a line containing a **Rem** statement. Execution continues with the first executable statement following the **Rem** statement.

As shown in syntax 2, you can use a single quotation mark or apostrophe (') instead of the **Rem** keyword. If the **Rem** keyword follows other statements on a line, it must be separated from the statements by a colon. However, when you use a single quotation mark, the colon is not required after other statements.

Example

This example illustrates the various forms of the **Rem** statement, which is used to include explanatory remarks in a program.

```
Rem This is the first form of the syntax.
' This is the second form of the syntax.
MyStr1 = "Hello" : Rem Comment after a statement separated by a colon.
MyStr2 = "Goodbye"  ' This is also a comment.
```

RemoveAllItems Method

Applies To

DrawingObjects Collection, **DropDown** Object, **DropDowns** Collection, **ListBox** Object, **ListBoxes** Collection.

Description

Removes all entries from a list box or drop-down list box.

Syntax

object.**RemoveAllItems**

object
Required. The object to which this method applies.

See Also

AddItem Method, **List** Property, **RemoveItem** Method.

Example

This example removes all entries from list box one on Dialog1.

```
DialogSheets("Dialog1").Listboxes(1).RemoveAllItems
```

RemoveItem Method

Applies To	**DrawingObjects** Collection, **DropDown** Object, **DropDowns** Collection, **ListBox** Object, **ListBoxes** Collection.
Description	Removes one or more items from a list box or drop-down list box.
Syntax	*object*.**RemoveItem**(*index*, *count*)

object
  Required. The object to which this method applies.

index
  Required. Specifies the number of the first item to remove. Valid values are from one to the number of items in the list (returned by the **ListCount** property).

count
  Optional. Specifies the number of items to remove starting at item *index*. If this argument is omitted, one item is removed. If *index* + *count* exceeds the number of items in the list, all items from *index* through the end of the list are removed without an error.

Remarks	This method fails if the object has a **ListFillRange** defined.
See Also	**AddItem** Method, **List** Property, **RemoveAllItems** Method.
Example	This example removes the first entry from list box one on Dialog1.

```
DialogSheets("Dialog1").Listboxes(1).RemoveItem index:=1
```

RemoveSubtotal Method

Applies To	**Range** Object.
Description	Removes subtotals from a list.
Syntax	*object*.**RemoveSubtotal**

object
  Required. The **Range** object.

See Also	**Subtotal** Method.
Example	This example removes subtotals for the range A1:G37 on Sheet1. The example should be run on a list that has subtotals.

```
Worksheets("Sheet1").Range("A1:G37").RemoveSubtotal
```

Repeat Method

Applies To	**Application** Object.
Description	Repeats the last user-interface action.
Syntax	*object*.**Repeat**

object
> Required. The **Application** object.

Remarks   This method can only be used to repeat the last action taken by the user before running the macro, and it must be the first line in the macro. It cannot be used to repeat Visual Basic commands.

Example   This example repeats the last user interface command. The example must be the first line in a macro.

```
Application.Repeat
```

Replace Method

Applies To   **Range** Object.

Description   Finds and replaces characters in cells within a range. Does not change the selection or active cell.

For help about using the **Replace** worksheet function in Visual Basic, see "Using Worksheet Functions in Visual Basic" in online Help.

Syntax   *object*.**Replace**(*what*, *replacement*, *lookAt*, *searchOrder*, *matchCase*, *matchByte*)

object
> Required. Replace characters or cells in this range.

what
> Required. A string indicating the contents for which you want to search.

replacement
> Required. A string indicating the text with which you want to replace *what*.

lookAt
> Optional. If **xlWhole**, *what* must match the entire contents of a cell. If **xlPart**, *what* must contain part of the contents of a cell.

searchOrder
Optional. Specifies whether to search by rows (**xlByRows**) or columns (**xlByColumns**).

matchCase
Optional. If **True**, search is case sensitive.

matchByte
Optional. Used only in Far East Microsoft Excel. If **True**, double-byte characters match only double-byte characters. If **False**, double-byte characters can match their single-byte equivalents.

Remarks

The settings for *lookAt*, *searchOrder*, *matchCase*, and *matchByte* are saved each time you use this method. If you do not specify values for these arguments the next time you call the method, the saved values are used. Setting these arguments changes the settings in the Find dialog box, and changing the settings in the Find dialog box changes the saved values that are used if you omit the arguments. To avoid problems, explicitly set these arguments each time you use this method.

If the contents of the *what* argument are found in at least one cell of the sheet, the method returns **True**.

See Also

Find Method, **FindNext** Method.

Example

This example replaces every occurrence of the function SIN with the function COS. The replacement range is column A on Sheet1.

```
Worksheets("Sheet1").Columns("A").Replace _
    what:="SIN", replacement:="COS", _
    searchOrder:=xlByColumns, matchCase:=True
```

ReplacementList Property

Applies To

AutoCorrect Object.

Description

Returns or sets the array of AutoCorrect replacements. This property is available only in Microsoft Excel for Windows 95. Read-write.

Syntax

object.**ReplacementList**(*index*)

object
Required. The **AutoCorrect** object.

index

Optional. Specifies which row of the array of AutoCorrect replacements to set or return. The row is returned as a one-dimensional array with two elements: the first element is the text in column 1, and the second element is the text in column 2. If *index* is out of range, the property fails.

If *index* is omitted, this property returns a two-dimensional array. Each row in the array contains one replacement, as shown in the following table.

Column	Contents
1	The text to replace
2	The replacement text

If *index* is omitted when you set this property, the entire replacement array is deleted and replaced.

Remarks

Be very careful when you set this property. If you don't specify the index argument, you'll delete the entire replacement array. It may be easier and safer to change a replacement by using the **AddReplacement** method.

Duplicate strings in column one of the array of replacements aren't allowed. If you attempt to modify or replace the array in a way that would create this condition, an error occurs.

See Also

AddReplacement Method, **DeleteReplacement** Method.

Example

This example searches the replacement list for "Temperature", sets the text to replace it with to "Temp.", and then writes the new array of AutoCorrect replacements to a worksheet.

```
With Application.AutoCorrect
    For x = 1 To UBound(.ReplacementList)
            repl = .ReplacementList(x)
            If repl(1) = "Temperature" Then
                repl(2) = "Temp."
                .ReplacementList(x) = repl
            End If
        Worksheets(1).Cells(x, 1) = repl(1)
        Worksheets(1).Cells(x, 2) = repl(2)
    Next
End With
```

ReplaceText Property

Applies To

AutoCorrect Object.

Description	**True** if text in the AutoCorrect replacements list is replaced automatically. This property is available only in Microsoft Excel for Windows 95. Read-write.
See Also	**ReplacementList** Property.
Example	This example turns off automatic text replacement.

```
With Application.AutoCorrect
    .CapitalizeNamesOfDays = True
    .ReplaceText = False
End With
```

Reply Method

Applies To	**Workbook** Object.
Description	Replies to the workbook by creating a copy of the workbook and pre-initializing the new workbook's mailer to send to the originator of the workbook. Valid only when the workbook has a received mailer attached (you can only reply to a workbook you have received). Available only in Microsoft Excel for the Apple Macintosh with the PowerTalk mail system extension installed.
Syntax	*object*.**Reply**
	object Required. The **Workbook** object.
Remarks	To reply to a workbook, use this method to set up the mailer, use the **Mailer** property to adjust the mailer settings (if necessary), and then use the **SendMailer** method to send the reply.
	This method generates an error if it is used in Microsoft Windows.
See Also	**Mailer** Property, **MailSystem** Property, **ReplyAll** Method, **SendMailer** Method.
Example	This example replies to the sender of the active workbook.

```
Set original = ActiveWorkbook
If original.HasMailer Then
    original.Reply
    original.Mailer.Subject = "Here's my reply"
    ActiveWorkbook.SendMailer
End If
```

ReplyAll Method

Applies To
Workbook Object.

Description
Replies to the workbook by creating a copy of the workbook and pre-initializing the new workbook's mailer to send to all recipients of the workbook. Valid only when the workbook has a received mailer attached (you can only reply to a workbook you have received). Available only in Microsoft Excel for the Apple Macintosh with the PowerTalk mail system extension installed.

Syntax
object.**ReplyAll**

object
    Required. The **Workbook** object.

Remarks
To reply to all recipients of a workbook, use this method to set up the mailer, use the **Mailer** property to adjust the mailer settings (if necessary), and then use the **SendMailer** method to send the reply.

This method generates an error if it is used in Microsoft Windows.

See Also
Mailer Property, **MailSystem** Property, **Reply** Method, **SendMailer** Method.

Example
This example replies to all recipients of the active workbook.

```
Set original = ActiveWorkbook
If original.HasMailer Then
    original.ReplyAll
    original.Mailer.Subject = "Here's my reply"
    ActiveWorkbook.SendMailer
End If
```

Reset Method

Applies To
MenuBar Object, **RoutingSlip** Object, **Toolbar** Object, **ToolbarButton** Object.

Description
Restores the built-in menu bar or toolbar to its original default configuration. Resets a toolbar button to its original face.

Resets the routing slip so that a new routing can be initiated with the same slip (using the same recipient list and delivery information). The routing must be completed before you use this method. Using this method at other times causes an error.

Syntax
object.**Reset**

object

Required. The object to which this method applies.

Remarks   Be careful when you reset a menu bar or toolbar—other macros may have added menu items or buttons, and resetting the menu bar or toolbar will remove those as well. To avoid conflicting with other macros, remove the menu items or buttons your macro has added without resetting the menu bar or toolbar.

This method cannot be used with a toolbar button that is a gap or a toolbar button that has a palette or list attached (such as the Font or Style buttons).

Example   This example resets the routing slip for BOOK1.XLS if routing is complete.

```
With Workbooks("BOOK1.XLS").RoutingSlip
    If .Status = xlRoutingComplete Then
        .Reset
    Else
        MsgBox "Cannot reset routing; not yet complete"
    End If
End With
```

Reset Statement

Description   Closes all disk files opened using the **Open** statement.

Syntax   **Reset**

Remarks   The **Reset** statement syntax closes all active files opened by the **Open** statement and writes the contents of all file buffers to disk.

See Also   **Close** Statement, **End** Statement, **Open** Statement.

Example   This example uses the **Reset** statement to close all open files and write the contents of all file buffers to disk.

```
For FileNumber = 1 To 5                   ' Loop 5 times.
    ' Open file for output.
    Open "TEST" & FileNumber For Output As #FileNumber
    Write #FileNumber, "Hello World"   ' Write data to file.
Next FileNumber
Reset                                     ' Close files and write contents
    ' to disk.
```

ResetTipWizard Method

Applies To   **Application** Object.

Description   Resets the TipWizard memory so that all tips will be shown. Normally tips that have been shown several times are disabled so that they do not become annoying.

Syntax   *object*.**ResetTipWizard**

object
    Required. The **Application** object.

See Also   **EnableTipWizard** Property.

Example   This example resets the TipWizard and then enables it.

```
With Application
   .ResetTipWizard
   .EnableTipWizard = True
End With
```

Reshape Method

Applies To   **Drawing** Object, **DrawingObjects** Collection, **Drawings** Collection.

Description   Reshapes the drawing by inserting, moving, or deleting vertices.

Syntax   *object*.**Reshape**(*vertex*, *insert*, *left*, *top*)

object
    Required. The object to which this method applies.

vertex
    Required. Specifies the vertex you want to insert, move, or delete.

insert
    Required. If **True**, Microsoft Excel inserts a vertex between the vertices *vertex* and *vertex* - 1. The number of the new vertex then becomes *vertex*. The number of the vertex previously identified by *vertex* becomes *vertex* + 1, and so on. If *insert* is **False**, Microsoft Excel deletes the vertex (if *top* and *left* are omitted) or moves the vertex to the position specified by the *top* and *left* arguments.

left
    Optional. The left position for the new or moved vertex, in points (1/72 inch) relative to the upper-left corner of cell A1 or the upper-left corner of the chart.

top
> Optional. The top position for the new or moved vertex, in points relative to the upper-left corner of cell A1 or the upper-left corner of the chart.

Remarks   You cannot delete a vertex if only two vertices remain.

See Also   **AddVertex** Method, **Vertices** Property.

Example   Assuming that drawing one on Sheet1 is a polygon with at least five vertices, this example reshapes the polygon by deleting vertex five.

```
Worksheets("Sheet1").Drawings(1).Reshape _
        vertex:=5, Insert:=False
```

Resize Method

Applies To   **Range** Object.

Description   Resizes the range.

Syntax   *object*.**Resize**(*rowSize*, *columnSize*)

object
> Required. The **Range** object to resize.

rowSize
> Optional. The number of rows in the new range. If omitted, the range will keep the same number of rows.

columnSize
> Optional. The number of columns in the new range. If omitted, the range will keep the same number of columns.

Example   This example resizes the selection on Sheet1 to extend it by one row and one column.

```
Worksheets("Sheet1").Activate
numRows = Selection.Rows.Count
numColumns = Selection.Columns.Count
Selection.Resize(numRows + 1, numColumns + 1).Select
```

This example assumes that you have a table on Sheet1 that has a header row. The example selects the table, without selecting the header row. The active cell must be somewhere in the table before you run the example.

```
Set tbl = ActiveCell.CurrentRegion
tbl.Offset(1, 0).Resize(tbl.Rows.Count - 1, tbl.Columns.Count).Select
```

Resume Statement

Description   Resumes execution after an error-handling routine is finished.

Syntax   **Resume [0]**

Resume Next

Resume *line*

The **Resume** statement syntax can have any of the following forms:

Statement	Description
Resume [0]	If the error occurred in the same procedure as the error handler, execution resumes with the one that caused the error. If the error occurred in another procedure, execution resumes at the statement that last called out of the procedure containing the error-handling routine.
Resume Next	If the error occurred in the same procedure as the error handler, execution resumes with the statement immediately following the statement that caused the error. If the error occurred in another procedure, execution resumes with the statement immediately following the statement that last called out of the procedure containing the error-handling routine.
Resume *line*	Execution resumes at *line*, which is a line label or line number. The argument *line* must be in the same procedure as the error handler.

Remarks   If you use a **Resume** statement anywhere except in an error-handling routine, an error occurs.

When an error-handling routine is active and the end of the procedure (an **End Sub**, **End Function**, or **End Property** statement) is encountered before a **Resume** statement is encountered, an error occurs because a logical error is presumed to have been made inadvertently. However, if an **Exit Sub**, **Exit Function**, or **Exit Property** statement is encountered while an error handler is active, no error occurs because it is considered a deliberate redirection of execution.

See Also   **On Error** Statement.

Example

This example uses the **Resume** statement to end error handling in a procedure and resume execution with the statement that caused the error. Error number 55 is generated to illustrate its usage.

```
Sub ResumeStatementDemo()
    On Error GoTo ErrorHandler   ' Enable error-handling routine.
    Open "TESTFILE" For Output As #1 ' Open file for output.
    Kill "TESTFILE" ' Attempt to delete open file.
    Exit Sub' Exit Sub before error handler.
ErrorHandler:    ' Error-handling routine.
    Select Case Err ' Evaluate Error Number.
        Case 55 ' "File already open" error.
            Close #1' Close open file.
        Case Else
            ' Handle other situations here...
    End Select
    Resume   ' Resume execution at same line
    ' that caused the error.
End Sub
```

ReturnWhenDone Property

Applies To   **RoutingSlip** Object.

Description   **True** if the workbook is returned to the sender when the routing is finished. Read-write before routing begins; read-only when routing is in progress.

Example   This example sends BOOK1.XLS to three recipients, one after the other, and returns the workbook to the sender when routing is complete.

```
Workbooks("BOOK1.XLS").HasRoutingSlip = True
With Workbooks("BOOK1.XLS").RoutingSlip
    .Delivery = xlOneAfterAnother
    .Recipients = Array("Adam Bendel", "Jean Selva", "Bernard Gabor")
    .Subject = "Here is BOOK1.XLS"
    .Message = "Here is the workbook. What do you think?"
    .ReturnWhenDone = True
End With
Workbooks("BOOK1.XLS").Route
```

ReversePlotOrder Property

Applies To   **Axis** Object.

Description   **True** if Microsoft Excel plots points from last to first. Read-write.

Remarks   This property is not available for radar charts.

Example   This example reverses the order in which points on the value axis in Chart1 are plotted.

```
Charts("Chart1").Axes(xlValue).ReversePlotOrder = True
```

RevisionNumber Property

Applies To   **Workbook** Object.

Description   Returns the number of times the workbook has been saved while open as a shared list. If the workbook is open in exclusive mode, this property returns 0 (zero). This property is available only in Microsoft Excel for Windows 95. Read-only.

Remarks   The **RevisionNumber** property is updated only when the local copy of the workbook is saved, not when remote copies are saved.

See Also   **MultiUserEditing** Property, **SaveAs** Method.

Example   This example uses the revision number to determine whether the active workbook is open in exclusive mode. If it is, the example saves the active workbook as a shared list.

```
If ActiveWorkbook.RevisionNumber = 0 then
    ActiveWorkbook.SaveAs filename := ActiveWorkbook.FullName, _
        accessMode:= xlShared, conflictResolution := _
        xlOtherSessionChanges
End If
```

This example displays the revision number of the active workbook.

```
MsgBox ActiveWorkbook.RevisionNumber
```

RGB Function

Description   Returns a whole number representing an RGB color value.

Syntax   **RGB** (*red*, *green*, *blue*)

The **RGB** function syntax has these named-argument parts:

Part	Description
red	Whole number in the range 0 to 255, inclusive, that represents the red component of the color.
green	Whole number in the range 0 to 255, inclusive, that represents the green component of the color.
blue	Whole number in the range 0 to 255, inclusive, that represents the blue component of the color.

Remarks   Application methods and properties that accept a color specification expect that specification to be a whole number representing an RGB color value. An RGB color value specifies the relative intensity of red, green, and blue, which combined cause a specific color to be displayed.

The value for any argument to **RGB** that exceeds 255 is assumed to be 255.

The following table lists some standard colors and the red, green and blue values they include:

Color	Red Value	Green Value	Blue Value
Black	0	0	0
Blue	0	0	255
Green	0	255	0
Cyan	0	255	255
Red	255	0	0
Magenta	255	0	255
Yellow	255	255	0
White	255	255	255

Note The RGB values returned by this function are incompatible with those used by the Macintosh operating system. They may be used within the context of Microsoft applications for the Macintosh, but should not be used when communicating color changes directly to the Macintosh operating system.

Example

This example shows how the **RGB** function is used to return a whole number representing an **RGB** color value. It is used for those application methods and properties that accept a color specification. The object `MyObject` and its property are used here for illustration purposes only.

```
Red = RGB(255, 0, 0)                 ' Return the value for Red.
I = 75                               ' Initialize offset.
RGBValue = RGB(I, 64 + I, 128 + I)   ' Same as RGB(75, 139, 203).
MyObject.Color = RGB(255, 0, 0)      ' Set the Color property of
    ' MyObject to Red.
```

This example sets the gridline color in the active window in BOOK1.XLS to red.

```
Workbooks("BOOK1.XLS").Worksheets("Sheet1").Activate
ActiveWindow.GridlineColor = RGB(255,0,0)
```

This example sets the color of the tick labels on the value axis in Chart1 to green.

```
Charts("Chart1").Axes(xlValue).TickLabels.Font.Color = RGB(0, 255, 0)
```

This example sets the marker background and foreground colors for the second point in series one in Chart1.

```
With Charts("Chart1").SeriesCollection(1).Points(2)
    .MarkerBackgroundColor = RGB(0,255,0) ' green
    .MarkerForegroundColor = RGB(255,0,0) ' red
End With
```

This example sets the interior pattern color for rectangle one on Sheet1 to red.

```
With Worksheets("Sheet1").Rectangles(1).Interior
    .Pattern = xlGrid
    .PatternColor = RGB(255,0,0)
End With
```

Right Function

Description   Returns a specified number of characters from the right side of a string.

Syntax   **Right**(*string*,*length*)

The **Right** function syntax has these named-argument parts:

Part	Description
string	String expression from which the rightmost characters are returned. If *string* contains no valid data, **Null** is returned.
length	Numeric expression indicating how many characters to return. If 0, a zero-length string is returned. If greater than or equal to the number of characters in *string*, the entire string is returned.

Remarks   To determine the number of characters in *string*, use the **Len** function.

Note   Another function (**RightB**) is provided for use with the double-byte character sets (DBCS) used in some Asian locales. Instead of specifying the number of characters to return, *length* specifies the number of bytes. In areas where DBCS is not used, **RightB** behaves the same as **Right**.

See Also   **Left** Function, **Len** Function, **Mid** Function.

Example   This example uses the **Right** function to return a specified number of characters from the right side of a string.

```
AnyString = "Hello World"          ' Define string.
MyStr = Right(AnyString, 1)        ' Returns "d".
MyStr = Right(AnyString, 6)        ' Returns " World".
MyStr = Right(AnyString, 20) ' Returns "Hello World".
```

RightAngleAxes Property

Applies To   **Chart** Object.

Description   **True** if the chart axes are at right angles, independent of chart rotation or elevation. Applies only to 3-D line, column, and bar charts. Read-write.

Remarks   If this property is **True**, the **Perspective** property is ignored.

See Also   **Elevation** Property, **Perspective** Property, **Rotation** Property.

Example   This example sets the axes in Chart1 to intersect at right angles. The example should be run on a 3-D chart.

```
Charts("Chart1").RightAngleAxes = True
```

RightFooter Property

Applies To	**PageSetup** Object.
Description	Returns or sets the right part of the footer. Read-write.
Remarks	Special format codes can be used in the footer text.
See Also	**CenterFooter** Property, **CenterHeader** Property, **LeftFooter** Property, **LeftHeader** Property, **RightHeader** Property.
Example	This example prints the page number in the lower-right corner of every page.

```
Worksheets("Sheet1").PageSetup.RightFooter = "&P"
```

RightHeader Property

Applies To	**PageSetup** Object.
Description	Returns or sets the right part of the header. Read-write.
Remarks	Special format codes can be used in the header text.
See Also	**CenterFooter** Property, **CenterHeader** Property, **LeftFooter** Property, **LeftHeader** Property, **RightFooter** Property.
Example	This example prints the filename in the upper-right corner of every page.

```
Worksheets("Sheet1").PageSetup.RightHeader = "&F"
```

RightMargin Property

Applies To	**PageSetup** Object.
Description	Returns or sets the size of the right margin, in points (1/72 inch). Read-write.
Remarks	Margins are set or returned in points. Use the **InchesToPoints** or **CentimetersToPoints** function to convert.

Example

This example sets the right margin of Sheet1 to 1.5 inches.

```
Worksheets("Sheet1").PageSetup.RightMargin = _
        Application.InchesToPoints(1.5)
```

This example sets the right margin of Sheet1 to 2 centimeters.

```
Worksheets("Sheet1").PageSetup.RightMargin = _
        Application.CentimetersToPoints(2)
```

This example displays the current right margin setting for Sheet1.

```
marginInches = Worksheets("Sheet1").PageSetup.RightMargin / _
    Application.InchesToPoints(1)
MsgBox "The current right margin is " & marginInches & " inches"
```

RmDir Statement

Description   Removes an existing directory or folder.

Syntax   **RmDir** *path*

The *path* named argument is a string expression that identifies the directory or folder to be removed—may include drive. If no drive is specified, **RmDir** removes the directory or folder on the current drive.

Remarks   An error occurs if you try to use **RmDir** on a directory or folder containing files. Use the **Kill** statement to delete all files before attempting to remove a directory or folder.

See Also   **ChDir** Statement, **CurDir** Function, **Kill** Statement, **MkDir** Statement.

Example   This example uses the **RmDir** statement to remove an existing directory or folder.

```
' Assume that MYDIR is an empty directory or folder.
RmDir "MYDIR"    ' Remove MYDIR.
```

Rnd Function

Description   Returns a random number.

Syntax   **Rnd**[(*number*)]

The *number* named argument can be any valid numeric expression.

Remarks

The **Rnd** function returns a value less than 1 but greater than or equal to 0.

The value of *number* determines how **Rnd** generates a random number:

If *number* is:	Rnd generates:
Less than zero	The same number every time, using *number* as the seed.
Greater than zero	The next random number in the sequence.
Equal to zero	The most recently generated number.
Not supplied	The next random number in the sequence.

For any given initial seed, the same number sequence is generated because each successive call to the **Rnd** function uses the previous number as a seed for the next number in the sequence.

Use the **Randomize** statement without an argument to provide a random seed based on the system timer to initialize the random-number generator before **Rnd** is called.

To produce random integers in a given range, use this formula:

Int((upperbound - lowerbound + 1) * **Rnd** + lowerbound)

Here, *upperbound* is the highest number in the range, and *lowerbound* is the lowest number in the range.

See Also

Randomize Statement, **Timer** Function.

Example

This example uses the **Rnd** function to generate a random integer value from 1 to 6.

```
MyValue = Int((6 * Rnd) + 1) ' Generate random value between 1 and 6.
```

Rotation Property

Applies To

Chart Object.

Description

Returns or sets the rotation of the 3-D chart view (the rotation of the plot area around the z-axis, in degrees). The value of this property must be between 0 and 360, except for 3-D Bar charts, where the value must be between 0 and 44. The default value is 20. Applies only to 3-D charts. Read-write.

See Also

Elevation Property, **Perspective** Property, **RightAngleAxes** Property.

Example

This example sets the rotation of Chart1 to 30 degrees. The example should be run on a 3-D chart.

```
Charts("Chart1").Rotation = 30
```

RoundedCorners Property

Applies To   **ChartObject** Object, **ChartObjects** Collection, **DrawingObjects** Collection, **GroupObject** Object, **GroupObjects** Collection, **Rectangle** Object, **Rectangles** Collection, **TextBox** Object, **TextBoxes** Collection.

Description   **True** if the drawing object has rounded corners. Read-write.

Example   This example adds rounded corners to rectangle one on Sheet1.

```
Worksheets("Sheet1").Rectangles(1).RoundedCorners = True
```

Route Method

Applies To   **Workbook** Object.

Description   Routes the workbook using the workbook's current routing slip.

Syntax   *object*.**Route**

object
     Required. The **Workbook** object.

Remarks   Routing a workbook sets the **Routed** property to **True**.

See Also   **Routed** Property, **RoutingSlip** Property, **SendMail** Method.

Example   This example creates a routing slip for BOOK1.XLS and then sends the workbook to three recipients, one after another.

```
Workbooks("BOOK1.XLS").HasRoutingSlip = True
With Workbooks("BOOK1.XLS").RoutingSlip
    .Delivery = xlOneAfterAnother
    .Recipients = Array("Adam Bendel", "Jean Selva", "Bernard Gabor")
    .Subject = "Here is BOOK1.XLS"
    .Message = "Here is the workbook. What do you think?"
End With
Workbooks("BOOK1.XLS").Route
```

Routed Property

Applies To   **Workbook** Object.

Description   **True** if the workbook has been routed to the next recipient; **False** if the workbook needs to be routed. Read-only.

Remarks   If the workbook was not routed to the current recipient, this property is always **False** (for example, if the document has no routing slip, or a routing slip was just created).

Example   This example sends the workbook to the next recipient.

```
If ActiveWorkbook.HasRoutingSlip And _
    Not ActiveWorkbook.Routed Then
        ActiveWorkbook.Route
End If
```

RoutingSlip Object

Description   Represents the routing slip for a workbook. The routing slip is used to send a workbook through the electronic mail system.

Accessors   The **RoutingSlip** property returns the routing slip for the workbook. The following example sets the delivery style for the routing slip attached to the active workbook. For a more detailed example, see the **RoutingSlip** property.

```
ActiveWorkbook.HasRoutingSlip = True
ActiveWorkbook.RoutingSlip.Delivery = xlOneAfterAnother
```

Remarks   The **RoutingSlip** object does not exist and cannot be accessed unless the **HasRoutingSlip** property for the workbook is **True**.

Properties   **Application** Property, **Creator** Property, **Delivery** Property, **Message** Property, **Parent** Property, **Recipients** Property, **ReturnWhenDone** Property, **Status** Property, **Subject** Property, **TrackStatus** Property.

Methods   **Reset** Method.

RoutingSlip Property

Applies To   **Workbook** Object.

Description   This example creates a routing slip for BOOK1.XLS and then sends the workbook to three recipients, one after another.

Accessor   Returns a **RoutingSlip** object that represents the routing slip for the workbook. Reading this property if there is no routing slip causes an error (check the **HasRoutingSlip** property first). Read-only.

Example

```
Workbooks("BOOK1.XLS").HasRoutingSlip = True
With Workbooks("BOOK1.XLS").RoutingSlip
    .Delivery = xlOneAfterAnother
    .Recipients = Array("Adam Bendel", "Jean Selva", "Bernard Gabor")
    .Subject = "Here is BOOK1.XLS"
    .Message = "Here is the workbook. What do you think?"
End With
Workbooks("BOOK1.XLS").Route
```

Row Property

Applies To   **Range** Object.

Description   Returns the number of the first row of the first area of the range. Read-only.

See Also   **Column** Property, **EntireColumn** Property, **EntireRow** Property, **Rows** Method.

Example   This example sets the row height of every other row on Sheet1 to 4 points.

```
For Each rw In Worksheets("Sheet1").Rows
    If rw.Row Mod 2 = 0 Then
        rw.RowHeight = 4
    End If
Next rw
```

RowDifferences Method

Applies To   **Range** Object.

Description   Accessor. Returns a **Range** object representing all the cells whose contents are different than the comparison cell in each of the rows. The comparison cell is a cell in the comparison column and is equal to the *comparison* argument.

Syntax	*object*.**RowDifferences**(*comparison*)

object
   Required. The object to which this method applies.

comparison
   Required. A cell in the comparison column. Use the **ActiveCell** property if you are finding the differences between the active cell's column and all rows in the range.

See Also	**ColumnDifferences** Method.
Example	This example selects the cells in row one on Sheet1 whose contents are different from cell D1.

```
Worksheets("Sheet1").Activate
Set c1 = ActiveSheet.Rows(1).RowDifferences( _
    comparison:=ActiveSheet.Range("D1"))
c1.Select
```

RowFields Method

Applies To	**PivotTable** Object.
Description	Accessor. Returns an object that represents a single pivot field (a **PivotField** object, Syntax 1) or a collection of the pivot fields (a **PivotFields** object, Syntax 2) that are currently showing as row fields. Read-only.
Syntax 1	*object*.**RowFields**(*index*)
Syntax 2	*object*.**RowFields**

object
   Required. The **PivotTable** object.

index
   Required for Syntax 1. The name or number of the pivot field to return (can be an array to specify more than one).

See Also	**ColumnFields** Method, **DataFields** Method, **HiddenFields** Method, **PageFields** Method, **PivotFields** Method, **VisibleFields** Method.

Example

This example adds the PivotTable row field names to a list box. The list box appears on Sheet1.

```
Set pvtTable = Worksheets("Sheet1").Range("A3").PivotTable
Set newListBox = Worksheets("Sheet1").ListBoxes.Add _
    (Left:=10, Top:=72, Width:=144, Height:=144)
For Each hdnField In pvtTable.RowFields
    newListBox.AddItem (hdnField.Name)
Next hdnField
Worksheets("Sheet1").Activate
```

RowGrand Property

Applies To

PivotTable Object.

Description

True if the PivotTable shows row grand totals. Read-write.

See Also

ColumnGrand Property.

Example

This example sets the PivotTable to show row grand totals.

```
Set pvtTable = Worksheets("Sheet1").Range("A3").PivotTable
pvtTable.RowGrand = True
```

RowHeight Property

Applies To

Range Object.

Description

Returns the height of all of the rows in the range specified, measured in points (1/72 inch). Read-write.

Remarks

For a single row, the value of the **Height** property is equal to the value of **RowHeight**. However, you can also use the **Height** property to return the total height of a range of cells.

Other differences between **RowHeight** and **Height** are the following:

- **Height** is read-only.
- If you return the **RowHeight** of several rows, you will either get the row height of each of the rows (if they are the same), or **Null** if they are different. If you return the **Height** property of several rows, you will get the total height of all the rows.

See Also   **ColumnWidth** Property, **Height** Property, **StandardHeight** Property.

Example   This example doubles the height of row one on Sheet1.

```
With Worksheets("Sheet1").Rows(1)
    .RowHeight = .RowHeight * 2
End With
```

RowRange Property

Applies To   **PivotTable** Object.

Description Accessor. Returns a **Range** object that represents the range that includes the PivotTable row area. Read-only.

See Also   **ColumnRange** Property, **DataBodyRange** Property, **DataLabelRange** Property, **PageRange** Property.

Example   This example selects the PivotTable row headers.

```
Worksheets("Sheet1").Activate
Range("A3").Select
ActiveCell.PivotTable.RowRange.Select
```

Rows Method

Applies To   **Application** Object, **Range** Object, **Worksheet** Object.

Description Accessor. Returns a **Range** object that represents a single row (Syntax 1) or a collection of rows (Syntax 2).

Syntax 1   *object*.**Rows(*index*)**

Syntax 2   *object*.**Rows**

object
Optional for **Application**, required for **Range** and **Worksheet**. The object that contains the rows. If you specify the **Application** object (or omit the object qualifier), this method applies to the active sheet in the active workbook. If the active sheet is not a worksheet, this method fails.

index
Required for Syntax 1. The name or number of the row.

Remarks   When applied to a **Range** object that is a multiple selection, this method returns rows from the first area of the range only. For example, if the **Range** object is a multiple selection with two areas, A1:B2 and C3:D4, `Selection.Rows.Count` returns 2, not 4. To use this method on a range that may contain a multiple selection, test `Areas.Count` to determine if the range is a multiple selection, and if it is, then loop over each area in the range; see the second example.

See Also   **Columns** Method, **Range** Method.

Example   This example deletes row three on Sheet1.

```
Worksheets("Sheet1").Rows(3).Delete
```

This example displays the number of rows in the selection on Sheet1. If more than one area is selected, the example loops through every area.

```
Worksheets("Sheet1").Activate
areaCount = Selection.Areas.Count
If areaCount <= 1 Then
    MsgBox "The selection contains " & _
        Selection.Rows.Count & " rows."
Else
    i = 1
    For Each a In Selection.Areas
        MsgBox "Area " & i & " of the selection contains " & _
            a.Rows.Count & " rows."
        i = i + 1
    Next a
End If
```

RSet Statement

Description   Right aligns a string within a string variable.

Syntax   **RSet** *stringvar* **=** *string*

The **RSet** statement syntax has these parts:

Part	Description
stringvar	Name of a string variable.
string	String expression to be right aligned within *stringvar*.

Remarks   **RSet** replaces any leftover characters in *stringvar* with spaces, back to its beginning.

RSet can't be used with user-defined types.

See Also	**LSet** Statement.
Example	This example uses the **RSet** statement to right align a string within a string variable.

```
MyString = "0123456789"              ' Initialize string.
RSet MyString = "Right->"   ' MyString contains "   Right->".
```

Run Method

Applies To	**Application** Object, **Range** Object.
Description	Syntax 1: Runs a macro or calls a function. This can be used to run a macro written in any language (Visual Basic, the Microsoft Excel 4.0 macro language, or a function in a DLL or XLL).
	Syntax 2: Runs the Microsoft Excel 4.0 macro at this location. The range must be on a macro sheet.
Syntax 1	*object*.**Run**(*macro*, *arg1*, *arg2*, ...)
Syntax 2	*object*.**Run**(*arg1*, *arg2*, ...)

object
> Optional for **Application**, required for **Range**. The application that contains the macro, or a range on a macro sheet that contains an Microsoft Excel 4.0 macro.

macro
> Required for Syntax 1 (not used with Syntax 2). The macro to run. This can be a string with the macro name, or a **Range** indicating where the function is, or a register ID for a registered DLL (XLL) function. If a string is used, the string will be evaluated in the context of the active sheet.

arg1, *arg2*, ...
> Optional. The arguments that should be passed to the function.

Remarks	The **Run** method returns whatever the called macro returns. Objects passed as arguments to the macro are converted to values (by applying the **Value** property to the object). This means you cannot pass objects to macros using the **Run** method.
Example	This example shows how to call the function macro My_Func_Sum, which is defined on the macro sheet MYCUSTOM.XLM (the macro sheet must be open). The function takes two numeric arguments—1 and 5, in this example.

```
mySum = Application.Run("MYCUSTOM.XLM!My_Func_Sum", 1, 5)
MsgBox "Macro result: " & mySum
```

RunAutoMacros Method

Applies To   **Workbook** Object.

Description   Runs the Auto_Open, Auto_Close, Auto_Activate, or Auto_Deactivate macros that are attached to the workbook.

These four auto macros do not run when workbooks are opened or closed (and when sheets are activated or deactivated) by a Visual Basic program. Use this method to run auto macros.

Syntax   *object*.**RunAutoMacros(*which*)**

object
    Required. The **Workbook** object.

which
    Required. Specifies which macros to run, as shown in the following table.

Value	Meaning
xlAutoOpen	Auto_Open macros.
xlAutoClose	Auto_Close macros.
xlAutoActivate	Auto_Activate macros.
xlAutoDeactivate	Auto_Deactivate macros.

Remarks   The Auto_Activate and Auto_Deactivate macros are included for backward compatibility with the Microsoft Excel 4.0 macro language. Use the **OnSheetActivate** and **OnSheetDeactivate** properties when you program in Visual Basic.

Example   This example opens the workbook ANALYSIS.XLS and then runs its Auto_Open macro.

```
Workbooks.Open "ANALYSIS.XLS"
ActiveWorkbook.RunAutoMacros xlAutoOpen
```

This example runs the Auto_Close macro for the active workbook and then closes the workbook.

```
With ActiveWorkbook
    .RunAutoMacros xlAutoClose
    .Close
End With
```

Save Method

Applies To	**Application** Object, **Workbook** Object.
Description	**Workbook** object (Syntax 1): Saves changes to the specified workbook. **Application** object (Syntax 2): Saves the current workspace.
Syntax 1	*object*.**Save**
Syntax 2	*object*.**Save**(*filename*)

object
   Required. The **Workbook** object (Syntax 1) or **Application** object (Syntax 2).

filename
   Optional. Specifies the name of the saved workspace file. If this argument is omitted, a default name is used.

Remarks	To open a workbook file, use the **Open** method.

To mark the workbook as saved without writing it to a disk, set its **Saved** property to **True**.

The first time you save a workbook, use the **SaveAs** method to specify a name for the file.

See Also	**Open** Method, **SaveAs** Method, **SaveCopyAs** Method, **Saved** Property.
Example	This example saves the active workbook.

```
ActiveWorkbook.Save
```

This example saves all open workbooks and then closes Microsoft Excel.

```
For Each w In Application.Workbooks
    w.Save
Next w
Application.Quit
```

SaveAs Method

Applies To	**Chart** Object, **DialogSheet** Object, **Module** Object, **Workbook** Object, **Worksheet** Object.
Description	Saves changes to the sheet or workbook in a different file.

Syntax	*object*.**SaveAs**(*filename*, *fileFormat*, *password*, *writeResPassword*, *readOnlyRecommended*, *createBackup*, *accessMode*, *conflictResolution*)

object
Required. The object to which this method applies.

filename
Optional. A string indicating the name of the file to save. You can include a full path; if you do not, Microsoft Excel saves the file in the current folder.

fileFormat
Optional. The file format to use when you save the file. See the **FileFormat** property for a list of valid choices.

password
Optional. A case-sensitive string indicating the protection password to be given to the file. Should be no more than 15 characters.

writeResPassword
Optional. A string indicating the write-reservation password for this file. If a file is saved with the password and the password is not supplied when the file is opened, the file is opened as read-only.

readOnlyRecommended
Optional. If **True**, when the file is opened, Microsoft Excel displays a message recommending that you open the file as read-only.

createBackup
Optional. If **True**, Microsoft Excel creates a backup file; if **False**, no backup file is created; if omitted, the status is unchanged.

accessMode
Optional. Specifies the workbook access mode. One of **xlShared** (shared list), **xlExclusive** (exclusive mode), or **xlNoChange** (do not change the access mode). If this argument is omitted, the access mode is not changed. This argument is ignored if you save a shared list without changing the filename. To change the access mode, use the **ExclusiveAccess** method.

conflictResolution
Optional. Specifies how change conflicts are resolved if the workbook is a shared list. One of **xlUserResolution** (display the conflict-resolution dialog box), **xlLocalSessionChanges** (automatically accept the local user's changes), or **xlOtherSessionChanges** (accept other changes in preference to the local user's changes). If this argument is omitted, the conflict-resolution dialog box is displayed.

See Also	**FileFormat** Property, **MultiUserEditing** Property, **Save** Method, **SaveCopyAs** Method, **Saved** Property.

Example

This example creates a new workbook, prompts the user for a filename, and then saves the workbook.

```
Set NewBook = Workbooks.Add
Do
     fName = Application.GetSaveAsFilename
Loop Until fName <> False
NewBook.SaveAs Filename:=fName
```

SaveCopyAs Method

Applies To   **Workbook** Object.

Description   Saves a copy of the workbook to a file but does not modify the open workbook in memory.

Syntax   *object*.**SaveCopyAs(*filename*)**

object
   Required. The **Workbook** object.

filename
   Required. Specifies the filename for the copy.

See Also   **Save** Method, **SaveAs** Method.

Example   This example saves a copy of the active workbook.

```
ActiveWorkbook.SaveCopyAs "C:\TEMP\XXXX.XLS"
```

This is the same example in Microsoft Excel for the Macintosh.

```
ActiveWorkbook.SaveCopyAs "HD:Temporary Folder:Temporary Workbook File"
```

Saved Property

Applies To   **Workbook** Object.

Description   **False** if changes have been made to a workbook since it was last saved. Read-write.

Remarks   If a workbook has never been saved, its **Path** will return an empty string ("").

You can set this property to **True** if you want to close a modified workbook without saving it or being prompted to save it.

See Also   **Save** Method, **SaveAs** Method, **SaveCopyAs** Method.

Example   This example displays a message if the active workbook contains unsaved changes.

```
If Not ActiveWorkbook.Saved Then
    MsgBox "This workbook contains unsaved changes."
End If
```

This example closes the workbook that contains the example code and discards any changes to the workbook by setting the **Saved** property to **True**.

```
ThisWorkbook.Saved = True
ThisWorkbook.Close
```

SaveData Property

Applies To   **PivotTable** Object.

Description   **True** if data for the PivotTable is saved with the workbook; **False** if only the PivotTable definition is saved. Read-write.

Example   This example sets the PivotTable to save data with the workbook.

```
Set pvtTable = Worksheets("Sheet1").Range("A3").PivotTable
pvtTable.SaveData = True
```

SaveLinkValues Property

Applies To   **Workbook** Object.

Description   **True** if Microsoft Excel will save external link values with this workbook. Read-write.

Example   This example causes Microsoft Excel to save external link values with the active workbook.

```
ActiveWorkbook.SaveLinkValues = True
```

ScaleType Property

Applies To   **Axis** Object.

Description   Returns or sets the value axis scale type (**xlLinear** or **xlLogarithmic**). Applies only to the value axis. Read-write.

Remarks   A logarithmic scale uses base ten logarithms.

Example   This example sets the value axis in Chart1 to use a logarithmic scale.

```
Charts("Chart1").Axes(xlValue).ScaleType = xlLogarithmic
```

Scenario Object

Description   Represents a scenario on a worksheet. A scenario is a group of input values (called changing cells) that is named and saved.

Accessors   The **Scenario** object is a member of the **Scenarios** collection. The **Scenarios** collection contains all of the defined scenarios for a worksheet. Use the **Add** method to create a new scenario and add it to the collection. To access a single member of the collection, use the **Scenarios** method with the index number or name of the scenario as an argument.

You assign a name to a scenario when you create it. Use the **Name** property to set or return the scenario name. The following example shows the scenario named "Typical" on the worksheet named "Options."

```
Worksheets("options").Scenarios("typical").Show
```

Scenario names are shown in the Scenario Manager dialog box and in the Scenarios box on the Workgroup toolbar. The first scenario created is at the top of the list; the last scenario is at the bottom (they are not sorted by alphabetical order). This is also the order used for the scenario index numbers. The first scenario created is Scenarios(1); the last scenario is Scenarios(Scenarios.Count). The following example hides scenario one for the worksheet named "Options." When the worksheet is protected, this scenario will not be visible in the Scenarios box or the Scenario Manager dialog box.

```
Worksheets("options").Scenarios(1).Hidden = True
```

Properties   **Application** Property, **ChangingCells** Property, **Comment** Property, **Creator** Property, **Hidden** Property, **Index** Property, **Locked** Property, **Name** Property, **Parent** Property, **Values** Property.

Methods   **ChangeScenario** Method, **Delete** Method, **Show** Method.

Scenarios Collection Object

Description   A collection of all the **Scenario** objects on the specified worksheet. A scenario is a group of input values (called changing cells) that is named and saved.

Accessors   Use the **Add** method to create a new scenario and add it to the collection. The following example adds a new scenario named "Typical" to the worksheet named "Options." The new scenario has two changing cells, A2 and A12, with the respective values of 55 and 60.

```
Worksheets("options").Scenarios.Add name:="Typical", _
    changingCells:=Worksheets("options").Range("A2,A12"), _
    values:=Array("55", "60")
```

Use the **Scenarios** method with an argument to access a single member of the collection or without an argument to access the entire collection at once. The following example creates a summary for the scenarios on the worksheet named "Options" using cells J10 and J20 as the result cells.

```
Worksheets("options").Scenarios.CreateSummary _
    resultCells:=Worksheets("options").Range("j10,j20")
```

Properties   **Application** Property, **Count** Property, **Creator** Property, **Parent** Property.

Methods   **Add** Method (**Scenarios** Collection), **CreateSummary** Method, **Item** Method, **Merge** Method.

Scenarios Method

Applies To   **Worksheet** Object.

Description   Accessor. Returns an object that represents a single scenario (a **Scenario** object, Syntax 1) or a collection of scenarios (a **Scenarios** object, Syntax 2) on the worksheet.

Syntax 1   *object*.**Scenarios(*index*)**

Syntax 2   *object*.**Scenarios**

object
    Required. The **Worksheet** object.

index

Required for Syntax 1. The name or number of the scenario (can be an array to specify more than one).

Example

This example sets the comment for the first scenario on Sheet1.

```
Worksheets("Sheet1").Scenarios(1).Comment = _
    "Worst-case July 1993 sales"
```

ScreenUpdating Property

Applies To

Application Object.

Description

True if screen updating is on. Read-write.

Remarks

Turn screen updating off to speed up your macro code. You will not be able to see what the macro is doing, but it will run faster.

Example

This example demonstrates how turning off screen updating can make your code run faster. The example hides every other column on Sheet1, while keeping track of the time it takes to do so. The first time it hides the columns, screen updating is on; the second time, screen updating is off. When you run this example, you can compare the two times that the example displays in the message box.

```
Dim elapsedTime(2)
Application.ScreenUpdating = True
For i = 1 To 2
    If i = 2 Then Application.ScreenUpdating = False
    startTime = Time
    Worksheets("Sheet1").Activate
    For Each c In ActiveSheet.Columns
        If c.Column Mod 2 = 0 Then
            c.Hidden = True
        End If
    Next c
    stopTime = Time
    elapsedTime(i) = (stopTime - startTime) * 24 * 60 * 60
Next i
Application.ScreenUpdating = True
MsgBox "Elapsed time, screen updating on: " & elapsedTime(1) & _
        " sec." & Chr(13) & _
        "Elapsed time, screen updating off: " & elapsedTime(2) & _
        " sec."
```

ScrollBar Object

Description   Represents a scroll bar control on a chart, dialogsheet, or worksheet. Window scroll bars are not **ScrollBar** objects. **ScrollBar** objects do not support border or pattern formatting.

Accessors   The **ScrollBar** object is a member of the **ScrollBars** collection. The **ScrollBars** collection contains all the **ScrollBar** objects on a single sheet. Use the **Add** method to create a new scroll bar and add it to the collection. Set the *width* argument to be greater than the *height* argument to create a horizontal scroll bar.

To access a single member of the collection, use the **ScrollBars** method with the index number or name of the scroll bar as an argument. The following example sets scroll bar one on the dialog sheet named "Dialog1" to the top or left of its range.

```
DialogSheets("dialog1").ScrollBars(1).Value = 0
```

The scroll bar name is shown in the Name Box when the scroll bar is selected. Use the **Name** property to set or return the scroll bar name. The following example sets the **OnAction** property for the scroll bar named "Scroll Bar 6." The Visual Basic procedure named "ScrollProc" is called whenever the scroll bar changes.

```
DialogSheets(1).ScrollBars("scroll bar 6").OnAction = "ScrollProc"
```

Properties   **Application** Property, **BottomRightCell** Property, **Creator** Property, **Display3DShading** Property, **Enabled** Property, **Height** Property, **Index** Property, **LargeChange** Property, **Left** Property, **LinkedCell** Property, **Locked** Property, **Max** Property, **Min** Property, **Name** Property, **OnAction** Property, **Parent** Property, **Placement** Property, **PrintObject** Property, **SmallChange** Property, **Top** Property, **TopLeftCell** Property, **Value** Property, **Visible** Property, **Width** Property, **ZOrder** Property.

Methods   **BringToFront** Method, **Copy** Method, **CopyPicture** Method, **Cut** Method, **Delete** Method, **Duplicate** Method, **Select** Method, **SendToBack** Method.

ScrollBars Collection Object

Description   A collection of all the **ScrollBar** objects on the specified chart sheet, dialog sheet, or worksheet (not including window scroll bars). **ScrollBar** objects do not support border or pattern formatting.

Accessors

Use the **Add** method to create a new scroll bar and add it to the collection. Set the *width* argument to be greater than the *height* argument to create a horizontal scroll bar. The following example adds a new scroll bar to the dialog sheet named "Dialog1." The new scroll bar is positioned relative to the upper-left corner of the dialog frame.

```
Dim df As DialogFrame
Set df = DialogSheets("dialog1").DialogFrame
DialogSheets("dialog1").ScrollBars.Add df.Left + 10, _
    df.Top + 20, 10, 100
```

Use the **ScrollBars** method with an argument to access a single member of the collection or without an argument to access the entire collection at once. The following example sets each of the scroll bars on the worksheet named "Sheet1" to the top or left of its range.

Properties

Application Property, **Count** Property, **Creator** Property, **Display3DShading** Property, **Enabled** Property, **Height** Property, **LargeChange** Property, **Left** Property, **LinkedCell** Property, **Locked** Property, **Max** Property, **Min** Property, **OnAction** Property, **Parent** Property, **Placement** Property, **PrintObject** Property, **SmallChange** Property, **Top** Property, **Value** Property, **Visible** Property, **Width** Property, **ZOrder** Property.

Methods

Add Method (Graphic Objects and Controls), **BringToFront** Method, **Copy** Method, **CopyPicture** Method, **Cut** Method, **Delete** Method, **Duplicate** Method, **Group** Method, **Item** Method, **Select** Method, **SendToBack** Method.

ScrollBars Method

Applies To

Chart Object, **DialogSheet** Object, **Worksheet** Object.

Description

Accessor. Returns an object that represents a single scroll bar control (a **ScrollBar** object, Syntax 1) or a collection of scroll bar controls (a **ScrollBars** object, Syntax 2) on the sheet.

Syntax 1

object.**ScrollBars**(*index*)

Syntax 2

object.**ScrollBars**

object
Required. The **Chart**, **DialogSheet**, or **Worksheet** object.

index
Required for Syntax 1. Specifies the name or number of the scroll bar (can be an array to specify more than one).

See Also	**Max** Property, **Min** Property.
Example	This example sets the minimum and maximum values for scroll bar one on Dialog1.

```
With DialogSheets("Dialog1").ScrollBars(1)
    .Min = 20
    .Max = 50
End With
```

ScrollColumn Property

Applies To	**Pane** Object, **Window** Object.
Description	Returns or sets the number of the column that appears at the left of the pane or window. Read-write.
Remarks	If the window is split, **Window.ScrollColumn** refers to the top left pane. If panes are frozen, **Window.ScrollColumn** excludes the frozen areas.
See Also	**ScrollRow** Property.
Example	This example moves column three to the left of the window.

```
Worksheets("Sheet1").Activate
ActiveWindow.ScrollColumn = 3
```

ScrollRow Property

Applies To	**Pane** Object, **Window** Object.
Description	Returns or sets the number of the row that appears at the top of the pane or window. Read-write.
Remarks	If the window is split, **Window.ScrollRow** refers to the top left pane. If panes are frozen, **Window.ScrollRow** excludes the frozen areas.
See Also	**ScrollColumn** Property.
Example	This example moves row 10 to the top of the window.

```
Worksheets("Sheet1").Activate
ActiveWindow.ScrollRow = 10
```

ScrollWorkbookTabs Method

Applies To   **Window** Object.

Description   Scrolls the workbook tabs at the bottom of the window. Does not affect the active sheet in the workbook.

Syntax   *object*.**ScrollWorkbookTabs**(*sheets*, *position*)

object
> Required. The **Window** object.

sheets
> Optional. The number of sheets to scroll. Positive means scroll forward, negative means scroll backward, zero means don't scroll. You must specify *sheets* if you do not specify *position*.

position
> Optional. **xlFirst** to scroll to the first sheet, or **xlLast** to scroll to the last sheet. You must specify *position* if you do not specify *sheets*.

Example   This example scrolls the workbook tabs to the last sheet in the workbook.

```
ActiveWindow.ScrollWorkbookTabs position:=xlLast
```

Second Function

Description   Returns a whole number between 0 and 59, inclusive, representing the second of the minute.

Syntax   **Second**(*time*)

The *time* named argument is limited to a time or numbers and strings, in any combination, that can represent a time. If *time* contains no valid data, **Null** is returned.

See Also   **Day** Function, **Hour** Function, **Minute** Function, **Now** Function, **Time** Function, **Time** Statement.

Example   This example uses the **Second** function to obtain the second of the minute from a specified time.

```
' In the development environment, the time (date literal) will display
' in short format using the locale settings of your code.
MyTime = #4:35:17 PM#                ' Assign a time.
MySecond = Second(MyTime)   ' MySecond contains 17.
```

Seek Function

Description

Returns the current read/write position within a file opened using the **Open** statement.

Syntax

Seek(*filenumber*)

The *filenumber* named argument is any valid file number.

Remarks

Seek returns a value between 1 and 2,147,483,647 (equivalent to 2^31-1), inclusive. For files open in **Random** mode, **Seek** returns the number of the next record read or written. For files opened in **Binary**, **Output**, **Append**, or **Input** mode, **Seek** returns the byte position at which the next operation is to take place. The first byte in a file is at position 1, the second byte is at position 2, and so on.

See Also

Get Statement, **Open** Statement, **Put** Statement, **Seek** Statement.

Example

This example uses the **Seek** function to return the current file position.

```
' For files opened in random-file mode, Seek returns number of next
' record. Assume TESTFILE is a file containing records of the
' user-defined type Record.
Type Record ' Define user-defined type.
    ID As Integer
    Name As String * 20
End Type
Dim MyRecord As Record              ' Declare variable.
' Open file in random-file mode.
Open "TESTFILE" For Random As #1 Len = Len(MyRecord)
Do While Not EOF(1)                  ' Loop until end of file.
    Get #1, , MyRecord               ' Read next record.
    Debug.Print Seek(1)              ' Print record number to Debug
            ' window.
Loop
Close #1' Close file.

' For files opened in modes other than random mode, Seek returns the
' byte position at which the next operation will take place. Assume
' TESTFILE is a file containing a few lines of text.
Open "TESTFILE" For Input As #1     ' Open file for reading.
Do While Not EOF(1)                  ' Loop until end of file.
    MyChar = Input(1,#1)            ' Read next character of data.
    Debug.Print Seek(1)              ' Print byte position to Debug
            ' window.
Loop
Close #1' Close file.
```

Seek Statement

Description   Sets the position for the next read or write within a file opened using the **Open** statement.

Syntax   **Seek** [#]*filenumber,position*

The **Seek** statement syntax has these parts:

Part	Description
filenumber	Any valid file number.
position	Number in the range 1 to 2,147,483,647, inclusive, that indicates where the next read or write should occur.

Remarks   Record numbers specified in **Get** and **Put** statements override file positioning done by **Seek**.

Performing a file write after doing a **Seek** operation beyond the end of a file extends the file. If you attempt a **Seek** operation to a negative or zero position, an error occurs.

See Also   **Get** Statement, **Open** Statement, **Put** Statement, **Seek** Function.

Example   This example uses the **Seek** statement to set the position for the next read or write within a file.

```
' For files opened in random-file mode, Seek sets the next
' record. Assume TESTFILE is a file containing records of the
' user-defined type Record.
Type Record                          ' Define user-defined type.
    ID As Integer
    Name As String * 20
End Type
Dim MyRecord As Record               ' Declare variable.
' Open file in random-file mode.
Open "TESTFILE" For Random As #1 Len = Len(MyRecord)
MaxSize = LOF(1) \ Len(MyRecord)     ' Get number of records in file.
' The loop reads all records starting from the last.
For RecordNumber = MaxSize To 1 Step - 1
    Seek #1, RecordNumber            ' Set position.
    Get #1, , MyRecord               ' Read record.
Next RecordNumber
Close #1                             ' Close file.
```

```
' For files opened in modes other than random mode, Seek sets the
' byte position at which the next operation will take place. Assume
' TESTFILE is a file containing a few lines of text.
Open "TESTFILE" For Input As #1      ' Open file for input.
MaxSize = LOF(1)                     ' Get size of file in bytes.
' The loop reads all characters starting from the last.
For NextChar = MaxSize To 1 Step -1
    Seek #1, NextChar                ' Set position.
    MyChar = Input(1,#1)             ' Read character.
Next NextChar
Close #1' Close file.
```

Select Case Statement

Description

Executes one of several groups of statements, depending on the value of an expression.

Syntax

Select Case *testexpression*
[**Case** *expressionlist-n*
    [*statements-n*]] . . .
[**Case Else**
    [*elsestatements*]]
End Select

The **Select Case** statement syntax has these parts:

Part	Description
testexpression	Any numeric or string expression.
expressionlist-n	Comma-delimited list of one or more of the following forms: *expression*, *expression* **To** *expression*, **Is** *comparisonoperator expression*. The **To** keyword specifies a range of values. If you use the **To** keyword, the smaller value must appear before **To**. Use the **Is** keyword with comparison operators (except **Is** and **Like**) to specify a range of values. If not supplied, the **Is** keyword is automatically inserted.
statements-n	One or more statements executed if *testexpression* matches any part of *expressionlist-n*.
elsestatements	One or more statements executed if *testexpression* doesn't match any of the **Case** clause.

Remarks

If *testexpression* matches any *expressionlist* expression associated with a **Case** clause, the *statements* following that **Case** clause are executed up to the next **Case** clause, or, for the last clause, up to the **End Select**. Control then passes to the statement following **End Select**. If *testexpression* matches an *expressionlist* expression in more than one **Case** clause, only the statements following the first match are executed.

The **Case Else** clause is used to indicate the *statements* to be executed if no match is found between the *testexpression* and an *expressionlist* in any of the other **Case** selections. When there is no **Case Else** statement and no expression listed in the **Case** clauses matches *testexpression*, execution continues at the statement following **End Select**.

Although not required, it is a good idea to have a **Case Else** statement in your **Select Case** block to handle unforeseen *testexpression* values.

You can use multiple expressions or ranges in each **Case** clause. For example, the following line is valid:

```
Case 1 To 4, 7 To 9, 11, 13, Is > MaxNumber
```

Note The **Is** comparison operator is not the same as the **Is** keyword used in the **Select Case** statement.

You also can specify ranges and multiple expressions for character strings. In the following example, **Case** matches strings that are exactly equal to everything, strings that fall between nuts and soup in alphabetical order, and the current value of TestItem:

```
Case "everything", "nuts" To "soup", TestItem
```

Select Case statements can be nested. Each **Select Case** statement must have a matching **End Select** statement.

See Also

If...**Then**...**Else** Statement; **On**...**GoSub**, **On**...**GoTo** Statements; **Option Compare** Statement.

Example

This example uses the **Select Case** statement to evaluate the value of a variable. The second **Case** clause contains the value of the variable being evaluated and therefore only the statement associated with it is executed.

```
Number = 8                          ' Initialize variable.
Select Case Number                  ' Evaluate Number.
Case 1 To 5                         ' Number between 1 and 5.
    MyString = "Between 1 and 5"
Case 6, 7, 8, 9, 10                 ' Number between 6 and 10.
    ' This is the only Case clause that evaluates to True.
    MyString = "Between 6 and 10"
Case Else                           ' Other values.
    MyString = "Not between 1 and 10"
End Select
```

This example displays the name of the mail system installed on the computer.

```
Sub foo()
Select Case Application.MailSystem
    Case Is = xlMAPI
        MsgBox "Mail system is Microsoft Mail"
    Case Is = xlPowerTalk
        MsgBox "Mail system is PowerTalk"
    Case Is = xlNoMailSystem
        MsgBox "No mail system installed"
End Select
End Sub
```

This example displays a message box that describes the location of the active cell in the PivotTable.

```
Worksheets("Sheet1").Activate
Select Case ActiveCell.LocationInTable
Case Is = xlRowHeader
    MsgBox "Active cell is part of a row header"
Case Is = xlColumnHeader
    MsgBox "Active cell is part of a column header"
Case Is = xlPageHeader
    MsgBox "Active cell is part of a page header"
Case Is = xlDataHeader
    MsgBox "Active cell is part of a data header"
Case Is = xlRowItem
    MsgBox "Active cell is part of a row item"
Case Is = xlColumnItem
    MsgBox "Active cell is part of a column item"
```

```
Case Is = xlPageItem
    MsgBox "Active cell is part of a page item"
Case Is = xlDataItem
    MsgBox "Active cell is part of a data item"
Case Is = xlTableBody
    MsgBox "Active cell is part of the table body"
End Select
```

This example displays a message if the active cell on Sheet1 contains a cell error value. You can use this example as a framework for a cell-error-value error handler.

```
Worksheets("Sheet1").Activate
If IsError(ActiveCell.Value) Then
    errval = ActiveCell.Value
    Select Case errval
        Case CVErr(xlErrDiv0)
            MsgBox "#DIV/0! error"
        Case CVErr(xlErrNA)
            MsgBox "#N/A error"
        Case CVErr(xlErrName)
            MsgBox "#NAME? error"
        Case CVErr(xlErrNull)
            MsgBox "#NULL! error"
        Case CVErr(xlErrNum)
            MsgBox "#NUM! error"
        Case CVErr(xlErrRef)
            MsgBox "#REF! error"
        Case CVErr(xlErrValue)
            MsgBox "#VALUE! error"
        Case Else
            MsgBox "This should never happen!!"
    End Select
End If
```

Select Method

Applies To Arc Object, **Arcs** Collection, **Axis** Object, **AxisTitle** Object, **Button** Object, **Buttons** Collection, **Chart** Object, **ChartArea** Object, **ChartObject** Object, **ChartObjects** Collection, **Charts** Collection, **ChartTitle** Object, **CheckBox** Object, **Corners** Object, **DataLabel** Object, **DataLabels** Collection, **DialogFrame** Object, **DialogSheet** Object, **DialogSheets** Collection, **DownBars** Object, **Drawing** Object, **DrawingObjects** Collection, **Drawings** Collection, **DropDown** Object, **DropDowns** Collection, **DropLines** Object, **EditBox** Object, **EditBoxes** Collection, **ErrorBars** Object, **Floor** Object, **Gridlines** Object, **GroupBox** Object, **GroupBoxes** Collection, **GroupObject** Object, **GroupObjects** Collection, **HiLoLines** Object, **Label** Object, **Labels** Collection, **Legend** Object, **LegendEntry** Object, **LegendKey** Object, **Line** Object, **Lines** Collection, **ListBox** Object, **ListBoxes** Collection, **Module** Object, **Modules** Collection, **OLEObject** Object, **OLEObjects** Collection, **OptionButton** Object, **OptionButtons** Collection, **Oval** Object, **Ovals** Collection, **Picture** Object, **Pictures** Collection, **PlotArea** Object, **Point** Object, **Range** Object, **Rectangle** Object, **Rectangles** Collection, **ScrollBar** Object, **ScrollBars** Collection, **Series** Object, **SeriesLines** Object, **Sheets** Collection, **Spinner** Object, **Spinners** Collection, **TextBox** Object, **TextBoxes** Collection, **TickLabels** Object, **Trendline** Object, **UpBars** Object, **Walls** Object, **Worksheet** Object, **Worksheets** Collection.

Description Selects the object.

Syntax *object*.**Select**(*replace*)

object
Required. The object to be selected.

replace
Optional (used only with drawing objects and sheets). If **True** or omitted, the current selection is replaced with a new selection consisting of the specified object. If **False**, the current selection is extended to include any previously selected objects and the specified object.

Remarks To select a cell or range of cells, use the **Select** method. To make a single cell the active cell, use the **Activate** method.

See Also **Activate** Method, **Goto** Method.

Example This example selects cells A1:B3 on Sheet1.

```
Worksheets("Sheet1").Activate
Range("A1:B3").Select
```

Selected Property

Applies To   **DrawingObjects** Collection, **ListBox** Object, **ListBoxes** Collection.

Description   Returns or sets an array of Boolean values indicating the selection state of items in the list box. Each entry in the array corresponds to an entry in the list box, and is **True** if the entry is selected or **False** if it is not selected. Use this property to obtain the selected items in a multi-select list box. Read-write.

Remarks   For single-selection list boxes, it is easier to use the **Value** or **ListIndex** properties to get and set the selection.

See Also   **ListIndex** Property, **Selection** Property, **Value** Property.

Example   This example selects every other item in list box one on Sheet1.

```
Dim items() As Boolean
Set lbox = Worksheets("Sheet1").ListBoxes(1)
ReDim items(1 To lbox.ListCount)
For i = 1 To lbox.ListCount
    If i Mod 2 = 1 Then
        items(i) = True
    Else
        items(i) = False
    End If
Next
lbox.MultiSelect = xlExtended
lbox.Selected = items
```

SelectedSheets Method

Applies To   **Window** Object.

Description   Accessor. Returns a **Sheets** collection that represents all the selected sheets in the specified window.

Syntax   *object*.**SelectedSheets**

object
    Required. The **Window** object.

Example   This example displays a message if Sheet1 is selected in BOOK1.XLS.

```
For Each sh In Workbooks("BOOK1.XLS").Windows(1).SelectedSheets
    If sh.Name = "Sheet1" Then
        MsgBox "Sheet1 is selected"
        Exit For
    End If
Next
```

Selection Property

Applies To   **Application** Object, **Window** Object.

Description   Accessor. If you specify the **Application** object (or omit the object qualifier), this property returns the selected object in the active window. If you specify a **Window** object, this property returns the selected object in the specified window. Read-only.

Remarks   The object type returned by the **Selection** property depends on the type of selection (for example, if a text box is selected, this property returns a **TextBox** object.)

The **Selection** property returns **Nothing** if nothing is selected.

See Also   **Activate** Method, **ActiveCell** Property, **Select** Method, **Selected** Property.

Example   This example clears the selection on Sheet1 (assuming that the selection is a range of cells).

```
Worksheets("Sheet1").Activate
Selection.Clear
```

This example displays the Visual Basic object type of the selection. Try running this example with cells selected, with a single oval selected, and with several different graphic objects selected.

```
Worksheets("Sheet1").Activate
MsgBox "The selection object type is " & TypeName(Selection)
```

SendDateTime Property

Applies To   **Mailer** Object.

Description	Returns the date and time that the mailer was sent. The mailer must be sent before this property is valid. Available only in Microsoft Excel for the Apple Macintosh with the PowerTalk mail system extension installed. Read-only.
See Also	**BCCRecipients** Property, **CCRecipients** Property, **Enclosures** Property, **Mailer** Property, **Received** Property, **Sender** Property, **SendMailer** Method, **Subject** Property, **ToRecipients** Property.
Example	This example displays the sender of the workbook, plus the date and time it was sent.

```
If ActiveWorkbook.HasMailer Then
    MsgBox "This workbook was sent by " & _
        ActiveWorkbook.Mailer.Sender & " at " & _
        Format(ActiveWorkbook.Mailer.SendDateTime, "General Date")
End If
```

Sender Property

Applies To	**Mailer** Object.
Description	Returns the name of the user (as text) who sent this workbook mailer. Available only in Microsoft Excel for the Apple Macintosh with the PowerTalk mail system extension installed. Read-only.
See Also	**BCCRecipients** Property, **CCRecipients** Property, **Enclosures** Property, **Mailer** Property, **Received** Property, **SendDateTime** Property, **SendMailer** Method, **Subject** Property, **ToRecipients** Property.
Example	This example displays the sender of the workbook, plus the date and time it was sent.

```
If ActiveWorkbook.HasMailer Then
    MsgBox "This workbook was sent by " & _
        ActiveWorkbook.Mailer.Sender & " at " & _
        Format(ActiveWorkbook.Mailer.SendDateTime, "General Date")
End If
```

SendKeys Method

Applies To	**Application** Object.

Description	Sends keystrokes to the active application. This method is not available on the Apple Macintosh.
Syntax	*object*.**SendKeys**(*keys*, *wait*)

object
> Optional. The **Application** object.

keys
> Required. The key or key combination you want to send to the application, as text.

wait
> Optional. If **True**, Microsoft Excel waits for the keys to be processed before returning control to the macro. If **False** or omitted, the macro continues to run without waiting for the keys to be processed.

Remarks

This method places keystrokes into a key buffer. In some cases, you must call this method before you call the method that will use the keystrokes. For example, to send a password to a dialog box, you must call the **SendKeys** method before you display the dialog box.

The *keys* argument can specify any single key, or any key combined with ALT, CTRL, or SHIFT, or any combination of those keys. Each key is represented by one or more characters, such as "a" for the character a, or "{ENTER}" for the ENTER key.

To specify characters that aren't displayed when you press the key, such as ENTER or TAB, use the codes shown in the following table. Each code in the table represents one key on the keyboard.

Key	Code
BACKSPACE	"{BACKSPACE}" or "{BS}"
BREAK	"{BREAK}"
CAPS LOCK	"{CAPSLOCK}"
CLEAR	"{CLEAR}"
DELETE or DEL	"{DELETE}" or "{DEL}"
DOWN ARROW	"
END	"{END}"
ENTER (numeric keypad)	"{ENTER}"
ENTER	"~" (tilde)
ESC	"{ESCAPE} or {ESC}"
HELP	"{HELP}"
HOME	"{HOME}"
INS	"{INSERT}"

Key	Code
LEFT ARROW	"{LEFT}"
NUM LOCK	"{NUMLOCK}"
PAGE DOWN	"{PGDN}"
PAGE UP	"{PGUP}"
RETURN	"{RETURN}"
RIGHT ARROW	"{RIGHT}"
SCROLL LOCK	"{SCROLLLOCK}"
TAB	"{TAB}"
UP ARROW	"{UP}"
F1 through F15	"{F1}" through "{F15}"

You can also specify keys combined with SHIFT and/or CTRL and/or ALT. To specify a key combined with another key or keys, use the following table.

To combine with	Precede the key code by
SHIFT	"+" (plus sign)
CTRL	"^" (caret)
ALT	"%" (percent sign)

Example

This example uses the **SendKeys** method to quit Microsoft Excel for Windows.

```
Application.SendKeys("%fx")
```

SendKeys Statement

Description

Sends one or more keystrokes to the active window as if typed at the keyboard; not available on the Macintosh.

Syntax

SendKeys *string*[,*wait*]

The **SendKeys** statement syntax has these named-argument parts:

Part	Description
string	String expression specifying the keystroke(s) to send.
wait	Boolean value specifying the wait mode. If **False** (default), control is returned to the procedure immediately after the keys are sent. If **True**, keystrokes must be processed before control is returned to the procedure.

Remarks

Each key is represented by one or more characters. To specify a single keyboard character, use the character itself. For example, to represent the letter A, use `"A"` for *string*. If you want to represent more than one character, append each additional character to the one preceding it. To represent the letters A, B, and C, use `"ABC"` for *string*.

The plus sign (+), caret (^), percent sign (%), tilde (~), and parentheses ( ) have special meanings to **SendKeys**. To specify one of these characters, enclose it within braces. For example, to specify the plus sign, use `{+}`. Brackets ([ ]) have no special meaning to **SendKeys**, but you must enclose them in braces as well, because in other applications, brackets do have a special meaning that may be significant when dynamic data exchange (DDE) occurs. To send brace characters, use `{{}` and `{}}`.

To specify characters that aren't displayed when you press a key (such as ENTER or TAB) and keys that represent actions rather than characters, use the codes shown below:

Key	Code
BACKSPACE	`{BACKSPACE}`, `{BS}`, or `{BKSP}`
BREAK	`{BREAK}`
CAPS LOCK	`{CAPSLOCK}`
DEL	`{DELETE}` or `{DEL}`
DOWN ARROW	`{DOWN}`
END	`{END}`
ENTER	`{ENTER}`
ESC	`{ESC}`
HELP	`{HELP}`
HOME	`{HOME}`
INS	`{INSERT}`
LEFT ARROW	`{LEFT}`
NUM LOCK	`{NUMLOCK}`
PAGE DOWN	`{PGDN}`
PAGE UP	`{PGUP}`
PRINT SCREEN	`{PRTSC}`
RIGHT ARROW	`{RIGHT}`
SCROLL LOCK	`{SCROLLLOCK}`
TAB	`{TAB}`
UP ARROW	`{UP}`
F1	`{F1}`
F2	`{F2}`

Key	Code
F3	{F3}
F4	{F4}
F5	{F5}
F6	{F6}
F7	{F7}
F8	{F8}
F9	{F9}
F10	{F10}
F11	{F11}
F12	{F12}
F13	{F13}
F14	{F14}
F15	{F15}
F16	{F16}

To specify keys combined with any combination of the SHIFT, CTRL, and ALT keys, precede the regular key code with one or more of the following codes:

Key	Code
SHIFT	+
CTRL (CONTROL)	^
ALT	%

To specify that any combination of SHIFT, CTRL, and ALT should be held down while several other keys are pressed, enclose the code for those keys in parentheses. For example, to specify to hold down SHIFT while E and C are pressed, use "+(EC)". To specify to hold down SHIFT while E is pressed, followed by C without SHIFT, use "+EC".

To specify repeating keys, use the form {*key number*}. You must put a space between *key* and *number*. For example, {LEFT 42} means press the LEFT ARROW key 42 times; {h 10} means press h 10 times.

Note **SendKeys** can't send keystrokes to an application that is not designed to run in Microsoft Windows. **Sendkeys** also can't send the PRINT SCREEN (PRTSC) key to any application.

See Also   **AppActivate** Statement, **DoEvents** Statement.

Example

This example uses the **Shell** function to run the Calculator application included with Microsoft Windows; it then uses the **SendKeys** statement to send keystrokes to add some numbers and then quit the Calculator. The **SendKeys** statement is not available on the Macintosh.

```
ReturnValue = Shell("Calc.exe", 1)  ' Run Calculator.
AppActivate ReturnValue             ' Activate the Calculator.
For I = 1 To 100                    ' Set up counting loop.
    SendKeys I & "{+}", True        ' Send keystrokes to Calculator
Next I                              ' to add each value of I.
SendKeys "=", True                  ' Get grand total.
SendKeys "%{F4}", True              ' Send Alt+F4 to close Calculator.
```

SendMail Method

Applies To

Workbook Object.

Description

Sends the workbook using the installed mail system.

Syntax

object.**SendMail**(*recipients*, *subject*, *returnReceipt*)

object
Required. The **Workbook** object.

recipients
Required. Specifies the name of the recipient as text, or an array of text strings if there are multiple recipients. At least one recipient must be specified, and all recipients are added as To recipients.

subject
Optional. Specifies the subject of the message. If omitted, the document name is used.

returnReceipt
Optional. If **True**, a return receipt is requested. If **False** or omitted, no return receipt is requested.

Remarks

Use the **SendMail** method on Microsoft Mail (MAPI or Microsoft Mail for the Apple Macintosh) email systems. Pass addressing information as parameters.

See Also

Mailer Object, **MailSystem** Property, **SendMailer** Method.

Example

This example sends the active workbook to a single recipient.

```
ActiveWorkbook.SendMail recipients:="Jean Selva"
```

Use the **SendMailer** method on PowerTalk email systems on the Apple Macintosh. The **Mailer** object contains the addressing information for PowerTalk.

SendMailer Method

Applies To   **Workbook** Object.

Description   Sends the workbook using the PowerTalk mailer. This method is available only on the Apple Macintosh with the PowerTalk system extension installed and can only be used on a workbook with a mailer attached.

Syntax   *object*.**SendMailer**(*fileFormat*, *priority*)

object
   Required. The **Workbook** object.

fileFormat
   Optional. Specifies the file format to use for the workbook that is sent. See the **FileFormat** property for a list of valid types.

priority
   Optional. Specifies the delivery priority of the message (one of **xlNormal**, **xlHigh**, or **xlLow**). The default value is **xlNormal**.

Remarks   Use the **SendMail** method on Microsoft Mail (MAPI or Microsoft Mail for the Apple Macintosh) email systems. Pass addressing information as parameters.

Use the **SendMailer** method on PowerTalk email systems on the Apple Macintosh. The **Mailer** object contains the addressing information for PowerTalk.

See Also   **BCCRecipients** Property, **CCRecipients** Property, **Enclosures** Property, **FileFormat** Property, **Mailer** Property, **Received** Property, **SendDateTime** Property, **Sender** Property, **SendMail** Method, **Subject** Property, **ToRecipients** Property.

Example   This example sets up the **Mailer** object for workbook one and then sends the workbook.

```
With Workbooks(1)
    .HasMailer = True
    With .Mailer
        .Subject = "Here is the workbook"
        .ToRecipients = Array("Jean")
        .CCRecipients = Array("Adam", "Bernard")
        .BCCRecipients = Array("Chris")
        .Enclosures = Array("TestFile")
    End With
    .SendMailer
End With
```

SendToBack Method

Applies To   Arc Object, **Arcs** Collection, **Button** Object, **Buttons** Collection, **ChartObject** Object, **ChartObjects** Collection, **CheckBox** Object, **Drawing** Object, **DrawingObjects** Collection, **Drawings** Collection, **DropDown** Object, **DropDowns** Collection, **EditBox** Object, **EditBoxes** Collection, **GroupBox** Object, **GroupBoxes** Collection, **GroupObject** Object, **GroupObjects** Collection, **Label** Object, **Labels** Collection, **Line** Object, **Lines** Collection, **ListBox** Object, **ListBoxes** Collection, **OLEObject** Object, **OLEObjects** Collection, **OptionButton** Object, **OptionButtons** Collection, **Oval** Object, **Ovals** Collection, **Picture** Object, **Pictures** Collection, **Rectangle** Object, **Rectangles** Collection, **ScrollBar** Object, **ScrollBars** Collection, **Spinner** Object, **Spinners** Collection, **TextBox** Object, **TextBoxes** Collection.

Description   Sends the object to the back of the z-order.

Syntax   *object*.**SendToBack**

object
> Required. The object to which this method applies.

See Also   **BringToFront** Method, **ZOrder** Property.

Example   This example sends rectangle one on Sheet1 to the back of the z-order.

```
Worksheets("Sheet1").Rectangles(1).SendToBack
```

Series Object

Description   Represents a series in a chart.

Accessors   The **Series** object is a member of the **SeriesCollection** collection. Use the **Add** method to create a new series and add it to the collection. To access a single member of the collection, use the **SeriesCollection** method with the index number or name of the series as an argument.

The series index number indicates the order in which the series were added to the chart. SeriesCollection(1) is the first series added to the chart; SeriesCollection(SeriesCollection.Count) is the last. The following example sets the interior color for series one in embedded chart one on the worksheet named "Sheet1."

```
Worksheets("sheet1").ChartObjects(1).Chart. _
    SeriesCollection(1).Interior.Color = RGB(255, 0, 0)
```

Use the **Name** property to set or return the series name. The default name given when a series is created has the form "Series*n*", where *n* is a number. The following example sets the chart type for the series named "Series2" in embedded chart one on the worksheet named "Sheet1."

```
Worksheets("sheet1").ChartObjects(1).Chart. _
    SeriesCollection("series2").Type = xlLine
```

Properties

Application Property, **AxisGroup** Property, **Border** Property, **Creator** Property, **ErrorBars** Property, **Explosion** Property, **Formula** Property, **FormulaLocal** Property, **FormulaR1C1** Property, **FormulaR1C1Local** Property, **HasDataLabels** Property, **HasErrorBars** Property, **Interior** Property, **InvertIfNegative** Property, **MarkerBackgroundColor** Property, **MarkerBackgroundColorIndex** Property, **MarkerForegroundColor** Property, **MarkerForegroundColorIndex** Property, **MarkerStyle** Property, **Name** Property, **Parent** Property, **PictureType** Property, **PictureUnit** Property, **PlotOrder** Property, **Smooth** Property, **Type** Property, **Values** Property, **XValues** Property.

Methods

ApplyDataLabels Method, **ClearFormats** Method, **Copy** Method, **DataLabels** Method, **Delete** Method, **ErrorBar** Method, **Paste** Method (**Point** or **Series** Object), **Points** Method, **Select** Method, **Trendlines** Method.

SeriesCollection Collection Object

Description

A collection of all the **Series** objects in the specified chart or chart group.

Accessors

Use the **Add** method to create a new series and add it to the chart. The following example adds the data from cells A1:A19 as a new series on the chart sheet named "Chart1."

```
Charts("chart1").SeriesCollection.Add _
    source:=Worksheets("sheet1").Range("a1:a19")
```

Use the **SeriesCollection** method with an argument to access a single member of the collection or without an argument to access the entire collection at once. The following example adds the data in cells C1:C10 on worksheet one to an existing series in the series collection in embedded chart one.

```
Worksheets(1).ChartObjects(1).Chart. _
    SeriesCollection.Extend Worksheets(1).Range("c1:c10")
```

Properties

Application Property, **Count** Property, **Creator** Property, **Parent** Property.

Methods	**Add** Method (**SeriesCollection** Collection), **Extend** Method, **Item** Method, **Paste** Method (**SeriesCollection** Object).

SeriesCollection Method

Applies To	**Chart** Object, **ChartGroup** Object.
Description	Accessor. Returns an object that represents a single series (a **Series** object, Syntax 1) or a collection of all the series (a **SeriesCollection** object, Syntax 2) in the chart or chart group.
Syntax 1	*object*.**SeriesCollection**(*index*)
Syntax 2	*object*.**SeriesCollection**

object
    Required. The **Chart** or **ChartGroup** object.

index
    Required for Syntax 1. The name or number of the series.

Example	This example turns on data labels for series one in Chart1.

```
Charts("Chart1").SeriesCollection(1).HasDataLabels = True
```

SeriesLines Object

Description	Represents series lines in a chart group. Series lines connect the data values from each series. Only 2-D stacked bar or column chart groups can have series lines. There is no singular SeriesLine object; you must turn series lines on or off for all points in a chart group at once.
Accessors	The **SeriesLines** property returns the series lines for a chart group. The following example adds series lines to chart group one in embedded chart one on worksheet one (the chart must be a 2-D stacked bar or column chart).

```
With Worksheets(1).ChartObjects(1).Chart.ChartGroups(1)
    .HasSeriesLines = True
    .SeriesLines.Border.Color = RGB(0, 0, 255)
End With
```

Remarks	If the **HasSeriesLines** property is **False**, most properties of the **SeriesLines** object are disabled.

Properties	**Application** Property, **Border** Property, **Creator** Property, **Name** Property, **Parent** Property.
Methods	**Delete** Method, **Select** Method.

SeriesLines Property

Applies To	**ChartGroup** Object.
Description	Accessor. Returns a **SeriesLines** object that represents the series lines for a stacked bar or stacked column chart. Applies only to stacked bar and stacked column charts. Read-only.
See Also	**HasSeriesLines** Property.
Example	This example turns on series lines for chart group one in Chart1 and then sets their line style, weight, and color. The example should be run on a 2-D stacked column chart that has two or more series.

```
With Charts("Chart1").ChartGroups(1)
    .HasSeriesLines = True
    With .SeriesLines.Border
        .LineStyle = xlThin
        .Weight = xlMedium
        .ColorIndex = 3
    End With
End With
```

Set Statement

Description	Assigns an object reference to a variable or property.
Syntax	**Set** *objectvar* = {*objectexpression*	**Nothing**}

The **Set** statement syntax has these parts:

Part	Description
objectvar	Name of the variable or property; follows standard variable naming conventions.
objectexpression	Expression consisting of the name of an object, another declared variable of the same object type, or a function or method that returns an object of the same object type.
Nothing	Discontinues association of *objectvar* with any specific object. Assigning *objectvar* to **Nothing** releases all the resources associated with the previously referenced object when no other variable refers to it.

Remarks

To be valid, *objectvar* must be an object type consistent with the object being assigned to it.

The **Dim**, **Private**, **Public**, **Redim** and **Static** statements only declare a variable that refers to an object. No actual object is referred to until you use **Set** statement to assign a specific object.

Generally, when you use **Set** to assign an object reference to a variable, no copy of the object is created for that variable. Instead, a reference to the object is created. More than one object variable can refer to the same object. Because these variables are references to (rather than copies of) the object, any change is reflected in all variables that refer to it.

See Also

Dim Statement, **Let** Statement, **Private** Statement, **Public** Statement, **ReDim** Statement, **Static** Statement.

Example

This example adds a new worksheet to the active workbook and then sets the name of the worksheet.

```
Set newSheet = Worksheets.Add
newSheet.Name = "1995 Budget"
```

This example creates a new worksheet and then inserts a list of all names in the active workbook, including their formulas in A1-style notation in the language of the user.

```
Set newSheet = ActiveWorkbook.Worksheets.Add
i = 1
For Each nm In ActiveWorkbook.Names
    newSheet.Cells(i, 1).Value = nm.NameLocal
    newSheet.Cells(i, 2).Value = "'" & nm.RefersToLocal
    i = i + 1
Next
```

SetAttr Statement

Description   Sets attribute information for a file.

Syntax   **SetAttr** *pathname*,*attributes*

The **SetAttr** statement syntax has these named-argument parts:

Part	Description
pathname	String expression that specifies a file name—may include directory or folder, and drive.
attributes	Constant or numeric expression, the sum of which specifies file attributes.

Constants and values for *attributes* are:

Constant	Value	File Attribute
vbNormal	0	Normal (default).
vbReadOnly	1	Read-only.
vbHidden	2	Hidden.
vbSystem	4	System—not available on the Macintosh.
vbArchive	32	File has changed since last backup—not available on the Macintosh.

Note   These constants are specified by Visual Basic. As a result, the names can be used anywhere in your code in place of the actual values.

Remarks   A run-time error occurs if you try to set the attributes of an open file.

See Also   **FileAttr** Function, **GetAttr** Function.

Example   This example uses the **SetAttr** statement to set attributes for a file.

```
SetAttr "TESTFILE", vbHidden                ' Set hidden attribute.
SetAttr "TESTFILE", vbHidden + vbReadOnly   ' Set hidden and Read-only
     ' attributes.
```

SetBackgroundPicture Method

Applies To   **Chart** Object, **Worksheet** Object.

Description	Sets the background graphic for a worksheet or chart. This method is available only in Microsoft Excel for Windows 95.
Syntax	*object*.**SetBackgroundPicture**(*fileName*)
	object Required. The **Worksheet** or **Chart** object.
	fileName Required. The graphic file to be displayed.
Example	This example sets the background graphic for worksheet one.

```
Worksheets(1).SetBackgroundPicture "c:\graphics\watrmark.bmp"
```

SetDefaultChart Method

Applies To	**Application** Object.
Description	Specifies the name of the chart template that Microsoft Excel will use when creating new charts.
Syntax	*object*.**SetDefaultChart**(*formatName*)
	object Required. The **Application** object.
	formatName Required. Specifies the name of a custom autoformat. This name can be a custom autoformat, as a string, or the special constant **xlBuiltIn** to specify the built-in chart template.
Example	This example sets the default chart template to the custom autoformat named "Monthly Sales."

```
Application.SetDefaultChart formatName:="Monthly Sales"
```

SetInfoDisplay Method

Applies To	**Window** Object.
Description	Sets the information displayed in the Info window (the specified window object must be the Info window).

| Syntax | *object*.**SetInfoDisplay**(*cell*, *formula*, *value*, *format*, *protection*, *names*, *precedents*, *dependents*, *note*) |

object
> Required. The **Window** object.

cell
> Optional. **True** to display the cell reference text.

formula
> Optional. **True** to display the cell formula.

value
> Optional. **True** to display the cell value.

format
> Optional. **True** to display cell formatting information.

protection
> Optional. **True** to display cell protection information.

names
> Optional. **True** to display cell name information.

precedents
> Optional. Sets whether precedents are displayed (one of **xlNone**, **xlDirect**, or **xlAll**).

dependents
> Optional. Sets whether dependents are displayed (one of **xlNone**, **xlDirect**, or **xlAll**).

note
> Optional. **True** to display notes.

Remarks   If this method is applied to any window other than Info window, an error occurs.

Example   This example displays the Info window and then sets it to display cell reference text and cell name information.

```
Application.DisplayInfoWindow = True
ActiveWindow.SetInfoDisplay cell:=True, Names:=True
```

SetLinkOnData Method

Applies To   **Workbook** Object.

Description   Sets the name of a macro or procedure that runs whenever a link is updated.

Syntax   *object*.**SetLinkOnData**(*name*, *procedure*)

object
> Required. The **Workbook** object.

name
> Required. Specifies the name of the Microsoft Excel or DDE/OLE link, as returned from the **LinkSources** method.

procedure
> Optional. Specifies the name of the procedure to run when the link is updated. This can be either a Microsoft Excel version 4.0 macro or a Visual Basic procedure. Set this argument to an empty string ("") to indicate that no procedure should run when the link is updated.

Remarks
> Use this method to set notification for a specific link. Use the **OnData** property if you wish to be notified when any link is updated.

See Also
> **OnData** Property.

Example
> This example sets the name of the procedure that runs whenever the DDE link is updated.

```
ActiveWorkbook.SetLinkOnData "WinWord|'C:\MSGFILE.DOC'!DDE_LINK1", _
    "my_Link_Update_Macro"
```

Sgn Function

Description
Returns an integer indicating the sign of a number.

Syntax
Sgn(*number*)

The *number* argument can be any valid numeric expression.

Return Values

If number is	Sgn returns
Greater than zero	1
Equal to zero	0
Less than zero	-1

Remarks
The sign of the *number* argument determines the return value of the **Sgn** function.

See Also
Abs Function.

Example
This example uses the **Sgn** function to determine the sign of a number.

```
MyVar1 = 12: MyVar2 = -2.4: MyVar3 = 0
MySign = Sgn(MyVar1)              ' Returns 1.
MySign = Sgn(MyVar2)              ' Returns -1.
MySign = Sgn(MyVar3) ' Returns 0.
```

Shadow Property

Applies To   **AxisTitle** Object, **ChartArea** Object, **ChartObject** Object, **ChartObjects** Collection, **ChartTitle** Object, **DataLabel** Object, **DataLabels** Collection, **Drawing** Object, **DrawingObjects** Collection, **Drawings** Collection, **Font** Object, **GroupObject** Object, **GroupObjects** Collection, **Legend** Object, **OLEObject** Object, **OLEObjects** Collection, **Oval** Object, **Ovals** Collection, **Picture** Object, **Pictures** Collection, **Rectangle** Object, **Rectangles** Collection, **TextBox** Object, **TextBoxes** Collection.

Description   **True** if the font is a shadow font or if the drawing object has a shadow. Read-write.

Remarks   For the **Font** object, this property has no effect in Microsoft Windows, but its value is retained (it can be set and returned).

Example   This example adds a shadow to the title of Chart1.

```
Charts("Chart1").ChartTitle.Shadow = True
```

Sheets Collection Object

Description   A collection of all the sheets in the specified or active workbook. The **Sheets** collection can contain **Chart**, **DialogSheet**, **Module**, or **Worksheet** objects.

The **Sheets** collection is useful when you want to access sheets of any type. If you need to work with sheets of only one type, see the object topic for that sheet type.

Accessors   Use the **Sheets** method with the sheet index number or name as an argument to access a single member of the collection or without an argument to access the entire collection at once.

The index number represents the position of the sheet on the tab bar of the workbook. Sheets(1) is the first (leftmost) sheet in the workbook; Sheets(Sheets.Count) is the last sheet. All sheets are included in the index count, even if they are hidden.

The following example hides the sheet one in the active workbook.

```
Sheets(1).Visible = False
```

The sheet name is shown on the workbook tab for the sheet. Use the **Name** property to set or return the sheet name (you cannot change the name of the sheet where the Visual Basic code is running, however). The following example protects the Visual Basic code on the sheet named "Sample Code."

```
Sheets("sample code").Protect password:="drowssap", contents:=True
```

You can also use an array to specify more than one sheet. The following example moves the sheets named "Module1" and "Sheet1" to the beginning of the workbook.

```
Sheets(Array("module1", "sheet1")).Move before:=Sheets(1)
```

Use the **Add** method to create a new sheet and add it to the collection. The following example adds two dialog sheets to the active workbook, placing them after sheet two in the workbook.

```
Sheets.Add type:=xlDialogSheet, count:=2, after:=Sheets(2)
```

Properties   **Application** Property, **Count** Property, **Creator** Property, **Parent** Property, **Visible** Property.

Methods   **Add** Method (**Sheets** Collection), **Copy** Method, **Delete** Method, **FillAcrossSheets** Method, **Item** Method, **Move** Method, **PrintOut** Method, **PrintPreview** Method, **Select** Method.

Sheets Method

Applies To   **Application** Object, **Workbook** Object.

Description   Accessor. Returns an object that represents a single sheet (Syntax 1) or a collection of sheets (Syntax 2) in the workbook. Read-only. A sheet can be a **Chart** object, **DialogSheet** object, **Module** object, or **Worksheet** object.

Syntax 1   *object*.**Sheets(*index*)**

Syntax 2   *object*.**Sheets**

object
Optional for **Application**, required for **Workbook**. The object to which this method applies.

index
Required for Syntax 1. The name or number of the sheet to return.

Remarks   Using this method with no object qualifier is equivalent to **ActiveWorkbook.Sheets**.

See Also	**DialogSheets** Method, **Modules** Method, **Worksheets** Method.
Example	This example creates a new worksheet and then places a list of the active workbook's sheet names in the first column.

```
Set newSheet = Sheets.Add(Type:=xlWorksheet)
For i = 1 To Sheets.Count
    newSheet.Cells(i, 1).Value = Sheets(i).Name
Next i
```

SheetsInNewWorkbook Property

Applies To	**Application** Object.
Description	Returns or sets the number of sheets Microsoft Excel automatically inserts in new workbooks. Read-write.
Example	This example displays the number of sheets automatically inserted into new workbooks.

```
MsgBox "Microsoft Excel inserts " & _
    Application.SheetsInNewWorkbook & _
    " sheet(s) in each new workbook"
```

Shell Function

Description	Runs an executable program.
Syntax	**Shell(*pathname*[,*windowstyle*])**

The **Shell** function syntax has these named-argument parts:

Part	Description
pathname	Name of the program to execute and any required arguments or command line switches; may include directory or folder and drive. May also be the name of a document that has been associated with an executable program.
	On the Macintosh, you can use the **MacID** function to specify an application's signature instead of its name. The following example uses the signature for Microsoft Word:
	`Shell MacID("MSWD")`
windowstyle	Number corresponding to the style of the window in which the program is to be run. In Microsoft Windows, if *windowstyle* is omitted, the program is started minimized with focus. On the Macintosh (System 7.0 or later), *windowstyle* only determines whether or not the application gets the focus when it is run.

The *windowstyle* named argument has these values:

Value	Window Style
1, 5, 9	Normal with focus.
2	Minimized with focus.
3	Maximized with focus.
4,8	Normal without focus.
6,7	Minimized without focus.

Remarks

If you use the **MacID** function with **Shell** in Microsoft Windows, an error occurs.

If the **Shell** function successfully executes the named file, it returns the task identification (ID) of the started program. The task ID is a unique number that identifies the running program. If the **Shell** function can't start the named program, an error occurs.

Note The **Shell** function runs other programs asynchronously. This means you can't depend on a program started with **Shell** to be finished executing before the statements following the **Shell** function in your application are executed.

See Also

AppActivate Statement, **MacID** Function.

Example   This example uses the **Shell** function to run an application specified by the user. On the Macintosh, using the **MacID** function ensures that the application can be launched even if the file name of the application has been changed. The **Shell** function is not available on the Macintosh prior to System 7.0.

```
' In Microsoft Windows.
' Specifying 1 as the second argument runs the application normally and
' gives it the focus.
RetVal = Shell("C:\WINDOWS\CALC.EXE", 1)  ' Run Calculator.

' On the Macintosh.
' Both statements launch Microsoft Excel.
RetVal = Shell("Microsoft Excel")          ' Specify file name.
RetVal = Shell(MacID("XCEL"))    ' Specify signature.
```

ShortcutKey Property

Applies To   **Name** Object.

Description   Returns or sets the shortcut key for a name defined as a custom Microsoft Excel version 4.0 macro command. Read-write.

Example   This example sets the shortcut key for name one in the active workbook. The example should be run on a workbook in which name one refers to a Microsoft Excel version 4.0 command macro.

```
ActiveWorkbook.Names(1).ShortcutKey = "K"
```

ShortcutMenus Method

Applies To   **Application** Object.

Description   Accessor. Returns a **Menu** object that represents a single shortcut menu. Read-only.

Syntax   *object*.**ShortcutMenus(*index*)**

object
    Optional. The **Application** object.

index

Required. Specifies the shortcut menu, as shown in the following list.

Constant	Description
xlAxis	Chart Axis
xlButton	Button
xlChartSeries	Chart Series
xlChartTitles	Chart Titles
xlColumnHeader	Column
xlDebugCodePane	Debug Code Pane
xlDesktop	Desktop
xlDialogSheet	Dialog Sheet
xlDrawingObject	Drawing Object
xlEntireChart	Entire Chart
xlFloor	Chart Floor
xlGridline	Chart Gridline
xlImmediatePane	Immediate Pane
xlLegend	Chart Legend
xlMacrosheetCell	Macro Sheet Cell
xlModule	Module
xlPlotArea	Chart Plot Area
xlRowHeader	Row
xlTextBox	Text Box
xlTitleBar	Title Bar
xlToolbar	Toolbar
xlToolbarButton	Toolbar Button
xlWatchPane	Watch Pane
xlWorkbookTab	Workbook Tab
xlWorksheetCell	Worksheet Cell

Example

This example adds a new menu item to the worksheet cells shortcut menu.

```
ShortcutMenus(xlWorksheetCell).MenuItems.Add _
    Caption:="More..."
```

This example deletes the new menu item.

```
ShortcutMenus(xlWorksheetCell).MenuItems("More...").Delete
```

Show Method

Applies To   **Dialog** Object, **DialogSheet** Object, **Range** Object, **Scenario** Object.

Description   **DialogSheet** object (Syntax 1): Runs the dialog box. This method will not return to the calling procedure until the dialog box is closed or hidden, but event procedures assigned to the dialog box controls will run while the calling procedure is suspended.

Range object (Syntax 1): Scrolls the active window to move the range into view. The range must consist of a single cell which is a part of the currently active document

Scenario object (Syntax 1): Shows the scenario by inserting the scenario's values onto the worksheet. The affected cells are the changing cells of the scenario.

Dialog object (Syntax 2): Displays the dialog box and waits for the user to input data.

Syntax 1   *object*.**Show**

Syntax 2   *object*.**Show**(*arg1*, *arg2*, ..., *arg30*)

object
   Required. For Syntax 1, the **DialogSheet**, **Range**, or **Scenario** object. For Syntax 2, the **Dialog** object.

arg1, *arg2*, ..., *arg30*
   Optional. For built-in dialog boxes only, provides the initial arguments for the command. For more information, see the following Remarks section.

Remarks   For built in dialog boxes, this method returns **True** if the user clicked OK, or **False** if the user clicked Cancel.

A single dialog box can change many properties at once. For example, the Format Cells dialog box can change all the properties of the **Font** object.

For some built-in dialog boxes (Open, for example), you can set initial values using *arg1*, *arg2*, ..., *arg30*.

Example   This example displays the custom dialog box Dialog1, and then it displays a message if you do not press the Cancel button. Before running this example, create a new default dialog sheet by pointing to Macro on the Insert menu and then clicking Dialog.

```
If DialogSheets("Dialog1").Show <> False Then
    MsgBox "You must have pressed the ""OK"" button"
End If
```

This example displays the Open dialog box and selects the Read-Only option.

```
Application.Dialogs(xlDialogOpen).Show arg3:=True
```

ShowAllData Method

Applies To   **Worksheet** Object.

Description   Makes all rows visible for the currently filtered list. If the AutoFilter is in use, this method changes the arrows to "All".

Syntax   *object*.**ShowAllData**

object
        Required. The **Worksheet** object.

See Also   **AdvancedFilter** Method, **AutoFilter** Method, **FilterMode** Property.

Example   This example makes all data on Sheet1 visible. The example should be run on a worksheet that contains a list that you filtered using the AutoFilter command on the Data menu.

```
Worksheets("Sheet1").ShowAllData
```

ShowConflictHistory Property

Applies To   **Workbook** Object.

Description   **True** if the Conflict History worksheet is visible in the workbook that's open as a shared list. This property is available only in Microsoft Excel for Windows 95. Read-write.

Remarks   If the specified workbook isn't open as a shared list, **ShowConflictHistory** fails. To determine whether a workbook is open as a shared list, use the **MultiUserEditing** property.

See Also   **MultiUserEditing** Property, **SaveAs** Method, **ShowConflictHistory** Property.

Example   This example determines whether the active workbook is open as a shared list. If it is, the example displays the Conflict History worksheet.

```
If ActiveWorkbook.MultiUserEditing Then
    ActiveWorkbook.ShowConflictHistory = True
End If
```

ShowDataForm Method

Applies To	**Worksheet** Object.
Description	Displays the data form associated with the worksheet.
Syntax	*object*.**ShowDataForm**

object
   Required. The **Worksheet** object.

Remarks	The macro pauses while you use the data form. When the user closes the data form, this macro will resume at the line following the **ShowDataForm** method.
	This method will run the custom data form, if one exists.
Example	This example displays the data form for Sheet1.

```
Worksheets(1).ShowDataForm
```

ShowDependents Method

Applies To	**Range** Object.
Description	Draws tracer arrows to the direct dependents of the range.
Syntax	*object*.**ShowDependents**(*remove*)

object
   Required. The **Range** object. Must be a single cell.

remove
   Optional. If **True**, removes one level of tracer arrows to direct dependents. If **False** or omitted, expands one level of tracer arrows.

See Also	**ClearArrows** Method, **Dependents** Property, **ShowErrors** Method, **ShowPrecedents** Method.
Example	This example draws tracer arrows to dependents of the active cell on Sheet1.

```
Worksheets("Sheet1").Activate
ActiveCell.ShowDependents
```

This example removes the tracer arrow for one level of dependents of the active cell on Sheet1.

```
Worksheets("Sheet1").Activate
ActiveCell.ShowDependents remove:=True
```

ShowDetail Property

Applies To   **PivotItem** Object, **Range** Object.

Description   **True** if the outline is expanded for the specified range (the detail of the column or row is visible). The specified range must be a single summary column or row in an outline. Read-write.

For the **PivotItem** object (or the **Range** object if the range is in a PivotTable), this property is **True** if the pivot item is showing detail.

Remarks   If the specified range is not in a PivotTable, the following comments apply:

- The range must be in a single summary row or column.
- This property returns **False** if *any* of the children of the row or column are hidden.
- Setting this property to **True** is equivalent to unhiding all the children on the summary row or column.
- Setting this property to **False** is equivalent to hiding all the children of the summary row or column.

If the specified range is in a PivotTable, it is possible to set this property for more than one cell at once if the range is contiguous. To return this property, the range must be a single cell.

Example   This example shows detail for the summary row of an outline on Sheet1. Before running this example, create a simple outline that contains a single summary row, and then collapse the outline so that only the summary row is showing. Select one of the cells in the summary row, and then run the example.

```
Worksheets("Sheet1").Activate
Set myRange = ActiveCell.CurrentRegion
lastRow = myRange.Rows.Count
myRange.Rows(lastRow).ShowDetail = True
```

ShowErrors Method

Applies To   **Range** Object.

Description   Draws tracer arrows through the precedents tree to the cell that is the source of the error, and returns the range that contains the source of the error.

Syntax   *object*.**ShowErrors**

object
    Required. The **Range** object.

See Also   **ClearArrows** Method, **ShowDependents** Method, **ShowPrecedents** Method.

Example   This example displays a red tracer arrow if there is an error in the active cell on Sheet1.

```
Worksheets("Sheet1").Activate
If IsError(ActiveCell.Value) Then
    ActiveCell.ShowErrors
End If
```

ShowLegendKey Property

Applies To   **DataLabel** Object, **DataLabels** Collection.

Description   **True** if the data label legend key is visible. Read-write.

Example   This example sets the data labels for series one in Chart1 to show values and the legend key.

```
With Charts("Chart1").SeriesCollection(1).DataLabels
    .ShowLegendKey = True
    .Type = xlShowValue
End With
```

ShowLevels Method

Applies To   **Outline** Object.

Description   Displays the specified number of row and/or column levels of an outline.

Syntax   *object*.**ShowLevels** (*rowLevels*, *columnLevels*)

object
    Required. The **Outline** object (`ActiveSheet.Outline`, for example).

rowLevels
    Optional. Specifies the number of row levels of an outline to display. If the outline has fewer levels than specified, Microsoft Excel shows all levels. If omitted or zero, no action is taken on rows.

columnLevels
> Optional. Specifies the number of column levels of an outline to display. If the outline has fewer levels than specified, Microsoft Excel shows all levels. If omitted or zero, no action is taken on columns.

Remarks   You must specify at least one argument.

Example   This example displays row levels one through three and column level one of the outline on Sheet1.

```
Worksheets("Sheet1").Outline.ShowLevels rowLevels:=3, columnLevels:=1
```

ShowPages Method

Applies To   **PivotTable** Object.

Description   Creates a new PivotTable for each item in the page field. Each new PivotTable is created on a new worksheet.

Syntax   *object*.**ShowPages(*pageField*)**

object
> Required. The **PivotTable** object.

pageField
> Required. A string that names a single page field in the PivotTable.

Example   This example creates a new PivotTable for each item in the page field, which is the field named "Country."

```
Set pvtTable = Worksheets("Sheet1").Range("A3").PivotTable
pvtTable.ShowPages "Country"
```

ShowPrecedents Method

Applies To   **Range** Object.

Description   Draws tracer arrows to the direct precedents of the range.

Syntax   *object*.**ShowPrecedents(*remove*)**

object
> Required. The **Range** object. Must be a single cell.

remove
> Optional. If **True**, removes one level of tracer arrows to direct precedents. If **False** or omitted, expands one level of tracer arrows.

See Also
> **ClearArrows** Method, **Precedents** Property, **ShowDependents** Method, **ShowErrors** Method.

Example
> This example draws tracer arrows to the precedents of the active cell on Sheet1.

```
Worksheets("Sheet1").Activate
ActiveCell.ShowPrecedents
```

This example removes the tracer arrow for one level of precedents of the active cell on Sheet1.

```
Worksheets("Sheet1").Activate
ActiveCell.ShowPrecedents remove:=True
```

ShowToolTips Property

Applies To
> **Application** Object.

Description
> **True** if ToolTips are turned on. Read-write.

Example
> This example causes Microsoft Excel to display ToolTips.

```
Application.ShowToolTips = True
```

Sin Function

Description
> Returns the sine of an angle.

Syntax
> **Sin(*number*)**

The ***number*** named argument can be any valid numeric expression that expresses an angle in radians.

Remarks
> The **Sin** function takes an angle and returns the ratio of two sides of a right triangle. The ratio is the length of the side opposite the angle divided by the length of the hypotenuse.

The result lies in the range -1 to 1.

To convert degrees to radians, multiply degrees by pi/180. To convert radians to degrees, multiply radians by 180/pi.

See Also   **Atn** Function, **Cos** Function, Derived Math Functions, **Tan** Function.

Example   This example uses the **Sin** function to return the sine of an angle.

```
MyAngle = 1.3                        ' Define angle in radians.
MyCosecant = 1 / Sin(MyAngle)    ' Calculate cosecant.
```

Single Data Type

Description   **Single** (single-precision floating-point) variables are stored as 32-bit (4-byte) numbers, ranging in value from -3.402823E38 to -1.401298E-45 for negative values and from 1.401298E-45 to 3.402823E38 for positive values. The type-declaration character for **Single** is **!** (character code 33).

See Also   **CSng** Function, Data Type Summary, **Def**type Statements, **Double** Data Type, **Variant** Data Type.

Size Property

Applies To   **Font** Object.

Description   Returns or sets the size of the font. Read-write.

Example   This example sets the font size for cells A1:D10 on Sheet1.

```
With Worksheets("Sheet1").Range("A1:D10")
    .Value = "Test"
    .Font.Size = 12
End With
```

SizeWithWindow Property

Applies To   **Chart** Object.

Description | **True** if chart resizes to match the size of the chart sheet window. **False** if the chart size is not attached to the window size. Applies only to charts that are sheets in a workbook, not to embedded charts. Read-write.

See Also | **ChartSize** Property.

Example | This example sets Chart1 to be sized to its window.

```
Charts("Chart1").SizeWithWindow = True
```

SmallChange Property

Applies To | **DrawingObjects** Collection, **ScrollBar** Object, **ScrollBars** Collection, **Spinner** Object, **Spinners** Collection.

Description | Returns or sets the amount that the scroll bar or spinner increments or decrements for a line scroll (when the user clicks an arrow). Read-write.

See Also | **LargeChange** Property.

Example | This example sets scroll bar one on Dialog1 to move two units for each line scroll and 20 units for each page scroll.

```
With DialogSheets("Dialog1").ScrollBars(1)
    .SmallChange = 2
    .LargeChange = 20
End With
```

SmallScroll Method

Applies To | **Pane** Object, **Window** Object.

Description | Scrolls the window by rows or columns.

Syntax | *object*.**SmallScroll**(*down*, *up*, *toRight*, *toLeft*)

object
Required. The window to scroll.

down
Optional. The number of rows to scroll the window down.

up
Optional. The number of rows to scroll the window up.

toRight
    Optional. The number of columns to scroll the window right.

toLeft
    Optional. The number of columns to scroll the window left.

Remarks

If *down* and *up* are both specified, the window is scrolled by the difference of the arguments. For example, if *down* is three and *up* is six, the window is scrolled up three rows.

If *toLeft* and *toRight* are both specified, the window is scrolled by the difference of the arguments. For example, if *toLeft* is three and *toRight* is six, the window is scrolled right three columns.

Any of the arguments can be a negative number.

See Also

LargeScroll Method.

Example

This example scrolls the active window of Sheet1 down three rows.

```
Worksheets("Sheet1").Activate
ActiveWindow.SmallScroll down:=3
```

Smooth Property

Applies To

LegendKey Object, **Series** Object.

Description

True if the line or scatter chart has curve smoothing on. Applies only to line and scatter charts. Read-write.

Example

This example turns on curve smoothing for series one in Chart1. The example should be run on a 2-D line chart.

```
Charts("Chart1").SeriesCollection(1).Smooth = True
```

SolverAdd Function

Description

Adds a constraint to the current problem. Equivalent to clicking Solver on the Tools menu and then clicking Add in the Solver Parameters dialog box.

Before you use this function, you must establish a reference to the Solver add-in. With a Visual Basic module active, click References on the Tools menu, and then select the Solver.xla check box in the Available References box. If Solver.xla doesn't appear in the Available References box, click Browse, click Solver in the \Excel\Library\Solver folder, and then click OK.

Syntax

SolverAdd(*cellRef*, *relation*, *formulaText*)

cellRef
  Required. Reference to a cell or a range of cells that forms the left side of a constraint.

relation
  Required. Specifies the arithmetic relationship between the left and right sides of the constraint. If 4 is chosen, *cellRef* must contain an integer, and *formulaText* should not be specified.

Relation	Arithmetic relationship
1	<=
2	=
3	>=
4	Cells referenced by *cellRef* must contain integers.

formulaText
  Optional. The right side of the constraint.

Remarks

After constraints are added, you can manipulate them with the **SolverChange** and **SolverDelete** functions.

See Also

SolverChange Function, **SolverDelete** Function, **SolverOk** Function.

Example

This example uses the Solver functions to maximize gross profit in a business problem. The **SolverAdd** function is used to add three constraints to the current problem.

```
Worksheets("Sheet1").Activate
SolverReset
SolverOptions precision:=0.001
SolverOK setCell:=Range("TotalProfit"), _
    maxMinVal:=1, _
    byChange:=Range("C4:E6")
SolverAdd cellRef:=Range("F4:F6"), _
    relation:=1, _
    formulaText:=100
SolverAdd cellRef:=Range("C4:E6"), _
    relation:=3, _
    formulaText:=0
SolverAdd cellRef:=Range("C4:E6"), _
    relation:=4
SolverSolve userFinish:=False
SolverSave saveArea:=Range("A33")
```

SolverChange Function

Description

Changes an existing constraint. Equivalent to clicking Solver on the Tools menu and then clicking Change in the Solver Parameters dialog box.

Before you use this function, you must establish a reference to the Solver add-in. With a Visual Basic module active, click References on the Tools menu, and then select the Solver.xla check box in the Available References box. If Solver.xla doesn't appear in the Available References box, click Browse, click Solver in the \Excel\Library\Solver folder, and then click OK.

Syntax

SolverChange(*cellRef*, *relation*, *formulaText*)

cellRef
Required. Reference to a cell or a range of cells that forms the left side of a constraint.

relation
Required. Specifies the arithmetic relationship between the left and right sides of the constraint. If 4 is chosen, *cellRef* must contain an integer, and *formulaText* should not be specified.

Relation	Arithmetic relationship
1	<=
2	=
3	>=
4	Cells referenced by *cellRef* must contain integers.

formulaText
Optional. The right side of the constraint.

Note If *cellRef* and *relation* do not match an existing constraint, you must use the **SolverDelete** and **SolverAdd** functions to change the constraint.

See Also   **SolverAdd** Function, **SolverOk** Function.

Example   This example loads the previously calculated Solver model stored on Sheet1, changes one of the constraints, and then solves the model again.

```
Worksheets("Sheet1").Activate
SolverLoad loadArea:=Range("A33:A38")
SolverChange cellRef:=Range("F4:F6"), _
    relation:=1, _
    formulaText:=200
SolverSolve userFinish:=False
```

SolverDelete Function

Description   Deletes an existing constraint. Equivalent to clicking Solver on the Tools menu and then clicking Delete in the Solver Parameters dialog box.

Before you use this function, you must establish a reference to the Solver add-in. With a Visual Basic module active, click References on the Tools menu, and then select the Solver.xla check box in the Available References box. If Solver.xla doesn't appear in the Available References box, click Browse, click Solver in the \Excel\Library\Solver folder, and then click OK.

Syntax   **SolverDelete**(*cellRef*, *relation*, *formulaText*)

cellRef
Required. Reference to a cell or a range of cells that forms the left side of a constraint.

relation
> Required. Specifies the arithmetic relationship between the left and right sides of the constraint. If 4 is chosen, *cellRef* must contain an integer, and *formulaText* should not be specified.

Relation	Arithmetic relationship
1	<=
2	=
3	>=
4	Cells referenced by *cellRef* must contain integers.

formulaText
> Optional. The right side of the constraint.

See Also
: **SolverAdd** Function, **SolverOk** Function.

Example
: This example loads the previously calculated Solver model stored on Sheet1, deletes one of the constraints, and then solves the model again.

```
Worksheets("Sheet1").Activate
SolverLoad loadArea:=Range("A33:A38")
SolverDelete cellRef:=Range("C4:E6"), _
    relation:=4
SolverSolve userFinish:=False
```

SolverFinish Function

Description
: Tells Microsoft Excel what to do with the results and what kind of report to create when the solution process is completed.

  Before you use this function, you must establish a reference to the Solver add-in. With a Visual Basic module active, click References on the Tools menu, and then select the Solver.xla check box in Available References box. If Solver.xla doesn't appear in the Available References box, click Browse, click Solver in the \Excel\Library\Solver folder, and then click OK.

Syntax
: **SolverFinish**(*keepFinal*, *reportArray*)

  keepFinal
  > Optional. Can be the number 1 or 2. If *keepFinal* is 1 or omitted, the final solution values are kept in the changing cells, replacing any former values. If *keepFinal* is 2, the final solution values are discarded, and the former values are restored.

reportArray
> Optional. Specifies what kind of report Microsoft Excel will create when Solver is finished: 1 creates an answer report, 2 creates a sensitivity report, and 3 creates a limit report. Use the **Array** function to specify the reports you want to display—for example, `ReportArray:= Array(1,3)`.

See Also   **SolverFinishDialog** Function, **SolverOk** Function.

Example   This example loads the previously calculated Solver model stored on Sheet1, solves the model again, and then generates an answer report on a new worksheet.

```
Worksheets("Sheet1").Activate
SolverLoad loadArea:=Range("A33:A38")
SolverSolve userFinish:=True
SolverFinish keepFinal:=1, reportArray:=Array(1)
```

SolverFinishDialog Function

Description   Tells Microsoft Excel what to do with the results and what kind of report to create when the solution process is completed. Displays the Solver Results dialog box after solving a problem. Equivalent to the **SolverFinish** function, but also displays the Solver Results dialog box after solving a problem.

Before you use this function, you must establish a reference to the Solver add-in. With a Visual Basic module active, click References on the Tools menu, and then select the Solver.xla check box in the Available References box. If Solver.xla doesn't appear in the Available References box, click Browse, click Solver in the \Excel\Library\Solver folder, and then click OK.

Syntax   **SolverFinishDialog**(*keepFinal*, *reportArray*)

keepFinal
> Optional. Can be the number 1 or 2. If *keepFinal* is 1 or omitted, the final solution values are kept in the changing cells, replacing any former values. If *keepFinal* is 2, the final solution values are discarded, and the former values are restored.

reportArray
> Optional. Specifies what kind of report Microsoft Excel will create when Solver is finished: 1 creates an answer report, 2 creates a sensitivity report, and 3 creates a limit report. Use the **Array** function to specify the reports you want to display—for example, `ReportArray:= Array(1,3)`.

See Also   **SolverFinish** Function, **SolverOk** Function.

Example   This example loads the previously calculated Solver model stored on Sheet1, solves the model again, and then displays the Finish dialog box with two preset options.

```
Worksheets("Sheet1").Activate
SolverLoad loadArea:=Range("A33:A38")
SolverSolve userFinish:=True
SolverFinishDialog keepFinal:=1, reportArray:=Array(1)
```

SolverGet Function

Description   Returns information about current settings for Solver. The settings are specified in the Solver Parameters and Solver Options dialog boxes.

Before you use this function, you must establish a reference to the Solver add-in. With a Visual Basic module active, click References on the Tools menu, and then select the Solver.xla check box in the Available References box. If Solver.xla doesn't appear in the Available References box, click Browse, click Solver in the \Excel\Library\Solver folder, and then click OK.

Syntax   **SolverGet(*typeNum*, *sheetName*)**

typeNum
Required. A number specifying the type of information you want. The following settings are specified in the Solver Parameters dialog box.

typeNum	Returns
1	The reference in the Set Target Cell box, or the #N/A error value if Solver hasn't been used on the active sheet.
2	A number corresponding to the Equal To option: 1 represents Max, 2 represents Min, and 3 represents Value Of.
3	The value in the Value Of box.
4	The reference (as a multiple reference, if necessary) in the By Changing Cells box.

typeNum	Returns
5	The number of constraints.
6	An array of the left sides of the constraints in text form.
7	An array of numbers corresponding to the relationships between the left and right sides of the constraints: 1 represents <=, 2 represents =, 3 represents >=, and 4 represents int.
8	An array of the right sides of the constraints in text form.

The following settings are specified in the Solver Options dialog box.

typenum	Returns
9	The maximum calculation time.
10	The maximum number of iterations.
11	The precision.
12	The integer tolerance value.
13	**True** if the Assume Linear Model check box is selected; **False** if it's cleared.
14	**True** if the Show Iteration Results check box is selected; **False** if it's cleared.
15	**True** if the Use Automatic Scaling check box is selected; **False** if it's cleared.
16	A number corresponding to the type of estimates: 1 represents Tangent, and 2 represents Quadratic.
17	A number corresponding to the type of derivatives: 1 represents Forward, and 2 represents Central.
18	A number corresponding to the type of search: 1 represents Quasi-Newton, and 2 represents Conjugate Gradient.

sheetName
Optional. The name of a sheet that contains the scenario for which you want information. If *sheetName* is omitted, this sheet is assumed to be the active sheet.

See Also   **SolverOk** Function.

Example

This example displays a message if you have not used Solver on Sheet1.

```
Worksheets("Sheet1").Activate
state = SolverGet(typeNum:=1)
If IsError(state) Then
    MsgBox "You have not used Solver on the active sheet"
End If
```

SolverLoad Function

Description

Loads parameters for an existing Solver model that have been saved to the worksheet.

Before you use this function, you must establish a reference to the Solver add-in. With a Visual Basic module active, click References on the Tools menu, and then select the Solver.xla check box in the Available References box. If Solver.xla doesn't appear in the Available References box, click Browse, click Solver in the \Excel\Library\Solver folder, and then click OK.

Syntax

SolverLoad(*loadArea*)

loadArea
  Required. A reference on the active worksheet to a range of cells from which you want to load a complete problem specification. The first cell in the *loadArea* contains a formula for the Set Target Cell box in the Solver Parameters dialog box; the second cell contains a formula for the By Changing Cells box; subsequent cells contain constraints in the form of logical formulas. The last cell optionally contains an array of Solver option values. For more information, see **SolverOptions**. The range represented by the argument *loadArea* can be on any worksheet, but you must specify the worksheet if it's not the active sheet. For example, SolverLoad("Sheet2!A1:A3") loads a model from Sheet2 even if it's not the active sheet.

See Also

SolverOk Function, **SolverSave** Function.

Example

This example loads the previously calculated Solver model stored on Sheet1, changes one of the constraints, and then solves the model again.

```
Worksheets("Sheet1").Activate
SolverLoad loadArea:=Range("A33:A38")
SolverChange cellRef:=Range("F4:F6"), _
    relation:=1, _
    formulaText:=200
SolverSolve userFinish:=False
```

SolverOk Function

Description   Defines a basic Solver model. Equivalent to clicking Solver on the Tools menu and then specifying options in the Solver Parameters dialog box.

Before you use this function, you must establish a reference to the Solver add-in. With a Visual Basic module active, click References on the Tools menu, and then select the Solver.xla check box in the Available References box. If Solver.xla doesn't appear in the Available References box, click Browse, click Solver in the \Excel\Library\Solver folder, and then click OK.

Syntax   **SolverOk**(*setCell*, *maxMinVal*, *valueOf*, *byChange*)

setCell
    Optional. Refers to a single cell on the active worksheet. Corresponds to the Set Target Cell box in the Solver Parameters dialog box.

maxMinVal
    Optional. Corresponds to the Max, Min, and Value Of options in the Solver Parameters dialog box.

maxMinVal	**Specifies**
1	Maximize
2	Minimize
3	Match specific value

valueOf
    Optional. If MaxMinVal is 3, you must specify the value to which the target cell is matched.

byChange
    Required. The cell or range of cells that will be changed in order to obtain the desired result in the target cell. Corresponds to the By Changing Cells box in the Solver Parameters dialog box.

See Also   **SolverOkDialog** Function.

Example

This example uses the Solver functions to maximize gross profit in a business problem. The **SolverOK** function defines a problem by specifying the *setCell*, *maxMinVal*, and *byChange* arguments.

```
Worksheets("Sheet1").Activate
SolverReset
SolverOptions precision:=0.001
SolverOK setCell:=Range("TotalProfit"), _
    maxMinVal:=1, _
    byChange:=Range("C4:E6")
SolverAdd cellRef:=Range("F4:F6"), _
    relation:=1, _
    formulaText:=100
SolverAdd cellRef:=Range("C4:E6"), _
    relation:=3, _
    formulaText:=0
SolverAdd cellRef:=Range("C4:E6"), _
    relation:=4
SolverSolve userFinish:=False
SolverSave saveArea:=Range("A33")
```

SolverOkDialog Function

Description

Same as the **SolverOK** function, but also displays the Solver dialog box.

Before you use this function, you must establish a reference to the Solver add-in. With a Visual Basic module active, click References on the Tools menu, and then select the Solver.xla check box in the Available References box. If Solver.xla doesn't appear in the Available References box, click Browse, click Solver in the \Excel\Library\Solver folder, and then click OK.

Syntax

SolverOkDialog(*setCell*, *maxMinVal*, *valueOf*, *byChange*)

setCell
Optional. Refers to a single cell on the active worksheet. Corresponds to the Set Target Cell box in the Solver Parameters dialog box.

maxMinVal
Optional. Corresponds to the Max, Min, and Value Of options in the Solver Parameters dialog box.

maxMinVal	Specifies
1	Maximize
2	Minimize
3	Match specific value

> *valueOf*
>> Optional. If MaxMinVal is 3, you must specify the value to which the target cell is matched.
>
> *byChange*
>> Optional. The cell or range of cells that will be changed in order to obtain the desired result in the target cell. Corresponds to the By Changing Cells box in the Solver Parameters dialog box.

See Also   **SolverOk** Function.

Example   This example loads the previously calculated Solver model stored on Sheet1, resets all Solver options, and then displays the Solver Parameters dialog box. From this point on, Solver can be used manually.

```
Worksheets("Sheet1").Activate
SolverLoad loadArea:=Range("A33:A38")
SolverReset
SolverOKDialog setCell:=Range("TotalProfit")
SolverSolve userFinish:=False
```

SolverOptions Function

Description   Allows you to specify advanced options for your Solver model. This function and its arguments correspond to the options in the Solver Options dialog box.

Before you use this function, you must establish a reference to the Solver add-in. With a Visual Basic module active, click References on the Tools menu, and then select the Solver.xla check box in the Available References box. If Solver.xla doesn't appear in the Available References box, click Browse, click Solver in the \Excel\Library\Solver folder, and then click OK.

Syntax   **SolverOptions(*maxTime*, *iterations*, *precision*, *assumeLinear*, *stepThru*, *estimates*, *derivatives*, *search*, *intTolerance*, *scaling*)**

> *maxTime*
>> Optional. The maximum time (in seconds) Microsoft Excel will spend solving the problem. The value must be a positive integer. The default value 100 is adequate for most small problems, but you can enter a value as high as 32,767.
>
> *iterations*
>> Optional. The maximum iterations Microsoft Excel will use in solving the problem. The value must be a positive integer. The default value 100 is adequate for most small problems, but you can enter a value as high as 32,767.

precision

Optional. A number between 0 and 1 that specifies the degree of precision to be used in solving the problem. The default precision is 0.000001. A lower precision is indicated if there are fewer decimal places—for example, 0.0001. In general, the higher the precision you specify (a smaller number), the more time Solver will take to reach solutions.

assumeLinear

Optional. If **True**, Solver assumes that the underlying model is linear. This speeds the solution process, but it should be used only if all the relationships in the model are linear. **False** is the default.

stepThru

Optional. If **True**, Solver pauses at each trial solution. You can pass Solver a macro to run at each pause by using the *showRef* argument of the **SolverSolve** function. If **False**, Solver doesn't pause at each trial solution. **False** is the default.

estimates

Optional. Specifies the approach used to obtain initial estimates of the basic variables in each one-dimensional search: 1 represents Tangent estimates, and 2 represents Quadratic estimates. Tangent uses linear extrapolation from a tangent vector. Quadratic uses quadratic extrapolation; this may improve the results on highly nonlinear problems. Tangent is the default.

derivatives

Optional. Specifies forward differencing or central differencing for estimates of partial derivatives of the objective and constraint functions: 1 represents forward differencing, and 2 represents central differencing. Central differencing requires more worksheet recalculations, but it may help with problems that generate a message saying that Solver couldn't improve the solution. With functions whose graphical representations aren't smooth and continuous, you should use the Central differencing option. Forward differencing is the default.

search

Optional. Use the Search options to specify which search algorithm will be used at each iteration to decide which direction to search in: 1 represents the Newton search method, and 2 represents the Conjugate search method. Newton, which uses a quasi-Newton method, is the default search method. This method typically requires more memory than the Conjugate search method, but it requires fewer iterations. Conjugate gradient searching requires less memory than the Newton search method, but it typically requires more iterations to reach a particular level of accuracy. You can try this method if you have a large problem and memory usage is a concern. Conjugate searching is especially useful if stepping through the iterations reveals slow progress between successive trial points.

intTolerance

Optional. A decimal number between 0 and 1 that specifies the integer tolerance. This argument applies only if integer constraints have been defined. You can adjust the Tolerance figure, which represents a percentage of error allowed in the optimal solution when an integer constraint is used on any element of the problem. A higher tolerance (allowable percentage of error) would tend to speed up the solution process.

scaling

Optional. If **True**, and if two or more constraints differ by several orders of magnitude, Solver scales the constraints to similar orders of magnitude during computation. This is useful when the inputs (in the By Changing Cells box in the Solver Parameters dialog box) and outputs (in the Set Target Cell and Subject To The Constraints boxes in the Solver Parameters dialog box) have large differences in magnitude—for example, maximizing percent profit based on million-dollar investments. If **False**, Solver calculates without scaling the constraints. **False** is the default.

See Also   **SolverOk** Function.

Example   This example sets the Precision option to .001.

```
Worksheets("Sheet1").Activate
SolverReset
SolverOptions precision:=0.001
SolverOK setCell:=Range("TotalProfit"), _
    maxMinVal:=1, _
    byChange:=Range("C4:E6")
SolverAdd cellRef:=Range("F4:F6"), _
    relation:=1, _
    formulaText:=100
SolverAdd cellRef:=Range("C4:E6"), _
    relation:=3, _
    formulaText:=0
SolverAdd cellRef:=Range("C4:E6"), _
    relation:=4
SolverSolve userFinish:=False
SolverSave saveArea:=Range("A33")
```

SolverReset Function

Description   Resets all cell selections and constraints in the Solver Parameters dialog box and restores all the settings in the Solver Options dialog box to their defaults. Equivalent to clicking Reset All in the Solver Parameters dialog box. The **SolverReset** function is called automatically when you call the **SolverLoad** function.

Before you use this function, you must establish a reference to the Solver add-in. With a Visual Basic module active, click References on the Tools menu, and then select the Solver.xla check box in the Available References box. If Solver.xla doesn't appear in the Available References box, click Browse, click Solver in the \Excel\Library\Solver folder, and then click OK.

Syntax   **SolverReset()**

Example   This example resets the Solver settings to their defaults before defining a new problem.

```
Worksheets("Sheet1").Activate
SolverReset
SolverOptions precision:=0.001
SolverOK setCell:=Range("TotalProfit"), _
    maxMinVal:=1, _
    byChange:=Range("C4:E6")
SolverAdd cellRef:=Range("F4:F6"), _
    relation:=1, _
    formulaText:=100
SolverAdd cellRef:=Range("C4:E6"), _
    relation:=3, _
    formulaText:=0
SolverAdd cellRef:=Range("C4:E6"), _
    relation:=4
SolverSolve userFinish:=False
SolverSave saveArea:=Range("A33")
```

SolverSave Function

Description   Saves the Solver problem specifications on the worksheet.

Before you use this function, you must establish a reference to the Solver add-in. With a Visual Basic module active, click References on the Tools menu, and then select the Solver.xla check box in the Available References box. If Solver.xla doesn't appear in the Available References box, click Browse, click Solver in the \Excel\Library\Solver folder, and then click OK.

Syntax

SolverSave(*saveArea*)

saveArea
   Required. The range of cells where the Solver model is to be saved. The range represented by the *saveArea* argument can be on any worksheet, but you must specify the worksheet if it's not the active sheet. For example, SolverSave("Sheet2!A1:A3") saves the model on Sheet2 even if Sheet2 isn't the active sheet.

See Also

SolverLoad Function.

Example

This example uses the Solver functions to maximize gross profit in a business problem. The **SolverSave** function saves the current problem to a range on the active worksheet.

```
Worksheets("Sheet1").Activate
SolverReset
SolverOptions precision:=0.001
SolverOK setCell:=Range("TotalProfit"), _
    maxMinVal:=1, _
    byChange:=Range("C4:E6")
SolverAdd cellRef:=Range("F4:F6"), _
    relation:=1, _
    formulaText:=100
SolverAdd cellRef:=Range("C4:E6"), _
    relation:=3, _
    formulaText:=0
SolverAdd cellRef:=Range("C4:E6"), _
    relation:=4
SolverSolve userFinish:=False
SolverSave saveArea:=Range("A33")
```

SolverSolve Function

Description

Begins a Solver solution run. The equivalent of clicking Solve in the Solver Parameters dialog box.

Before you use this function, you must establish a reference to the Solver add-in. With a Visual Basic module active, click References on the Tools menu, and then select the Solver.xla check box in the Available References box. If Solver.xla doesn't appear in the Available References box, click Browse, click Solver in the \Excel\Library\Solver folder, and then click OK.

Syntax   **SolverSolve**(*userFinish*, *showRef*)

userFinish
Optional. If **True**, returns the results without displaying the Solver Results dialog box. If **False** or omitted, returns the results and displays the Solver Results dialog box.

showRef
Optional. Used only if **True** is passed to the *stepThru* argument of the *solverOptions* function. You can pass the name of a macro (as a string) as the *showRef* argument. This macro is then called whenever Solver returns an intermediate solution.

See Also   **SolverOk** Function.

Example   This example uses the Solver functions to maximize gross profit in a business problem. The **SolverSolve** function begins the Solver solution run.

```
Worksheets("Sheet1").Activate
SolverReset
SolverOptions precision:=0.001
SolverOK setCell:=Range("TotalProfit"), _
    maxMinVal:=1, _
    byChange:=Range("C4:E6")
SolverAdd cellRef:=Range("F4:F6"), _
    relation:=1, _
    formulaText:=100
SolverAdd cellRef:=Range("C4:E6"), _
    relation:=3, _
    formulaText:=0
SolverAdd cellRef:=Range("C4:E6"), _
    relation:=4
SolverSolve userFinish:=False
SolverSave saveArea:=Range("A33")
```

Sort Method

Applies To   **Range** Object.

Description	Syntax 1: Sorts the range, or sorts the current region if the range contains only one cell.

Syntax 2: Sorts a PivotTable; see the argument list for more information.

Syntax 1   *object*.**Sort**(*key1*, *order1*, *key2*, *order2*, *key3*, *order3*, *header*, *orderCustom*, *matchCase*, *orientation*)

Syntax 2   *object*.**Sort**(*key1*, *order1*, *type*, *orderCustom*, *orientation*)

object
> Required. The **Range** object.

key1
> Optional. The first sort field, as text (a pivot field or range name) or a **Range** object ("Dept" or Cells(1, 1), for example).

order1
> Optional. If **xlAscending** or omitted, *key1* is sorted in ascending order. If **xlDescending**, *key1* is sorted in descending order.

key2
> Optional. The second sort field, as text (a pivot field or range name) or a **Range** object. If omitted, there is no second sort field. Not used when sorting PivotTables.

type
> Optional. Only used when sorting PivotTables. Specifies which elements are sorted, either **xlSortValues** or **xlSortLabels**.

order2
> Optional. Sort order for *key2* (**xlAscending** or **xlDescending**); if omitted, **xlAscending** is assumed. Not used when sorting PivotTables.

key3
> Optional. The third sort field, as text (a range name) or a **Range** object. If omitted, there is no third sort field. Not used when sorting PivotTables.

order3
> Optional. Sort order for *key3* (**xlAscending** or **xlDescending**); if omitted, **xlAscending** is assumed. Not used when sorting PivotTables.

header
> Optional. If **xlYes**, the first row contains headers (it is not sorted). If **xlNo** or omitted, no headers exist (the entire range is sorted). If **xlGuess**, Microsoft Excel guesses if there is a header, and where it is if there is one. Not used when sorting PivotTables.

orderCustom
> Optional. One-based integer offset into the list of custom sort orders. If omitted, one (Normal) is used.

matchCase
>   Optional. If **True**, the sort is case sensitive. If **False**, the sort is not case
>   sensitive. Not used when sorting PivotTables.

orientation
>   Optional. If **xlTopToBottom** or omitted, the sort is done from top to bottom
>   (sort rows). If **xlLeftToRight**, the sort is done from left to right (sort columns).

Example   This example sorts the range A1:C20 on Sheet1, using cell A1 as the first sort key
and cell B1 as the second sort key. The sort is done in ascending order by row, and
there are no headers.

```
Worksheets("Sheet1").Range("A1:C20").Sort _
    key1:=Worksheets("Sheet1").Range("A1"), _
    key2:=Worksheets("Sheet1").Range("B1")
```

This example sorts the current region that contains cell A1 on Sheet1, sorting by the
data in the first column and automatically using a header row if one exists. The
Sort method determines the current region automatically.

```
Worksheets("Sheet1").Range("A1").Sort _
    key1:=Worksheets("Sheet1").Columns("A"), _
    header:=xlGuess
```

SortSpecial Method

Applies To   **Range** Object.

Description   Syntax 1: Uses Far-East sorting methods to sort the range, or the current region if
the range contains only one cell.

Syntax 2: Uses Far-East sorting methods to sort a PivotTable; see the argument list
for more information.

Syntax 1   *object*.**SortSpecial**(*sortMethod*, *key1*, *order1*, *key2*, *type*, *order2*, *key3*, *order3*,
header, *orderCustom*, *matchCase*, *orientation*)

Syntax 2   *object*.**SortSpecial**(*sortMethod*, *key1*, *order1*, *type*, *orderCustom*, *orientation*)

object
>   Required. The **Range** object.

sortMethod
>   Optional. Specifies how to sort (**xlSyllabary** to sort phonetically or
>   **xlCodePage** to sort by code page). The default value is **xlSyllabary**.

key1
> Optional. The first sort field, as text (a pivot field or range name) or a **Range** object ("Dept" or `Cells(1, 1)`, for example).

order1
> Optional. If **xlAscending** or omitted, *key1* is sorted in ascending order. If **xlDescending**, *key1* is sorted in descending order.

key2
> Optional. The second sort field, as text (a pivot field or range name) or a **Range** object. If omitted, there is no second sort field. Not used when sorting PivotTables.

type
> Optional. Only used when sorting PivotTables. Specifies which elements are sorted, either **xlSortValues** or **xlSortLabels**.

order2
> Optional. Sort order for *key2* (**xlAscending** or **xlDescending**); if omitted, **xlAscending** is assumed. Not used when sorting PivotTables.

key3
> Optional. The third sort field, as text (a range name) or a **Range** object. If omitted, there is no third sort field. Not used when sorting PivotTables.

order3
> Optional. Sort order for *key3* (**xlAscending** or **xlDescending**); if omitted, **xlAscending** is assumed. Not used when sorting PivotTables.

header
> Optional. If **xlYes**, the first row contains headers (it is not sorted). If **xlNo** or omitted, no headers exist (the entire range is sorted). If **xlGuess**, Microsoft Excel guesses if there is a header, and where it is if there is one. Not used when sorting PivotTables.

orderCustom
> Optional. One-based integer offset into the list of custom sort orders. If omitted, one (Normal) is used.

matchCase
> Optional. If **True**, the sort is case sensitive. If **False**, the sort is not case sensitive. Not used when sorting PivotTables.

orientation
> Optional. If **xlTopToBottom** or omitted, the sort is done from top to bottom (sort rows). If **xlLeftToRight**, the sort is done from left to right (sort columns).

Example   This example sorts the range A1:G37 on Sheet1, using cell A1 as the first sort key and cell C1 as the second key. The sort is done in ascending code page order by row, and there are no headers.

```
Worksheets("Sheet1").Range("A1:G37").SortSpecial _
    sortMethod:=xlCodePage, _
    key1:=Range("A1"), order1:=xlAscending, _
    key2:=Range("C1"), order2:=xlAscending
```

SoundNote Object

Description   Represents a sound note in a cell (a cell is a **Range** object). Your computer may need additional hardware to play and record sound notes.

Accessors   The **SoundNote** property returns the sound note for a cell. The following example records a sound note if the computer is capable of recording.

```
If Application.CanRecordSounds Then
    With Worksheets(1).Range("a1").SoundNote
        .Delete
        .Record
    End With
Else
    MsgBox "This machine cannot record sound notes."
End If
```

Properties   **Application** Property, **Creator** Property, **Parent** Property.

Methods   **Delete** Method, **Import** Method, **Play** Method, **Record** Method.

SoundNote Property

Applies To   **Range** Object.

Description   Accessor. Returns a **SoundNote** object that represents the sound note associated with the top left cell in the specified range. Read-only.

Remarks   Your computer may require optional hardware to record and play sound notes.

See Also   **Import** Method, **Play** Method, **Record** Method.

Example

This example deletes the sound note in cell A1 on Sheet1, records a new sound note for the same cell, and then plays the sound note.

```
With Worksheets("Sheet1").Range("A1").SoundNote
    .Delete
    .Record
    .Play
End With
```

SourceData Property

Applies To

PivotTable Object.

Description

Returns the data source for the **PivotTable**, as shown in the following table.

Data Source	Return Value
Microsoft Excel list or database	The cell reference as text.
External data source	An array. Each row consists of a SQL connection string with the remaining elements as the query string broken down into 200-character segments.
Multiple Consolidation ranges	A two-dimensional array. Each row consists of a reference and associated page field items.
Another PivotTable	One of the above three kinds of information.

Example

Assume that you used an external data source to create a PivotTable on Sheet1. This example inserts the SQL connection string and query string into a new worksheet.

```
Set newSheet = ActiveWorkbook.Worksheets.Add
sdArray = Worksheets("Sheet1").UsedRange.PivotTable.SourceData
For i = LBound(sdArray) To UBound(sdArray)
    newSheet.Cells(i, 1) = sdArray(i)
Next i
```

SourceName Property

Applies To

PivotField Object, **PivotItem** Object.

Description   Returns the object name (a string) as it appears in the original source data for the PivotTable. This might be different from the current item name if the user renamed the item after creating the PivotTable. Read-only.

Example   This example displays the original name (the name from the source database) of the item that contains the active cell.

```
Worksheets("Sheet1").Activate
MsgBox("The original item name is " & _
    ActiveCell.PivotItem.SourceName)
```

Space Function

Description   Returns a string consisting of the specified number of spaces.

Syntax   **Space(*number*)**

The *number* named argument is the number of spaces you want in the string.

Remarks   The **Space** function is useful for formatting output and clearing data in fixed-length strings.

See Also   **Spc** Function, **String** Function.

Example   This example uses the **Space** function to return a string consisting of a specified number of spaces.

```
' Returns a string with 10 spaces.
MyString = Space(10)
' Insert 10 spaces between 2 strings.
MyString = "Hello" & Space(10) & "World"
```

Spc Function

Description Used with the **Print #** statement or the **Print** method to position output.

Syntax **Spc**(*n*)

The *n* argument is the number of spaces to insert before displaying or printing the next expression in a list.

Remarks If *n* is less than the output-line width, the next print position immediately follows the number of spaces printed. If *n* is greater than the output-line width, **Spc** calculates the next print position using the formula:

currentprintposition + (*n* **Mod** *width*)

For example, if the current print position is 24, the output-line width is 80 and you specify **Spc**(90), the next print will start at position 34 (current print position + the remainder of 90/80). If the difference between the current print position and the output-line width is less than *n* (or *n* **Mod** *width*), the **Spc** function skips to the beginning of the next line and generates a number of spaces equal to *n* - (*width* - *currentprintposition*).

Note Make sure your tabular columns are wide enough to accommodate wider letters.

When you use the **Print** method with a proportionally spaced font, the width of space characters printed using the **Spc** function is always an average of the width of all characters in the point size for the chosen font. However, there is no correlation between the number of characters printed and the number of fixed-width columns those characters occupy. For example, the uppercase letter W occupies more than one fixed-width column and the lowercase letter I occupies less.

See Also **Print #** Statement, **Print** Method, **Space** Function, **Tab** Function, **Width #** Statement.

Example This example uses the **Spc** function to position output in a file and in the Debug window.

```
' The Spc function can be used with the Print # statement.
Open "TESTFILE" For Output As #1    ' Open file for output.
Print #1, "10 spaces between here"; Spc(10); "and here."
Close #1                            ' Close file.
' The following statement causes the text to be printed in the Debug
' window, preceded by 30 spaces.
Debug.Print Spc(30); "Thirty spaces later..."
```

SpecialCells Method

Applies To   **Range** Object.

Description   Accessor. Returns a **Range** object that represents all the cells that match the specified type and value.

Syntax   *object*.**SpecialCells**(*type, value*)

object
Required. The **Range** object.

type
Required. The types of cells to include, as shown in the following table.

Value	Meaning
xlNotes	Cells containing notes.
xlConstants	Cells containing constants.
xlFormulas	Cells containing formulas.
xlBlanks	Empty cells.
xlLastCell	Last cell of the used range.
xlVisible	All visible cells.

value
Optional. If *type* is **xlConstants** or **xlFormulas**, the *value* argument is used to determine which types of cells to include in the result. These values may be added together to return more than one type. The default is to select all constants or formulas, no matter what the type.

Value	Meaning
xlNumbers	Numbers
xlTextValues	Text
xlLogical	Logical values
xlErrors	Error values

Example   This example selects the last cell in the used range of Sheet1.

```
Worksheets("Sheet1").Activate
ActiveSheet.Cells.SpecialCells(xlLastCell).Activate
```

Spinner Object

Description   Represents a spinner, which is often linked to edit boxes so that the user can select a numeric value without having to type in a number. Spinners are very similar to scroll bars (**ScrollBar** object), but spinners do not have the **LargeChange** property.

Edit boxes do not have spinners by default. If you want an edit box to have a spinner, you must create a separate **Spinner** object and add the Visual Basic code to link the spinner value to the edit box. The following example links the value of the spinner named "spnTest" to the text displayed in the edit box named "edtTest," so that changing the value of one control simultaneously changes the value of the other.

```
Sub spnTest_Change()
    ActiveDialog.EditBoxes("edtTest").Text = _
        ActiveDialog.Spinners("spnTest").Value
End Sub

Sub edtTest_Change()
    ActiveDialog.Spinners("spnTest").Value = _
        ActiveDialog.EditBoxes("edtTest").Text
End Sub
```

Accessors   The **Spinner** object is a member of the **Spinners** collection. The **Spinners** collection contains all the **Spinner** objects on a single sheet. Use the **Add** method to create a new spinner and add it to the collection.

To access a single member of the collection, use the **Spinners** method with the index number or name of the spinner as an argument.

The following example sets the **OnAction** property for spinner one on the worksheet named "Sheet1." The SpinnerProc Visual Basic procedure runs when the user clicks the spinner.

```
Worksheets("sheet1").Spinners(1).OnAction = "SpinnerProc"
```

The spinner name is shown in the Name Box when the spinner is selected. Use the **Name** property to set or return the spinner name. The following example disables the spinner named "Spinner 5" on the worksheet named "Sheet1."

```
Worksheets("sheet1").Spinners("spinner 5").Enabled = False
```

Properties   **Application** Property, **BottomRightCell** Property, **Creator** Property,
Display3DShading Property, **Enabled** Property, **Height** Property, **Index** Property,
Left Property, **LinkedCell** Property, **Locked** Property, **Max** Property, **Min**
Property, **Name** Property, **OnAction** Property, **Parent** Property, **Placement**
Property, **PrintObject** Property, **SmallChange** Property, **Top** Property,
TopLeftCell Property, **Value** Property, **Visible** Property, **Width** Property,
ZOrder Property.

Methods   **BringToFront** Method, **Copy** Method, **CopyPicture** Method, **Cut** Method,
Delete Method, **Duplicate** Method, **Select** Method, **SendToBack** Method.

Spinners Collection Object

Description   A collection of all the **Spinner** objects on the specified chart sheet, dialog sheet, or
worksheet. Spinners are often linked to edit boxes so that the user can select a
numeric value without having to type in a number. Spinners are very similar to
scroll bars (**ScrollBar** objects), but spinners do not have the **LargeChange**
property.

Accessors   Use the **Add** method to create a new spinner and add it to the collection. The
following example adds a new spinner to the worksheet named "Sheet1." The new
spinner is 10 points wide and is located at the left edge of cell C5.

```
Dim r As Range
Set r = Worksheets("sheet1").Range("c5")
Worksheets("sheet1").Spinners.Add r.Left, r.Top, 10, r.Height
```

Use the **Spinners** method with an argument to access a single member of the
collection or without an argument to access the entire collection at once. The
following example deletes all of the spinners on the worksheet named "Sheet1."

```
Worksheets("sheet1").Spinners.Delete
```

Properties   **Application** Property, **Count** Property, **Creator** Property, **Display3DShading**
Property, **Enabled** Property, **Height** Property, **Left** Property, **LinkedCell** Property,
Locked Property, **Max** Property, **Min** Property, **OnAction** Property, **Parent**
Property, **Placement** Property, **PrintObject** Property, **SmallChange** Property,
Top Property, **Value** Property, **Visible** Property, **Width** Property, **ZOrder**
Property.

Methods   **Add** Method (Graphic Objects and Controls), **BringToFront** Method, **Copy**
Method, **CopyPicture** Method, **Cut** Method, **Delete** Method, **Duplicate** Method,
Group Method, **Item** Method, **Select** Method, **SendToBack** Method.

Spinners Method

Applies To
Chart Object, **DialogSheet** Object, **Worksheet** Object.

Description
Accessor. Returns an object that represents a single spinner control (a **Spinner** object, Syntax 1) or a collection of spinner controls (a **Spinners** object, Syntax 2) on the sheet.

Syntax 1
object.**Spinners**(*index*)

Syntax 2
object.**Spinners**

object
Required. The **Chart**, **DialogSheet**, or **Worksheet** object.

index
Required for Syntax 1. Specifies the name or number of the spinner (can be an array to specify more than one).

Example
This example displays the current value of spinner one on Dialog1. This example can be used in the event procedure for the spinner, in which case the message box appears every time you click the spinner.

```
MsgBox DialogSheets("Dialog1").Spinners(1).Value
```

Split Property

Applies To
Window Object.

Description
True if the window is split. Read-write.

Remarks
It is possible for **FreezePanes** to be **True** and **Split** to be **False**, or vice versa.

This property applies only to worksheets and macro sheets.

Example
This example splits the active window in BOOK1.XLS at cell B2, without freezing panes. This causes the **Split** property to return **True**.

```
Workbooks("BOOK1.XLS").Worksheets("Sheet1").Activate
With ActiveWindow
    .SplitColumn = 2
    .SplitRow = 2
End With
```

There are two ways to remove the split added by the previous example.

```
Workbooks("BOOK1.XLS").Worksheets("Sheet1").Activate
ActiveWindow.Split = False                    'method one

Workbooks("BOOK1.XLS").Worksheets("Sheet1").Activate
ActiveWindow.SplitColumn = 0          'method two
ActiveWindow.SplitRow = 0
```

This example removes the window split. Before you can remove the split, you must set **FreezePanes** to **False** to remove frozen panes.

```
Workbooks("BOOK1.XLS").Worksheets("Sheet1").Activate
With ActiveWindow
    .FreezePanes = False
    .Split = False
End With
```

SplitColumn Property

Applies To   **Window** Object.

Description   Returns or sets the column number where the window is split into panes (the number of columns to the left of the split line). Read-write.

See Also   **SplitHorizontal** Property, **SplitRow** Property, **SplitVertical** Property.

Example   This example splits the window and leaves 1.5 columns to the left of the split line.

```
Workbooks("BOOK1.XLS").Worksheets("Sheet1").Activate
ActiveWindow.SplitColumn = 1.5
```

SplitHorizontal Property

Applies To   **Window** Object.

Description   Returns or sets the location of the horizontal window split, in points (1/72 inch). Read-write.

See Also   **SplitColumn** Property, **SplitRow** Property, **SplitVertical** Property.

Example   This example sets the horizontal split for the active window to 216 points (3 inches).

```
Workbooks("BOOK1.XLS").Worksheets("Sheet1").Activate
ActiveWindow.SplitHorizontal = 216
```

SplitRow Property

Applies To   **Window** Object.

Description   Returns or sets the row number where the window is split into panes (the number of rows above the split). Read-write.

See Also   **SplitColumn** Property, **SplitHorizontal** Property, **SplitVertical** Property.

Example   This example splits the active window so that there are 10 rows above the split line.

```
Workbooks("BOOK1.XLS").Worksheets("Sheet1").Activate
ActiveWindow.SplitRow = 10
```

SplitVertical Property

Applies To   **Window** Object.

Description   Returns or sets the location of the vertical window split, in points (1/72 inch). Read-write.

See Also   **SplitColumn** Property, **SplitHorizontal** Property, **SplitRow** Property.

Example   This example sets the vertical split for the active window to 216 points (3 inches).

```
Workbooks("BOOK1.XLS").Worksheets("Sheet1").Activate
ActiveWindow.SplitVertical = 216
```

SQLBind Function

Description
In Microsoft Excel for Windows 95, do not use **SQLBind** and the other ODBC functions in the XLODBC.XLA add-in; use the objects, methods, and properties in the Data Access Objects (DAO) library instead.

SQLBind specifies where results are placed when they are retrieved using **SQLRetrieve** or **SQLRetrieveToFile**. Use **SQLBind** to change the column order of the result set from a query, or to place the result set columns in non-adjacent worksheet columns.

This function is contained in the XLODBC.XLA add-in (ODBC Add-In on the Macintosh). Before you use the function, you must establish a reference to the add-in using the References command (Tools menu).

Syntax
SQLBind(*connectionNum, column, reference*)

connectionNum
Required. The unique connection ID of the data source, returned by **SQLOpen**, for which you want to bind results.

column
Optional. The column number of the result set that you want to bind. Columns in the result set are numbered from left to right starting with 1. If you omit *column*, all bindings for *connectionNum* are removed.

Column number 0 (zero) contains row numbers for the result set. You can return the row numbers by binding column number 0 (zero).

reference
Optional. The location of a single cell on a worksheet where you want the results bound, as a **Range** object. If *reference* is omitted, binding is removed for the column.

Return Value
This function returns an array listing the bound columns for the current connection by column number.

If **SQLBind** is unable to bind the column to the cell in the specified reference, it returns Error 2042.

If *connectionNum* is not valid or if you try to bind a cell that is not available, **SQLBind** returns Error 2015.

If *reference* refers to more than a single cell, **SQLBind** returns Error 2023.

If **SQLRetrieve** does not have a destination parameter, **SQLBind** places the result set in the location indicated by reference.

Remarks
SQLBind tells the ODBC Control Panel Administrator where to place results when they are received using **SQLRetrieve** The results are placed in the reference cell and cells immediately below it.

Use **SQLBind** if you want the results from different columns to be placed in disjoint worksheet locations.

Use **SQLBind** for each column in the result set. A binding remains valid as long as the connection specified by *connectionNum* is open.

Call **SQLBind** after calling **SQLOpen** and **SQLExecQuery**, but before calling **SQLRetrieve** or **SQLRetrieveToFile**. Calls to **SQLBind** do not affect results that have already been retrieved.

See Also

SQLClose Function, **SQLError** Function, **SQLExecQuery** Function, **SQLGetSchema** Function, **SQLOpen** Function, **SQLRequest** Function, **SQLRetrieve** Function, **SQLRetrieveToFile** Function.

Example

This example runs a query on the NWind sample database, and then it uses the **SQLBind** function to display only the fourth and ninth columns of the query result set (the product name and the quantity on order) on Sheet1.

```
If Application.OperatingSystem Like "*Win*" Then
    databaseName = "NWind"
Else            'Macintosh
    databaseName = "NorthWind"
End If
queryString = "SELECT * FROM product.dbf WHERE (product.ON_ORDER<>0)"
chan = SQLOpen("DSN=" & databaseName)
SQLExecQuery chan, queryString
Set output1 = Worksheets("Sheet1").Range("A1")
Set output2 = Worksheets("Sheet1").Range("B1")
SQLBind chan, 4, output1
SQLBind chan, 9, output2
SQLRetrieve chan
SQLClose chan
```

SQLClose Function

Description

In Microsoft Excel for Windows 95, do not use **SQLClose** and the other ODBC functions in the XLODBC.XLA add-in; use the objects, methods, and properties in the Data Access Objects (DAO) library instead.

SQLClose closes a connection to an external data source.

This function is contained in the XLODBC.XLA add-in (ODBC Add-In on the Macintosh). Before you use the function, you must establish a reference to the add-in using the References command (Tools menu).

Syntax

SQLClose(*connectionNum*)

connectionNum
> Required. The unique connection ID of the data source from which you want to disconnect.

Return Value   If the connection is successfully closed, this function returns 0 (zero) and the connection ID is no longer valid.

If *connectionNum* is not valid, this function returns Error 2015.

If **SQLClose** is unable to disconnect from the data source, it returns Error 2042.

See Also   **SQLBind** Function, **SQLError** Function, **SQLExecQuery** Function, **SQLGetSchema** Function, **SQLOpen** Function, **SQLRequest** Function, **SQLRetrieve** Function, **SQLRetrieveToFile** Function.

Example   This example runs a query on the NWind sample database. The result of the query, displayed on Sheet1, is a list of all products that are currently on order.

```
If Application.OperatingSystem Like "*Win*" Then
    databaseName = "NWind"
Else            'Macintosh
    databaseName = "NorthWind"
End If
queryString = "SELECT * FROM product.dbf WHERE (product.ON_ORDER<>0)"
chan = SQLOpen("DSN=" & databaseName)
SQLExecQuery chan, queryString
Set output = Worksheets("Sheet1").Range("A1")
SQLRetrieve chan, output, , , True
SQLClose chan
```

SQLError Function

Description   In Microsoft Excel for Windows 95, do not use **SQLError** and the other ODBC functions in the XLODBC.XLA add-in; use the objects, methods, and properties in the Data Access Objects (DAO) library instead.

SQLError returns detailed error information when called after one of the other ODBC functions fails. If **SQLError** itself fails, it cannot return error information.

Error information is defined and stored in memory whenever an ODBC function fails. To make the error information available, call the **SQLError** function.

SQLError provides detailed error information only about errors that occur when an ODBC function fails. It does not provide information about Microsoft Excel errors.

This function is contained in the XLODBC.XLA add-in (ODBC Add-In on the Macintosh). Before you use the function, you must establish a reference to the add-in using the References command (Tools menu).

Syntax

SQLError()

Return Value

If there are errors, **SQLError** returns detailed error information in a two-dimensional array in which each row describes one error.

Each row has the following three fields for information obtained through the **SQLError** function call in ODBC:

A character string indicating the ODBC error class and subclass.

A numeric value indicating the data source native error code.

A text message describing the error.

If a function call generates multiple errors, **SQLError** creates a row for each error.

If there are no errors from a previous ODBC function call, this function returns only Error 2042.

See Also

SQLBind Function, **SQLClose** Function, **SQLExecQuery** Function, **SQLGetSchema** Function, **SQLOpen** Function, **SQLRequest** Function, **SQLRetrieve** Function, **SQLRetrieveToFile** Function.

Example

This example generates an intentional error by attempting to open a connection to the NWind sample database using an incorrect connection string (NWind is misspelled). The error information is displayed on Sheet1.

```
chan = SQLOpen("DSN=NWin")
returnArray = SQLError()
For i = LBound(returnArray, 1) To UBound(returnArray, 1)
    Worksheets("Sheet1").Cells(1, i).Formula = returnArray(i)
Next i
SQLClose chan
```

SQLExecQuery Function

Description

In Microsoft Excel for Windows 95, do not use **SQLExecQuery** and the other ODBC functions in the XLODBC.XLA add-in; use the objects, methods, and properties in the Data Access Objects (DAO) library instead.

SQLExecQuery executes a query on a data source with a connection that has been established using **SQLOpen**.

SQLExecQuery executes only the query. Use **SQLRetrieve** or **SQLRetrieveToFile** to get the results.

This function is contained in the XLODBC.XLA add-in (ODBC Add-In on the Macintosh). Before you use the function, you must establish a reference to the add-in using the References command (Tools menu).

Syntax

SQLExecQuery(*connectionNum*, *queryText*)

connectionNum
> Required. The unique connection ID returned by **SQLOpen** that identifies the data source you want to query.

queryText
> Required. The query to be executed on the data source. The query must follow the SQL syntax guidelines for the specific driver.

Return Value

The value returned by **SQLExecQuery** depends on the type of SQL statement executed, as shown in the following table.

SQL statement executed	Return Value
SELECT	The number of columns in the result set.
UPDATE, INSERT or DELETE	The number of rows affected by the statement.
Any other valid SQL statement	0 (zero)

If **SQLExecQuery** is unable to execute the query on the specified data source, it returns Error 2042.

If *connectionNum* is not valid, **SQLExecQuery** returns Error 2015.

Remarks

Before calling **SQLExecQuery** you must establish a connection to a data source using **SQLOpen** The unique connection ID returned by **SQLOpen** is used by **SQLExecQuery** to send queries to the data source.

If you call **SQLExecQuery** using a previously used connection ID, any pending results on that connection are replaced by the new results.

See Also

SQLBind Function, **SQLClose** Function, **SQLError** Function, **SQLGetSchema** Function, **SQLOpen** Function, **SQLRequest** Function, **SQLRetrieve** Function, **SQLRetrieveToFile** Function.

Example

This example runs a query on the NWind sample database. The result of the query, displayed on Sheet1, is a list of all products that are currently on order.

```
If Application.OperatingSystem Like "*Win*" Then
    databaseName = "NWind"
Else            'Macintosh
    databaseName = "NorthWind"
End If
queryString = "SELECT * FROM product.dbf WHERE (product.ON_ORDER<>0)"
chan = SQLOpen("DSN=" & databaseName)
SQLExecQuery chan, queryString
Set output = Worksheets("Sheet1").Range("A1")
SQLRetrieve chan, output, , , True
SQLClose chan
```

SQLGetSchema Function

Description

In Microsoft Excel for Windows 95, do not use **SQLGetSchema** and the other ODBC functions in the XLODBC.XLA add-in; use the objects, methods, and properties in the Data Access Objects (DAO) library instead.

SQLGetSchema returns information about the structure of the data source on a particular connection.

This function is contained in the XLODBC.XLA add-in (ODBC Add-In on the Macintosh). Before you use the function, you must establish a reference to the add-in using the References command (Tools menu).

Syntax

SQLGetSchema(*connectionNum*, *typeNum*, *qualifierText***)**
connectionNum

Required. The unique connection ID of the data source you connected to using **SQLOpen** and for which you want information.

typeNum

Required. Specifies the type of information you want returned, as shown in the following table.

Value	Meaning
1	A list of available data sources.
2	A list of databases on the current connection.
3	A list of owners in a database on the current connection.
4	A list of tables for a given owner and database on the current connection.

Value	Meaning
5	A list of columns in a particular table and their ODBC SQL data types in a two-dimensional array. The first field contains the name of the column and the second field is the ODBC SQL data type of the column.
6	The user ID of the current user.
7	The name of the current database.
8	The name of the data source defined during setup or by using the ODBC Control Panel Administrator.
9	The name of the DBMS the data source uses, for example, ORACLE or SQL Server.
10	The server name for the data source.
11	The terminology used by the data source to refer to the owners, for example "owner", "Authorization ID", or "Schema".
12	The terminology used by the data source to refer a table, for example, "table" or "file".
13	The terminology used by the data source to refer to a qualifier, for example, "database" or "directory".
14	The terminology used by the data source to refer to a procedure, for example, "database procedure", "stored procedure", or "procedure".

qualifierText
Optional. Included only for *typeNum* values of 3, 4 and 5. A string that qualifies the search, as shown in the following table.

typeNum	qualifierText
3	The name of the database in the current data source. **SQLGetSchema** returns the names of the table owners in that database.
4	Both a database name and an owner name. The syntax consists of the database name followed by the owner's name with a period separating the two; for example, "DatabaseName.OwnerName". This function returns an array of table names that are located in the given database and owned by the given owner.
5	The name of a table. **SQLGetSchema** returns information about the columns in the table.

Return Value

The return value from a successful call to **SQLGetSchema** depends on the type of information that is requested.

If **SQLGetSchema** cannot find the requested information, it returns Error 2042.

If *connectionNum* is not valid, this function returns Error 2015.

Remarks

SQLGetSchema uses the ODBC API functions SQLGetInfo and SQLTables to find the requested information.

See Also

SQLBind Function, **SQLClose** Function, **SQLError** Function, **SQLExecQuery** Function, **SQLOpen** Function, **SQLRequest** Function, **SQLRetrieve** Function, **SQLRetrieveToFile** Function.

Example

This example retrieves the database name and DBMS name for the NWind sample database and then displays them in a message box.

```
If Application.OperatingSystem Like "*Win*" Then
    databaseName = "NWind"
Else            'Macintosh
    databaseName = "NorthWind"
End If
chan = SQLOpen("DSN=" & databaseName)
dsName = SQLGetSchema(chan, 8)
dsDBMS = SQLGetSchema(chan, 9)
MsgBox "Database name is " & dsName & ", and its DBMS is " & dsDBMS
SQLClose chan
```

SQLOpen Function

Description
In Microsoft Excel for Windows 95, do not use **SQLOpen** and the other ODBC functions in the XLODBC.XLA add-in; use the objects, methods, and properties in the Data Access Objects (DAO) library instead.

SQLOpen establishes a connection to a data source.

This function is contained in the XLODBC.XLA add-in (ODBC Add-In on the Macintosh). Before you use the function, you must establish a reference to the add-in using the References command (Tools menu)..

Syntax
SQLOpen(*connectionStr, outputRef, driverPrompt*)

connectionStr
Required. Supplies the information required by the driver being used to connect to a data source and must follow the driver's format.

The *connectionStr* supplies the data source name and other information, such as user ID and passwords, that is required by the driver to make a connection.

You must define the data source name (DSN) used in *connectionStr* before you try to connect to it.

outputRef
Optional. A single cell, as a **Range** object, that contains the completed connection string.

Use *outputRef* when you want **SQLOpen** to return the completed connection string to a worksheet.

driverPrompt
Optional. Specifies when the driver dialog box is displayed and which options are available. Use one of the numbers described in the following table. If *driverPrompt* is omitted, **SQLOpen** uses 2 as the default.

Value	Meaning
1	Driver dialog box is always displayed.
2	Driver dialog box is displayed only if information provided by the connection string and the data source specification are not sufficient to complete the connection. All dialog box options are available.

Value	Meaning
3	The same as 2 except that dialog box options that are not required are dimmed and unavailable.
4	Driver dialog box is not displayed. If the connection is not successful, **SQLOpen** returns an error.

Return Value

If successful, **SQLOpen** returns a unique connection ID number. Use the connection ID number with the other ODBC functions.

If **SQLOpen** is unable to connect using the information you provide, it returns Error 2042. Additional error information is placed in memory for use by **SQLError**.

See Also

SQLBind Function, **SQLClose** Function, **SQLError** Function, **SQLExecQuery** Function, **SQLGetSchema** Function, **SQLRequest** Function, **SQLRetrieve** Function, **SQLRetrieveToFile** Function.

Example

This example runs a query on the NWind sample database. The result of the query, displayed on Sheet1, is a list of all products that are currently on order.

```
If Application.OperatingSystem Like "*Win*" Then
    databaseName = "NWind"
Else            'Macintosh
    databaseName = "NorthWind"
End If
queryString = "SELECT * FROM product.dbf WHERE (product.ON_ORDER<>0)"
chan = SQLOpen("DSN=" & databaseName)
SQLExecQuery chan, queryString
Set output = Worksheets("Sheet1").Range("A1")
SQLRetrieve chan, output, , , True
SQLClose chan
```

SQLRequest Function

Description

In Microsoft Excel for Windows 95, do not use **SQLRequest** and the other ODBC functions in the XLODBC.XLA add-in; use the objects, methods, and properties in the Data Access Objects (DAO) library instead.

SQLRequest connects to an external data source and runs a query from a worksheet, and then returns the result as an array.

This function is contained in the XLODBC.XLA add-in (ODBC Add-In on the Macintosh). Before you use the function, you must establish a reference to the add-in using the References command (Tools menu).

SQLRequest(*connectionStr, queryText, outputRef, driverPrompt, colNamesLogical*)

connectionStr
>   Required. Supplies information, such as the data source name, user ID, and passwords, required by the driver being used to connect to a data source and must follow the driver's format.
>
>   You must define the data source name (DSN) used in *connectionStr* before you try to connect to it.
>
>   If **SQLRequest** is unable to access the data source using *connectionStr*, it returns Error 2042.

queryText
>   Required. The SQL statement that you want to execute on the data source.
>
>   If **SQLRequest** is unable to execute *queryText* on the specified data source, it returns Error 2042.

outputRef
>   Optional. A single worksheet cell, as a **Range** object, where you want the completed connection string placed.

driverPrompt
>   Optional. Specifies when the driver dialog box is displayed and which options are available. Use one of the numbers described in the following table. If *driverPrompt* is omitted, **SQLRequest** uses 2 as the default.

Value	Meaning
1	Driver dialog box is always displayed.
2	Driver dialog box is displayed only if information provided by the connection string and the data source specification is not sufficient to complete the connection. All dialog box options are available.
3	Driver dialog box is displayed only if information provided by the connection string and the data source specification is not sufficient to complete the connection. Dialog box options are dimmed and unavailable if they are not required.
4	Dialog box is not displayed. If the connection is not successful, it returns an error.

colNamesLogical

Optional. **True** if you want the column names to be returned as the first row of results. It should contain **False** if you do not want the column names returned. The default value, if *colNamesLogical* is omitted, is **False**.

Remarks   The arguments to the **SQLRequest** function are in a different order than the arguments to the SQL.REQUEST macro function.

Return Value   If this function completes all of its actions, it returns an array of query results or the number of rows affected by the query.

If **SQLRequest** is unable to complete all of its actions, it returns an error value and places the error information in memory for **SQLError**

If **SQLRequest** is unable to access the data source using *connectionStr*, it returns Error 2042.

See Also   **SQLBind** Function, **SQLClose** Function, **SQLError** Function, **SQLExecQuery** Function, **SQLGetSchema** Function, **SQLOpen** Function, **SQLRetrieve** Function, **SQLRetrieveToFile** Function.

Example   This example runs a query on the NWind sample database. The result of the query, displayed on Sheet1, is a list of all products that are currently on order. The **SQLRequest** function also writes the full connection string to Sheet2.

```
If Application.OperatingSystem Like "*Win*" Then
    databaseName = "NWind"
Else       'Macintosh
    databaseName = "NorthWind"
End If
queryString = "SELECT * FROM product.dbf WHERE (product.ON_ORDER<>0)"
returnArray = SQLRequest("DSN=" & databaseName, _
        queryString, _
        Worksheets("Sheet1").Range("A1"), _
        2, True)
For i = LBound(returnArray, 1) To UBound(returnArray, 1)
    For j = LBound(returnArray, 2) To UBound(returnArray, 2)
        Worksheets("Sheet1").Cells(i, j).Formula = returnArray(i, j)
    Next j
Next i
```

SQLRetrieve Function

Description   In Microsoft Excel for Windows 95, do not use **SQLRetrieve** and the other ODBC functions in the XLODBC.XLA add-in; use the objects, methods, and properties in the Data Access Objects (DAO) library instead.

SQLRetrieve retrieves all or part of the results from a previously executed query.

Before using **SQLRetrieve**, you must establish a connection with **SQLOpen**, execute a query with **SQLExecQuery**, and have the results pending.

This function is contained in the XLODBC.XLA add-in (ODBC Add-In on the Macintosh). Before you use the function, you must establish a reference to the add-in using the References command (Tools menu).

Syntax   **SQLRetrieve**(*connectionNum*, *destinationRef*, *maxColumns*, *maxRows*, *colNamesLogical*, *rowNumsLogical*, *namedRngLogical*, *fetchFirstLogical*)

connectionNum
Required. The unique connection ID returned by **SQLOpen** and for which you have pending query results generated by **SQLExecQuery**.

If *connectionNum* is not valid, **SQLExecQuery** returns Error 2015.

destinationRef
Optional. A Range object that specifies where the results should be placed. This function overwrites any values in the cells without confirmation.

If *destinationRef* refers to a single cell, **SQLRetrieve** returns all of the pending results in that cell and in the cells to the right and below it.

If *destinationRef* is omitted, the bindings established by previous calls to **SQLBind** are used to return results. If no bindings exist for the current connection, **SQLRetrieve** returns Error 2023.

If a particular result column has not been bound and *destinationRef* is omitted, the results are discarded.

maxColumns
Optional. The maximum number of columns returned to the worksheet starting at *destinationRef*.

If *maxColumns* specifies more columns than are available in the result, **SQLRetrieve** places data in the columns for which data is available and clears the additional columns.

If *maxColumns* specifies fewer columns than are available in the result, **SQLRetrieve** discards the rightmost result columns until the results fit the specified size.

The order in which the data source returns the columns determines column position.

All of the results are returned if *maxColumns* is omitted.

maxRows
Optional. The maximum number of rows to be returned to the worksheet starting at *destinationRef*.

If *maxRows* specifies more rows than are available in the results, **SQLRetrieve** places data in the rows for which data is available and clears the additional rows.

If *maxRows* specifics fewer rows than are available in the results, **SQLRetrieve** places data in the selected rows but does not discard the additional rows. Extra rows are retrieved by using **SQLRetrieve** again and by setting *fetchFirstLogical* to **False**.

All of the rows in the results are returned if *maxRows* is omitted.

colNamesLogical
Optional. **True** if you want the column names to be returned as the first row of results. **False** or omitted if you do not want the column names returned.

rowNumsLogical
Optional. Used only when *destinationRef* is included in the function call. If *rowNumsLogical* is **True**, the first column in the result set contains row numbers. If *destinationRef* is **False** or omitted, the row numbers are not returned. You can also retrieve row numbers by binding column number 0 (zero) with **SQLBind**.

namedRngLogical
Optional. **True** if you want each column of the results to be declared as a named range on the worksheet. The name of each range is the result column name. The named range includes only the rows that are returned with **SQLRetrieve**. The default is **False**.

fetchFirstLogical
Optional. Allows you to request results from the beginning of the result set. If *fetchFirstLogical* is **False**, **SQLRetrieve** can be called repeatedly to return the next set of rows until all the result rows are returned. When there are no more rows in the result set, **SQLRequest** returns 0 (zero). If you want to retrieve results from the beginning of the result set, set *fetchFirstLogical* to **True**. To retrieve additional rows from the result set, set *fetchFirstLogical* to **False** in subsequent calls. The default is **False**.

Return Value

SQLRetrieve returns the number of rows in the result set.

If **SQLRetrieve** is unable to retrieve the results on the specified data source or if there are no results pending, it returns Error 2042. If no data is found, it returns 0 (zero).

Remarks

Before calling **SQLRetrieve**, you must do the following:

1. Establish a connection with a data source using **SQLOpen**.
2. Use the connection ID returned in **SQLOpen** to send a query with **SQLExecQuery**.

See Also

SQLBind Function, **SQLClose** Function, **SQLError** Function, **SQLExecQuery** Function, **SQLGetSchema** Function, **SQLOpen** Function, **SQLRequest** Function, **SQLRetrieveToFile** Function.

Example

This example runs a query on the NWind sample database. The result of the query, displayed on Sheet1, is a list of all products that are currently on order.

```
If Application.OperatingSystem Like "*Win*" Then
    databaseName = "NWind"
Else            'Macintosh
    databaseName = "NorthWind"
End If
queryString = "SELECT * FROM product.dbf WHERE (product.ON_ORDER<>0)"
chan = SQLOpen("DSN=" & databaseName)
SQLExecQuery chan, queryString
Set output = Worksheets("Sheet1").Range("A1")
SQLRetrieve chan, output, , , True
SQLClose chan
```

SQLRetrieveToFile Function

Description

In Microsoft Excel for Windows 95, do not use **SQLRetrieveToFile** and the other ODBC functions in the XLODBC.XLA add-in; use the objects, methods, and properties in the Data Access Objects (DAO) library instead.

SQLRetrieveToFile retrieves all of the results from a previously executed query and places them in a file.

To use this function you must have established a connection with a data source using **SQLOpen**, executed a query using **SQLExecQuery**, and have the results of the query pending.

This function is contained in the XLODBC.XLA add-in (ODBC Add-In on the Macintosh). Before you use the function, you must establish a reference to the add-in using the References command (Tools menu).

Syntax

SQLRetrieveToFile(*connectionNum, destination, colNamesLogical, columnDelimiter***)**

connectionNum
> Required. The unique connection ID returned by **SQLOpen** and for which you have pending query results generated by **SQLExecQuery**.

> If *connectionNum* is not valid, **SQLExecQuery** returns Error 2015.

destination

Required. A string that specifies the name and path of the file where you want to place the results. If the file exists, its contents are replaced with the query results. If the file does not exist, **SQLRetrieveToFile** creates and opens the file and fills it with the results.

The format of the data in the file is compatible with the Microsoft Excel .CSV (comma-separated value) file format.

Columns are separated by the character specified by *columnDelimiter*, and the individual rows are separated by a carriage return.

If the file specified by *destination* cannot be opened, **SQLRetrieveToFile** returns Error 2042.

colNamesLogical

Optional. **True** if you want the column names to be returned as the first row of data. **False** or omitted if you do not want the column names returned.

columnDelimiter

Optional. A string that specifies the character used to separate the elements in each row. For example, use "," to specify a comma delimiter or ";" to specify a semicolon delimiter. If you omit *columnDelimiter*, the list separator character is used.

Return Value

If successful, **SQLRetrieveToFile** returns the query results, writes them to a file, and then returns the number of rows that were written to the file.

If **SQLRetrieveToFile** is unable to retrieve the results, it returns Error 2042, and does not write the file.

If there are no pending results on the connection, **SQLRetrieveToFile** returns Error 2042.

Remarks

Before calling **SQLRetrieveToFile**, you must do the following:

1. Establish a connection with a data source using **SQLOpen**.

2. Use the connection ID returned by **SQLOpen** to send a query with **SQLExecQuery**.

See Also

SQLBind Function, **SQLClose** Function, **SQLError** Function, **SQLExecQuery** Function, **SQLGetSchema** Function, **SQLOpen** Function, **SQLRequest** Function, **SQLRetrieve** Function.

Example   This example runs a query on the NWind sample database. The result of the query, which is a list of all products that are currently on order, is written as a delimited text file, OUTPUT.TXT, in the current directory or folder.

```
If Application.OperatingSystem Like "*Win*" Then
    databaseName = "NWind"
Else            'Macintosh
    databaseName = "NorthWind"
End If
queryString = "SELECT * FROM product.dbf WHERE (product.ON_ORDER<>0)"
chan = SQLOpen("DSN=" & databaseName)
SQLExecQuery chan, queryString
SQLRetrieveToFile chan, "OUTPUT.TXT", True
SQLClose chan
```

Sqr Function

Description   Returns the square root of a number.

Syntax   **Sqr(*number*)**

The *number* named argument can be any valid numeric expression greater than or equal to 0.

Example   This example uses the **Sqr** function to calculate the square root of a number.

```
MySqr = Sqr(4)                    ' Returns 2.
MySqr = Sqr(23)                   ' Returns 4.795832.
MySqr = Sqr(0)                    ' Returns 0.
MySqr = Sqr(-4) ' Generates run-time error.
```

StandardFont Property

Applies To   **Application** Object.

Description   Returns or sets the standard font name as a string. Read-write.

Remarks   If you change the standard font using this property, the change does not take effect until you restart Microsoft Excel.

See Also   **StandardFontSize** Property.

Example

This example sets the standard font to Arial (in Windows) or Geneva (on the Macintosh).

```
If Application.OperatingSystem Like "*Macintosh*" Then
    Application.StandardFont = "Geneva"
Else
    Application.StandardFont = "Arial"
End If
```

StandardFontSize Property

Applies To   **Application** Object.

Description   Returns or sets the standard font size in points (1/72 inch). Read-write.

Remarks   If you change the standard font size using this property, the change does not take effect until you restart Microsoft Excel.

See Also   **StandardFont** Property.

Example   This example sets the standard font size to 12 points.

```
Application.StandardFontSize = 12
```

StandardHeight Property

Applies To   **Worksheet** Object.

Description   Returns the standard (default) height of all the rows in the worksheet, measured in points (1/72 inch). Read-only.

See Also   **Height** Property, **RowHeight** Property, **StandardWidth** Property.

Example   This example sets the height of row one on Sheet1 to the standard height.

```
Worksheets("Sheet1").Rows(1).RowHeight = _
    Worksheets("Sheet1").StandardHeight
```

StandardWidth Property

Applies To   **Worksheet** Object.

Description   Returns or sets the standard (default) width of all the columns in the worksheet, measured in characters of the normal font. Read-write.

Remarks   If the normal font is a proportional font, this property returns the column width measured in characters of the zero (0) character in the normal font.

See Also   **ColumnWidth** Property, **StandardHeight** Property, **Width** Property.

Example   This example sets the width of column one on Sheet1 to the standard width.

```
Worksheets("Sheet1").Columns(1).ColumnWidth = _
    Worksheets("Sheet1").StandardWidth
```

StartupPath Property

Applies To   **Application** Object.

Description   Returns the complete path of the startup directory, not including the final separator. Read-only.

Example   This example displays the full path to the Microsoft Excel startup folder.

```
MsgBox Application.StartupPath
```

Static Statement

Description   Used at the procedure level to declare variables and allocate storage space. Variables declared with the **Static** statement retain their value as long as the code is running.

Syntax	**Static** *varname*[([*subscripts*])][**As** *type*][,*varname*[([*subscripts*])][**As** *type*]] . . .

The **Static** statement syntax has these parts:

Part	Description
varname	Name of the variable; follows standard variable naming conventions.
subscripts	Dimensions of an array variable; up to 60 multiple dimensions may be declared. The *subscripts* argument uses the following syntax:
	[*lower* **To**] *upper* [,[*lower* **To**] *upper*] . . .
type	Data type of the variable; may be **Boolean**, **Integer**, **Long**, **Currency**, **Single**, **Double**, **Date**, **String** (for variable-length strings), **String** * *length* (for fixed-length strings), **Object**, **Variant**, a user-defined type, or an object type. Use a separate **As** *type* clause for each variable being defined.

Remarks

Once the module code is running, variables declared with the **Static** statement retain their value until the module is reset or restarted. Use the **Static** statement in nonstatic procedures to explicitly declare **Static** variables.

Use a **Static** statement within a procedure to declare the data type of a **Static** variable. For example, the following statement declares a fixed-size array of integers:

```
Static EmployeeNumber(200) As Integer
```

If you do not specify a data type or object type, and there is no **Def**type statement in the module, the variable is **Variant** by default.

Note The **Static** statement and the **Static** keyword affect the lifetime of variables differently. If you declare a procedure using the **Static** keyword (as in `Static Sub CountSales ()`), the storage space for all local variables within the procedure is allocated once and the value of the variables is preserved for the entire time the code is running. For nonstatic procedures, storage space for variables is allocated each time the procedure is called and released when the procedure is exited. The **Static** statement is used to declare variables within nonstatic procedures to preserve their value as long as the program is running.

When variables are initialized, a numeric variable is initialized to 0, a variable-length string is initialized to a zero-length string, and a fixed-length string is filled with zeros. **Variant** variables are initialized to **Empty**. Each element of a user-defined type variable is initialized as if it was a separate variable. A variable that refers to an object must be assigned an existing object using the **Set** statement before it can be used. Until it is assigned an object, the declared object variable has the special value **Nothing**, which indicates that it does not refer to any particular instance of an object.

> **Tip** When you use the **Static** statement in a procedure, it is a generally accepted programming practice to put the **Static** statement at the beginning of the procedure with any **Dim** statements.

See Also

Array Function, **Dim** Statement, **Function** Statement, **Option Base** Statement, **Private** Statement, **Public** Statement, **ReDim** Statement, **Sub** Statement.

Example

This example uses the **Static** statement to retain the value of a variable as long as module code is running.

```
' Function definition.
Function KeepTotal(Number)
    ' Only the variable Accumulate preserves its value between calls.
    Static Accumulate
    Accumulate = Accumulate + Number
    KeepTotal = Accumulate
End Function

' Static function definition.
Static Function MyFunction(Arg1, Arg2, Arg3)
    ' All local variables preserve value between function calls.
    Accumulate = Arg1 + Arg2 + Arg3
    Half = Accumulate / 2
    MyFunction = Half
End Function
```

This example uses the worksheet function **Pmt** to calculate a home mortgage loan payment. Note that this example uses the **InputBox** method instead of the **InputBox** function so that the method can perform type checking. The **Static** statements cause Visual Basic to retain the values of the three variables; these are displayed as default values the next time you run the example.

```
Static loanAmt
Static loanInt
Static loanTerm
loanAmt = Application.InputBox _
    (Prompt:="Loan amount (100,000 for example)", _
        Default:=loanAmt, Type:=1)
loanInt = Application.InputBox _
    (Prompt:="Annual interest rate (8.75 for example)", _
        Default:=loanInt, Type:=1)
loanTerm = Application.InputBox _
    (Prompt:="Term in years (30 for example)", _
        Default:=loanTerm, Type:=1)
payment = Application.Pmt(loanInt / 1200, loanTerm * 12, loanAmt)
MsgBox "Monthly payment is " & Format(payment, "Currency")
```

Status Property

Applies To   **RoutingSlip** Object.

Description   Indicates the status of the routing slip (one of **xlNotYetRouted**, **xlRoutingInProgress**, or **xlRoutingComplete**). Read-only.

Example   This example resets the routing slip for BOOK1.XLS if routing is complete.

```
With Workbooks("BOOK1.XLS").RoutingSlip
    If .Status = xlRoutingComplete Then
        .Reset
    Else
        MsgBox "Cannot reset routing; not yet complete."
    End If
End With
```

StatusBar Property

Applies To   **Application** Object, **MenuItem** Object, **ToolbarButton** Object.

Description   Returns or sets the text in the status bar. Read-write.

Remarks   For the **Application** object, this property returns **False** if Microsoft Excel has control of the status bar; set the property to **False** to restore the default status bar text. This works even if the status bar is hidden.

You can return or set the status bar text of custom menu items only, not built-in menu items.

Changing the macro assigned to a toolbar button with the **OnAction** property or the Assign Macro command (Tools menu) will reset the value of this property to match the status bar text of the macro.

See Also   **DisplayStatusBar** Property, **HelpContextID** Property, **HelpFile** Property.

Example   This example sets the status bar text to "Please be patient..." before it opens the workbook LARGE.XLS, and then it restores the text to the default.

```
oldStatusBar = Application.DisplayStatusBar
Application.DisplayStatusBar = True
Application.StatusBar = "Please be patient..."
Workbooks.Open filename:="LARGE.XLS"
Application.StatusBar = False
Application.DisplayStatusBar = oldStatusBar
```

This example adds a new menu item to the Help menu in the Visual Basic Module menu bar and then sets the status bar text, the Help filename, and the Help context ID for the new menu item (note that the **HelpFile** and **HelpContextId** properties are available only in Windows).

```
Set menuObj = MenuBars(xlModule).Menus("Help")
Set newMenuItem = menuObj.MenuItems.Add(Caption:="&Read Me First", _
        OnAction:="readmeMacro", _
        Before:=1)
newMenuItem.StatusBar = "Read this topic before you begin"
newMenuItem.HelpFile = "C:\xl5\vba_xl.hlp"
newMenuItem.HelpContextID = 65535
```

Stop Statement

Description   Suspends execution.

Syntax   **Stop**

Remarks   You can place **Stop** statements anywhere in procedures to suspend execution. Using the **Stop** statement is similar to setting a breakpoint in the code.

The **Stop** statement suspends execution, but unlike **End**, it doesn't close any files or clear variables.

See Also   **End** Statement.

Example   This example uses the **Stop** statement to suspend execution for each iteration through the **For**...**Next** loop.

```
For I = 1 To 10                    ' Start For...Next loop.
    Debug.Print I                  ' Print I to Debug window.
    Stop                           ' Stop each time through.
Next I
```

Str Function

Description   Returns a string representation of a number.

Syntax   **Str(*number*)**

The ***number*** named argument is any valid numeric expression.

Remarks
When numbers are converted to strings, a leading space is always reserved for the sign of *number*. If *number* is positive, the returned string contains a leading space and the plus sign is implied.

Use the **Format** function to convert numeric values you want formatted as dates, times, or currency or in other user-defined formats. Unlike **Str**, the **Format** function doesn't include a leading space for the sign of *number*.

Note The **Str** function recognizes only the period (.) as a valid decimal separator. When a possibility exists that different decimal separators may be used (for example, in international applications), you should use **CStr** to convert a number to a string.

See Also   **Format** Function.

StrComp Function

Description   Returns a value indicating the result of a string comparison.

Syntax   **StrComp**(*string1*,*string2*[,*compare*])

The **StrComp** function syntax has these parts:

Part	Description
string1	Any valid string expression.
string2	Any valid string expression.
compare	Number specifying the type of string comparison. Specify a **1** to perform a textual comparison. Specify a **0** (default) to perform a binary comparison. If *compare* is **Null**, an error occurs. If *compare* is omitted, the setting of **Option Compare** is used to determine the type of comparison.

Return Values

Value	Description
-1	*string1* is less than *string2*.
0	*string1* is equal to *string2*.
1	*string1* is greater than *string2*.
Null	*string1* or *string2* is **Null**.

Remarks

Note When **Option Compare Text** is specified, comparisons are textual and case-insensitive. When **Option Compare Binary** is specified, comparisons are strictly binary.

See Also

Option Compare Statement.

Example

This example uses the **StrComp** function to return the results of a string comparison. If 1 is supplied as the third argument, a textual comparison is performed; whereas, if the third argument is 0 or omitted, a binary comparison is performed.

```
MyStr1 = "ABCD": MyStr2 = "abcd"      ' Define variables.
MyComp = StrComp(MyStr1, MyStr2, 1)   ' Returns 0.
MyComp = StrComp(MyStr1, MyStr2, 0)   ' Returns -1.
MyComp = StrComp(MyStr2, MyStr1) ' Returns 1.
```

Strikethrough Property

Applies To

Font Object.

Description

True if the font is struck through. Read-write.

Example

This example sets the font in the active cell on Sheet1 to strikethrough.

```
Worksheets("Sheet1").Activate
ActiveCell.Font.Strikethrough = True
```

String Data Type

Description

There are two kinds of strings:

- Variable-length strings, which can contain up to approximately 2 billion (2^{31}) characters (approximately 64K (2^{16}) characters for Microsoft Windows version 3.1 and earlier).

- Fixed-length strings, which contain a declared number of characters (less than 64K).

The type-declaration character for **String** is **$** (character code 36). The codes for **String** characters range from 0 to 255. The first 128 characters (0-127) of the character set correspond to the letters and symbols on a standard U.S. keyboard. These first 128 characters are the same as those defined by the ASCII character set. The second 128 characters (128-255) represent special characters, such as letters in international alphabets, accents, currency symbols, and fractions.

See Also

CStr Function, Data Type Summary, **Def**type Statements, **String** Function, **Variant** Data Type.

String Function

Description

Returns a repeating character string of the length specified.

Syntax

String(*number*,*character*)

The **String** function syntax has these named-argument parts:

Part	Description
number	Length of the returned string. If *number* contains no valid data, **Null** is returned.
character	Character code specifying the character or string expression whose first character is used to build the return string. If *character* contains no valid data, **Null** is returned.

Remarks

If you specify a number for *character* greater than 255, **String** converts the number to a valid character code using the formula:

character **Mod** 256

See Also

Space Function, **String Data** Type.

Example

This example uses the **String** function to return repeating character strings of the length specified.

```
MyString = String(5, "*")       ' Returns "*****".
MyString = String(5, 42)        ' Returns "*****".
MyString = String(10, "ABC") ' Returns "AAAAAAAAAA".
```

Style Object

Description   Represents a range style description. The **Style** object contains all style attributes (font, number format, alignment, and so on) as properties. There are several built-in styles, including Normal, Currency, and Percent, which are listed in the Style Name box of the Style dialog box (Format menu). The **Style** object is a fast and efficient way to change several cell formatting properties on many cells at once.

Accessors   For a **Range** object, the **Style** property sets or returns the style used for that range. The following example applies the Percent style to cells A1:A10 on the worksheet named "Sheet1."

```
Worksheets("sheet1").Range("a1:a10").Style = "percent"
```

You can change the appearance of a cell by changing properties of the style applied to that cell. Keep in mind, however, that changing a style property will affect all cells already formatted with that style.

For the **Workbook** object, the **Style** object is a member of the **Styles** collection. The **Styles** collection contains all the defined styles for the workbook. Use the **Add** method to create a new style and add it to the collection. To access a single member of the collection, use the **Styles** method with the index number or name of the style as an argument.

Styles are sorted alphabetically by style name. The style index number represents the position of the specified style in the sorted list of style names. Styles(1) is the first style in the alphabetical list; Styles(Styles.Count) is the last. The following example creates a list of style names on worksheet one in the active workbook.

```
For i = 1 To ActiveWorkbook.Styles.Count
    Worksheets(1).Cells(i, 1) = ActiveWorkbook.Styles(i).Name
Next
```

You assign a name to a style when you create it. Use the **Name** property to return the style name. The following example changes the Normal style by setting its **Bold** property.

```
ActiveWorkbook.Styles("Normal").Font.Bold = True
```

For more information about creating and modifying a style, see the **Styles** object.

Properties	**AddIndent** Property, **Application** Property, **Creator** Property, **Font** Property, **FormulaHidden** Property, **HorizontalAlignment** Property, **IncludeAlignment** Property, **IncludeBorder** Property, **IncludeFont** Property, **IncludeNumber** Property, **IncludePatterns** Property, **IncludeProtection** Property, **Interior** Property, **Locked** Property, **Name** Property, **NameLocal** Property, **NumberFormat** Property, **NumberFormatLocal** Property, **Orientation** Property, **Parent** Property, **Value** Property, **VerticalAlignment** Property, **WrapText** Property.
Methods	**Borders** Method, **Delete** Method.

Style Property

Applies To	**Range** Object.
Description	Accessor. Returns a **Style** object that represents the style of the specified range. Read-only.
Example	This example applies the Normal style to cell A1 on Sheet1.

```
Worksheets("Sheet1").Range("A1").Style.Name = "Normal"
```

If cell B4 on Sheet1 currently has the Normal style applied, this example applies the Percent style.

```
If Worksheets("Sheet1").Range("B4").Style.Name = "Normal" Then
    Worksheets("Sheet1").Range("B4").Style.Name = "Percent"
End If
```

Styles Collection Object

Description	A collection of all the **Style** objects in the specified or active workbook. Each **Style** object represents a range style description. The **Style** object contains all style attributes (font, number format, alignment, and so on) as properties. There are several built-in styles, including Normal, Currency, and Percent, which are listed in the Style Name box of the Style dialog box (Format menu).

Accessors	Use the **Add** method to create a new style and add it to the collection. The following example creates a new style based on the Normal style, modifies the border and font, and then applies the new style to cells A25:A30.

```
Dim newStyle as Style
Set newStyle = ActiveWorkbook.Styles.Add(name:="bookman top border")
newStyle.Borders(xlTop).LineStyle = xlDouble
newStyle.Font.Bold = True
newStyle.Font.Name = "bookman"
Worksheets(1).Range("a25:a30").Style = "bookman top border"
```

Use the **Styles** method with an argument to access a single member of the collection or without an argument to access the entire collection at once.

Properties	**Application** Property, **Count** Property, **Creator** Property, **Parent** Property.
Methods	**Add** Method (**Styles** Collection), **Item** Method, **Merge** Method.

Styles Method

Applies To	**Workbook** Object.
Description	Accessor. Returns an object that represents a single style (a **Style** object, Syntax 1) or a collection of all the styles (a **Styles** object, Syntax 2) in the workbook. Read-only.
Syntax 1	*object*.**Styles**(*index*)
Syntax 2	*object*.**Styles**

object
   Required. The **Workbook** object.

index
   Required for Syntax 1. The name or number of the style to return.

Example	This example deletes the user-defined style "Stock Quote Style" from the active workbook.

```
ActiveWorkbook.Styles("Stock Quote Style").Delete
```

Sub Statement

Description	Declares the name, arguments, and code that form the body of a **Sub** procedure.

Syntax

[**Private** | **Public**][**Static**] **Sub** *name* [(*arglist*)]
    [*statements*]
    [**Exit Sub**]
    [*statements*]
End Sub

The **Sub** statement syntax has these parts:

Part	Description
Public	Indicates that the **Sub** procedure is accessible to all other procedures in all modules. If used in a private module (one that contains an **Option Private** statement) the procedure is not available outside the project.
Private	Indicates that the **Sub** procedure is accessible only to other procedures in the module where it is declared.
Static	Indicates that the **Sub** procedure's local variables are preserved between calls. The **Static** attribute doesn't affect variables that are declared outside the **Sub**, even if they are used in the procedure.
name	Name of the **Sub**; follows standard variable naming conventions.
arglist	List of variables representing arguments that are passed to the **Sub** procedure when it is called. Multiple variables are separated by commas.
statements	Any group of statements to be executed within the body of the **Sub** procedure.

The *arglist* argument has the following syntax and parts:

[[**Optional**][**ByVal** | **ByRef**][**ParamArray**] *varname*[( )] **As** *type*]

Part	Description
Optional	Indicates that an argument is not required. If used, all subsequent arguments in *arglist* must also be optional and declared using the **Optional** keyword. All **Optional** arguments must be **Variant**. **Optional** can't be used for any argument if **ParamArray** is used.
ByVal	Indicates that the argument is passed by value.
ByRef	Indicates that the argument is passed by reference.
ParamArray	Used only as the last argument in *arglist* to indicate that the final argument is an **Optional** array of **Variant** elements. The **ParamArray** keyword allows you to provide an arbitrary number of arguments. May not be used with **ByVal**, **ByRef**, or **Optional**.
varname	Name of the variable representing the argument; follows standard variable naming conventions.
type	Data type of the argument passed to the procedure; may be **Boolean**, **Integer**, **Long**, **Currency**, **Single**, **Double**, **Date**, **String** (variable length only), **Object**, **Variant**, a user-defined type, or an object type.

Remarks   If not explicitly specified using either **Public** or **Private**, **Sub** procedures are **Public** by default. If **Static** is not used, the value of local variables is not preserved between calls.

All executable code must be in procedures. You can't define a **Sub** procedure inside another **Sub**, **Function**, or **Property** procedure.

The **Exit Sub** keyword causes an immediate exit from a **Sub** procedure. Program execution continues with the statement following the statement that called the **Sub** procedure. Any number of **Exit Sub** statements can appear anywhere in a **Sub** procedure.

Like a **Function** procedure, a **Sub** procedure is a separate procedure that can take arguments, perform a series of statements, and change the value of its arguments. However, unlike a **Function** procedure, which returns a value, a **Sub** procedure can't be used in an expression.

You call a **Sub** procedure using the procedure name followed by the argument list. See the **Call** statement for specific information on how to call **Sub** procedures.

Caution **Sub** procedures can be recursive; that is, they can call themselves to perform a given task. However, recursion can lead to stack overflow. The **Static** keyword usually is not used with recursive **Sub** procedures.

Variables used in **Sub** procedures fall into two categories: those that are explicitly declared within the procedure and those that are not. Variables that are explicitly declared in a procedure (using **Dim** or the equivalent) are always local to the procedure. Other variables used but not explicitly declared in a procedure are also local unless they are explicitly declared at some higher level outside the procedure.

Caution A procedure can use a variable that is not explicitly declared in the procedure, but a name conflict can occur if anything you have defined at the module level has the same name. If your procedure refers to an undeclared variable that has the same name as another procedure, constant or variable, it is assumed that your procedure is referring to that module-level name. Explicitly declare variables to avoid this kind of conflict. You can use an **Option Explicit** statement to force explicit declaration of variables.

Note You can't use **GoSub**, **GoTo**, or **Return** to enter or exit a **Sub** procedure.

See Also   **Call** Statement, **Dim** Statement, **Function** Statement, **Option Explicit** Statement, **Property Get** Statement, **Property Let** Statement, **Property Set** Statement, **Static** Statement.

Example

This example uses the **Sub** statement to declare the name, arguments and code that form the body of a **Sub** procedure.

```
' Sub procedure definition.
Sub SubComputeArea(Length, Width)   ' Sub with two arguments.
    Dim Area As Double              ' Declare local variable.
    If Length = 0 Or Width = 0 Then ' If either argument = 0.
        Exit Sub                    ' Exit Sub immediately.
    End If
    Area = Length * Width           ' Calculate area of rectangle.
    Debug.Print Area                ' Print Area to Debug window.
End Sub
```

Subject Property

Applies To

AddIn Object, **Mailer** Object, **RoutingSlip** Object, **Workbook** Object.

Description

Returns or sets the subject for the object, as a string. Read-only for **AddIn**, read-write for **RoutingSlip** and **Workbook**.

Remarks

In Microsoft Excel for Windows 95, this property has been replaced by a built-in OLE document property. For more information about OLE document properties, see **BuiltinDocumentProperties**.

The subject for the **RoutingSlip** object is used as the subject of mail messages used to route the workbook. PowerTalk requires that a subject be present before the mailer can be sent.

You cannot use this property with an **AddIn** object that represents an XLL file or an add-in that was created with the Microsoft Excel 4.0 macro language.

See Also

Author Property, **Comments** Property, **Keywords** Property, **Title** Property.

Example

This example sets the subject for the active workbook.

```
ActiveWorkbook.Subject = "Data for my presentation in April"
```

This example sets the subject for a routing slip for the workbook BOOK1.XLS. To run this example, you must have Microsoft Mail for Windows or Microsoft Mail for the Macintosh installed.

```
Workbooks("BOOK1.XLS").HasRoutingSlip = True
With Workbooks("BOOK1.XLS").RoutingSlip
    .Delivery = xlOneAfterAnother
    .Recipients = Array("Adam Bendel", "Jean Selva", "Bernard Gabor")
    .Subject = "Here is BOOK1.XLS"
    .Message = "Here is the workbook. What do you think?"
End With
Workbooks("BOOK1.XLS").Route
```

This example sets the subject for a mailer in the PowerTalk mail system (Macintosh only). To run this example, you must have the PowerTalk mail system installed.

```
With Workbooks(1)
    .HasMailer = True
    With .Mailer
        .Subject = "Here is the workbook"
        .ToRecipients = Array("Jean")
        .CCRecipients = Array("Adam", "Bernard")
        .BCCRecipients = Array("Chris")
        .Enclosures = Array("TestFile")
    End With
    .SendMailer
End With
```

SubscribeTo Method

Applies To   **Range** Object.

Description   Apple Macintosh (running System 7 or later) only. Subscribes to a published edition.

Syntax   *object*.**SubscribeTo**(*edition*, *format*)

object
  Required. The **Range** object.

edition
  Required. The name of the edition, as a string, to which you want to subscribe.

format
  Optional. **xlPicture** to subscribe to a picture, **xlText** to subscribe to text.

See Also   **CreatePublisher** Method.

Example

This example subscribes to the "stock data" publisher.

```
Worksheets("Sheet1").Range("D1").SubscribeTo "stock data"
```

Subscript Property

Applies To	**Font** Object.
Description	**True** if the font is subscripted. Read-write.
Remarks	This property is **False** by default.
See Also	**Characters** Object, **Superscript** Property.
Example	This example makes the second character in cell A1 a subscript.

```
Worksheets("Sheet1").Range("A1").Characters(2, 1).Font.Subscript = True
```

Subtotal Method

Applies To

Range Object.

Description

Creates subtotals for the range (or current region if the range is a single cell).

For help about using the Subtotal worksheet function in Visual Basic, see "Using Worksheet Functions in Visual Basic" in online Help.

Syntax

object.**Subtotal**(*groupBy*, *function*, *totalList*, *replace*, *pageBreaks*, *summaryBelowData*)

object
　　Required. The **Range** object.

groupBy
　　Required. The field to group by, as a one-based integer offset. For more information, see the example.

function
　　Required. The subtotal function. Can be one of **xlAverage**, **xlCount**, **xlCountNums**, **xlMax**, **xlMin**, **xlProduct**, **xlStDev**, **xlStDevP**, **xlSum**, **xlVar**, or **xlVarP**.

totalList
　　Required. An array of one-based field offsets, indicating the fields to which the subtotals are added. For more information, see the example.

replace

Optional. If **True**, existing subtotals are replaced. If **False** or omitted, existing subtotals are not replaced.

pageBreaks

Optional. **True** to create page breaks after each group, **False** or omitted if no page breaks are created.

summaryBelowData

Optional. If **xlBelow** or omitted, the summary goes below detail. If **xlAbove**, the summary goes above detail.

See Also   **RemoveSubtotal** Method.

Example   This example creates subtotals for the selection on Sheet1. The subtotals are sums grouped by each change in field one, with the subtotals added to fields two and three.

```
Worksheets("Sheet1").Activate
Selection.Subtotal groupBy:=1, function:=xlSum, _
    totalList:=Array(2, 3)
```

Subtotals Property

Applies To   **PivotField** Object.

Description   Returns or sets an array of Boolean values corresponding to the subtotals showing with the specified field. This property is valid only for non-data fields. Read-write.

Remarks   This property returns an array of Boolean values, as shown in the following table.

Array element	Meaning
1	Automatic
2	Sum
3	Count
4	Average
5	Max
6	Min
7	Product
8	Count Nums

Array element	Meaning
9	StdDev
10	StdDevp
11	Var
12	Varp

If an element is **True**, the field shows that subtotal. If element one (Automatic) is **True**, all other values are set to **False**.

Example

This example sets the field that contains the active cell to show Sum subtotals.

```
Worksheets("Sheet1").Activate
ActiveCell.PivotField.Subtotals = _
    Array(False, True, False, False, False, False, _
    False, False, False, False, False, False)
```

SubType Property

Applies To

Chart Object, **ChartGroup** Object.

Description

Returns or sets the subtype for a single chart group or for all chart groups in the chart. Read-write.

Remarks

Set the **SubType** property *after* you set the **Type** property. Each type supports different subtypes (for example, a column chart type can have clustered, stacked, or percent subtypes). The easiest way to obtain the number of the subtype is to record the subtype formatting using the macro recorder.

Example

This example sets the subtype for radar group one in Chart1. The example should be run on a 2-D chart.

```
Charts("Chart1").RadarGroups(1).SubType = 2
```

Summary Property

Applies To

Range Object.

Description

True if the range is an outlining summary row or column. The range should be a row or a column. Read-only.

Example

This example formats row four on Sheet1 as bold and italic if it is an outlining summary column.

```
With Worksheets("Sheet1").Rows(4)
    If .Summary = True Then
        .Font.Bold = True
        .Font.Italic = True
    End If
End With
```

SummaryColumn Property

Applies To   **Outline** Object.

Description   Returns or sets the location of the summary columns in the outline, as shown in the following table. Read-write.

Value	Meaning
xlLeft	The summary column will be to the left of the detail columns in the outline.
xlRight	The summary column will be to the right of the detail columns in the outline.

Example

This example creates an outline with automatic styles, the summary row above the detail rows, and the summary column to the right of the detail columns.

```
Worksheets("Sheet1").Activate
Selection.AutoOutline
With ActiveSheet.Outline
    .SummaryRow = xlAbove
    .SummaryColumn = xlRight
    .AutomaticStyles = True
End With
```

SummaryRow Property

Applies To   **Outline** Object.

Description	Returns or sets the location of the summary rows in the outline, as shown in the following table. Read-write.

Value	Meaning
xlAbove	The summary row will be above the detail columns in the outline.
xlBelow	The summary row will be below the detail columns in the outline.

Remarks	Set **SummaryRow** to **xlAbove** for Microsoft Word-style outlines, where category headers are above the detail. Set **SummaryRow** to **xlBelow** for accounting-style outlines, where summations are below the detailed information.
Example	This example creates an outline with automatic styles, the summary row above the detail rows, and the summary column to the right of the detail columns.

```
Worksheets("Sheet1").Activate
Selection.AutoOutline
With ActiveSheet.Outline
    .SummaryRow = xlAbove
    .SummaryColumn = xlRight
    .AutomaticStyles = True
End With
```

Superscript Property

Applies To	**Font** Object.
Description	**True** if the font is superscripted. Read-write.
Remarks	This property is **False** by default.
See Also	**Characters** Object, **Subscript** Property.
Example	This example makes the last character in cell A1 a superscript.

```
n = Worksheets("Sheet1").Range("A1").Characters.Count
Worksheets("Sheet1").Range("A1").Characters(n, 1).Font.Superscript = _
        True
```

SurfaceGroup Property

Applies To	**Chart** Object.

Description   Accessor. Returns a **ChartGroup** object that represents the surface chart group of a 3-D chart. Read-only.

Example   This example converts the 3-D surface group in Chart1 to a 3-D area group. The example should be run on a 3-D chart.

```
Charts("Chart1").SurfaceGroup.Type = xl3DArea
```

Tab Function

Description   Used with the **Print #** statement or the **Print** method to position output.

Syntax   **Tab**[(*n*)]

The *n* argument is the column number to tab to before displaying or printing the next expression in a list. If omitted, **Tab** moves the cursor to the beginning of the next print zone. This allows **Tab** to be used instead of a comma in locales where the comma is used as a decimal separator.

Remarks   If the current print position on the current line is greater than *n*, **Tab** skips to the *n*th column on the next output line. If *n* is less than 1, **Tab** moves the print position to column 1. If *n* is greater than the output-line width, **Tab** calculates the next print position using the formula:

n **Mod** *width*

For example, if width is 80 and you specify **Tab**(90), the next print will start at column 10 (the remainder of 90/80). If *n* is less than the current print position, printing begins on the next line at the calculated print position. If the calculated print position is greater than the current print position, printing begins at the calculated print position on the same line.

The leftmost print position on an output line is always 1. When you use the **Print #** statement to print to files, the rightmost print position is the current width of the output file, which you can set using the **Width #** statement.

Note Make sure your tabular columns are wide enough to accommodate wider letters.

When you use the **Tab** function with the **Print** method, the print surface is divided into uniform, fixed-width columns. The width of each column is an average of the width of all characters in the point size for the chosen font. However, there is no correlation between the number of characters printed and the number of fixed-width columns those characters occupy. For example, the uppercase letter W occupies more than one fixed-width column and the lowercase letter I occupies less.

See Also

Print # Statement, **Print** Method, **Space** Function, **Spc** Function, **Width #** Statement.

Example

This example uses the **Tab** function to position output in a file or in the Debug window.

```
' The Tab function can be used with the Print # statement.
Open "TESTFILE" For Output As #1     ' Open file for output.
' The second word prints at column 20.
Print #1, "Hello"; Tab(20); "World."
' If the argument is omitted, cursor is moved to the next print zone.
Print #1, "Hello"; Tab ; "World"
Close #1                            ' Close file.

' The Tab function can also be used with the Print method.
' The following statement prints text starting at column 10.
Debug.Print Tab(10); "10 columns from start."
```

Table Method

Applies To

Range Object.

Description

Creates a data table based on input values and formulas that you define on a worksheet.

Syntax

object.**Table**(*rowInput*, *columnInput*)

object
  Required. The object to which this method applies.

rowInput
  Optional. A single cell to use as the row input for your table.

columnInput
  Optional. A single cell to use as the column input for your table.

Remarks

Use data tables to perform a what-if analysis by changing certain constant values on your worksheet to see how values in other cells are affected.

Example   This example creates a formatted multiplication table in cells A1:K11 on Sheet1.

```
Set dataTableRange = Worksheets("Sheet1").Range("A1:K11")
Set rowInputCell = Worksheets("Sheet1").Range("A12")
Set columnInputCell = Worksheets("Sheet1").Range("A13")

Worksheets("Sheet1").Range("A1").Formula = "=A12*A13"
For i = 2 To 11
    Worksheets("Sheet1").Cells(i, 1) = i - 1
    Worksheets("Sheet1").Cells(1, i) = i - 1
Next i
dataTableRange.Table rowInputCell, columnInputCell
With Worksheets("Sheet1").Range("A1").CurrentRegion
    .Rows(1).Font.Bold = True
    .Columns(1).Font.Bold = True
    .Columns.AutoFit
End With
```

TableRange1 Property

Applies To   **PivotTable** Object.

Description   Accessor. Returns a **Range** object that represents the range that contains the entire PivotTable, but does not include page fields. Read-only.

Remarks   The **TableRange2** property includes page fields.

Example   This example selects the PivotTable, except that its page fields are not selected.

```
Worksheets("Sheet1").Activate
Range("A3").PivotTable.TableRange1.Select
```

TableRange2 Property

Applies To   **PivotTable** Object.

Description   Accessor. Returns a **Range** object that represents the range that includes the entire PivotTable, including page fields. Read-only.

Remarks   The **TableRange1** property does not include page fields.

Example   This example selects the PivotTable, including its page fields.

```
Worksheets("Sheet1").Activate
Range("A3").PivotTable.TableRange2.Select
```

TabRatio Property

Applies To   **Window** Object.

Description   Returns or sets the ratio of the width of the workbook tab area to the width of the window horizontal scroll bar (as a number between 0 (zero) and 1; the default value is 0.75). Read-write.

Remarks   This property has no effect when **DisplayWorkbookTabs** is set to **False** (its value is retained, but it has no effect on the display).

See Also   **DisplayHorizontalScrollBar** Property, **DisplayWorkbookTabs** Property.

Example   This example makes the workbook tabs half the width of the horizontal scroll bar.

```
ActiveWindow.TabRatio = 0.5
```

Tan Function

Description   Returns the tangent of an angle.

Syntax   **Tan(*number*)**

The ***number*** named argument can be any valid numeric expression that expresses an angle in radians.

Remarks   **Tan** takes an angle and returns the ratio of two sides of a right triangle. The ratio is the length of the side opposite an angle divided by the length of the side adjacent to the angle.

To convert degrees to radians, multiply degrees by pi/180. To convert radians to degrees, multiply radians by 180/pi.

See Also   **Atn** Function, **Cos** Function, Derived Math Functions, **Sin** Function.

Example   This example uses the **Tan** function to return the tangent of an angle.

```
MyAngle = 1.3                          ' Define angle in radians.
MyCotangent = 1 / Tan(MyAngle)        ' Calculate cotangent.
```

TemplatesPath Property

Applies To   **Application** Object.

Description   Returns the local path where templates are stored. This property is available only in Microsoft Excel for Windows 95. Read-only.

Example   This example returns the path where templates are stored.

```
Msgbox Application.TemplatesPath
```

Text Property

Applies To   **AxisTitle** Object, **Button** Object, **Buttons** Collection, **Characters** Object, **ChartTitle** Object, **CheckBox** Object, **DataLabel** Object, **DialogFrame** Object, **DrawingObjects** Collection, **DropDown** Object, **DropDowns** Collection, **EditBox** Object, **EditBoxes** Collection, **GroupBox** Object, **GroupBoxes** Collection, **Label** Object, **Labels** Collection, **OptionButton** Object, **OptionButtons** Collection, **Range** Object, **TextBox** Object, **TextBoxes** Collection.

Description   Returns or sets the text for the specified object, as shown in the following table. Read-write, except for the **Range** object, where this property is read-only. The **Text** property will not work with a drop-down, but it will work with a combination drop-down edit.

Object	Text
AxisTitle, **ChartTitle**	The title text.
Button	The button text.
Characters	The text of this range of characters.
Controls	The control text (check box, dialog frame, drop down, edit box, group box, label, and option button).
DataLabel	The data label text.
Range	The actual text appearing in a cell, as a string. For example, if a cell is formatted to show dollar signs, returning the text of a cell will show the dollar sign. This can be used to create readable text representations of the values on a worksheet. Read-only.
TextBox	The text in the text box.

Example   This example sets the text in text box one on Sheet1. Existing text, if any, is deleted before the new text is set.

```
Worksheets("Sheet1").TextBoxes(1).Text = "This is a test"
```

This example sets the text for the chart title of Chart1.

```
With Charts("Chart1")
    .HasTitle = True
    .ChartTitle.Text = "First Quarter Sales"
End With
```

This example sets the axis title text for the category axis in Chart1.

```
With Charts("Chart1").Axes(xlCategory)
    .HasTitle = True
    .AxisTitle.Text = "Month"
End With
```

This example replaces the text of the label named "Label 1" on the dialog sheet Dialog1 with the current date and time.

```
DialogSheets("Dialog1").Labels("Label 1").Text = Now()
```

This example erases the text on every button on Sheet1.

```
Worksheets("Sheet1").Buttons.Text = ""
```

This example illustrates the difference between the **Text** and **Value** properties of cells that contain formatted numbers.

```
Set c = Worksheets("Sheet1").Range("B14")
c.Value = 1198.3
c.NumberFormat = "$#,##0_);($#,##0)"
MsgBox c.Value
MsgBox c.Text
```

For help about using the **Text** worksheet function in Visual Basic, see "Using Worksheet Functions in Visual Basic" in online Help.

TextBox Object

Description   Represents a text box graphic object (a rectangle with text in it) on a chart sheet, dialog sheet, or worksheet.

Accessors

The **TextBox** object is a member of the **TextBoxes** collection. The **TextBoxes** collection contains all the **TextBox** objects on a single sheet. Use the **Add** method to create a new text box and add it to the collection.

To access a single member of the collection, use the **TextBoxes** method with the index number or name of the text box as an argument.

The following example sets the formula for text box one on the worksheet named "Sheet1." This links the text box to cell A10 on the worksheet. When the contents of cell A10 change, the new contents are placed in the text box.

```
Worksheets("sheet1").TextBoxes(1).Formula = "=a10"
```

The text box name is shown in the Name Box when the text box is selected. Use the **Name** property to set or return the name. The following example places a dashed border around the text box named "Text 1" on the worksheet named "Sheet1."

```
Worksheets("sheet1").TextBoxes("text 1").Border.LineStyle = xlDash
```

Properties

AddIndent Property, **Application** Property, **AutoSize** Property, **Border** Property, **BottomRightCell** Property, **Caption** Property, **Creator** Property, **Enabled** Property, **Font** Property, **Formula** Property, **Height** Property, **HorizontalAlignment** Property, **Index** Property, **Interior** Property, **Left** Property, **Locked** Property, **LockedText** Property, **Name** Property, **OnAction** Property, **Orientation** Property, **Parent** Property, **Placement** Property, **PrintObject** Property, **RoundedCorners** Property, **Shadow** Property, **Text** Property, **Top** Property, **TopLeftCell** Property, **VerticalAlignment** Property, **Visible** Property, **Width** Property, **ZOrder** Property.

Methods

BringToFront Method, **Characters** Method, **CheckSpelling** Method, **Copy** Method, **CopyPicture** Method, **Cut** Method, **Delete** Method, **Duplicate** Method, **Select** Method, **SendToBack** Method.

TextBoxes Collection Object

Description

A collection of all the **TextBox** objects (rectangles with text inside) on the specified chart sheet, dialog sheet, or worksheet.

Accessors

Use the **Add** method to create a new text box and add it to the collection. The following example creates a new text box on the worksheet named "Sheet1." The new text box is twice as wide and three times as high as cell C5; its upper-left corner is positioned at the upper-left corner of cell C5.

```
Dim r As Range
Set r = Worksheets("sheet1").Range("c5")
Worksheets("sheet1").TextBoxes.Add r.Left, r.Top, _
    2 * r.Width, 3 * r.Height
```

Use the **TextBoxes** method with an argument to access a single member of the collection or without an argument to access the entire collection at once. The following example deletes all of the text boxes on the worksheet named "Sheet1."

```
Worksheets("sheet1").TextBoxes.Delete
```

Properties

AddIndent Property, **Application** Property, **AutoSize** Property, **Border** Property, **Caption** Property, **Count** Property, **Creator** Property, **Enabled** Property, **Font** Property, **Formula** Property, **Height** Property, **HorizontalAlignment** Property, **Interior** Property, **Left** Property, **Locked** Property, **LockedText** Property, **OnAction** Property, **Orientation** Property, **Parent** Property, **Placement** Property, **PrintObject** Property, **RoundedCorners** Property, **Shadow** Property, **Text** Property, **Top** Property, **VerticalAlignment** Property, **Visible** Property, **Width** Property, **ZOrder** Property.

Methods

Add Method (Graphic Objects and Controls), **BringToFront** Method, **Characters** Method, **CheckSpelling** Method, **Copy** Method, **CopyPicture** Method, **Cut** Method, **Delete** Method, **Duplicate** Method, **Group** Method, **Item** Method, **Select** Method, **SendToBack** Method.

TextBoxes Method

Applies To

Chart Object, **DialogSheet** Object, **Worksheet** Object.

Description

Accessor. Returns an object that represents a single text box (a **TextBox** object, Syntax 1) or a collection of text boxes (a **TextBoxes** object, Syntax 2) on the sheet. Read-only.

Syntax 1

object.**TextBoxes**(*index*)

Syntax 2

object.**TextBoxes**

object
Required. The object containing the text boxes.

index
    Required for Syntax 1. The name or number of the text box.

Example   This example sets the text that appears in text box one on Sheet1.

```
Worksheets("Sheet1").TextBoxes(1).Caption = "Text Box One"
```

This example deletes all text boxes on Sheet1.

```
Worksheets("Sheet1").TextBoxes.Delete
```

TextToColumns Method

Applies To   **Range** Object.

Description   Parses a column of cells containing text into several columns

Syntax   *object*.**TextToColumns**(*destination*, *dataType*, *textQualifier*, *consecutiveDelimiter*, *tab*, *semicolon*, *comma*, *space*, *other*, *otherChar*, *fieldInfo*)

object
    Required. The **Range** object.

destination
    Optional. A range that specifies where Microsoft Excel will place the results. If the range is larger than a single cell, the top leftmost cell is used.

dataType
    Optional. Specifies the format of the text to split into columns. Can be either **xlDelimited** or **xlFixedWidth**. The default is **xlDelimited**.

textQualifier
    Optional. Specifies the text qualifier. Can be one of **xlDoubleQuote**, **xlSingleQuote**, or **xlNone**. The default is **xlDoubleQuote**.

consecutiveDelimiter
    Optional. **True** if consecutive delimiters should be considered as one delimiter. The default is **False**.

tab
    Optional. **True** if *dataType* is **xlDelimited** and the tab character is a delimiter. The default is **False**.

semicolon
    Optional. True if *dataType* is **xlDelimited** and the semicolon character is a delimiter. The default is **False**.

comma

Optional. True if *dataType* is **xlDelimited** and the comma character is a delimiter. The default is **False**.

space

Optional. True if *dataType* is **xlDelimited** and the space character is a delimiter. The default is **False**.

other

Optional. **True** if *dataType* is **xlDelimited** and the character specified by the *otherChar* argument is a delimiter. The default is **False**.

otherChar

Optional (required if *other* is **True**). Specifies the delimiter character when *other* is True. If more than one character is specified, only the first character of the string is used, remaining characters are ignored.

fieldInfo

Optional. An array containing parse information for the individual columns of data. The interpretation depends on the value of *dataType*.

When the data is delimited, this argument is an array of two-element arrays, with each two-element array specifying the conversion options for a particular column. The first element is the column number (one based), and the second element is one of the following numbers specifying how the column is parsed:

1   General

2   Text

3   MDY date

4   DMY date

5   YMD date

6   MYD date

7   DYM date

8   YDM date

9   Skip the column

The column specifiers may be in any order. If a column specifier is not present for a particular column in the input data, the column is parsed using the General setting. This example causes the third column to be skipped, the first column to be parsed as text, and the remaining columns in the source data to be parsed with the General setting.

```
Array(Array(3, 9), Array(1, 2))
```

If the source data has fixed-width columns, the first element of each two-element array specifies the starting character position in the column (as an integer; character zero is the first character). The second element of the two-element array specifies the parse option for the column as a number from one through nine, as listed above.

The following example parses two columns from a fixed-width file, with the first column starting at the beginning of the line and extending for 10 characters. The second column starts at position 15 and goes to the end of the line. To avoid including the characters between position 10 and position 15, a skipped column entry is added.

```
Array(Array(0, 1), Array(10, 9), Array(15, 1))
```

See Also   **OpenText** Method.

Example   This example converts the contents of the Clipboard, which contains a space-delimited text table, into separate columns on Sheet1. You can create a simple space-delimited table in Notepad or WordPad (or another text editor), copy the text table to the Clipboard, switch to Microsoft Excel, and then run this example.

```
Worksheets("Sheet1").Activate
ActiveSheet.Paste
Selection.TextToColumns DataType:=xlDelimited, _
    consecutiveDelimiter:=True, Space:=True
```

ThisWorkbook Property

Applies To   **Application** Object.

Description   Accessor. Returns a **Workbook** object that represents the workbook where the current macro code is running. Read-only.

Remarks   Use this property to refer to the workbook containing your macro code. **ThisWorkbook** is the only way to refer to an add-in workbook from inside the add-in itself. The **ActiveWorkbook** property does not return the add-in workbook (it returns the workbook *calling* the add-in), and the **Workbooks** method may fail because the workbook name probably changed when you created the add-in. **ThisWorkbook** always returns the workbook where the code is running.

For example, use the following code to activate a dialog sheet stored in your add-in workbook.

```
ThisWorkbook.DialogSheets(1).Show
```

This property can be used only from inside Microsoft Excel. You cannot use this property to access a workbook from another application.

Example   This example closes the workbook that contains the example code. Changes to the workbook, if any, are not saved.

```
ThisWorkbook.Close savechanges:=False
```

TickLabelPosition Property

Applies To   **Axis** Object.

Description   Describes the position of tick labels on the specified axis (one of **xlNone**, **xlLow**, **xlHigh**, or **xlNextToAxis**). Read-write.

See Also   **MajorTickMark** Property, **MinorTickMark** Property, **TickLabels** Property, **TickLabelSpacing** Property, **TickMarkSpacing** Property.

Example   This example sets tick labels on the category axis in Chart1 to the high position (above the chart).

```
Charts("Chart1").Axes(xlCategory).TickLabelPosition = xlHigh
```

TickLabels Object

Description   Represents the tick-mark labels associated with tick marks on a chart axis. There is no single **TickLabel** object; you must access all of the tick-mark labels at once.

Tick-mark label text for the category (x) axis comes from the name of the associated category in the chart. The default tick-mark label text for the category (x) axis is the number indicating the position of the category from the left. To change the number of unlabelled tick marks between tick-mark labels, you must change the **TickLabelSpacing** property for the category (x) axis.

Tick-mark label text for the value (y) axis is calculated based on the **MajorUnit**, **MinimumScale**, and **MaximumScale** properties of the value (y) axis. You must change the values of these properties to change the tick-mark label text for the value (y) axis.

Accessors   Use the **TickLabels** property to return the tick-mark labels for an axis. The following example sets the number format for the tick-mark labels on the value (y) axis in embedded chart one on the worksheet named "Sheet1."

```
Worksheets("sheet1").ChartObjects(1).Chart _
    .Axes(xlValue).TickLabels.NumberFormat = "0.00"
```

Properties   **Application** Property, **Creator** Property, **Font** Property, **Name** Property, **NumberFormat** Property, **NumberFormatLinked** Property, **Orientation** Property, **Parent** Property.

Methods   **Delete** Method, **Select** Method.

TickLabels Property

Applies To   **Axis** Object.

Description   Accessor. Returns a **TickLabels** object that represents the tick labels for the specified axis. Read-only.

See Also   **MajorTickMark** Property, **MinorTickMark** Property, **TickLabelPosition** Property, **TickLabelSpacing** Property, **TickMarkSpacing** Property.

Example   This example sets the color of the tick label font for the value axis in Chart1.

```
Charts("Chart1").Axes(xlValue).TickLabels.Font.ColorIndex = 3
```

TickLabelSpacing Property

Applies To   **Axis** Object.

Description   Returns or sets the number of categories or series between tick labels. Applies only to category and series axes. Read-write.

Remarks   This property applies to the category and series axes only. Label spacing on the value axis is always calculated by Microsoft Excel.

See Also   **MajorTickMark** Property, **MinorTickMark** Property, **TickLabelPosition** Property, **TickLabels** Property, **TickMarkSpacing** Property.

Example   This example sets the number of categories between tick labels on the category axis in Chart1.

```
Charts("Chart1").Axes(xlCategory).TickLabelSpacing = 10
```

TickMarkSpacing Property

Applies To   **Axis** Object.

Description   Returns or sets the number of categories or series between tick marks. Applies only to category and series axes. Read-write.

Remarks   This property applies to the category and series axes only. Use the **MajorUnit** and **MinorUnit** properties to set tick mark spacing on the value axis.

See Also   **MajorTickMark** Property, **MajorUnit** Property, **MinorTickMark** Property, **MinorUnit** Property, **TickLabelPosition** Property, **TickLabels** Property, **TickLabelSpacing** Property.

Example   This example sets the number of categories between tick marks on the category axis in Chart1.

```
Charts("Chart1").Axes(xlCategory).TickMarkSpacing = 10
```

Time Function

Description   Returns the current system time.

Syntax   **Time**

Remarks   To set the system time, use the **Time** statement.

See Also   **Date** Function, **Date** Statement, **Time** Statement, **Timer** Function.

Example   This example uses the **Time** function to return the current system time.

```
MyTime = Time    ' Return current system time.
```

Time Statement

Description   Sets the system time.

Syntax   **Time** = *time*

The *time* argument is limited to expressions that can represent a time. If *time* contains no valid data, **Null** is returned.

Remarks   If *time* is a string, **Time** attempts to convert it to a time using the time separators you specified for your system. If it can't be converted to a valid time, an error occurs.

> **Note** If you use the **Time** statement to set the time on computers using versions of MS-DOS earlier than version 3.3, the change remains in effect only until you change it again or turn off your computer. Many computers have a battery-powered CMOS RAM that retains date and time information when the computer is turned off. However, to permanently change the time on computers running earlier versions of MS-DOS, you may have to use your Setup disk or perform some equivalent action. Refer to the documentation for your particular system.

See Also   **Date** Function, **Date** Statement, **Time** Function.

Example   This example uses the **Time** statement to set the computer system time to a user-defined time.

```
MyTime = #4:35:17 PM#                 ' Assign a time.
Time = MyTime    ' Set system time to MyTime.
```

Timer Function

Description   Returns the number of seconds elapsed since midnight.

Syntax   **Timer**

Remarks   The return value of the **Timer** function is automatically used with the **Randomize** statement to generate a seed for the **Rnd** (random-number) function.

See Also   **Randomize** Statement, **Rnd** Function, **Time** Function.

Example   This example uses the **Timer** function to record the number of seconds taken to print output to the Debug window.

```
Start = Timer                         ' Set start time.
For I = 1 to 50                       ' Loop 50 times.
    Debug.Print I                     ' Print to Debug window.
Next I
Finish = Timer                        ' Set end time.
TotalTime = Finish - Start   ' Calculate total time.
```

TimeSerial Function

Description   Returns a date containing the time for a specific hour, minute, and second.

Syntax   **TimeSerial**(*hour*,*minute*,*second*)

The **TimeSerial** function syntax has these named-argument parts:

Part	Description
hour	Number between 0 (12:00 A.M.) and 23 (11:00 P.M.), inclusive, or a numeric expression.
minute	Number between 0 and 59, inclusive, or a numeric expression.
second	Number between 0 and 59, inclusive, or a numeric expression.

Remarks   To specify a time, such as 11:59:59, the range of numbers for each **TimeSerial** argument should be in the normally accepted range for the unit; that is, 0-23 for hours and 0-59 for minutes and seconds. However, you can also specify relative times for each argument using any numeric expression that represents some number of hours, minutes, or seconds before or after a certain time. The following example uses expressions instead of absolute time numbers. The **TimeSerial** function returns a time for 15 minutes before (0 - 15) six hours before noon (12 - 6), or 5:45:00 A.M.

```
TimeSerial(12 - 6, 0 - 15, 0)
```

If the time specified by the three arguments, either directly or by expression, falls outside the acceptable range of times, an error occurs.

See Also   **DateSerial** Function, **DateValue** Function, **Hour** Function, **Minute** Function, **Now** Function, **Second** Function, **TimeValue** Function.

Example   This example uses the **TimeSerial** function to return a time for the specified hour, minute and second.

```
' MyTime contains the time for 4:35:17 PM
MyTime = TimeSerial(16, 35, 17)  ' Return time.
```

TimeValue Function

Description   Returns a time.

Syntax   **TimeValue**(*time*)

The *time* named argument is normally a string expression representing a time from 0:00:00 (12:00:00 A.M.) to 23:59:59 (11:59:59 P.M.), inclusive. However, *time* can also be any expression that represents a time in that range. If *time* contains no valid data, **Null** is returned.

Remarks   You can enter valid times using a 12- or 24-hour clock. For example, `"2:24PM"` and `"14:24"` are both valid time arguments.

If the *time* argument contains date information, **TimeValue** doesn't this information. However, if *time* includes invalid date information, an error occurs.

See Also   **DateSerial** Function, **DateValue** Function, **Hour** Function, **Minute** Function, **Now** Function, **Second** Function, **TimeSerial** Function.

Example   This example uses the **TimeValue** function to convert a string to a time. In general, it is bad programming practice to hard code dates/ times as strings as shown in this example. Use date literals instead.

```
MyTime = TimeValue("4:35:17 PM") ' Return time.
```

Title Property

Applies To   **AddIn** Object, **Workbook** Object.

Description   Returns or sets the long, descriptive title for the object, as a string. Read-only for **AddIn**, read-write for **Workbook**.

See Also   **Author** Property, **AxisTitle** Property, **ChartTitle** Property, **Comments** Property, **Keywords** Property.

Example   This example displays the title and filename of every add-in.

```
For Each a In AddIns
    MsgBox a.Title & " has the filename " & a.Name
Next a
```

This example sets the title of the active workbook.

```
ActiveWorkbook.Title = "Weekly Sales Summary"
```

In Microsoft Excel for Windows 95, this property has been replaced by a built-in OLE document property. For more information about OLE document properties, see **BuiltinDocumentProperties**.

Toolbar Object

Description   Represents a toolbar, either built-in or custom.

Accessors   The **Toolbar** object is a member of the **Toolbars** collection. Use the **Add** method to create a new toolbar and add it to the collection. To access a single member of the collection, use the **Toolbars** method with the index number or name of the toolbar as an argument.

The toolbar index number represents the position of the toolbar name in the list shown in the Toolbars dialog box (Toolbars command, View menu). Toolbars(1) is at the top of the list; Toolbars(Toolbars.Count) is at the bottom. Built-in toolbars are shown first, with custom toolbars arranged alphabetically after the last built-in toolbar.

The following example moves the Standard toolbar to the bottom of the Microsoft Excel window.

```
Toolbars(1).Position = xlBottom
```

The **Name** property returns the toolbar name (as shown in the Toolbars dialog box). The **Name** property is read-only; you cannot change the name of a built-in or custom toolbar. The following example makes the Forms toolbar visible.

```
Toolbars("forms").Visible = True
```

The following example creates a table on worksheet one in the active workbook that contains the names of all the **ToolbarButton** objects in all the **Toolbar** objects in the application. The column headings are the **Toolbar** object names, and the column entries under each heading are the names of the **ToolbarButton** objects in that **Toolbar** object. **ToolbarButton** objects that represent gaps (extended spaces between buttons) have no name; their corresponding cells are therefore blank.

```
Sub EnumerateToolbars()
    Worksheets(1).Activate
    For col = 1 To Toolbars.Count
        Cells(1, col) = Toolbars(col).Name
        For rw = 2 To Toolbars(col).ToolbarButtons.Count + 1
            Cells(rw, col) = Toolbars(col).ToolbarButtons(rw - 1).Name
        Next
    Next
End Sub
```

Properties   **Application** Property, **BuiltIn** Property, **Creator** Property, **Height** Property, **Left** Property, **Name** Property, **Parent** Property, **Position** Property, **Protection** Property, **Top** Property, **Visible** Property, **Width** Property.

Methods   **Delete** Method, **Reset** Method, **ToolbarButtons** Method.

ToolbarButton Object

Description   Represents a button or a gap (an extended space between buttons) on a toolbar. Do not confuse the **ToolbarButton** object with the **Button** object, which is a custom button graphic object on a chart sheet, dialog sheet, or worksheet.

Accessors   The **ToolbarButton** object is a member of the **ToolbarButtons** collection. The **ToolbarButtons** collection contains all the **ToolbarButton** objects on a single toolbar. Use the **Add** method to create a new toolbar button and add it to the collection. For a complete list of available toolbar buttons, see "Toolbar Button ID Values" in online Help.

To access a single member of the collection, use the **ToolbarButtons** method with the toolbar button index number as an argument.

The index number represents the position of the toolbar button on the toolbar. ToolbarButtons(1) is the first (leftmost) button on the toolbar; ToolbarButtons(ToolbarButtons.Count) is the last. The following example deletes the last button on the Standard toolbar.

```
With Toolbars("standard")
    .ToolbarButtons(.ToolbarButtons.Count).Delete
End With
```

The following example creates a table on worksheet one in the active workbook. The table contains the names of all the **ToolbarButton** objects in all the **Toolbar** objects in the application. The column headings are the **Toolbar** object names, and the column entries under each heading are the names of the **ToolbarButton** objects in that **Toolbar** object. **ToolbarButton** objects that represent gaps (extended spaces between buttons) have no name; their corresponding cells are therefore blank.

```
Sub EnumerateToolbars()
    Worksheets(1).Activate
    For col = 1 To Toolbars.Count
        Cells(1, col) = Toolbars(col).Name
        For rw = 2 To Toolbars(col).ToolbarButtons.Count + 1
            Cells(rw, col) = Toolbars(col).ToolbarButtons(rw - 1).Name
        Next
    Next
End Sub
```

Remarks   The **Name** property sets or returns the toolbar button tool tip text (the text displayed when the user moves the mouse cursor over the toolbar button).

Properties	**Application** Property, **BuiltIn** Property, **BuiltInFace** Property, **Creator** Property, **Enabled** Property, **HelpContextID** Property, **HelpFile** Property, **Id** Property, **IsGap** Property, **Name** Property, **OnAction** Property, **Parent** Property, **Pushed** Property, **StatusBar** Property, **Width** Property.
Methods	**Copy** Method, **CopyFace** Method, **Delete** Method, **Edit** Method, **Move** Method, **PasteFace** Method, **Reset** Method.

ToolbarButtons Collection Object

Description   A collection of all the **ToolbarButton** objects on the specified toolbar. Each **ToolbarButton** object represents a button or a gap (an extended space between buttons) on a toolbar. Do not confuse the **ToolbarButton** object with the **Button** object, which is a custom button graphic object on a chart sheet, dialog sheet, or worksheet.

Accessors   Use the **ToolbarButtons** method with an argument to access a single member of the collection or without an argument to access the entire collection at once. The following example sets the cButtons variable to the number of toolbar buttons and gaps on the Standard toolbar.

```
cButtons = Toolbars("standard").ToolbarButtons.Count
```

Use the **Add** method to add a toolbar button to a toolbar. The following example adds the Insert Module button to the end of the Standard toolbar.

```
Toolbars("standard").ToolbarButtons.Add button:=190
```

For a complete list of available toolbar buttons, see "Toolbar Button ID Values" in online Help.

To add a gap instead of a button, omit the *button* argument for the **Add** method.

Properties   **Application** Property, **Count** Property, **Creator** Property, **Parent** Property.

Methods   **Add** Method (**ToolbarButtons** Collection), **Item** Method.

ToolbarButtons Method

Applies To   **Toolbar** Object.

Description	Accessor. Returns an object that represents a single toolbar button (a **ToolbarButton** object, Syntax 1) or a collection of toolbar buttons (a **ToolbarButtons** object, Syntax 2) on the specified toolbar.
Syntax 1	*object*.**ToolbarButtons**(*index*)
Syntax 2	*object*.**ToolbarButtons**

object
    Required. The **Toolbar** object.

index
    Required for Syntax 1. The number of the button.

Example   This example deletes the New Workbook button from the Standard toolbar.

```
Application.Toolbars("Standard").ToolbarButtons(1).Delete
```

Toolbars Collection Object

Description   A collection of all the **Toolbar** objects in the Microsoft Excel application. Each **Toolbar** object represents a toolbar, either built-in or custom.

Accessors   Use the **Add** method to create a new toolbar and add it to the collection. The following example creates a new toolbar called "small VBA," adds the Insert Module button (190) and the Run Macro button (100) to it, makes the new toolbar visible, and moves it to the top of the Microsoft Excel window.

```
Dim tb As Toolbar
Set tb = Toolbars.Add("small VBA")
tb.ToolbarButtons.Add 190 'Insert Module button
tb.ToolbarButtons.Add 100 'Run Macro button
tb.Visible = True
tb.Position = xlTop
```

Use the **Toolbars** method with an argument to access a single member of the collection or without an argument to access the entire collection at once. The following example displays the total number of toolbars currently available in Microsoft Excel and the number of built-in toolbars.

```
cToolbars = Toolbars.Count
cBuiltIn = 0
For i = 1 To cToolbars
    If Toolbars(i).BuiltIn Then cBuiltin = cBuiltin + 1
Next
MsgBox cToolbars & " toolbars, " & cBuiltin & " built in."
```

Properties	**Application** Property, **Count** Property, **Creator** Property, **Parent** Property.
Methods	**Add** Method (**Toolbars** Collection), **Item** Method.

Toolbars Method

Applies To	**Application** Object.
Description	Accessor. Returns an object that represents a single toolbar (a **Toolbar** object, Syntax 1) or a collection of toolbars (a **Toolbars** object, Syntax 2) in the current instance of Microsoft Excel. Read-only.
Syntax 1	*object*.**Toolbars**(*index*)
Syntax 2	*object*.**Toolbars**

object
> Optional. The **Application** containing the toolbars.

index
> Required for Syntax 1. The name or number of the toolbar.

Example	This example adds a new toolbar button to the first position on the Standard toolbar and then assigns the macro myNewButtonMacro to the button.

```
Set newButton = Toolbars("Standard").ToolbarButtons.Add _
    (Button:=210, Before:=1)
newButton.OnAction = "myNewButtonMacro"
```

This example resets all toolbars to their default configurations.

```
For Each tb In Application.Toolbars
    tb.Reset
Next tb
```

Top Property

Applies To   **Application** Object, **Arc** Object, **Arcs** Collection, **AxisTitle** Object, **Button** Object, **Buttons** Collection, **ChartArea** Object, **ChartObject** Object, **ChartObjects** Collection, **ChartTitle** Object, **CheckBox** Object, **DataLabel** Object, **DialogFrame** Object, **Drawing** Object, **DrawingObjects** Collection, **Drawings** Collection, **DropDown** Object, **DropDowns** Collection, **EditBox** Object, **EditBoxes** Collection, **GroupBox** Object, **GroupBoxes** Collection, **GroupObject** Object, **GroupObjects** Collection, **Label** Object, **Labels** Collection, **Legend** Object, **Line** Object, **Lines** Collection, **ListBox** Object, **ListBoxes** Collection, **OLEObject** Object, **OLEObjects** Collection, **OptionButton** Object, **OptionButtons** Collection, **Oval** Object, **Ovals** Collection, **Picture** Object, **Pictures** Collection, **PlotArea** Object, **Range** Object, **Rectangle** Object, **Rectangles** Collection, **ScrollBar** Object, **ScrollBars** Collection, **Spinner** Object, **Spinners** Collection, **TextBox** Object, **TextBoxes** Collection, **Toolbar** Object, **Window** Object.

Description   Returns or sets the position of the specified object, in points (1/72 inch). Read-write, except for the **Range** object.

Remarks   The **Top** property has several different meanings, depending on the object to which it is applied.

Object	Meaning
Application	The distance from the top edge of the physical screen to the top edge of the main Microsoft Excel window, in points. In Windows, if the application window is minimized, this property controls the position of the icon (anywhere on the screen). On the Apple Macintosh the value is always zero; setting the value to something else will have no effect.
Button	The top position of the object, in points, measured from the top of row 1.
Range	The distance from the top edge of row one to the top edge of the range, in points. If the range is discontinuous, the first area is used. If the range is more than one row high, the top (lowest numbered) row in the range is used. Read-only.
Toolbar	If the toolbar is docked (the **Position** property of the Toolbar object is not **xlFloating**), the number of points from the top edge of the toolbar to the top edge of the toolbar docking area. If the toolbar is floating, the number of points from the top edge of the toolbar to the top edge of the Microsoft Excel workspace.

Object	Meaning
Window	The top position of the window, in points, measured from the top edge of the usable area (below the menus, top-docked toolbars, and/or the formula bar). You cannot set this property for a maximized window. Use the **WindowState** property to return or set the state of the window.
Arc, **AxisTitle**, **ChartArea**, **ChartTitle**, **CheckBox**, **DataLabel**, **DialogFrame**, **Drawing**, **DrawingObjects**, **DropDown**, **EditBox**, **GroupBox**, **GroupObject**, **Label**, **Legend**, **Line**, **ListBox**, **OLEObject**, **OptionButton**, **Oval**, **Picture**, **PlotArea**, **Rectangle**, **ScrollBar**, **Spinner**, **TextBox**, **Title**	The top position of the object, in points, measured from the top of row one (on a worksheet) or the top of the chart area (on a chart).

See Also   **Height** Property, **Left** Property, **Width** Property.

Example   This example moves oval one on Sheet1 so that it is aligned with the top edge of row 4.

```
Worksheets("Sheet1").Ovals(1).Top = _
    Worksheets("Sheet1").Rows(4).Top
```

This example aligns the top of every button on Sheet1 with the top of row 2.

```
topEdge = Worksheets("Sheet1").Rows(2).Top
For Each b In Worksheets("Sheet1").Buttons
    b.Top = topEdge
Next b
```

This example expands the active window to the maximum size available (assuming that the window is not already maximized).

```
With ActiveWindow
    .WindowState = xlNormal
    .Top = 1
    .Left = 1
    .Height = Application.UsableHeight
    .Width = Application.UsableWidth
End With
```

TopLeftCell Property

Applies To   **Arc** Object, **Button** Object, **ChartObject** Object, **CheckBox** Object, **Drawing** Object, **DropDown** Object, **EditBox** Object, **GroupBox** Object, **GroupObject** Object, **Label** Object, **Line** Object, **ListBox** Object, **OLEObject** Object, **OptionButton** Object, **Oval** Object, **Picture** Object, **Rectangle** Object, **ScrollBar** Object, **Spinner** Object, **TextBox** Object.

Description   Accessor. Returns a **Range** object that represents the cell that lies under the top left corner of this object. For drawing objects, this property applies only when the drawing object is on a worksheet. Read only.

See Also   **BottomRightCell** Property.

Example   This example displays the address of the cell beneath the upper-left corner of rectangle one on Sheet1.

```
MsgBox "The top left corner is over cell " & _
    Worksheets("Sheet1").Rectangles(1).TopLeftCell.Address
```

TopMargin Property

Applies To   **PageSetup** Object.

Description   Returns or sets the size of the top margin, in points (1/72 inch). Read-write.

Remarks   Margins are set or returned in points. Use the **InchesToPoints** or **CentimetersToPoints** function to convert.

Example   These two examples set the top margin of Sheet1 to 0.5 inch (36 points).

```
Worksheets("Sheet1").PageSetup.TopMargin = _
        Application.InchesToPoints(0.5)

Worksheets("Sheet1").PageSetup.TopMargin = 36
```

This example displays the current top margin setting.

```
marginInches = ActiveSheet.PageSetup.TopMargin / _
    Application.InchesToPoints(1)
MsgBox "The current top margin is " & marginInches & " inches"
```

ToRecipients Property

Applies To
: **Mailer** Object.

Description
: Returns or sets the direct recipients of the mailer. Available only in Microsoft Excel for the Apple Macintosh with the PowerTalk mail system extension installed. Read-write.

Remarks
: This property is an array of strings specifying the address, in one of the following formats:

- A record in the Preferred Personal Catalog. These names are one level deep ("Fred" or "June").
- A full path specifying either a record in a personal catalog ("HD:Excel Folder:My Catalog:Barney") or a plain record ("HD:Folder:Martin").
- A relative path from the current working folder specifying either a personal catalog record ("My Catalog:Barney") or a plain record ("Martin").
- A path in a PowerShare catalog tree of the form "CATALOG_NAME:<node>:RECORD_NAME" where <node> is a path to a PowerShare catalog. An example of a complete path is "AppleTalk:North Building Zone:George's Mac".

See Also
: **BCCRecipients** Property, **CCRecipients** Property, **Enclosures** Property, **Mailer** Property, **Received** Property, **SendDateTime** Property, **Sender** Property, **SendMailer** Method, **Subject** Property.

Example
: This example sets up the **Mailer** object for workbook one and then sends the workbook.

```
With Workbooks(1)
    .HasMailer = True
    With .Mailer
        .Subject = "Here is the workbook"
        .ToRecipients = Array("Jean")
        .CCRecipients = Array("Adam", "Bernard")
        .BCCRecipients = Array("Chris")
        .Enclosures = Array("TestFile")
    End With
    .SendMailer
End With
```

TotalLevels Property

Applies To   **PivotField** Object.

Description   Returns the total number of fields in the current field grouping. If the field is not grouped, **TotalLevels** returns the value 1. Read-only.

Remarks   All fields in a set of grouped fields have the same **TotalLevels** value.

Example   This example displays the total number of fields in the group that contains the active cell.

```
Worksheets("Sheet1").Activate
MsgBox "This group has " & _
    ActiveCell.PivotField.TotalLevels & " levels."
```

TrackStatus Property

Applies To   **RoutingSlip** Object.

Description   **True** if status tracking is enabled for the routing slip. Read-write before routing begins; read-only when routing is in progress.

Example   This example sends BOOK1.XLS to three recipients, with status tracking enabled.

```
Workbooks("BOOK1.XLS").HasRoutingSlip = True
With Workbooks("BOOK1.XLS").RoutingSlip
    .Delivery = xlOneAfterAnother
    .Recipients = Array("Adam Bendel", "Jean Selva", "Bernard Gabor")
    .Subject = "Here is BOOK1.XLS"
    .Message = "Here is the workbook. What do you think?"
    .ReturnWhenDone = True
    .TrackStatus = True
End With
Workbooks("BOOK1.XLS").Route
```

TransitionExpEval Property

Applies To   **Worksheet** Object.

Description   **True** if Microsoft Excel will use Lotus 1-2-3 expression evaluation rules for this worksheet. Read-write.

Example	This example causes Microsoft Excel to use Lotus 1-2-3 expression evaluation rules for Sheet1.

```
Worksheets("Sheet1").TransitionExpEval = True
```

TransitionFormEntry Property

Applies To	**Worksheet** Object.
Description	**True** if Microsoft Excel will use Lotus 1-2-3 formula entry rules for this worksheet. Read-write.
Remarks	This property is not available on the Apple Macintosh.
Example	This example causes Microsoft Excel to use Lotus 1-2-3 formula entry rules for Sheet1.

```
Worksheets("Sheet1").TransitionFormEntry = True
```

TransitionMenuKey Property

Applies To	**Application** Object.
Description	Returns or sets the alternate menu or help key, which is usually "/". Read-write.
Example	This example sets the transition menu key to "/" (which is the default).

```
Application.TransitionMenuKey = "/"
```

TransitionMenuKeyAction Property

Applies To	**Application** Object.
Description	Returns or sets the action taken when the alternate menu key is pressed (one of **xlExcelMenus** or **xlLotusHelp**). This property cannot be set to **xlLotusHelp** on the Apple Macintosh. Read-write.
See Also	**TransitionMenuKey** Property.

Example

This example sets the alternate menu key to run Lotus 1-2-3 Help when it is pressed. This property cannot be set to **xlLotusHelp** on the Macintosh.

```
Application.TransitionMenuKeyAction = xlLotusHelp
```

TransitionNavigKeys Property

Applies To   **Application** Object.

Description   **True** if alternate navigation keys are active. Read-write.

Example   This example displays the current state of the Transition Navigation Keys option.

```
If Application.TransitionNavigKeys Then
    keyState = "On"
Else
    keyState = "Off"
End If
MsgBox "The Transition Navigation Keys option is " & keyState
```

Trappable Errors

Trappable errors can occur while an application is running. Some of these can also occur during development or compile time. You can test and respond to trappable errors using the **On Error** statement and the **Err** function.

Code	Message
3	Return without GoSub
5	Invalid procedure call
6	Overflow
7	Out of memory
9	Subscript out of range
10	Duplicate definition
11	Division by zero
13	Type mismatch
14	Out of string space
16	String formula too complex
17	Can't perform requested operation

Code	Message
18	User interrupt occurred
20	Resume without error
28	Out of stack space
35	Sub or Function not defined
48	Error in loading DLL
49	Bad DLL calling convention
51	Internal error
52	Bad file name or number
53	File not found
54	Bad file mode
55	File already open
57	Device I/O error
58	File already exists
59	Bad record length
61	Disk full
62	Input past end of file
63	Bad record number
67	Too many files
68	Device unavailable
70	Permission denied
71	Disk not ready
74	Can't rename with different drive
75	Path/File access error
76	Path not found
91	Object variable not set
92	For loop not initialized
93	Invalid pattern string
94	Invalid use of Null
95	User-defined error
323	Can't load module; invalid format
423	Property or method not found
424	Object required
430	Class does not support OLE Automation
438	Object doesn't support this property or method
440	OLE Automation error

Code	Message
445	Object doesn't support this action
446	Object doesn't support named arguments
447	Object doesn't support current locale setting
448	Named argument not found
449	Argument not optional
450	Wrong number of arguments
451	Object not a collection
452	Invalid ordinal
453	Specified DLL function not found
454	Code resource not found
455	Code resource lock error

You can also work with Microsoft Excel cell error values in Visual Basic. For more information, see Cell Error Values.

Code	Message
1000	**'[Object]' does not have '[property name]' property**
	The property doesn't exist for this object. For more information, see the entry for the object name.
1001	**'[Object]' does not have '[method name]' method**
	The method doesn't exist for this object. For more information, see the entry for the object name.
1002	**Missing required argument '[argument]'**
	The method expected a required argument that wasn't specified. Add the argument to the code. To see a list of required arguments, see the entry for the method name.
1003	**Invalid number of arguments**
	The method has the wrong number of arguments. This usually occurs when you specify arguments by position instead of by name and you have too many arguments. To see the valid arguments for the method, see the entry for the method name.

Code	Message
1004	**'[Method name]' method of '[object]' class failed**
	The method cannot be used on the object. Possible reasons include the following:
	An argument contains a value that isn't valid. A common cause of this problem is an attempt to access an object that doesn't exist (for example, you tried to use Workbooks(5) when there were only three workbooks open).
	The method cannot be used in the applied context. For example, some **Range** object methods require that the range contain data; if the range doesn't contain data, the method fails.
	An external error occurred, such as a failure to read or write from a file.
	For more information about the method, see the entry for the method name.
1005	**Unable to set the '[property name]' property of the '[object]' class**
	The property cannot be changed. Possible reasons include the following:
	The value you're using for the property isn't valid (for example, you set a property to a string value, but the property requires a Boolean value).
	The property is read-only.
	For more information about the property, see the entry for the property name.
1006	**Unable to get the '[property name]' property of the '[object]' class**
	The property cannot be read. A possible reason is that the property cannot be used in the applied context. For example, the code `ActiveChart.Legend.Font.Color = RGB(255, 0, 0)` will cause this error if the active chart doesn't contain a legend.
	For more information about the property, see the entry for the property name.

Trendline Object

Description   Represents a trendline in a chart. A trendline shows the trend, or direction, of data in a series.

Accessors   The **Trendline** object is a member of the **Trendlines** collection. The **Trendlines** collection contains all the **Trendline** objects for a single series. Use the **Add** method to create a new trendline and add it to the series.

To access a single member of the collection, use the **Trendlines** method with the trendline index number as an argument.

The index number represents the order in which the trendlines were added to the series. Trendlines(1) is the first trendline added; Trendlines(Trendlines.Count) is the last. The following example changes the trendline type for series one in embedded chart one on worksheet one. If the series has no trendline, this example will fail.

```
Worksheets(1).ChartObjects(1).Chart. _
    SeriesCollection(1).Trendlines(1).Type = xlMovingAvg
```

Properties   **Application** Property, **Backward** Property, **Border** Property, **Creator** Property, **DataLabel** Property, **DisplayEquation** Property, **DisplayRSquared** Property, **Forward** Property, **Index** Property, **Intercept** Property, **InterceptIsAuto** Property, **Name** Property, **NameIsAuto** Property, **Order** Property, **Parent** Property, **Period** Property, **Type** Property.

Methods   **ClearFormats** Method, **Delete** Method, **Select** Method.

Trendlines Collection Object

Description   A collection of all the **Trendline** objects for the specified series. Each **Trendline** object represents a trendline in a chart. A trendline shows the trend, or direction, of data in a series.

Accessors   Use the **Add** method to create a new trendline and add it to the series. The following example adds a linear trendline to series one in embedded chart one on the worksheet named "Sheet1."

```
Worksheets("sheet1").ChartObjects(1).Chart.SeriesCollection(1) _
    .Trendlines.Add type:=xlLinear, name:="Linear Trend"
```

Use the **Trendlines** method with an argument to access a single member of the collection or without an argument to access the entire collection at once.

Properties   **Application** Property, **Count** Property, **Creator** Property, **Parent** Property.

Methods   **Add** Method (**Trendlines** Collection), **Item** Method.

Trendlines Method

Applies To   **Series** Object.

Description   Accessor. Returns an object that represents a single trendline (a **Trendline** object, Syntax 1) or a collection of all the trendlines (a **Trendlines** object, Syntax 2) for the series.

Syntax 1   *object*.**Trendlines(*index*)**

Syntax 2   *object*.**Trendlines**

object
    Required. The **Series** object.

index
    Required for Syntax 1. The name or number of the trendline.

Example   This example adds a linear trendline to series one in Chart1.

```
Charts("Chart1").SeriesCollection(1).Trendlines.Add Type:=xlLinear
```

TwoInitialCapitals Property

Applies To   **AutoCorrect** Object.

Description   **True** if words that begin with two initial capital letters are corrected automatically. This property is available only in Microsoft Excel for Windows 95. Read-write.

Example   This example sets Microsoft Excel to correct words that begin with two initial capital letters.

```
With Application.AutoCorrect
    .TwoInitialCapitals = True
    .ReplaceText = True
End With
```

Type Property (DocumentProperty Object)

Applies To   **DocumentProperty** Object.

Description

Returns or sets the document property type (can be one of **offPropertyTypeBoolean**, **offPropertyTypeDate**, **offPropertyTypeFloat**, **offPropertyTypeNumber**, or **offPropertyTypeString**). Read-only for built-in document properties; read-write for custom document properties.

To use this property, you should establish a reference to the Microsoft Office 95 Object Library by using the References command (Tools menu).

Example

This example displays the name, type, and value of a document property. You must pass a **DocumentProperty** object to the procedure.

```
Sub DisplayPropertyInfo(dp As DocumentProperty)
    MsgBox "value = " & dp.Value & Chr(13) & _
        "type = " & dp.Type & Chr(13) & _
        "name = " & dp.Name
End Sub
```

This example displays the type of custom document property one in the active workbook.

```
MsgBox ActiveWorkbook.CustomDocumentProperties(1).Type
```

Type Property

Applies To

Axis Object, **Chart** Object, **ChartGroup** Object, **DataLabel** Object, **DataLabels** Collection, **Series** Object, **Trendline** Object, **Window** Object, **Worksheet** Object.

Description

Returns the object type, as shown in the following table. Read-write except as noted.

Object	Type
Axis	Axis type. Can be one of **xlCategory**, **xlValue**, or **xlSeries** (only 3-D charts use **xlSeries**).
Chart	Chart type. Can be one of **xl3DArea**, **xl3DBar**, **xl3DColumn**, **xl3DLine**, **xl3DPie**, **xl3DSurface**, **xlArea**, **xlBar**, **xlColumn**, **xlDoughnut**, **xlLine**, **xlPie**, **xlRadar**, or **xlXYScatter**. If the chart has chart groups of more than one type, this property returns **Null**, but setting the property sets all the chart groups.
ChartGroup	Chart group type. Can be one of the values shown for the **Chart** object. If you set the chart group type to a type that is not on the chart, Microsoft Excel creates a new chart group.

Object	Type
DataLabel	Data label type (one of **xlNone**, **xlShowValue**, **xlShowLabel**, **xlShowPercent**, or **xlShowLabelAndPercent**).
Series	Series type. Can be one of the values shown for the **Chart** object. If you set the series type to a type that is not on the chart, Microsoft Excel creates a new chart group.
Trendline	Trendline type. Can be one of **xlLinear**, **xlLogarithmic**, **xlExponential**, **xlPolynomial**, **xlMovingAvg**, or **xlPower**.
Window	Window type. Can be one of **xlChartInPlace**, **xlChartAsWindow**, **xlWorkbook**, **xlInfo**, or **xlClipboard**. Read-only.
Worksheet	Worksheet type. Can be one of **xlWorksheet**, **xlExcel4MacroSheet**, or **xlExcel4IntlMacroSheet**. Read-only.

See Also   **SubType** Property.

Example   This example changes the 3-D line group in Chart1 to an area group. The example should be run on a 3-D chart.

```
Charts("Chart1").Line3DGroup.Type = xl3DArea
```

Type Statement

Description   Used at module level to define a user-defined data type containing one or more elements.

Syntax   [**Private** | **Public**] **Type** *varname*
    elementname [([*subscripts*])] **As** *type*
    [*elementname* [([*subscripts*])] **As** *type*]

    . . .

End Type

The **Type** statement syntax has these parts:

Part	Description
Public	Used to declare user-defined types that are available to all procedures in all modules in all projects.
Private	Used to declare user-defined types that are available only within the module where the declaration is made.

Part	Description
varname	Name of the user-defined type; follows standard variable naming conventions.
elementname	Name of an element of the user-defined type. Element names also follow standard variable naming conventions, except that reserved words can be used.
subscripts	Dimensions of an array element. Use only parentheses when declaring an array whose size can change.
type	Data type of the element; may be **Boolean**, **Integer**, **Long**, **Currency**, **Single**, **Double**, **Date**, **String**, **String** * *length* (for fixed-length strings), **Object**, **Variant**, another user-defined type, or an object type.

Remarks

The **Type** statement can be used only at module level. Once you have declared a user-defined type using the **Type** statement, you can declare a variable of that type anywhere within the scope of the declaration. Use **Dim**, **Private**, **Public**, **ReDim**, or **Static** to declare a variable of a user-defined type.

Line numbers and line labels aren't allowed in **Type**...**End Type** blocks. User-defined types are often used with data records, which frequently consist of a number of related elements of different data types.

The following example shows the use of fixed-size arrays in a user-defined type:

```
Type StateData
    CityCode (1 To 100) As Integer ' Declare a static array.
    County As String * 30
End Type
Dim Washington(1 To 100) As StateData
```

In the preceding example, StateData includes the CityCode static array, and the record Washington has the same structure as StateData.

When you declare a fixed-size array within a user-defined type, its dimensions must be declared with numeric literals or constants rather than variables.

The setting of the **Option Base** statement determines the lower bound for arrays within user-defined types.

See Also

Dim Statement, **Private** Statement, **Public** Statement, **ReDim** Statement, **Static** Statement.

TypeName Function

Description   Returns a string that provides information about a variable.

Syntax   **TypeName(*varname*)**

The ***varname*** named argument can be any variable except a variable of a user-defined type.

Remarks   The string returned by **TypeName** can be any one of the following:

String Returned	Variable contains
objecttype	An OLE Automation object whose type is *objecttype*.
Integer	An integer.
Long	A long integer.
Single	A single-precision floating point number.
Double	A double-precision floating point number.
Currency	A currency value.
Date	A date.
String	A string.
Boolean	A Boolean value.
Error	An error value.
Empty	Uninitialized.
Null	No valid data.
Object	An object that doesn't support OLE Automation.
Unknown	An OLE Automation object whose type is unknown.
Nothing	An object variable that doesn't refer to an object.

If ***varname*** is an array, the returned string can be any one of the possible returned strings (or **Variant**) with empty parentheses appended. For example, if ***varname*** is an array of integers, **TypeName** returns "`Integer()`".

See Also   Data Type Summary, **IsArray** Function, **IsDate** Function, **IsEmpty** Function, **IsError** Function, **IsMissing** Function, **IsNull** Function, **IsNumeric** Function, **IsObject** Function, **Variant Data** Type, **VarType** Function.

Example   This example uses the **TypeName** function to return information about a variable.

```
' Declare variables.
Dim StrVar As String, IntVar As Integer, CurVar As Currency
Dim ArrayVar (1 To 5) As Integer
NullVar = Null                          ' Assign Null value.
MyType = TypeName(StrVar)               ' Returns "String".
MyType = TypeName(IntVar)               ' Returns "Integer".
MyType = TypeName(CurVar)               ' Returns "Currency".
MyType = TypeName(NullVar)              ' Returns "Null".
MyType = TypeName(ArrayVar)  ' Returns "Integer()".
```

This example displays the Visual Basic object type of the selection. You can run this example with cells selected, with a single oval selected, or with several different graphic objects selected.

```
Worksheets("Sheet1").Activate
MsgBox "The selection object type is " & TypeName(Selection)
```

UBound Function

Description   Returns the largest available subscript for the indicated dimension of an array.

Syntax   **UBound**(*arrayname*[,*dimension*])

The **UBound** function syntax has these parts:

Part	Description
arrayname	Name of the array variable; follows standard variable naming conventions.
dimension	Whole number indicating which dimension's upper bound is returned. Use 1 for the first dimension, 2 for the second, and so on. If *dimension* is omitted, 1 is assumed.

Remarks   The **UBound** function is used with the **LBound** function to determine the size of an array. Use the **LBound** function to find the lower limit of an array dimension.

UBound returns the values listed in the table below for an array with these dimensions:

```
Dim A(1 To 100, 0 To 3, -3 To 4)
```

Statement	Return Value
UBound(A, 1)	100
UBound(A, 2)	3
UBound(A, 3)	4

See Also

Dim Statement, **LBound** Function, **Option Base** Statement, **Public** Statement, **ReDim** Statement, **Static** Statement.

Example

This example uses the **UBound** function to determine the largest available subscript for the indicated dimension of an array.

```
Dim MyArray(1 To 10, 5 To 15, 10 To 20) ' Declare array variables.
Dim AnyArray(10)
Upper = UBound(MyArray, 1)              ' Returns 10.
Upper = UBound(MyArray, 3)              ' Returns 20.
Upper = UBound(AnyArray)                ' Returns 10.
```

This example writes the elements of the first custom list in column one on Sheet1.

```
Sub foo()
On Error GoTo err_handler
listArray = Application.GetCustomListContents(1)
For i = LBound(listArray, 1) To UBound(listArray, 1)
    Worksheets("sheet1").Cells(i, 1).Value = listArray(i)
Next i
Exit Sub

err_handler:
    MsgBox "Custom list does not exist"
End Sub
```

This example assumes that you used an external data source to create a PivotTable on Sheet1. The example inserts the SQL connection string and query string into a new worksheet.

```
Set newSheet = ActiveWorkbook.Worksheets.Add
sdArray = Worksheets("Sheet1").UsedRange.PivotTable.SourceData
For i = LBound(sdArray) To UBound(sdArray)
    newSheet.Cells(i, 1) = sdArray(i)
Next i
```

UCase Function

Description

Returns a string that has been converted to uppercase.

Syntax	**UCase**(*string*)
	The *string* named argument is any valid string expression. If *string* contains no valid data, **Null** is returned.
Remarks	Only lowercase letters are converted to uppercase; all uppercase letters and nonletter characters remain unchanged.
See Also	**LCase** Function.
Example	This example uses the **UCase** function to return an uppercase version of a string.

```
LowerCase = "Hello World 1234"     ' String to convert.
UpperCase = UCase(LowerCase)       ' Returns "HELLO WORLD 1234".
```

Underline Property

Applies To	**Font** Object.
Description	Returns or sets the type of underline applied to the font, as shown in the following table. Read-write.

Value	Meaning
xlNone	No underline.
xlSingle	Single underline.
xlDouble	Double underline.
xlSingleAccounting	Single accounting underline.
xlDoubleAccounting	Double accounting underline.

Example	This example sets the font in the active cell on Sheet1 to single underline.

```
Worksheets("Sheet1").Activate
ActiveCell.Font.Underline = xlSingle
```

Undo Method

Applies To	**Application** Object.
Description	Cancels the last user-interface action.
Syntax	*object*.**Undo**

object
> Required. The **Application** object.

Remarks   This method can only be used to undo the last action taken by the user before running the macro, and it must be the first line in the macro. It cannot be used to undo Visual Basic commands.

Example   This example cancels the last user interface action. The example must be the first line in a macro.

```
Application.Undo
```

Ungroup Method

Applies To   **DrawingObjects** Collection, **GroupObject** Object, **GroupObjects** Collection, **Range** Object.

Description   **Range** object: Promotes a range in an outline level (in other words, decreases its outline level). The specified range must be a row or column, or a range of rows or columns. If the range is in a PivotTable, ungroups the items contained in the range.

> **GroupObject**: Ungroups a group of drawing objects. Returns a **DrawingObjects** collection containing the objects in the group.

Syntax   *object*.**Ungroup**

object
> Required. The object to which this method applies.

Remarks   If the active cell is in a field header of a parent field, all the groups in that field are ungrouped and the field is removed from the PivotTable. When the last group in a parent field is ungrouped, the entire field is removed from the PivotTable.

See Also   **Group** Method, **OutlineLevel** Property.

Example   This example ungroups drawing object group one on Sheet1.

```
Worksheets("Sheet1").GroupObjects(1).Ungroup
```

This example ungroups the field named "ORDER_DATE."

```
Set pvtTable = Worksheets("Sheet1").Range("A3").PivotTable
Set groupRange = pvtTable.PivotFields("ORDER_DATE").DataRange
groupRange.Cells(1).Ungroup
```

Union Method

Applies To	**Application** Object.
Description	Returns the union of two or more ranges.
Syntax	*object*.**Union(*arg1*, *arg2*, ...)**

object
    Optional. The **Application** object.

arg1, *arg2*, ...
    Required. Return the union of these ranges. At least two **Range** objects must be specified.

See Also	**Intersect** Method.
Example	This example fills the union of two named ranges, Range1 and Range2, with the formula =RAND().

```
Worksheets("Sheet1").Activate
Set bigRange = Application.Union(Range("Range1"), Range("Range2"))
bigRange.Formula = "=RAND()"
```

Unprotect Method

Applies To	**Chart** Object, **DialogSheet** Object, **Module** Object, **Workbook** Object, **Worksheet** Object.
Description	Removes protection from a sheet or workbook. This method has no effect if the sheet or workbook is not protected.
Syntax	*object*.**Unprotect(*password*)**

object
    Required. The object to which this method applies.

password
    Optional. A string giving the case-sensitive password to use to unprotect the sheet or workbook. If the sheet or workbook is not protected with a password, this argument is ignored. On a sheet, if you omit this argument and the sheet was protected with a password, you will be prompted for the password. On a workbook, if you omit this argument and the workbook was protected with a password, the method fails.

Remarks	If you forget the password, you cannot unprotect the sheet or workbook. It's a good idea to keep a list of your passwords and their corresponding document names in a safe place.
See Also	**Locked** Property, **Protect** Method, **ProtectContents** Property, **ProtectDrawingObjects** Property.
Example	This example removes protection from the active workbook.

```
ActiveWorkbook.Unprotect
```

UpBars Object

Description	Represents the up bars in a chart group. Up bars connect points on series one with higher values on the last series in the chart group (the lines go up from series one). Only 2-D line groups that contain at least two series can have up bars. There is no singular UpBar object; you must turn up bars and down bars on or off for all points in a chart group at once.
Accessors	The **UpBars** property returns the up bars for a chart group. The following example turns on up and down bars for chart group one in embedded chart one on the worksheet named "Sheet5." The example then sets the up bar color to blue and the down bar color to red.

```
With Worksheets("sheet5").ChartObjects(1).Chart.ChartGroups(1)
    .HasUpDownBars = True
    .UpBars.Interior.Color = RGB(0, 0, 255)
    .DownBars.Interior.Color = RGB(255, 0, 0)
End With
```

Remarks	If the **HasUpDownBars** property is **False**, most properties of the **UpBars** object are disabled.
See Also	**DownBars** Object
Properties	**Application** Property, **Border** Property, **Creator** Property, **Interior** Property, **Name** Property, **Parent** Property.
Methods	**Delete** Method, **Select** Method.

UpBars Property

Applies To   **ChartGroup** Object.

Description   Accessor. Returns an **UpBars** object that represents the up bars on a line chart. Applies only to line charts. Read-only.

See Also   **DownBars** Property, **HasUpDownBars** Property.

Example   This example turns on up and down bars for chart group one in Chart1 and then sets their colors. The example should be run on a 2-D line chart containing two series that cross each other at one or more data points.

```
With Charts("Chart1").ChartGroups(1)
    .HasUpDownBars = True
    .DownBars.Interior.ColorIndex = 3
    .UpBars.Interior.ColorIndex = 5
End With
```

Update Method

Applies To   **OLEObject** Object.

Description   Updates the link.

Syntax   *object*.**Update**

                    object
                        Required. The **OLEObject** object.

Example   This example updates the link to OLE object one on Sheet1.

```
Worksheets("Sheet1").OLEObjects(1).Update
```

UpdateFromFile Method

Applies To   **Workbook** Object.

Description   Updates a read-only workbook from the saved disk file version of the workbook if the disk version is more recent than the current copy of the workbook in memory. If the disk copy has not changed since the workbook was loaded, the in-memory copy of the workbook is not reloaded.

Syntax	*object*.**UpdateFromFile**
	object Required. The **Workbook** object.
Remarks	This method is useful when a workbook is opened as read-only by user A and read-write by user B. If user B saves a newer version of the workbook to disk while user A still has the workbook open, user A cannot get the updated copy without closing and reopening the workbook and losing view settings. The **UpdateFromFile** method updates the in-memory copy of the workbook from the disk file.
See Also	**ChangeFileAccess** Method.
Example	This example updates the active workbook.

```
ActiveWorkbook.UpdateFromFile
```

UpdateLink Method

Applies To	**Workbook** Object.
Description	Updates a Microsoft Excel, DDE, or OLE link (or links).
Syntax	*object*.**UpdateLink**(*name*, *type*)
	object Required. The **Workbook** object.
	name Required. Specifies the name of the Microsoft Excel or DDE/OLE link to update, as returned from the **LinkSources** method.
	type Optional. Specifies the link type. Can be either **xlExcelLinks** or **xlOLELinks** (also used for DDE links). **xlExcelLinks** if omitted.
Example	This example updates all links in the active workbook.

```
ActiveWorkbook.UpdateLink name:=ActiveWorkbook.LinkSources
```

UpdateRemoteReferences Property

Applies To	**Workbook** Object.
Description	**True** if remote references will be updated for the workbook. Read-write.

Example   This example causes remote references to be updated on the active workbook.

```
ActiveWorkbook.UpdateRemoteReferences = True
```

UsableHeight Property

Applies To   **Application** Object, **Window** Object.

Description   Returns the height of the space that can be used by a window in the application window area (the window is not maximized). The height is returned in points (1/72 inch). Read-only.

Remarks   Adding a toolbar reduces the usable height.

See Also   **UsableWidth** Property.

Example   This example expands the active window to the maximum size available (assuming that the window is not already maximized).

```
With ActiveWindow
    .WindowState = xlNormal
    .Top = 1
    .Left = 1
    .Height = Application.UsableHeight
    .Width = Application.UsableWidth
End With
```

UsableWidth Property

Applies To   **Application** Object, **Window** Object.

Description   Returns the width of the space that can be used by a window in the application window area (the window is not maximized). The width is returned in points (1/72 inch). Read-only.

See Also   **UsableHeight** Property.

Example

This example expands the active window to the maximum size available (assuming that the window is not already maximized).

```
With ActiveWindow
    .WindowState = xlNormal
    .Top = 1
    .Left = 1
    .Height = Application.UsableHeight
    .Width = Application.UsableWidth
End With
```

UsedRange Property

Applies To

Worksheet Object.

Description

Accessor. Returns a **Range** object that represents the used range on the specified worksheet. Read-only.

Example

This example selects the used range on Sheet1.

```
Worksheets("Sheet1").Activate
ActiveSheet.UsedRange.Select
```

User-Defined Data Type

Description

Any data type you define using the **Type** statement. User-defined data types can contain one or more elements of any data type, array, or a previously defined user-defined type. For example:

```
Type MyType
    MyName As String          ' String variable stores a name.
    MyBirthDate As Date       ' Date variable stores a birthdate.
    MySex as Integer          ' Integer variable stores sex (0 for
End Type                      ' female, 1 for male.
```

See Also

Data Type Summary, **Type** Statement.

UserName Property

Applies To	**Application** Object.
Description	Returns or sets the name of the current user (as a string). Read-write.
Example	This example displays the current user name.

```
MsgBox "Current user is " & Application.UserName
```

UserStatus Property

Applies To   **Workbook** Object.

Description   Returns a one-based, two-dimensional array specifying information about each user who has the workbook open as a shared list. The first element of the second dimension is the name of the user; the second element is the date and time when the user opened the workbook; and the third element is a number indicating the type of list (1 indicates exclusive, and 2 indicates shared). This property is available only in Microsoft Excel for Windows 95. Read-only.

Remarks   The **UserStatus** property doesn't return information about users who have the specified workbook open as read-only.

See Also   **MultiUserEditing** Property, **SaveAs** Method.

Example   This example creates a new workbook and inserts information about all users who have the active workbook open as a shared list.

```
users = ActiveWorkbook.UserStatus
With Workbooks.Add.Sheets(1)
    For row = 1 To ubound(users, 1)
        .Cells(row, 1) = users(row, 1)
        .Cells(row, 2) = users(row, 2)
        Select Case users(row, 3)
            Case 1
                .Cells(row, 3).Value = "Exclusive"
            Case 2
                .Cells(row, 3).Value = "Shared"
        End Select
    Next
End With
```

UseStandardHeight Property

Applies To   **Range** Object.

Description   **True** if the row height of the **Range** object equals the standard height of the sheet. Read-write.

See Also   **RowHeight** Property, **StandardHeight** Property, **UseStandardWidth** Property.

Example   This example sets the height of row one on Sheet1 to the standard height.

```
Worksheets("Sheet1").Rows(1).UseStandardHeight = True
```

UseStandardWidth Property

Applies To   **Range** Object.

Description   **True** if the column width of the **Range** object equals the standard width of the sheet. Read-write.

See Also   **ColumnWidth** Property, **StandardWidth** Property, **UseStandardHeight** Property.

Example   This example sets the width of column A on Sheet1 to the standard width.

```
Worksheets("Sheet1").Columns("A").UseStandardWidth = True
```

Val Function

Description   Returns the numbers contained in a string.

Syntax   **Val(*string*)**

The *string* named argument is any valid string expression.

Remarks   The **Val** function stops reading the string at the first character it can't recognize as part of a number. Symbols and characters that are often considered parts of numeric values, such as dollar signs and commas, are not recognized. However, the function recognizes radix prefixes &O (for octal) and &H (for hexadecimal). Blanks, tabs, and linefeeds are stripped from the argument.

The following returns the value 1615198:

```
Val("    1615 198th Street N.E.")
```

In the code below, **Val** returns the decimal value -1 for the hexadecimal value shown:

```
Val("&HFFFF")
```

Note The **Val** function recognizes only the period (.) as a valid decimal separator. When a possibility exists that different decimal separators may be used (for example, in international applications), you should use **CDbl** instead to convert a string to a number.

Value Property

Applies To

Application Object, **Borders** Collection, **CheckBox** Object, **DrawingObjects** Collection, **DropDown** Object, **DropDowns** Collection, **ListBox** Object, **ListBoxes** Collection, **Name** Object, **OptionButton** Object, **OptionButtons** Collection, **PivotField** Object, **PivotItem** Object, **PivotTable** Object, **Range** Object, **ScrollBar** Object, **ScrollBars** Collection, **Spinner** Object, **Spinners** Collection, **Style** Object.

Description

The meaning of the **Value** property depends on the object to which it is applied, as shown in the following table.

Object	Value
Application	Always returns "Microsoft Excel". Read-only.
Borders	Synonym for **Borders.LineStyle**.
CheckBox	Indicates check box status (**xlOn**, **xlOff**, or **xlMixed**).
DropDown, **ListBox**	Indicates the selected item in the list (the value is always between one and the number of items in the list). This method cannot be used with multi-select list boxes; use the **Selected** method instead.
Name	A string containing the formula that the name is defined to refer to, in A1-style notation, in the language of the macro, beginning with an equal sign. Read-only.
OptionButton	Indicates button status (one of **xlOn** or **xlOff**).
PivotField	The name of the field in the PivotTable.
PivotItem	The name of the item in the PivotTable field.

Object	Value
PivotTable	The name of the PivotTable.
Range	The value of a cell. If the cell is empty, returns the value **Empty**. Use the **IsEmpty** function to test for this case. If the **Range** object contains more than one cell, returns an array of values. Use the **IsArray** function to test for this case.
ScrollBar	The position of the scroll box.
Spinner	A value between the minimum and maximum range limit.
Style	The name of the style.

See Also   **LineStyle** Property, **MultiSelect** Property, **Selected** Property.

Example   This example sets the value of cell A1 on Sheet1 to 3.14159.

```
Worksheets("Sheet1").Range("A1").Value = 3.14159
```

This example loops on cells A1:D10 on Sheet1. If one of the cells has a value less than 0.001, the code replaces the value with 0 (zero).

```
For Each c in Worksheets("Sheet1").Range("A1:D10")
    If c.Value < .001 Then
        c.Value = 0
    End If
Next c
```

This example is a simple event procedure for a list box on a custom dialog box, Dialog1. The example sets the variable itemNum to the index of the selected item in the list box.

```
itemNum = DialogSheets("Dialog1").ListBoxes(1).Value
```

Value Property (DocumentProperty Object)

Applies To   **DocumentProperty** Object.

Description   Returns or sets the document property value. Read-write.

To use this property, you should establish a reference to the Microsoft Office 95 Object Library by using the References command (Tools menu).

Remarks   If the application doesn't define a value for one of the built-in document properties, reading the **Value** property for that document property causes an error.

Example

This example displays the name, type, and value of a document property. You must pass a **DocumentProperty** object to the procedure.

```
Sub DisplayPropertyInfo(dp As DocumentProperty)
    MsgBox "value = " & dp.Value & Chr(13) & _
        "type = " & dp.Type & Chr(13) & _
        "name = " & dp.Name
End Sub
```

This example displays the value of custom document property one in the active workbook.

```
MsgBox ActiveWorkbook.CustomDocumentProperties(1).Value
```

Values Property

Applies To   **Scenario** Object, **Series** Object.

Description   **Scenario** object: Returns an array containing the current values for the scenario changing cells. Read-only.

Series object: Returns or sets a collection of all the values in the series. This can be a range on a worksheet or an array of constant values (but not a combination of both). See the examples for details. Read-write.

Example   This example sets the series values from a range. The example uses the **Set** statement because the right-hand side of the expression is an object, not a value.

```
Set Charts("Chart1").SeriesCollection(1).Values = _
    Worksheets("Sheet1").Range("C5:T5")
```

To assign a constant value to each individual data point, you must use an array. This example does not require the **Set** statement.

```
Charts("Chart1").SeriesCollection(1).Values = _
    Array(1, 3, 5, 7, 11, 13, 17, 19)
```

Variant Data Type

Description   The **Variant** data type is the data type that all variables become if not explicitly declared as some other type (using statements such as **Dim**, **Private**, **Public**, or **Static**). The **Variant** data type has no type-declaration character.

The **Variant** is a special data type that can contain any kind of data as well as the special values **Empty**, **Error**, and **Null**. You can determine how the data in a **Variant** is treated using the **VarType** or **TypeName** function.

Numeric data can be any integer or real number value ranging from -1.797693134862315E308 to -4.94066E-324 for negative values and from 4.94066E-324 to 1.797693134862315E308 for positive values. Generally, numeric **Variant** data is maintained in its original data type within the **Variant**. For example, if you assign an **Integer** to a **Variant**, subsequent operations treat the **Variant** as if it were an **Integer**. However, if an arithmetic operation is performed on a **Variant** containing an **Integer**, a **Long**, or a **Single**, and the result exceeds the normal range for the original data type, the result is promoted within the **Variant** to the next larger data type. An **Integer** is promoted to a **Long**, and a **Long** and a **Single** are promoted to a **Double**. An error occurs when **Variant** variables containing **Currency** and **Double** values exceed their respective ranges.

You can use the **Variant** data type in place of any data type to work with data in a more flexible way. If the contents of a **Variant** variable are digits, they may be either the string representation of the digits or their actual value, depending on the context. For example:

```
Dim MyVar As Variant
MyVar = 98052
```

In the example shown above, MyVar contains a numeric representation—the actual value 98052. Arithmetic operators work as expected on **Variant** variables that contain numeric values or string data that can be interpreted as numbers. If you use the + operator to add MyVar to another **Variant** containing a number or to a variable of a numeric data type, the result is an arithmetic sum. See the information about addition and concatenation operators for complete information on how to use them with **Variant** data.

The value **Empty** denotes a **Variant** variable that hasn't been initialized (assigned an initial value). A **Variant** containing **Empty** is 0 if it is used in a numeric context and a zero-length string ("") if it is used in a string context.

Don't confuse **Empty** with **Null**. **Null** indicates that the **Variant** variable intentionally contains no valid data.

In a **Variant**, **Error** is a special value used to indicate that an error condition has occurred in a procedure. However, unlike for other kinds of errors, normal application-level error handling does not occur. This allows the programmer, or the application itself, to take some alternative based on the error value. **Error** values are created by converting real numbers to error values using the **CVErr** function.

See Also

CVar Function, **CVErr** Function, Data Type Summary, **Def**type Statements, **Dim** Statement, **Private** Statement, **Public** Statement, **Static** Statement, **TypeName** Function, **VarType** Function.

VarType Function

Description   Returns a value indicating the subtype of a variable.

Syntax   **VarType(*varname*)**

The ***varname*** named argument can be any variable except a variable of a user-defined type.

Return Values

Value Returned	Constant	Variable Type
0	vbEmpty	Empty (uninitialized).
1	vbNull	Null (no valid data).
2	vbInteger	Integer.
3	vbLong	Long integer.
4	vbSingle	Single-precision floating point number.
5	vbDouble	Double-precision floating point number.
6	vbCurrency	Currency.
7	vbDate	Date.
8	vbString	String.
9	vbObject	OLE Automation object.
10	vbError	Error.
11	vbBoolean	Boolean.
12	vbVariant	Variant (used only with arrays of Variants).
13	vbDataobject	Non-OLE Automation object.
8192	vbArray	Array.

Note These constants are specified by Visual Basic. As a result, the names can be used anywhere in your code in place of the actual values.

Remarks   The **VarType** function never returns the value for vbArray by itself. It is always added to some other value to indicate an array of a particular type. The constant vbVariant is only returned in conjunction with vbArray to indicate that the argument to the **VarType** function is an array of type **Variant**. For example, the value returned for an array of integers is calculated as vbInteger + vbArray, or 8194.

See Also   Data Type Summary, **IsArray** Function, **IsDate** Function, **IsEmpty** Function, **IsError** Function, **IsMissing** Function, **IsNull** Function, **IsNumeric** Function, **IsObject** Function, **TypeName** Function, **Variant Data** Type.

Example	This example uses **VarType** to determine the subtype of a variable.

```
' Initialize variables.
IntVar = 459: StrVar = "Hello World": DateVar = #2/12/69#
MyCheck = VarType(IntVar)          ' Returns 2.
MyCheck = VarType(DateVar)         ' Returns 7.
MyCheck = VarType(StrVar)          ' Returns 8.
```

VaryByCategories Property

Applies To	**ChartGroup** Object.
Description	If this property is **True**, Microsoft Excel assigns a different color or pattern to each data marker. The chart must contain only one series. Read-write.
Example	This example assigns a different color or pattern to each data marker in chart group one. The example should be run on a 2-D line chart that has data markers on a series.

```
Charts("Chart1").ChartGroups(1).VaryByCategories = True
```

Verb Method

Applies To	**OLEObject** Object.
Description	Sends a verb to the server of the specified OLE object.
Syntax	*object*.**Verb**(*verb*)
	object Required. The **OLEObject** object.
	verb Optional. The verb that the server of the OLE object should act upon. If this argument is omitted, the default verb is sent. The available verbs are determined by the object's source application. Typical verbs for an OLE object are Open and Primary (represented by the **xlOpen** and **xlPrimary** constants).
Example	This example sends the default verb to the server for OLE object one on Sheet1.

```
Worksheets("Sheet1").OLEObjects(1).Verb
```

Version Property

Applies To   **Application** Object.

Description   Returns the version number of Microsoft Excel. Read-only.

Example   This example displays a message box with the Microsoft Excel version number and the name of the operating system.

```
MsgBox "Welcome to Microsoft Excel version " & _
    Application.Version & " running on " & _
    Application.OperatingSystem & "!"
```

VerticalAlignment Property

Applies To   **AxisTitle** Object, **Button** Object, **Buttons** Collection, **ChartTitle** Object, **DataLabel** Object, **DataLabels** Collection, **DrawingObjects** Collection, **GroupObject** Object, **GroupObjects** Collection, **Range** Object, **Style** Object, **TextBox** Object, **TextBoxes** Collection.

Description   Returns or sets the vertical alignment of the object (can be one of **xlBottom**, **xlCenter**, **xlDistributed**, **xlJustify**, or **xlTop**). Read-write.

Remarks   The **xlDistributed** alignment style works only in Far East versions of Microsoft Excel.

See Also   **AddIndent** Property, **HorizontalAlignment** Property.

Example   This example sets the height of row two on Sheet1 to twice the standard height and then centers the vertical alignment.

```
Worksheets("Sheet1").Rows(2).RowHeight = _
    2 * Worksheets("Sheet1").StandardHeight
Worksheets("Sheet1").Rows(2).VerticalAlignment = xlCenter
```

Vertices Property

Applies To   **Drawing** Object, **DrawingObjects** Collection.

Description

Returns or sets the vertices of a polygon or freehand drawing, as a two-dimensional array of vertex coordinates in points (1/72 inch) relative to the upper-left corner of cell A1. The x coordinate is in column one of the array, the y coordinate is in column two. Every drawing and polygon will have at least two vertices. Read-only.

See Also

AddVertex Method, **Reshape** Method.

Example

This example creates a new worksheet and then inserts a list of the vertex coordinates for drawing one on Sheet1.

```
Set newSheet = ActiveWorkbook.Worksheets.Add
allVertices = Worksheets("Sheet1").Drawings(1).Vertices
newSheet.Range("A1:C1").Font.Bold = True
newSheet.Range("A1").Value = "Vertex"
newSheet.Range("B1").Value = "X value"
newSheet.Range("C1").Value = "Y value"
for i = LBound(allVertices, 1) to UBound(allVertices, 1)
    newSheet.Cells(i + 1, 1) = i
    newSheet.Cells(i + 1, 2) = allVertices(i, 1)
    newSheet.Cells(i + 1, 3) = allVertices(i, 2)
Next i
```

Assuming that drawing one on Sheet1 is a polygon with at least six vertices, this example reshapes the polygon by moving vertex five 12 points (1/6 inch) in the X direction.

```
With Worksheets("Sheet1").Drawings(1)
    vX = .Vertices(5, 1)
    vY = .Vertices(5, 2)
    .Reshape vertex:=5, Insert:=False, Left:=vX + 12, Top:=vY
End With
```

Visible Property

Applies To
Application Object, **Arc** Object, **Arcs** Collection, **Button** Object, **Buttons** Collection, **Chart** Object, **ChartObject** Object, **ChartObjects** Collection, **Charts** Collection, **CheckBox** Object, **DialogSheet** Object, **DialogSheets** Collection, **Drawing** Object, **DrawingObjects** Collection, **Drawings** Collection, **DropDown** Object, **DropDowns** Collection, **EditBox** Object, **EditBoxes** Collection, **GroupBox** Object, **GroupBoxes** Collection, **GroupObject** Object, **GroupObjects** Collection, **Label** Object, **Labels** Collection, **Line** Object, **Lines** Collection, **ListBox** Object, **ListBoxes** Collection, **Module** Object, **Modules** Collection, **Name** Object, **OLEObject** Object, **OLEObjects** Collection, **OptionButton** Object, **OptionButtons** Collection, **Oval** Object, **Ovals** Collection, **Picture** Object, **Pictures** Collection, **PivotItem** Object, **Rectangle** Object, **Rectangles** Collection, **ScrollBar** Object, **ScrollBars** Collection, **Sheets** Collection, **Spinner** Object, **Spinners** Collection, **TextBox** Object, **TextBoxes** Collection, **Toolbar** Object, **Window** Object, **Worksheet** Object, **Worksheets** Collection.

Description
True if the object is visible. For a chart, dialog sheet, module or worksheet, this property can be set to **xlVeryHidden**. This hides the object so that it can only be made visible by setting this property to **True** (the user cannot make the object visible). Read-write.

Remarks
The **Visible** property for a pivot item is **True** if the item is currently showing on the table.

If you set the **Visible** property for a name to **False**, the name will not appear in the Define Name dialog box.

Example
This example hides Sheet1.

```
Worksheets("Sheet1").Visible = False
```

This example makes Sheet1 visible.

```
Worksheets("Sheet1").Visible = True
```

This example makes every sheet in the active workbook visible.

```
For Each sh In Sheets
    sh.Visible = True
Next sh
```

This example creates a new worksheet and then sets its **Visible** property to **xlVeryHidden**. To refer to the sheet, use its object variable, `newSheet`, as shown in the last line of the example. To use the `newSheet` object variable in another procedure, you must declare it as a public variable (`Public newSheet As Object`) in the first line of the module preceding any **Sub** or **Function** procedure.

```
Set newSheet = Worksheets.Add
newSheet.Visible = xlVeryHidden
newSheet.Range("A1:D4").Formula = "=RAND()"
```

VisibleFields Method

Applies To   **PivotTable** Object.

Description   Accessor. Returns an object that represents a single pivot field (a **PivotField** object, Syntax 1) or a collection of the visible pivot fields (a **PivotFields** object, Syntax 2). Visible pivot fields are showing as row, column, page or data fields. Read-only.

Syntax 1   *object*.**VisibleFields**(*index*)

Syntax 2   *object*.**VisibleFields**

object
> Required. The **PivotTable** object.

index
> Required for Syntax 1. The name or number of the pivot field to return (can be an array to specify more than one).

See Also   **ColumnFields** Method, **DataFields** Method, **HiddenFields** Method, **PageFields** Method, **PivotFields** Method, **RowFields** Method.

Example   This example adds the visible field names to a list box. The list box appears on Sheet1.

```
Set pvtTable = Worksheets("Sheet1").Range("A3").PivotTable
Set newListBox = Worksheets("Sheet1").ListBoxes.Add _
    (Left:=10, Top:=72, Width:=144, Height:=144)
For Each hdnField In pvtTable.VisibleFields
    newListBox.AddItem (hdnField.Name)
Next hdnField
Worksheets("Sheet1").Activate
```

VisibleItems Method

Applies To   **PivotField** Object.

Description   Accessor. Returns an object that represents one visible pivot item (a **PivotItem** object, Syntax 1) or a collection of all the visible pivot items (a **PivotItems** object, Syntax 2) in the specified field. Read-only.

Syntax 1   *object*.**VisibleItems**(*index*)

Syntax 2   *object*.**VisibleItems**

object
    Required. The **PivotField** object.

index
    Required for Syntax 1. The number or name of the pivot item to return (can be an array to specify more than one).

See Also   **ChildItems** Method, **HiddenItems** Method, **ParentItems** Method, **PivotItems** Method.

Example   This example adds the names of all visible items in the field named "COMPANY" to a list box. The list box appears on Sheet1.

```
Set pvtTable = Worksheets("Sheet1").Range("A3").PivotTable
Set newListBox = Worksheets("Sheet1").ListBoxes.Add _
    (Left:=10, Top:=72, Width:=144, Height:=144)
Set pvtField = pvtTable.PivotFields("COMPANY")
For Each pvtItem In pvtField.VisibleItems
    newListBox.AddItem (pvtItem.Name)
Next pvtItem
Worksheets("Sheet1").Activate
```

VisibleRange Property

Applies To   **Pane** Object, **Window** Object.

Description   Accessor. Returns a **Range** object that represents the range of cells that are visible in the window or pane. If a column or row is partially visible, it is included in the range. Read-only.

Example   This example displays the number of cells visible on Sheet1.

```
Worksheets("Sheet1").Activate
MsgBox "There are " & Windows(1).VisibleRange.Cells.Count _
    & " cells visible"
```

Volatile Method

Applies To   **Application** Object.

Description   Marks a user-defined function as volatile. A volatile function must be recalculated whenever calculation occurs in any cells of the worksheet. A non-volatile function is recalculated only when the input variables change. This method has no effect if it is not inside a user-defined function used to calculate a worksheet cell.

Syntax   *object*.**Volatile**(*volatile*)

object
    Required. The **Application** object.

volatile
    Optional. If **True** or omitted, the function is marked as volatile. If **False**, the function is marked as non-volatile.

Example   This example marks the user-defined function "My_Func" as volatile. The function will be recalculated whenever calculation occurs in any cells on the worksheet where this function appears.

```
Function My_Func()
    Application.Volatile
    '
    '   Remainder of the function
    '
End Function
```

Wait Method

Applies To   **Application** Object.

Description   Pauses a macro that is running until a specified time is reached.

Important   The **Wait** method suspends all Microsoft Excel activity and may prevent you from performing other operations on your computer. Background processes, such as printing and recalculation, are continued.

Syntax   *object*.**Wait**(*time*)

object
    Required. The **Application** object.

time
>   Required. The time you want the macro to resume, in Microsoft Excel date format.

Example   This example pauses a running macro until 6:23 P.M. today.

```
Application.Wait "18:23:00"
```

This example pauses a running macro for approximately 10 seconds.

```
newHour = Hour(Now())
newMinute = Minute(Now())
newSecond = Second(Now()) + 10
waitTime = TimeSerial(newHour, newMinute, newSecond)
Application.Wait waitTime
```

Walls Object

Description   Represents the walls of a 3-D chart. There is no singular Wall object; you must access all the walls at once.

Accessors   The **Walls** property returns the walls for the specified chart. The following example sets the pattern on the walls for embedded chart one on the worksheet named "Sheet1." The example will fail if the chart is not a 3-D chart.

```
Worksheets("Sheet1").ChartObjects(1).Chart _
    .Walls.Interior.Pattern = xlGray75
```

Properties   **Application** Property, **Border** Property, **Creator** Property, **Interior** Property, **Name** Property, **Parent** Property.

Methods   **ClearFormats** Method, **Select** Method.

Walls Property

Applies To   **Chart** Object.

Description   Accessor. Returns a **Walls** object that represents the walls of the 3-D chart. Read-only.

Remarks   This property does not apply to 3-D pie charts.

Example   This example sets the wall border color of Chart1 to red. The example should be run on a 3-D chart.

```
Charts("Chart1").Walls.Border.ColorIndex = 3
```

WallsAndGridlines2D Property

Applies To   **Chart** Object.

Description   **True** if gridlines are drawn in 2-D on a 3-D chart. Read-write.

Example   This example causes Microsoft Excel to draw 2-D gridlines on Chart1.

```
Charts("Chart1").WallsAndGridlines2D = True
```

Weekday Function

Description   Returns a whole number representing the day of the week.

Syntax   **Weekday(*date*)**

The *date* named argument is limited to numbers or strings, in any combination, that can represent a date. If *date* contains no valid data, **Null** is returned.

Return Values

Value	Description
1	Sunday
2	Monday
3	Tuesday
4	Wednesday
5	Thursday
6	Friday
7	Saturday

See Also   **Date** Function, **Date** Statement, **Day** Function, **Month** Function, **Now** Function, **Year** Function.

Example   This example uses the **Weekday** function to obtain the day of the week from a specified date.

```
MyDate = #February 12, 1969#        ' Assign a date.
MyWeekDay = Weekday(MyDate)         ' MyWeekDay contains 4 since it
    ' was a Wednesday.
```

Weight Property

Applies To   **Border** Object, **Borders** Collection.

Description   Returns or sets the weight of the border (one of **xlHairline**, **xlThin**, **xlMedium**, or **xlThick**). Read-write.

Example   This example sets the border weight for oval one on Sheet1.

```
Worksheets("Sheet1").Ovals(1).Border.Weight = xlMedium
```

While...Wend Statement

Description   Executes a series of statements as long as a given condition is **True**.

Syntax   **While** *condition*
    [*statements*]
Wend

The **While**...**Wend** statement syntax has these parts:

Part	Description
condition	Numeric or string expression that evaluates to **True** or **False**.
statements	One or more statements executed while condition is **True**.

Remarks   If *condition* is **True**, all statements in *statements* are executed until the **Wend** statement is encountered. Control then returns to the **While** statement and *condition* is again checked. If *condition* is still **True**, the process is repeated. If it is not **True**, execution resumes with the statement following the **Wend** statement.

While...Wend loops can be nested to any level. Each **Wend** matches the most recent **While**.

Caution Do not branch into the body of a **While**...**Wend** loop without executing the **While** statement. Doing so may cause run-time errors or other problems that are difficult to locate.

Tip The **Do**...**Loop** statement provides a more structured and flexible way to perform looping.

See Also

Do...**Loop** Statement, **With** Statement.

Example

This example uses the **While**...**Wend** statement to increment a counter variable. The statements in the loop are executed as long as the condition evaluates to **True**.

```
Counter = 0                          ' Initialize variable.
While Counter < 20                   ' Test value of Counter.
    Counter = Counter + 1            ' Increment Counter.
Wend
Debug.Print Counter                  ' Prints 20 in Debug window.
```

Width Property

Applies To

Application Object, **Arc** Object, **Arcs** Collection, **Button** Object, **Buttons** Collection, **ChartArea** Object, **ChartObject** Object, **ChartObjects** Collection, **CheckBox** Object, **DialogFrame** Object, **Drawing** Object, **DrawingObjects** Collection, **Drawings** Collection, **DropDown** Object, **DropDowns** Collection, **EditBox** Object, **EditBoxes** Collection, **GroupBox** Object, **GroupBoxes** Collection, **GroupObject** Object, **GroupObjects** Collection, **Label** Object, **Labels** Collection, **Legend** Object, **Line** Object, **Lines** Collection, **ListBox** Object, **ListBoxes** Collection, **OLEObject** Object, **OLEObjects** Collection, **OptionButton** Object, **OptionButtons** Collection, **Oval** Object, **Ovals** Collection, **Picture** Object, **Pictures** Collection, **PlotArea** Object, **Range** Object, **Rectangle** Object, **Rectangles** Collection, **ScrollBar** Object, **ScrollBars** Collection, **Spinner** Object, **Spinners** Collection, **TextBox** Object, **TextBoxes** Collection, **Toolbar** Object, **ToolbarButton** Object, **Window** Object.

Description

Returns or sets an object's width in points (1/72 inch). Read-write for all objects, except **Range**, which is read-only.

Remarks

The **Width** property has several different meanings, depending on the object to which it is applied.

Object	Description
Application	The distance from the left edge of the application window to the right edge of the application window.
Range	The width of the range.
Toolbar	The width of the toolbar. When you set the width, Microsoft Excel snaps both the width and the height to match the nearest allowable size.
Window	The width of the window. Use the **UsableWidth** property to determine the maximum size for the window.
	You cannot set this property if the window is maximized or minimized. Use the **WindowState** property to determine the window state.
Arc, **Button**, **ChartArea**, **CheckBox**, **DialogFrame**, **Drawing**, **DrawingObjects**, **DropDown**, **EditBox**, **GroupBox**, **GroupObject**, **Label**, **Legend**, **Line**, **ListBox**, **OLEObject**, **OptionButton**, **Oval**, **Picture**, **PlotArea**, **Rectangle**, **ScrollBar**, **Spinner**, **TextBox**, **ToolbarButton**, **Window**	The width of the object. If you set the width for an entire collection of objects (using `Ovals.Width = 100`, for example), the width of each object changes in proportion to its existing width (this mimics the behavior of selecting all the objects and then dragging a handle to change the width of the selection). This means that the width of each object changes, but they are *not* all set to the same width. To set every object in the collection to the same width, you must iterate the collection and set the width of each individual object.

On the Apple Macintosh, **Application.Width** is always equal to the total width of the screen, in points. Setting this value to any other value will have no effect.

In Microsoft Windows, if the window is minimized, **Application.Width** is read-only and returns the width of the icon.

You can use negative numbers to set the **Height** and **Width** properties of the following drawing objects: **Arc**, **Button**, **CheckBox**, **Drawing**, **DropDown**, **EditBox**, **GroupBox**, **GroupObject**, **Label**, **Line**, **ListBox**, **OLEObject**, **OptionButton**, **Oval**, **Picture**, **Rectangle**, **ScrollBar**, **Spinner**, and **TextBox**. This causes the object to reflect or translate (the behavior depends on the object), after which the **Top** and **Left** properties change to describe the new position. The **Height** and **Width** properties always return positive numbers.

See Also

Top Property.

Example

This example sets the width of oval one on Sheet1 to 1 inch (72 points).

```
Worksheets("Sheet1").Ovals(1).Width = 72
```

This example sets the width of every button on Sheet1 to 36 points.

```
For Each b In Worksheets("Sheet1").Buttons
    b.Width = 36
Next b
```

This example expands the active window to the maximum size available (assuming that the window is not maximized).

```
With ActiveWindow
    .WindowState = xlNormal
    .Top = 1
    .Left = 1
    .Height = Application.UsableHeight
    .Width = Application.UsableWidth
End With
```

Width # Statement

Description   Assigns an output-line width to a file opened using the **Open** statement.

Syntax   **Width #**_filenumber_,_width_

The **Width** statement syntax has these parts:

Part	Description
filenumber	Any valid file number.
width	Numeric expression in the range 0 to 255, inclusive, that indicates how many characters appear on a line before a new line is started. If _width_ equals 0, there is no limit to the length of a line. The default value for _width_ is 0.

See Also   **Open** Statement, **Print #** Statement.

Example   This example uses the **Width** statement to set the output-line width for a file.

```
Open "TESTFILE" For Output As #1     ' Open file for output.
Width #1, 5                          ' Set output-line width to 5.
For I = 0 To 9                       ' Loop 10 times.
    Print #1, Chr(48 + I);           ' This prints 5 characters per line.
Next I
Close #1' Close file.
```

Window Object

Description

Represents a window. Many worksheet characteristics, such as scroll bars and gridlines, are actually properties of the window.

Accessors

The **Window** object is a member of the **Windows** collection. The **Windows** collection for the **Application** object contains all the windows in the application, whereas the **Windows** collection for the **Workbook** object contains only the windows in the specified workbook. Use the **NewWindow** method to create a new window and add it to the collection.

To access a single member of the collection, use the **Windows** method with the index number or caption of the window as an argument. Using the **Windows** method with no object qualifier returns the collection of windows for the application (this is equivalent to **Application.Windows**). The active window is always Windows(1).

The following example maximizes the active window.

```
Windows(1).WindowState = xlMaximized
```

The window caption is the text shown in the title bar at the top of the window when the window is not maximized. The caption is also shown in the list of open files on the bottom of the Windows menu. Use the **Caption** property to set or return the window caption. Changing the window caption does not change the name of the workbook. The following example turns off cell gridlines for the worksheet shown in the BOOK1.XLS:1 window.

```
Windows("book1.xls:1").DisplayGridlines = False
```

Properties

ActiveCell Property, **ActiveChart** Property, **ActivePane** Property, **ActiveSheet** Property, **Application** Property, **Caption** Property, **Creator** Property, **DisplayFormulas** Property, **DisplayGridlines** Property, **DisplayHeadings** Property, **DisplayHorizontalScrollBar** Property, **DisplayOutline** Property, **DisplayRightToLeft** Property, **DisplayVerticalScrollBar** Property, **DisplayWorkbookTabs** Property, **DisplayZeros** Property, **FreezePanes** Property, **GridlineColor** Property, **GridlineColorIndex** Property, **Height** Property, **Index** Property, **Left** Property, **OnWindow** Property, **PageSetup** Property, **Parent** Property, **RangeSelection** Property, **ScrollColumn** Property, **ScrollRow** Property, **Selection** Property, **Split** Property, **SplitColumn** Property, **SplitHorizontal** Property, **SplitRow** Property, **SplitVertical** Property, **TabRatio** Property, **Top** Property, **Type** Property, **UsableHeight** Property, **UsableWidth** Property, **Visible** Property, **VisibleRange** Property, **Width** Property, **WindowNumber** Property, **WindowState** Property, **Zoom** Property.

Methods	**Activate** Method, **ActivateNext** Method, **ActivatePrevious** Method, **Close** Method, **LargeScroll** Method, **NewWindow** Method, **Panes** Method, **PrintOut** Method, **PrintPreview** Method, **ScrollWorkbookTabs** Method, **SelectedSheets** Method, **SetInfoDisplay** Method, **SmallScroll** Method.

WindowNumber Property

Applies To	**Window** Object.
Description	Returns the window number. For example, a window entitled "BOOK1.XLS:2" has a window number of two. Most windows have a window number of one. Read-only.
Remarks	The window number is not the same as the window **Index**, which is the position of the window within the **Windows** collection.
See Also	**Index** Property.
Example	This example creates a new window of the active window and then displays the window number of the new window.

```
ActiveWindow.NewWindow
MsgBox ActiveWindow.WindowNumber
```

Windows Collection Object

Description	A collection of all the **Window** objects in the Microsoft Excel application. The **Windows** collection for the **Application** object contains all the windows in the application, whereas the **Windows** collection for the **Workbook** object contains only the windows in the specified workbook.
Accessors	Use the **NewWindow** method to create a new window and add it to the collection. The following example creates a new window for the active workbook.

```
ActiveWorkbook.NewWindow
```

Use the **Windows** method with an argument to access a single member of the collection or without an argument to access the entire collection at once. The following example cascades all the windows currently showing in Microsoft Excel.

```
Windows.Arrange arrangeStyle:=xlCascade
```

Properties	**Application** Property, **Count** Property, **Creator** Property, **Parent** Property.
Methods	**Arrange** Method, **Item** Method.

Windows Method

Applies To	**Application** Object, **Workbook** Object.
Description	Accessor. Returns an object that represents a single window (a **Window** object, Syntax 1) or a collection of windows (the **Windows** object, Syntax 2). Read-only.
Syntax 1	*object*.**Windows**(*index*)
Syntax 2	*object*.**Windows**

object
> Optional for **Application**, required for **Workbook**. If **Application** (or omitted) this method returns a window (or windows) from any open workbook. If **Workbook**, this method returns a window (or windows) in the specified workbook.

index
> Required for Syntax 1. The name or number of the window.

Remarks	Syntax 2 returns a collection of both visible and hidden windows.
Example	This example closes the first open or hidden window in Microsoft Excel.

```
Application.Windows(1).Close
```

This example sets the name of window one in the active workbook to Consolidated Balance Sheet. This name is then used as the index to the **Windows** method.

```
ActiveWorkbook.Windows(1).Caption = "Consolidated Balance Sheet"
ActiveWorkbook.Windows("Consolidated Balance Sheet") _
    .ActiveSheet.Calculate
```

WindowsForPens Property

Applies To	**Application** Object.
Description	**True** if the computer is running under Microsoft Windows for Pen Computing. Read-only.

Example

This example shows how to limit handwriting recognition to numbers and punctuation only if Microsoft Windows for Pen Computing is running.

```
If Application.WindowsForPens Then
    Application.ConstrainNumeric = True
End If
```

WindowState Property

Applies To

Application Object, **Window** Object.

Description

Returns or sets the state of the window, as shown in the following table. Read-write.

Value	Meaning
xlNormal	Window is not maximized or minimized.
xlMaximized	Window is maximized (Microsoft Windows only). Maximizing a window maximizes all windows on the Microsoft Excel desktop.
xlMinimized	Window is minimized (Microsoft Windows only).

Example

This example maximizes the application window in Microsoft Excel for Windows. (This property cannot be set on the Macintosh.)

```
Application.WindowState = xlMaximized
```

This example expands the active window to the maximum size available (assuming that the window is not already maximized).

```
With ActiveWindow
    .WindowState = xlNormal
    .Top = 1
    .Left = 1
    .Height = Application.UsableHeight
    .Width = Application.UsableWidth
End With
```

With Statement

Description

Executes a series of statements on a single object or a user-defined type.

Syntax

With *object*
    [*statements*]
End With

The **With** statement syntax has these parts:

Part	Description
object	Name of an object or a user-defined type.
statements	One or more statements to be executed on *object*.

Remarks

The **With** statement allows you to perform a series of statements on a specified object without requalifying the name of the object. For example, if you have a number of different properties to change on a single object, it is more convenient to place the property assignment statements within the **With** control structure, referring to the object once instead of referring to it with each property assignment. The following example illustrates use of the **With** statement to assign values to several properties of the same object.

```
With MyLabel
    .Height = 2000
    .Width = 2000
    .Caption = "This is MyLabel"
End With
```

You can nest **With** statements by placing one **With** loop within another. Each *object* must be unique.

See Also

Do...**Loop** Statement, **While**...**Wend** Statement.

Example

This example uses the **With** statement to execute a series of statements on a single object. The object MyObject and its properties are generic names used for illustration purposes only.

```
With MyObject
    ' Same as MyObject.Height = 100
    .Height = 100
    .Caption = "Hello World"
    With .Font
        ' Same as MyObject.Font.Color = Red.
        .Color = Red
        .Bold = True
    End With
End With
```

The following example adds a new menu bar and then activates it. After running the example, you can use `MenuBars(xlModule).Activate` to restore the Visual Basic Module menu.

```
With MenuBars.Add("Stock Chart")
    With .Menus.Add("File")
        .MenuItems.Add "Update", "UpdateProc"
        .MenuItems.Add "Print", "PrintProc"
    End With
End With
MenuBars("Stock Chart").Activate
```

This example creates a formatted multiplication table in cells A1:K11 on Sheet1.

```
Set dataTableRange = Worksheets("Sheet1").Range("A1:K11")
Set rowInputCell = Worksheets("Sheet1").Range("A12")
Set columnInputCell = Worksheets("Sheet1").Range("A13")

Worksheets("Sheet1").Range("A1").Formula = "=A12*A13"
For i = 2 To 11
    Worksheets("Sheet1").Cells(i, 1) = i - 1
    Worksheets("Sheet1").Cells(1, i) = i - 1
Next i
dataTableRange.Table rowInputCell, columnInputCell
With Worksheets("Sheet1").Range("A1").CurrentRegion
    .Rows(1).Font.Bold = True
    .Columns(1).Font.Bold = True
    .Columns.AutoFit
End With
```

Workbook Object

Description

Represents a Microsoft Excel workbook.

Accessors

The **Workbook** object is a member of the **Workbooks** collection. The **Workbooks** collection contains all the **Workbook** objects currently open in Microsoft Excel. Use the **Open** method to open a file. Use the **Add** method to create a new empty workbook and add it to the collection.

To access a single member of the collection, use the **Workbooks** method with the index number or name of the workbook as an argument.

The index number represents the order in which the workbooks were opened or created. Workbooks(1) is the first workbook created; Workbooks(Workbooks.Count) is the last. Activating a workbook does not change its index number. All workbooks are included in the index count, even if they are hidden. The following example activates workbook one.

```
Workbooks(1).Activate
```

The **Name** property returns the workbook name. You cannot set the name using this property. Use the **SaveAs** method to save the workbook under a different name if you need to change the name. The following example activates the worksheet named "Sheet1" in the workbook named COGS.XLS (the workbook must already be open in Microsoft Excel).

```
Workbooks("cogs.xls").Worksheets("sheet1").Activate
```

Using ActiveWorkbook

The **ActiveWorkbook** property returns the currently active workbook. The following example sets the name of the author for the active workbook.

```
ActiveWorkbook.Author = "Jean Selva"
```

Using ThisWorkbook

The **ThisWorkbook** property returns the workbook where the Visual Basic code is running. In most cases, this is the same as the active workbook. However, if the Visual Basic code is part of an add-in, the **ThisWorkbook** property will not return the active workbook. In this case, the active workbook is the workbook calling the add-in, while the **ThisWorkbook** property returns the add-in workbook.

If you will be creating an add-in from your Visual Basic code, you should use the **ThisWorkbook** property to qualify any statement which must run on the workbook you compile into the add-in.

Properties

ActiveChart Property, ActiveSheet Property, Application Property, Author Property, BuiltinDocumentProperties Property, Colors Property, Comments Property, Container Property, CreateBackup Property, Creator Property, CustomDocumentProperties Property, Date1904 Property, DisplayDrawingObjects Property, FileFormat Property, FullName Property, HasMailer Property, HasPassword Property, HasRoutingSlip Property, Keywords Property, Mailer Property, MultiUserEditing Property, Name Property, OnSave Property, OnSheetActivate Property, OnSheetDeactivate Property, Parent Property, Path Property, PrecisionAsDisplayed Property, ProtectStructure Property, ProtectWindows Property, ReadOnly Property, ReadOnlyRecommended Property, RevisionNumber Property, Routed Property, RoutingSlip Property, Saved Property, SaveLinkValues Property, ShowConflictHistory Property, Subject Property, Title Property, UpdateRemoteReferences Property, UserStatus Property, WriteReserved Property, WriteReservedBy Property.

Methods

Activate Method, ChangeFileAccess Method, ChangeLink Method, Charts Method, Close Method, DeleteNumberFormat Method, DialogSheets Method, EditionOptions Method, Excel4IntlMacroSheets Method, Excel4MacroSheets Method, ExclusiveAccess Method, ForwardMailer Method, LinkInfo Method, LinkSources Method, Modules Method, Names Method, NewWindow Method, OpenLinks Method, Post Method, PrintOut Method, PrintPreview Method, Protect Method, Reply Method, ReplyAll Method, Route Method, RunAutoMacros Method, Save Method, SaveAs Method, SaveCopyAs Method, SendMail Method, SendMailer Method, SetLinkOnData Method, Sheets Method, Styles Method, Unprotect Method, UpdateFromFile Method, UpdateLink Method, Windows Method, Worksheets Method.

Workbooks Collection Object

Description

A collection of all the **Workbook** objects currently open in the Microsoft Excel application.

Accessors

Use the **Open** method to open a file. Use the **Add** method to create a new empty workbook and add it to the collection. The following example adds a new empty workbook to Microsoft Excel (this is equivalent to clicking the New command on the File menu).

```
Workbooks.Add
```

The following example opens the file ARRAY.XLS as a read-only workbook.

```
Workbooks.Open fileName:="array.xls", readOnly:=True
```

Use the **Workbooks** method with an argument to access a single member of the collection or without an argument to access the entire collection at once. The following example closes all open workbooks.

```
Workbooks.Close
```

Properties	**Application** Property, **Count** Property, **Creator** Property, **Parent** Property.
Methods	**Add** Method (**Workbooks** Collection), **Close** Method, **Item** Method, **Open** Method, **OpenText** Method.

Workbooks Method

Applies To	**Application** Object.
Description	Accessor. Returns an object that represents a single open workbook (a **Workbook** object, Syntax 1) or a collection of all open workbooks (the **Workbooks** object, Syntax 2). Read-only.
Syntax 1	*object*.**Workbooks**(*index*)
Syntax 2	*object*.**Workbooks**

object
> Optional. The **Application** object.

index
> Required for Syntax 1. The name or number of the workbook.

Remarks	The collection returned by syntax 2 of the **Workbooks** method does not include open add-ins, which are a special kind of hidden workbook.

You can, however, return a single open add-in if you know the filename. For example `Workbooks("OSCAR.XLA")` will return the open add-in named "OSCAR.XLA" as a **Workbook** object.

Example	This example activates workbook BOOK1.

```
Workbooks("BOOK1").Activate
```

This example opens the workbook LARGE.XLS.

```
Workbooks.Open filename:="LARGE.XLS"
```

This example closes and saves changes to all workbooks except the one that is running the example.

```
For Each w In Workbooks
    If w.Name <> ThisWorkbook.Name Then
        w.Close savechanges:=True
    End If
Next w
```

Worksheet Object

Description

Represents a worksheet, a Microsoft Excel version 4.0 macro sheet, or a Microsoft Excel version 4.0 international macro sheet.

Accessors

The **Worksheet** object is a member of the **Worksheets** collection. The **Worksheets** collection contains all the **Worksheet** objects in a workbook. Use the **Add** method to create a new worksheet and add it to the collection. To access a single member of the collection, use the **Worksheets** method with the index number or name of the worksheet as an argument.

The worksheet index number represents the position of the worksheet on the tab bar of the workbook. Worksheets(1) is the first (leftmost) worksheet in the workbook; Worksheets(Worksheets.Count) is the last. All worksheets are included in the index count, even if they are hidden.

The following example hides worksheet one in the active workbook.

```
Worksheets(1).Visible = False
```

The worksheet name is shown on the tab for the worksheet. Use the **Name** property to set or return the worksheet name. The following example protects the scenarios on the worksheet named "Sheet1."

```
Worksheets("sheet1").Protect password:="drowssap", scenarios:=True
```

The **Worksheet** object is also a member of the **Sheets** collection. The **Sheets** collection contains all of the sheets in the workbook (chart sheets, dialog sheets, modules, and worksheets). To access a single member of the collection, use the **Sheets** method with the index number or name of the sheet as an argument.

Using ActiveSheet

When a worksheet is the active sheet, you can use the **ActiveSheet** property to refer to it. The following example uses the **Activate** method to activate the worksheet named "Sheet 1," sets the page orientation to landscape mode, and then prints the worksheet.

```
Worksheets("sheet1").Activate
ActiveSheet.PageSetup.Orientation = xlLandscape
ActiveSheet.PrintOut
```

Properties

Application Property, **AutoFilterMode** Property, **CircularReference** Property, **ConsolidationFunction** Property, **ConsolidationOptions** Property, **ConsolidationSources** Property, **Creator** Property, **DisplayAutomaticPageBreaks** Property, **EnableAutoFilter** Property, **EnableOutlining** Property, **EnablePivotTable** Property, **FilterMode** Property, **Index** Property, **Name** Property, **Next** Property, **OnCalculate** Property, **OnData** Property, **OnDoubleClick** Property, **OnEntry** Property, **OnSheetActivate** Property, **OnSheetDeactivate** Property, **Outline** Property, **PageSetup** Property, **Parent** Property, **Previous** Property, **ProtectContents** Property, **ProtectDrawingObjects** Property, **ProtectionMode** Property, **ProtectScenarios** Property, **StandardHeight** Property, **StandardWidth** Property, **TransitionExpEval** Property, **TransitionFormEntry** Property, **Type** Property, **UsedRange** Property, **Visible** Property.

Methods

Activate Method, **Arcs** Method, **Buttons** Method, **Calculate** Method, **Cells** Method, **ChartObjects** Method, **CheckBoxes** Method, **CheckSpelling** Method, **ClearArrows** Method, **Columns** Method, **Copy** Method, **Delete** Method, **DrawingObjects** Method, **Drawings** Method, **DropDowns** Method, **Evaluate** Method, **GroupBoxes** Method, **GroupObjects** Method, **Labels** Method, **Lines** Method, **ListBoxes** Method, **Move** Method, **Names** Method, **OLEObjects** Method, **OptionButtons** Method, **Ovals** Method, **Paste** Method (**DialogSheet** or **Worksheet** Object), **PasteSpecial** Method (**DialogSheet** or **Worksheet** Object), **Pictures** Method, **PivotTables** Method, **PivotTableWizard** Method, **PrintOut** Method, **PrintPreview** Method, **Protect** Method, **Range** Method, **Rectangles** Method, **Rows** Method, **SaveAs** Method, **Scenarios** Method, **ScrollBars** Method, **Select** Method, **SetBackgroundPicture** Method, **ShowAllData** Method, **ShowDataForm** Method, **Spinners** Method, **TextBoxes** Method, **Unprotect** Method.

Worksheet Property

Applies To   **Range** Object.

Description   Accessor. Returns a **Worksheet** object that represents the worksheet containing the specified range. Read-only.

Example   This example displays the name of the worksheet containing the active cell. The example must be run from a worksheet.

```
MsgBox ActiveCell.Worksheet.Name
```

This example displays the name of the worksheet containing the range named "testRange."

```
MsgBox Range("testRange").Worksheet.Name
```

Worksheets Collection Object

Description   A collection of all the **Worksheet** objects in the specified or active workbook. Each **Worksheet** object represents a worksheet, a Microsoft Excel version 4.0 macro sheet, or a Microsoft Excel version 4.0 international macro sheet.

Use the **Add** method to create a new worksheet and add it to the collection. The following example adds two new worksheets before sheet one of the active workbook.

```
Worksheets.Add count:=2, before:=Sheets(1)
```

Use the **Worksheets** method with an argument to access a single member of the collection or without an argument to access the entire collection at once. The following example moves all the worksheets to the end of the workbook.

```
Worksheets.Move after:=Sheets(Sheets.Count)
```

The **Sheets** collection contains all of the sheets in the workbook (chart sheets, dialog sheets, modules, and worksheets). Use the **Sheets** method with an argument to access a single member of the collection or without an argument to access the entire collection at once.

Properties   **Application** Property, **Count** Property, **Creator** Property, **Parent** Property, **Visible** Property.

Methods   **Add** Method (**Worksheets** Collection), **Copy** Method, **Delete** Method, **FillAcrossSheets** Method, **Item** Method, **Move** Method, **PrintOut** Method, **PrintPreview** Method, **Select** Method.

Worksheets Method

Applies To   **Application** Object, **Workbook** Object.

Description   Accessor. Returns an object that represents a worksheet (a **Worksheet** object, Syntax 1) or a collection of all worksheets (a **Worksheets** object, Syntax 2) in the workbook. Read-only.

Syntax 1   *object*.**Worksheets(***index***)**

Syntax 2   *object*.**Worksheets**

object
    Optional for **Application**, required for **Workbook**. The object that contains worksheets.

index
    Required for Syntax 1. The name or number of the worksheet to return.

Remarks   This method returns worksheets with the **Type** property equal to **xlWorksheet**, not **xlExcel4MacroSheet** or **xlExcel4IntlMacroSheet**; use the **Excel4MacroSheets** method or the **Excel4IntlMacroSheets** method to return those types.

Using this method with no object qualifier is a shortcut for **ActiveWorkbook.Worksheets**.

Example   This example displays the value in cell A1 on Sheet1 in the active workbook.

```
MsgBox Worksheets("Sheet1").Range("A1").Value
```

This example displays the name of each worksheet in the active workbook.

```
For Each ws In Worksheets
    MsgBox ws.Name
Next ws
```

This example adds a new worksheet to the active workbook and then sets the name of the worksheet.

```
Set newSheet = Worksheets.Add
newSheet.Name = "1995 Budget"
```

WrapText Property

Applies To	**Range** Object, **Style** Object.
Description	**True** if Microsoft Excel wraps the text in the object. Read-write.
Remarks	Microsoft Excel will change the row height of the range, if necessary, to display the text in the range.
Example	This example formats cell B2 on Sheet1 so that the text in it wraps.

```
Worksheets("Sheet1").Range("B2").Value = _
    "This text should wrap in a cell."
Worksheets("Sheet1").Range("B2").WrapText = True
```

Write # Statement

Description   Writes raw data to a sequential file.

Syntax   **Write #**_filenumber_[,_outputlist_]

The **Write** statement syntax has these parts:

Part	Description
filenumber	Any valid file number.
outputlist	One or more comma-delimited numeric or string expressions to write to a file.

Remarks

If you omit _outputlist_ and include a comma after _filenumber_, a blank line prints to the file. Multiple expressions can be separated with a space, a semicolon, or a comma. A space has the same effect as a semicolon.

When **Write #** is used to output data to a file, several universal assumptions are followed so the data can always be read and correctly interpreted using **Input #**, regardless of locale:

- Numeric data is always output using the period (.) as the decimal separator.

- For Boolean data, either #TRUE# or #FALSE# is printed. The **True** and **False** keywords are not translated, regardless of locale.

- Date data is written to the file using the universal date format. When either the date or the time component is missing or zero, only the provided part gets written to the file.

- Nothing is written to the file if *outputlist* data is **Empty**. However, for **Null** data, #NULL# is output.

- For error data, the output appears as #ERROR *errorcode*#. The **Error** keyword is not translated, regardless of locale.

Unlike the **Print #** statement, the **Write #** statement inserts commas between items and quotation marks around strings as they are written to the file. You don't have to put explicit delimiters in the list. **Write #** inserts a newline character (carriage return or carriage return-linefeed) after it has written the final character in *outputlist* to the file.

See Also   **Input #** Statement, **Open** Statement, **Print #** Statement.

Example   This example uses the **Write #** statement to write raw data to a sequential file.

```
Open "TESTFILE" For Output As 1        ' Open file for output.
Write #1, "Hello World", 234           ' Written data is comma delimited.
Write #1,                              ' Write blank line.

' Assign Boolean, Date, Null and Error values.
MyBool = False : MyDate = #February 12, 1969# : MyNull = Null
MyError = CVErr(32767)
' Boolean data is written as #TRUE# or #FALSE#. Date literals are
' written in universal date format. Null data is written as #NULL#.
' Error data is written as #ERROR errorcode#.
Write #1, MyBool ; " is a Boolean value"
Write #1, MyDate ; " is a date"
Write #1, MyNull ; " is a null value"
Write #1, MyError ; " is an error value"
Close #1                               ' Close file.
```

WriteReserved Property

Applies To   **Workbook** Object.

Description   **True** if the workbook is write reserved. Read-only.

Remarks   Use the **SaveAs** method to set this property.

Example   If the active workbook is write-reserved, this example displays a message that contains the name of the user who saved the workbook as write-reserved.

```
With ActiveWorkbook
    If .WriteReserved = True Then
        MsgBox "Please contact " & .WriteReservedBy & Chr(13) & _
            " if you need to insert data in this workbook."
    End If
End With
```

WriteReservedBy Property

Applies To   **Workbook** Object.

Description   Returns a string that names the user with current write permission for the workbook. Read-only.

Example   If the active workbook is write-reserved, this example displays a message that contains the name of the user who saved the workbook as write-reserved.

```
With ActiveWorkbook
    If .WriteReserved = True Then
        MsgBox "Please contact " & .WriteReservedBy & Chr(13) & _
            " if you need to insert data in this workbook."
    End If
End With
```

Xor Operator

Description   Used to perform a logical exclusion on two expressions.

Syntax   *result* = *expression1* **Xor** *expression2*

The **Xor** operator syntax has these parts:

Part	Description
result	Any numeric variable.
expression1	Any expression.
expression2	Any expression.

Remarks

If one, and only one, of the expressions evaluates **True**, *result* is **True**. However, if either expression is a **Null**, *result* is also a **Null**. When neither expression is a **Null**, *result* is determined according to the following table:

If *expression1* is	And *expression2* is	The *result* is
True	True	False
True	False	True
False	True	True
False	False	False

The **Xor** operator also performs a bit-wise comparison of identically positioned bits in two numeric expressions and sets the corresponding bit in *result* according to the following truth table:

If bit in *expression1* is	And bit in *expression2* is	The *result* is
0	0	0
0	1	1
1	0	1
1	1	0

See Also

Operator Precedence.

Example

This example uses the **Xor** operator to perform logical exclusion on two expressions.

```
A = 10: B = 8: C = 6 : D = Null    ' Initialize variables.
MyCheck = A > B Xor B > C           ' Returns False.
MyCheck = B > A Xor B > C           ' Returns True.
MyCheck = B > A Xor C > B           ' Returns False.
MyCheck = B > D Xor A > B           ' Returns Null.
MyCheck = A Xor B    ' Returns 2 (bit-wise comparison).
```

XValues Property

Applies To

Series Object.

Description

Returns or sets an array of x values for a chart series. The **XValues** property can be set to a range on a worksheet or an array of values, but it may not be a combination of both. Read-write.

Example

This example sets the x values for series one in Chart1 to the range B1:B5 on Sheet1.

```
Set Charts("Chart1").SeriesCollection(1).XValues = _
        Worksheets("Sheet1").Range("B1:B5")
```

This example uses an array to set values for the individual points in series one in Chart1.

```
Charts("Chart1").SeriesCollection(1).XValues = _
        Array(5.0, 6.3, 12.6, 28, 50)
```

XYGroups Method

Applies To

Chart Object.

Description

Accessor. On a 2-D chart, returns an object that represents a single scatter chart group (a **ChartGroup** object, Syntax 1), or a collection of the scatter chart groups (a **ChartGroups** collection, Syntax 2).

Syntax 1

object.**XYGroups**(*index*)

Syntax 2

object.**XYGroups**

object
    Required. The **Chart** object.

index
    Required for Syntax 1. Specifies the chart group.

Example

This example converts X-Y group (scatter group) one to an area group. The example should be run on a 2-D chart.

```
Charts("Chart1").XYGroups(1).Type = xlArea
```

Year Function

Description

Returns a whole number representing the year.

Syntax

Year(*date*)

The *date* named argument is limited to a date or numbers and strings, in any combination, that can represent a date. If *date* contains no valid data, **Null** is returned.

See Also   **Date** Function, **Date** Statement, **Day** Function, **Month** Function, **Now** Function, **Weekday** Function.

Example   This example uses the **Year** function to obtain the year from a specified date.

```
' In the development environment, the date literal will display in short
' format using the locale settings of your code.
MyDate = #February 12, 1969#        ' Assign a date.
MyYear = Year(MyDate)               ' MyYear contains 1969.
```

Zoom Property

Applies To   **PageSetup** Object, **Window** Object.

Description   **PageSetup** object:

Returns or sets a percentage to scale the worksheet for printing, between 10 and 400 percent. Read-write.

If this property is **False**, the **FitToPagesWide** and **FitToPagesTall** properties control how the worksheet is scaled.

Window object:

Returns or sets the display size of the window, in percent (100 means show at normal size; 200 means the window is double size, etc.).

The property can also be set to **True** to set the window size to fit the current selection.

Remarks   **PageSetup** object:

This property applies only to worksheets.

All scaling retains the aspect ratio of the original document.

Window object:

This function will only affect the sheet that is currently active in the window. To use this property on other sheets, you must first activate them.

Example   This example scales Sheet1 by 150 percent when the worksheet is printed.

```
Worksheets("Sheet1").PageSetup.Zoom = 150
```

ZOrder Property

Applies To   Arc Object, **Arcs** Collection, **Button** Object, **Buttons** Collection, **ChartObject** Object, **ChartObjects** Collection, **CheckBox** Object, **Drawing** Object, **DrawingObjects** Collection, **Drawings** Collection, **DropDown** Object, **DropDowns** Collection, **EditBox** Object, **EditBoxes** Collection, **GroupBox** Object, **GroupBoxes** Collection, **GroupObject** Object, **GroupObjects** Collection, **Label** Object, **Labels** Collection, **Line** Object, **Lines** Collection, **ListBox** Object, **ListBoxes** Collection, **OLEObject** Object, **OLEObjects** Collection, **OptionButton** Object, **OptionButtons** Collection, **Oval** Object, **Ovals** Collection, **Picture** Object, **Pictures** Collection, **Rectangle** Object, **Rectangles** Collection, **ScrollBar** Object, **ScrollBars** Collection, **Spinner** Object, **Spinners** Collection, **TextBox** Object, **TextBoxes** Collection.

Description   Returns the z-order position of the object. Read only.

Remarks   For any collection of objects, the object at the back of the z-order is *collection*(1), and the object at the front of the z-order is *collection*(*collection*.Count). For example, if there are three ovals on the active sheet, the oval at the back of the z-order is `ActiveSheet.Ovals(1)`, and the oval at the front of the z-order is `ActiveSheet.Ovals(ActiveSheet.Ovals.Count)`.

See Also   **BringToFront** Method, **SendToBack** Method.

Example   This example displays the z-order position of oval one on Sheet1.

```
MsgBox "The oval's z-order position is " & _
    Worksheets("Sheet1").Ovals(1).ZOrder
```

APPENDIX

Microsoft Excel Object Model Graphics

Whenever you want to work with an object in Microsoft Excel, you must first build an expression that returns the object. To build the expression, you must understand where the object fits into the object hierarchy, or *object model*. This appendix contains a graphical representation of the Microsoft Excel object model.

Microsoft Excel Objects

drawing objects

Subitem of Worksheet, Chart, and DialogSheet objects

ChartObjects (ChartObject)

Chart

GroupObjects (GroupObject)

OLEObjects (OLEObject)

Arcs (Arc)

Drawings (Drawing)

Lines (Line)

Ovals (Oval)

Pictures (Picture)

Rectangles (Rectangle)

TextBoxes (TextBox)

Buttons (Button)

CheckBoxes (CheckBox)

DropDowns (DropDown)

GroupBoxes (GroupBox)

Labels (Label)

ListBoxes (ListBox)

OptionButtons (OptionButton)

ScrollBars (ScrollBar)

Spinners (Spinner)

EditBoxes (EditBox)

On DialogSheet objects only

DrawingObjects

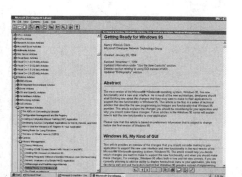